Kawasaki
ER-6f and ER-6n
Service and Repair Manual

by Phil Mather

Models covered

(4874-320)

ER650 (ER-6n). 649cc. 2006 to 2010
EX650 (ER-6f). 649cc. 2006 to 2010
ABS versions included

© Haynes Publishing 2010

ABCDE
FGHIJ
KLMNO
PQRST

A book in the Haynes Service and Repair Manual Series

Printed in the USA

Haynes Publishing
Sparkford, Yeovil, Somerset BA22 7JJ, England

ISBN 978 1 84425 874 1

Library of Congress Control Number 2009932064

Haynes North America, Inc
861 Lawrence Drive, Newbury Park, California 91320, USA

Haynes Publishing Nordiska AB
Box 1504, 751 45 Uppsala, Sweden

Contents

LIVING WITH YOUR KAWASAKI

Introduction

Pre-ride checks

MAINTENANCE

Routine maintenance and servicing

Contents

REPAIRS AND OVERHAUL

REFERENCE

Kawasaki
The Green Meanies

by Julian Ryder

Kawasaki Heavy Industries

Kawasaki is a company of contradictions. It is the smallest of the big four Japanese manufacturers but the biggest company, it was the last of the four to make and market motorcycles yet it owns the oldest name in the Japanese industry, and it was the first to set up a factory in the USA. Kawasaki Heavy Industries, of which the motorcycle operation is but a small component, is a massive company with its heritage firmly in the old heavy industries like shipbuilding and railways; nowadays it is as much involved in aerospace as in motorcycles.

In fact it may be because of this that Kawasaki's motorcycles have always been quirky, you get the impression that they are designed by a small group of enthusiasts who are given an admirably free hand. More realistically, it may be that Kawasaki's designers have experience with techniques and materials from other engineering disciplines. Either way, Kawasaki have managed to be the factory who surprise us more than the rest. Quite often, they do this by totally ignoring a market segment the others are scrabbling over, but more often they hit us with pure, undiluted performance.

The origins of the company, and its name, go back to 1878 when Shozo Kawasaki set up a dockyard in Tokyo. By the late 1930s, the company was making its own steel in massive steelworks and manufacturing railway locos and rolling stock. In the run up to war, the Kawasaki Aircraft Company was set up in 1937 and it was this arm of the now giant operation that would look to motorcycle engine manufacture in post-war Japan.

They bought their high-technology experience to bear first on engines which were sold on to a number of manufacturers as original equipment. Both two- and four-stroke units were made, a 58 cc and 148 cc OHC unit. One of the customer companies was Meihatsu Heavy Industries, another company within the Kawasaki group, which in 1961 was shaken up and renamed Kawasaki Auto Sales. At the same time, the Akashi factory which was to be Kawasaki's main production facility until the Kobe earthquake of 1995, was opened.

Shortly afterwards, Kawasaki took over the ailing Meguro company, Japan's oldest motorcycle maker, thus instantly obtaining a range of bigger bikes which were marketed as Kawasaki Meguros. The following year, the first bike to be made and sold as a Kawasaki was produced, a 125 cc single called the B8 and in 1963 a motocross version, the B8M appeared.

Model development

Kawasaki's first appearance on a road-race circuit came in 1965 with a batch of disc-valve 125 twins. They were no match for the opposition from Japan in the shape of Suzuki and Yamaha or for the fading force of the factory MZs from East Germany. Only after the other Japanese factories had pulled out of the class did Kawasaki win, with British rider Dave Simmonds becoming World 125 GP Champion in 1969 on a bike that looked astonishingly similar to the original racer. That same year Kawasaki reorganised once again, this time merging three companies to form Kawasaki Heavy Industries. One of the new organisation's objectives was to take motorcycle production forward and exploit markets outside Japan.

KHI achieved that target immediately and set out their stall for the future with the astonishing and frightening H1. This three-cylinder air-cooled 500 cc two-stroke was arguably the first modern pure performance bike to hit the market. It hypnotised a whole generation of motorcyclists who'd never before encountered such a ferocious, wheelie inducing power band or such shattering straight-line speed allied to questionable handling. And as for the 750 cc version ...

The triples perfectly suited the late '60s, fitting in well with the student demonstrations of 1968 and the anti-establishment ethos of the Summer of Love. Unfortunately, the oil crisis would put an end to the thirsty strokers but Kawasaki had another high-performance ace up their corporate sleeve. Or rather they thought they did.

The 1968 Tokyo Show saw probably the single most significant new motorcycle ever made unveiled: the Honda CB750. At Kawasaki it caused a major shock, for they also had a 750 cc four, code-named New

The three cylinder two-stroke 750

The first Superbike, Kawasaki's 900 cc Z1

no major difference between that first Z1 and the air-cooled GPz range. Add water-cooling and you have the GPZ900, which in turn metamorphosed into the GPZ1000RX and then the ZX-10 and the ZZ-R1100. Indeed, the last three models share the same 58 mm stroke. The bikes are obviously very different but it's difficult to put your finger on exactly why.

Other models have remained effectively untouched for over a decade: the KH and KE single-cylinder air-cooled two-stroke learner bikes, the GT550 and 750 shaft-drive hacks favoured by big city despatch riders and the GPz305 being prime examples. It's only when they step outside the performance field that Kawasakis seems less sure. Their first factory customs were dire, you simply got the impression that the team that designed them didn't have their heart in the job. Only when the Classic range appeared in 1995 did they get it right.

Racing success

Kawasaki also have a more focused approach to racing than the other factories. The policy has always been to race the road bikes and with just a couple of exceptions that's what they've done. Even Simmonds' championship winner bore a strong resemblance to the twins they were selling in the late '60s and racing versions of the 500 and 750 cc triples were also sold as over-the-counter racers, the H1R and H2R. The 500 was in the forefront of the two-stroke assault on MV Agusta but wasn't a Grand Prix

York Steak, almost ready to roll and it was a double, rather than single, overhead cam motor. Bravely, they took the decision to go ahead - but with the motor taken out to 900 cc. The result was the Z1, unveiled at the 1972 Cologne Show. It was a bike straight out of the same mould as the H1, scare stories spread about unmanageable power, dubious straight-line stability and frightening handling, none of which stopped the sales graph

rocketing upwards and led to the coining of the term 'superbike'. While rising fuel prices cut short development of the big two-strokes, the Z1 went on to found a dynasty, indeed its genes can still be detected in Kawasaki's latest products like the ZZ-R1100 (Ninja ZX-11).

This is another characteristic of the way Kawasaki operates. Models quite often have very long lives, or gradually evolve. There is

One of the two-stroke engined KH and KE range - the KE100B

The GT750 - a favourite hack for despatch riders

The high-performance ZXR750

winner. It was the 750 that made the impact and carried the factory's image in F750 racing against the Suzuki triples and Yamaha fours.

The factory's decision to use green, usually regarded as an unlucky colour in sport, meant its bikes and personnel stood out and the phrase 'Green Meanies' fitted them perfectly. The Z1 motor soon became a full 1000 cc and powered Kawasaki's assault in F1 racing, notably in endurance which Kawasaki saw as being most closely related to its road bikes.

That didn't stop them dominating 250 and 350 cc GPs with a tandem twin two-stroke in the late '70s and early '80s, but their path-breaking monocoque 500 while a race winner never won a world title. When Superbike arrived, Kawasaki's road 750s

weren't as track-friendly as the opposition's out-and-out race replicas. This makes Scott Russell's World title on the ZXR750 in 1993 even more praiseworthy, for the homologation bike, the ZXR750RR, was much heavier and much more of a road bike than the Italian and Japanese competition.

The company's Supersport 600 contenders have similarly been more sports-tourers than race-replicas, yet they too have been competitive on the track. Indeed, the flagship bike, the ZZ-R1100, is most definitely a sports tourer capable of carrying two people and their luggage at high speed in comfort all day and then doing it again the next day. Try that on one of the race replicas and you'll be in need of a course of treatment from a chiropractor.

Through doing it their way Kawasaki developed a brand loyalty for their performance bikes that kept the Z1's derivatives in production until the mid-'80s and turned the bike into a classic in its model life. You could even argue that the Z1 lives on in the shape of the 1100 Zephyr's GPz1100-derived motor. And that's another Kawasaki invention, the retro bike. But when you look at what many commentators refer to as the retro boom, especially in Japan, you find that it is no such thing. It is the Zephyr boom. Just another example of Japan's most surprising motorcycle manufacturer getting it right again.

Clever Revver

Kawasaki do not bring out new lightweights very often. Unlike cutting-edge sports bikes, their design life tends to be longer than three years. Consider the predecessor to the ER-6, the ER-5. That bike, or at least its engine, could trace its ancestry back to the EN450 factory custom, and that bike's motor was basically two cylinders off the original GPZ900, the first Ninja which has just celebrated its twenty-fifth birthday.

So when the 5 turned into a 6, the new bike bears very careful examination because it is going to be around for a while. Not surprisingly, Kawasaki stuck with a twin and a parallel twin at that. A four would have been too wide and too expensive and Kawasaki reserve their V-twin designs for the cruiser range. There is no doubt, though, that the fuel-injected parallel twin tuned for usability not outright power is much smoother at small throttle openings than most V-twins which have a tendency to be lumpy in that rev range. However, it's not the engine that's the star of this bike, efficient and responsive as it is: It's the packaging. The ER-6n, where the 'n' stands for 'naked' packs a lot of character into a small, manageable package that

The 2008 ER-6n

The 2009 ER-6n

The 2007 ER-6f

The 2009 ER-6f

attracts newly-qualified riders as well as more experienced bikers who don't want, or can't afford, to go the full-on supersports route.

The designers decided to make a feature of the frame – it looks like ladder or lattice chassis but there's a substantial spine hiding in there as well. The rear suspension is offset to the right, a major styling cue, and the body work is both minimalist and modern. Or it was until the ER-6f arrived. The 'f', you won't be surprised to hear, stands for 'faired.' Kawasaki decided that northern European riders, specifically the ones in the UK, Germany, Holland, Belgium and Luxembourg, need some weather protection. With minimal alterations to the 'n', the only significant one being a slightly longer front fork, the ER-6

suddenly becomes an even more practical all-rounder. It doesn't look anywhere near as sharp as the 'n' but retains all the character of the original design. That's a clever trick.

The trouble with most bikes that are built down to a price is that they look like it. Not the ER. The engine may be basic by today's standards but Kawasaki have been clever enough to incorporate enough elements of their Ninjas to make sure the customer doesn't feel short-changed. For instance, the triangular relative layout of the crankshaft and gearbox shafts make the engine very short front to back. That means the swingarm can be relatively long without giving the bike a long wheelbase overall: very MotoGP.

The surprise in the specification of a bike

like this is that ABS brakes are offered as an option. However, as one major customer sector for the ER is the learner and newly qualified rider, the non-ABS machine provides a cheaper option. More experienced riders will probably spend their extra cash on Kawasaki's accessories, luggage, crash mushrooms, flip-up screen, mini indicator kit, etc. The petal brake discs are standard fitment by the way.

Both models received a makeover for 2009, three years after their introduction, which resulted in a much sharper look. Mechanically, the most significant modification was the introduction of rubber mountings for the rear upper engine mountings, handlebars and footrests, a revised swingarm and new instrumentation.

Acknowledgements

Our thanks are due to Bridge Motorcycles of Exeter and Taylors Motorcycles of Crewkerne who supplied the machines featured in the illustrations throughout this manual. We would also like to thank NGK Spark Plugs (UK) Ltd for supplying the colour spark plug condition photographs, the Avon Rubber Company for supplying information on tyre fitting and Draper Tools Ltd for some of the workshop tools shown.

Thanks are also due to Julian Ryder who wrote the introduction and to Kawasaki Motors Europe who supplied model photographs.

About this Manual

The aim of this manual is to help you get the best value from your motorcycle. It can do so in several ways. It can help you decide what work must be done, even if you choose to have it done by a dealer; it provides information and procedures for routine maintenance and servicing; and it offers diagnostic and repair procedures to follow when trouble occurs.

We hope you use the manual to tackle the work yourself. For many simpler jobs, doing it yourself may be quicker than arranging an appointment to get the motorcycle into a dealer and making the trips to leave it and pick it up. More importantly, a lot of money can be saved by avoiding the expense the shop must pass on to you to cover its labour and overhead costs. An added benefit is the sense of satisfaction and accomplishment that you feel after doing the job yourself.

References to the left or right side of the motorcycle assume you are sitting on the seat, facing forward.

We take great pride in the accuracy of **information given in this manual, but motorcycle manufacturers make alterations and design changes during the production run of a particular motorcycle of which they do not inform us. No liability can be accepted by the authors or publishers for loss, damage or injury caused by any errors in, or omissions from, the information given.**

Illegal Copying

ER-6n (ER650) 2005 to 2008

Introduced in October 2005, the 'naked' ER650 features a compact parallel twin cylinder engine unit housed in a tubular steel frame with offset single-shock rear suspension and conventional telescopic front forks.

The engine is a liquid cooled twin-cylinder with double overhead camshafts driven by chain off the crankshaft. There are four valves per cylinder and valve adjustment is by a bucket and shim arrangement.

The compression ratio is 11.3:1 and cylinder dimensions of 83 mm bore x 60 mm stroke give an engine capacity of 649 cc. The aluminium cylinder block houses plated cylinders and is separate from the crankcase. A balancer shaft is mounted in front of the crankshaft.

The transmission shafts and selector drum are designed as a cassette assembly that can be removed without taking the engine out of the frame. Drive to the six-speed gearbox is by a cable operated, wet multi-plate clutch; drive to the rear wheel is by chain and sprockets, with a cush drive in the rear hub.

Kawasaki's fuel injection system supplies fuel and air to the engine via twin 38 mm Keihin dual valve throttle bodies. An electronic engine management system controls both the injection system and the ignition system. The exhaust system is a two-into-one design with the silencer mounted centrally underneath the engine unit. Kawasaki's 'clean air system' introduces filtered air into the exhaust ports via an electronically controlled valve to promote the burning of excess fuel in the exhaust gases. An oxygen sensor is located in the silencer front pipe and a catalytic converter is located inside the silencer itself.

The engine is housed in a diamond-section steel frame which utilises the engine as a stressed member. Front suspension is by conventional, non-adjustable oil-damped telescopic forks. Rear suspension is by a single shock absorber with adjustable spring pre-load and square-section steel swingarm. The shock is offset to the right-hand side of the machine.

Cast alloy wheels mount twin, floating front discs with a single, conventionally mounted disc at the rear. The discs are of the 'petal' pattern. The front brakes feature dual piston sliding calipers, while a single piston sliding caliper is used at the back. ABS is available as an option.

Although designated a 'naked' machine, the ER650 features a small headlight fairing, two separately mounted side fairings and a belly panel. The instrumentation is located in a pod above the headlight fairing, incorporating an analogue tachometer, digital speedometer and LCD display for fuel, odometer, trip and clock.

ER-6n (ER650) 2009-on

A revised model was introduced in 2009. Visually more angular, it featured a new headlight and LED tail light design, two-piece front mudguard, revised fuel tank, passenger grab-handles and tubular footrest brackets. A number of items, such as the front fork outer tubes, front brake master cylinder reservoir, mirrors and rear turn signal assemblies were re-styled. A D-section steel swingarm was fitted and the design of the chain adjusters was revised.

The upper rear engine mounting and handlebars were rubber mounted and the footrests had rubber grips. A larger front mudguard was fitted and a hugger was located on the swingarm.

Instrumentation featured an analogue speedometer and a digital tachometer. A fuel gauge was added with the addition of a fuel level sensor inside the tank, and a wider radiator was fitted. On all models except those intended for sale in the US and Canada, an oxygen sensor was located in the silencer front pipe and a revised design of catalytic converter was located inside the silencer itself.

ER-6f (EX650) 2006 to 2008

Introduced in January 2006, the EX650 is a fully faired version of the ER650. The engine, transmission and chassis are identical, the only exceptions being minor changes to the steering head angle, longer front forks and stronger fork springs.

The front fairing is a five-piece assembly with windshield, incorporating dual headlights, turn signals and the instrument cluster. The speedometer and tachometer are both analogue instruments with LCD display for fuel, odometer, trip and clock. On all models except those intended for sale in the US and Canada, an oxygen sensor was located in the silencer front pipe and a catalytic converter is located inside the silencer itself.

ER-6f (EX650) 2009-on

A revised model was introduced in 2009, adopting more angular features along similar lines to the 2009 ER650. The modifications to such items as the front forks, swingarm and front brake master cylinder reservoir are all incorporated on the EX650, as are the larger front mudguard and rear hugger.

The fairing belly panel was extended rearwards, a lip was added to the top of the windshield to deflect air away from the rider and an air duct beneath the centre of the windshield was fitted to reduce wind buffeting.

The instrument cluster was fully digitalised, all information being presented by LCD displays. The clock and fuel level are permanent displays.

Dimensions and weights

Overall length
ER650 . . . . .2100 mm
EX650 (2006 to 2008 models) . . . . .2105 mm
EX650 (2009-on models) . . . . .2100 mm
Overall width. . . . . .760 mm
Overall height
ER650 (2006 to 2008 models) . . . . .1095 mm
ER650 (2009-on models) . . . . .1105 mm
EX650 (2006 to 2008 models) . . . . .1210 mm
EX650 (2009-on models) . . . . .1200 mm
Wheelbase
ER650 . . . . .1405 mm
EX650 . . . . .1410 mm
Seat height
ER650 . . . . .785 mm
EX650 . . . . .790 mm
Ground clearance
ER650 . . . . .140 mm
EX650 . . . . .145 mm
Dry weight
ER650A (2006 to 2008 models) . . . . .174 kg (178 kg B model)
ER650C (2009-on models) . . . . .178 kg (180 kg D model)
EX650A (2006 to 2008 models) . . . . .178 kg (182 kg B model)
EX650C (2009-on models) . . . . .182 kg (186 kg D model)

Engine

Type . . . . Four-stroke parallel twin
Capacity . . . . .649 cc
Bore . . . . .83 mm
Stroke . . . . .60 mm
Compression ratio . . . . 11.3 to 1
Cooling system. . . . . Liquid cooled
Clutch . . . . Wet multi-plate
Transmission. . . . . .Six-speed constant mesh
Final drive . . . . .Chain and sprockets
Camshafts . . . . DOHC, chain-driven
Fuel system . . . . .Keihin fuel injection
Ignition system . . . . Computer-controlled digital transistorised
with electronic advance

Chassis

Frame type . . . . Diamond-section steel
Rake . . . . 24.5 mm
Trail . . . . .102 mm
Fuel tank capacity (including reserve) . . . . 15.5 litres
Front suspension
Type .41 mm oil-damped telescopic forks
Travel . . . . .120 mm
Adjustment . . . . None
Rear suspension
Type . . . . . . Single offset shock absorber, tubular steel swingarm
Travel (at rear wheel axle) . . . . .125 mm
Adjustment . . . . .Spring pre-load
Wheels . . . . 17 inch alloys
Tyres
Front 120/70-ZR17 (58W)
Rear 160/60-ZR17 (69W)
Front brake . . . . Twin 300 mm floating discs with twin-piston
sliding calipers
Rear brake . . . .Single 220 mm disc with a single-piston sliding caliper

Professional mechanics are trained in safe working procedures. However enthusiastic you may be about getting on with the job at hand, take the time to ensure that your safety is not put at risk. A moment's lack of attention can result in an accident, as can failure to observe simple precautions.

There will always be new ways of having accidents, and the following is not a comprehensive list of all dangers; it is intended rather to make you aware of the risks and to encourage a safe approach to all work you carry out on your bike.

Asbestos

● Certain friction, insulating, sealing and other products - such as brake pads, clutch linings, gaskets, etc. - contain asbestos. Extreme care must be taken to avoid inhalation of dust from such products since it is hazardous to health. If in doubt, assume that they do contain asbestos.

Fire

● Remember at all times that petrol is highly flammable. Never smoke or have any kind of naked flame around, when working on the vehicle. But the risk does not end there - a spark caused by an electrical short-circuit, by two metal surfaces contacting each other, by careless use of tools, or even by static electricity built up in your body under certain conditions, can ignite petrol vapour, which in a confined space is highly explosive. Never use petrol as a cleaning solvent. Use an approved safety solvent.

● Always disconnect the battery earth terminal before working on any part of the fuel or electrical system, and never risk spilling fuel on to a hot engine or exhaust.

● It is recommended that a fire extinguisher of a type suitable for fuel and electrical fires is kept handy in the garage or workplace at all times. Never try to extinguish a fuel or electrical fire with water.

Fumes

● Certain fumes are highly toxic and can quickly cause unconsciousness and even death if inhaled to any extent. Petrol vapour comes into this category, as do the vapours from certain solvents such as trichloro-ethylene. Any draining or pouring of such volatile fluids should be done in a well ventilated area.

● When using cleaning fluids and solvents, read the instructions carefully. Never use materials from unmarked containers - they may give off poisonous vapours.

● Never run the engine of a motor vehicle in an enclosed space such as a garage. Exhaust fumes contain carbon monoxide which is extremely poisonous; if you need to run the engine, always do so in the open air or at least have the rear of the vehicle outside the workplace.

The battery

● Never cause a spark, or allow a naked light near the vehicle's battery. It will normally be giving off a certain amount of hydrogen gas, which is highly explosive.

● Always disconnect the battery ground (earth) terminal before working on the fuel or electrical systems (except where noted).

Electricity

● When using an electric power tool, inspection light etc., always ensure that the appliance is correctly connected to its plug and that, where necessary, it is properly grounded (earthed). Do not use such appliances in damp conditions and, again, beware of creating a spark or applying excessive heat in the vicinity of fuel or fuel vapour. Also ensure that the appliances meet national safety standards.

● A severe electric shock can result from touching certain parts of the electrical system, such as the spark plug wires (HT leads), when the engine is running or being cranked, particularly if components are damp or the insulation is defective. Where an electronic ignition system is used, the secondary (HT) voltage is much higher and could prove fatal.

Remember...

✗ **Don't** start the engine without first ascertaining that the transmission is in neutral.

✗ **Don't** suddenly remove the pressure cap from a hot cooling system - cover it with a cloth and release the pressure gradually first, or you may get scalded by escaping coolant.

✗ **Don't** attempt to drain oil until you are sure it has cooled sufficiently to avoid scalding you.

✗ **Don't** grasp any part of the engine or exhaust system without first ascertaining that it is cool enough not to burn you.

✗ **Don't** allow brake fluid or antifreeze to contact the machine's paintwork or plastic components.

✗ **Don't** siphon toxic liquids such as fuel, hydraulic fluid or antifreeze by mouth, or allow them to remain on your skin.

✗ **Don't** inhale dust - it may be injurious to health (see Asbestos heading).

✗ **Don't** allow any spilled oil or grease to remain on the floor - wipe it up right away, before someone slips on it.

✗ **Don't** use ill-fitting spanners or other tools which may slip and cause injury.

✗ **Don't** lift a heavy component which may be beyond your capability - get assistance.

✗ **Don't** rush to finish a job or take unverified short cuts.

✗ **Don't** allow children or animals in or around an unattended vehicle.

✗ **Don't** inflate a tyre above the recommended pressure. Apart from overstressing the carcass, in extreme cases the tyre may blow off forcibly.

✔ **Do** ensure that the machine is supported securely at all times. This is especially important when the machine is blocked up to aid wheel or fork removal.

✔ **Do** take care when attempting to loosen a stubborn nut or bolt. It is generally better to pull on a spanner, rather than push, so that if you slip, you fall away from the machine rather than onto it.

✔ **Do** wear eye protection when using power tools such as drill, sander, bench grinder etc.

✔ **Do** use a barrier cream on your hands prior to undertaking dirty jobs - it will protect your skin from infection as well as making the dirt easier to remove afterwards; but make sure your hands aren't left slippery. Note that long-term contact with used engine oil can be a health hazard.

✔ **Do** keep loose clothing (cuffs, ties etc. and long hair) well out of the way of moving mechanical parts.

✔ **Do** remove rings, wristwatch etc., before working on the vehicle - especially the electrical system.

✔ **Do** keep your work area tidy - it is only too easy to fall over articles left lying around.

✔ **Do** exercise caution when compressing springs for removal or installation. Ensure that the tension is applied and released in a controlled manner, using suitable tools which preclude the possibility of the spring escaping violently.

✔ **Do** ensure that any lifting tackle used has a safe working load rating adequate for the job.

✔ **Do** get someone to check periodically that all is well, when working alone on the vehicle.

✔ **Do** carry out work in a logical sequence and check that everything is correctly assembled and tightened afterwards.

✔ **Do** remember that your vehicle's safety affects that of yourself and others. If in doubt on any point, get professional advice.

● If in spite of following these precautions, you are unfortunate enough to injure yourself, seek medical attention as soon as possible.

Frame and engine numbers

The frame number is stamped into the right-hand side of the steering head. The engine number is stamped into the upper crankcase half at the front. Both of these numbers should be recorded and kept in a safe place so they can be given to law enforcement officials in the event of a theft. The VIN plate is on the outside of the right-hand frame beam. The throttle bodies also have an ID number stamped into them.

The frame and engine numbers should also be kept in a handy place (such as with your driving licence) so they are always available when purchasing or ordering parts for your machine.

Model	Year	Initial frame number
ER650-A6	2006	JKAER650AAA000001
ER650-B6 (ABS)	2006	JKAER650ABA000001
ER650-A7	2007	JKAER650AAA030001
ER650-B7 (ABS)	2007	JKAER650ABA030001
ER650-A8	2008	JKAER650AADA00007
ER650-B8 (ABS)	2008	JKAER650ABDA00407
ER650-C9	2009	JKAER650CCDA00001
ER650-D9 (ABS)	2009	JKAER650CDDA00001
ER650-CA	2010	JKAER650CCDA47087
ER650-DA (ABS)	2010	JKAER650CDDA47087
EX650-A6	2006	JKAEX650AAA000001
EX650-B6 (ABS)	2006	JKAEX650ABA000001
EX650-A7	2007	JKAEX650AAA018001
EX650-B7 (ABS)	2007	JKAEX650ABA018001
EX650-A8	2008	JKAEX650AAA036001
EX650-B8 (ABS)	2008	JKAEX650ABA036001
EX650-C9	2009	JKAEX650CCDA21538
EX650-D9 (ABS)	2009	JKAEX650CDDA23433
EX650-CA	2010	JKAEX650CCDA47198
EX650-DA (ABS)	2010	JKAEX650CDDA47258

The procedures in this manual identify models by their production year (e.g. ER650 2006), or where further identification is required, by their model code e.g. ER650-A6.

Buying spare parts

Once you have found all the identification numbers, record them for reference when buying parts. Since the manufacturers change specifications, parts and vendors (companies that manufacture various components on the machine), providing the ID numbers is the only way to be reasonably sure that you are buying the correct parts.

Whenever possible, take the worn part to the dealer so direct comparison with the new component can be made. Along the trail from the manufacturer to the parts shelf, there are numerous places that the part can end up with the wrong number or be listed incorrectly.

The two places to purchase new parts for your motorcycle – the franchised or main dealer and the parts/accessories store – differ in the type of parts they carry. While dealers can obtain every single genuine part for your motorcycle, the accessory store is usually limited to normal high wear items such as chains and sprockets, brake pads, spark plugs and cables, and to tune-up parts and various engine gaskets, etc. Rarely will an accessory outlet have major suspension components, camshafts, transmission gears, or engine cases.

Used parts can be obtained from breakers yards for roughly half the price of new ones, but you can't always be sure of what you're getting. Once again, take your worn part to the breaker for direct comparison, or when ordering by mail order make sure that you can return it if you are not happy.

Whether buying new, used or rebuilt parts, the best course is to deal directly with someone who specialises in your particular make.

The engine number is stamped into the upper front crankcase half

The VIN plate is riveted to the right-hand side of the frame

The frame number is stamped into the right-hand side of the steering head

Note: *These checks are outlined in the owner's manual and covers those items which Kawasaki advise be inspected before you ride the motorcycle.*

Coolant level

> ⚠️ **Warning: DO NOT remove the radiator pressure cap to add coolant. Topping up is done via the coolant reservoir tank filler. DO NOT leave open containers of coolant about, as it is poisonous.**

Before you start

✔ Make sure you have a supply of coolant available (a mixture of 50% distilled or soft water and 50% corrosion inhibited ethylene glycol anti-freeze is needed).

✔ Always check the coolant level when the engine is cold.

✔ Support the motorcycle upright on level ground.

✔ The coolant reservoir is behind the right-hand fairing side panel. On ER650 models the level lines are visible behind the front fork leg. On EX650 models the level lines are visible via the cut-out in the panel. If topping-up is necessary remove the cockpit trim panel or fairing side panel (see Chapter 7).

Bike care

● Use only the specified coolant mixture. It is important that anti-freeze is used in the system all year round, and not just in the winter. Do not top the system up using only water, as the system will become too diluted.

● Do not overfill the reservoir. If the coolant is significantly above the F level line at any time, the surplus should be siphoned or drained off to prevent the possibility of it being expelled out of the overflow hose.

● If the coolant level falls steadily, check the system for leaks (see Chapter 1). If no leaks are found and the level continues to fall, it is recommended that the machine is taken to a Kawasaki dealer for a pressure test.

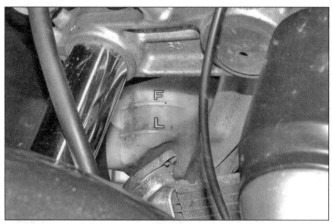

1 The coolant level should lie between the F (FULL) and L (LOW) level lines marked on the reservoir.

2 On EX650 models, the L line is visible via panel cut-out.

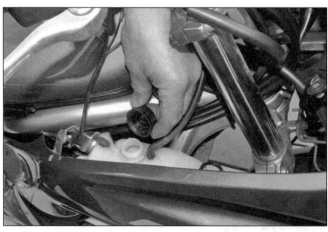

3 If the coolant level is on or below the L line, remove the reservoir filler cap.

4 Top the reservoir up with the recommended coolant mixture almost to the F level line, using a suitable funnel if required. Fit the cap securely.

Engine oil level

Before you start
✔ Support the motorcycle upright on level ground. If the engine has been run allow it to stand undisturbed for a few minutes to allow the oil level to stabilise.
✔ The oil level inspection window is located on the right-hand side of the engine in the bottom of the clutch cover. If necessary wipe the window so that it is clean.

The correct oil
● Modern, high-revving engines place great demands on their oil. It is very important that the correct oil for your bike is used.
● Always top up with a good quality motorcycle oil of the specified type and viscosity, that matches the type and viscosity of the oil already in the engine – do not use car oils and do not overfill the engine.
Caution: Do not use chemical additives or oils labelled "ENERGY CONSERVING". Such additives or oils could cause clutch slip.

Oil type	API grade SE, SF, SG, or API SH, SJ, SL, SM with JASO MA, MA1 or MA2
Oil viscosity	SAE 10W40

Bike care
● If you have to add oil frequently, check whether you have any oil leaks from the engine joints, oil seals and gaskets. If not, the engine could be burning oil, in which case there will be white smoke coming out of the exhaust (see *Fault Finding* at the end of this manual).

1 The oil level should lie between the upper and lower level lines.

2 If the level is on or below the lower line, unscrew the oil filler cap from the clutch cover.

3 Top up the engine with the recommended grade and type of oil almost up to the upper line on the inspection window. Do not overfill. On completion, make sure the filler cap is secure in the cover.

Brake fluid levels

> ⚠ **Warning: Brake fluid can harm your eyes and damage painted surfaces, so use extreme caution when handling and pouring it and cover surrounding surfaces with rag. Do not use fluid that has been standing open for some time, as it is hygroscopic (absorbs moisture from the air) which can cause a dangerous loss of braking effectiveness.**

Before you start:

✔ The front brake fluid reservoir is on the right-hand handlebar. The rear brake fluid reservoir is located below the seat on the right-hand side.

✔ Make sure you have a supply of DOT 4 brake fluid.

✔ Wrap a rag around the reservoir being worked on to ensure that any spillage does not come into contact with painted surfaces.

✔ When checking the fluid in the front reservoir turn the handlebars so the reservoir is level.

✔ When checking the fluid in the rear reservoir support the motorcycle upright.

Bike care:

● The fluid in the front and rear brake fluid reservoirs will drop very gradually as the brake pads wear down. If the fluid level is low check the brake pads for wear (see Chapter 1), and replace them with new ones if necessary (see Chapter 6). Do not top the reservoir(s) up until the new pads have been fitted, and then check to see if topping up is still necessary – this is because when the caliper pistons are pushed back to accommodate the extra thickness of the pads some fluid will be displaced back into the reservoir.

● If either fluid reservoir requires repeated topping-up there could be a leak somewhere in the system, which must be investigated immediately.

● Check for signs of fluid leakage from the brake hoses and/or brake system components – if found, rectify immediately (see Chapter 6).

● Check the operation of both brakes before taking the machine on the road; if there is evidence of air in the system (spongy feel to lever or pedal), it must be bled (see Chapter 6).

FRONT

1 The front brake fluid level is visible through the sightglass in the reservoir – it must be above the LOWER level line.

2 If the level is on or below the LOWER line, undo the reservoir cover screws and remove the cover, diaphragm plate and diaphragm.

3 Top up with new clean DOT 4 hydraulic fluid, until the level is up to the upper level line on the inside of the reservoir. Do not overfill and take care to avoid spills (see **Warning** above).

4 Wipe any moisture off the diaphragm with an absorbent lint-free cloth.

5 Ensure that the diaphragm is correctly seated before installing the plate and cover. Secure the cover with the screws.

REAR

1 The rear brake fluid level is visible through the reservoir body – it must be between the UPPER and LOWER level lines.

2 If the level is on or below the LOWER line, unscrew the cap and remove the diaphragm plate and diaphragm.

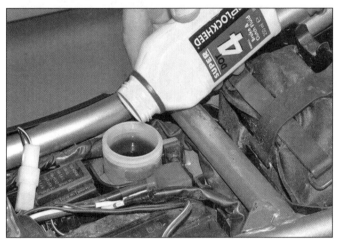

3 Top up with new clean DOT 4 hydraulic fluid, until the level is up to the UPPER line. Do not overfill and take care to avoid spills (see **Warning** on page 0•14).

4 Wipe any moisture off the diaphragm with an absorbent lint-free cloth. Ensure that the diaphragm is correctly seated before installing the plate and tightening the cap securely.

Legal and safety checks

Lighting and signalling:
● Take a minute to check that the headlights, sidelights, tail light, brake light, licence plate light, instrument lights and turn signals all work correctly.
● Check that the horn sounds when the button is pressed.
● A working speedometer, graduated in mph, is a statutory requirement in the UK.

Safety:
● Check that the throttle grip rotates smoothly when opened and snaps shut when released, in all steering positions. Also check for the correct amount of freeplay (see Chapter 1).
● Check that the brake lever and pedal, clutch lever and gearchange lever operate smoothly. Lubricate them at the specified intervals or when necessary (see Chapter 1).
● Check that the engine shuts off when the kill switch is operated. Check the starter interlock circuit (see Chapter 1).

● Check that sidestand return springs hold the stand up securely when retracted.

Fuel:
● This may seem obvious, but check that you have enough fuel to complete your journey. If you notice signs of fuel leakage – rectify the cause immediately.
● Ensure you use the correct grade fuel – see Chapter 4 Specifications.

Tyres

The correct pressures
● The tyres must be checked when **cold**, not immediately after riding. Note that incorrect tyre pressures will cause abnormal tread wear and unsafe handling. Very low tyre pressures may cause the tyre to slip on the rim or come off.
● Use an accurate pressure gauge. Spend as much as you can justify on a quality gauge.
● Proper air pressure will increase tyre life and provide maximum stability and ride comfort.

Front	Rear
32 psi (2.25 Bar)	36 psi (2.50 Bar)

Tyre care
● Check the tyres carefully for cuts, tears, embedded nails or other sharp objects and excessive wear. Operation of the motorcycle with excessively worn tyres is extremely hazardous, as traction and handling are directly affected.
● Check the condition of the tyre valve and ensure the dust cap is in place.
● Pick out any stones or nails which may have become embedded in the tyre tread. If left, they will eventually penetrate through the casing and cause a puncture.
● If tyre damage is apparent, or unexplained loss of pressure is experienced, seek the advice of a tyre fitting specialist without delay.

Tyre tread depth
● At the time of writing UK law requires that tread depth must be at least 1 mm over 3/4 of the tread breadth all the way around the tyre, with no bald patches. Many riders, however, consider 2 mm tread depth minimum to be a safer limit. Kawasaki recommend a minimum of 1 mm on the front and 2 mm on the rear for normal speeds, but note that German law requires a minimum of 1.6 mm for each tyre.
● Many tyres now incorporate wear indicators in the tread. Identify the location marking on the tyre sidewall (either an arrow, triangle, the letters TWI, or the manufacturer's logo) to locate the indicator bar and replace the tyre if the tread has worn down to the bar.

1 Remove the dust cap from the valve, and do not forget to fit the cap after checking the pressure.

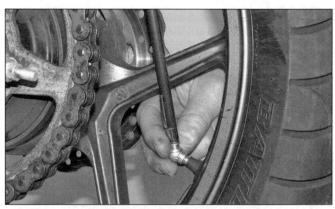

2 Use an accurate gauge and make sure the tyres are **cold**.

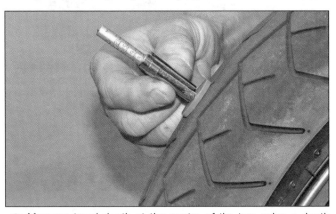

3 Measure tread depth at the centre of the tyre using a depth gauge.

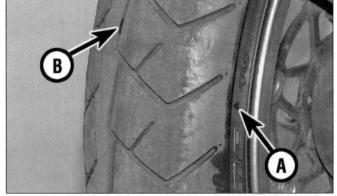

4 Tyre tread wear indicator (B) and its location marking (A).

Suspension, steering and drive chain

Suspension and steering
● Check that the front and rear suspension operates smoothly without binding (see Chapter 1). Adjust the rear shock absorber if necessary (Chapter 5).
● Check that the steering moves smoothly from lock-to-lock.

Drive chain
● Check that the chain isn't too loose or too tight, and adjust it if necessary (see Chapter 1).
● If the chain looks dry, lubricate it (see Chapter 1).

Chapter 1
Routine maintenance and servicing

Contents

Degrees of difficulty

| Easy, suitable for novice with little experience | Fairly easy, suitable for beginner with some experience | Fairly difficult, suitable for competent DIY mechanic | Difficult, suitable for experienced DIY mechanic | Very difficult, suitable for expert DIY or professional 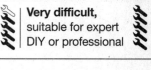 |

Engine

Cylinder numbering	1 left, 2 right
Spark plug type	NGK CR9EIA-9
Spark plug electrode gap	0.8 to 0.9 mm
Engine idle speed	1300 ± 50 rpm
Valve clearances (COLD engine)	
Intake valves	0.15 to 0.21 mm
Exhaust valves	0.22 to 0.31 mm
Throttle body bypass screw setting	0 to 2 1/2 turns out
Throttle body vacuum range at idle speed	255 to 275 mmHg

Cycle parts

Drive chain slack	
2006 to 2008 models	30 to 40 mm
2009-on models	25 to 35 mm
Drive chain 20-link length	
Standard	317.5 to 318.2 mm
Stretch limit	323 mm
Clutch cable freeplay	2 to 3 mm
Throttle cable freeplay	2 to 3 mm
Tyre pressures (cold)	
Front	32 psi (2.25 Bar)
Rear	36 psi (2.50 Bar)
Brake pad friction material minimum thickness	1 mm
Rear brake pedal position (see text)	approx 40 mm below footrest

Lubricants and fluids

Air filter oil	SE, SF or SG class SAE 30
Engine oil	see Pre-ride checks
Engine oil capacity	
Oil and filter change	1.9 litres
Following engine overhaul – dry engine, new filter	2.4 litres
Coolant type	50% distilled or soft water, 50% corrosion inhibited ethylene glycol anti-freeze
Coolant capacity	1.2 litres
Brake fluid	DOT 4
Drive chain	Chain lubricant suitable for O-ring chains or SAE 90 gear oil
Steering head bearings	Multi-purpose grease with EP2 rating
Swingarm pivot bearings	Multi-purpose grease with EP2 rating
Bearing seal lips	Multi-purpose grease
Rear brake pedal/footrest pivots	Multi-purpose grease
Clutch lever pivot	Multi-purpose grease
Sidestand pivot	Multi-purpose grease
Throttle twistgrip	Multi-purpose grease
Front brake lever pivot and piston tip	Silicone grease
Cables	Aerosol cable lubricant

Torque settings

Engine oil drain bolt	30 Nm
Engine oil filter	18 Nm
Rear axle nut	108 Nm
Spark plugs	15 Nm

Note: *Perform the pre-ride inspection at every maintenance interval (in addition to the procedures listed). The intervals listed below are the intervals recommended by the manufacturer for the models covered in this manual.*

Pre-ride

☐ See *'Pre-ride checks'* at the beginning of this manual.

After the initial 600 miles (1000 km)

Note: *This check is usually performed by a Kawasaki dealer after the first 600 miles (1000 km) from new. Thereafter, maintenance is carried out according to the following intervals of the schedule.*

Every 400 miles (600 km)

☐ Check, adjust, clean and lubricate the drive chain (Section 1)

Every 3750 miles (6000 km) or 6 months

☐ Check the brake system and brake light switch operation (Section 2)
☐ Check the brake pads for wear (Section 2)

Every 7500 miles (12,000 km) or 12 months

Carry out all the items under the 3750 mile (6000 km) check, plus the following:

☐ Check the drive chain and sprocket wear and chain stretch (Section 1)
☐ Clean the air filter element (Section 3)
☐ Check the fuel system and hoses (Section 4)
☐ Check the clean air system and EVAP system (Section 5)
☐ Check and adjust the throttle cables (Section 6)
☐ Check and adjust the clutch cable freeplay (Section 7)
☐ Change the spark plugs (Section 8)
☐ Change the engine oil and fit a new filter (Section 9)
☐ Check the cooling system (Section 10)
☐ Check and adjust the engine idle speed (Section 11)
☐ Check throttle body synchronisation (Section 12)
☐ Check the sidestand and starter interlock circuit (Section 13)
☐ Check the headlight and handlebar switches (Section 14)

Every 7500 miles (12,000 km) or 12 months (continued)

☐ Lubricate the sidestand pivot, clutch and brake lever pivots, and the clutch and throttle cables (Section 15)
☐ Check and adjust the steering head bearings (Section 16)
☐ Check the front and rear suspension (Section 17)
☐ Check the condition of the wheels, wheel bearings and tyres (Section 18)
☐ Check the tightness of all nuts, bolts and fasteners (Section 19)

Every 15,000 miles (24,000 km) or two years

Carry out all the items under the 7500 mile (12,000 km) check, plus the following:

☐ Check and adjust the valve clearances – US and Canada models only (Section 20)
☐ Fit a new air filter element (Section 3)
☐ Change the brake fluid (Section 2)
☐ Change the coolant (Section 11)
☐ Re-grease the steering head bearings (Section 16)

Every 26,000 miles (42,000 km)

Carry out all the items under the 7500 mile (12,000 km) check, plus the following:

☐ Check and adjust the valve clearances – Europe models (Section 20)

Every three years

☐ Fit new cooling system hoses (Section 10)

Every four years

☐ Fit new brake hoses (Section 2)
☐ Fit new brake master cylinder and caliper seals (Section 2)
☐ Fit new fuel system hoses (Section 4)

Non-scheduled maintenance

☐ Check the battery (Section 21)
☐ Change the front fork oil (Section 17 and Chapter 5)
☐ Re-grease the swingarm bearings (Section 17 and Chapter 5)

ER650 right side

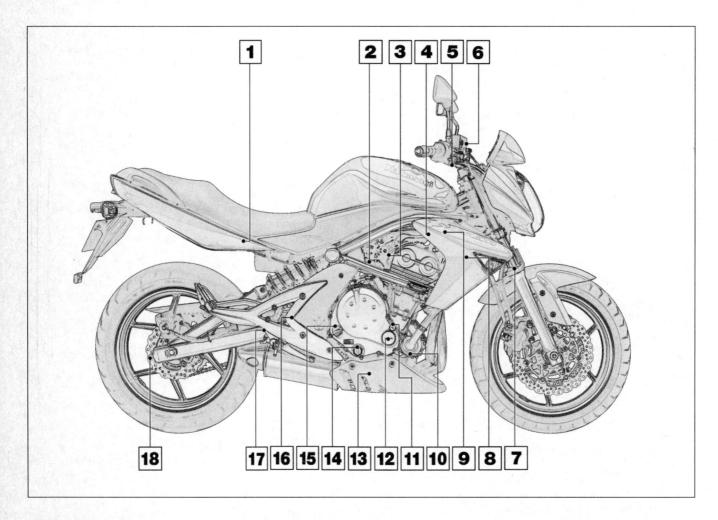

1 Rear brake fluid reservoir
2 Idle speed adjuster
3 Clutch cable in-line adjuster
4 Throttle decelerator cable in-line adjuster
5 Throttle accelerator cable in-line adjuster
6 Front brake fluid reservoir

7 Front fork seal
8 Radiator pressure cap
9 Coolant reservoir
10 Coolant drain bolt
11 Timing mark inspection cap
12 Timing rotor cap

13 Engine oil drain plug
14 Engine oil level inspection window
15 Engine oil filler cap
16 Rear brake light switch
17 Rear brake pedal height adjuster
18 Drive chain adjuster

ER650 left side

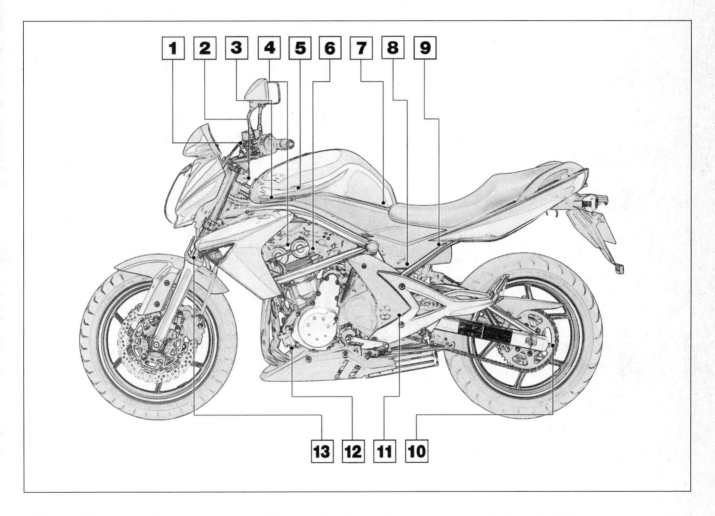

1 Clutch cable upper adjuster
2 Steering head bearing adjuster
3 Clean air system control valve
4 Spark plugs
5 Air filter

6 EVAP canister and separator
  (where fitted)
7 Fuel filter
8 ABS control unit
9 Battery

10 Drive chain adjuster
11 Drive chain slider
12 Engine oil filter
13 Front fork seal

EX650 right side

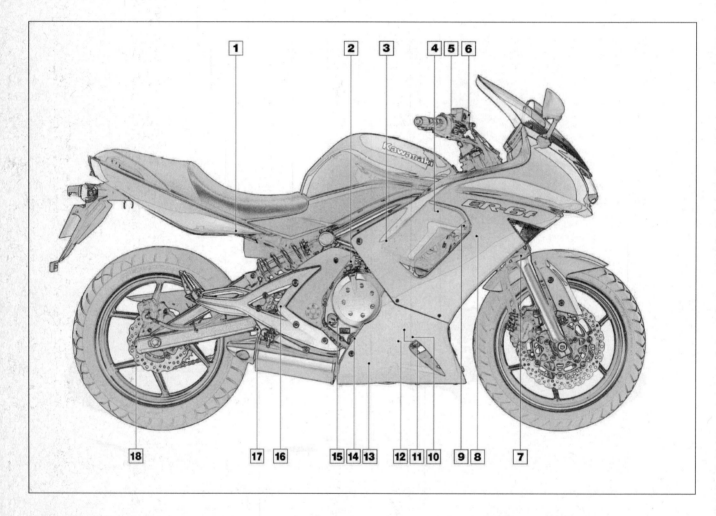

1 Rear brake fluid reservoir
2 Idle speed adjuster
3 Clutch cable in-line adjuster
4 Throttle decelerator cable in-line adjuster
5 Throttle accelerator cable in-line adjuster
6 Front brake fluid reservoir

7 Front fork seal
8 Radiator pressure cap
9 Coolant reservoir
10 Coolant drain bolt
11 Timing mark inspection cap
12 Timing rotor cap

13 Engine oil drain plug
14 Engine oil level inspection window
15 Engine oil filler cap
16 Rear brake light switch
17 Rear brake pedal height adjuster
18 Drive chain adjuster

EX650 left side

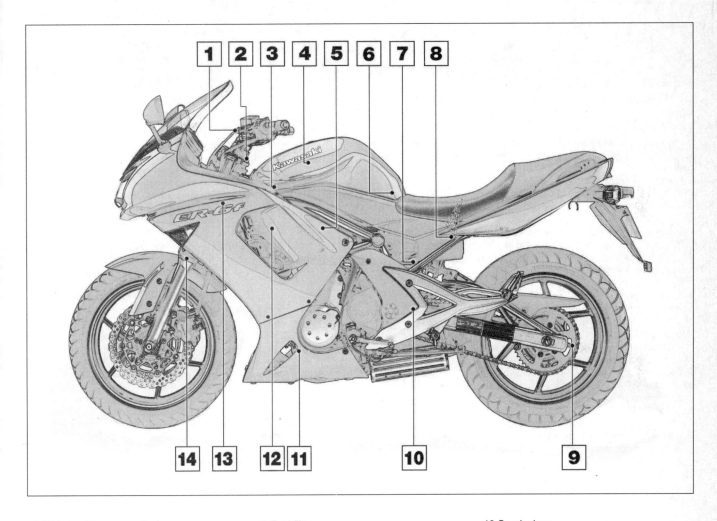

1 Clutch cable upper adjuster
2 Steering head bearing adjuster
3 Clean air system control valve
4 Air filter
5 EVAP canister and separator
  2006 to 2008 (where fitted)

6 Fuel filter
7 ABS control unit
8 Battery
9 Drive chain adjuster
10 Drive chain slider
11 Engine oil filter

12 Spark plugs
13 EVAP canister and separator
  2009-on (where fitted)
14 Front fork seal

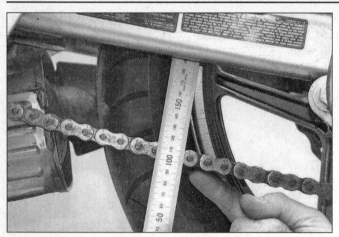

1.3a Hold a ruler midway between the two sprockets . . .

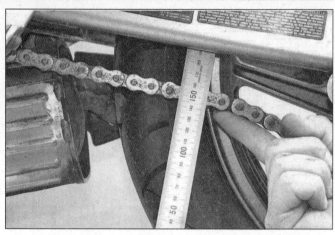

1.3b . . . then push the chain up to measure the slack

1 This Chapter is designed to help the home mechanic maintain his/her motorcycle for safety, economy, long life and peak performance.

2 Deciding where to start or plug into the routine maintenance schedule depends on several factors. If your motorcycle has been maintained according to the warranty standards and has just come out of warranty, start routine maintenance as it coincides with the next mileage or calendar interval. If you have owned the machine for some time but have never performed any maintenance on it, start at the nearest interval and include some additional procedures to ensure that nothing important is overlooked. If you have just had a major engine overhaul, then start the maintenance routine from the beginning. If you have a used machine and have no knowledge of its history or maintenance record, combine all the checks into one large service initially and then settle into the specified maintenance schedule.

3 Before beginning any maintenance or repair, the machine should be cleaned thoroughly, especially around the oil filter, valve cover, body panels, drive chain, suspension, wheels, etc. Cleaning will help ensure that dirt does not contaminate the engine and will allow you to detect wear and damage that could otherwise easily go unnoticed.

4 Certain maintenance information is sometimes printed on labels attached to the motorcycle. If the information on the labels differs from that included here, use the information on the label.

1 Drive chain and sprockets

Check and adjust the chain

Check chain slack

1 A neglected drive chain won't last long and will quickly damage the sprockets. Routine chain adjustment and lubrication isn't difficult and will ensure maximum chain and sprocket life.

2 To check the chain, support the bike on its sidestand and shift the transmission into neutral.

3 Push up on the bottom run of the chain midway between the two sprockets and measure the slack, then compare your measurement to that listed in this Chapter's Specifications **(see illustrations)**. As the chain stretches with wear, periodic adjustment will be necessary (see below).

4 Since the chain will rarely wear evenly, roll the bike forward so that another section of chain can be checked – having an assistant to do this makes the task a lot easier. Do this several times to check the entire length of chain, and mark the tightest spot.

Caution: Riding the bike with excess slack in the chain could lead to damage.

5 In some cases where lubrication has been neglected, corrosion and dirt may cause the links to bind and kink, which effectively shortens the chain's length and makes it tight **(see illustration)**. Thoroughly clean and work free any such links, then highlight them with a marker pen or paint. Take the bike for a ride.

6 After the bike has been ridden, repeat the measurement for slack in the highlighted area. If the chain has kinked again and is still tight, replace it with a new one (see Chapter 6). A rusty, kinked or worn chain will damage the sprockets and can damage transmission bearings. If in any doubt as to the condition of a chain, it is far better to install a new one than risk damage to other components and possibly yourself.

7 Check the entire length of the chain for damaged rollers, loose links and pins, and missing O-rings and replace it with a new one if necessary. **Note:** *Never install a new chain on old sprockets, and never use the old chain if you install new sprockets – replace the chain and sprockets as a set.*

8 Inspect the drive chain slider on the front of the swingarm for excessive wear and damage and replace it with a new one if necessary (see Chapter 5).

Adjust chain slack

9 Move the bike so that the chain is positioned with the tightest point at the centre of its bottom run, then support the bike on its sidestand.

10 Straighten and remove the split pin from the left-hand end of the axle **(see illustration)**. Discard it as a new one must be used. Slacken the rear axle nut.

11 Loosen the locknut on the left and right-hand chain adjusters, then turn both adjuster nuts evenly and a little at a time until the amount of freeplay specified at the beginning of the Chapter is obtained at the centre of the bottom run of the chain **(see**

1.5 Neglect has caused the links in this chain to kink

1.10 Straighten and remove the split pin then slacken the axle nut (arrowed)

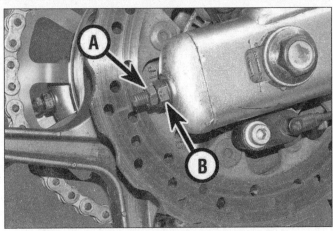

1.11 Adjuster locknut (A) and adjuster nut (B)

1.12a Adjustment index marks – 2006 to 2008 models

1.12b Adjustment index marks – 2009-on models

1.14 Counter-hold the adjuster nut and tighten the locknut

illustration). If the chain was slack turn the adjuster nuts clockwise; if the chain was tight turn them anti-clockwise, then move the wheel forwards in the swingarm to take up the gap between the nuts and the swingarm end caps.

12 Following adjustment, check that the chain adjusters are in the same position on both sides. On 2006 to 2008 models, ensure that the same number of index marks are visible through the axle slots (see illustration). On 2009-on models, ensure that the adjuster plates align with the same index marks on the swingarm (see illustration).

13 If the adjustment is not the same on both sides the rear wheel will be out of alignment with the front (see Wheel alignment in Chapter 6). If there is a difference in the positions of the chain adjusters, adjust one so that its position is exactly the same as the other, then check the chain freeplay again and readjust if necessary.

14 When adjustment is complete, counter-hold the adjuster nuts to prevent them turning and tighten the locknuts (see illustration). Tighten the axle nut to the torque setting specified at the beginning of the Chapter. Recheck the chain adjustment as above.

15 Check the alignment of the hole in the end of the axle with the slots in the nut – they must align to allow the split pin to be fitted (see illustration). If necessary tighten the nut further until the nearest slot aligns with the hole. Fit a new split pin and bend it around the nut as shown (see illustration).

Clean and lubricate the chain

16 Clean the chain using a dedicated aerosol cleaner that will not damage the O-rings, or paraffin (kerosene), using a soft brush to work out any dirt (see illustration). Wipe the cleaner off the chain and allow it to dry,

1.15a Fit the new split pin . . .

1.15b . . . and bend it around the nut as shown

1.16 Using a dedicated chain cleaner and brush

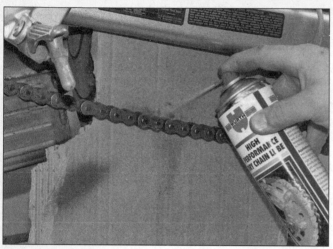

1.17 Apply the lubricant to the area where the sideplates overlap

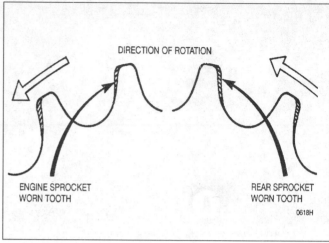

1.19 Check the sprockets in the area indicated to see if they are worn excessively

using compressed air if available. If the chain is excessively dirty, follow the procedure in Chapter 6 to remove it from the machine and allow it to soak in the paraffin or solvent.

Caution: Don't use petrol (gasoline), an unsuitable solvent or other cleaning fluids which might damage the internal sealing properties of the chain. Don't use high-pressure water to clean the chain. The entire process shouldn't take longer than ten minutes, otherwise the O-rings could be damaged.

17 The best time to lubricate the chain is after the motorcycle has been ridden. When the chain is warm, the lubricant will penetrate the joints between the sideplates better than when cold. **Note:** *Kawasaki specifies SAE 90 gear oil or an aerosol chain lube that it is suitable for O-ring chains; do not use any other chain lubricants – the solvents could damage the sealing O-rings.* Apply the lubricant to the area where the sideplates overlap – not the middle of the rollers **(see illustration)**.

HAYNES HINT *Apply the lubricant to the top of the lower chain run, so centrifugal force will work the oil into the chain when the bike is moving. After applying the lubricant, let it soak in for a few minutes before wiping off any excess.*

⚠ *Warning: Take care not to get any lubricant on the tyre or brake components. If any of the lubricant inadvertently contacts them, clean it off thoroughly using a suitable solvent or dedicated brake cleaner before riding the machine.*

Check sprocket wear and drive chain stretch

18 Remove the front sprocket cover and the chainguard (see Chapter 6).
19 Check the teeth on the front and the rear sprockets for wear **(see illustration)**. If the

sprocket teeth are worn excessively, replace the chain and both sprockets with a new set.
20 Measure the amount of chain stretch as follows. Ensure that the chain is clean and lubricated (see above). Support the machine upright on an auxiliary stand, then hang a 10 kg or 20 lb weight from the centre of the bottom run of the chain **(see illustration)**.
21 Measure along the top run the length of 20 links (from the centre of the 1st pin to the centre of the 21st pin) and compare the result to the stretch limit specified at the beginning of this Chapter. Rotate the rear wheel so that several sections of the chain can be measured, then calculate the average. If the chain stretch measurement exceeds the service limit the chain must be replaced with a new one (see Chapter 6). **Note:** *Never fit a new chain on old sprockets, and never use the old chain if you fit new sprockets – renew the chain and sprockets as a set.*
22 Install the chainguard and front sprocket cover (see Chapter 6).

2 Brake system

Brake system check

1 A routine check of the brake system will ensure that any problems are discovered and remedied before the rider's safety is put at risk.
2 Check the brake lever and pedal for loose fixings, improper or rough action, excessive play, bends, and other damage. Replace any damaged parts with new ones (see Chapter 6). Clean and lubricate the lever and pedal pivots if their action is stiff or rough (see Section 15). If the lever or pedal action is spongy, bleed the brakes (see Chapter 6).
3 Check the brake pads for wear (see below) and make sure the fluid level in the reservoirs is correct (see *Pre-ride checks*). Examine the

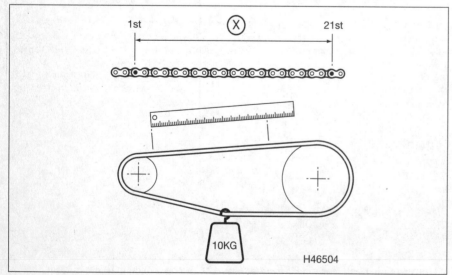

1.20 Measure a 20-link section (X) as shown to determine chain stretch

2.5a Inspect the hose unions (A) and brake hoses (B)

2.5b Check areas of potential hose wear (arrowed)

surface of the brake discs for scoring and check the disc runout (see Chapter 6).

4 Make sure all brake fasteners are tight (see *Torque settings* at the beginning of Chapter 6).

5 Look for leaks at the hose unions and check for cracks in the hoses **(see illustration)**. Check potential areas for hose wear **(see illustration)**.

6 On models with ABS, remove the right-hand fairing side panel and the left-hand frame cover and fuel tank side panel (see Chapters 7 and 4). Check the brake pipes, the pipe joints and the ABS control unit for signs of fluid leakage and for any dents or cracks in the pipes **(see illustrations)**.

7 Make sure the brake light operates when the front brake lever is pulled in. The front brake light switch is located on the underside of the lever bracket **(see illustration)**. The switch is not adjustable – if it fails to operate properly, check it (see Chapter 8).

8 Make sure the brake light is activated after about 10 mm of pedal travel and just before

2.6a ABS system brake pipes (arrowed) are routed below the fuel tank

2.6b Location of the ABS control unit (arrowed)

the rear brake takes effect. The switch is located behind the right-hand footrest bracket – if adjustment is necessary, undo the bolts securing the bracket and displace the bracket (see Chapter 5). Secure the bracket with a cable tie to avoid straining the rear brake hoses. Hold the switch and turn the adjuster nut in the retaining bracket **(see illustration)**. If the brake light comes on too late, turn the

nut anti-clockwise. If the brake light comes on too soon or is permanently on, turn the nut clockwise. If the switch doesn't operate the brake light, check the bulb (2006 to 2008 models), the switch and the circuit (see Chapter 8).

9 The front brake lever has a span adjuster which alters the distance of the lever from the handlebar **(see illustration)**. Each setting

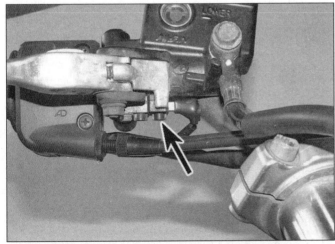

2.7 Location of the front brake light switch (arrowed)

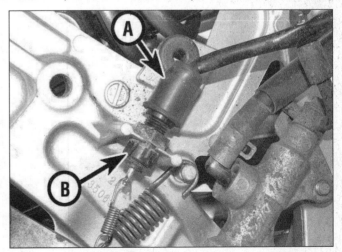

2.8 Rear brake light switch (A) and adjuster nut (B)

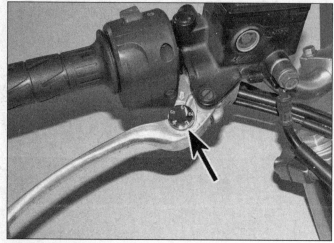

2.9 Front brake lever span adjuster (arrowed)

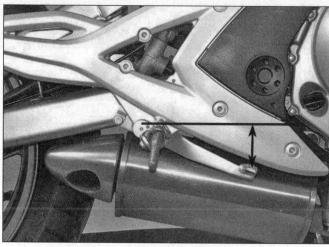

2.10a Measure brake pedal height as indicated

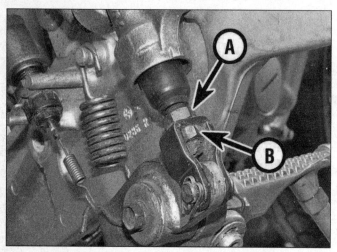

2.10b Pushrod locknut (A) and captive nut (B)

2.11 Location of the brake pad wear indicator (arrowed)

is identified by a number on the adjuster which must align with the arrow on the lever. Push the lever away from the handlebar and turn the adjuster until the setting which best suits the rider is obtained. Setting 1 gives the maximum span and setting 5 the minimum. When making adjustment, ensure that the pin set in the lever bracket is engaged in its detent in the adjuster.

10 Check the position of the rear brake pedal.

2.14 Measuring the thickness of the brake pad friction material

The distance between the top edge of the brake pedal and the top of the rider's footrest should be as specified at the beginning of this Chapter (see illustration). To adjust the pedal position, loosen the locknut on the top of the master cylinder pushrod clevis, then turn the pushrod in or out of the captive nut inside the clevis until the pedal is at the correct height (see illustration). Tighten the locknut securely and check the setting of the rear brake light switch (see Step 8). Note: *Kawasaki give an alternative measurement for adjusting the brake pedal – the distance between the bottom mounting bolt for the master cylinder and the clevis pin (measured centre-to-centre and parallel to the master cylinder centre line) that should be 69 to 71 mm.*

Brake pad wear check

11 Each brake pad has wear indicator cut-outs in the friction material adjacent to the backing plate (see illustration). If the pads are worn down to or beyond the wear indicators, they must be replaced with new ones. Note: *The grooves in the front brake pad friction material are not wear indicators.*

12 Since the wear indicators are difficult to see when the pads are in place it is advisable either to displace the calipers or remove the pads for inspection (see Chapter 6). Note: *Some after-market pads may use different indicators to those on the original equipment pads.*

13 Clean off any accumulation of road dirt and brake dust and examine the friction material as described in Chapter 6.

14 Kawasaki specify a minimum thickness of 1 mm for the friction material (see illustration).

15 If any of the pads are excessively worn, check the corresponding brake disc for scoring (see Chapter 6). If the pads appear to be wearing unevenly, disassemble the caliper and check the operation of the pistons and the condition of the slider pins (see Chapter 6).

Brake fluid change

16 The brake fluid should be changed at the specified service interval or whenever a master cylinder or caliper overhaul is carried out. Refer to Chapter 6, Section 11 for details.

3.2 Disconnect the air system hose from the housing

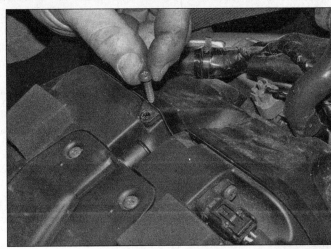

3.3a Undo the screw . . .

Ensure that all the old fluid is pumped from the system and that the level in the fluid reservoir is checked and the brakes tested before riding the motorcycle.

Brake hoses

17 The hoses will deteriorate with age and should be replaced with new ones at the specified service interval regardless of their apparent condition (see Chapter 6).
18 Always renew the banjo union sealing washers when fitting new hoses. Refill the system with new brake fluid and bleed the system as described in Chapter 6.

Brake caliper and master cylinder seals

19 Brake system seals will deteriorate with age and lose their effectiveness. They should be replaced with new ones at the specified service interval and particularly if fluid leakage or a sticking action is apparent.
20 Renew all the seals in each caliper as a set – a rebuild kit for each caliper is available. Master cylinder seals are supplied as a kit

along with a new piston and spring (see Chapter 6).

3 Air filter

Caution: If the machine is continually ridden in wet or dusty conditions, the filter should be replaced more frequently.
1 Remove the fuel tank (see Chapter 4).
2 Disconnect the secondary air system hose from the air filter housing **(see illustration)**.
3 Undo the screw securing the air filter element assembly, then withdraw the assembly from the housing, noting how it fits **(see illustrations)**.
4 Prise off the upper half of the element holder and lift out the filter element **(see illustrations)**. Do not remove the wire screen from the lower half of the element holder.
5 To clean the element, spray it with a dedicated cleaner or wash it in a bath of solvent suitable for foam filters. Next, dry it

3.3b . . . then withdraw the air filter element assembly

carefully using compressed air directed at the rear surface or by pressing it between sheets of absorbent paper.
6 If the element is damaged or ingrained with dirt that cannot be removed, or has reached the end of its service life according to the schedule, replace it with a new one.
7 Once the element is dry, saturate a clean, lint-free cloth with the oil specified at the

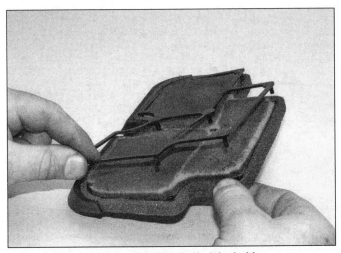

3.4a Remove the upper half of the holder . . .

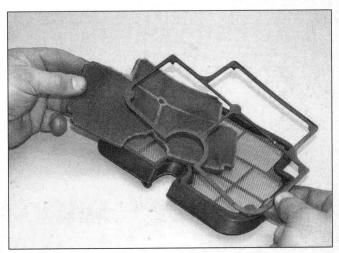

3.4b . . . and lift out the filter element

3.7a Pour filter oil into a shallow tray . . .

3.7b . . . then soak the filter in the oil

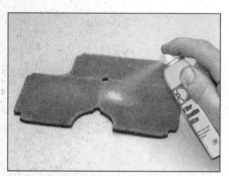

3.7c Apply aerosol filter oil

beginning of this Chapter. Lay the element flat, then press the cloth onto it so that the oil is absorbed into the element. Alternatively, pour a small amount of filter oil into a shallow tray and soak the filter in the oil, or apply aerosol filter oil as directed by the manufacturer **(see illustrations)**.

8 Ensure that the wire screen in the lower half of the element holder is clean and dry, position the element on it then install the upper half of the element holder **(see illustration 3.4b and a)**.

9 Slide the filter assembly into the housing with the wire screen facing rearwards. Make sure the assembly is properly seated and secure it with the screw **(see illustration 3.3b and a)**.

10 Connect the secondary air system hose from the air filter housing **(see illustration 3.2)**.

11 Install the fuel tank (see Chapter 4).

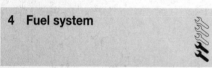

4 Fuel system

  Warning: Petrol (gasoline) is extremely flammable, so take extra precautions when you work on any part of the fuel system.

Don't smoke or allow open flames or bare light bulbs near the work area, and don't work in a garage where a natural gas-type appliance is present. If you spill any fuel on your skin, rinse it off immediately with soap and water. When you perform any kind of work on the fuel system, wear safety glasses and have a fire extinguisher suitable for a Class B type fire (flammable liquids) on hand.

Check the fuel hoses and system components

1 Remove the fuel tank (see Chapter 4) and check the tank, the fuel hose and the tank drain and breather hoses (as applicable) for damage and deterioration. On California models, inspect the EVAP emission control system hoses (see Section 5).

2 Replace any hose that is cracked or deteriorated with a new one. Where appropriate, secure each new hose to its unions using new clips.

3 In particular check that there are no leaks from the fuel hose unions. There are O-ring seals inside the elbows at both ends of the fuel hose – if they damaged or hardened a new fuel hose must be fitted (see Chapter 4, Section 14).

4 Inspect the joints between the fuel rail, the injectors and the throttle body assembly. If there are any leaks, remove the fuel rail and fit new seals and O-rings to the injectors (see Chapter 4).

5 If the joint between the fuel pump mounting plate and the tank is leaking, or, on 2009-on models, the fuel level gauge sensor mounting plate and the tank is leaking, ensure the mounting bolts are tightened to the specified torque setting. If the leak persists, remove the pump or level gauge sensor, and fit a new gasket (see Chapter 4).

Fuel filter

6 Cleaning and inspection of the fuel filter is advised after a particularly high mileage has been covered, although no service interval is

specified by Kawasaki. It is also necessary if fuel starvation is suspected.

7 The filter is integral with the fuel pump – remove the pump from the fuel tank for access (see Chapter 4). It is not available as a separate component. If, after checking all other possibilities, a blocked filter is the cause of fuel starvation a new pump assembly must be installed (see Chapter 4).

5 Clean air system and EVAP system

Clean air system

1 The Kawasaki clean air system is a secondary air system designed to reduce the amount of unburned hydrocarbons released in the exhaust gases. The system consists of the control valve (mounted in front of the air filter housing), the reed valves (fitted in the valve cover) and the hoses linking them. The control valve is actuated by the electronic control unit (ECU).

2 Under certain operating conditions the control valve allows filtered air to be drawn through it to the reed valves and then, via passages in the cylinder head, into the exhaust ports. There the air mixes with the exhaust gases, allowing any remaining particles of fuel in the exhaust to be burnt. This process changes a considerable amount of hydrocarbons and carbon monoxide into relatively harmless carbon dioxide and water. When the control valve closes the air supply is cut off – this prevents exhaust popping when the throttle is closed with high engine revs. The reed valves prevent the flow of exhaust gases back into the control valve and air filter housing.

3 To check the clean air system, first remove the fuel tank (see Chapter 4).

4 Ensure that the hose between the air filter housing and the control valve is in good condition and is securely connected

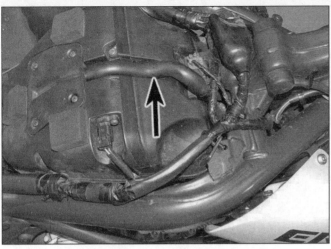

5.4 Check the air system hose (arrowed)

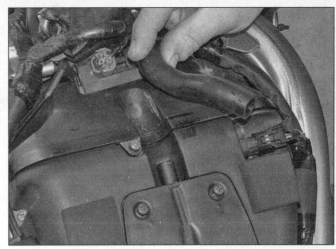

5.5a Disconnect the hose and route it to one side . . .

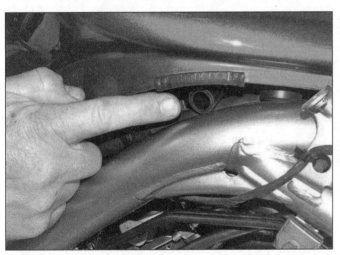

5.5b . . . so that the open end is accessible with the fuel tank installed

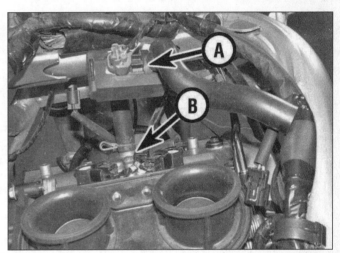

5.7 Location of the control valve (A) and reed valve cover (B)

(see illustration). If the hose is cracked or deteriorated it should be renewed.

5 If the control valve is thought to be faulty, disconnect the hose from the air filter housing and route it to one side so that the open end is accessible once the fuel tank is installed (see illustrations).

6 Install the fuel tank (see Chapter 4). Start the engine and let it run at idle speed, then place a finger into the end of the hose and check for pulsing suction (see illustration 5.5b). If there is no suction, remove the control valve and test it as described in Chapter 4, Section 10 or 11. Note: A failure in the control valve's electric circuit will be identified as a fuel injection system fault (code 64) – see Chapter 4.

7 To check the hose between the control valve and the reed valve cover, first remove the air filter housing (see Chapter 4). The hose should be in good condition and secured to the reed valve cover with a clip (see illustration).

8 The reed valves should be checked for any build-up of carbon by removing the cover

and lifting out the reed valve assembly (see Chapter 2, Section 6). If any carbon deposits are found, clean up the valves and their housings

EVAP system (California models)

Check

9 California models are fitted with an EVAP emission control system that prevents the escape of fuel vapour into the atmosphere by storing it in a charcoal-filled canister. When the engine is not running, excess fuel vapour from the tank passes, via a separator, into the canister. When the engine is started, intake manifold depression to draws the vapour from the canister into the throttle bodies to be burned during the normal combustion process (see illustration). The separator prevents fuel spilling in the event of the bike falling over.

10 Remove the left-hand fairing side-panel (see Chapter 7). Check that the retaining straps for the canister and separator are secure and that the canister and separator are not

damaged. Ensure that the system hoses are in good condition and are securely connected. If any hose is cracked or deteriorated it should be renewed. Note: The separator may contain residual fuel – hold it upright while

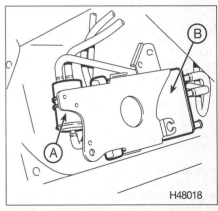

H48018

5.9 Components of the EVAP system

A Separator   B Cannister

6.5 Throttle cable freeplay is measured in terms of twistgrip rotation

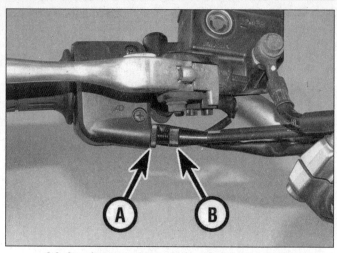

6.6 Accelerator cable lockring (A) and adjuster (B)

6.7 Location of the decelerator cable adjuster (arrowed)

disconnecting it to prevent fuel flowing into the canister.

11 To check the operation of the separator, first disconnect the breather hose from the separator and inject approximately 20 ml of fuel into the separator via the hose union. Now disconnect the return hose from the fuel tank, place the open end in a suitable container, and hold the container level with the top of the tank. Start the engine and let it run at idle speed – if the separator is working correctly, the fuel should come out of the return hose into the container. If not, replace the separator with a new one.

Caution: Fuel vapour is toxic. A small amount of vapour will be present in the system when it is removed from the bike. Take care not to inhale the vapour when checking the separator and canister.

Removal and installation

12 Remove the left-hand fairing side panel (see Chapter 7).

13 Release the clips securing the hoses to the unions on the separator and disconnect the hoses, noting how they fit. Unclip the strap securing the separator to the mounting bracket and remove the separator.

14 Release the clips securing the hoses to the unions on the canister and disconnect the hoses, noting how they fit. Unclip the strap

securing the canister to the mounting bracket and remove the canister.

15 Installation is the reverse of removal

6 Throttle cables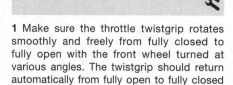

1 Make sure the throttle twistgrip rotates smoothly and freely from fully closed to fully open with the front wheel turned at various angles. The twistgrip should return automatically from fully open to fully closed when released.

2 If the throttle sticks, this is probably due to a cable fault. Remove the cables (see Chapter 4) and lubricate them (see Section 15). Check that the inner cables slide freely and easily in the outer cables. If not, replace the cables with new ones.

3 With the cables removed, check that the twistgrip turns smoothly around the handlebar – dirt combined with a lack of lubrication can cause the action to be stiff. Remove, clean and lightly grease the twistgrip pulley and the inside of the twistgrip housing if necessary. Note: *To remove the twistgrip it will first be necessary to remove the right-hand bar end – see Chapter 5, Section 5).*

4 Install the lubricated or new cables, making sure they are correctly routed (see Chapter 4). If this fails to improve the operation of the throttle, the fault could lie in the throttle bodies. Remove the air filter housing and check the action of the throttle pulley (see Chapter 4).

5 With the throttle operating smoothly, check for a small amount of freeplay in the cables, measured in terms of the amount of twistgrip rotation before the throttle opens, and compare the amount to that listed in this Chapter's Specifications **(see illustration)**. If it's incorrect, adjust the cables as follows.

6 Loosen the lockring on the accelerator (throttle opening) cable and turn the adjuster

in to increase freeplay in the cable **(see illustration)**.

7 Remove the right-hand fairing side panel (see Chapter 7). Displace the coolant reservoir (see Section 10). Locate the adjuster on the decelerator (throttle closing) cable **(see illustration)**. **Note:** *On models equipped with ABS it may be necessary to displace the brake system pipes to access the decelerator cable adjuster (see Section 2).* Ensure the throttle twistgrip is fully closed, then loosen the lockring and turn the adjuster to remove all freeplay in the cable. Tighten the lockring.

8 Now turn the accelerator cable adjuster out until the specified amount of freeplay is obtained, then retighten the lockring.

9 If the cables cannot be adjusted as specified, install a new set (see Chapter 4).

⚠️ *Warning: Turn the handlebars all the way through their travel with the engine idling. Idle speed should not change. If it does, the cables may be routed incorrectly. Correct this condition before riding the bike.*

10 Check that the throttle twistgrip operates smoothly and snaps shut quickly when released. Install the right-hand fairing side panel (see Chapter 7).

7 Clutch cable

1 Check that the clutch lever operates smoothly and easily.

2 If the clutch lever operation is heavy or stiff, remove the cable (see Chapter 2) and lubricate it (see Section 15). If the cable is still stiff, replace it with a new one. Install the lubricated or new cable (see Chapter 2).

3 With the cable operating smoothly, check that it is correctly adjusted. Periodic

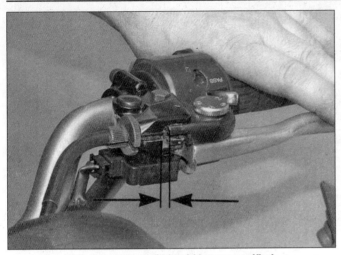

7.3 Gap (arrowed) should be as specified

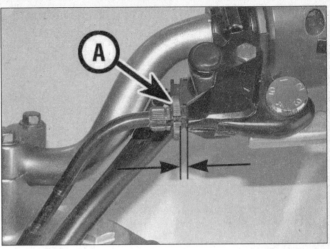

7.4 Turn the adjuster (A) to expose thread (arrowed)

adjustment is necessary to compensate for wear in the clutch plates and stretch of the cable. Pull lightly on the clutch lever until freeplay is taken up, then measure the gap between the inner front edge of the lever and the lever bracket **(see illustration)**. Check that the gap is as specified at the beginning of the Chapter.

4 If adjustment is required, first loosen the lockring on the adjuster at the handlebar end, then turn the adjuster so that 5 to 6 mm of thread is exposed **(see illustration)**.

5 Locate the in-line adjuster on the clutch cable behind the cylinder head **(see illustration)**. On EX650 models first remove the right-hand fairing side panel (see Chapter 7). Loosen the locknut and turn the adjuster until the specified amount of freeplay is obtained at the lever, then tighten the locknut. On EX650 models, install the right-hand fairing side panel (see Chapter 7).

6 When required, further adjustment can be

made with the adjuster at the handlebar end. Don't forget to tighten the adjuster lockring. **Note:** *Ensure the slot in the adjuster is not aligned with the slot in the lever bracket. These slots are to facilitate cable removal – if they are aligned while the bike is in use the cable could jump out. Also ensure the adjuster is not threaded too far out of the handlebar bracket – this will leave it unstable and the threads could be damaged.*

7 The clutch lever has a span adjuster which alters the distance of the lever from the handlebar **(see illustration)**. Each setting is identified by a number on the adjuster which must align with the arrow on the lever. Push the lever away from the handlebar and turn the adjuster until the setting which best suits the rider is obtained. Setting 1 gives the maximum span and setting 5 the minimum. When making adjustment, ensure that the pin set in the lever bracket is engaged in its detent in the adjuster.

8 Spark plugs

Note: *The spark plug caps are integral with the ignition coils. To avoid damaging the wiring, always disconnect the wiring connectors before removing the coils. Do not attempt to lever the coils off the plugs or pull them off with pliers. Do not drop the coils.*

Special tool: *A wire-type feeler gauge is necessary for this job (see Step 10).*

Removal

1 Make sure your spark plug socket is the correct size before attempting to remove the plugs – a suitable one is supplied in the motorcycle's tool kit which is stored under the seat (see Step 5). Make sure the ignition is switched OFF.

2 To access the spark plugs, first remove the

7.5 Location of the in-line clutch cable adjuster

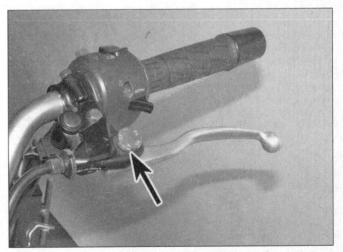

7.7 Clutch lever span adjuster (arrowed)

8.3a Check cylinder numbering on the connector wiring (arrowed)

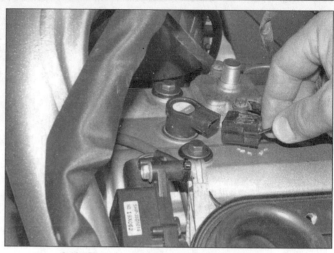

8.3b Disconnect the coil wiring connectors

fuel tank and the air filter housing (see Chapter 4).

3 Check that the cylinder location is marked on both coil wiring connectors and mark them accordingly if not, then disconnect the connectors **(see illustrations)**.

4 Clean the area around the coil seals to prevent any dirt falling into the spark plug channels, then pull the coils off the spark plugs **(see illustration)**. **Note:** *If the coils are stuck in the plug channels squirt penetrating fluid into the gap between the coils and the valve cover, then twist them carefully and ease them out.* .

5 Using either the plug socket supplied in the

bike's toolkit or a 16 mm deep socket type wrench, unscrew the plugs from the cylinder head **(see illustrations)**.

Check

6 New spark plugs should be fitted at the specified service interval (see Steps 11 to 16). However, if a running problem develops between services, check the plugs as follows.

7 Keep note of which cylinder each plug came from, then if either plug shows up a problem it will then be easy to identify the troublesome cylinder.

8 Look for excessive deposits and evidence of a cracked or chipped insulator around the

centre electrode. Compare your spark plugs to the colour spark plug reading chart on the inside rear cover. Inspect the ceramic insulator body for cracks and other damage. Check the threads and the sealing washer.

9 Make sure the plugs are the correct type and heat range as specified at the beginning of this Chapter. Examine the pointed iridium-tipped centre electrode; if the tip has rounded off, the plug is worn **(see illustration)**.

10 Measure the gap between the two electrodes with a wire type gauge only **(see illustration)** – do not use blade type feeler gauges because the iridium tip might be damaged. The gap should be as specified; if the electrodes have worn and the gap is wider, or if the gap is narrower (if the plug has been dropped for instance) a new plug must be installed. Do not bend the outer electrode to adjust the gap.

Installation

11 Always install the correct type and heat range of spark plug for your machine (see *Specifications* at the beginning of this Chapter).

12 Check the gap between the electrodes (see Step 10) and make sure the sealing washer is in place on the plug.

13 Fit the plug into the end of the tool, then use the tool to insert the plug **(see illustration 8.5b)**.

8.4 Pull the coils off the spark plugs

8.5a Using the toolkit plug socket . . .

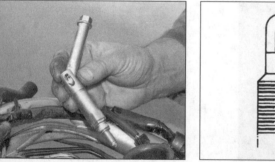

8.5b . . . to unscrew the spark plug

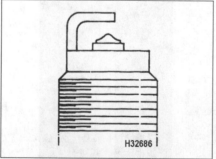

8.9 If the iridium centre electrode has rounded-off the plug is worn

8.10 Using a wire-type gauge to measure the electrode gap

Since the cylinder head is made of aluminium, which is soft and easily damaged, thread the plugs as far as possible into the head turning the tool by hand. Once the plugs are finger-tight, the job can be finished with a spanner on the tool supplied or a socket drive.

HAYNES HiNT *As the plugs are quite recessed, slip a short length of hose over the end of the plug to use as a tool to thread it into place. The hose will grip the plug well enough to turn it, but will start to slip if the plug begins to cross-thread in the hole – this will prevent damaged threads.*

14 If a torque wrench is available, tighten the spark plugs to the torque setting specified at the beginning of the Chapter. Otherwise, tighten them according the instructions on the box – generally if new plugs are being used, tighten them by 1/2 a turn after the washer has seated, and if the old plugs are being reused, tighten them by 1/8 to 1/4 turn after they have seated. Do not over-tighten the spark plugs.
15 Install the ignition coils and connect the wiring. **Note:** *Smear the outside of the coils with copper-based grease to ease future removal because this will prevent corrosion between the coil and cylinder head.*

HAYNES HiNT *Stripped plug threads in the cylinder head can be repaired with a Heli-Coil insert – see 'Tools and Workshop Tips' in the Reference section.*

16 Install the remaining components in the reverse order of removal.

9 Engine oil and filter

Special tool: A filter removing tool is necessary for this job (see Step 6).

⚠️ *Warning: Be careful when draining the oil, as the exhaust pipes, the engine, and the oil itself can cause severe burns.*

1 Regular oil and filter changes are the single most important maintenance procedure you can perform on a motorcycle. The oil not only lubricates the internal parts of the engine, transmission and clutch, but it also acts as a coolant, a cleaner, a sealant, and a protector. Because of these demands, the oil takes a terrific amount of abuse and should be drained and the engine refilled with new oil of the correct type and grade at the specified

Note: *It is antisocial and illegal to dump oil down the drain. To find the location of your local oil recycling bank, call this number free.*

In the USA, note that any oil supplier must accept used oil for recycling.

OIL CARE

0800 66 33 66
www.oilbankline.org.uk

service interval. A new oil filter should be fitted at the same time.
2 Remove the belly panel (see Chapter 7). Warm up the engine so the oil will drain easily.
3 Support the bike in an upright position on level ground and place a drain tray below the engine. Unscrew the oil filler cap from the clutch cover to vent the crankcase and to act as a reminder that there is no oil in the engine **(see illustration)**. Check the condition of the O-ring on the filler cap and replace it with a new one if it is damaged or worn.
4 Next, unscrew the oil drain plug from the sump on the bottom of the engine and allow the oil to flow into the drain tray **(see illustrations)**. Note the sealing washer on the drain plug and discard it as a new one must be fitted – you will probably need to cut the old one off **(see illustration)**.

9.3 Unscrew the oil filler cap

9.4a Unscrew the drain plug (arrowed) . . .

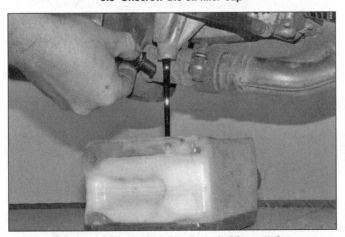

9.4b . . . and drain the oil into a suitable container

9.4c Cut the old washer off with tin snips

To help determine whether any abnormal or excessive engine wear is occurring, place a strainer between the engine and the drain tray so that any debris in the oil is filtered out and can be examined. If there are flakes or chips of metal in the oil or on the drain plug magnet, then something is drastically wrong internally and the engine will have to be disassembled for inspection and repair. If there are pieces of fibre-like material in the oil, the clutch is wearing excessively and should be checked.

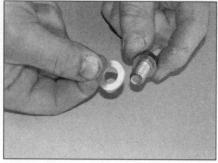

9.5 Always fit a new sealing washer to the drain plug

5 When the oil has completely drained, fit a new sealing washer to the drain plug **(see illustration)**, screw the plug into the sump and tighten it to the torque setting specified at the beginning of this Chapter. Do not overtighten it as the threads in the sump are easily damaged.
6 Place the drain tray below the oil filter on the front of the engine. Clean the crankcase around the filter, then unscrew the filter using

a filter adapter (Kawasaki service tool Part No. 57001-1249, or an aftermarket alternative) **(see illustration)**.
7 Tip any residual oil into the drain tray. Clean any oil off the exhaust pipes to prevent smoking when the engine is started.
8 Lubricate the seal of the new filter with clean engine oil, then screw it onto the engine by hand until the seal seats **(see illustrations)**. Using the filter adapter (DO NOT use a strap or

chain type removing tool), tighten the filter to the specified torque setting **(see illustration)**. **Note:** *Kawasaki stress that the filter must be tightened using the tools described – hand-tightening is not sufficient.*
9 Refill the engine with the correct amount and type of oil (see *Specifications*). With the motorcycle supported upright on level ground, the oil level should lie between the upper and lower level lines on the inspection window (see *Pre-ride checks*). Install the filler cap.

Saving a little money on the difference between good and cheap oils won't pay off if the engine is damaged as a result.

10 Start the engine and let it run for two or three minutes (make sure that the oil pressure warning display and the warning light extinguish after a few seconds). Shut it off, wait a few minutes, then recheck the oil level. If necessary, add more oil to bring the level up to the upper level line on the window but avoid over-filling the engine.

9.6 Use a filter adapter to unscrew the oil filter

9.8a Lubricate the filter seal . . .

9.8b . . . then screw the new filter on by hand

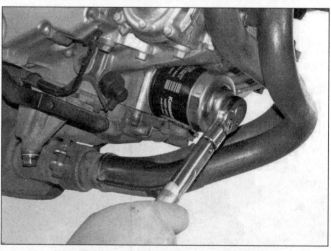

9.8c Tighten the filter to the specified torque

10.3 Inspect all the coolant hoses and clips (arrowed)

10.5 Check the underside of the water pump (arrowed) for leaks

11 Check that there are no leaks from around the drain plug and oil filter. Ensure the filler cap is tightened securely **(see illustration 9.3)**.
12 Install the belly panel (see Chapter 7).
13 The old oil drained from the engine cannot be re-used and should be disposed of properly. Check with your local refuse disposal company, disposal facility or environmental agency to see whether they will accept the used oil for recycling. Don't pour used oil into drains or onto the ground.

10 Cooling system

Check

> ⚠️ **Warning: The engine must be cool before beginning this procedure.**

1 Remove the fairing side panels (see Chapter 7).

2 Check the coolant level in the reservoir (see *Pre-ride checks*).
3 The coolant hoses will deteriorate with age – examine each hose along its length, looking for cracks, abrasions and other damage **(see illustration)**. Squeeze each hose at various points. They should feel firm, yet pliable, and return to their original shape when released. If they are cracked or hard, fit new ones (see Chapter 3).
4 Check for evidence of leaks at each cooling system joint and ensure the hose clips are tightened securely **(see illustration 10.3)**.
5 Check around the bottom of the water pump, which is on the right-hand side of the engine **(see illustration)**. If the pump cover is leaking, check that the bolts are tight – if they are, remove the cover and replace the seal with a new one (see Chapter 3). If the pump-to-crankcase joint is leaking, remove the pump and replace the body O-ring and seal with new ones (see Chapter 3).
6 If coolant is leaking from the drain hole on the underside of the pump, the internal

mechanical seal has failed and should be replaced with a new one (see Chapter 3).
7 Check the radiator for leaks and other damage **(see illustration)**. Leaks in the radiator leave tell-tale scale deposits or coolant stains on the outside of the core below the leak. If leaks are noted, remove the radiator (see Chapter 3) and have it repaired by a specialist. *Caution: Do not use a liquid leak stopping compound to try to repair leaks.*
8 Check the radiator fins for mud, dirt and insects, which may impede the flow of air through the radiator. If the fins are dirty, remove the radiator (see Chapter 3) and clean it using water or low pressure compressed air directed through the fins from the back. If the fins are bent or distorted, straighten them carefully with a screwdriver. If airflow is restricted by bent or damaged fins over more than 20% of the radiator's surface area, replace the radiator with a new one.
9 On 2006 to 2008 models, undo the bolts securing the coolant reservoir and displace the reservoir **(see illustration)**. Locate the

10.7 Inspect the radiator for leaks and damage

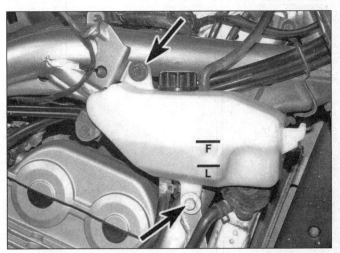

10.9a Undo the bolts (arrowed) securing the reservoir

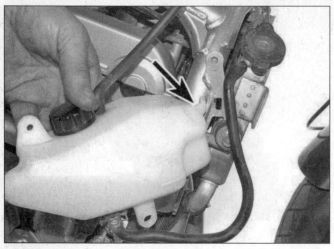

10.9b Locate the projection (arrowed) in the hole in the frame bracket . . .

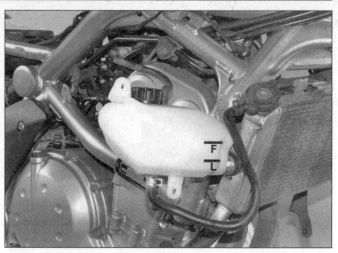

10.9c . . . to temporarily support the reservoir. Note the F and L level lines

10.10 Remove the radiator pressure cap (arrowed) as described

projection on the reservoir in the hole in the frame bracket to temporarily support the reservoir **(see illustrations)**.

10 Remove the pressure cap from the radiator filler neck by turning it anti-clockwise until it reaches the stop. Now press down on the cap and continue turning it until it can be removed **(see illustration)**.

 Warning: Do not remove the pressure cap when the engine is hot. It is good practice to cover the cap with a heavy cloth and turn the cap slowly anti-clockwise. If you hear a hissing sound (indicating that there is still pressure in the system), wait until it stops, then continue turning the cap until it can be removed.

11 Check the condition of the coolant in the system. If it is rust-coloured or if accumulations of scale are visible, drain, flush and refill the system with new coolant (see below). Check the antifreeze content of the coolant with an antifreeze hydrometer **(see illustration)**. If the system has not been topped-up with the correct coolant mixture (see *Pre-ride checks*) the coolant will be too weak to offer adequate protection. If the hydrometer indicates a weak mixture, drain, flush and refill the system (see below).

12 Check the cap seal for cracks and other damage. If in doubt about the pressure cap's condition, have it tested by a Kawasaki dealer or fit a new one.

13 To fit the cap, align the tabs with the cut-outs in the filler neck **(see illustration)**. Press down on the cap and turn it clockwise until it is tight.

14 Start the engine and let it reach normal operating temperature, then check that there are no leaks. As the coolant temperature increases, the electric fan (mounted on the back of the radiator) should come on automatically and the temperature should begin to drop. If it does not, refer to Chapter 3 and check the fan motor and fan circuit carefully. Also, if necessary, check the operation of the thermostat.

15 If the coolant level is consistently low, and no evidence of leaks can be found, have the entire system pressure checked by a Kawasaki dealer.

Change the coolant

 Warning: Allow the engine to cool completely before performing this maintenance operation. Also, don't allow anti-freeze to

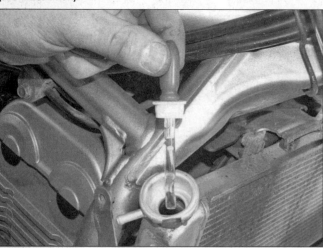

10.11 Checking the coolant antifreeze content with an antifreeze hydrometer

10.13 Align the cap with the cut-outs in the filler neck

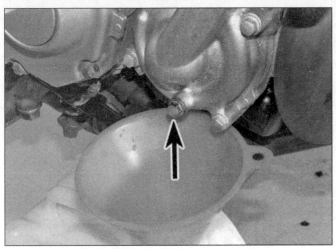

10.18a Unscrew the drain bolt (arrowed) . . .

10.18b . . . and drain the coolant into a suitable container

come into contact with your skin or the painted surfaces of the motorcycle. Rinse off spills immediately with plenty of water. Anti-freeze is highly toxic if ingested. Never leave anti-freeze lying around in an open container or in puddles on the floor; children and pets are attracted by its sweet smell and may drink it. Check with local authorities (councils) about disposing of anti-freeze. Many communities have collection centres which will see that anti-freeze is disposed of safely. Anti-freeze is also combustible, so don't store it near open flames.

Draining

16 Support the motorcycle securely in an upright position. Remove the right-hand fairing side panel and the belly panel (see Chapter 7).
17 Displace the coolant reservoir on all models (see Step 9). Follow the procedure in Step 10 to remove the radiator pressure cap – note the **Warning**.
18 Position a suitable container beneath the water pump. Unscrew the drain bolt and allow the coolant to completely drain from

the system **(see illustrations)**. Retain the old sealing washer for use during flushing.
19 Release the clip securing the overflow hose to the union on the radiator filler neck and disconnect the hose, then unscrew the reservoir cap and drain the coolant into the container **(see illustration)**. Rinse the inside of the reservoir with clean water.

Flushing

20 Flush the system with clean tap water by inserting a hose in the radiator filler neck. Allow the water to run through the system until it is clear and flows out cleanly. If the radiator is extremely corroded, remove it (see Chapter 3) and have it cleaned by a specialist.
21 Ensure the drain hole in the water pump is clear, then install the drain bolt using the old sealing washer **(see illustration 10.18a)**.
22 Fill the cooling system with clean water mixed with a flushing compound **(see illustration)**. Make sure the flushing compound is compatible with aluminium components, and follow the manufacturer's instructions carefully. Fit the radiator cap.

23 Secure the overflow hose to the union on the radiator filler neck, then fill the coolant reservoir to the F level line with clean water and fit the cap **(see illustration 10.9a)**.
24 Start the engine and allow it to reach normal operating temperature. Let it run for about ten minutes, then stop the engine and let it cool.
25 Drain the system (see Steps 17 to 19).
26 Refill the system with clean water only, repeat the flushing procedure, then drain the system, including the coolant reservoir.

Refilling

27 Install the drain bolt using a new sealing washer and tighten it to the torque setting specified at the beginning of Chapter 3 **(see illustration 10.18a)**.
28 Fill the system to the base of the radiator filler neck with the specified coolant mixture **(see illustration 10.22)**. **Note:** *Pour the coolant in slowly to minimise the amount of air entering the system. Squeeze the coolant hoses to expel any trapped air and check the system for leaks. Top-up the radiator if necessary and fit the pressure cap.*

10.19 Drain the coolant from the reservoir

10.22 Filling the cooling system via the radiator filler neck

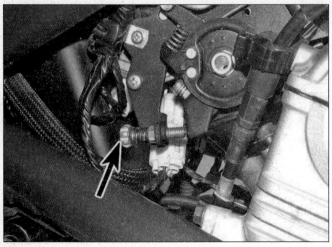

11.3a Location of the idle speed adjuster – ER650 models   **11.3b Location of the idle speed adjuster – EX650 models**

29 Install the reservoir and tighten the mounting bolts securely. Fill the reservoir to the F level line and fit the cap **(see illustration 10.9a)**.

30 Start the engine and allow it to reach normal operating temperature. Let it run until the cooling fan comes on, then stop the engine and let it cool.

31 Check the coolant level in the reservoir and top-up if necessary.

32 Install the fairing side panels (see Chapter 7).

33 Do not dispose of the old coolant by pouring it down the drain. Instead pour it into a heavy plastic container, cap it tightly and take it into an authorised disposal site or service station – see *Warning* above.

Hose renewal

34 The hoses will deteriorate with age and should be replaced with new ones at the specified interval regardless of their apparent condition (see Chapter 3).

11 Idle speed

1 The engine idle speed should be checked and adjusted before and after synchronising the throttle bodies and after checking the valve clearances, and when it is obviously too high or too low. Before adjusting the idle speed, ensure that the valve clearances were checked at the previous service interval, the spark plugs are in good condition and the air filter is clean. Also, turn the handlebars from side-to-side and check the idle speed does not change. If it does, the throttle cables may not be adjusted or routed correctly, or may be worn out. This is a dangerous condition that can cause loss of control of the bike. Be sure to correct this problem before proceeding.

2 The engine should be at normal operating temperature, which is usually reached after 10 to 15 minutes of stop-and-go riding. Place the motorcycle on its sidestand, and make sure the transmission is in neutral.

3 On ER650 models, the idle speed adjuster is located on the right-hand end of the throttle body assembly; on EX650 models, the adjuster is held in a bracket retained by one of the clutch cover screws **(see illustrations)**.

4 With the engine running, turn the adjuster knob until the engine idles at the speed specified at the beginning of the Chapter. Turn the knob clockwise to increase idle speed, and anti-clockwise to decrease it.

5 Snap the throttle open and shut a few times, then recheck the idle speed. If necessary, repeat the adjustment procedure.

6 If a smooth, steady idle can't be achieved, first check the throttle body synchronisation, then the clean air system reed valves and then the valve clearances (see Sections 12, 5 and 20).

12 Throttle body synchronisation

⚠️ **Warning: Petrol (gasoline) is extremely flammable, so take extra precautions when you work on any part of the fuel system.** *Don't smoke or allow open flames or bare light bulbs near the work area, and don't work in a garage where a natural gas-type appliance is present. If you spill any fuel on your skin, rinse it off immediately with soap and water. When you perform any kind of work on the fuel system, wear safety glasses and have a fire extinguisher suitable for a Class B type fire (flammable liquids) on hand.*

⚠️ *Warning: Do not allow exhaust gases to build up in the work area; either perform the check outside or use an exhaust gas extraction system.*

Special tools: *Two vacuum gauges (or a manometer) are necessary for this job. A special screwdriver is required to adjust the throttle body bypass screws (see Step 6). Ideally an auxiliary tachometer with inductive*

pickup is required, although the machine's own tachometer in the instruments should suffice.

1 Throttle body synchronisation ensures each throttle body passes the same amount of fuel/air mixture to each cylinder. This is done by measuring the vacuum produced in each cylinder. Throttle bodies that are out of synchronisation will result in increased fuel consumption, higher engine temperature, less than ideal throttle response and higher vibration levels. Before synchronising the throttle bodies, ensure that the idle speed is properly adjusted (Section 11) and that the valve clearances were checked at the previous service interval (Section 20).

2 Start the engine and let it run until it reaches normal operating temperature, then shut it off. Support the machine upright on level ground using an auxiliary stand.

3 On EX650 models, remove the fairing side panels (see Chapter 7).

4 Temporarily remove the air filter housing (see Chapter 4).

5 Remove the blanking caps from the unions on both throttle bodies and connect the vacuum gauge hoses to the unions **(see illustration)**. Make sure the No. 1 gauge is attached to the No. 1 (left-hand) throttle body. If using an auxiliary tachometer, connect its pickup to one ignition coil primary connector.

12.5 Remove the blanking caps from the unions (arrowed)

12.6a Identify the bypass screws (arrowed)

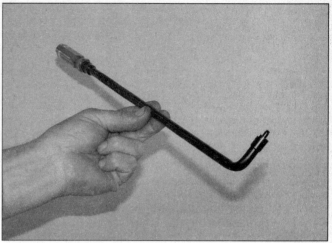

12.6b The screwdriver required to adjust the throttle bodies

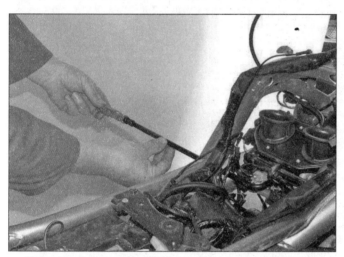

12.6c Aligning the screwdriver from the side of the machine

12.9 Adjusting the vacuum gauge readings

6 Identify the bypass screws on the throttle bodies and ensure that the special screwdriver can reach the screws for adjustment when the fuel tank is installed **(see illustrations)**. Kawasaki produce a service tool (Part No. 57001-1603) to do this.

7 Install the air filter housing and the fuel tank (see Chapter 4).

8 Start the engine and let it idle, making sure the speed is still correct. If the vacuum gauges being used have damping adjustment, set them so that the needle flutter is just eliminated yet they can still respond to small changes in pressure.

9 The vacuum readings for both cylinders should be the same and within the range specified at the beginning of this Chapter **(see illustration)**.

10 If one reading is out of the specified range, use the special screwdriver to turn the appropriate bypass screw in until it seats lightly, then turn it out to achieve the correct vacuum reading.

11 If one reading is slightly higher than the

other, turn the appropriate bypass screw out to reduce the reading until it matches the lower one.

12 When both throttle bodies are synchronised, open and close the throttle quickly to settle the linkage, and recheck the gauge readings, readjusting if necessary.

13 If satisfactory adjustment is not possible, remove the bypass screws as follows and clean them with fuel system cleaner. Remove the air filter housing. Ensure that the area around the screws is clean. Working on one screw at a time, unscrew it all the way. Note the spring, washer and O-ring on the bypass screw.

14 If any of the components are damaged or deteriorated they should be renewed. On installation, turn the screws all the way in until they seat lightly, then follow the procedure in Steps 7 to 12 to synchronise the throttle bodies.

15 When the adjustment is complete, remove the gauges and refit the blanking caps **(see illustration 12.5)**.

16 Install the air filter housing and fuel tank (see Chapter 4), then check the idle speed (see Section 11).

17 Check the output voltage of the main throttle position sensor (see Chapter 4).

18 On EX650 models, install the fairing side panels (see Chapter 7).

13 Sidestand and starter safety interlock circuit

1 Check the stand springs for damage and distortion. The springs must be capable of retracting the stand fully and holding it retracted when the motorcycle is in use. If a spring is sagged or broken it must be replaced with a new one (see Chapter 5, Section 4).

2 Lubricate the stand pivot regularly (see Section 15).

3 Check the stand and its mount for bends and cracks. Stands can often be repaired by welding.

Sidestand	Gear position	Clutch lever	Engine starts	Engine runs
UP	NEUTRAL	RELEASED	YES	YES
UP	NEUTRAL	PULLED IN	YES	YES
UP	IN GEAR	RELEASED	NO	
UP	IN GEAR	PULLED IN	YES	YES
DOWN	NEUTRAL	RELEASED	YES	YES
DOWN	NEUTRAL	PULLED IN	YES	YES
DOWN	IN GEAR	RELEASED	NO	NO
DOWN	IN GEAR	PULLED IN	NO	NO

4 Check the operation of the starter safety interlock system according to the conditions shown in the table.
5 If the system does not operate as described, check the sidestand switch, neutral switch and the clutch switch, and the circuit between them (see *Wiring Diagrams* at the end of Chapter 8), then check the starter circuit relay and diodes (see Chapter 8).

14 Headlight and handlebar switches

Headlight

1 Start the engine and check the operation

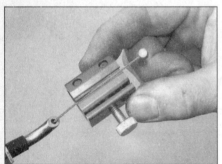

15.5a Fitting the cable lubricating adapter onto the inner cable

of the headlight high and low beams. If one or both lights fail to work, refer to Chapter 8, Section 6, and rectify the fault.
2 Check the headlight aim. An improperly adjusted headlight may cause problems for oncoming traffic or provide poor, unsafe illumination of the road ahead. The headlight beams can be adjusted both horizontally and vertically – refer to Chapter 8, Section 7, for details.

Handlebar switches

3 Check the operation of the handlebar switches, including the engine stop switch. If a switch is thought to be faulty, follow the inspection procedure in Chapter 8, Section 15.

15 Sidestand, lever pivots and cable lubrication

Pivot points

1 Since the controls and components of a motorcycle are exposed to the elements, they should be checked, cleaned and lubricated periodically to ensure safe and trouble-free operation.
2 The footrest pivots, clutch and brake lever pivots, brake pedal pivot and linkage and sidestand pivot should be lubricated frequently. In order for the lubricant to be

applied where it will do the most good, the component should be disassembled (see Chapter 5).
3 The lubricant recommended by Kawasaki for each application is listed at the beginning of this Chapter. If an aerosol lubricant is used, it can be applied to the pivot joint gaps and will usually work its way into the areas where friction occurs, so less disassembly of the component is needed (however it is always better to do so and clean off all corrosion, dirt and old lubricant first). If motor oil or light grease is being used, apply it sparingly as it may attract dirt (which could cause the controls to bind or wear at an accelerated rate).

Cables

Special tool: *A cable lubricating adapter is necessary for this procedure.*
4 Disconnect the cable at its upper end – see Chapter 2 for the clutch cable removal procedure and Chapter 4 for the throttle cables.
5 Attach the pressure adapter and aerosol cable lube **(see illustrations)**. Apply the lubricant – if the adapter leaks, check the installation of the cable and ensure the adapter is tightened securely.

16 Steering head bearings

Freeplay check and adjustment

1 Steering head bearings can become dented, rough or loose during normal use of the machine. In extreme cases, worn or loose steering head bearings can cause steering wobble – a condition that is potentially dangerous.

Check

2 Support the motorcycle upright using an auxiliary stand, then position an additional

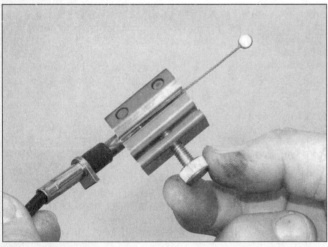

15.5b Ensure the adapter grips the inner and outer cables firmly

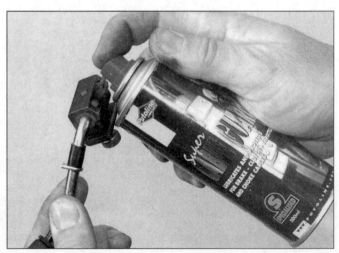

15.5c Connect the can of cable lubricant to the adapter

16.4 Checking for play in the steering head bearings

16.7a Bend the upward-pointing tabs out of the notches in the locknut (arrowed)

support under the engine so that the front wheel is off the ground. Ensure the bike is held securely.

3 Point the front wheel straight-ahead and slowly move the handlebars from lock to lock. Any dents or roughness in the bearing races will be felt and if the bearings are too tight the bars will not move smoothly and freely. If the bearings are damaged they should be replaced with new ones (see Chapter 5). If the bearings are too tight, adjust them as described below.

4 Next, grasp the bottom of the forks and try to move them forwards and backwards **(see illustration)**. Any looseness or freeplay in the steering head bearings will be felt as front-to-rear movement of the forks. If play is felt, adjust the bearings as described below.

Adjustment

Special tool: *A suitably sized C-spanner is required for this procedure (see Step 8).*

5 As a precaution, remove the fuel tank (see Chapter 4) – though not actually necessary, this will prevent the possibility of damage should a tool slip.

6 Follow the procedure in Chapter 5 to displace the handlebars, then displace the front fork top yoke. Note the routing of all cables and wiring around the frame steering head and fork legs

7 Bend the upward-pointing lockwasher tabs out of the notches in the locknut **(see illustration)**. Unscrew the locknut using either your fingers (it shouldn't be tight) or a C-spanner, then remove the lockwasher **(see illustrations)**. Discard the lockwasher as a new one must be used.

16.7b Unscrew the locknut . . .

8 Using a C-spanner, either loosen or tighten the adjuster nut according to whether the bearings were too tight or too loose **(see illustration)**. The object is to set the adjuster nut so that the bearings are under a very light loading, just enough to remove any front-to-rear freeplay (see Step 4). Turn the nut only a little at a time, and after each adjustment check the freeplay.

HAYNES HiNT *Make sure you are not mistaking any movement between the bike and stand, or between the stand and the ground, for freeplay in the bearings. Do not pull and push the forks too hard – a gentle movement is all that is needed. Freeplay between the fork tubes due to worn bushes can also be misinterpreted as steering head bearing play – do not confuse the two.*

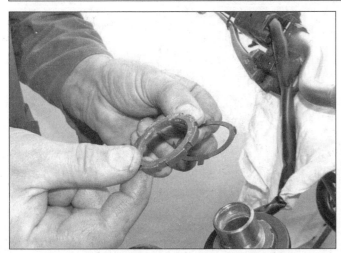

16.7c . . . and remove the locknut and lockwasher

16.8 Adjust the bearings using a C-spanner

Caution: Take great care not to apply excessive pressure because this will cause premature failure of the bearings.

9 Once the bearings seem to be correctly adjusted, turn the steering from lock to lock several times to settle the bearings, then recheck the adjustment.

10 If the bearings cannot be correctly adjusted, remove the steering stem and check the bearings and races (see Chapter 5).

11 With the bearings correctly adjusted, fit the new lockwasher onto the underside of the locknut – align the upward pointing tabs with the slots in the locknut **(see illustration 16.7c)**.

12 Install the locknut on the steering stem and tighten it finger-tight. Now tighten the nut just enough to align its notches with the notches in the adjuster nut, ensuring the adjuster nut does not turn at the same time **(see illustration)**. Secure the locknut in position by bending the outward pointing lockwasher tabs down into the notches in the adjuster nut **(see illustration)**.

13 Follow the procedure in Chapter 5 to install the front fork top yoke and the handlebars. Ensure all cables and wiring are correctly routed around the frame steering head and fork legs

14 Check the bearing adjustment as

16.12a Align the notches in the locknut and adjuster nut

described above and re-adjust if necessary. Install the remaining components in the reverse order of removal.

Lubrication

15 Over a considerable time the grease in the bearings will be dispersed or will harden allowing the ingress of dirt and water.

16 The steering stem should be disassembled periodically and the bearings cleaned and re-greased (see Chapter 5).

17 Suspension

1 The suspension components must be maintained in top operating condition to ensure rider safety. Loose, worn or damaged suspension parts decrease the motorcycle's stability and control.

Front suspension check

2 While standing alongside the motorcycle, apply the front brake and push on the handlebars to compress the forks several times. They should move up-and-down smoothly without binding. If binding is felt, the forks should be disassembled and inspected (see Chapter 5).

3 Inspect the surface of the fork inner tubes for scratches, corrosion and pitting which will cause premature seal failure – if the damage is excessive, new tubes should be installed (see Chapter 5).

4 Carefully lever up the dust seals using a flat-bladed screwdriver and inspect the area around the top of the fork seals. If oil leaks are evident, the fork seals must be replaced with new ones (see Chapter 5). Press the dust seals back into the tops of the fork outer tubes on completion.

5 Check the tightness of all suspension nuts and bolts to be sure none have worked loose,

referring to the torque settings specified at the beginning of Chapter 5.

Rear suspension check

6 Inspect the rear shock absorber for fluid leaks and tightness of its mountings. If leakage is found, the shock must be replaced with a new one or rebuilt by a suspension specialist (see Chapter 5).

7 With the aid of an assistant to support the bike, compress the rear suspension several times. It should move up and down freely without binding. If any binding is felt, the worn or faulty component must be identified and renewed. The problem could be caused by the shock absorber or the swingarm components.

8 Support the motorcycle on an auxiliary stand so that the rear wheel is off the ground. Grasp the top of the rear wheel and pull it upwards – there should be no discernible freeplay before the shock absorber begins to compress **(see illustration)**. Any freeplay indicates a worn spring or shock absorber mountings. The worn components must be replaced with new ones (see Chapter 5).

9 Grasp the rear of the swingarm and rock it from side-to-side – there should be no discernible movement. If there's a little movement or a slight clicking can be heard, check the tightness of the swingarm pivot bolt nut, referring to the torque setting specified at the beginning of Chapter 5. If there is still movement with the pivot bolt tightened correctly it is likely the swingarm bearings are worn..

10 To make an accurate assessment of the swingarm bearings, first remove the rear wheel (see Chapter 6). Remove the lower shock mounting bolt and secure the shock clear of the swingarm (see Chapter 5).

11 Grasp the rear of the swingarm with one hand and place your other hand at the junction of the swingarm and the frame. Try to move the rear of the swingarm from side-to-side. Any wear (play) in the bearings should be felt as movement between the swingarm and

16.12b Bend the outward pointing tabs down

17.8 Checking for play in the shock absorber mountings

the frame at the front. If there is any play the swingarm will be felt to move forward and backward at the front (not from side-to-side).

12 Next, move the swingarm up and down through its full travel. It should move freely, without any binding or rough spots.

13 If the swingarm bearings are worn or if the swingarm does not move freely, new bearings must be fitted (see Chapter 5).

Front fork oil change

14 Although there is no set interval for changing the fork oil, note that the oil will degrade over a period of time and lose its damping qualities. Refer to Chapter 5 for details of front fork removal, draining and refilling. The forks do not need to be completely disassembled to change the oil.

Rear suspension bearing lubrication

15 Although there is no specific service interval for lubricating the bearing in the lower shock mounting and the swingarm bearings, over a considerable mileage the grease in them will be washed out or will harden allowing the ingress of dirt and water.

16 The shock and the swingarm should be removed periodically and the bearings cleaned and re-greased (see Chapter 5).

18 Wheels, wheel bearings and tyres

Wheels

1 Cast wheels are virtually maintenance free, but they should be kept clean and checked periodically for cracks and other damage. Also check the wheel runout and alignment (see Chapter 6). Never attempt to repair damaged cast wheels; they must be renewed if damaged.

2 Check that the wheel balance weights are

18.2 Check the security of the wheel balance weight (arrowed)

fixed firmly to the wheel rim **(see illustration)**. If you suspect that a weight has fallen off, have the wheel rebalanced by a motorcycle tyre specialist.

Wheel bearings

3 Wheel bearings will wear over a considerable mileage and should be checked periodically to avoid handling problems.

4 Support the motorcycle upright using an auxiliary stand so that the wheel being examined is off the ground. Check for any play in the bearings by pushing and pulling the wheel against the hub **(see illustrations)**. Also rotate the wheel and check that it turns smoothly and without any grating noises.

5 If any play is detected in the hub, or if the wheel does not rotate smoothly (and this is not due to brake or drive chain drag), the wheel should be removed and the bearings inspected for wear or damage (see Chapter 6).

Tyres

6 Check the tyre condition and tread depth thoroughly – see *Pre-ride checks*. Check the valve rubber for signs of damage or deterioration and have it renewed if necessary by a tyre fitting specialist. Also, make sure the valve stem cap is in place and tight.

19 Nuts and bolts

1 Since vibration of the machine tends to loosen fasteners, all nuts, bolts, screws, etc. should be periodically checked for proper tightness.

2 Pay particular attention to the following, referring to the relevant Chapter:
- Exhaust system bolts/nuts
- Engine mounting bolts
- Engine oil and coolant drain bolts
- Front axle and axle clamp bolt
- Rear axle nut and split pin
- Handlebar clamp bolts
- Lever and pedal bolts
- Brake caliper and master cylinder mounting bolts
- Brake hose banjo bolts and caliper bleed valves
- Brake disc bolts
- Front fork clamp bolts (top and bottom yoke)
- Steering stem bolt
- Swingarm pivot bolt nut
- Shock absorber and mounting bolts
- Footrest and sidestand bolts
- Front mudguard mounting bolts

3 If a torque wrench is available, use it along with the torque settings given at the beginning of this and other Chapters.

20 Valve clearances

Special tool: *A set of blade-type feeler gauges is necessary for this job* **(see illustration 20.10)**.

Check

1 The engine must be completely cold for this maintenance procedure.

18.4a Checking for play in the front wheel bearings

18.4b Checking for play in the rear wheel bearings

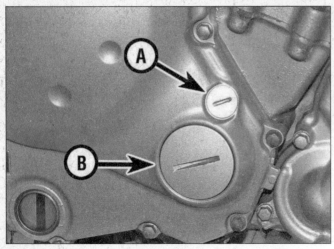

20.6 Timing inspection cap (A) and rotor cap (B)

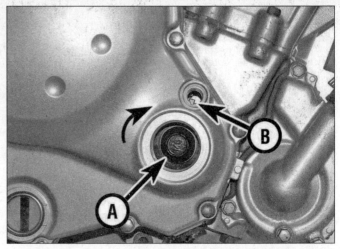

20.8a Turn the rotor (A) clockwise. Align timing mark with notch (B)

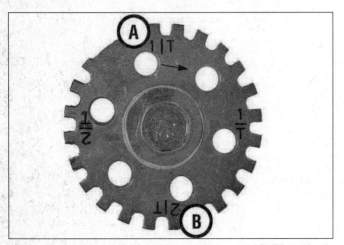

20.8b Timing mark 1/T (A) for No. 1 cylinder and 2/T (B) for No. 2 cylinder

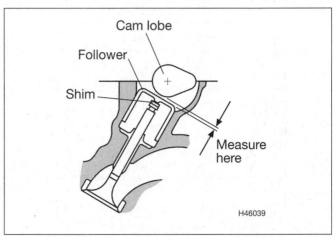

20.8c Camshaft lobe should point away so that clearance can be measured between base circle and follower

2 On EX650 models remove the right-hand half of the belly panel (see Chapter 7).

3 Remove the spark plugs (see Section 8).

4 Displace the throttle body assembly (see Chapter 4).

5 Remove the valve cover (see Chapter 2).

6 Unscrew the timing inspection cap and timing rotor cap in the clutch cover **(see illustration)**. Note the location of the O-rings and discard them if they are damaged or distorted.

7 Make a chart or sketch of all valve positions so that a note of each clearance can be made against the relevant valve. The cylinders are numbered 1 and 2 from left to right, viewed as normally seated on the bike. The intake valves are in the back of the cylinder head and the exhaust valves are in the front.

8 Using a socket spanner on the timing rotor bolt, turn the engine in the normal direction of rotation (clockwise) until the '1/T' timing mark on the rotor aligns with the notch in the lower edge of the timing inspection cap **(see illustrations)**. The No. 1 piston should now be at top dead centre (TDC) with all valves for that cylinder closed – the camshaft lobes should point away from each other **(see illustration)**.

9 With the engine in this position, check the clearances on the No. 1 cylinder intake and exhaust valves.

10 Insert a feeler gauge of the same thickness as the correct valve clearance (see *Specifications* at the beginning of this Chapter) between the camshaft lobe and the follower of each valve and check that it is a firm sliding fit – you should feel a slight drag when the you pull the gauge out **(see illustration)**. If not, use the feeler gauges to obtain the exact clearance. Record the measured clearances on the chart. Note: *The intake and exhaust valve clearances are different.*

11 Now rotate the engine 180° clockwise until the '2/T' mark on the rotor aligns with the notch in the lower edge of the timing inspection cap (see illustrations 20.8a and b). The No. 2 piston should now be at TDC with all valves closed – the camshaft lobes should point away from each other. Check the clearances on the No. 2 cylinder intake and exhaust valves and record them on the chart.

Adjustment

12 When all clearances have been measured and recorded, identify whether the clearance on any valve falls outside the specified range. If it

20.10 Insert the feeler gauge between the base of the cam lobe and the top of the follower as shown

20.15a Lift out the cam follower

20.15b Retrieve the shim from inside the follower . . .

20.15c . . . or from the top of the valve

does, the shim between the cam follower and the valve must be replaced with one of a thickness which will restore the correct clearance.

13 Changing the shims requires removal of the camshafts (see Chapter 2). There is no need to remove both camshafts if shims from only intake or exhaust valves need changing.

14 Place rags over the spark plug holes and the cam chain tunnel to prevent a shim from dropping into the engine on removal. Work on one valve at a time to prevent the possibility of mixing up the cam followers, which must be returned to their original locations.

15 With the camshaft removed, lift out the cam follower of the valve in question **(see illustration)**. If necessary, use a magnet or suction tool (such as a valve lapping tool). Retrieve the shim from the inside of the follower or pick it out of the top of the valve using either a magnet or a screwdriver with a dab of grease on it (the shim will stick to the grease) **(see illustrations)**. Do not allow the shim to fall into the engine.

20.16a The shim size is marked on one face . . .

16 One face of the shim should be marked with a size code **(see illustration)**. A shim marked 95 is 2.95 mm thick **(see illustration 20.17a or b)**. Measure the thickness of the shim with a micrometer to check that it has not worn – if it is undersize, this must be taken into account and the valve clearance adjusted accordingly.

20.16b . . . but check the thickness using a micrometer

17 Using the appropriate shim selection chart, find where the measured valve clearance and existing shim thickness values intersect and read off the shim size required **(see illustrations)**. New shims are available from 2.50 mm to 3.50 mm thick in increments of 0.05 mm. **Note:** *If the required replacement*

	PRESENT SHIM																				
PART No. (92180-)	1014	1016	1018	1020	1022	1024	1026	1028	1030	1032	1034	1036	1038	1040	1042	1044	1046	1048	1050	1052	1054
MARK	50	55	60	65	70	75	80	85	90	95	00	05	10	15	20	25	30	35	40	45	50
THICKNESS (mm)	2.50	2.55	2.60	2.65	2.70	2.75	2.80	2.85	2.90	2.95	3.00	3.05	3.10	3.15	3.20	3.25	3.30	3.35	3.40	3.45	3.50
CLEARANCE																					
0.00 - 0.01	-	-	-	-	2.50	2.55	2.60	2.65	2.70	2.75	2.80	2.85	2.90	2.95	3.00	3.05	3.10	3.15	3.20	3.25	3.30
0.02 - 0.06	-	-	-	2.50	2.55	2.60	2.65	2.70	2.75	2.80	2.85	2.90	2.95	3.00	3.05	3.10	3.15	3.20	3.25	3.30	3.35
0.07 - 0.11	-	-	2.50	2.55	2.60	2.65	2.70	2.75	2.80	2.85	2.90	2.95	3.00	3.05	3.10	3.15	3.20	3.25	3.30	3.35	3.40
0.12 - 0.14	-	2.50	2.55	2.60	2.65	2.70	2.75	2.80	2.85	2.90	2.95	3.00	3.05	3.10	3.15	3.20	3.25	3.30	3.35	3.40	3.45
0.15 - 0.21	CORRECT INTAKE VALVE CLEARANCE																				
0.22 - 0.24	2.55	2.60	2.65	2.70	2.75	2.80	2.85	2.90	2.95	3.00	3.05	3.10	3.15	3.20	3.25	3.30	3.35	3.40	3.45	3.50	
0.25 - 0.29	2.60	2.65	2.70	2.75	2.80	2.85	2.90	2.95	3.00	3.05	3.10	3.15	3.20	3.25	3.30	3.35	3.40	3.45	3.50		
0.30 - 0.34	2.65	2.70	2.75	2.80	2.85	2.90	2.95	3.00	3.05	3.10	3.15	3.20	3.25	3.30	3.35	3.40	3.45	3.50			
0.35 - 0.39	2.70	2.75	2.80	2.85	2.90	2.95	3.00	3.05	3.10	3.15	3.20	3.25	3.30	3.35	3.40	3.45	3.50				
0.40 - 0.44	2.75	2.80	2.85	2.90	2.95	3.00	3.05	3.10	3.15	3.20	3.25	3.30	3.35	3.40	3.45	3.50					
0.45 - 0.49	2.80	2.85	2.90	2.95	3.00	3.05	3.10	3.15	3.20	3.25	3.30	3.35	3.40	3.45	3.50						
0.50 - 0.54	2.85	2.90	2.95	3.00	3.05	3.10	3.15	3.20	3.25	3.30	3.35	3.40	3.45	3.50							
0.55 - 0.59	2.90	2.95	3.00	3.05	3.10	3.15	3.20	3.25	3.30	3.35	3.40	3.45	3.50								
0.60 - 0.64	2.95	3.00	3.05	3.10	3.15	3.20	3.25	3.30	3.35	3.40	3.45	3.50									
0.65 - 0.69	3.00	3.05	3.10	3.15	3.20	3.25	3.30	3.35	3.40	3.45	3.50										
0.70 - 0.74	3.05	3.10	3.15	3.20	3.25	3.30	3.35	3.40	3.45	3.50											
0.75 - 0.79	3.10	3.15	3.20	3.25	3.30	3.35	3.40	3.45	3.50												
0.80 - 0.84	3.15	3.20	3.25	3.30	3.35	3.40	3.45	3.50													
0.85 - 0.89	3.20	3.25	3.30	3.35	3.40	3.45	3.50														
0.90 - 0.94	3.25	3.30	3.35	3.40	3.45	3.50															
0.95 - 0.99	3.30	3.35	3.40	3.45	3.50																
1.00 - 1.04	3.35	3.40	3.45	3.50																	
1.05 - 1.09	3.40	3.45	3.50																		
1.10 - 1.14	3.45	3.50																			
1.15 - 1.19	3.50																				

Example: Present shim is **2.85 mm**
Measured clearance is **0.37 mm**
Replace **2.85 mm** shim with **3.05 mm** shim

20.17a Shim selection chart – intake valves

PART No. (92180-)	PRESENT SHIM																				
PART No. (92180-)	1014	1016	1018	1020	1022	1024	1026	1028	1030	1032	1034	1036	1038	1040	1042	1044	1046	1048	1050	1052	1054
MARK	50	55	60	65	70	75	80	85	90	95	00	05	10	15	20	25	30	35	40	45	50
THICKNESS (mm)	2.50	2.55	2.60	2.65	2.70	2.75	2.80	2.85	2.90	2.95	3.00	3.05	3.10	3.15	3.20	3.25	3.30	3.35	3.40	3.45	3.50
CLEARANCE																					
0.00 - 0.04	-	-	-	-	-	2.50	2.55	2.60	2.65	2.70	2.75	2.80	2.85	2.90	2.95	3.00	3.05	3.10	3.15	3.20	3.25
0.05 - 0.09	-	-	-	-	2.50	2.55	2.60	2.65	2.70	2.75	2.80	2.85	2.90	2.95	3.00	3.05	3.10	3.15	3.20	3.25	3.30
0.10 - 0.14	-	-	-	2.50	2.55	2.60	2.65	2.70	2.75	2.80	2.85	2.90	2.95	3.00	3.05	3.10	3.15	3.20	3.25	3.30	3.35
0.15 - 0.19	-	-	2.50	2.55	2.60	2.65	2.70	2.75	2.80	2.85	2.90	2.95	3.00	3.05	3.10	3.15	3.20	3.25	3.30	3.35	3.40
0.20 - 0.21	-	2.50	2.55	2.60	2.65	2.70	2.75	2.80	2.85	2.90	2.95	3.00	3.05	3.10	3.15	3.20	3.25	3.30	3.35	3.40	3.45
0.22 - 0.31	CORRECT EXHAUST VALVE CLEARANCE																				
0.32 - 0.34	2.55	2.60	2.65	2.70	2.75	2.80	2.85	2.90	2.95	3.00	3.05	3.10	3.15	3.20	3.25	3.30	3.35	3.40	3.45	3.50	
0.35 - 0.39	2.60	2.65	2.70	2.75	2.80	2.85	2.90	2.95	3.00	3.05	3.10	3.15	3.20	3.25	3.30	3.35	3.40	3.45	3.50		
0.40 - 0.44	2.65	2.70	2.75	2.80	2.85	2.90	2.95	3.00	3.05	3.10	3.15	3.20	3.25	3.30	3.35	3.40	3.45	3.50			
0.45 - 0.49	2.70	2.75	2.80	2.85	2.90	2.95	3.00	3.05	3.10	3.15	3.20	3.25	3.30	3.35	3.40	3.45	3.50				
0.50 - 0.54	2.75	2.80	2.85	2.90	2.95	3.00	3.05	3.10	3.15	3.20	3.25	3.30	3.35	3.40	3.45	3.50					
0.55 - 0.59	2.80	2.85	2.90	2.95	3.00	3.05	3.10	3.15	3.20	3.25	3.30	3.35	3.40	3.45	3.50						
0.60 - 0.64	2.85	2.90	2.95	3.00	3.05	3.10	3.15	3.20	3.25	3.30	3.35	3.40	3.45	3.50							
0.65 - 0.69	2.90	2.95	3.00	3.05	3.10	3.15	3.20	3.25	3.30	3.35	3.40	3.45	3.50								
0.70 - 0.74	2.95	3.00	3.05	3.10	3.15	3.20	3.25	3.30	3.35	3.40	3.45	3.50									
0.75 - 0.79	3.00	3.05	3.10	3.15	3.20	3.25	3.30	3.35	3.40	3.45	3.50										
0.80 - 0.84	3.05	3.10	3.15	3.20	3.25	3.30	3.35	3.40	3.45	3.50											
0.85 - 0.89	3.10	3.15	3.20	3.25	3.30	3.35	3.40	3.45	3.50												
0.90 - 0.94	3.15	3.20	3.25	3.30	3.35	3.40	3.45	3.50													
0.95 - 0.99	3.20	3.25	3.30	3.35	3.40	3.45	3.50														
1.00 - 1.04	3.25	3.30	3.35	3.40	3.45	3.50															
1.05 - 1.09	3.30	3.35	3.40	3.45	3.50																
1.10 - 1.14	3.35	3.40	3.45	3.50																	
1.15 - 1.19	3.40	3.45	3.50																		
1.20 - 1.24	3.45	3.50																			
1.25 - 1.29	3.50																				

Example: Present shim is **3.00 mm**.
Measured clearance is **0.37 mm**.
Replace **3.00 mm** shim with **3.10 mm** shim.

20.17b Shim selection chart – exhaust valves

shim is greater than 3.50 mm (the largest available), the valve is probably not seating correctly due to a build-up of carbon deposits or valve damage. Remove the valve for checking (see Chapter 2).

18 When installing a shim, lubricate it with engine oil or molybdenum disulphide oil (a 50/50 mixture of molybdenum disulphide grease and engine oil) and fit it into its recess in the top of the valve with the size code facing up.

19 Check that the shim is correctly seated, then lubricate the cam follower with molybdenum disulphide grease and install it onto the valve.

20 Repeat the process for any other valves as required, then install the camshafts (see Chapter 2).

21 Rotate the crankshaft clockwise several turns to seat the new shim(s), then check the valve clearances again.

22 Install the valve cover (see Chapter 2).

23 If necessary, fit a new O-ring onto the timing rotor cap. Lubricate the O-ring with a smear of engine oil, then tighten the cap securely **(see illustration)**. Lubricate the timing inspection cap O-ring with a smear of engine oil, fit it into the recess for the cap then install the cap **(see illustrations)**.

24 Install the remaining components in the reverse order of removal.

25 On completion, check and adjust the idle speed (see Section 11).

21 Battery

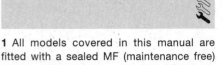

1 All models covered in this manual are fitted with a sealed MF (maintenance free) battery. **Note:** *Do not attempt to remove the battery caps to check the electrolyte level or battery specific gravity. Removal will damage the caps, resulting in electrolyte leakage and battery damage.*

2 All that should be done is to check that the terminals are clean and tight and that the casing is not damaged or leaking. Smear the battery terminals with battery terminal grease or petroleum jelly to deter corrosion.

3 See Chapter 8 for details of battery removal and installation, and charging information.

4 If the machine is not in regular use, remove the battery and give it a refresher charge every month to six weeks.

20.23a Fit the O-ring to the timing rotor cap

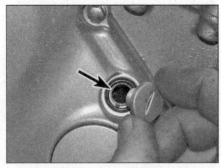

20.23b Install the inspection cap O-ring (arrowed) then fit the cap

Chapter 2
Engine, clutch and transmission

Contents

Degrees of difficulty

Easy, suitable for novice with little experience	**Fairly easy,** suitable for beginner with some experience	**Fairly difficult,** suitable for competent DIY mechanic	**Difficult,** suitable for experienced DIY mechanic	**Very difficult,** suitable for expert DIY or professional

Specifications

General

Type	Four-stroke parallel twin
Capacity	649 cc
Bore	83.0 mm
Stroke	60.0 mm
Compression ratio	11.3 to 1
Cylinder numbering	1 left, 2 right
Camshafts	DOHC, chain-driven
Clutch	Wet multi-plate
Transmission	Six-speed constant mesh cassette type
Final drive	Chain
Cooling system	Liquid cooled
Lubrication	Wet sump pressure fed

Camshafts and followers

Intake lobe height
  Standard... 36.543 to 36.657 mm
  Service limit (min)................................. 36.44 mm
Exhaust lobe height
  Standard... 35.843 to 35.957 mm
  Service limit (min)................................. 35.74 mm
Camshaft journal diameter
  Standard... 23.950 to 23.972 mm
  Service limit (min)................................. 23.92 mm
Camshaft holder bore diameter
  Standard... 24.000 to 24.021 mm
  Service limit (min)................................. 24.08 mm
Oil clearance
  Standard... 0.028 to 0.071 mm
  Service limit (max)................................ 0.16 mm
Runout
  Standard... 0.02 mm
  Service limit (max)................................ 0.10 mm

Cylinder head

Warpage (max).. 0.05 mm

Valves, guides and springs

Valve clearances..................................... see Chapter 1
Stem diameter
  Intake valve
    Standard... 4.475 to 4.490 mm
    Service limit (min)............................... 4.46 mm
  Exhaust valve
    Standard... 4.455 to 4.470 mm
    Service limit (min)............................... 4.44 mm
Guide bore diameter – intake and exhaust valves
  Standard... 4.500 to 4.512 mm
  Service limit (max)................................ 4.58 mm
Stem-to-guide clearance – wobble method (see text)
  Intake valve
    Standard... 0.02 to 0.08 mm
    Service limit..................................... 0.22 mm
  Exhaust valve
    Standard... 0.07 to 0.14 mm
    Service limit..................................... 0.27 mm
Valve margin thickness
  Intake
    Standard... 0.5 mm
    Service limit (min)............................... 0.25 mm
  Exhaust
    Standard... 0.8 mm
    Service limit (min)............................... 0.5 mm
Seat and face width – 2006 to 2008 models
  Intake .... 0.5 to 1.0 mm
  Exhaust.. 0.8 to 1.2 mm
Seat and face width – 2009-on models................. 0.5 to 1.0 mm
Valve seating surface outer diameter
  Intake valve....................................... 32.6 to 32.8 mm
  Exhaust valve...................................... 27.6 to 27.8 mm
Valve spring free length – intake and exhaust valves
  Standard... 41.91 mm
  Service limit (min)................................. 40.3 mm
Stem runout – intake and exhaust valves
  Standard... 0.01 mm
  Service limit (max)................................ 0.05 mm

Cylinder bores

Bore
  Standard... 82.994 to 83.006 mm
  Service limit (max)................................ 83.10 mm
Cylinder compression................................. 139 to 213 psi (9.8 to 15.0 Bar) @ 400 rpm

Pistons

Piston diameter (measured 18 mm up from the bottom of the skirt, at 90° to piston pin axis)
    Standard . . . . 82.969 to 82.984 mm
    Service limit (min) . . . . 82.82 mm
Piston-to-bore clearance . . . . 0.010 to 0.037 mm
Piston ring groove width
  Top ring
    Standard . . . . 0.92 to 0.94 mm
    Service limit (max) . . . . 1.02 mm
  Second ring
    Standard . . . . 1.01 to 1.03 mm
    Service limit (max) . . . . 1.11 mm

Piston rings

Ring end gap (installed)
  Top ring
    Standard . . . . 0.25 to 0.40 mm
    Service limit (max) . . . . 0.70 mm
  Second ring
    Standard . . . . 0.40 to 0.55 mm
    Service limit (max) . . . . 0.80 mm
Ring-to-groove clearance
  Top ring
    Standard . . . . 0.03 to 0.07 mm
    Service limit (max) . . . . 0.17 mm
  Second ring
    Standard . . . . 0.02 to 0.06 mm
    Service limit (max) . . . . 0.16 mm
Ring thickness
  Top ring
    Standard . . . . 0.87 to 0.89 mm
    Service limit (max) . . . . 0.80 mm
  Second ring
    Standard . . . . 0.97 to 0.99 mm
    Service limit (max) . . . . 0.90 mm

Clutch

Friction plate thickness
    Standard . . . . 2.92 to 3.08 mm
    Service limit (min) . . . . 2.8 mm
Plate warpage (max)
    Standard . . . . 0.15 mm
    Service limit . . . . 0.3 mm
Spring free length
    Standard . . . . 33.6 mm
    Service limit (min) . . . . 32.6 mm

Oil pump

Oil pressure (at main gallery, with engine warm) . . . . 31 to 43 psi (2.2 to 3.0 Bar) @ 4000 rpm, oil @ 90°C

Selector drum and forks

Selector fork end thickness
    Standard . . . . 5.9 to 6.0 mm
    Service limit (min) . . . . 5.8 mm
Gear groove width
    Standard . . . . 6.05 to 6.15 mm
    Service limit (max) . . . . 6.25 mm
Selector fork guide pin OD
    Standard . . . . 6.9 to 7.0 mm
    Service limit (min) . . . . 6.8 mm
Selector drum track width
    Standard . . . . 7.05 to 7.20 mm
    Service limit (max) . . . . 7.30 mm

Crankshaft and bearings

Crankshaft side clearance
    Standard... 0.05 to 0.20 mm
    Service limit (max) .... 0.40 mm
Main bearing oil clearance
    Standard... 0.012 to 0.036 mm
    Service limit (max) .... 0.07 mm
Main bearing journal diameter
    Standard
        No mark on crank web .... 37.984 to 37.992 mm
        '1' mark on crank web .... 37.993 to 38.000 mm
    Service limit (min) .... 37.96 mm
Crankcase main bearing bore diameter
    'O' mark on crankcase .... 41.000 to 41.008 mm
    No mark on crankcase .... 41.009 to 41.016 mm
Big-end journal diameter
    No mark on crank web .... 37.984 to 37.992 mm
    'O' mark on crank web .... 37.993 to 38.000 mm
    Service limit (min) .... 37.97 mm
Runout (max)
    Standard... 0.02 mm
    Service limit .... 0.05 mm

Connecting rods

Big-end side clearance
    Standard... 0.13 to 0.38 mm
    Service limit (max) .... 0.58 mm
Big-end oil clearance
    Standard... 0.017 to 0.041 mm
    Service limit (max) .... 0.08 mm
Connecting rod big-end inside diameter
    No mark on side of rod............................. 41.000 to 41.008 mm
    'O' mark on side of rod............................. 41.009 to 41.016 mm

Balancer shaft

Bearing oil clearance
    Standard... 0.011 to 0.033 mm
    Service limit (max) .... 0.08 mm
Bearing journal diameter
    No mark on crankcase .... 27.987 to 27.993 mm
    'O' mark on crankcase .... 27.994 to 28.000 mm
    Service limit (min) .... 27.96 mm
Bearing bore diameter
    'O' mark on crankcase .... 31.000 to 31.008 mm
    No mark on crankcase .... 31.009 to 31.016 mm

Transmission

Gear ratios (no. of teeth)
    Primary reduction .... 2.095 to 1 (88/42)
    Final reduction .... 3.067 to 1 (46/15)
    1st gear... 2.438 to 1 (39/16)
    2nd gear .... 1.714 to 1 (33/21)
    3rd gear .... 1.333 to 1 (32/24)
    4th gear .... 1.111 to 1 (30/27)
    5th gear .... 0.966 to 1 (28/29)
    6th gear .... 0.852 to 1 (23/27)

Torque settings

Alternator cover bolts.................................. 10 Nm
Cam chain tensioner blade pivot bolt .... 20 Nm
Cam chain tensioner cap bolt .... 20 Nm
Cam chain tensioner mounting bolts................... 10 Nm
Camshaft holder bolts................................. 12 Nm
Camshaft sprocket bolts .... 15 Nm
Clutch cover bolts.................................... 10 Nm
Clutch centre nut .... 132 Nm
Clutch spring bolts................................... 10 Nm

Torque settings (continued)

Connecting rod bolt nuts
New con-rod* with attached new bolts and nuts.	18 Nm +120°
New con-rod* with attached new bolts and separate new nuts	20 Nm +120°
Old con-rod with new bolts and new nuts.	25 Nm +120°
Old con-rod with new bolts and old nuts.	24 Nm +120°

New con-rods are supplied either with the bolts attached and the nuts threaded loosely onto them, or with the bolts attached and the nuts separate.

Crankcase bolts	
Lower crankcase 9 mm bolts.	44 Nm
Lower crankcase balancer shaft journal 8 mm bolts	35 Nm
Lower crankcase 8 mm bolts.	27 Nm
Lower crankcase 6 mm bolts.	20 Nm
Upper crankcase bolts	27 Nm
Cylinder block 10 mm nut	49 Nm
Cylinder block 8 mm bolt	28 Nm
Cylinder block 6 mm bolts	12 Nm
Cylinder head 10 mm bolts	
Initial setting	25 Nm
Final setting	
Used bolts.	54 Nm
New bolts	60 Nm
Cylinder head 6 mm bolts	12 Nm
Engine mountings	
Engine bracket bolts.	25 Nm
Front mounting bolts	44 Nm
Rear mounting bolt nuts	44 Nm
Gearchange mechanism cover bolts	10 Nm
Gearchange shaft return spring pin	29 Nm
Gearchange stopper arm bolt	12 Nm
Oil gallery plug (oil pressure check take-off point).	20 Nm
Oil pipe retainer bolt.	10 Nm
Oil gallery bolts.	10 Nm
Oil pressure relief valve	15 Nm
Oil pressure switch.	15 Nm
Oil filter mounting.	25 Nm
Oil internal filter plate bolts.	10 Nm
Oil pump chain guide bolts	12 Nm
Oil pump cover bolts	10 Nm
Oil pump sprocket bolt.	12 Nm
Oil sump bolts	12 Nm
Selector pin/neutral contact plate screw	5 Nm
Selector drum cam bolt	12 Nm
Selector fork shaft retainer plate bolt.	10 Nm
Starter clutch bolts.	34 Nm
Reed valve housing bolts	10 Nm
Timing rotor bolt.	40 Nm
Transmission cover bolts	20 Nm
Valve cover bolts	10 Nm

1 General information

The engine is a liquid-cooled, parallel twin cylinder unit. The valves, four per cylinder, are operated by double overhead camshafts which are chain driven off the right-hand end of the crankshaft. A gear driven balancer shaft is located in the front of the crankcases.

The crankcase incorporates a wet sump and pressure-fed lubrication system which uses a dual rotor trochoidal pump. The pump is chain-driven off the back of the clutch. The system has an oil strainer in the pick-up, a pressure relief valve in the feed from the pump to the filter and an oil pressure switch off the main gallery.

The alternator is on the left-hand end of the crankshaft and the rotor incorporates the starter clutch. The water pump is on the right-hand side of the crankcase and is driven by the balancer shaft.

Power from the crankshaft is routed to the transmission via the clutch. The clutch is of the wet, multi-plate type and is gear-driven off the crankshaft. The clutch is operated by cable. The transmission is a six-speed, constant-mesh type housed within the crankcases. The cassette type transmission assembly can be removed from the right-hand side of the engine unit without having to split the crankcases.

Final drive to the rear wheel is by chain and sprockets.

2 Component access

Operations possible with the engine in the frame

The components and assemblies listed below can be removed without having to remove the engine from the frame. If however, a number of areas require attention at the same time, removal of the engine is recommended.

Valve cover
Cam chain tensioner and blades
Camshafts
Cylinder head
Cylinder bock
Pistons
Starter motor and alternator (see Chapter 8)
Starter clutch and idler gear
Clutch
Gearchange mechanism
Transmission shafts and gears
Selector drum and forks
Oil sump, oil strainer and oil pressure
    relief valve
Oil pump
Water pump (see Chapter 3)

Operations requiring engine removal

It is necessary to remove the engine from the frame to gain access to the following components.

Connecting rods
Crankshaft and bearings
Cam chain
Balancer shaft

3 Engine wear assessment

Cylinder compression check

Special tool: *A compression gauge with a suitable adaptor (10 mm x 1.0 pitch) is required for this test (see Step 4). Kawasaki produces a gauge and adapter (Part Nos. 57001-221 and 57001-1317) for this purpose.*

1 Poor engine performance, exhaust smoke, heavy oil consumption and poor starting are indications of low compression. This may be caused by leaking valve stem seals, incorrect valve clearances, a leaking head gasket, or worn pistons, rings and/or cylinder walls.
2 Before you start, make sure the valve clearances are correctly set (see Chapter 1).
3 Run the engine until it reaches normal operating temperature. Stop the engine, then follow the procedure in Chapter 1 to remove the spark plugs, taking care not to burn your hands on the hot components.
4 Fit the adaptor and gauge into the No. 1 cylinder spark plug hole **(see illustration)**. Place a rag over the open No. 2 cylinder spark plug hole to prevent atomised fuel escaping. Temporarily connect the intake air temperature sensor wiring connector.
5 Turn the ignition ON and open the throttle fully. Crank the engine over on the starter motor for a few seconds until the gauge reading stabilises and take a note of the reading. Turn the ignition OFF. Transfer the compression gauge and adaptor to the other cylinder and repeat the procedure.
6 Compare the readings obtained with those in the *Specifications* at the beginning of this Chapter. If they fall within the specified range and are relatively equal, the engine is in good condition. Install the components in the reverse order of removal.
7 If the readings are close to or below the minimum limit, or one cylinder differs markedly from the other, further investigation is required. To determine the cause of low compression, inject a small quantity of engine oil into the spark plug hole of the suspect cylinder with a pump-type oil can – this will temporarily seal the piston rings. Repeat the compression test. If the result shows a noticeable increase in pressure this confirms that the cylinder bore, piston or rings are worn (see Sections 12 to 14). If there is no change in the reading, the cylinder head gasket or valves are leaking (see Sections 10 and 11).
8 Although unlikely with the use of modern fuels, a high compression reading indicates excessive carbon deposits in the combustion chamber area. Remove the cylinder head and clean all carbon off the pistons, head and valves (see Sections 10 and 11).

Engine oil pressure check

Special tool: *An oil pressure gauge and adapter (PT 3/8x10) are required for this test. Kawasaki produces a gauge and adapter (Part Nos. 57001-164 and 57001-1233) for this purpose.*
Note: *Always ensure that the recommended grade and type of oil are used in your motorcycle (see Pre-ride checks).*
9 The oil pressure warning light should come on when the ignition switch is turned ON, and should go out when the engine is started – this serves as a check that the LED is sound. If the light does not go out when the engine is started, or if it comes on when the engine is running, low oil pressure is indicated – stop the engine immediately and firstly carry out an oil level check (see *Pre-ride checks*).
10 If the oil level is good, check the operation of the oil pressure switch (see Chapter 8). If the switch is good, check the oil pressure as follows. **Note:** *An oil pressure check will provide useful information about the condition of the engine's lubrication system.*
11 Remove the belly panel (see Chapter 7).
12 Position a suitable container below the main oil gallery plug on the right-hand side of the engine to catch any residual oil **(see illustration)**. Unscrew the plug and screw the gauge adapter into the crankcase threads, then connect the hose and gauge to the adapter **(see illustration)**. If much oil is lost, top-up to the correct level before proceeding (see **Note** above).
13 Warm the engine up to normal operating temperature (between 10 and 20 minutes running at 2000 rpm) then increase the engine speed to 4000 rpm whilst watching the gauge reading. The oil pressure should be similar to that given in *Specifications* at the beginning of this Chapter.
14 If the pressure is significantly lower than standard, the oil filter or strainer is blocked, the pressure relief valve is stuck open, the oil pump is faulty, or there is other engine damage. Begin diagnosis by checking the oil filter, strainer and relief valve, then the oil pump (see Sections 19 and 20). If those items are good, it is likely the crankshaft bearing oil clearances are excessive and the engine needs to be overhauled.
15 If the pressure is too high, an oil passage

3.4 Compression check set-up

3.12a Location of the main oil gallery plug (arrowed)

3.12b Oil pressure check set-up

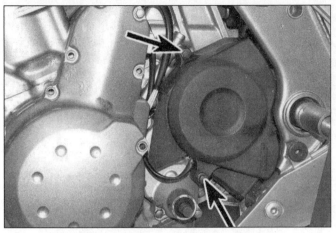

4.4 Bolts (arrowed) secure front sprocket cover

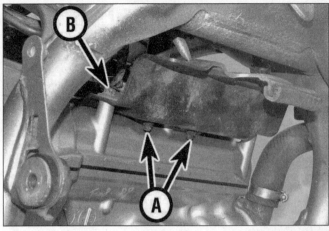

4.10a Release the wiring clips (A). Undo the right-hand mounting bolt (B)

is clogged, the relief valve is stuck closed or the wrong grade of oil is being used.

16 Turn the engine OFF. Disconnect the hose and gauge from the adapter and unscrew the adapter from the crankcase.

⚠️ *Warning: Be careful when removing the pressure gauge adapter as the exhaust pipes, the engine and the oil itself can cause severe burns.*

17 Apply a suitable non-permanent silicone sealant to the oil gallery plug threads, then screw it into the engine and tighten it to the torque setting specified at the beginning of this Chapter.

18 Check the engine oil level (see *Pre-ride checks*).

19 Install the belly panel (See Chapter 7).

4 Engine removal and installation

Caution: The engine is very heavy. Engine removal and installation should be carried out with the aid of at least one assistant; personal injury or damage could occur if the engine falls or is dropped. If available, an hydraulic or mechanical floor jack should be used to support and lower or raise the engine.

Removal

1 Support the bike securely in an upright position using the centre stand or an auxiliary stand. Work can be made easier by raising the machine to a suitable working height on an hydraulic ramp or a suitable platform.

2 Remove the seat, belly panel, fairing side panels and frame covers (see Chapter 7).

3 Disconnect the negative (-ve) lead from the battery (see Chapter 8).

4 Undo the bolts securing the front sprocket cover and remove the cover **(see illustration)**.

5 Remove the gearchange lever (see Section 18).

6 If the engine is dirty, particularly around its

4.10b Undo the left-hand mounting bolt

mountings, clean it thoroughly before starting any major dismantling. This will make work much easier and rule out the possibility of dirt falling into some vital component.

7 Drain the engine oil – if required remove the oil filter (see Chapter 1).

8 Remove the exhaust system (see Chapter 4).

9 Drain the coolant and remove the reservoir tank (see Chapter 1).

10 Remove the radiator and the radiator hoses (see Chapter 3). Release the wiring loom clips from the baffle plate, then undo the bolts securing the baffle plate to the front of the valve cover and lift the baffle plate off **(see illustrations)**.

11 Remove the fuel tank, the air filter housing and the throttle bodies (see Chapter 4). Plug

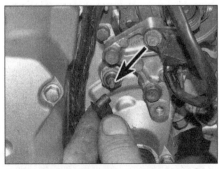

4.15 Disconnect the connector from the neutral switch (arrowed)

4.10c Lift the baffle plate off

the engine intake manifolds with clean rag.

12 Remove the clean air system control valve (see Chapter 4).

13 Check that the cylinder location is marked on both ignition coil wiring connectors and mark them accordingly if not. Disconnect the connectors and pull the coils off the spark plugs (see Chapter 1).

14 Refer to Section 17 and detach the clutch cable from the clutch actuating arm and the cable stop on the top of the engine unit. Position the cable clear of the engine unit.

15 Disconnect the neutral switch wiring connector **(see illustration)**.

16 Undo the bolts securing the speed sensor bracket and displace the bracket **(see illustration)**.

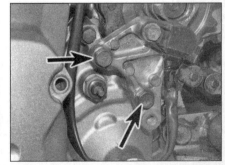

4.16 Speed sensor bracket bolts (arrowed)

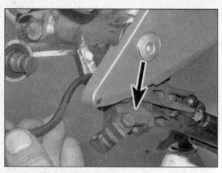

4.18a Trace the wiring from the sidestand switch (arrowed) . . .

4.18b . . . and disconnect it at the connector

4.18c Disconnect the alternator wiring connector

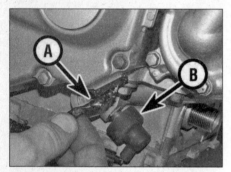

4.19a Wiring for the crankshaft position sensor (A) and oil pressure switch (B)

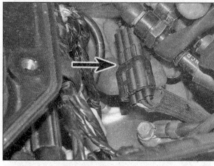

4.19b Crankshaft position sensor and oil pressure switch wiring connector

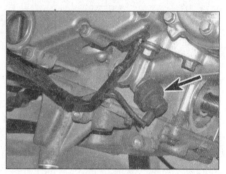

4.19c Displace the rubber boot (arrowed) . . .

4.19d . . . and disconnect the wiring connector

4.19e Unscrew the oil pressure switch

17 Remove the front sprocket (see Chapter 6). Rest the drive chain over the chain slider on the swingarm.
18 Remove the ducting from the wiring on the left-hand side of the engine so that the individual wires can be more easily identified. Trace the

wiring from the sidestand switch and disconnect it at the connector (see illustrations). Free the wiring from any clips or ties and secure it clear of the engine. Trace the alternator wiring from the rear of the alternator cover and disconnect it at the connector (see illustration).

19 Trace the wiring from the crankshaft position sensor and oil pressure switch on the right-hand side of the engine and disconnect it at the connector (see illustrations). Free the wiring from any clips or ties and secure it clear of the frame. To avoid damaging the switch, pull back the rubber boot, loosen the screw and disconnect the wiring connector (see illustrations). Unscrew the switch from the crankcase (see illustration).
20 Disconnect the coolant temperature sensor wiring connector (see illustration).
21 On machines with engine numbers up to AE046804, follow the procedure in Chapter 8 and remove the starter motor. On machines with engine numbers from AE046805-on, peel back the rubber boot, undo the nut securing the starter lead and disconnect the lead (see illustrations).
22 Undo the bolt securing the earth (ground) lead to the crankcase and detach the lead

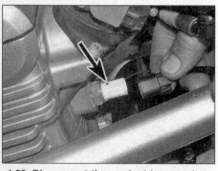

4.20 Disconnect the coolant temperature sensor (arrowed)

4.21a Displace the rubber boot (arrowed) . . .

4.21b . . . and undo the starter motor terminal nut

4.22 Disconnect the earth lead (arrowed)

4.23 Support the weight of the engine on a jack

4.24a Undo the front left-hand . . .

4.24b . . . and front right-hand mounting nuts and bolts

4.24c Note the location of the spacer on the right-hand bolt

4.25a Undo the bolts (arrowed) . . .

(see illustration). Temporarily install the bolt.
23 At this point, position an hydraulic or mechanical jack under the engine with a block of wood between the jack head and sump. Make sure the jack is centrally positioned so the engine will not topple in any direction when the last mounting bolt is removed. Take the weight of the engine on the jack **(see illustration)**.
24 Undo the front left and right-hand mounting bolts and remove the nuts retained in the engine casings **(see illustrations)**. As the right-hand mounting bolt is withdrawn, remove the spacer located between the frame and the engine **(see illustration)**.
25 Undo the bolts securing the front left and right-hand mounting brackets and remove the brackets, noting how they fit **(see illustrations)**.

4.25b . . . and remove the left-hand bracket

4.25c Undo the bolts (arrowed) and remove the right-hand bracket

26 Undo the nuts on the rear upper and lower mounting bolts **(see illustrations)**.
27 Withdraw the upper and lower rear

mounting bolts from the left-hand side **(see illustration)**.
28 Make sure the engine is properly

4.26a Undo the nuts on the rear upper . . .

4.26b . . . and lower mounting bolts (arrowed)

4.27 Withdraw the upper and lower rear mounting bolts (arrowed)

4.28 Manoeuvre the engine out of the frame

4.31 Install the rear mounting bolts from the left-hand side

supported on the jack and have an assistant support it as well. Check that all wiring, cables and hoses are disconnected and clear of the engine. Carefully lower the engine and draw it forwards out of the frame (see illustration).

Installation

Note: *The mounting bolt nuts are self-locking and should only be used once. If new nuts are not available, apply a suitable non-permanent locking compound to the bolt threads before installation.*

29 Clean the threads of the engine mounting bolts.

30 With the aid of an assistant, place the engine unit on top of the jack and block of wood and carefully raise it into position in the frame (see illustration 4.28). Ensure no wires, cables or hoses become trapped between the engine and the frame.

31 Align the bolt holes and slide the upper and lower rear mounting bolts through from the left-hand side (see illustration).

32 Install the right-hand engine mounting bracket and tighten the bolts finger-tight (see illustration 4.25c). Install the right-hand mounting bolt, spacer and nut and tighten the bolt finger-tight.

33 Install the left-hand engine mounting bracket and tighten the bolts finger-tight (see illustration 4.25a). Install the left-hand mounting bolt and nut and tighten the bolt finger-tight.

34 Hand tighten the nuts on the rear mounting bolts (see illustrations 4.26a and b).

35 Once the engine unit, frame and mounting brackets are all correctly aligned, tighten the nuts and bolts in the following order to the torque settings specified at the beginning of his Chapter. **Note:** *Counter-hold the rear mounting bolts when tightening the nuts.*

● Rear mounting bolt nuts
● Right-hand mounting bracket bolts
● Right-hand front mounting bolt
● Left-hand mounting bracket bolts
● Left-hand front mounting bolt

36 The remainder of the installation procedure

is the reverse of removal, noting the following points.

● Make sure all wires, cables and hoses are correctly routed and connected, and secured by the relevant clips or ties
● Tighten all bolts to the specified torque settings where given
● Adjust the throttle and clutch cable freeplay (see Chapter 1)
● Adjust the drive chain (see Chapter 1)
● Refilll the engine with oil and coolant to the correct levels (see Chapter 1 and *Pre-ride checks*)
● Start the engine and check that there is no coolant or oil leakage. **Note:** *Perform this check before installing the belly panel or fairing side panels.*
● Adjust the idle speed if necessary (see Chapter 1)

5 Engine overhaul information

1 Before disassembling the engine, the external surfaces of the unit should be thoroughly cleaned and degreased. This will prevent contamination of the engine internals, and will also make working a lot easier and cleaner. A high flash-point solvent, such as paraffin (kerosene) can be used, or better still, a proprietary engine cleaner such as Gunk. Use a paraffin brush or old paintbrush to work the solvent into the recesses of the engine casings. Take care to exclude solvent or water from the electrical components and intake and exhaust ports.

 Warning: The use of petrol (gasoline) as a cleaning agent should be avoided because of the risk of fire.

2 When the engine is clean and dry, clear a suitable area for working – a workbench is desirable for all operations once a component has been removed from the machine. Gather a selection of small containers and plastic bags so that parts can be grouped together in

an easily identifiable manner. Some paper and a pen should be at hand so that notes can be made and labels attached where necessary. A supply of clean rag is also required. If the engine has been removed from the bike (see Section 4), have an assistant help you lift it onto the workbench.

3 Before commencing work, read through the appropriate section so that some idea of the necessary procedure can be gained. When removing components it should be noted that great force is seldom required. In many cases, a component's reluctance to be removed is indicative of an incorrect approach or removal method – if in any doubt, re-check with the text. In cases where fasteners have corroded, apply penetrating oil or WD-40 before disassembly.

4 When disassembling the engine, keep 'mated' parts together (e.g. camshafts and followers, valve assemblies, pistons and connecting rods, clutch plates etc. that have been in contact with each other during engine operation). These 'mated' parts must be reused or renewed as assemblies.

5 A complete engine/transmission disassembly should be done in the following general order with reference to the appropriate Sections.

Remove the water pump (see Chapter 3)
Remove the valve cover
Remove the cam chain tensioner
Remove the camshafts
Remove the cam chain guide and tensioner blades
Remove the cylinder head
Remove the cylinder block
Remove the pistons
Remove the alternator and starter motor (see Chapter 8)
Remove the starter clutch and drive gears
Remove the clutch
Remove the gearchange mechanism
Remove the transmission assembly
Remove the oil pump
Remove the oil sump
Separate the upper crankcase from the lower crankcase

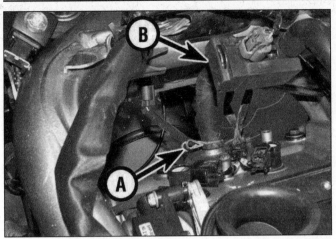

6.3 Release the clip (A) and remove the control valve assembly

6.7 Release the clip (arrowed) securing the clutch cable

Remove the balancer shaft
Remove the crankshaft and connecting rod assemblies
Remove the cam chain

Reassembly

6 Reassembly is accomplished by reversing the general disassembly sequence.

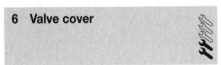

6 Valve cover

Note: *The valve cover can be removed with the engine in the frame. If the engine has been removed, ignore the steps which do not apply.*

Removal

1 Remove the left and right-hand fairing side panels (see Chapter 7).
2 Remove the fuel tank and the air filter housing and displace the throttle body assembly (see Chapter 4).
3 Disconnect the clean air system control valve wiring connector, then release the clip securing the control valve hose and remove the control valve assembly **(see illustration)**.
4 Remove the ignition coils (see Chapter 1, Section 8). Release the coil wiring from the clip on the valve cover.
5 Undo the bolts securing the baffle plate to

the front of the valve cover and lift the baffle plate off **(see illustrations 4.10a, b and c)**.
6 If required, the clean air system reed valves can be removed at this stage (see Steps 11 and 12). Alternatively, remove the reed valves once the valve cover is off the machine.
7 Release the clip securing the clutch cable to the rear, right-hand side of the valve cover **(see illustration)**.
8 Undo the valve cover bolts, noting the location of the sealing washers **(see illustration)**. Discard the washers as new ones must be fitted on reassembly.
9 Lift the valve cover off the cylinder head **(see illustration)**. If it is stuck, tap around the joint with a soft-faced mallet to dislodge it – don't try to lever it off with a screwdriver as

the sealing surfaces will be damaged. Discard the cover gasket as a new one must be fitted on reassembly.
10 Remove the spark plug hole gaskets and discard them as new ones must be fitted **(see illustration)**. Note the two dowels that link the air system passages between the valve cover and cylinder head and remove them for safekeeping if they are loose.
11 Undo the bolts securing the reed valve cover, noting the location of the wiring clip, and lift the cover off **(see illustration)**. Lift out the reed valves, noting which way round they are fitted **(see illustration)**. Take care not to damage the sealing surface of the valves as no gasket is fitted.

6.8 Undo the valve cover bolts

6.9 Lift off the valve cover

6.10 Remove the spark plug hole gaskets. Note the air system passage dowels (arrowed)

6.11a Note the wiring clip (arrowed) on the reed valve cover

6.11b Lift out the reed valves

6.12a Location of the reed valve stopper plates (arrowed)

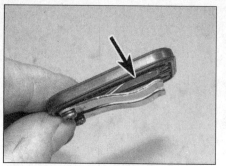

6.12b The reeds (arrowed) should lay flat against the valve body

6.16a Ensure the new gasket is correctly located

6.16b Apply non-permanent sealant . . .

6.16c . . . to the camshaft end cap cut-outs (arrowed)

a criss-cross sequence to the specified torque setting.

18 Install the remaining components in the reverse order of removal.

---

7 Cam chain tensioner

Note: *The cam chain tensioner can be removed with the engine in the frame. If the engine has been removed, ignore the steps which do not apply.*

Removal

1 On EX650 models, remove the right-hand fairing side panel and the right-hand half of the belly panel (see Chapter 7).

2 Remove the spark plugs (see Chapter 1).

3 Remove the valve cover (see Section 6).

4 Unscrew the timing inspection cap and timing rotor cap in the clutch cover (see illustration). Note the location of the O-rings and discard them if they are damaged or distorted.

5 Using a socket spanner on the timing rotor bolt, turn the engine in the normal direction of rotation (clockwise) until the '2/T' mark on the rotor aligns with the notch in the lower edge of the timing inspection cap (see illustrations). Check the alignment of the timing marks on the camshaft sprockets (see illustration 8.31).

6 Unscrew the tensioner cap bolt and

12 Inspect the reed valves for damage and gum and carbon deposits. If necessary, clean the reeds and stopper plates carefully with a suitable solvent (see illustration). The reeds should lay flat against the valve body – if the reeds have become distorted, fit a new valve assembly (see illustration).

Installation

13 Clean the mating surfaces of the cylinder head and valve cover with a suitable solvent to remove all traces of old sealant and gasket. If a scraper is used, take care not to scratch or gouge the soft aluminium. Ensure none of the old gasket material falls into the engine.

14 Install the reed valves reed side down (see illustration 6.11b). Clean the threads of the cover bolts and apply a suitable non-permanent thread-locking compound,

then install the cover and tighten the bolts to the torque setting specified at the beginning of this Chapter – don't forget to fit the wiring clip to the rear bolt (see illustration 6.11a).

15 If removed, install the air system dowels, then fit spark plug hole gaskets, making sure they locate around the rim of each hole (see illustration 6.10).

16 Lay the new gasket onto the valve cover, making sure it locates correctly in its groove – if necessary, apply dabs of grease to hold it in place (see illustration). Apply a suitable, non-permanent sealant to the camshaft end cap cut-outs in the cylinder head (see illustrations).

17 Position the valve cover on the cylinder head carefully, making sure the gasket stays in position (see illustration 6.9). Install the cover bolts with new sealing washers metal face upwards. Tighten the bolts evenly and in

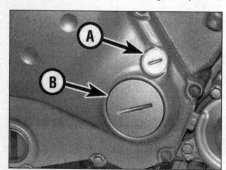

7.4 Timing inspection cap (A) and rotor cap (B)

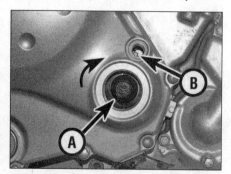

7.5a Turn the rotor (A) clockwise. Align timing mark with notch (B)

7.5b Timing mark 2/T (arrowed) on timing rotor

7.6a Unscrew the tensioner cap bolt (arrowed) . . .

7.6b . . . and remove the cap bolt, sealing washer and spring

7.7a Unscrew the tensioner mounting bolts (arrowed) . . .

remove the sealing washer and spring **(see illustrations)**. Discard the sealing washer as a new one must be used.

7 Unscrew the tensioner mounting bolts, then withdraw the tensioner from the cylinder head **(see illustrations)**.

8 Remove and discard the O-ring as a new one must be fitted on installation **(see illustration)**. Do not attempt to dismantle the tensioner.

 Warning: Do not rotate the crankshaft with the tensioner removed.

Inspection

9 Examine the cam chain tensioner and spring for signs of wear or damage. Install the spring and check that the tensioner pushrod extends under pressure and that the teeth on the push rod are not worn or damaged **(see illustration)**.

10 Release the catch and ensure that the pushrod retracts into the tensioner body **(see illustration)**. If any components are worn or damaged fit a new cam chain tensioner or spring.

Installation

11 Ensure the pushrod is fully retracted into the tensioner body (see Step 10). Fit a new

7.7b . . . then withdraw the tensioner from the cylinder head

O-ring onto the body and lubricate it with a smear of engine oil.

12 Install the tensioner with the release catch facing up **(see illustration 7.7b)**. Tighten the mounting bolts to the torque setting specified at the beginning of this Chapter.

13 Check the alignment of the timing marks on the timing rotor and camshaft sprockets (see Step 5). Install the spring and the cap bolt with a new sealing washer and tighten the bolt to the specified torque **(see illustration 7.6b)**. Note that a clicking noise will be heard as the cap bolt is tightened.

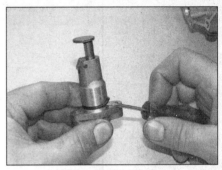

7.8 Remove the old O-ring

14 Using a socket spanner on the timing rotor bolt, turn the engine clockwise through two full turns to set the tensioner, then check the alignment of the timing marks on the camshaft sprockets (see Step 5). If the sprockets do not align correctly the cam chain has slipped. Remove the tensioner, lift the chain off the sprockets and reposition them correctly, then install the tensioner again.

15 Install the remaining components in the reverse order of removal. Lubricate the timing rotor and inspection cap O-rings with a smear of engine oil before installation.

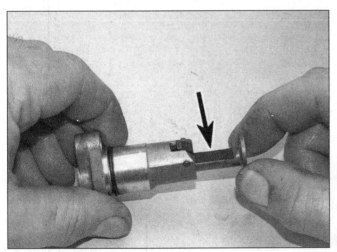

7.9 Check the teeth (arrowed) on the pushrod

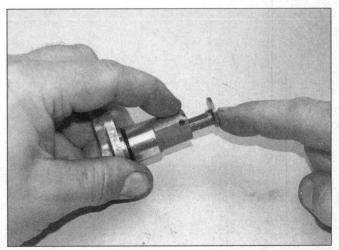

7.10 Ensure the pushrod retracts into the tensioner body

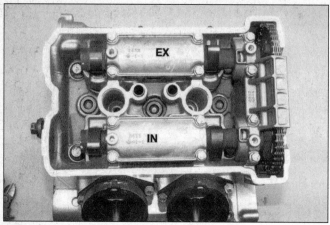

8.2 Camshaft holder identification

8.3a Note how the holders locate on the dowels (arrowed)

8.3b Lift off the right-hand holder . . .

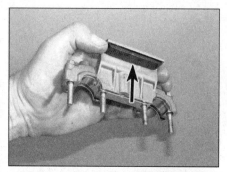

8.3c . . . noting the location of the cam chain guide (arrowed)

8.3d Remove the dowels for safekeeping if they are loose

8 Camshafts and followers

Note: *The camshafts can be removed with the engine in the frame. Plug the spark plug holes and the cam chain tunnel with clean rag to prevent any component from dropping into the engine.*

Removal

1 Follow the procedure in Section 7 and remove the cam chain tensioner.
2 Before disturbing the camshaft holders, check for identification markings. The exhaust camshaft holder is marked 'EX' and the intake camshaft holder is marked 'IN' **(see illustration)**. These markings ensure that the holders can be matched to their original positions on installation. **Note:** *If no markings are visible, make your own using a felt pen.*
3 Unscrew the camshaft holder bolts evenly and a little at a time in a **reverse** of the tightening sequence **(see illustration 8.32)**. Remove the bolts and lift off the holders carefully, noting how they locate on dowels **(see illustration)**. Note the location of the upper cam chain guide on the underside of the right-hand holder **(see illustrations)**. Remove the dowels for safekeeping if they are loose **(see illustration)**.

Caution: Make sure the camshaft holders lift up squarely and do not stick on a dowel or distort because the bolts are being slackened unevenly. If a holder is damaged the complete cylinder head assembly must be renewed; the holders are matched to the cylinder head and cannot be renewed separately.
4 Lift the cam chain off the intake camshaft sprocket and lift the camshaft out of the head, then remove the exhaust camshaft **(see illustration)**. **Note:** *Secure the cam chain to some convenient point with wire or a cable-tie to prevent it falling into the engine.*
5 The camshafts are marked for identification. The intake camshaft is marked 'IN' and

8.4 Lift out the intake and exhaust camshafts

the exhaust camshaft is marked 'EX' **(see illustration)**.
6 While the camshafts are out do not rotate the crankshaft unless necessary – the chain may bind around the crankshaft. If you do need to turn the crankshaft, pull the chain up taut as you do.
7 If the cam followers and shims are being removed, obtain a container which is divided into eight compartments, and label each compartment with the location of its corresponding valve in the cylinder head. If a container is not available, use labelled plastic bags. **Note:** *It is essential that the followers and shims are stored according to their position in the head and fitted back on their original*

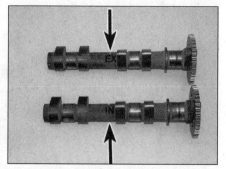

8.5 Camshaft identification markings (arrowed)

8.7a Lift out the cam followers . . .

8.7b . . . and retrieve the shims from inside the followers . . .

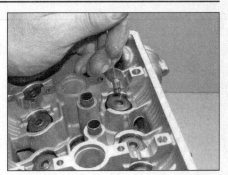

8.7c . . . or from the tops of the valves

valves otherwise all the valve clearances will be wrong. Lift each cam follower out of the cylinder head **(see illustration)**. If necessary use a magnet or suction tool (such as a valve lapping tool). Retrieve the shim from either the inside of the follower or pick it out of the top of the valve, using a magnet or a small screwdriver with a dab of grease on it (the shim will stick to the grease) **(see illustrations)**. Do not allow the shim to fall into the engine.

8 Cover the cylinder head to prevent anything falling into the engine.

Inspection

9 Inspect the bearing surfaces of the camshaft holders and cylinder head and the corresponding journals on the camshafts **(see illustrations)**. Look for score marks, deep scratches and evidence of spalling (a pitted appearance) **(see illustrations)**.

10 Check the camshaft lobes for heat discoloration (blue appearance), score marks,

chipped areas, flat spots and spalling **(see illustration)**. Measure the height of each lobe with a micrometer and compare the results to the *Specifications* at the beginning of this Chapter **(see illustration)**. If damage is noted or wear is excessive, the camshaft must be replaced with a new one.

11 Check camshaft runout by supporting each end on V-blocks and measuring any runout at the journals using a dial gauge (see *Tools and Workshop Tips* in the *Reference* section). If the runout exceeds the specified limit the camshaft must be replaced with a new one.

12 If removed, inspect the outer surfaces of the cam followers for evidence of wear, scoring or other damage. If the surface of a follower is in poor condition, it is probable that the bore in which it works is also damaged. Remove the valves (see Section 11) and measure the internal diameter of the follower bore in different places to determine wear. If

the bore is seriously out-of-round the cylinder head will have to be replaced with a new one.

> **HAYNES HiNT** *Refer to Tools and Workshop Tips in the Reference section for details of how to read a micrometer and dial gauge.*

13 The camshaft journal oil clearance should now be checked. There are two possible ways of doing this, either by direct measurement (see Steps 14 to 16) or by the use of a product known as Plastigauge (see Steps 17 to 23).

14 If direct measurement is to be used, make sure the camshaft holder dowels are in position then fit the holders, making sure they are in their correct locations **(see illustration 8.2)**. Tighten the holder bolts evenly to the torque setting specified at the beginning of this Chapter.

15 Make a chart or sketch of the cylinder head so that a note of each measurement can be

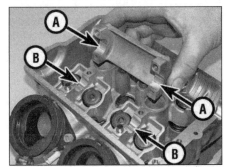

8.9a Inspect the bearing surfaces of the camshaft holders (A), cylinder head (B) . . .

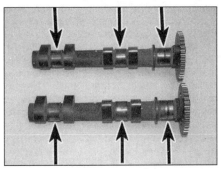

8.9b . . . and the camshaft journals (arrowed)

8.9c Look for score marks and deep scratches

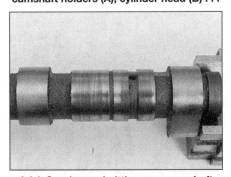

8.9d Scoring and pitting on a camshaft journal

8.10a Extreme wear on a camshaft lobe

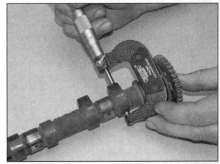

8.10b Measuring the camshaft lobe height

8.15a Measuring the internal diameter of the holder journals

8.15b Measuring the camshaft journal diameter

8.19 Lay a strip of Plastigauge across each journal, along the camshaft centreline

made against the appropriate bearing surface. Using telescoping gauges and a micrometer (see *Tools and Workshop Tips*), measure the internal diameter of each holder journal and record it on the chart **(see illustration)**. Now measure the diameter of the corresponding camshaft journals with a micrometer and record them on the chart **(see illustration)**.

16 To determine the journal oil clearance, subtract the camshaft journal diameter from the holder journal diameter. Compare the result with the *Specifications* at the beginning of this Chapter. If any oil clearance is greater than specified, compare the individual measurements of the camshaft and holder journals to the *Specifications* and renew whichever component is beyond its service limit. **Note:** *If a holder journal is worn beyond its service limit a new cylinder head will have to be fitted.*

17 If the Plastigauge method is to be used, first remove the cylinder head, then remove the valves (see Sections 10 and 11). This will negate the probability of the camshaft rotating due to pressure from the valves as the holder bolts are tightened – *it is essential that the camshaft does not rotate during this procedure.*

18 Clean the camshaft and the bearing surfaces in the cylinder head and camshaft holder with a clean, lint-free cloth.

19 Working on one camshaft at a time, lay the camshaft in its correct location in the cylinder head (see Step 5). Cut strips of Plastigauge and lay one piece on each camshaft journal, along the camshaft centreline **(see illustration)**.

20 Make sure the camshaft holder dowels are in position then fit the holders, making

sure they are in their correct locations **(see illustration 8.2)**. Tighten the holder bolts to the torque setting specified at the beginning of this Chapter – tighten the bolts evenly and a little at a time, ensuring that the holders come down squarely onto the cylinder head and do not stick on the locating dowels.

21 Now unscrew the bolts evenly and a little at a time in the reverse order and carefully lift off the camshaft holders.

22 To determine the oil clearance, compare the crushed Plastigauge (at its widest point) on each journal to the scale printed on the Plastigauge container **(see illustration)**.

23 Compare the results to this Chapter's *Specifications*. If any oil clearance is greater than specified, measure the internal diameter of the appropriate holder journal and corresponding camshaft journal **(see illustrations 8.15a and b)**. Compare the results with the *Specifications* and renew whichever component is worn beyond its service limit. **Note:** *If a holder journal is worn beyond its service limit a new cylinder head will have to be fitted.*

24 Check the camshaft sprockets for wear, chipped teeth and other damage (see illustration). If necessary, undo the bolts securing the sprockets and lift them off, noting which way round they are fitted. Prior to installation, clean the threads of the sprocket bolts and apply a suitable thread locking compound. Ensure the new sprockets are fitted the correct way round with the timing marks facing out. On the intake camshaft use the bolt holes marked 'IN' and on the exhaust camshaft use the bolt holes marked

'EX'. Tighten the bolts to the torque setting specified at the beginning of this Chapter.

25 If the sprockets on the camshafts are worn, the chain and the drive sprocket on the crankshaft are probably worn as well and should be checked (see Sections 9 and 27).

26 Inspect the cam chain guides and tensioner blade (see Section 9).

Installation

27 Make sure the bearing surfaces on the camshafts and in the cylinder head and holders are clean, then lubricate them with molybdenum disulphide oil (a 50/50 mixture of molybdenum disulphide grease and engine oil). If a new camshaft is being fitted, lubricate the cam lobes with a smear of molybdenum disulphide grease.

28 If removed, fit each shim into its recess in the top of the valve, with the size marking on the shim facing up. Check that the shim is correctly seated, then install the follower **(see illustration 8.7a)**. **Note:** *It is most important that the shims and followers are returned to their original valves otherwise the valve clearances will be inaccurate.*

29 Ensure that the '2/T' mark on the timing rotor aligns with the notch in the lower edge of the timing inspection cap **(see illustrations 7.5a and b)**. If it is necessary to turn the crankshaft to restore the alignment, pull the cam chain up taut to prevent it binding on the crankshaft.

30 Keeping the front run of the cam chain taut, lay the exhaust (EX) camshaft into the cylinder head with the 'I EX' mark on the camshaft sprocket at the front, level with the top surface on the cylinder head **(see illustration)**. Engage

8.22 Compare the width of the crushed Plastigauge with the scale provided

8.24 Inspect the camshaft sprockets for wear and chipped teeth

8.30 Install the exhaust camshaft – note the 'I EX' mark (arrowed)

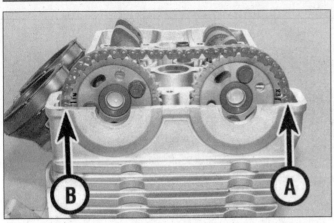

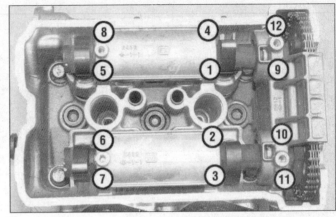

8.31 Count from the No. 1 pin (A) and ensure (B) is the 32nd pin

8.32 Camshaft holder bolt TIGHTENING sequence

the chain on the sprocket, ensuring there is no slack in the front run between the crankshaft and the sprocket on the camshaft.

31 Lay the intake (IN) camshaft into the cylinder head with the 'I IN' mark on the camshaft sprocket at the back, level with the top surface on the cylinder head. Starting with the cam chain pin that is directly below the 'I EX' mark on the **exhaust** camshaft sprocket, count 32 pins back along the chain towards the intake side and engage the chain on the **intake** camshaft sprocket so that the 32nd pin is directly below the 'I IN' mark **(see illustration)**. Check that the '2/T' mark on the timing rotor still aligns with the notch in the lower edge of the timing inspection cap.

32 Make sure the camshaft holder dowels are in position then fit the holders, ensuring they are in their correct locations **(see illustrations 8.3b, 3a and 2)**. To begin with, tighten the holder bolts evenly and a little at a time, ensuring that the holders come down squarely onto the cylinder head and do not stick on the locating dowels. Next, tighten the holder bolts to the specified torque setting in the numerical sequence shown **(see illustration)**.
Caution: The camshaft holders are likely to break if they are not tightened evenly and squarely. Also, a camshaft could

be damaged if the holder bolts are not tightened evenly and the pressure on a depressed valve causes the shaft to bend.

33 Any slack in the cam chain must lie in the rear run of the chain between the intake camshaft sprocket and the crankshaft where it will be taken up by the tensioner. Using a length of wooden dowel inserted through the tensioner hole, press on the back of the tensioner blade to take up the slack, then check that all the timing marks are still in **exact** alignment as described in Step 31. If the marks are out of alignment, verify which camshaft is misaligned, then remove the wooden dowel. Disengage the chain from the camshaft sprocket, then move the camshaft round as required. Refit the cam chain and check the marks again.
Caution: If the marks are not aligned exactly as described, the valve timing will be incorrect and the valves may strike the pistons, causing extensive damage to the engine.

34 Install the cam chain tensioner (see Section 7).

35 Check the valve clearances and adjust them if necessary (see Chapter 1).

36 Install the remaining components in the reverse order of removal.

9 Cam chain, tensioner blade and guide blades

Tensioner and guide blades

Note: *The tensioner and guide blades can be removed with the engine in the frame.*

Removal

1 Remove the camshafts (see Section 8).
2 Note the location of the upper cam chain guide on the underside of the right-hand camshaft holder **(see illustration 8.3c)**.
3 Remove the clutch cover (see Section 16).
4 Although not essential, it is advisable to remove the timing rotor to ensure the correct location of the front guide blade on reassembly. To undo the rotor bolt the crankshaft must be locked using one of the following methods:
● If the engine is in the frame, engage 1st gear and have an assistant sit on the bike and hold the rear brake on hard with the rear tyre in firm contact with the ground.
● Remove the alternator cover and counter-hold the alternator bolt (see Chapter 8).
● Undo the rotor bolt and lift off the timing rotor, noting how it fits (see illustrations).

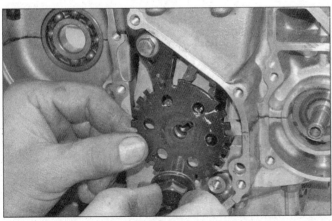

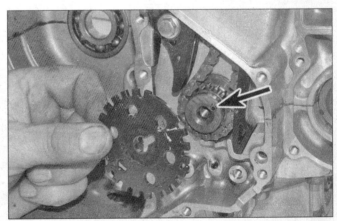

9.4a Undo the timing rotor bolt . . .

9.4b . . . and remove the rotor – note the locating peg (arrowed)

9.5a Note location of front guide blade (arrowed) . . .

9.5b . . . then lift the guide blade out

9.6a Undo the tensioner blade pivot bolt (arrowed) . . .

5 Note the location of the lower end of the front guide blade, then lift it out **(see illustrations)**.

6 Undo the tensioner blade pivot bolt and lift the blade out, noting the location of the sleeves in both sides of the bolt hole **(see illustrations)**.

Inspection

7 Examine the sliding surfaces of the guide and tensioner blades for signs of wear or damage. Check them carefully for cracks in the surface and along the edges. Install new components if necessary.

Installation

8 Clean the threads of the tensioner blade pivot bolt and apply a suitable non-permanent thread-locking compound. Ensure both sleeves are fitted to the blade, then install it, making sure it is the correct way round **(see illustrations 9.6c and b)**. Fit the pivot bolt and

tighten it to the torque setting specified at the beginning of this Chapter **(see illustration)**.

9 Install the front guide blade, making sure the lower end is correctly located **(see illustrations 9.5b and a)**.

10 If removed, install the timing rotor and tighten the rotor bolt to the specified torque setting.

11 Install the remaining components in the reverse order of removal.

Cam chain

Note: *To remove the cam chain the engine must be removed from the frame.*

12 Except in cases of oil starvation, the cam chain wears very little. If the chain has stretched excessively and can no longer be correctly tensioned by the cam chain tensioner, it is likely that the chain guide and tensioner blades will be worn and in need of renewal as well. Also check the condition

of the camshaft sprockets (see Section 8) and crankshaft sprocket (see Step 14). **Note:** *Check the operation of the cam chain tensioner if the chain is slack but appears to be in good condition.*

Inspection

13 Check all round the chain – if there is any discernible slack between the links, or if there is any doubt about its condition, fit a new chain **(see illustration)**.

14 Follow the procedure in Steps 4 to 6 and remove the timing rotor, front guide blade and tensioner blade. Inspect the teeth of the crankshaft sprocket. If there are any signs of wear or damage, a new crankshaft will have to be fitted.

Removal and installation

15 Remove the engine (see Section 4). Separate the crankcase halves (see Section 24).

16 Lift the cam chain off the crankshaft sprocket **(see illustration)**.

17 Installation is the reverse of removal.

10 Cylinder head removal and installation

Note: *The cylinder head can be removed with the engine in the frame. If the engine has been removed, ignore the steps which do not apply.*

Removal

1 Drain the coolant, disconnect the coolant hose from the thermostat housing on the

9.6b . . . and lift out the blade

9.6c Note the location of the sleeves in the bolt hole

9.8 Thread-lock the tensioner blade pivot bolt

9.13 Check for discernible slack between the chain links

9.16 Removing the cam chain from the crankshaft

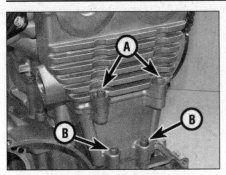

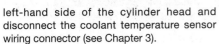

10.6a Cylinder head 6 mm bolts (A) and cylinder block bolts (B)

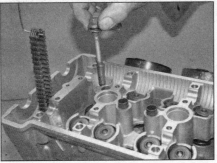

10.6b Lift out the cylinder head bolts and washers

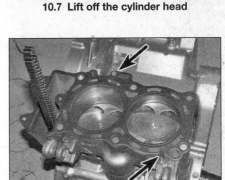

10.7 Lift off the cylinder head

10.8 Remove the head gasket

10.9 Note the location of the dowels (arrowed)

left-hand side of the cylinder head and disconnect the coolant temperature sensor wiring connector (see Chapter 3).

2 Remove the throttle bodies and the exhaust system (see Chapter 4).

3 Remove the camshafts, cam followers and shims (see Section 8).

4 Remove the cam chain tensioner blade and front guide blade (see Section 9).

5 The cylinder head is secured by two 6 mm bolts and six 10 mm bolts with washers. In addition, when undoing the cylinder head bolts, the bolts and nut securing the cylinder block must be loosened. **Note:** *bolt sizes relate to their thread diameters, not head sizes.*

6 First loosen the 6 mm bolts – remove the two bolts securing the cylinder head **(see illustration)**. Next, loosen the 8 mm bolt located in the rear of the cam chain tunnel and the nut at the rear, right-hand side of the cylinder block **(see illustrations 12.4a and b)**. Now loosen the cylinder head bolts evenly and a little at a time in a **reverse** of the tightening sequence shown until they are all loose **(see illustration 10.19)**. Lift out the bolts and their washers noting where they fit **(see illustration)**.

7 Lift the head off the cylinder block, passing the cam chain down through the tunnel as you do **(see illustration)**. If the head is stuck, tap

around the joint with a soft-faced mallet to free it. Do not attempt to free the head by levering it off – you'll damage the sealing surfaces.

8 Secure the cam chain to prevent it falling into the engine and stuff a clean rag into the cam chain tunnel to prevent any debris falling in. Remove the cylinder head gasket **(see illustration)**.

9 If they are loose, remove the dowels from the front and rear edges of the cylinder block for safekeeping **(see illustration)**. If either appears to be missing it is probably stuck in the underside of the cylinder head.

10 Inspect the cylinder head gasket and the mating surfaces on the cylinder head and block for signs of leakage, which could indicate

that the head is distorted. If necessary, check the cylinder head with a straight-edge (see Section 11). Discard the old head gasket as a new one must be fitted on reassembly.

11 If required, loosen the clamps on the intake manifolds and remove the clamps, noting how they fit **(see illustration)**. Undo the screws securing the manifolds and draw them out carefully, noting their positions in the cylinder head **(see illustration)**. Discard the manifold O-rings as new ones must be fitted on reassembly.

12 Clean all traces of old gasket material from the cylinder head and block with a suitable solvent. If a scraper is used, take care not to scratch or gouge the soft aluminium.

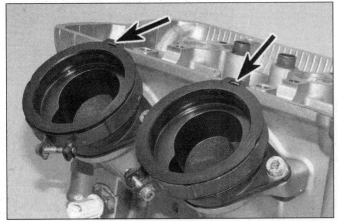

10.11a Note the location of the tabs (arrowed) on the manifold clamps

10.11b Location of the manifold screws (arrowed)

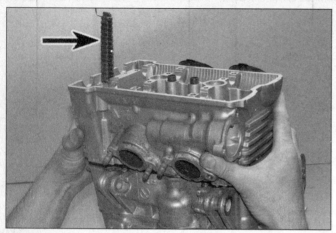

10.18 Lower the cylinder head, keeping the cam chain (arrowed) taut

10.19 TIGHTENING sequence for the 10 mm cylinder head bolts

Be careful not to let any of the old gasket material fall into the cylinder bores or the oil and coolant passages.

HAYNES HiNT *Refer to Tools and Workshop Tips for details of gasket removal methods.*

Installation

13 If removed, fit new O-rings smeared with grease onto the intake manifolds, then install the manifolds. Apply a suitable non-permanent thread-locking compound to the mounting screws and tighten them securely **(see illustration 10.11b)**. Install the clamps as noted on disassembly.

14 If removed, install the two dowels into the cylinder block **(see illustration 10.9)**.

15 Remove any rag from the cam chain tunnel and check that the lower end of the cam chain guide blade is properly located (see Section 9).

16 Temporarily remove the 8 mm bolt and washer located in the rear of the cam chain tunnel and the nut and washer at the rear, right-hand side of the cylinder block **(see illustrations 12.4a and b)**. Apply some molybdenum disulphide oil (a 50/50 mixture of molybdenum disulphide grease and

engine oil) to both sides of the washers, then reinstall the washers, bolt and nut and tighten them finger-tight. Ensure the two 6 mm bolts securing the cylinder block are finger-tight **(see illustration 10.6a)**.

17 Lay the new head gasket onto the block, locating it over the dowels and making sure all the holes are correctly aligned **(see illustration 10.8)**.

18 With the help of an assistant, keep the cam chain taut and pass it up through the tunnel in the head while the head is lowered onto the block **(see illustration)**. Ensure the head locates onto the dowels, then secure the cam chain.

19 Apply some molybdenum disulphide oil to both sides of the washers on the 10 mm cylinder head bolts **(see illustration 10.6b)**. Install the 10 mm bolts and tighten them all finger-tight at first, then tighten them following the numerical sequence, first to the initial torque setting specified at the beginning of this Chapter, then to the final torque setting specified, noting the different settings for new and used bolts **(see illustration)**.

20 Tighten the nut at the rear of the cylinder block and the 8 mm bolt inside the cam chain tunnel to the specified torque setting.

21 Install the 6 mm cylinder head bolts, then

tighten all the 6 mm bolts to the specified torque setting **(see illustration 10.6a)**.

22 Install the remaining components in the reverse order of removal.

11 Cylinder head and valve overhaul

1 Because of the complex nature of this job and the special tools and equipment required, most owners leave servicing of the valves, valve seats and valve guides to a professional. However, you can make an initial assessment of whether the valves are seating correctly, and therefore sealing, by pouring a small amount of solvent into each of the valve ports. If the solvent leaks past any valve into the combustion chamber area the valve is not seating correctly and sealing.

2 With the correct tools (a valve spring compressor is essential – make sure it is suitable for motorcycle work), you can also remove the valves and associated components from the cylinder head, clean them and check them for wear to assess the extent of the work needed, and, unless seat cutting or guide replacement is required, grind in the valves and reassemble them in the head.

3 A dealer service department or specialist can renew the guides and re-cut the valve seats.

4 After the valve service has been performed, be sure to clean it very thoroughly before installation on the engine to remove any metal particles or abrasive grit that may still be present from the valve service operations. Use compressed air, if available, to blow out all the holes and passages.

Disassembly

Special tool: *A valve spring compressor suitable for motorcycle work is absolutely necessary for this procedure (see Step 7).*

5 Before proceeding, arrange to label and store the valves along with their related components in such a way that they can be returned to their original locations without getting mixed up **(see illustration)**. Either

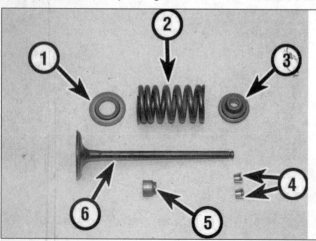

11.5 Valve components

1 Spring seat
2 Spring
3 Spring retainer
4 Collets
5 Valve stem seal
6 Valve

11.7a Install the valve spring compressor . . .

11.7b . . . making sure it is a good fit on the top . . .

11.7c . . . and the bottom of the valve assembly

use the same container as the cam followers and shims are stored in (see Section 8), or obtain a separate container and label each compartment accordingly. Alternatively, labelled plastic bags will do just as well.

6 If required, remove the thermostat housing and thermostat from the left-hand side of the cylinder head, and unscrew the coolant temperature sensor (see Chapter 3).

7 Compress the valve spring on the first valve with a spring compressor, making sure it is correctly located onto each end of the valve assembly **(see illustration)**. On the top of the valve the adaptor needs to be about the same size as the spring retainer – if too big it will contact the follower bore and mark it, and if it is too small it will be difficult to remove and install the collets **(see illustration)**. On the underside of the head make sure the plate on the compressor only contacts the valve and not the soft aluminium of the head **(see illustration)** – if the plate is too big for the valve, use a spacer between them. Do not compress the spring any more than is absolutely necessary.

Caution: Take great care not to mark the cam follower bore with the spring compressor.

8 Remove the collets, using a magnet or a screwdriver with a dab of grease on it **(see illustration)**.

9 Carefully release the valve spring compressor and remove the spring retainer, the spring and the spring seat, noting which way up each component fits **(see illustrations)**.

10 Pull the valve out from the underside of the

head **(see illustration)**. If the valve binds in the guide and won't pull through, push it back into the head and deburr the area around the collet groove with a very fine file **(see illustration)**.

11 Pull the valve stem seal off the top of the valve guide with pliers and discard it

(the old seals should never be reused) **(see illustration)**.

12 Repeat the procedure for the remaining valves. Remember to keep the parts for each valve together so they can be reinstalled in the same location.

11.8 Remove the collets

11.9a Remove the spring retainer . . .

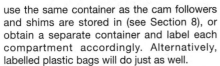

11.9b . . . the valve spring . . .

11.9c . . . and the spring seat

11.10a Pull out the valve

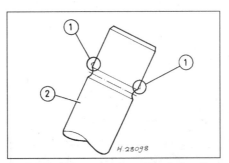

11.10b If the valve stem (2) won't pull through the guide deburr the area above the collet groove (1)

11.11 Pull the old stem seals off with pliers

11.17 Check the head gasket mating surface for warpage

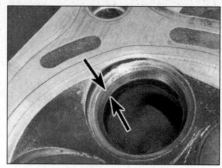

11.18 Measure the valve seat width

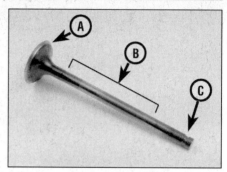

11.19 Examine the valve head (A), stem (B) and collet groove (C)

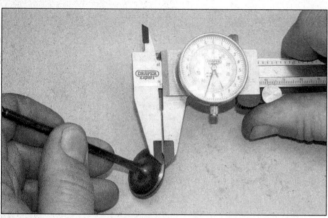

11.20a Measure the valve face width

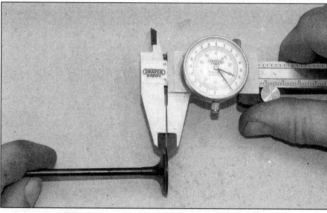

11.20b Measure the valve margin thickness

13 Clean the cylinder head with solvent and dry it thoroughly. Compressed air will speed the drying process and ensure that all holes and recessed areas are clean. **Note:** *Do not use a wire brush mounted in a drill motor to clean the combustion chambers as the head material is soft and may be scratched or eroded away by the wire brush.*

14 Clean all of the valve springs, collets, retainers and spring seats with solvent and dry them thoroughly. Do the parts from one valve at a time so that no mixing of parts between valves occurs.

15 Remove any carbon deposits that may have formed on the valve head using a scraper or a motorised wire brush. Again, make sure the valves do not get mixed-up.

Inspection

16 Inspect the head very carefully for cracks and other damage. If cracks are found, a new head will be required. Check the camshaft bearing surfaces for wear and evidence of seizure. Check the camshafts and holder for wear as well (see Section 8).

17 Using a precision straight-edge and a feeler gauge, check the head gasket mating surface for warpage **(see illustration)**. Refer to *Tools and Workshop Tips* in the Reference section for details of how to use the straight-edge. If the head is warped beyond the limit specified at the beginning of this Chapter, consult your Kawasaki dealer or take it to a specialist repair shop for rectification.

18 Examine the valve seats in the combustion chamber. If they are pitted, cracked or burned, the head will require work beyond the scope of the home mechanic. Measure the outer diameter of the seating surface and compare it to this Chapter's *Specifications*. Also measure the seat width and compare it to the specification **(see illustration)**. If either exceeds the service limit, or varies around the circumference, consult your Kawasaki dealer or take the head to a specialist repair shop for rectification.

19 Examine the head of each valve for cracks, pits and burned spots, then check the valve stem and the collet groove area for wear and damage **(see illustration)**. Rotate the valve and check for any obvious indication that it

is bent. Check the end of the stem for pitting and excessive wear.

20 Measure the face width on each valve and compare it to this Chapter's *Specifications* **(see illustration)**. Measure the valve margin thickness and compare it to the specification **(see illustrations)**. If either exceeds the service limit, replace the valve with a new one.

21 Using V-blocks and a dial gauge, measure the valve stem runout and compare the results to the specification **(see illustration)**. If the measurement exceeds the service limit a new valve must be fitted.

22 Measure the valve stem diameter **(see illustration)**. Clean the valve guides to remove any carbon build-up, then measure the inside

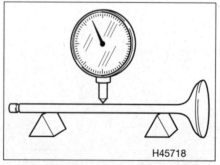

11.21 Measuring the valve stem runout

H45718

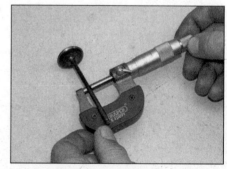

11.22a Measuring the valve stem diameter with a micrometer

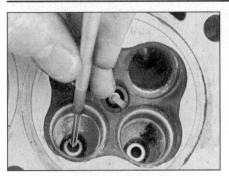

11.22b Measuring the valve guide inside diameter with a small hole gauge

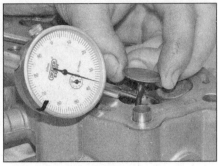

10.23 Measure the amount of 'wobble' as shown

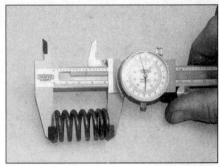

11.24 Measuring valve spring free length

diameter of the guide with a small hole gauge and micrometer **(see illustration)**. Measure the guides at each end and at the centre to determine if they are worn unevenly.

23 Install each valve in its guide in turn so that its face is 10 mm above the seat. Mount a dial gauge against the side of the valve face and measure the amount of side clearance (wobble) between the valve stem and its guide in two directions **(see illustration)**.

24 Check the end of each valve spring for wear. Measure the spring free length and compare it to that listed in *Specifications* **(see illustration)**. If any spring is shorter than specified it has sagged and must be renewed.

25 Place each spring upright on a flat surface and check it for bend with a set square **(see illustration)**. If the bend in any spring is excessive, it must be replaced with a new one.

26 Check the spring seats, retainers and

collets for wear and damage. Any questionable parts should not be reused, as extensive damage will occur in the event of failure during engine operation.

27 If the inspection indicates that no overhaul work is required, the valve components can be reinstalled in the head.

Reassembly

28 Before installing the valves in the head they should be ground in (lapped) to ensure a positive seal between the valves and seats. This procedure requires coarse and fine valve grinding compound and a valve grinding tool (hand-held is preferred). If a grinding tool is not available, a piece of rubber or plastic hose can be slipped over the valve stem (after the valve has been installed in the guide) and used to turn the valve.

29 Apply a small amount of coarse grinding

compound to the valve face **(see illustration)**. Smear some molybdenum disulphide oil (a 50/50 mixture of molybdenum disulphide grease and engine oil) to the valve stem, then slip the valve into the guide **(see illustration)**. **Note:** *Make sure each valve is installed in its correct guide and be careful not to get any grinding compound on the valve stem.*

30 Rotate the tool between the palms of your hands. Use a back-and-forth motion (as though rubbing your hands together) rather than a circular motion (i.e. so that the valve rotates alternately clockwise and anti-clockwise rather than in one direction only) **(see illustration)**. Lift the valve off the seat and turn it at regular intervals to distribute the grinding compound properly. Continue the grinding procedure until the valve face and seat contact area is of uniform width, and unbroken around the entire circumference **(see illustrations)**.

11.25 Check that the springs are not bent

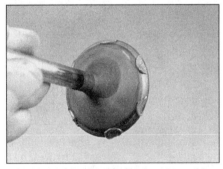

11.29a Apply the grinding compound in small dabs to the valve face only

11.29b Insert the vale into the guide

11.30a Rotate the grinding tool back-and-forth between the palms of your hands

11.30b The grinding process should leave the valve face (arrowed) . . .

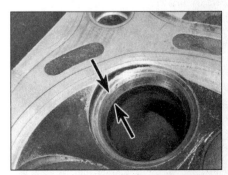

11.30c . . . and seat (arrowed) as an unbroken ring of uniform width

11.35 Use a suitably-sized socket to install the stem seal

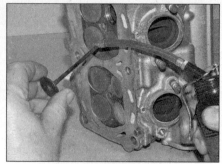

11.36 Lubricate the valve stem before installation

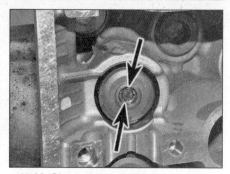

11.38 Check the correct location of the collets (arrowed)

31 Carefully remove the valve and wipe off all traces of grinding compound, making sure none gets in the guide. Use solvent to clean the valve and wipe the seat area thoroughly with a solvent soaked cloth.

32 Repeat the procedure with fine valve grinding compound, then repeat the entire procedure for the remaining valves.

33 On completion, thoroughly clean the head making sure all traces of the grinding compound have been removed. As a final precaution, blow through all passages with compressed air.

34 When installing the valves, work on one at a time so that no mixing of parts occurs.

35 Lubricate the new valve stem seal with molybdenum disulphide oil and fit it onto the top of the valve guide. Use an appropriate size deep socket to push the seal squarely over the end of the guide until it is felt to clip into place (see illustration).

36 Lubricate the valve stem with molybdenum disulphide oil, then slip it into its guide, rotating it slowly to avoid damaging the seal (see illustration). Check that the valve moves up and down freely in the guide.

37 Install the valve spring seat, then the valve spring with its closer-wound coils facing down into the cylinder head, followed by the spring retainer, with its shouldered side facing down into the top of the spring (see illustrations 11.9c, b and a).

38 Apply a small amount of grease to the collets to help hold them in place. Compress the spring with the valve spring compressor and install the collets (see illustration 11.8). When compressing the spring, depress it only as far as is absolutely necessary to slip the collets into place, taking care not to mark the follower bore (see Step 7). Make certain that the collets are securely located in the collet groove and release the spring compressor (see illustration).

39 Repeat the procedure for the remaining valves. Remember to keep the parts for each valve together and separate from the other valves so they can be reinstalled in the correct location.

40 Support the cylinder head on blocks so the valves can't contact the work surface, then tap the end of each valve stem lightly with a suitable punch to seat the collets in their grooves (see illustration).

HAYNES HiNT *Check for proper sealing of the valves by pouring a small amount of solvent into each of the valve ports. If the solvent leaks past any valve into the combustion chamber the valve grinding operation on that valve should be repeated.*

41 If removed, install the thermostat and thermostat housing and the coolant temperature sensor.

42 After the cylinder head and camshafts have been installed, check the valve clearances and adjust as required (see Chapter 1).

12 Cylinder block

Note: *The cylinder block can be removed with the engine in the frame. If the engine has been removed, ignore the steps which do not apply.*

Removal

1 Remove the cylinder head (see Section 10).

2 Follow the procedure in Section 4, Steps 24 and 25, and remove the front engine mounting bolts and mounting brackets.

3 Remove the two 6 mm bolts securing the cylinder block (see illustration 10.6a).

4 Remove the 8 mm bolt and washer located in the rear of the cam chain tunnel and the nut and washer at the rear, right-hand side of the cylinder block (see illustrations).

5 Ease the cylinder up off the crankcase. If it is stuck, tap around the joint face between the cylinder and the crankcase with a soft-faced mallet to free it. Do not attempt to free the cylinder by levering with a screwdriver between the cylinder and crankcase – you'll damage the sealing surfaces. Once the cylinder has separated from the crankcase, secure the cam chain so that it passes through the tunnel as the cylinder is lifted off and support the pistons to prevent the connecting

11.40 Tap each valve stem lightly to seat the collets

12.4a Location of the bolt (arrowed) in the cam chain tunnel

12.4b Nut and washer at the rear of the cylinder block

12.5a Secure the cam chain (arrowed) . . .

12.5b . . . and support the pistons as the cylinder is lifted

12.7 Remove the cylinder base gasket

rods or piston skirts hitting the crankcase **(see illustrations)**.

6 Once the cylinder has been removed, stuff clean rag around the connecting rods to protect them and to prevent anything falling into the crankcase. Secure the cam chain to prevent it slipping into the crankcase.

7 Remove the cylinder base gasket **(see illustration)**.

8 If they are loose, remove the dowels from the front and rear edges of the crankcase for safekeeping **(see illustration)**. If either appears to be missing it is probably stuck in the underside of the cylinder block.

9 Clean all traces of old gasket material from the cylinder block and crankcase with a suitable solvent. If a scraper is used, take care not to scratch or gouge the soft aluminium. Be careful not to let any of the gasket material fall into the engine.

Inspection

10 Check the cylinder walls carefully for scratches and score marks **(see illustration)**.

11 Using a telescoping bore gauge and a micrometer, check the dimensions of the cylinders to assess the amount of wear, taper and ovality. Measure 10 mm and 60 mm from the top of the bore, both parallel to and across the crankshaft axis **(see illustrations)**. Compare the results with *Specifications* at the beginning of this Chapter. If either cylinder is worn beyond the service limit, is oval or

12.8 Location of the cylinder block dowels (arrowed)

tapered, replace the block with a new one – reboring is not possible.

12 If the precision measuring tools are not available, take the cylinder block to a Kawasaki dealer or specialist motorcycle repair shop for assessment and advice.

Installation

13 If removed, fit the two dowels into the crankcase **(see illustration 12.8)**. Remove the rags from around the pistons, taking care not to let the connecting rods fall against the crankcase, and lay the new base gasket in place, locating it over the dowels.

14 If available, screw two lengths of threaded bar into two outer and diagonally opposite cylinder head bolt holes in the crankcase – these will act as guides to keep the cylinder

12.10 Inspect the cylinder walls (arrowed) for damage

block aligned as it is lowered **(see illustration)**. Ensure the bars are long enough to protrude above the top of the block once it is installed to facilitate their removal.

15 Ensure the piston ring end gaps are correctly staggered (see Section 14), then lubricate the pistons, rings and cylinder bores with clean engine oil.

16 Pull the cam chain up taut and rotate the crankshaft so that the piston positions are staggered, then lower the cylinder block down over the chain – and the threaded bars, if applicable **(see illustrations 12.5a and b)**.

17 Have an assistant support the cylinder with the top of the highest piston in the bottom of its cylinder bore, then carefully compress and feed the top ring into the bore

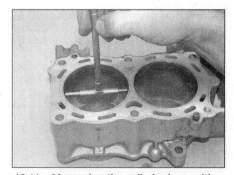

12.11a Measuring the cylinder bore with a telescoping gauge . . .

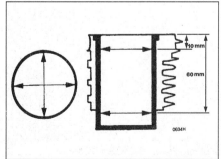

12.11b . . . in the directions shown

12.14 Screw two lengths of threaded bar into the holes (arrowed)

12.17a Locate the top of the piston in the cylinder bore . . .

12.17b . . . then feed the piston rings into the cylinder carefully

12.20a Check that the dowel (arrowed) at the front . . .

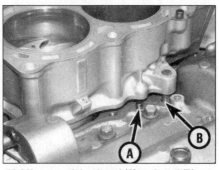

12.20b . . . and the dowel (A) and stud (B) are correctly aligned

as the cylinder is pressed down – use your finger-tips and a small screwdriver to do this **(see illustrations)**. Don't press the cylinder down too hard as this will only

cause the ring to snag and take care not to score the surface of the piston skirt with the screwdriver.

18 Gradually lower the cylinder over the

13.2 Mark the cylinder identity on the top of each piston. Note the indents (arrowed)

13.3a Prise out the circlip . . .

13.3b . . . then push out the piston pin . . .

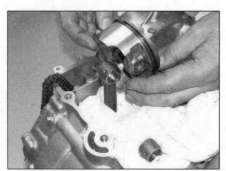

13.3c . . . to free the piston from the connecting rod

piston and feed the second ring and oil ring in using the same method.

19 Once all the rings are safely inside the cylinder, carefully rotate the crankshaft to position the top of the second piston in the bottom of its bore, then feed in the piston rings as before.

20 Lower the bores into the opening in the crankcase – ensure the dowels at the front and rear are aligned with their holes in the cylinder block and the threaded stud at the rear of the block is aligned with its hole **(see illustrations)**. Keep the cam chain taught so that it does not become trapped between the crankshaft and the crankcase, then press the block down onto the crankcase. Secure the cam chain.

21 Install the two 6 mm bolts finger-tight **(see illustration 10.6a)**. Install the 8 mm bolt and washer and the nut and washer securing the cylinder block to the crankcase finger-tight **(see illustrations 12.4a and b)**. If fitted, remove the threaded bars (see Step 14).

22 Install the cylinder head (see Section 10).

23 Follow the procedure in Section 4, Steps 30, 33, 34 and 36 and install the front engine mounting brackets and bolts.

13 Pistons

Note: *This procedure can be carried out with the engine in the frame. If the engine has been removed, ignore the steps which do not apply.*

Removal

1 Remove the cylinder block (see Section 12). Once the cylinder block has been removed, stuff clean rag around the connecting rods to protect them and to prevent anything falling into the crankcase.

2 Before removing a piston from its connecting rod, ensure it is marked with its cylinder identity. Cylinders are numbered 1 and 2, from the left to right side of the engine **(see illustration)**. If the piston is going to be cleaned, scratch the identity lightly on the inside of the piston skirt. The pistons must be installed in their original cylinders on reassembly. Note the indent on the top of each piston which faces the front (exhaust side) of the engine. If this is not visible, mark the piston accordingly so that it can be installed the correct way round.

3 Working on one piston at a time, carefully prise out the circlip on one side of the piston using needle-nose pliers or a small flat-bladed screwdriver inserted into the notch **(see illustration)**. Push the piston pin out from the other side to free the piston from the connecting rod **(see illustrations)**. Remove the other circlip and discard them as new ones must be used. When the piston has been removed, slide its pin back into its bore so that related parts do not get mixed up.

13.4a Remove the piston rings using your thumbs . . .

13.4b . . . or a thin blade

13.10 Measuring the piston diameter

HAYNES HINT *If a piston pin is a tight fit in the piston bosses, heat the piston gently with a hot air gun – this will expand the alloy piston sufficiently to release its grip on the pin. If the piston pin is particularly stubborn, extract it using a drawbolt tool, but be careful to protect the piston's working surfaces – see Tools and Workshop Tips in the Reference section.*

4 Using your thumbs or a thin blade, carefully remove the rings from the piston **(see illustrations)**. Do not nick or gouge the pistons in the process. Note which way up each ring fits and in which groove as they must be installed in their original positions if being re-used (see Section 14). The oil control ring (lowest on the piston) is composed of three separate components – the expander and the upper and lower side rails (see Section 14). **Note:** *It is good practice to fit new piston rings when an engine is being overhauled.*

5 Clean all traces of carbon from the top of the piston. A hand-held wire brush or a piece of fine emery cloth can be used once most of the deposits have been scraped away. Do not, under any circumstances, use a wire brush mounted in a drill motor; the piston material is soft and will be eroded away by the wire brush.

6 Use a piston ring groove cleaning tool to remove any carbon deposits from the ring grooves. If a tool is not available, a piece broken off an old ring will do the job. Be very careful to remove only the carbon deposits.

Do not remove any metal and do not nick or gouge the sides of the ring grooves.

7 Once the carbon has been removed, clean the piston with a suitable solvent and dry it thoroughly. If the identification previously marked on the piston is cleaned off, be sure to re-mark it with the correct identity. Make sure the oil return holes at the back of the oil ring groove are clear.

Inspection

8 Carefully inspect each piston for cracks around the skirt, at the pin bosses and at the ring lands (between the ring grooves). Also check that the circlip grooves are not damaged. Normal piston wear appears as even, vertical wear on the thrust surfaces of the piston. If the skirt is scored or scuffed, the engine may have been suffering from overheating and/or abnormal combustion, which causes excessively high operating temperatures. The oil pump should be checked thoroughly. If wear is apparent on just one piston, check that the piston oil jet in the front of the connecting rod for that piston/cylinder is not blocked (see Section 28).

9 In extreme cases, a hole in the top of the piston or burned areas around the edge of the piston crown indicate that pre-ignition or knocking under load have occurred, although the electronic control unit should detect problems with the fuel or ignition systems long before serious damage takes place. Check the symptoms of poor running in *Fault Finding* in the *Reference* section and refer to Chapter 4, Section 9, for full details of the engine management system fault codes.

10 Check the piston-to-bore clearance by measuring the bore (see Section 12) and the piston diameter. Make sure the piston is matched to its correct cylinder. Measure the piston 18 mm up from the bottom of the skirt and at 90° to the piston pin axis **(see illustration)**. Subtract the piston diameter from the bore diameter to obtain the clearance. If it is greater than the figure specified at the beginning of this Chapter, check whether it is the bore or piston that is worn. If the piston diameter is less than the service limit, new pistons and rings should be fitted. Note that the bore is electro-plated and its surface is unlikely to wear.

11 Measure the groove widths for the top and second piston rings with a feeler gauge – check the clearance at three or four locations around the each groove, then compare the results with *Specifications* at the beginning of this Chapter **(see illustration)**. If the grooves are worn, new pistons and rings will have to be fitted. **Note:** *New piston rings should always be fitted with new pistons.*

12 Measure the piston ring-to-groove clearance by fitting each ring in its groove and slipping a feeler gauge in beside it **(see illustration)**. If new piston rings are being used, measure the clearance using the new rings. Make sure you have the correct ring for the groove (see Section 14). Check the clearance at three or four locations around the groove. If the clearance is greater than specified, measure the width of each ring with a micrometer and compare the results with *Specifications* **(see illustration)**. Renew whichever components are worn.

13.11 Measuring the piston ring grooves

13.12a Measuring the ring-to-groove clearance

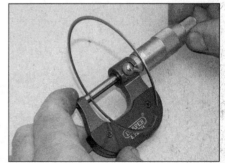

13.12b Measuring piston ring width

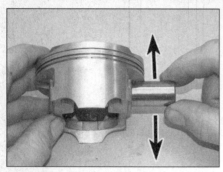

13.13a Checking the piston pin for freeplay

13.13b Measuring the external diameter of the pin at both ends . . .

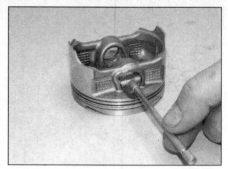

13.13c . . . and the internal diameter of the pin bore

13.13d Measuring the external diameter of the pin at the centre

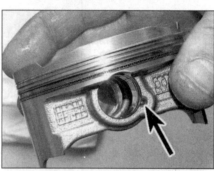

13.15 Position open end of circlip away from removal notch (arrowed)

13.17a Always use new circlips . . .

13.17b . . . and install them carefully with a small screwdriver

13 Apply clean engine oil to the piston pin, insert it into the piston and check for any freeplay between the two **(see illustration)**. Measure the pin external diameter and the pin bore in the piston and compare the

results to the *Specifications* at the beginning of this Chapter **(see illustrations)**. Repeat the measurements between the pin **(see illustration)** and the connecting rod small-end (see Section 28). Renew components that

are worn beyond the specified limits. **Note:** *If the connecting rod small-end is worn a new connecting rod will have to be fitted (see Section 28).*

Installation

14 Inspect and install the piston rings (see Section 14).
15 Working on one piston at a time, install a **new** circlip into one side of the piston – never re-use old circlips. When installing the circlips, compress them only just enough to fit them in the piston, and make sure they are properly seated in their grooves with the open end away from the removal notch **(see illustration)**.
16 Lubricate the piston pin, the piston pin bore and the connecting rod small-end bore with clean engine oil, then install the piston on its correct connecting rod. Ensure the indent on the top of the piston faces the front (exhaust side) of the engine **(see illustration 13.2)**.
17 Insert the piston pin from the side without the circlip and push it all the way in. Secure the pin with the other **new** circlip **(see illustrations)**.
18 Remove the rag from around the connecting rods and install the cylinder block (see Section 12).

14 Piston rings

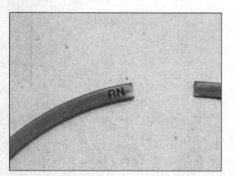

14.2a Marking RN on second piston ring

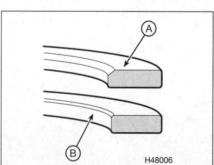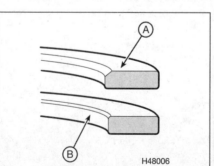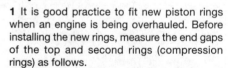

14.2b Piston ring cross-sections – (A) top ring, (B) second ring

Inspection

1 It is good practice to fit new piston rings when an engine is being overhauled. Before installing the new rings, measure the end gaps of the top and second rings (compression rings) as follows.
2 Lay out each piston with its ring set so the rings will be matched with the same piston and cylinder during the measurement procedure. The upper surface of the top and second rings should have a manufacturer's mark at one end – the top ring is marked 'R' and the second ring is marked 'RN' **(see illustration)**. Also note that the rings can be identified by their different cross-sections **(see illustration)**.
3 The end gaps are measured with the rings

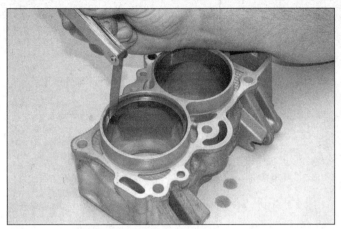

14.3 Measuring piston ring installed end gap

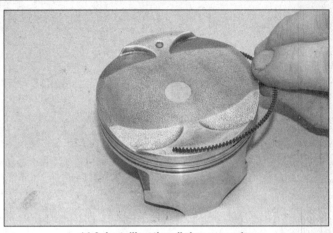

14.6 Installing the oil ring expander

fitted inside the cylinder bore – insert a ring into the bottom of the bore and square it up with the cylinder walls by pushing it down with the top of the piston. The ring should be about 15 mm below the edge of the cylinder. Slip a feeler gauge between the ends of the ring to measure the gap and compare the result to *Specifications* at the beginning of this Chapter **(see illustration)**. Note that the gaps for the first and second rings are different.

4 If the gap is larger or smaller than specified, check that you have the correct rings before proceeding. Excess end gap is not critical unless it exceeds the service limit.

5 Repeat the procedure for all the compression rings. Remember to keep the rings together with their matched pistons.

Installation

6 The oil control ring (lowest on the piston) is installed first. It is composed of three separate components – the expander and the upper and lower side rails. Slip the expander into the groove, positioning its ends so that they touch but do not overlap **(see illustration)**.

7 Install the lower side rail. Do not use a piston ring installation tool on the oil ring side rails as they may be damaged. Instead, place one end of the side rail into the groove between the expander and the ring land **(see illustration)**. Hold it firmly in place and slide a finger or thin blade around the piston while pushing the rail into the groove. Next, install the upper side rail in the same manner.

14.9b . . . and install it using a thin blade

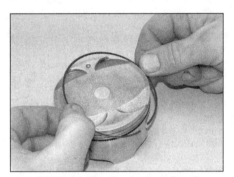

14.7 Installing the lower side rail

8 After the oil control ring has been installed, check that both its upper and lower side rails can be turned smoothly in the ring groove.

9 Fit the second ring into the middle groove in the piston with its mark facing up (see Step 2). Do not expand the ring any more than is necessary to slide it into place **(see illustrations)**. If required, use a piston ring installation tool to avoid breaking the ring.

10 Follow the same procedure to install the top ring into the top groove in the piston

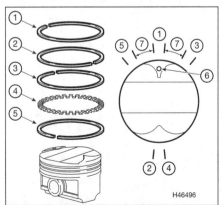

14.11 Stagger the ring end gaps as shown

1 Top ring
2 Second ring
3 Oil ring top side rail
4 Oil ring expander
5 Oil ring lower side rail
6 Indent
7 30 to 40°

14.9a Fit the second ring over the top of the piston . . .

11 Once the rings are correctly installed, check they move freely without snagging and stagger their end gaps as shown **(see illustration)**.

15 Starter clutch and gears

Note: *The starter clutch can be removed with the engine in the frame. If the engine has been removed, ignore the steps which do not apply.*

Check

1 The operation of the starter clutch can be checked while it is in situ. First remove the starter motor (see Chapter 8). Check that the reduction gear, located inside the starter motor aperture, rotates freely clockwise (as you look at the bike from the left-hand side), but locks when rotated anti-clockwise. If not, the starter clutch is faulty and should be removed for inspection.

Removal

2 Remove the left-hand frame cover, belly panel and, on EX650 models, the left-hand fairing side panel (see Chapter 7).

3 Drain the engine oil (see Chapter 1). Position

15.5a Undo the alternator cover bolts . . .

15.5b . . . noting the location of the guide (arrowed) . . .

15.5c . . . and lift the cover off

a suitable receptacle underneath the alternator cover to catch any residual oil when the cover is removed.

4 Remove the ducting from the wiring on the left-hand side of the engine so that the individual wires can be more easily identified.

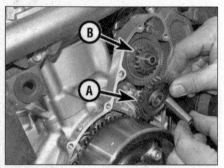

15.7a Remove the idler gear (A). Note the reduction gear (B)

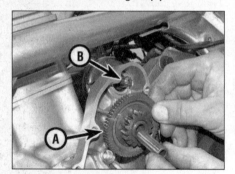

15.7b Remove the reduction gear (A). Note the starter motor pinion (B)

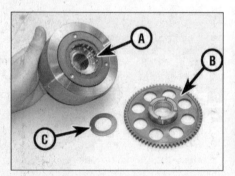

15.10b Starter clutch (A), starter driven gear (B) and plain washer (C)

Trace the alternator wiring from the rear of the alternator cover and disconnect it at the connector (see Section 4, Step 18).

5 Undo the alternator cover bolts, noting the location of the guide for the fuel tank breather hose and oxygen sensor wiring, and lift the cover off (see illustrations).

6 Remove the cover gasket and discard it; note the position of the cover dowels and remove them for safe-keeping if they are loose (see illustrations 15.21c and a).

7 Withdraw the idler gear shaft and remove the gear, noting how it engages with the smaller pinion on the reduction gear (see illustration). Withdraw the reduction gear shaft and remove the gear, noting how the larger pinion engages with the starter motor pinion (see illustration).

8 Before proceeding further, the operation of the starter clutch can be checked while it is in situ. Check that the driven gear on the back

15.8 Driven gear should rotate freely in a clockwise direction only

15.10c Remove the plain washer . . .

of the starter clutch is able to rotate freely clockwise as you look at it, but locks when rotated anti-clockwise (see illustration). If not the starter clutch is faulty and should be removed for inspection.

9 Remove the alternator rotor – the starter clutch is mounted on the back of it (see Chapter 8). Note: If the starter clutch is going to be removed, slacken the three starter clutch bolts while holding the rotor centre bolt before removing the alternator rotor.

10 If the starter driven gear comes off with the alternator rotor, lay the rotor face down on the work bench, then lift the gear off the back of the rotor, rotating it anti-clockwise as you do to release it from the starter clutch (see illustrations). Note the location of the large plain washer between the rotor and the gear. If the starter driven gear remains on the crankshaft, remove the large plain washer, then draw the gear off, noting how it fits (see illustrations).

15.10a Draw the gear off, rotating it anti-clockwise

15.10d . . . then draw the driven gear off the crankshaft

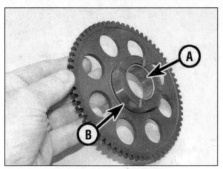

15.12 Inspect the internal (A) and external (B) bearing surfaces

15.13 Inspect the sprags (arrowed) and the sprag cage inside the clutch housing

15.14 Starter clutch is retained by three bolts (arrowed)

Inspection

11 Inspect the teeth on the idler and reduction gear pinions and renew the gears if any are chipped or worn (see illustrations 15.7a and b). Check the gear shafts and bearing surfaces for signs of wear or damage, and renew if necessary.

12 Inspect the driven gear bearing surfaces for signs of wear and scoring (see illustration). If the bearing surfaces show signs of excessive wear, replace the gear with a new one and inspect the surface of the crankshaft for damage. Inspect the teeth of the driven gear and renew the gear if they are worn or damaged.

13 Inspect the condition of the sprags and the sprag cage inside the starter clutch housing (see illustration). Clean the assembly with a suitable solvent, dry it thoroughly, then lubricate it with clean engine oil. The sprags

should turn freely inside the cage – if they are damaged or worn, the starter clutch should be renewed. Note: If the clutch sprags are worn, the external bearing surface on the driven gear hub is likely to be worn also. Renew the clutch assembly and driven gear as a set.

14 Unscrew the starter clutch bolts and remove the clutch housing from the back of the alternator rotor (see illustration).

Installation

15 Position the housing on the back of the alternator rotor and align the bolt holes (see illustration 15.14). Clean the threads of the starter clutch bolts and apply a suitable non-permanent thread-locking compound, then install the bolts and tighten them to the torque setting specified at the beginning of this Chapter.

16 Prior to installation, lay the rotor face down and install the starter driven gear,

rotating it anti-clockwise (see illustration 15.10a). Holding the rotor assembly as shown, ensure that the driven gear rotates freely in a clockwise direction and locks against the rotor in an anti-clockwise direction (see illustration). Withdraw the driven gear (see Step 10).

17 Clean any traces of oil off the tapered section of the crankshaft and the taper inside the rotor with solvent and clean rag.

18 Lubricate the bearing surface of the crankshaft with molybdenum disulphide grease, then install the starter driven gear and the large plain washer (see illustrations 15.10d and c). Ensure the tapered section of the crankshaft remains clean.

19 Install the alternator rotor (see Chapter 8).

20 Lubricate the reduction gear shaft with molybdenum disulphide grease, then install the gear and shaft (see illustration 15.7b). Follow the same procedure to install the idler gear (see illustration 15.7a).

21 Clean all old gasket and sealant from the alternator cover and crankcase. If removed, install the cover dowels, then apply a smear of suitable sealant across the crankcase joints and the alternator wiring grommet (see illustrations). Fit the new cover gasket, making sure it locates correctly onto the dowels (see illustration).

22 Install the cover and cover bolts – don't forget to fit the guide for the breather hose and wiring (see illustration 15.5b). Tighten the bolts evenly in a criss-cross pattern to the specified torque setting.

23 Refill the engine oil (see Chapter 1). Install the remaining components in the reverse order of removal. Ensure the alternator wiring is correctly routed and secured.

15.16 Check the operation of the starter clutch

15.21a Install the dowels (A) and apply sealant across the joints (B) . . .

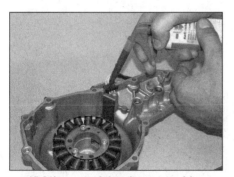

15.21b . . . and the alternator wiring grommet

15.21c Ensure the gasket locates onto the dowels

16 Clutch

Note 1: The clutch can be removed with the engine in the frame. If the engine has been removed, ignore the steps which do not apply.
Note 2: The clutch nut must be discarded and a new one used on installation – it is best to obtain the new nut in advance.

16.3 Note the location of the return spring (arrowed)

16.4a Bolts (arrowed) secure the clutch cover

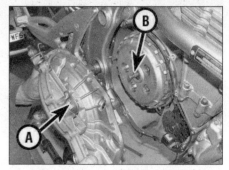

16.4b Clutch actuating shaft (A) and pull-rod (B)

Special tool: *A clutch holding tool will be required for this procedure (see Step 8).*

Removal

1 Remove the right-hand frame cover, belly panel and, on EX650 models, the right-hand fairing side panel (see Chapter 7).

2 Drain the engine oil (see Chapter 1). Position a suitable receptacle underneath the clutch cover to catch any residual oil when the cover is removed.

3 Detach the clutch cable from the clutch actuating arm (see Section 17). Note the location of the return spring on the clutch arm **(see illustration)**.

4 Undo the clutch cover bolts **(see illustration)**. On EX650 models, note the location of the idle speed adjuster bracket. Pull the clutch arm back (anti-clockwise) towards the rear of

the bike and remove the cover, noting how the lower end of the actuating shaft engages on the pull-rod **(see illustration)**. Remove the cover gasket and discard it; note the position of the cover dowels and remove them for safe-keeping if they are loose **(see illustration 16.38c and a)**.

5 Undo the clutch spring bolts a little at a time in a criss-cross pattern, then remove the bolts, washers and the springs **(see illustrations)**. **Note:** *The washers are integral with the bolts.*

6 Lift off the pressure plate and remove the pull-rod, either from the back of the pressure plate or the end of the transmission input shaft **(see illustration)**. Note the location of the pull-rod bearing in the pressure plate **(see illustration 16.22)**.

7 Note the location of the outer friction plate tabs, then withdraw the clutch plates from

the clutch housing **(see illustrations)**. Keep the plates in their original order, even if they are being replaced with new ones. There are seven friction plates and six plain plates. Note that the innermost plain plate is thicker than the other plain plates.

8 To loosen the clutch centre nut the input shaft must be locked using one of the following methods:

● If the engine is in the frame, engage 1st gear and have an assistant sit on the bike and hold the rear brake on hard with the rear tyre in firm contact with the ground.

● Use the Kawasaki service tool (Part No. 57001-1243) to engage the clutch centre splines.

● Use a commercially available clutch holding tool which will engage the clutch centre splines **(see illustration)**.

16.5a Undo the clutch spring bolts (arrowed) . . .

16.5b . . . and remove the bolts, washers and springs

16.6 Remove the pressure plate and pull-rod

16.7a Note the location of the outer friction plate tabs (arrowed) . . .

16.7b . . . then withdraw the plates from the clutch housing

16.8 Using a commercially available tool to hold the clutch. Note the location of the bar (arrowed)

16.10a Remove the clutch centre nut . . .

16.10b . . . and the dished washer noting how it fits

16.11a Remove the clutch centre . . .

Caution: The clutch centre nut is extremely tight. If a clutch holding tool is used, ensure it does not slip and damage the clutch.

9 If required, insert a long bar through the frame tube to the rear of the clutch and rest the holding tool against it while loosening the clutch nut **(see illustration 16.8)**.

10 Unscrew the centre nut and remove the dished washer from the input shaft, noting which way round the washer fits **(see illustrations)**. Discard the nut as a new one must be used on installation.

11 Draw the clutch centre off the shaft then remove the outer thrust washer **(see illustrations)**.

12 Undo the oil pump sprocket bolt by turning it clockwise – the bolt has a left-hand thread **(see illustration)**.

13 Using circlip pliers inserted into the two

holes in the end of the input shaft sleeve, withdraw the sleeve from the centre of the clutch housing **(see illustration)**. Disengage the primary driven gear on the back of the clutch housing from the primary drive gear on the crankshaft and draw the housing off, together with the oil pump drive chain and sprocket **(see illustrations)**.

14 Note the location of the inner thrust washer and remove it if required **(see illustration)**.

Inspection

15 After an extended period of service the clutch friction plates will wear and promote clutch slip. Measure the thickness of each friction plate using a Vernier caliper **(see illustration)**. If any plate has worn to or beyond the service limits given in the *Specifications* at

16.11b . . . and the outer thrust washer

the beginning of this Chapter, or if any of the plates smell burnt or are glazed, the friction plates must be replaced with a new set.

16.12 Oil pump sprocket bolt (arrowed) has a left-hand thread

16.13a Withdraw the sleeve . . .

16.13b . . . then manoeuvre the clutch housing out . . .

16.13c . . . together with the oil pump drive chain and sprocket

16.14 Remove the inner thrust washer

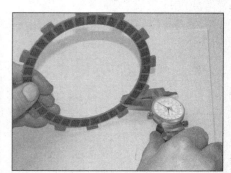

16.15 Measure the thickness of the friction plates

16.16 Check the plain plates for warpage

16.17a Inspect the slots in the housing . . .

16.17b . . . and the corresponding tabs on the friction plates

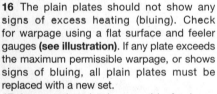

16.17c Inspect the slots in the clutch centre . . .

16.17d . . . and the inner tongues on the plain plates

16.19 Inspect the bearing surfaces of the clutch housing and input shaft sleeve

16 The plain plates should not show any signs of excess heating (bluing). Check for warpage using a flat surface and feeler gauges **(see illustration)**. If any plate exceeds the maximum permissible warpage, or shows signs of bluing, all plain plates must be replaced with a new set.

17 Inspect the clutch assembly for burrs and indentations in the slots in the housing and on the corresponding tabs on the friction plates **(see illustrations)**. Similarly check for wear between the slots in the clutch centre and the inner tongues of the plain plates **(see illustrations)**. Wear of this nature will cause clutch drag and slow disengagement during gear changes, since the plates will snag when

the pressure plate is lifted. With care, a small amount of wear can be corrected by dressing with a fine file, but if this is excessive the worn components should be renewed.

18 Ensure the threads for the spring bolts in the clutch centre are in good condition.

19 Inspect the bearing surfaces of the clutch housing and the input shaft sleeve for wear **(see illustration)**.

20 The clutch housing incorporates a cush-drive mechanism – check that the springs are not loose or broken and that there is no backlash between the housing and the primary driven gear, otherwise replace the housing with a new one **(see illustration)**.

21 Check the teeth of the primary driven gear

on the back of the clutch housing and the corresponding teeth of the primary drive gear on the crankshaft **(see illustration 16.29a)**. Replace the clutch housing with a new one if any teeth are worn or chipped. The primary drive gear is an integral part of the crankshaft – if the gear is damaged take the crankshaft to a Kawasaki dealer or specialist engineer for assessment (see Section 27 for removal of the crankshaft).

22 Check the surface of the pressure plate and the pull-rod bearing for signs of wear, damage or roughness and renew any parts as necessary **(see illustration)**. Refer to *Tools and Workshop Tips* in the *Reference* section for details of bearing removal and installation.

16.20 Check the cush-drive mechanism

16.22 Inspect the pressure plate and bearing (arrowed)

16.23a Check the pull-rod and clutch actuating shaft for wear

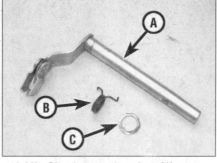

16.23b Clutch actuating shaft (A), return spring (B) and thrust washer (C)

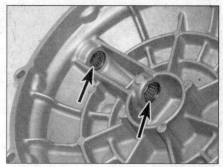

16.23c Location of the needle bearings (arrowed)

23 Inspect the outer end of the pull-rod and the slot it engages in on the lower end of the clutch actuating shaft for wear **(see illustration)**. If there is freeplay between the shaft and its bearings in the clutch cover, or evidence of oil leakage at the top of the shaft, pull the shaft out of the cover, noting the location of the return spring and thrust washer **(see illustration)**. Inspect the shaft and the needle bearings in the cover for wear and damage and renew any parts as necessary **(see illustration)**.
24 Carefully lever out the seal in the cover with a flat-bladed screwdriver to avoid damaging the casing **(see illustration)**. Lubricate the new seal with a smear of engine oil, then press it into place with a suitably-sized socket **(see illustration)**.
25 Measure the free length of each clutch spring using a Vernier caliper **(see illustration)**.

Stand each spring upright on a flat surface and check it for bend by placing a set square against it. If any spring is shorter than the specified service limit, or if the bend in any spring is excessive, replace all the springs as a set.

Installation

26 Remove all traces of old gasket from the crankcase and clutch cover surfaces.
27 Ensure the inner thrust washer is located on the transmission input shaft **(see illustration 16.14)**.
28 Lubricate the clutch housing bearing surface with clean engine oil, then assemble the clutch housing, oil pump drive chain and sprocket as shown **(see illustration 16.13c)**.
29 Manoeuvre the clutch housing over the end of the input shaft and engage the primary driven gear with the drive gear on the

crankshaft **(see illustration)**. Note the two oil holes in the bearing surface of the input shaft sleeve and fit the sleeve with the hole furthest from the end innermost **(see illustration)**. Ensure that the two holes used to withdraw the sleeve are facing out, then press the sleeve all the way in **(see illustration 16.13a)**.
30 Install the oil pump sprocket on the pump shaft **(see illustration)**. Clean the threads of the sprocket bolt and apply a suitable non-permanent thread-locking compound, then install the bolt by turning it anti-clockwise. Tighten the bolt to the torque setting specified at the beginning of this Chapter.
31 Install the outer thrust washer and the clutch centre **(see illustrations 16.11b and a)**.
32 Slide on the dished washer with the side marked OUT SIDE facing out **(see illustration 16.10b)**.

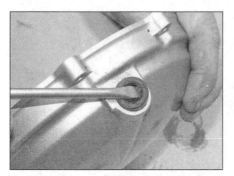

16.24a Lever out the seal in the cover carefully

16.24b Lubricate the new seal prior to installation

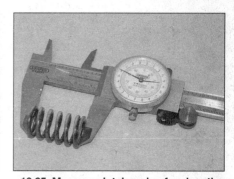

16.25 Measure clutch spring free length

16.29a Primary driven gear teeth (A) and crankshaft drive gear teeth (B)

16.29b Location of oil holes (arrowed) in input shaft sleeve

16.30 Fit the oil pump sprocket on the pump shaft (arrowed)

16.33a Ensure the holding tool is firmly secured . . .

16.33b . . . then tighten the clutch nut to the specified torque

33 Thread the new clutch nut onto the shaft with the shoulder facing out **(see illustration 16.10a)**. Using the method employed on removal to lock the input shaft (see Step 8), tighten the nut to the torque setting specified at the beginning of this Chapter **(see illustrations)**.

34 Arrange the clutch plates in the correct order on the work surface (see Step 7). Coat each plate with clean engine oil before installing it.

35 First install the innermost friction plate, then install the thicker plain plate **(see illustrations)**. Continue to alternate friction

and plain plates to build up the clutch, finishing with the outermost friction plate, locating its tabs in the shallow slots in the housing **(see illustration 16.7b and a)**.

36 Lubricate the pull-rod bearing with oil and each end of the pull-rod with molybdenum grease. Fit the pull-rod into its bearing, then install the pressure plate locating its castellations in the slots in the clutch centre **(see illustration)**. Install the springs and the bolts with their washers, then tighten the bolts evenly in a criss-cross pattern to the specified torque setting **(see illustrations 16.5b and a)**.

37 If removed, fit the return spring and washer on the clutch arm shaft. Lubricate the seal in the clutch cover with a smear of grease, and the shaft bearings with clean engine oil. Insert the shaft carefully to avoid damaging the seal and press it all the way in. Align the ends of the spring as noted on disassembly (see Step 3).

38 If removed, install the clutch cover dowels **(see illustration)**. Apply a smear of suitable sealant across the crankcase joints then fit the new cover gasket, making sure it locates correctly onto the dowels **(see illustrations)**.

39 Install the cover – pull the clutch arm

16.35a First install the innermost friction plate . . .

16.35b . . . then install the thicker plain plate

16.36 Install the pressure plate over the end of the clutch centre

16.38a Install the cover dowels (arrowed)

16.38b Smear sealant across the crankcase joints (arrowed) . . .

16.38c . . . and fit a new cover gasket

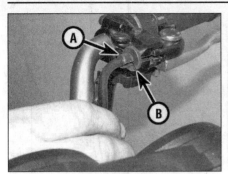

17.1 Clutch cable adjuster (A) and lockring (B)

17.2a Pull the cable out of the adjuster . . .

17.2b . . . and pass it through the slot in the bracket

17.3 Release the cable end from the lever

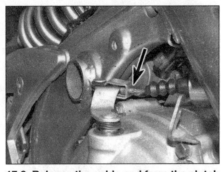

17.6 Release the cable end from the clutch arm (arrowed)

17.7 Pull the lower end of the cable out of the cable stop

back (anti-clockwise), then rotate it forwards so that it engages behind the end of the pull-rod as the cover is pressed into position **(see illustration 16.4b)**. Tighten the cover bolts evenly in a criss-cross sequence to the specified torque **(see illustration 16.4a)**. On EX650 models, don't forget to secure the idle speed adjuster bracket.

40 Connect the clutch cable to the actuating arm (see Section 17). Check the operation of the clutch (see Chapter 1).

41 Refilll the engine with oil (see Chapter 1 and *Pre-ride Checks*)

42 Install the remaining components in the reverse order of removal.

17 Clutch cable

Removal

1 Start at the handlebar end of the cable. Loosen the adjuster lockring, then thread the adjuster fully into the lever bracket to make freeplay in the cable **(see illustration)**.

2 Align the slots in the adjuster and lockring with the slot in the lever bracket, then pull the cable out of the adjuster and pass it through the slot in the bracket **(see illustrations)**.

3 Release the inner cable end from the lever **(see illustration)**.

4 On EX650 models, remove the right-hand fairing side panel (see Chapter 7). On all

models, remove the fuel tank (see Chapter 4).

5 Release the cable from the clip on the rear of the valve cover **(see illustration 6.7)**.

6 Release the inner cable end from the clutch arm, then draw off the protective boot **(see illustration)**.

7 Pull the lower end of the cable out of the cable stop on the top of the engine unit **(see illustration)**.

8 Remove the cable from the machine, noting its routing.

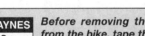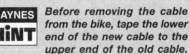

HAYNES HiNT *Before removing the cable from the bike, tape the lower end of the new cable to the upper end of the old cable. Slowly pull the lower end of the old cable out, guiding the new cable down into position. Using this method will ensure the cable is routed correctly.*

Installation

9 Installation is the reverse of removal. Apply grease to the cable ends. Make sure the cable is correctly routed. Adjust the clutch lever freeplay (see Chapter 1).

18 Gearchange mechanism

Note 1: *The gearchange mechanism can be removed with the engine in the frame. If the*

engine has been removed, ignore the steps which do not apply.

Note 2: *Due to their location on the machine, inspection of the gearchange mechanism components is divided into two separate procedures.*

External gearchange mechanism

Removal

1 Remove the left-hand frame cover and the belly panel and, on EX650 models, remove the left-hand fairing side panel (see Chapter 7).

2 Drain the engine oil (see Chapter 1).

3 Make sure the transmission is in neutral. Undo the bolts securing the front sprocket cover and remove the cover **(see illustration)**.

4 Unscrew the pinch bolt on the gearchange

18.3 Remove the front sprocket cover

18.4a Undo the pinch bolt

18.4b Note the alignment of the register marks (arrowed)

18.5 Disconnect the neutral switch wiring connector

lever, then pull the lever off the gearchange shaft, noting the alignment of the register marks **(see illustrations)**.

5 Disconnect the neutral switch wiring connector **(see illustration)**.

6 Remove the front sprocket (see Chapter 6). Rest the drive chain over the chain slider on the swingarm.

7 Clean the area around the transmission output shaft and gearchange mechanism

cover thoroughly, then undo the cover bolts and Phillips-head screw and draw the cover off **(see illustrations)**. Remove the cover gasket and discard it; note the location of the cover dowels and remove them for safe-keeping if they are loose **(see illustration)**.

8 Withdraw the gearchange shaft from the cover, noting the location of the thrust washer **(see illustration)**.

Inspection

9 Inspect the gearchange shaft return spring **(see illustration)**. If is fatigued, worn or damaged it must be renewed. To remove the spring, first ease the retaining circlip out of its groove and slide it off the shaft, then slide off the collar and spring, noting which way round the spring is fitted **(see illustration)**. On installation, ensure the ends of the spring are correctly located either side of the tab on the selector arm. Secure the spring with a new circlip.

10 When the gearchange shaft is installed on the engine casing, the two ends of the return spring fit on each side of the locating pin **(see illustration)**. Check that the pin is tight – if not, unscrew it, clean the threads and apply a suitable locking compound. Install the pin and tighten it to the torque setting specified at the beginning of this Chapter.

11 Check the gearchange shaft splines for damage **(see illustration 18.9a)**. If the splines are damaged the shaft must be renewed.

12 Check the condition of the seal in the cover – if it is damaged or deteriorated, or there is evidence of leakage, lever it out

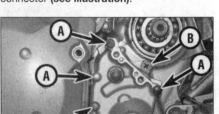

18.7a Undo the bolts (A) and Phillips-head screw (B) . . .

18.7b . . . and draw the gearchange cover off

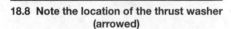

18.7c Location of the cover dowels (arrowed)

18.8 Note the location of the thrust washer (arrowed)

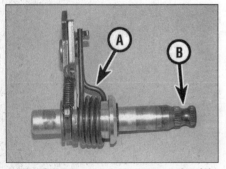

18.9a Gearchange shaft return spring (A). Note the splines (B)

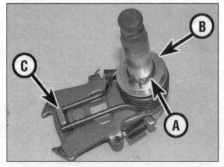

18.9b Circlip (A) and spring collar (B). Note the tab (C) on the selector arm

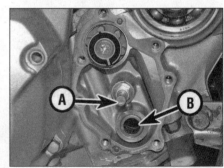

18.10 Return spring locating pin (A). Note the gearchange shaft bearing (B)

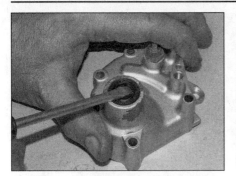

18.12a Lever out the seal in the cover carefully

18.12b Location of the shaft needle bearing (arrowed)

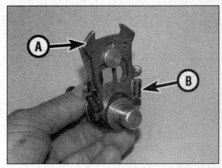

18.13 Selector arm pawls (A) and the pawl springs (B)

carefully with a flat-bladed screwdriver **(see illustration)**. Prior to installing the new seal, check the condition of the gearchange shaft needle bearing in the cover **(see illustration)**. Also check the shaft bearing in the engine casing **(see illustration 18.10)**. If the bearings are worn or pitted, a special puller will be required to remove them – refer to *Tools and Workshop Tips* in the *Reference* section for more information. To fit the new oil seal, first lubricate it with a smear of engine oil, then press it into place with a suitably-sized socket.

13 Inspect the selector arm pawls and the pawl springs **(see illustration)**. If the pawls are worn, or if the springs are fatigued or damaged, renew them. The shaft and pawls are available as an assembly. Note the location of the collar on the inner side of the shaft.

14 Inspect the gearchange selector pins and the contact plate of the neutral position switch for wear and damage **(see illustration)**. If necessary, undo the centre screw and withdraw the selector pin/contact plate assembly, noting how the drive pin locates in the end of the selector drum **(see illustrations)**. Also note how a pin inside the body of the selector pin holder locates the contact plate in position **(see illustrations)**.

15 Prior to assembly, clean the threads of the centre screw and apply a suitable thread-locking compound. Ensure the drive pin is installed in the end of the selector drum, then fit the selector pin holder onto the drive pin. Install the neutral position switch contact plate, aligning it with the pin inside the body of the selector pin holder, then install the screw and tighten it to the specified torque setting.

Installation

16 Remove all traces of old gasket from the crankcase and gearchange mechanism cover surfaces.

17 If removed, install the cover dowels, then fit the new cover gasket, making sure it locates correctly onto the dowels **(see illustration)**.

18 Lubricate the inside of the gearchange shaft seal with a smear of grease, ensure that the thrust washer is in place on the shaft, then install the shaft in the cover **(see illustration 18.8)**.

19 Align the two ends of the return spring with the locating pin in the engine casing, then install the gearchange mechanism cover **(see illustration 18.7b)**. Install the cover bolts and Phillips-head screw and tighten them to the torque setting specified at the beginning of this Chapter **(see illustration 18.7a)**.

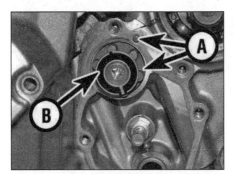

18.14a Gearchange selector pins (A) and neutral position switch contact plate (B)

18.14b Remove the centre screw . . .

18.14c . . . then withdraw the selector pin/contact plate assembly . . .

18.14d . . . noting the location of the drive pin (arrowed)

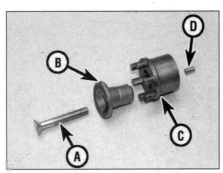

18.14e Centre screw (A), neutral switch contact plate (B), selector pin holder (C) and locating pin (D)

18.17 Install a new cover gasket

18.22 Gearchange stopper arm (A) and selector cam (B)

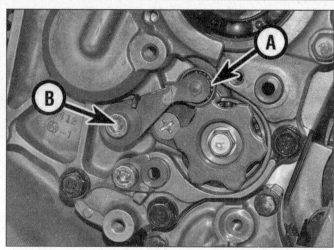

18.23 Gearchange stopper arm roller (A) and pivot bolt (B)

18.24a Undo the pivot bolt

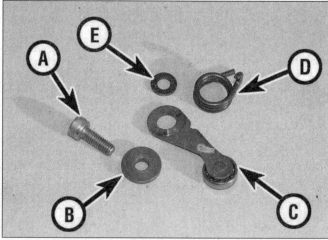

18.24b Stopper arm assembly – pivot bolt (A), collar (B), stopper arm (C), spring (D) and washer (E)

20 Install the remaining components in the reverse order of removal.

Gearchange stopper arm and selector cam

Removal and inspection

21 Remove the clutch (see Section 16).
22 Note the location of the gearchange stopper arm roller in the neutral detent on the gearchange selector cam (see illustration).
23 Check that the stopper arm roller turns freely. The stopper arm should be a light fit on the pivot bolt with no appreciable freeplay between them (see illustration). Inspect the stopper arm return spring – if it is fatigued, worn or damaged it must be renewed.
24 If required, undo the pivot bolt and draw the stopper arm assembly off (see illustrations).
25 Inspect the lobes on the gearchange cam and renew it if necessary. Don't forget to install the locating pin in the end of the selector drum before installing the cam. Clean the threads of the retaining bolt and apply a

suitable locking compound, then tighten the bolt to the specified torque setting. **Note:** *For further details of renewing the gearchange cam see Section 22.*

Installation

26 Fit the collar onto the pivot bolt, then fit the stopper arm, washer and spring (see illustration 18.24b).

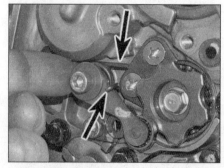

18.27a Position the ends of the spring as shown . . .

27 Install the pivot bolt loosely, ensure that the ends of the return spring are correctly positioned, then lift the roller onto the neutral detent on the gearchange selector cam (see illustrations). Tighten the pivot bolt to the specified torque setting.
28 Install the remaining components in the reverse order of removal.

18.27b . . . then lift the roller onto the selector cam

19.2 Bolts (arrowed) secure chain guide

19 Oil pump

Note 1: *The oil pump can be removed with the engine in the frame. If the engine has been removed, ignore the steps which don't apply.*
Note 2: *Two designs of oil pump body are fitted to the machines covered in this manual. Check your engine number before proceeding.*
Note 3: *When removing the pump rotors note which way round they fit, so that they can be returned to their original position on reassembly, thus ensuring that the mated surfaces between the two rotors continue to run together.*

Removal

1 On all models, first remove the clutch (see Section 16).
2 Undo the bolts securing the oil pump drive chain guide and remove the guide **(see illustration)**.

Engine numbers up to ER650AE039871

3 Undo the bolts securing the pump cover and remove the cover – note the location of the cover dowel and remove it if it is loose **(see illustration)**.
4 Draw out the inner and outer rotors of the scavenge pump. Note the location of the drive pin for the scavenge pump inner rotor in the pump shaft.
5 Draw out the pump shaft and pump body. Note the location of the drive pin for the feed pump inner rotor in the pump shaft. Remove the rotor drive pins and draw the shaft out of the pump body, noting which way round it fits.
6 Draw the inner and outer rotors of the feed pump out from the engine casing.
7 Lay the parts out in the proper order to aid reassembly **(see illustration 19.3)**. Note that the scavenge pump rotors are wider than the feed pump rotors.

Engine numbers from ER650AE039872-on

8 Undo the bolts securing the pump cover **(see illustration)**. Temporarily install the pump

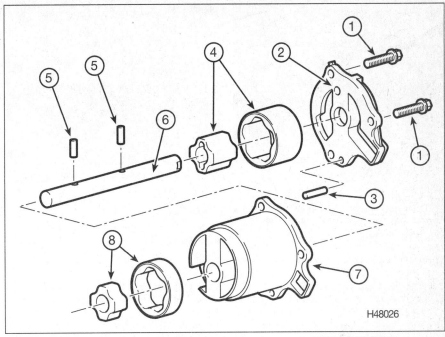

19.3 Oil pump components – engine numbers up to ER650AE039871

1 Cover bolts
2 Pump cover
3 Cover dowel
4 Scavenge pump rotors
5 Drive pin
6 Pump shaft
7 Pump body
8 Feed pump rotors

sprocket bolt by turning it anti-clockwise, then draw out the oil pump **(see illustration)**.
9 Draw the outer rotor of the feed pump out from the engine casing **(see illustration)**.

10 Unscrew the pump sprocket bolt and remove the pump cover **(see illustration)**. Note the location of the cover dowel and remove it if it is loose.

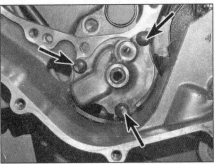

19.8a Undo the bolts (arrowed) . . .

19.8b . . . then draw out the oil pump

19.9 Remove the feed pump outer rotor

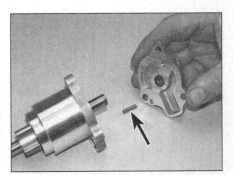

19.10 Remove the cover noting the dowel (arrowed)

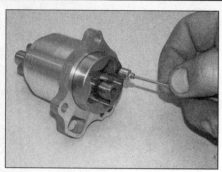

19.11a Draw out the outer . . .

19.11b . . . and inner scavenge pump rotors

19.11c Remove the scavenge pump drive pin

11 Draw out the outer and inner rotors of the scavenge pump **(see illustrations)**. Remove the drive pin for the scavenge pump inner rotor from the pump shaft **(see illustration)**.
12 Remove the drive pin for the feed pump inner rotor, then slide off the inner rotor and withdraw the shaft **(see illustrations)**.
13 Lay the parts out in the proper order to aid reassembly. Note that the scavenge pump rotors are wider than the feed pump rotors.

Inspection

14 Inspect the inside of the pump body for wear and damage **(see illustration)**. Check that the shaft rotates freely inside the body without any side-to-side play or binding. Inspect the shaft and rotors for wear and scoring – if new rotors are required they should be renewed in matching pairs **(see illustration)**.

Installation

Note: *Prior to installation, lubricate the rotors with clean engine oil.*

Engine numbers up to ER650AE039871

15 Install the outer and inner feed pump rotors into the engine casing **(see illustration 19.3)**.
16 Lubricate the bearing sections of the pump shaft with molybdenum disulphide grease. Fit the drive pin for the feed pump inner rotor into the shaft, then install the shaft, aligning the drive pin with the slot in the inner rotor.
17 Install the pump body. If removed, install the cover dowel to ensure the body is correctly aligned with the casing.
18 Fit the drive pin for the scavenge pump inner rotor into the shaft, then install the inner rotor, aligning the slot in the rotor with the drive pin.

19 Install the scavenge pump outer rotor.
20 Align the pump cover with the body and dowel. Clean the threads of the cover bolts, then apply a suitable thread-locking compound and tighten the bolts to the torque setting specified at the beginning of this Chapter.
21 Install the oil pump drive chain guide, noting how it locates in the slot in the input shaft selector fork shaft **(see illustration)**. Clean the threads of the mounting bolts, then apply a suitable thread-locking compound and tighten the bolts to the torque setting specified at the beginning of this Chapter.
22 Install the remaining components in the reverse order of removal.

Engine numbers from ER650AE039872-on

23 Install the feed pump outer rotor into the engine casing **(see illustration 19.9)**.
24 Fit the drive pin for the feed pump inner rotor into the shaft, then install the rotor and slide it down the shaft, aligning the slot in the rotor with the drive pin.
25 Lubricate the bearing sections of the pump shaft with molybdenum disulphide oil (a 50/50 mixture of molybdenum disulphide grease and engine oil), then install the shaft into the body **(see illustration 19.12a)**.
26 Fit the drive pin for the scavenge pump inner rotor into the shaft, then install the inner rotor, aligning the slot in the rotor with the drive pin **(see illustrations 19.11c and b)**. Install the scavenge pump outer rotor.
27 If removed, install the cover dowel, then install the cover **(see illustration 19.10)**.

19.12a Remove the feed pump drive pin . . .

19.12b . . . then the inner rotor and pump shaft

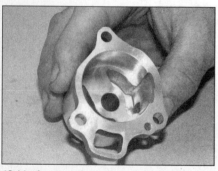

19.14a Inspect the inside of the pump body

19.14b Keep rotors together in matched pairs

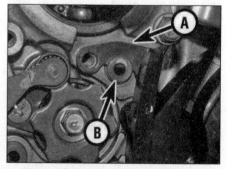

19.21 Drive chain guide (A) locates in selector fork shaft (B)

28 Align the feed pump inner rotor with the outer rotor in the engine casing and install the pump assembly **(see illustration 19.8b)**. Clean the threads of the cover bolts, then apply a suitable thread-locking compound and tighten the bolts to the torque setting specified at the beginning of this Chapter **(see illustration 19.8a)**.

29 Install the oil pump drive chain guide (see Step 21).

30 Install the remaining components in the reverse order of removal.

20 Oil sump, oil strainer and pressure relief valve

Note: *The oil sump, strainer and pressure relief valve can be removed with the engine in the frame. If the engine has been removed, ignore the steps which do not apply.*

Removal

1 Drain the engine oil (see Chapter 1).

2 Remove the exhaust system (see Chapter 4).

3 If required, undo the bolts securing the belly panel brackets and remove the brackets **(see illustrations)**.

4 Unscrew the ten sump bolts, loosening them evenly in a criss-cross pattern to prevent distortion, and remove the sump **(see illustration)**. Remove the gasket and discard it as a new one must be fitted on reassembly **(see illustration 20.21)**. Note the location of the sleeve on the end of the breather pipe and remove it if it is loose **(see illustration)**.

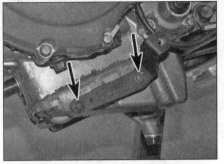
20.3a Undo the bolts (arrowed) . . .

20.3b . . . securing the belly panel brackets

20.4a Remove the sump

20.4b Note the sleeve (arrowed) on the breather pipe

5 Pull the oil strainer out of its socket in the crankcase and discard the seal as a new one must be fitted **(see illustrations)**.

6 Undo the bolt securing the oil pipe retainer and remove the retainer **(see illustration 20.5b)**. Ease the large diameter oil pipe out of its sockets **(see illustration)**. Ease the small diameter oil pipe out of its sockets **(see**

illustration). Note the location of the O-rings on the oil pipe unions and discard them as new ones should be used.

7 Unscrew the pressure relief valve **(see illustration)**.

8 Undo the bolts securing the gauze filter plate in the sump and remove the filter **(see illustration)**.

20.5a Remove the oil strainer . . .

20.5b . . . and pull out the seal. Note the oil pipe retainer bolt (arrowed)

20.6a Ease out the large diameter oil pipe

20.6b Ease out the small diameter oil pipe

20.7 Unscrew the pressure relief valve

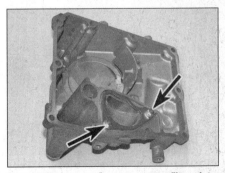
20.8 Bolts (arrowed) secure gauze filter plate

20.12 Plunger should move freely inside body

20.14a Location of oil pipe below alternator rotor

20.14b Note O-rings on oil pipe unions

20.15a Undo the bolts . . .

20.15b . . . and draw the oil gallery off

20.15c Note the O-rings (arrowed) on the gallery . . .

9 Remove all traces of old gasket from the sump and crankcase mating surfaces with a suitable solvent. If a scraper is used, take care not to scratch or gouge the soft aluminium.

Inspection

10 Clean the sump thoroughly and wash the gauze filter with a suitable solvent. Renew the gauze if it is damaged.

11 Wash the oil strainer with solvent and remove any debris caught in the mesh, using compressed air if available. Inspect the strainer for any signs of wear or damage and renew it if necessary.

12 Clean the pressure relief valve. Push the plunger into the regulator body and check that it moves freely against the spring pressure (see illustration). If required, the pressure relief valve can be disassembled for cleaning, but no component parts are available – if the valve is worn or damaged, a new one must be fitted.

13 Wash the oil pipes in solvent and blow them through with compressed air if available. If a blocked oilway is suspected, also clean and check the oil pipe located below the alternator rotor and the external oil gallery located behind the front sprocket cover as follows.

14 Remove the alternator cover (see Section 15). Ease the oil pipe out of its sockets (see illustration). Note the location of the O-rings on the pipe unions and discard them as new ones should be used (see illustration). On installation, lubricate the new O-rings with a smear of grease and press the pipe unions into the sockets firmly. Install the alternator cover (see Section 15).

15 Remove the front sprocket cover (see Section 18). Clean the area around the oil gallery thoroughly, then undo the mounting bolts and lift the gallery off (see illustrations). Note the location of the O-rings at both ends of the gallery and on the crankcase union and

discard them as new ones should be used (see illustrations). On installation, lubricate the new O-rings with a smear of grease and press the gallery firmly over the O-ring on the crankcase union. Clean the threads of the mounting bolts and apply a suitable non-permanent thread-locking compound, then tighten the bolts to the torque setting specified at the beginning of this Chapter. Install the front sprocket cover.

Installation

16 Clean the threads of the pressure relief valve and apply a suitable non-permanent thread-locking compound, then install the valve and tighten it to the torque setting specified at the beginning of this Chapter (see illustration 20.7).

17 Lubricate the new O-rings on the oil pipe unions with a smear of grease (see illustrations). Press the pipe unions into their sockets firmly (see illustrations 20.6b and a).

20.15d . . . and on the crankcase union

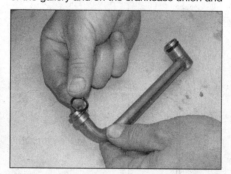

20.17a Fit new O-rings onto the unions on the large . . .

20.17b . . . and small diameter oil pipes

20.17c Thread-lock the pipe retainer bolt

20.21 Install a new sump gasket

21.2 Draw off the spacer . . .

21.3 . . . then lever out the shaft seal . . .

Clean the threads of the pipe retainer bolt and apply a suitable non-permanent thread-locking compound, then install retainer and tighten the bolt to the specified torque (see illustration).

18 Smear the new oil strainer seal with grease and install it in the crankcase (see illustration 20.5b). Ensure the strainer is correctly aligned, then press it into the seal firmly (see illustration 20.5a).

19 Clean the threads of the filter plate bolts and apply a suitable non-permanent thread-locking compound, then install the gauze filter and plate and tighten the bolts to the specified torque (see illustration 20.8).

20 Ensure the sleeve is in place on the end of the breather pipe (see illustration 20.4b).

21 Install a new sump gasket then fit the sump onto the crankcase, making sure the bolt holes align (see illustration). Install the sump bolts, then tighten them evenly in a criss-cross pattern to the specified torque setting (see illustration 20.4a).

22 Install the remaining components in the reverse order of removal.

23 Don't forget to refill the engine oil (see Chapter 1 and *Pre-ride checks*). Start the engine and check that there are no leaks around the sump, then install the belly panel (see Chapter 7).

21 Transmission assembly removal and installation

Note: *The transmission assembly can be removed with the engine in the frame. If the engine has been removed, ignore the steps which do not apply.*

Removal

1 Remove the front sprocket (see Chapter 6).
2 Draw the spacer off the transmission output shaft (see illustration).
3 Lever out the shaft seal with a flat-bladed screwdriver, noting how it is fitted (see illustration). Discard the seal as a new one must be fitted on installation.

4 Remove the O-ring from the groove in the shaft (see illustration). Discard the O-ring as a new one must be fitted.
5 Remove the external gearchange mechanism, including the selector pin holder and neutral position switch contact plate assembly (see Section 18).
6 Remove the clutch (see Section 16).
7 Undo the bolts securing the oil pump drive chain guide and remove the guide (see illustration 19.2).
8 Undo the bolts securing the transmission cover and remove them, noting their locations (see illustration).
9 Withdraw the cover and transmission assembly from the crankcase (see illustration).

21.8 Location of the transmission cover bolts

21.9 Withdraw the cover and transmission assembly

21.4 . . . and remove the O-ring

21.10a Note the location of the O-ring

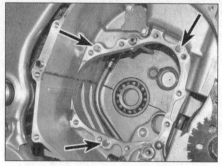

21.10b Note the location of the cover dowels (arrowed)

21.16a Fit the O-ring into the groove in the shaft

21.16b Install the new output shaft seal . . .

21.16c . . . and press it into its housing

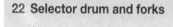

22 Selector drum and forks

Note: *The selector drum and forks can be removed with the engine in the frame. If the engine has been removed, ignore the steps which do not apply.*

Removal

1 Remove the transmission assembly (see Section 21).
2 Before removing the selector forks, note which way round they are fitted **(see illustration)**. Mark the forks with paint or a felt pen according to their location to aid installation.
3 Note how the guide pin on the transmission input shaft selector fork locates in the centre groove on the selector drum and how the fork locates in the groove on the 3rd/4th gear pinion, then support the fork and withdraw the fork shaft **(see illustration)**. Slide the fork back on its shaft.
4 Undo the bolt securing the transmission output shaft selector fork shaft retainer and remove the retainer **(see illustration)**.
5 Note how the guide pins on the transmission output shaft selector forks locate in the outside grooves on the selector drum and how the forks locate in the grooves on the 5th and 6th gear pinions, then support the forks and withdraw the fork shaft **(see illustration)**. Slide the forks back on their shaft.
6 Support the transmission shafts as an

10 Note the location of the oil gallery O-ring and remove it as a new one must be fitted **(see illustration)**. Note the location of the cover dowels and remove them for safekeeping if they are loose **(see illustration)**.
11 If required, the transmission shafts can be disassembled and inspected for wear or damage (see Sections 22 and 23).

Installation

12 If removed, install the cover dowels. Lubricate the new oil gallery O-ring with grease and install it on the union **(see illustration 21.10a)**.
13 Ensure the mating surfaces of the transmission cover and casing are clean. Align the transmission output shaft, input shaft and selector drum with their bearings in the left-had side of the casing, then install the transmission assembly. Install the cover bolts

finger-tight, then check that the output and input shafts rotate freely.
14 Tighten the cover bolts evenly in a criss-cross pattern to the torque setting specified at the beginning of this Chapter **(see illustration 21.8)**.
15 Install the oil pump drive chain guide (see Section 19, Step 21).
16 Install the remaining components in the reverse order of removal, noting the following:
● Fit a new O-ring into the groove in the transmission output shaft **(see illustration)**. Lubricate the O-ring with a smear of grease.
● Lubricate the new output shaft seal with grease, then slide it carefully over the end of the shaft making sure it is the correct way round **(see illustration)**. Press the seal into its housing with a suitably-sized socket **(see illustration)**.

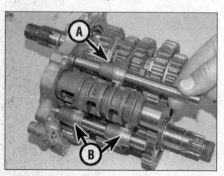

22.2 Note the selector forks on the input (A) and output shafts (B)

22.3 Removing the input shaft selector fork

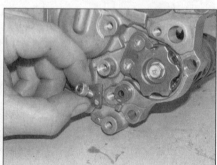

22.4 Remove the selector fork shaft retainer

22.5 Removing the output shaft selector forks

22.6a Support the transmission shafts as an assembly . . .

22.6b . . . and withdraw them from the transmission cover

assembly and withdraw them from the transmission cover **(see illustrations)**.

7 To remove the selector drum from its bearing in the cover, first remove the gearchange cam. Pass a steel rod through the drum to hold it, then undo the centre bolt **(see illustrations)**. Lift off the cam and draw the drum out of the bearing **(see illustrations)**. The cam locates on a pin in the end of the selector drum – remove it for safekeeping **(see illustration)**.

Inspection

8 Inspect the selector forks for any signs of wear or damage, especially around the fork ends where they engage with the groove in the pinion. Measure the thickness of the fork ends and the width of the pinion grooves and compare the results with the specifications at the beginning of this Chapter **(see illustrations)**. Renew the forks and/or gear pinions if they are worn beyond the service limits.

9 Inspect the selector drum grooves and selector fork guide pins for signs of wear or damage **(see illustration)**. Measure the width of each groove and the diameter of the guide pins and compare the results with the

specifications **(see illustration)**. Renew the forks and/or selector drum if they are worn beyond the service limits.

10 Check closely to see if the forks are bent. Ensure that the forks fit correctly on their

22.7a Undo the gearchange cam centre bolt

22.7b Lift off the gearchange cam . . .

22.7c . . . and draw the drum out of the bearing

22.7d Remove the pin from the end of the selector drum

22.8a Measuring the thickness of the selector fork ends

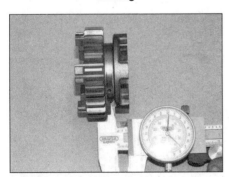

22.8b Measuring the width of the pinion grooves

22.9a Check the drum grooves and corresponding selector fork guide pins

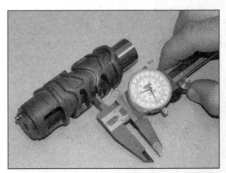

22.9b Measuring the width of the selector drum grooves

22.10 Forks should slide freely on their shafts

22.13b Location of the selector drum needle bearing

shafts – they should move freely but with no appreciable freeplay (see illustration). If the forks are in any way damaged they must be replaced with new ones.

11 Inspect both selector fork shafts for signs of wear or damage. Check each shaft is straight by rolling it along a flat surface. A bent shaft will cause difficulty in selecting gears and make the gearchange action heavy. Renew either shaft if it is bent.

12 Check that the fork shaft holes in the casing and the transmission cover are neither worn nor damaged.

13 Check that the selector drum bearings rotate freely – a caged ball bearing is located in the transmission cover and a needle bearing in the left-hand side of the engine casing (see illustrations). Only remove the bearings if they are going to be renewed. The ball bearing is retained by a plate on the outside of the cover (see illustration 22.13a). Undo the screws and remove the plate, then heat the bearing housing with a hot air gun and press the

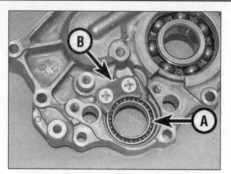

22.13a Selector drum ball bearing (A) is retained by plate (B)

22.16 Slotted end (arrowed) of the selector forks shaft

bearing out from the other side. On installation, clean the screw threads and apply a suitable non-permanent thread locking compound, then tighten the screws securely. Before removing the needle bearing, note its location in the housing. Press the new bearing in carefully to avoid damage. Refer to *Tools and Workshop Tips* in the *Reference* section for more details of bearing removal and installation.

Installation

Note: *During installation, lubricate the components with clean engine oil.*

14 If removed, locate the selector drum in its bearing in the transmission cover. Fit the pin into the end of the selector drum and install the gearchange cam (see illustrations 22.7c and b). Clean the threads of the centre bolt and apply a suitable non-permanent thread locking compound, then tighten the bolt to the torque setting specified at the beginning of this Chapter (see illustration 22.7a).

15 Align the gear pinions on the transmission

shafts and install the shafts as an assembly (see illustration 22.6b and a).

16 Install the output shaft selector forks in the grooves on the 5th and 6th gear pinions, align the outside grooves on the selector drum with the fork guide pins, then secure the forks with the fork shaft (see illustration 22.5). The slotted end of the shaft should locate in the transmission cover (see illustration). Clean the threads of the retainer bolt and apply a suitable non-permanent thread locking compound, then install the retainer and tighten the bolt to the specified torque setting (see illustration 22.4).

17 Install the input shaft selector fork in the groove on the 3rd/4th gear pinion and align the fork guide pin with the centre groove on the selector drum, then secure the fork with the fork shaft (see illustration 22.3). Position the fork shaft so that the slot in the cover end aligns with the bracket on the oil pump drive chain guide when it is installed (see Section 19, Step 21).

18 Install the transmission assembly (see Section 21).

23 Transmission shaft overhaul

Note: *References to the right and left-hand ends of the transmission shafts are made as though they are installed in the engine and the engine is the correct way up.*

1 Remove the transmission assembly (see Section 21), then follow the procedure in Section 22 to remove the transmission shafts.

2 Always disassemble the transmission shafts separately to avoid mixing up the components.

 HAYNES HINT *When disassembling the transmission shafts, place the parts on a long rod or thread a wire through them to keep them in order and facing the proper direction.*

Input shaft disassembly

3 Remove the circlip from the left-hand end of the shaft, then remove the needle bearing and the plain washer (see illustrations).

23.3a Remove the circlip . . .

23.3b . . . the needle bearing . . .

23.3c . . . and the plain washer

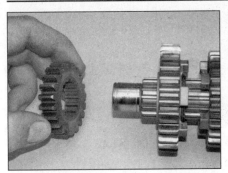

23.4a Slide off the 2nd gear pinion . . .

23.4b . . . the 6th gear pinion . . .

23.4c . . . and the 6th gear pinion bush. Note the oil holes (arrowed)

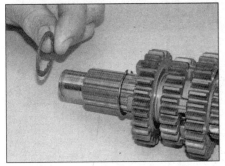

23.5a Slide off the splined washer . . .

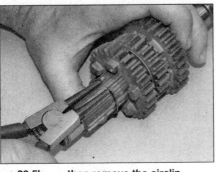

23.5b . . . then remove the circlip . . .

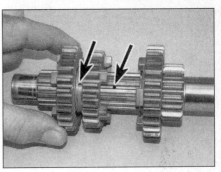

23.5c . . . and slide off the 3rd/4th gear pinion. Note the oil holes (arrowed)

4 Slide the 2nd gear pinion and the 6th gear pinion and bush off the shaft **(see illustrations)**.

5 Slide off the splined washer, then remove the circlip securing the combined 3rd/4th gear pinion and slide the pinion off the shaft **(see illustrations)**.

6 Remove the circlip securing the 5th gear pinion, then slide the splined washer, 5th gear pinion and its bush off the shaft **(see illustrations)**.

7 The 1st gear pinion is integral with the shaft **(see illustration)**.

Input shaft inspection

8 Wash all the components in solvent and dry them off.

9 Check the gear teeth for cracking, chipping, pitting and other obvious wear or damage **(see illustration)**. Any pinion that is damaged must

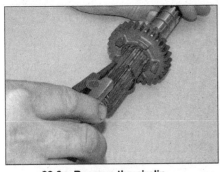

23.6a Remove the circlip . . .

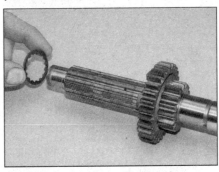

23.6b . . . and the splined washer . . .

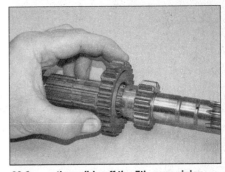

23.6c . . . then slide off the 5th gear pinion . . .

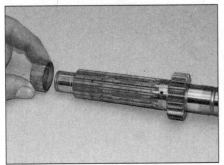

23.6d . . . and the 5th gear pinion bush

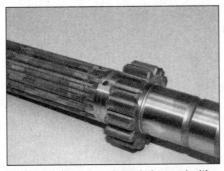

23.7 The 1st gear pinion is integral with the shaft

23.9a Check the gear teeth for signs of wear or damage

23.9b Inspect mating dogs as sets

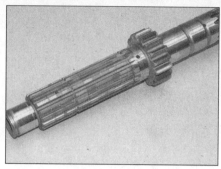

23.13 Inspect the bearing surfaces and splines for wear

23.15a Input shaft ball bearing (A), output shaft needle bearing outer race (B), retaining plate (C)

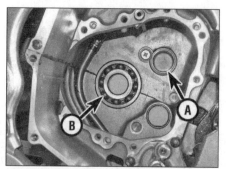

23.15b Input shaft needle bearing outer race (A), output shaft ball bearing (B)

side. On installation, clean the screw threads and apply a suitable non-permanent thread locking compound, then tighten the screw securely. The needle bearing on the left-hand end of the shaft runs in a race in the upper half of the crankcase – the race is retained by a screw and washer (see illustration). Extract the old bearing race with a knife-edged puller and press the new one in carefully to avoid damage. On installation, apply non-permanent thread locking compound to the screw.

Input shaft reassembly

16 During reassembly, apply clean engine oil to the mating surfaces of the shaft, pinions and bushes. When installing the circlips, do not expand their ends any further than is necessary. Install the stamped circlips so that the chamfered side faces the pinion it secures (see Correct fitting of a stamped circlip illustration in Tools and Workshop Tips of the Reference Section).

17 Slide the 5th gear bush all the way on the shaft from the left-hand end, then slide the 5th gear pinion onto the bush, with its dogs facing away from the integral 1st gear (see illustrations 23.6d and c). Slide on the splined washer (see illustration 23.6b), then install the stamped circlip, making sure it is properly seated in its groove (see illustration).

18 Slide on the combined 3rd/4th gear pinion so that the smaller (3rd gear) pinion faces the 5th gear (see illustration 23.5c). Ensure the oil holes in the combined pinion and shaft are aligned

19 Install the stamped circlip (see illustration 23.5b).

20 Slide on the splined washer (see illustration 23.5a). Slide on the 6th gear pinion splined bush, aligning the oil hole in the bush with the hole in the shaft (see illustration 23.4c). Fit the 6th gear pinion onto the bush, with its dogs facing the dogs on the 4th gear pinion (see illustration 23.4b).

21 Slide on the 2nd gear pinion, the plain washer and the needle bearing (see illustrations 23.4a, 3c and b).

22 Secure the bearing with the circlip, making sure it is properly seated in its groove (see illustration 23.3a).

23 Check that all components have been correctly installed (see illustration).

be replaced with a new one. Inspect the dogs in the pinions for cracks, chips, and excessive wear especially in the form of rounded edges. Make sure mating gear dogs engage properly – replace the paired gears with a new set if necessary (see illustration).

10 Measure the selector fork groove width (see Section 22).

11 Check for signs of scoring or bluing on the pinions, bushes and shaft. This could be caused by overheating due to inadequate lubrication. Check that all the oil holes and passages are clear. Replace any damaged pinions or bushes with new ones.

12 Check that each pinion moves freely on the shaft or bush but without undue freeplay. Check that each bush moves freely on the shaft but without undue freeplay.

13 The shaft is unlikely to sustain damage

unless the engine has seized, placing an unusually high loading on the transmission, or the machine has covered a very high mileage. Check the surface of the shaft, especially where a pinion turns on it, and replace the shaft with a new one if it has scored or picked up, or if there is any wear (see illustration).

14 Check the washers and replace any that are bent or worn with new ones. Discard the circlips as new ones must be fitted on reassembly.

15 Refer to Tools and Workshop Tips in the Reference Section to check the input shaft bearings and renew any bearing if it is worn, loose or damaged. The large ball bearing in the transmission cover is retained by a plate on the inside of the cover (see illustration). Undo the screw and remove the plate, then heat the bearing housing with a hot air gun and press the bearing out from the other

23.17 Ensure the circlip is seated in its groove

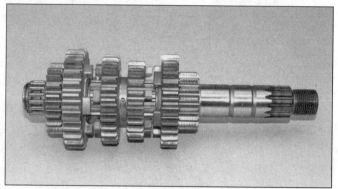

23.23 The assembled input shaft should look like this

23.24 Remove the plain washer

23.25a Slide off the 2nd gear pinion . . .

23.25b . . . and the 6th gear pinion. Note the oil holes (arrowed)

23.26a Remove the circlip . . .

23.26b . . . the needle bearing . . .

23.26c . . . and the plain washer

Output shaft disassembly

24 Remove the plain washer from the left-hand end of the shaft **(see illustration)**.
25 Slide the 2nd and 6th gear pinions off the shaft **(see illustrations)**.
26 Remove the circlip from the right-hand end of the shaft, then remove the needle bearing and the plain washer **(see illustrations)**.
27 Slide off the 1st gear pinion and the plain washer **(see illustrations)**.
28 The 5th gear pinion has three steel balls inside it for the positive neutral finder mechanism. The balls lock the pinion to the shaft unless it is spun rapidly enough to fling the balls outward by centrifugal force. To remove the 5th gear pinion, hold the shaft

23.27a Slide off the 1st gear pinion . . .

23.27b . . . and the plain washer

vertical by the 4th gear pinion, then spin the 5th gear while pulling it up **(see illustration)**. It may take several attempts to release the 5th

gear pinion, but it will come off easily once disengaged – take care not to loose the steel balls **(see illustration)**.

23.28a Spin the 5th gear and pull it up and off . . .

23.28b . . . taking care not to loose the balls (arrowed)

23.29a Remove the circlip . . .

23.29b . . . and the splined washer

23.30a Slide off the 3rd gear pinion . . .

Caution: Don't pull the gear up too hard or fast – the balls will fly out of the gear.

29 Remove the circlip securing the 3rd gear pinion, then slide off the splined washer (see illustrations).

30 Note which way round the 3rd and 4th gear pinions are fitted, then slide the pinions off the shaft (see illustrations).

31 Slide off the bush for the 3rd and 4th gear pinions, then remove the plain washer (see illustration).

Output shaft inspection

32 Refer to Steps 8 to 14 above. In addition, examine the positive neutral finder mechanism balls for damage and pitting, and examine the ball recesses in the shaft for wear and damage (see Illustration). Renew any components as necessary.

33 Refer to *Tools and Workshop Tips* in the *Reference* Section to check the output shaft

bearings and renew any bearing if it is worn, loose or damaged. The large ball bearing in the crankcase is secured by a half ring retainer in the upper crankcase half (see illustration 23.15b). The bearing can only be removed once the crankcase halves have been separated (see Sections 24 and 25). The needle bearing on the right-hand end of the shaft runs in a race in the transmission cover – the race is retained by a plate (see illustration 23.15a). Remove the plate (see Step 15). Extract the old bearing race with a knife-edged puller and press the new one in carefully to avoid damage. On installation, apply non-permanent thread locking compound to the screw.

Output shaft reassembly

34 Lubricate mating surfaces with clean engine oil and ensure the circlips are installed correctly (see Step 16).

35 Slide the plain washer all the way onto the shaft from the right-hand end, then slide on the bush for the 3rd and 4th gear pinions (see illustration 23.31).

36 Slide on the 4th gear pinion, ensuring it is fitted the correct way round, then slide on the 3rd gear pinion (see illustrations 23.30b and a).

37 Slide on the splined washer, then install the stamped circlip, making sure it is properly seated in its groove (see illustrations 23.29b and a). Note the space between the installed pinions (see illustration).

38 Install the three balls in the recesses inside the 5th gear pinion – use oil to hold them in position, not grease as it will impair the action of the positive neutral finder mechanism (see illustration). Hold the shaft vertical, align the large holes in the pinion selector fork groove with the oil holes in the shaft, then slide the gear pinion onto the shaft (see illustration).

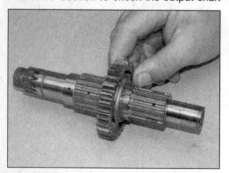

23.30b . . . and the 4th gear pinion

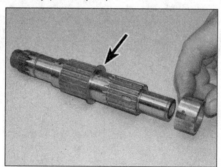

23.31 Slide off the bush and the plain washer (arrowed)

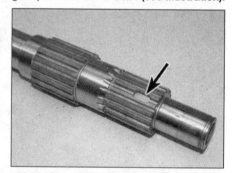

23.32 Check the recesses for the neutral finder mechanism balls

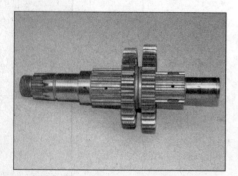

23.37 The installed 4th and 3rd gear pinions should look like this

23.38a Install the three balls in the recesses inside the 5th gear pinion

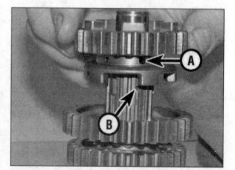

23.38b Align the large holes (A) with the oil holes (B) in the shaft and slide the gear on

23.43 The assembled output shaft should look like this

24.4a Release the clip (arrowed) . . .

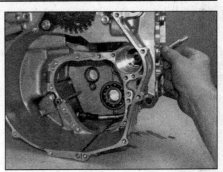

24.4b . . . and remove the breather pipe

Check that the balls are correctly engaged by sliding the pinion up-and-down – it should not come off the end of the shaft.

39 Slide on the plain washer and the 1st gear pinion **(see illustration 23.27b and a)**.

40 Slide on the plain washer and the needle bearing, then secure the bearing with the circlip, making sure it is properly seated in its groove **(see illustration 23.26c, b and a)**.

41 Slide the 6th gear pinion onto the left-hand end of the shaft, aligning the oil hole in the pinion with the hole in the shaft **(see illustration 23.25b)**.

42 Slide on the 2nd gear pinion (dished side towards 6th gear) and the plain washer **(see illustrations 23.25a and 23.24)**.

43 Check that all components have been correctly installed **(see illustration)**.

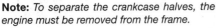

24 Crankcase separation and reassembly

Note: *To separate the crankcase halves, the engine must be removed from the frame.*

Separation

1 To gain access to the connecting rods, crankshaft and bearings and balancer shaft, the crankcase must be split into two parts.

2 Remove the engine from the frame (see Section 4).

3 Before the crankcases can be separated the following components must be removed:

Cylinder head (Section 10)
Cylinder block (Section 12)
Pistons (Section 13)
Water pump (Chapter 3)
Alternator and starter motor (Chapter 8)
Clutch (Section 16)
Gearchange mechanism (Section 18)
Transmission assembly (Section 21)
Oil pump, if required (Section 19)
Oil sump, strainer and pressure relief valve (Section 20)

4 If required, release the clip securing the breather pipe and withdraw the pipe through the lower crankcase half **(see illustrations)**.

5 Make a cardboard template punched with holes to match all the bolts in each crankcase half – as each bolt is removed, store it in its relative position in the template **(see**

24.5 An example of a template for storing crankcase bolts

illustration). This will ensure all bolts and washers are installed in the correct location on reassembly. **Note:** *New copper-plated sealing washers should be used on reassembly where fitted – keep the old ones with the bolts to be used for the main bearing and balancer shaft bearing oil clearance checks and as a guide to reassembly.*

6 Unscrew the three upper crankcase bolts **(see illustration)**.

7 Turn the engine upside down.

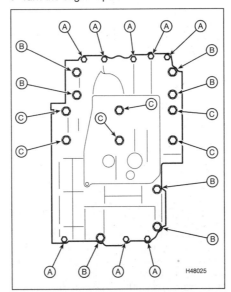

24.8 Lower crankcase 6 mm bolts (A), 8 mm bolts (B) and 9 mm bolts (C)

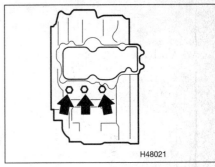

24.6 Location of upper crankcase bolts (arrowed)

8 Unscrew the eight 6 mm bolts along the front and rear edges evenly, a little at a time, then unscrew the seven 8 mm bolts evenly, a little at a time **(see illustration)**.

9 Unscrew the six 9 mm crankshaft journal bolts evenly, a little at a time in a **reverse** of the numerical sequence marked on the crankcase **(see illustrations 24.8 and 24.25)**.

10 Carefully lift the lower crankcase half off the upper half, using a soft-faced hammer to tap around the joint to initially separate the halves if necessary **(see illustration)**. **Note:** *If the halves do not separate easily, make sure all fasteners have been removed. Do not try and separate the halves by levering between the crankcase mating surfaces as they are easily damaged and will leak on reassembly.*

11 The lower crankcase will come away leaving the crankshaft, balancer shaft and left-hand transmission output shaft bearing in

24.10 Carefully separate the crankcase halves

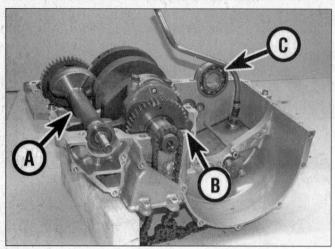

24.11a Balancer shaft (A), crankshaft (B) and transmission output shaft bearing (C)

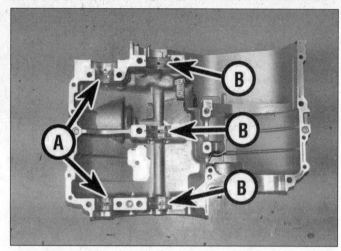

24.11b Balancer shaft shells (A) and lower main bearing shells (B)

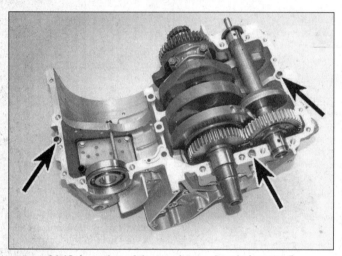

24.12 Location of the crankcase dowels (arrowed)

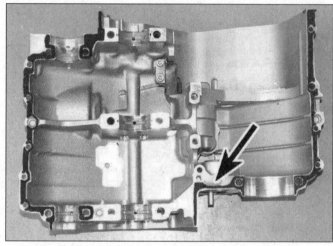

24.19 Apply sealant to the area shown – avoid oil passage (arrowed)

the upper crankcase (see illustration). Take care not to dislodge the lower main bearing shells and balancer shaft shells which should remain in their seats in the lower crankcase (see illustration). Remove the shells if they are loose, but keep them in order.

12 Note the location of the crankcase dowels and remove them for safekeeping if they are loose (see illustration).

13 Refer to Sections 25, 27 and 29 for inspection of the crankcases, and removal and installation of the crankshaft and balancer shaft.

Reassembly

14 Remove all traces of old sealant from the crankcase mating surfaces with a suitable solvent and clean the threads of all the crankcase bolts.

15 Support the upper crankcase securely on the work surface. Ensure that all components and their bearings are in place in the upper crankcase, including the cam chain and

transmission output shaft bearing (see illustration 24.11a).

16 If removed, fit the locating dowels into the upper crankcase (see illustrations 24.12).

17 Check that the lower main bearing shells are correctly located in the lower crankcase (see illustration 24.11b).

18 Lubricate the crankshaft big-end and main bearings, and the balancer shaft bearings, with clean engine oil.

19 Wipe the mating surfaces of both crankcase halves with a rag soaked in high flash-point solvent to remove all traces of oil. Apply a thin coating of suitable sealant to the mating surface of the upper crankcase (see illustration).

Caution: Apply the sealant only to the areas indicated in the photo. Do not apply an excessive amount of sealant as it will ooze out when the case halves are assembled and may obstruct oil passages. Do not apply the sealant on or too close to any of the bearing shells or surfaces.

20 Carefully fit the lower crankcase onto the upper crankcase, making sure the dowels all align correctly. If it hasn't been removed, ensure that the breather pipe is correctly located through the hole in the lower crankcase (see illustration).

21 Check that the lower crankcase is correctly seated. Note: *The crankcases should fit together*

24.20 Ensure breather pipe (arrowed) is correctly located

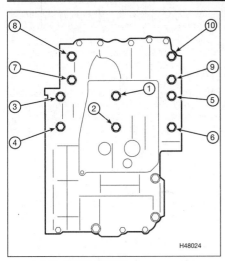

24.25 TIGHTENING sequence for crankshaft and balancer shaft journal bolts

without being forced. If the casings are not correctly seated, remove the lower crankcase and investigate the problem. Do not attempt to pull the casings together using the crankcase bolts as they will crack and be ruined.

22 Fit new copper-plated sealing washers to the six 9 mm crankshaft journal bolts **(see illustration 24.8)**. Lubricate both sides of the washers and the bolt threads with molybdenum sulphide oil (a 50/50 mixture of molybdenum disulphide grease and engine oil), then install the bolts finger-tight.
23 Lubricate the underside of the flanges and the threads of the 8 mm balancer shaft journal

25.3 Note the alignment of the hose clips (arrowed)

25.4b ... and on oil pipe (arrowed)

25.2a Lift out the output shaft bearing ...

bolts, numbered 7 to 10 on the crankcase, with molybdenum sulphide oil **(see illustration 24.25)**. Install the bolts finger-tight.
24 Install the remaining 8 and 6 mm bolts in the lower crankcase without lubrication.
25 Tighten the crankshaft and balancer shaft journal bolts in the numerical sequence marked in the crankcase, to the torque settings specified at the beginning of this Chapter **(see illustration)**.
26 Tighten the remaining 8 mm bolts to the specified torque, then tighten the 6 mm bolts to the specified torque **(see illustration 24.8)**.
27 Turn the engine the right way up. Install the upper crankcase bolts, not forgetting the new sealing washers, then tighten the bolts to the specified torque **(see illustration 24.6)**.
28 With all the crankcase bolts tightened, check that the crankshaft and balancer shaft rotate smoothly and easily. If there are any signs of undue stiffness, tight or rough spots,

25.4a O-ring on gallery union ...

25.5a Selector drum needle bearing ...

25.2b ... and the bearing half ring retainer

or of any other problem, the fault must be rectified before proceeding further.
29 Install the remaining components in the reverse order of removal.

25 Crankcases

1 After the crankcase halves have been separated, follow the procedures in Sections 27 and 29 for the removal of the crankshaft and balancer shaft and their bearing shells.
2 Lift out the transmission output shaft bearing, noting which way round it fits, and the bearing half ring retainer **(see illustrations)**. Refer to *Tools and Workshop Tips* in the *Reference* Section to check the bearing and renew it if necessary.
3 If not already done, release the clips securing the breather pipe, noting their alignment, and remove the pipe **(see illustration)**. Examine the flexible hose – if it is cracked or perished renew it.
4 Refer to Section 20, Step 15 and remove the external oil gallery. Discard the gallery O-rings and the O-rings on the union and the oil pipe in the upper crankcase **(see illustrations)**.
5 If not already done, examine the needle bearings for the selector drum and gearchange shaft in the lower crankcase and renew them if necessary **(see illustrations)**.
6 The crankcases should be cleaned thoroughly with a suitable solvent and dried with compressed air. All oil passages and the oil gallery should be blown through with compressed air.

25.5b ... and gearchange shaft needle bearing (arrowed)

7 Remove all traces of old sealant from the mating surfaces with a suitable solvent. Minor damage to the surfaces can be cleaned up with a fine file.

Caution: Be very careful not to nick or gouge the crankcase mating surfaces or oil leaks will result. Check the crankcases very carefully for cracks and other damage.

8 Small cracks or holes in aluminium castings may be repaired with an epoxy resin adhesive as a temporary measure. Permanent repairs can only be effected by argon-arc welding, and only a specialist in this process is in a position to advise on the economy or practical aspect of such a repair, although low-temperature DIY weld kits are available for small repairs. If any damage is found that can't be repaired, renew the crankcase halves as a set.

9 Damaged threads can be economically reclaimed by using a diamond section wire insert, of the Heli-Coil type, which is easily fitted after drilling and re-tapping the affected thread.

10 Sheared studs or screws can usually be removed with stud extractors, which consist of a tapered, left-hand threaded screw of very hard steel. These are inserted into a pre-drilled hole in the stud, and usually succeed in dislodging the most stubborn stud or screw.

 HAYNES HiNT *Refer to Tools and Workshop Tips for details of installing a thread insert and using screw extractors.*

11 Always clean the crankcases thoroughly after any repair work to ensure no dirt or metal swarf is trapped inside when the engine is rebuilt.

12 Fit new O-rings onto the oil pipe and oil gallery union in the upper crankcase (see Step 4). Fit new O-rings into both ends of the oil gallery. Lubricate all O-rings with a smear of grease. Follow the procedure in Section 20, Step 15, to install the oil gallery.

13 If required, install the breather pipe and secure it with the clips **(see illustration 25.3)**. Alternatively, install the pipe once the crankcases have been assembled (see Section 24, Step 4).

14 Install the half ring retainer and transmission output shaft bearing **(see illustrations 25.2b and a)**. Note that the shaft seal should be fitted after the transmission assembly has been installed (see Section 21, Step 16).

15 Install the remaining components in the reverse order of removal.

26 Connecting rod and main bearing information

1 Even though new main and connecting rod bearings are generally fitted during engine overhaul, the old bearings should be retained for close examination as they may reveal valuable information about the condition of the engine.

2 Bearing failure occurs mainly because of lack of lubrication, the presence of dirt or other foreign particles, overloading the engine and/or corrosion. Regardless of the cause of bearing failure, it must be corrected before the engine is reassembled to prevent it from happening again.

3 When examining the bearings, lay them out on a clean surface in the same general position as their location on the crankshaft journals. This will enable you to match any noted bearing problems with the corresponding crankshaft journal.

4 Dirt and other foreign particles get into the engine in a variety of ways. They may be left in the engine during assembly or they may pass through filters or breathers, then get into the oil and from there into the bearings. Metal chips from machining operations and normal engine wear are often present. Abrasives are sometimes left in engine components after reconditioning operations, especially when parts are not thoroughly cleaned using the proper cleaning methods. Whatever the source, foreign objects often end up imbedded in the soft bearing material and are easily recognised. Large particles will not embed in the bearing and will score or gouge the bearing and journal. The best prevention for this cause of bearing failure is to clean all parts thoroughly and keep everything spotlessly clean during engine reassembly. Regular oil and filter changes are also recommended.

5 Lack of lubrication or lubrication breakdown has a number of interrelated causes. Excessive heat (which thins the oil), overloading (which squeezes the oil from the bearing face) and oil leakage or throw off (from excessive bearing clearances, worn oil pump or high engine speeds) all contribute to lubrication breakdown. Blocked oil passages will starve a bearing of lubrication and destroy it. When lack of lubrication is the cause of bearing failure, the bearing material is wiped or extruded from the steel backing of the bearing. Temperatures may increase to the point where the steel backing and the journal turn blue from overheating. Refer to *Tools and Workshop Tips* in the Reference section at the end of this manual for bearing fault finding.

6 Riding habits can have a definite effect on bearing life. Full throttle low, speed operation, or labouring the engine, puts very high loads on

bearings, which tend to squeeze out the oil film. These loads cause the bearings to flex, which produces fine cracks in the bearing face (fatigue failure). Eventually the bearing material will loosen in pieces and tear away from the steel backing. Short trip riding leads to corrosion of bearings, as insufficient engine heat is produced to drive off the condensed water and corrosive gases produced. These products collect in the engine oil, forming acid and sludge. As the oil is carried to the engine bearings, the acid attacks and corrodes the bearing material.

7 Incorrect bearing installation during engine assembly will lead to bearing failure as well. Tight fitting bearings which leave insufficient bearing oil clearances result in oil starvation. Dirt or foreign particles trapped behind a bearing shell result in high spots on the bearing which lead to failure.

8 To avoid bearing problems, clean all parts thoroughly before reassembly, double check all bearing clearance measurements and lubricate the new bearings with clean engine oil during installation.

27 Crankshaft and main bearings

Note: *To remove the crankshaft the engine must be removed from the frame and the crankcase halves separated.*

Removal

1 Remove the engine from the frame (see Section 4) and separate the crankcase halves (see Section 24).

2 Before removing the crankshaft, insert a feeler gauge between the crankshaft web and the No. 2 main bearing journal and check the side clearance **(see illustration)**. Compare the result with this Chapter's *Specifications*. If the clearance exceeds the service limit replace the crankcase halves as a set.

3 Note the alignment between the driven gear on the balancer shaft and the drive gear on the crankshaft, then lift out the balancer shaft (see Section 29).

4 Lift out the crankshaft together with the connecting rods and the cam chain, taking care not to dislodge the main bearing shells **(see illustration)**. Lift off the cam chain and detach the connecting rods (see Section 28).

27.2 Measuring the crankshaft side clearance

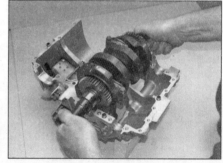

27.4 Lift the crankshaft out of the crankcase

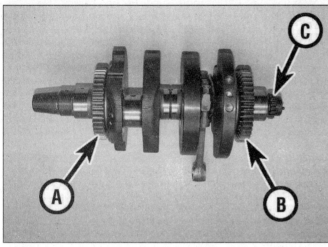

27.6 Balancer shaft drive gear (A), the primary drive gear (B) and the cam chain sprocket (C)

27.9 Check crankshaft runout at the points arrowed

Inspection

5 Clean the crankshaft with a suitable solvent, paying particular attention to flush out the oil passages. If available, blow the crank dry with compressed air, and also blow through the oil passages.

6 Inspect the balancer shaft drive gear, the primary drive gear and the cam chain sprocket for wear or damage (see illustration). If any of the gear or sprocket teeth are excessively worn, chipped or broken, the crankshaft must be renewed. Note: *If wear or damage is found, also inspect the primary driven gear on the back of the clutch housing (see Section 16), the driven gear on the balancer shaft (see Section 29) or the cam chain and camshaft sprockets (see Sections 8 and 9).*

7 Refer to Section 26 and examine the main bearing shells (see illustration 27.10). If they are scored, badly scuffed or appear to have been seized, new shells must be installed. Always renew the main bearing shells as a set. If any are badly damaged, check the corresponding crankshaft journals. Evidence of extreme heat, such as discoloration, indicates that lubrication failure has occurred. Be sure to check the oil pump (see Section 19), pressure relief valve and all oil holes and passages (see Section 20) thoroughly before reassembling the engine.

8 The crankshaft journals should be given a close visual examination, paying particular attention where damaged bearings have been discovered. If the journals are scored or pitted in any way, a new crankshaft will be required.

9 Place the crankshaft on V-blocks and check the runout at the centre main bearing journal using a dial gauge (see *Tools and Workshop Tips* in the *Reference* Section) (see illustration). Compare the result with the specifications at the beginning of this Chapter – if the runout exceeds the service limit, a new crankshaft must be fitted.

10 Remove the bearing shells from both crankcase halves by pushing their centres to the side, then lifting them out (see illustration). Keep the shells in order so that they can be fitted in their original locations for the oil clearance check.

Oil clearance check

11 Whether new bearing shells are being fitted or the original ones are being reused, the main bearing oil clearance should be checked before the engine is reassembled. Main bearing oil clearance is measured with a product known as Plastigauge.

12 Clean the backs of the bearing shells, the bearing seats in both crankcase halves, and the main bearing journals on the crankshaft. Remove all traces of old sealant from the

crankcase mating surfaces with a suitable solvent and clean the threads of the crankcase bolts.

13 Press the bearing shells into their seats, ensuring that the tab on each shell engages in the notch in the crankcase (see illustration). Make sure the bearings are fitted in the correct locations and take care not to touch bearing surfaces with your fingers.

14 Lay the crankshaft in position in the upper crankcase half. If removed, fit the dowels into the crankcase (see illustration 24.12).

15 Cut three lengths of the appropriate size Plastigauge – they should be slightly shorter than the width of the crankshaft journals – then place a length of Plastigauge along the centreline of each journal (see illustration). Do not place Plastigauge over the oil holes in the crankshaft.

16 Carefully fit the lower crankcase half onto the upper crankcase, ensuring that the Plastigauge is not disturbed (see illustration 24.10). Note: *It is essential that, throughout this procedure, the crankshaft does not rotate in the crankcase.* Make sure the dowels locate correctly and that the lower crankcase half is correctly seated. Note: *Do not tighten the crankcase bolts if the casing is not correctly seated.*

17 Follow the procedure in Section 24 to

27.10 Removing a bearing shell from its seat

27.13 Ensure the tab (arrowed) locates correctly

27.15 Lay a strip of Plastigauge along the centreline of each journal

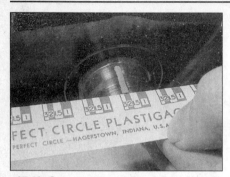

27.19 Compare the width of the crushed Plastigauge with the scale provided

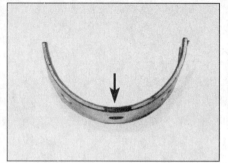

27.22 The colour code is marked on the side of the shell (arrowed)

27.23 Measuring the crankshaft journal diameter

install and tighten the crankcase bolts – use the old sealing washers for the purpose of the check.

18 Unscrew the crankcase bolts in the **reverse** order of the tightening sequence and remove them. Carefully lift off the lower crankcase half, making sure the Plastigauge is not disturbed.

19 Compare the width of the crushed Plastigauge on each crankshaft journal to the printed Plastigauge scale to obtain the main bearing oil clearance **(see illustration)**. Compare the oil clearance to the specifications at the beginning of this Chapter.

20 If the oil clearance measurements are within the standard specified range and the bearings are in perfect condition, they can be reused.

21 Carefully scrape away all traces of the Plastigauge from the crankshaft journals and bearing shells using a fingernail or other object which will not score the bearing surfaces.

22 If the oil clearance is between the standard specified maximum and the service limit, replace all the old bearing shells with new shells that are colour coded blue **(see illustration)**, then check the oil clearance once again. The new clearance may exceed the standard specified maximum slightly, but it must not be less than the standard specified minimum, otherwise bearing seizure may occur.

23 If the oil clearance exceeds the service limit, measure the diameter of the main bearing journals with a micrometer and compare the results with the specifications

(see illustration). If any journal has worn down past the service limit, replace the crankshaft with a new one.

24 If the journal diameters are above the service limit, but differ from their original size according to the markings on the crankshaft webs, apply new marks with a hammer and punch **(see illustration)**. Use these new marks when selecting new main bearing shells.

25 Remove the main bearing shells, assemble the crankcase halves, then install and tighten the crankcase bolts as before (see Step 17). Using a telescoping gauge and micrometer, measure the diameters of the main bearing bores, then compare the measurements with the specifications. The measurements in the specifications and the marks on the front of the upper crankcase half should correspond **(see illustration)**. Use these marks when selecting new main bearing shells.

Main bearing shell selection

26 Marks stamped on the crankshaft webs and upper crankcase half are used to identify the correct bearing selection. The mark for each main bearing journal is stamped on the crankshaft web adjacent to the journal – the web will either be unmarked or marked '1' **(see illustration 27.24)**. The mark for the corresponding main bearing bore is stamped into the front of the upper crankcase half – the crankcase will either be unmarked or marked 'O' **(see illustration 27.25)**. The left-hand mark (as seated on the bike) corresponds to the left-hand housing (viewed upside down), and so on.

27 Using the table below, cross-reference

the main bearing journal mark with the main bearing bore mark to select the correct bearing. The bearings are colour coded – the colour is marked on the side of the bearing shell **(see illustration 27.22)**.

Main bearing journal	Main bearing bore	Bearing colour code
1	O	Brown
1	None	Black
None	O	Black
None	None	Blue

Installation

28 Follow the procedure in Section 28 to install the connecting rods.

29 Ensure that the backs of the bearing shells, the bearing seats in the crankcase halves and the crankshaft journals are clean. If new shells are being fitted, ensure that all traces of the protective grease are cleaned off using paraffin (kerosene). Dry the shells, seats and journals with a clean, lint-free cloth.

30 Install the bearing shells, making sure the tab on each shell engages the notch in the

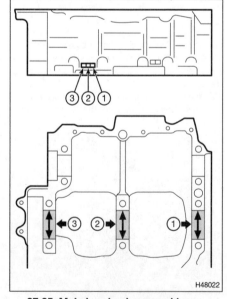

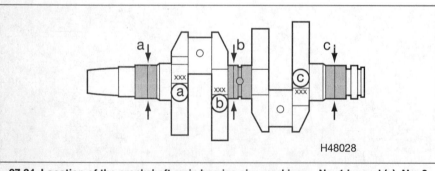

27.24 Location of the crankshaft main bearing size markings – No. 1 journal (a), No. 2 journal (b) and No. 3 journal (c)

27.25 Main bearing bore markings – numbered 1 to 3 from the left

28.2 Measuring the big-end side clearance

28.3 Mark the cylinder identity on each connecting rod (A) and cap (B)

28.4a Unscrew the connecting rod cap nuts

bearing seat (see illustration 27.13). Ensure the shells are fitted in their correct locations and take care not to touch any bearing surfaces with your fingers.

31 Lubricate the shells with molybdenum disulphide oil (a 50/50 mixture of molybdenum disulphide grease and clean engine oil).

32 Fit the cam chain over the crankshaft sprocket, then lay the crankshaft in position in the upper crankcase half.

33 Install the balancer shaft (see Section 29).

34 Reassemble the crankcase halves (see Section 24).

28 Connecting rods and bearings

Note 1: *To remove the connecting rods the engine must be removed from the frame and the crankcase halves separated.*

Note 2: *The connecting rod bolts can only be used in a running engine once, though they can be used when performing the oil clearance check. If new connecting rods are fitted they will come with nuts and bolts.*

Removal

1 Remove the engine from the frame (see Section 4). Separate the crankcase halves and lift out the crankshaft (see Sections 24 and 27).

2 Before detaching the connecting rods from the crankshaft, measure the big-end side

clearance on each rod with a feeler gauge **(see illustration)**. If the clearance on either rod is greater than the service limit listed in the Specifications at the beginning of this Chapter, renew the rod and check the clearance again. If the clearance is still excessive, replace the crankshaft with a new one.

3 Using paint or a felt marker pen, mark the cylinder identity on each connecting rod and cap across the cap-to-connecting rod join to ensure that the cap and rod are fitted the correct way around on reassembly **(see illustration)**. Note the piston oil jet on the lower front edge of each connecting rod. **Note:** *The markings already across the rod and cap indicate rod weight and bearing size, not cylinder number. The letter indicating rod weight should be the same for both rods.*

4 Working on one connecting rod at a time, unscrew the cap nuts **(see illustration)**. Remove the cap, complete with the lower bearing shell, from the crankshaft, then detach the rod, complete with the upper bearing shell **(see illustration)**. If the cap appears stuck, tap it on one end with a hammer while pulling it.

5 Keep the rod, cap, nuts, bolts (the old bolts should be used for an oil clearance check), and the bearing shells together as a matched set for inspection – fit the caps back onto the rods and finger-tighten the nuts to make sure. **Caution: The connecting rod bolts are designed to stretch when they are tightened. NEVER use the old bolts for final installation.**

Inspection

6 Check the connecting rods for cracks and other obvious damage. Have the rods checked for twist and bend by a Kawasaki dealer if you are in doubt about their straightness.

7 If not already done, follow the procedure in Section 13 and check for freeplay between each piston pin its connecting rod small-end **(see illustration 13.13a)**. If there is freeplay, measure the pin external diameter **(see illustration 13.13d)** and the small-end bore diameter and compare the measurements to the specifications at the beginning of this Chapter **(see illustration)**. Renew components that are worn beyond the service limit.

8 Refer to Section 26 and examine the connecting rod big-end bearing shells. If they are scored, badly scuffed or appear to have seized, new shells must be installed. Always renew the shells as a set. If any are badly damaged, check the corresponding crankshaft journal. Evidence of extreme heat, such as discoloration, indicates that lubrication failure has occurred. Be sure to check the oil pump, pressure relief valve and all oil holes and passages thoroughly before reassembling the engine. Remove the bearing shells by pushing their centres out to the side then lifting them out **(see illustration)**.

Oil clearance check

9 Whether new bearing shells are being fitted or the original ones are being re-used, the connecting rod big-end bearing oil clearance should be checked prior to reassembly. Bearing oil clearance is measured with a product known as Plastigauge.

28.4b Detach the cap and connecting rod from the crankshaft

28.7 Measuring the small-end bore diameter

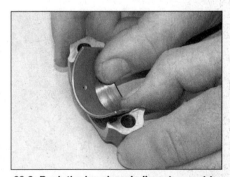

28.8 Push the bearing shell centres out to the side

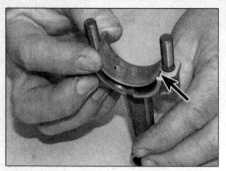

28.11 Ensure the tab (arrowed) locates correctly

28.20 Measuring the big-end journal diameter

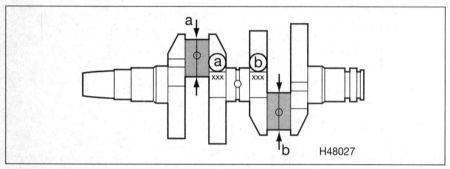

28.21 Location of the big-end journal size markings – No. 1 journal (a), No. 2 journal (b)

10 Remove the bearing shells from the rods and caps, keeping them in order. Clean the backs of the bearing shells, the bearing locations in both the connecting rod and cap, and the crankshaft big-end journal with a suitable solvent.

11 Press the bearing shells into their locations, ensuring that the tab on each shell engages the notch in the connecting rod or cap **(see illustration)**. Make sure the bearings are fitted in the correct locations and take care not to touch any shell's bearing surface with your fingers.

12 Support the crankshaft. Cut a length of appropriate size Plastigauge – it should be slightly shorter than the width of the big-end journal – and place it on the centreline of the journal to be checked **(see illustration 27.15)**. Do not place Plastigauge over the oil holes in the journal.

13 Fit the connecting rod and cap onto the journal, ensuring that the rod is fitted the

correct way round and that the previously made markings align (see Step 3). **Note:** *It is essential that, throughout this procedure, the connecting rod does not rotate on the crankshaft.*

14 Lubricate the threads of the connecting bolts and the seating surfaces of the nuts with molybdenum sulphide oil (a 50/50 mixture of molybdenum disulphide grease and clean engine oil), then install the nuts and tighten them to the appropriate torque setting followed by tightening through 120° (see the Specifications at the beginning of this Chapter).

15 Undo the nuts and remove the cap and connecting rod from the crankshaft, again taking great care that the rod does not rotate on the crankshaft.

16 Compare the width of the crushed Plastigauge on the big-end journal to the printed Plastigauge scale to obtain the big-end bearing oil clearance **(see illustration 27.19)**.

Compare the oil clearance to the specifications at the beginning of this Chapter.

17 If the oil clearance is within the standard specified range and the bearings are in perfect condition, they can be reused.

18 Carefully scrape away all traces of the Plastigauge from the big-end journal and bearing shells using a fingernail or other object which will not score the bearing surfaces.

19 If the oil clearance is between the standard specified maximum and the service limit, replace all the old bearing shells with new shells that are colour coded blue **(see illustration 27.22)**, then check the oil clearance once again. The new clearance may exceed the standard specified maximum slightly, but it must not be less than the standard specified minimum, otherwise bearing seizure may occur.

20 If the oil clearance exceeds the service limit, measure the diameter of the big-end journals with a micrometer and compare the results with the specifications **(see illustration)**. If any journal has worn down past the service limit, replace the crankshaft with a new one.

21 If the journal diameters are above the service limit, but differ from their original size according to the markings on the crankshaft webs, apply new marks with a hammer and punch **(see illustration)**. Use these new marks when selecting new big-end bearing shells.

22 Remove the big-end bearing shells, assemble the connecting rod and cap and tighten the nuts as before (see Step 14). Using a telescoping gauge and micrometer, measure the internal diameter of the connecting rod big-end **(see illustration)**. Compare the measurements with the specifications. The measurements in the specifications and the marks on the connecting rod should correspond **(see illustration)**. Use these marks when selecting new big-end bearing shells.

Big-end bearing shell selection

23 Marks stamped on the crankshaft webs and the connecting rods are used to identify the correct bearing selection. The mark for each big-end bearing journal is stamped on the crankshaft web adjacent to the journal – the web will either be unmarked or marked 'O' **(see illustration 28.21)**. The mark for the corresponding connecting rod is stamped across the flat face of the connecting rod and cap – the rod will either be unmarked or marked 'O' **(see illustration 28.22b)**.

24 Using the table below, cross-reference the big-end bearing journal mark with the connecting rod mark to select the correct bearing. The bearings are colour coded – the colour is marked on the side of the bearing shell **(see illustration 27.22)**.

28.22a Measuring the internal diameter of the big-end

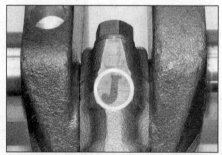

28.22b Connecting rod big-end size marking (circle or no circle) and weight code (letter)

Big-end bearing journal	Connecting rod big-end	Bearing colour code
O	None	Brown
None	None	Black
O	O	Black
None	O	Blue

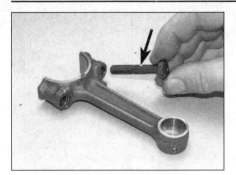

28.26a DO NOT twist the bolts – splines (arrowed) will damage rod

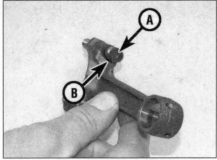

28.26b Align bolt head (A) with recess (B) carefully . . .

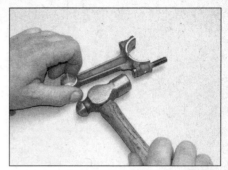

28.26c . . . then tap the bolts all the way in

Installation

25 Work on one connecting rod at a time. If new rods are being fitted they will be supplied with caps, bolts and nuts – use all the new components. Clean the new rods, bolts and nuts with solvent to remove the anti-rust coating, then dry them using compressed air.

26 If the old rods are being used, lay each rod on a flat surface and gently tap out the old bolts – DO NOT twist the bolts as they are removed from the rod **(see illustration)**. Clean the new bolts (and nuts if used) with solvent to remove the anti-rust coating. Align the heads of the new bolts with the recesses in the rod and press them in carefully, check that the heads are aligned with the recesses, then tap the bolts all the way in **(see illustrations)**.

28.29a Tightening the nuts with a torque angle gauge

27 Ensure that the backs of the bearing shells, the bearing seats in the caps and rods and the crankshaft journals are clean. If new shells are being fitted, ensure that all traces of protective grease are removed using paraffin (kerosene). Dry the shells, with a clean, lint-free cloth. Install the shells, making sure the tab on each shell engages the notch in the cap or rod **(see illustration 28.11)**. Make sure the shells are fitted in their correct locations and take care not to touch any bearing surfaces with your fingers.

28 Lubricate the shells and crankshaft journal with molybdenum disulphide oil. Fit the connecting rod and cap onto the journal, ensuring that the rod is fitted the correct way round and that the previously made markings align (see Step 3).

29 Lubricate the threads of the connecting bolts and the seating surfaces of the nuts with molybdenum sulphide oil, then install the nuts and tighten them to the torque setting specified at the beginning of this Chapter. Now tighten each nut in one continuous movement through the specified angle using a torque angle gauge **(see illustration)**. If tightening is paused between the torque setting and angle setting, slacken the bolt to below the torque setting and repeat the procedure. If a torque angle gauge is not available, paint a small reference mark on the cap and a second mark on the edge of the nut 120° anti-clockwise from the first mark **(see illustration). Note:** *There are six points on each*

nut, so the angle between each point is 60°. Ensure you can see the mark on the nut with the spanner installed, then tighten the nut until the marks align **(see illustration)**.

30 Check that the rods rotate smoothly and freely on the crankshaft. If there are any signs of roughness or tightness, remove the rod and re-check the bearing clearance. Sometimes tapping the connecting rod cap bolts will relieve tightness.

31 Install the remaining components in the reverse order of disassembly.

32 Turn the rod on the crankshaft. If it feels tight, tap on the cap with a hammer – this should relieve stress and free it up. If it doesn't, recheck the bearing clearance. Fit the other rod.

33 Install the crankshaft (see Section 27) and reassemble the crankcase halves (see Section 24).

29 Balancer shaft

Note: *To remove the balancer shaft the engine must be removed from the frame and the crankcase halves separated.*

Removal

1 Remove the engine from the frame (see Section 4) and separate the crankcase halves (see Section 24).

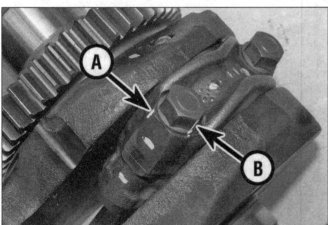

28.29b First mark (A) on the cap, second mark (B) on the nut

28.29c Marks (arrowed) align when nut is tightened sufficiently

29.2a Note the alignment marks on the crankshaft (A) and balancer shaft (B) gears . . .

2 Note the alignment between the driven gear on the balancer shaft and the drive gear on the crankshaft, then lift out the balancer shaft **(see illustrations)**. Lift out the crankshaft (see Section 27).

Inspection

3 Clean the balancer shaft with a suitable solvent, paying particular attention to flush out the oil passages. If available, blow the shaft dry with compressed air, and also blow through the oil passages.

4 Inspect the shaft driven gear for wear or damage **(see illustration)**. If any of the gear teeth are excessively worn, chipped or broken, the shaft must be renewed. **Note:** *If wear or damage is found, also inspect the drive gear on the crankshaft (see Section 27).*

5 The driven gear incorporates a cush-drive mechanism – check that the springs are not loose or broken and that there is no backlash between the shaft and the gear, otherwise replace the shaft with a new one.

6 Refer to Section 26 and examine the bearing shells **(see illustration)**. If they are scored, badly scuffed or appear to have been seized, new shells must be installed. Always renew the bearing shells as a set. If any are badly damaged, check the corresponding balancer shaft journals. Evidence of extreme heat, such as discoloration, indicates that lubrication failure has occurred. Be sure to

29.2b . . . then lift out the balancer shaft

check the oil pump (see Section 19), pressure relief valve and all oil holes and passages (see Section 20) thoroughly before reassembling the engine.

7 The balancer journals should be given a close visual examination, paying particular attention where damaged bearings have been discovered **(see illustration 29.4)**. If the journals are scored or pitted in any way, a new shaft will be required.

8 Remove the bearing shells from both crankcase halves by pushing their centres to the side, then lifting them out **(see illustration 27.10)**. Keep the shells in order so that they can be fitted in their original locations for the oil clearance check.

Oil clearance check

9 Whether new bearing shells are being fitted or the original ones are being reused, the balancer shaft bearing oil clearance should be checked before the engine is reassembled. Bearing oil clearance is measured with a product known as Plastigauge.

10 Clean the backs of the bearing shells, the bearing seats in both crankcase halves, and the bearing journals on the shaft. Remove all traces of old sealant from the crankcase mating surfaces with a suitable solvent and clean the threads of the crankcase bolts.

11 Press the bearing shells into their seats, ensuring that the tab on each shell engages in the notch in the crankcase **(see illustration 27.13)**. Make sure the bearings are fitted in the

correct locations and take care not to touch bearing surfaces with your fingers.

12 Lay the balancer shaft in position in the upper crankcase half. If removed, fit the dowels into the crankcase **(see illustration 24.12)**.

13 Cut two lengths of the appropriate size Plastigauge – they should be slightly shorter than the width of the shaft journals – then place a length of Plastigauge along the centreline of each journal **(see illustration 27.15)**. Do not place Plastigauge over the oil holes in the shaft.

14 Carefully fit the lower crankcase half onto the upper crankcase, ensuring that the Plastigauge is not disturbed **(see illustration 24.10)**. **Note:** *It is essential that, throughout this procedure, the balancer shaft does not rotate in the crankcase.* Make sure the dowels locate correctly and that the lower crankcase half is correctly seated. **Note:** *Do not tighten the crankcase bolts if the casing is not correctly seated.*

15 Follow the procedure in Section 24 to install and tighten the crankcase bolts – use the old sealing washers for the purpose of the check.

16 Unscrew the crankcase bolts in the **reverse** order of the tightening sequence and remove them. Carefully lift off the lower crankcase half, making sure the Plastigauge is not disturbed.

17 Compare the width of the crushed Plastigauge on both balancer shaft journals to the printed Plastigauge scale to obtain the bearing oil clearance **(see illustration 27.19)**. Compare the oil clearance to the specifications at the beginning of this Chapter.

18 If the oil clearance measurements are within the standard specified range and the bearings are in perfect condition, they can be reused.

19 Carefully scrape away all traces of the Plastigauge from the shaft journals and bearing shells using a fingernail or other object which will not score the bearing surfaces.

20 If the oil clearance is between the standard specified maximum and the service limit, replace all the old bearing shells with new shells

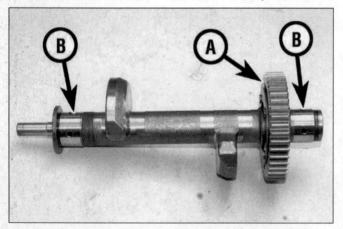

29.4 Inspect the driven gear (A) and bearing journals (B)

29.6 Location of the balancer shaft shells – upper crankcase half

29.21 Measuring the balancer shaft journal diameter

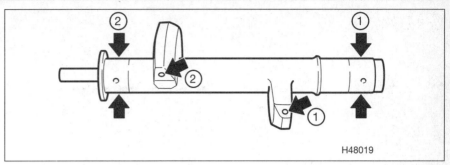

H48019

29.22 Location of the balancer shaft journal size markings
Journals are numbered 1 (left), 2 (right)

that are colour coded blue **(see illustration 27.22)**, then check the oil clearance once again. The new clearance may exceed the standard specified maximum slightly, but it must not be less than the standard specified minimum, otherwise bearing seizure may occur.

21 If the oil clearance exceeds the service limit, measure the diameter of the bearing journals with a micrometer and compare the results with the specifications **(see illustration)**. If any journal has worn down past the service limit, replace the balancer shaft with a new one.

22 If the journal diameters are above the service limit, but differ from their original size according to the markings on the shaft webs, apply new marks with a hammer and punch **(see illustration)**. Use these new marks when selecting new main bearing shells.

23 Remove the bearing shells, assemble the crankcase halves, then install and tighten the crankcase bolts as before (see Steps 14 and 15). Using a telescoping gauge and micrometer, measure the diameters of the bearing bores, then compare the measurements with the specifications. The measurements in the specifications and the marks on the front of

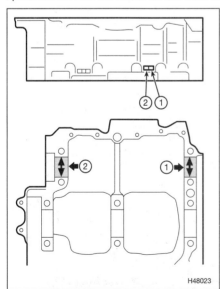

H48023

29.23 Balancer shaft bearing bore markings – numbered 1 (left) and 2 (right)

the upper case half should correspond **(see illustration)**. Use these marks when selecting new bearing shells.

Balancer shaft bearing shell selection

24 Marks stamped on the shaft weights and upper crankcase half are used to identify the correct bearing selection. The mark for each bearing journal is stamped on the shaft weight adjacent to the journal – the weight will either be unmarked or marked 'O' **(see illustration 29.22)**. The mark for the corresponding bearing bore is stamped into the front of the upper crankcase half – the crankcase will either be unmarked or marked 'O' **(see illustration 29.23)**. The left-hand mark (as seated on the bike) corresponds to the left-hand housing (viewed upside down).

25 Using the table below, cross-reference the bearing journal mark with the bearing bore mark to select the correct bearing. The bearings are colour coded – the colour is marked on the side of the bearing shell **(see illustration 27.22)**.

Bearing journal	Bearing bore	Bearing colour code
O	O	Brown
None	O	Black
O	None	Black
None	None	Blue

Installation

26 Ensure that the backs of the bearing shells, the bearing seats in the crankcase halves and the balancer shaft journals are clean. If new shells are being fitted, ensure that all traces of the protective grease are cleaned off using paraffin (kerosene). Dry the shells, seats and journals with a clean, lint-free cloth.

27 Install the bearing shells, making sure the tab on each shell engages the notch in the bearing seat **(see illustration 27.13)**. Ensure the shells are fitted in their correct locations and take care not to touch any bearing surfaces with your fingers.

28 Lubricate the shells with molybdenum disulphide oil (a 50/50 mixture of molybdenum disulphide grease and clean engine oil).

29 Install the crankshaft (see Section 27).

30 Lower the balancer shaft into the upper crankcase half, ensuring the register marks on

the driven gear and the crankshaft drive gear align **(see illustration 29.2a)**. Ensure the shaft journals locate fully into the bearings.

31 Reassemble the crankcase halves (see Section 24).

30 Running-in procedure

1 Make sure the engine oil and coolant levels are correct (see *Pre-ride checks*). Make sure there is fuel in the tank.

2 Turn the engine kill switch to the ON position and shift the gearbox into neutral. Turn the ignition ON.

3 Start the engine and allow it to run at a moderately fast idle until it reaches operating temperature.

⚠️ *Warning: If the oil pressure warning light doesn't go off, or if it comes on while the engine is running, stop the engine immediately.*

4 If a lubrication failure is suspected, stop the engine immediately and try to find the cause. If an engine is run without oil, even for a short period of time, severe damage will occur.

5 Check carefully that there are no oil or coolant leaks and make sure the transmission and controls, especially the brakes, function properly before road testing the machine.

6 Treat the machine gently for the first few miles to make sure oil has circulated throughout the engine and any new parts installed have started to seat.

7 Upon completion of the road test, and after the engine has cooled down completely, check the engine oil and coolant levels (see *Pre-ride checks*).

8 If new pistons/rings, a new cylinder block or a new crankshaft have been fitted, the bike will have to be run in as when new. This means greater use of the transmission and a restraining hand on the throttle, keeping engine speed below 4000 rpm until at least 500 miles (800 km) have been covered. There's no point in keeping to any set speed limit – the main idea is to keep from labouring the engine. Between 500 and 1000 miles (800 and 1600 km) keep engine speeds below 6000 rpm. Experience is the best guide, since it's easy to tell when an engine is running freely.

Notes

Chapter 3
Cooling system

Contents

Degrees of difficulty

Easy, suitable for novice with little experience | **Fairly easy,** suitable for beginner with some experience | **Fairly difficult,** suitable for competent DIY mechanic | **Difficult,** suitable for experienced DIY mechanic | **Very difficult,** suitable for expert DIY or professional

Specifications

Coolant

Mixture type and capacity .... see Chapter 1

Cooling fan switch

Switch closes (fan ON) .... 93 to 103°C
Switch opens (fan OFF) .... 91°C

Coolant temperature (ECT) sensor

Resistance @ 0°C .... 6.54 K-ohms approx
Resistance @ 40°C .... 1.04 to 1.23 K-ohms
Resistance @ 100°C .... 0.15 to 0.16 K-ohms

Thermostat

Opening temperature .... 80.5 to 83.5°C
Fully open .... 95°C
Valve lift .... 8 mm (min)

Torque settings

Coolant drain bolt
  Aluminium washer .... 7 Nm
  Plated copper washer .... 10 Nm
Engine coolant temperature (ECT) sensor .... 12 Nm
Radiator mounting bolt .... 14 Nm
Thermostat housing bolts .... 10 Nm
Water pump cover bolts .... 10 Nm
Water pump impeller bolt .... 10 Nm

1 General information

The cooling system uses a water/anti-freeze coolant to carry away excess heat from the engine and maintain as constant a temperature as possible. The cylinders are surrounded by a water jacket through which the coolant is circulated by thermo-syphonic action in conjunction with a water pump. The pump is located on the right-hand side of the crankcase and is driven by the balancer shaft.

Hot coolant passes upwards through the water jacket to the cylinder head and through to the radiator. The coolant flows across the core of the radiator, then to the water pump and back to the engine where the cycle is repeated.

A thermostat is fitted in the system to prevent the coolant flowing through the radiator when the engine is cold, therefore accelerating the speed at which the engine reaches normal operating temperature. The thermostat is located on the left-hand side of the cylinder head

An engine coolant temperature (ECT) sensor located in the rear of the cylinder head transmits information to the ECU (electronic control unit). If the coolant temperature rises sufficiently, the ECU switches on the cooling fan fitted to the back of the radiator. The ECU also illuminates the warning light and coolant symbol in the instrument cluster when necessary.

The cooling system is partially sealed and pressurised, the pressure being controlled by a valve in the radiator cap. An overflow hose from the radiator is connected to a reservoir into which coolant is expelled under pressure when the engine is hot. The discharged coolant is automatically returned to the radiator by the vacuum created when the engine cools.

⚠️ *Warning: Do not remove the pressure cap from the radiator when the engine is hot. Scalding hot coolant and steam may be blown out under pressure, which could cause serious injury. When the engine has cooled, place a thick rag, such as a hand towel, over the pressure cap; slowly rotate the cap anti-clockwise to the first stop. This procedure allows any residual pressure to escape. When the steam has stopped escaping, press down on the cap while turning it anti-clockwise and remove it.*

Caution: Do not allow anti-freeze to come in contact with your skin or painted surfaces of the motorcycle. Rinse off any spills immediately with plenty of water. Anti-freeze is highly toxic if ingested. Never leave anti-freeze lying around in an open container or in puddles on the floor; children and pets are attracted by its sweet smell and may drink it. Check with the local authorities about disposing of used anti-freeze. Many communities will have collection centres which will see that anti-freeze is disposed of safely.

Caution: At all times use the specified type of anti-freeze, and always mix it with

distilled water in the correct proportion. The anti-freeze contains corrosion inhibitors which are essential to avoid damage to the cooling system. A lack of these inhibitors could lead to a build-up of corrosion which would block the coolant passages, resulting in overheating and severe engine damage. Distilled water must be used as opposed to tap water to avoid a build-up of scale which would also block the passages.

2 Cooling fan and fan relay

1 If the engine is overheating and the cooling fan isn't coming on, first check the coolant level (see *Pre-ride checks*). If the level is correct, check the fan fuse (see Chapter 8). If the fuse is blown, check the fan circuit for a short to earth (see *Wiring Diagrams* at the end of Chapter 8). If the fuse is good, check the fan relay, then the fan motor, and then the ECT sensor, which acts as the fan switch via the ECU (see Section 3).

Cooling fan relay

Note: *A failure of the relay signal to the ECU will be identified as a fuel injection system fault (code 56) – see Chapter 4.*

2 To access the relay box, remove the fuel tank and the fuel tank bracket (see Chapter 4). Release the clips securing the relay box, lift it out of its rubber holder and disconnect the wiring connectors **(see illustrations)**.

3 Using a multimeter, check for continuity between terminals 17 and 20 on the relay **(see illustration)**. There should be no continuity. Now use jumper wires to connect the positive (+ve) terminal of a fully charged 12 volt battery to terminal 18 on the relay and the negative (-ve) battery terminal to relay terminal 19. There should now be continuity between terminals 17 and 20. If the relay fails either of the checks the relay box must be replaced with a new one – individual relays are not available.

4 If the relay is good, check for battery voltage between the green and pink/blue wire terminals on the loom side of the wiring

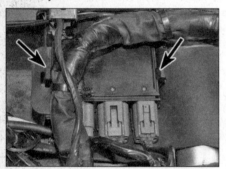
2.2a Release the clips (arrowed) . . .

2.2b . . . and lift out the relay box . . .

2.2c . . . and disconnect the wiring connectors

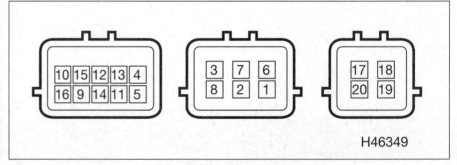
2.3 Relay box terminal numbering

H46349

2.6 Disconnect the fan wiring connector

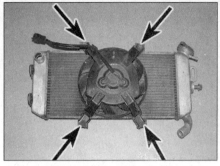

2.12 Location of the cooling fan mounting bolts

connector with the ignition and kill switch ON. If there is no voltage, check the circuit and its components, referring to the relevant wiring diagram at the end of Chapter 8. If voltage is present, check the wiring between the relay and the fan wiring connector and between the relay and the ECU for continuity.

5 If all the wiring is good, check the fan motor, then the ECT sensor (see Section 3). Check the ECU (see Chapter 4).

Cooling fan motor

Check

6 To test the cooling fan motor, first remove the left-hand fairing side panel (see Chapter 7). Trace the wiring from the back of the fan assembly and disconnect it at the connector **(see illustration)**.

7 Using a 12 volt battery and two insulated jumper wires, connect the battery positive (+) lead to the blue wire terminal on the fan side of the wiring connector, and the battery negative (–) lead to the black wire terminal. Once connected the fan should operate. If it does not, and the wiring and connectors are all good, then the fan motor is faulty. Individual components are not available for the fan assembly.

8 If the fan works when connected to a battery, check for continuity in the blue/white wire between the loom side of the connector and the fan relay, and in the black/yellow wire to earth.

9 If the fan works but is suspected of cutting in at the wrong temperature, check the ECT sensor (see Section 3).

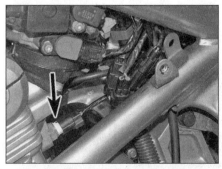

3.1 Location of the engine coolant temperature sensor

10 If the fan operates all the time, test the relay (see above). If the relay is good, it is likely either the ECT sensor or the ECU is faulty.

Removal and installation

⚠ **Warning: The engine must be completely cool before carrying out this procedure.**

11 Remove the radiator (see Section 7).

12 Unscrew the fan mounting bolts and detach the fan from the radiator, noting how it is fitted **(see illustration)**.

13 Installation is the reverse of removal. Tighten the mounting bolts securely, then install the radiator (see Section 7).

---

3 Engine coolant temperature (ECT) sensor

Check

1 The engine coolant temperature (ECT) sensor is located in the rear of the cylinder head **(see illustration)**. If a sensor fault

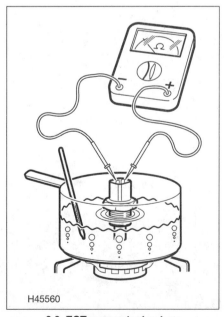

H45560

3.3 ECT sensor test set-up

is indicated by the fuel injection system diagnostic process (fault code 14), carry out the preliminary checks as described in Chapter 4, Section 10 or 11.

2 To check the sensor resistance remove it from the cylinder head (see Steps 5 to 8).

3 Fill a small heatproof container with coolant and place it on a stove. Using an ohmmeter set to the K-ohms scale, connect the meter probes to the sensor terminals, and using some wire or other support, suspend the sensor in the coolant so that just the sensing portion and the threads are submerged **(see illustration)**. Also place a thermometer capable of reading temperatures up to 100°C in the coolant so that its bulb is close to the switch. **Note:** *None of the components should be allowed to touch the container directly.*

4 Check the meter reading and compare the result with the specifications at the beginning of this Chapter, then heat the coolant slowly, stirring it gently.

⚠ **Warning: This must be done very carefully to avoid the risk of personal injury.**

As the temperature of the coolant rises, the sensor resistance should fall. Check that the specified resistance is obtained at the correct temperature (see *Specifications*). If the readings obtained are different, or are obtained at different temperatures, the sensor is faulty and must be renewed. If the readings are as specified, the fault could lie in the coolant temperature display circuit in the instrument cluster (see Chapter 8).

Removal and installation

⚠ **Warning: The engine must be completely cool before carrying out this procedure.**

5 Note the location of the ECT sensor (see Step 1). On EX650 models, remove the left-hand fairing side panel for access (see Chapter 7).

6 Drain the cooling system (see Chapter 1).

7 Disconnect the sensor wiring connector **(see illustration)**.

8 Place a rag on the crankcase underneath the sensor to soak-up any residual coolant, then unscrew the sensor from the cylinder head. Discard the O-ring as a new one must be fitted on reassembly.

3.7 Disconnecting the ECT wiring

4.2 Location of the thermostat housing

9 Installation is the reverse of removal, noting the following:
● Lubricate the new O-ring with a smear of grease.
● Tighten the sensor to the torque setting specified at the beginning of this Chapter.
● Refill the cooling system (see Chapter 1).

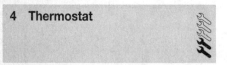

4 Thermostat

1 The thermostat is automatic in operation and shouldn't require attention. In the event of a failure, the valve will probably jam open, in which case the engine will take much longer than normal to warm up. Conversely, if the valve jams shut, the coolant will be unable to circulate and the engine will overheat. Neither condition is acceptable, and the fault must be investigated promptly.

4.7 Thermostat should be closed at room temperature

4.11 Bleed hole (arrowed) should be at the top

4.5 Thermostat housing bolts (arrowed)

Removal

 Warning: The engine must be completely cool before carrying out this procedure.

2 The thermostat is located in the thermostat housing which is mounted on the left-hand side of the cylinder head **(see illustration)**. Remove the left-hand fairing side panel for access (see Chapter 7).
3 Drain the cooling system (see Chapter 1).
4 Loosen both clips on the coolant hose between the thermostat housing and the radiator, then disconnect the hose from the housing.
5 Place a rag underneath the housing to soak-up any residual coolant, then undo the housing bolts and lift it off carefully – the thermostat may come away with the housing or it may remain in the cylinder head **(see illustration)**.
6 Discard the O-ring as a new one must be fitted on reassembly **(see illustration)**.

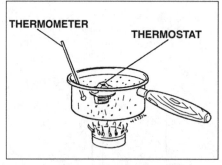

THERMOMETER   THERMOSTAT

4.8 Set-up for testing the thermostat

5.1 Location of the water pump (arrowed)

4.6 Note the location of the O-ring

Check

7 Examine the thermostat visually before carrying out the test. If it remains in the open position at room temperature, it should be replaced with a new one **(see illustration)**.
8 Fill a small heatproof container with cold water and place it on a stove. Using a piece of wire, suspend the thermostat in the water. Place a thermometer in the water so that its bulb is close to the thermostat **(see illustration)**. **Note:** *None of the components should be allowed to touch the container directly.*
9 Heat the water, noting the temperature when the thermostat opens, and compare the result with the specifications given at the beginning of this Chapter. Also check the amount the valve opens after it has been heated at 95°C for a few minutes and compare the measurement to the specifications. If the readings obtained differ from those given, the thermostat is faulty and must be renewed.
10 In the event of thermostat failure, as an emergency measure only, it can be removed and the machine used without it. **Note:** *Take care when starting the engine from cold as it will take much longer than usual to warm up.* Ensure that a new unit is installed as soon as possible.

Installation

11 Installation is the reverse of removal, noting the following:
● Lubricate the new O-ring with a smear of grease.
● Install the thermostat with the bleed hole at the top **(see illustration)**.
● Tighten the housing bolts to the specified torque setting.
● Ensure the coolant hose is correctly aligned before tightening the clips.
● Refill the cooling system (see Chapter 1).

5 Water pump

Check

1 The water pump is located on the lower right-hand side of the engine **(see illustration)**. On EX650 models, remove the belly panel for access (see Chapter 7).
2 Check the area around the pump for signs of leakage.

5.3 Location of the water pump drain hole (arrowed)

5.5 Detach the hose (arrowed) from the pump

3 To prevent internal leakage of water from the pump into the crankcase, a mechanical seal is fitted on the back of the pump impeller. To prevent oil entering the pump from the crankcase, an impeller shaft oil seal is installed on the back of the pump body. If either seal fails, a drain hole in the underside of the pump body allows the coolant or oil to escape **(see illustration)**. Look for telltale signs of leakage around the drain hole.

Removal

4 Drain the cooling system (see Chapter 1).
5 Loosen the clip securing the coolant hose to the pump and detach the hose **(see illustration)**.

6 Undo the bolts securing the pump cover, noting their locations, and lift the cover off **(see illustrations)**. Note the location of the dowels and remove them for safekeeping if they are loose **(see illustration)**. Discard the cover seal as a new one must be fitted.
7 Undo the impeller bolt, noting the location of the washer **(see illustration)**. Draw the impeller off the shaft, noting the location of the outer half of the two-part mechanical seal **(see illustration)**.
8 Note the location of the inner half of the two-part mechanical seal, then draw off the pump body – note the location of the dowel and remove it for safekeeping if it is loose **(see illustrations)**.

5.6a Undo the pump cover bolts (arrowed)

5.6b Lift off the cover noting the location of the seal (arrowed) . . .

5.6c . . . and the cover dowels (arrowed)

5.7a Note the washer (arrowed) on the impeller bolt

5.7b Note the outer half of the mechanical seal (arrowed)

5.8a Note the inner half of the mechanical seal (arrowed) then draw off the pump body . . .

5.8b . . . noting the location of the dowel (arrowed)

5.9a Discard the coolant gallery seal . . .

5.9b . . . and the pump body O-ring

5.10 Water pump impeller shaft (arrowed)

9 Discard the coolant gallery seal and O-ring from the back of the pump body **(see illustrations)**.

10 The impeller shaft is an extension of the engine balancer shaft **(see illustration)**. Check the shaft for up-and-down movement – in the unlikely event that the shaft bearings are worn, the crankcases will have to be separated and new bearing shells fitted (see Chapter 2).

Overhaul

11 Inspect the impeller for damage and clean off any corrosion **(see illustration)**. If the impeller is damaged a new one will have to be fitted.

12 Clean the ceramic seal on the back of the impeller carefully – if the surface is worn or pitted a new two-part seal will have to be fitted **(see illustration 5.7b)**.

13 The ceramic seal is a press fit in its rubber seat and should pull out easily – take care not to damage the inside surface of the impeller **(see illustration)**. Lubricate the new seal and seat with coolant and press them all the way in by hand.

14 To remove the inner half of the mechanical seal in the pump body, first prise out the oil seal, noting which way round it fits **(see illustration)**.

15 Support the pump body on wooden blocks on the work surface, mechanical seal side down, then press the mechanical seal out with a bearing driver or suitably-sized socket **(see illustrations)**.

16 Lubricate the new oil seal with a smear of water pump grease, then press it into the pump body until the outer edge is level with the housing **(see illustration)**.

17 Turn the body over. Now press in the new mechanical seal in until the flange on the seal is level with the housing **(see illustration)**.

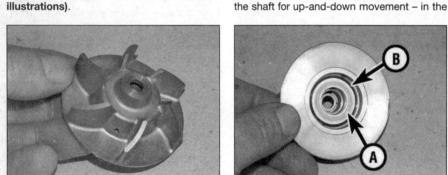

5.11 Inspect the impeller for damage and corrosion

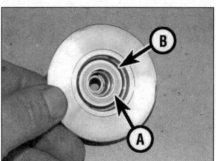

5.13 Ease out the ceramic seal (A) and rubber seat (B)

5.14 Remove the oil seal (arrowed) on the back of the pump body

5.15a To remove the inner half of the mechanical seal (arrowed) . . .

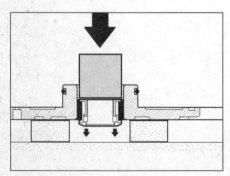

5.15b . . . press it out from the opposite side with a bearing driver

5.16 Level outer edge of oil seal (arrowed) with the housing

5.17 Level flange on mechanical seal (arrowed) with the housing

Installation

18 Installation is the reverse of removal, noting the following:

● If removed, install the dowels **(see illustrations 5.8b and 6c)**.
● Lubricate the new coolant gallery seal and pump body O-ring with a smear of grease **(see illustrations 5.9a and b)**.
● Fit the washer onto the impeller bolt, then tighten the bolt to the specified torque setting.
● Lubricate the new cover seal with a smear of grease **(see illustration 5.6b)**.
● Tighten the cover bolts to the specified torque setting.
● Ensure the coolant hose is correctly aligned before tightening the clip.
● Refill the cooling system (see Chapter 1 and *Pre-ride checks*).

6 Coolant reservoir

Removal

1 The coolant reservoir is located on the right-hand side of the machine behind the fairing side panel – remove the side panel for access (see Chapter 7).
2 Release the clip securing the radiator overflow hose to the union on the radiator filler neck, disconnect the hose and place the end in a suitable container **(see illustrations)**.
3 Unscrew the reservoir cap and drain the coolant into the container.
4 Release the reservoir breather hose from any clips, then undo the bolts securing the reservoir and lift it off **(see illustrations)**.

Installation

5 Installation is the reverse of removal, noting the following:
● Make sure the breather hose is correctly routed and secured.
● Tighten the mounting bolts securely.
● Make sure the overflow hose is correctly routed and secured.
● Refill the reservoir to the 'F' level line with the specified coolant mixture (see Chapter 1 and *Pre-ride checks*).

6.2a Release the clip (arrowed)

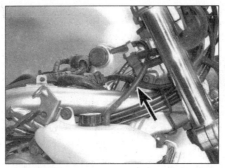

6.4a Note the routing of the breather hose (arrowed)

7 Radiator and pressure cap

Note: *If the radiator is being removed as part of the engine removal procedure, detach the hoses from their unions on the engine rather than on the radiator and remove the radiator with the hoses attached. Note the routing of the hoses.*

Removal

⚠ **Warning: The engine must be completely cool before carrying out this procedure.**

1 Remove the fairing side panels (see Chapter 7).
2 Drain the cooling system (see Chapter 1).

6.2b Place the hose in a suitable container

6.4b Bolts (arrowed) secure coolant reservoir

3 Remove the coolant reservoir (see Section 6).
4 Disconnect the cooling fan motor wiring connector **(see illustration 2.6)**
5 Loosen both clips on the coolant hoses between the radiator and the thermostat housing and water pump, then disconnect the hoses from the radiator **(see illustrations 4.2 and 5.5)**.
6 Undo the radiator mounting bolt on the right-hand side, noting the collar and bush in the mounting bracket **(see illustration)**.
7 Ease the radiator off the brackets on the left-hand side of the frame and remove it **(see illustration)**. Note the location of the baffle plate on the front edge of the valve cover **(see illustration)**.

Inspection

8 Note the location of the bushes in the

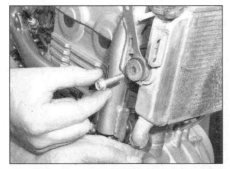

7.6 Undo the right-hand radiator mounting bolt

7.7a Left-hand radiator mounting brackets (arrowed)

7.7b Location of the baffle plate (arrowed)

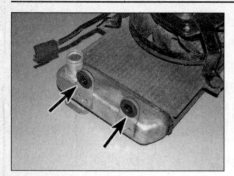

7.8 Inspect the radiator mounting bushes (arrowed)

8.2a Larger-bore hoses are secured by hose clips (arrowed)

8.2b Smaller-bore hoses are secured by spring clamps (arrowed)

radiator mounts **(see illustration)**. Renew any of the bushes if they are damaged, deformed or deteriorated.

9 If required, remove the cooling fan from the radiator (see Section 2). Check the radiator for signs of damage and clear any dirt or debris that might obstruct airflow and inhibit cooling. Damaged fins can be straightened carefully using a flat-bladed screwdriver. However, if more than 20% of the radiator surface has been damaged its cooling efficiency will be seriously affected and a new radiator should be fitted.

10 Check the condition of the coolant hoses and the hose clips (see Chapter 1).

Installation

11 Installation is the reverse of removal, noting the following:
- Ensure the bushes are in place and the collar is fitted in the bush on the right-hand mounting bracket **(see illustrations 7.8 and 7.6)**.
- Tighten the mounting bolt to the specified torque setting.
- Ensure the fan motor wiring is securely connected.
- Ensure the coolant hoses are correctly aligned before tightening the clips.
- Refill the cooling system (see Chapter 1 and *Pre-ride checks*).

Pressure cap check

12 If problems such as overheating or loss of coolant occur, check the entire system as described in Chapter 1. The radiator cap opening pressure should be checked by a Kawasaki dealer with the special tester required to do the job. If the cap is defective, replace it with a new one.

8 Coolant hoses

Removal

1 Before removing a hose, drain the coolant (see Chapter 1). **Note:** *When removing components of the cooling system, be prepared to catch any residual coolant.*

2 Use a screwdriver or a small socket to slacken the larger-bore hose clips, then slide them back along the hose and clear of the union spigot **(see illustration)**. The smaller-bore hoses are secured by spring clamps which can be expanded by squeezing their ears together with pliers **(see illustration)**.

Caution: The radiator unions are fragile. Do not use excessive force when attempting to remove the hoses.

3 If a hose proves stubborn, release it by rotating it on its union before working it off. If

8.4a Note the shoulder (arrowed) on the hose union

all else fails, cut the hose with a sharp knife, then slit it lengthways at the union so that it can be peeled off (see *Tools and Workshop Tips* in the reference Section). Whilst this means replacing the hose with a new one, it is preferable to buying a new radiator.

Installation

4 Slide the clips onto the hose and then work the hose on to its union as far as the shoulder **(see illustrations)**.

> **HAYNES HINT** *If the hose is difficult to push on its union, soften it by soaking it in very hot water, or alternatively a little soapy water on the union can be used as a lubricant.*

5 Rotate the hose on its unions to settle it in position before sliding the clips into place and tightening them securely.

6 Refill the cooling system (see Chapter 1 and *Pre-ride checks*).

8.4b Position the hose then install the clip (arrowed)

Chapter 4
Engine management system

Contents

Degrees of difficulty

Easy, suitable for novice with little experience	Fairly easy, suitable for beginner with some experience	Fairly difficult, suitable for competent DIY mechanic	Difficult, suitable for experienced DIY mechanic	Very difficult, suitable for expert DIY or professional

Specifications

General information
Cylinder numbering .... 1 and 2 from left to right
Spark plugs .... see Chapter 1

Fuel
Type .... Unleaded. Minimum 91 RON
Fuel tank capacity (including reserve) .... 15.5 litres

Fuel supply system
Fuel pressure 2006 to 2008 models
  Ignition ON, fuel pump running .... 47 psi (3.3 Bar)
  Ignition ON, fuel pump off, system pressurised .... 38 psi (2.7 Bar)
  Engine idling .... 48 psi (3.4 Bar)
Fuel pressure 2009-on models
  Engine idling .... 43 psi (3.0 Bar)
Minimum fuel flow rate .... 60 ml every 3 seconds

Component test data

Clean air system control valve
Resistance . . . . 18 to 22 ohms at 20°C (68°F)
Crankshaft position (CKP) sensor
Resistance . . . . 376 to 564 ohms
Minimum peak voltage output . . . . 1.9 volts
Engine coolant temperature (ECT) sensor
Output voltage . . . . 2.8 to 2.97 volts at 20°C (68°F)
Fuel injector resistance. . . . . 11.7 to 12.3 ohms at 20°C (68°F)
Fuel level gauge sensor resistance (2009-on models)
Tank full. . . . . 5 to 7 ohms
Tank empty. . . . . 204 to 210 ohms
Intake air pressure (IAP) sensor
Input voltage. . . . . 4.75 to 5.25 volts
Output voltage . . . . 3.8 to 4.2 volts at standard atmospheric pressure
Intake air temperature (IAT) sensor resistance
At 0°C (32°F). . . . . 5.4 to 6.6 K-ohms
At 80°C (176°F). . . . . 0.29 to 0.39 K-ohms
Output voltage . . . . approx. 2.25 to 2.5 volts at 20°C (68°F)
Oxygen sensor
Output voltage
With air system blocked . . . . min 0.7 volts
With air system open . . . . max. 0.2 volts
Heater resistance . . . . 11.7 to 14.5 ohms at 20°C (68°F)
Secondary throttle position (STP) sensor
Input voltage. . . . . 4.75 to 5.25 volts
Output voltage . . . . approx. 0.4 to 3.9 volts as throttle is opened
Resistance . . . . 4 to 6 K-ohms
Secondary throttle valve actuator
Resistance . . . . approx. 5.5 to 7.5 ohms
Input voltage. . . . . 8.5 to 10.5 volts
Speed sensor
Input voltage. . . . . 9 to 11 volts
Output voltage . . . . 0.05 to 0.07 volts to 4.5 to 4.9 volts approx.
Throttle position (TP) sensor
Input voltage. . . . . 4.75 to 5.25 volts
Output voltage . . . . 1.0 rising to 4.4 volts as throttle is opened
Resistance . . . . 4 to 6 K-ohms
Tip-over (TO) sensor
Input voltage. . . . . 4.75 to 5.25 volts
Output voltage
Sensor upright . . . . 3.55 to 4.45 volts
Sensor tilted (see text) . . . . 0.65 to 1.35 volts

Ignition coils

Primary winding resistance . . . . 1.1 to 1.5 ohms
Secondary winding resistance . . . . 10.8 to 16.2 K-ohms
Primary peak voltage (see text)
2006 to 2008 models . . . . 88 volts
2009-on models . . . . 117 volts

Torque settings

Crankshaft position (CKP) sensor bolts . . . . 6 Nm
Engine coolant temperature (ECT) sensor . . . . 12 Nm
Exhaust system
Header pipe nuts . . . . 17 Nm
Silencer mounting bolts . . . . 20 Nm
Fuel level gauge sensor screws (2009-on) . . . . 7 Nm
Fuel pump mounting bolts . . . . 10 Nm
Oxygen sensor . . . . 44 Nm
Speed sensor mounting bolt . . . . 8 Nm
Speed sensor bracket bolts . . . . 10 Nm

1 General information and precautions

General information

The engine management system combines the operations of the fuel and ignition systems. Together they are controlled by the electronic control unit which ensures that the engine is running at optimum efficiency under all riding conditions.

Fuel system

The fuel system consists of the fuel tank, an integrated fuel pump, pressure regulator, low level sender and filter, the fuel hose, fuel rail, injectors, throttle bodies, and control cables.

Fuel is pumped under pressure from the tank to the fuel rail, from which the individual injectors are fed. The fuel pump is switched on and off by the ignition switch, via a relay. Operating pressure is maintained by the pressure regulator.

When they open, the injectors spray fuel into the throttle bodies where it mixes with air and vaporises, before entering the cylinder where it is compressed and ignited. Fuel supply varies according to the engine's needs for starting, warming-up, idling, cruising and acceleration. The timing and duration of fuel delivery is determined by the ECU using the information obtained from the various sensors it monitors (see Section 8).

The exhaust system is a two-into-one design. On all models except those intended for sale in the US and Canada, an oxygen sensor is located in the silencer front pipe and a catalytic converter is located inside the silencer itself. The Kawasaki clean air system introduces filtered air into the exhaust ports to promote the burning of excess fuel in the exhaust gases.

On California models an EVAP emission control system prevents fuel vapour escaping into the atmosphere from the fuel tank (see Chapter 1 for more information).

Ignition system

The ignition system consists of a timing rotor, crankshaft position sensor (CKP sensor), ignition coils and spark plugs.

The triggers on the rotor, which is fitted to the right-hand end of the crankshaft, generate signals in the CKP sensor as the crankshaft rotates. The sensor sends those signals to the ECU which, in conjunction with information received from the throttle position and engine coolant temperature sensors, calculates the ignition timing and supplies the ignition coils with the power necessary to produce a spark at the plugs. There is no provision for checking or adjusting the ignition timing.

The ignition coils for both spark plugs are incorporated in the spark plug caps.

The system incorporates a safety interlock circuit which will cut the ignition if the sidestand is extended whilst the engine is running and in gear. It also prevents the engine from being started if the sidestand is down

and the engine is in gear. Refer to Chapter 8 for full component details.

Note: *Individual engine management system components can be checked but not repaired. If system troubles occur, and the faulty component can be isolated, the only cure for the problem in most cases is to replace the part with a new one. Keep in mind that most electronic parts, once purchased, cannot be returned. To avoid unnecessary expense, make very sure the faulty component has been positively identified before buying a new part.*

Precautions

⚠️ **Warning: Petrol (gasoline) is extremely flammable, so take extra precautions when you work on any part of the fuel system. Always remove the battery (see Chapter 8). Don't smoke or allow open flames or bare light bulbs near the work area, and don't work in a garage where a natural gas-type appliance is present. If you spill any fuel on your skin, rinse it off immediately with soap and water. When you perform any kind of work on the fuel system, wear safety glasses and have a fire extinguisher suitable for a class B type fire (flammable liquids) on hand.**

Ensure the ignition is switched OFF before disconnecting or reconnecting any fuel injection system wiring connector. If a connector is disconnected or reconnected with the ignition switched ON, the electronic control unit (ECU) may be damaged.

Always perform service procedures in a well-ventilated area to prevent a build-up of fumes.

Never work in a building containing a gas appliance with a pilot light, or any other form of naked flame. Ensure that there are no naked light bulbs or any sources of flame or sparks nearby.

Do not smoke (or allow anyone else to smoke) while in the vicinity of petrol (gasoline) or of components containing it. Remember the possible presence of vapour from these sources and move well clear before smoking.

Check all electrical equipment belonging to the house, garage or workshop where work is being undertaken (see the *Safety first!* section of this manual). Remember that certain electrical appliances such as drills, cutters etc, create sparks in the normal course of operation and must not be used near petrol (gasoline) or any component containing it. Again, remember the possible presence of

fumes before using electrical equipment.

Always mop up any spilt fuel and safely dispose of the rag used.

Any stored fuel that is drained off during servicing work must be kept in sealed containers that are suitable for holding petrol (gasoline), and clearly marked as such; the containers themselves should be kept in a safe place. Note that this last point applies equally to the fuel tank if it is removed from the machine; also remember to keep its filler cap closed at all times.

Read the *Safety first!* section of this manual carefully before starting work.

Owners of machines used in the US, particularly California, should note that their machines must comply at all times with Federal or State legislation governing the permissible levels of noise and of pollutants such as unburnt hydrocarbons, carbon monoxide etc. that can be emitted by those machines. All vehicles offered for sale must comply with legislation in force at the date of manufacture and must not subsequently be altered in any way which will affect their emission of noise or of pollutants.

In practice, this means that adjustments may not be made to any part of the fuel, ignition or exhaust systems by anyone who is not authorised or mechanically qualified to do so, or who does not have the tools, equipment and data necessary to properly carry out the task. Also if any part of these systems is to be renewed it must be renewed with only genuine Kawasaki components or by components which are approved under the relevant legislation. The machine must never be used with any part of these systems removed, modified or damaged.

2 Fuel tank

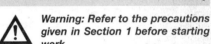

⚠️ **Warning: Refer to the precautions given in Section 1 before starting work.**

Note: *Try to time the removal procedure with a near empty tank, which makes it much easier to lift.*

Removal

1 Ensure the ignition is switched OFF.
2 Remove the seat (see Chapter 7).
3 Undo the bolts securing the front seat bracket and lift it off **(see illustrations)**.

2.3a Undo the bolts (arrowed) . . .

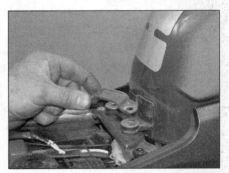

2.3b . . . and lift off the bracket

2.5a Open the hose connector clip . . .

2.5b . . . and pull the connector off the pump union

2.6a Trace the fuel pump wiring (arrowed) . . .

2.6b . . . to the connector

2.8 Disconnect any ancillary hoses

2.10 Draw the tank back and off

4 Remove the fuel tank side panels (see Chapter 7).

5 Temporarily open the fuel cap to release any pressure inside the tank, then raise the rear of the tank to access the fuel hose connector on the fuel pump. Place some rag under the hose connector to catch any residual fuel. Insert a flat-bladed screwdriver under the hose connector clip and twist the screwdriver to open the clip **(see illustration)**. Pull the connector off the pump union **(see illustration)**. **Note:** *A small amount of residual*

pressure will remain in the fuel hose after the motorcycle has been used. Close the fuel cap securely.

6 Trace the wiring from the fuel pump and disconnect it at the connector **(see illustrations)**.

7 On California models, disconnect the EVAP system red (fuel return) and blue (tank breather) hoses from the underside of the tank, noting where they fit.

8 On all other models, disconnect the breather and/or drain hose **(see illustration)**.

9 On 2009-on models, trace the wiring from the fuel level sensor on the underside of the tank and disconnect it at the connector.

10 Draw the tank back so the front mounting cups clear the rubbers on the frame, and lift the tank off **(see illustration)**. Support the rear of the tank on a block of wood to avoid it resting on the fuel pump union.

11 If required, unscrew the fuel tank bracket bolts, unclip the wiring loom from the bracket and remove it **(see illustrations)**.

12 Check all the tank mounting rubbers

2.11a Unscrew the fuel tank bracket bolts . . .

2.11b . . . and unclip the wiring loom

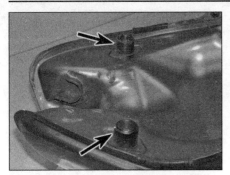

2.12a Inspect the mounting rubbers (arrowed) at the front . . .

2.12b . . . and rear of the tank . . .

2.12c . . . and on the frame

for signs of damage or deterioration and replace them with new ones if necessary **(see illustrations)**. Note the location of the collars in the rear mounting rubbers.

13 On 2009-on models, inspect the catch-tank on the lower end of the breather hose **(see illustration)**. If required, release the clip securing the tank and empty out any fluid.

Installation

14 Installation is the reverse of removal, noting the following:

● Make sure all mounting rubbers and collars are in place.
● Ensure the front mounting cups are pushed firmly onto the rubbers on the frame.
● Connect the hoses as noted on removal (see Steps 7 and 8).
● Connect the fuel pump wiring connector and, on 2009-on models, the fuel level sensor wiring connector, securely.
● Push the fuel hose connector all the way on its union until it clicks into place, then lock it in position with the clip.
● Make sure the fuel hose is secure by pulling and pushing the joint on the union – the hose should not come off, but there should be a small amount of movement. If the joint does not slide, remove and refit it.
● Lower the tank, install the front seat bracket and tighten the mounting bolts securely.
● Start the engine and check that there is no sign of fuel leakage, then turn it OFF.
● Install the remaining components in the reverse order of removal.

2.13 Location of the breather hose catch tank

Repair

15 All repairs to the fuel tank should be carried out by a professional who has experience in this critical and potentially dangerous work. Even after cleaning and flushing of the fuel system, explosive fumes can remain and ignite during repair of the tank.

16 If the fuel tank is removed from the bike, it should not be placed in an area where sparks or open flames could ignite the fumes coming out of the tank. Be especially careful inside garages where a natural gas-type appliance is located, because the pilot light could cause an explosion.

3 Fuel pressure check

Special Tool: *A fuel pressure gauge, hose and adapter are required for this procedure (see Step 2).*

1 The fuel pump is located inside the fuel tank. When the ignition is switched ON, it should be possible to hear the pump run for approximately 3 seconds until the system is up to pressure. If you can't hear anything, first check the pump relay (see Section 4). If the relay is good, check the wiring and terminals for physical damage or loose or corroded connections and rectify as necessary (see the *Wiring Diagrams* at the end of Chap-

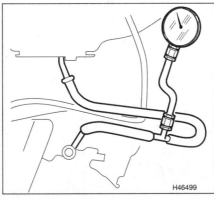

3.3 Fuel pressure gauge and hose set-up

ter 8). If the pump still will not run, check the tip-over (TO) sensor (see Section 10 or 11 as appropriate). If that is good, and assuming the ECU is OK, fit a new pump assembly.

2 To check the fuel pressure, a suitable gauge, gauge adapter and hose are needed. Kawasaki provides service tools (Part Nos. 57001-125, 57001-1593 and 57001-1607) for this purpose.

3 Raise the fuel tank, then disconnect the fuel hose from the pump union **(see illustrations 2.5a and b)**. Use the service tools to connect the gauge between the fuel tank and the fuel rail **(see illustration)**.

4 On 2006 to 2008 models, turn the ignition switch ON and note the pressure reading on the gauge as the pump runs for 3 seconds and pressurises the system, then with the system pressurised when the pump has stopped. The system should hold the fuel pressure for approximately 30 seconds.

5 On all models, now start the engine and note the fuel pressure with the engine idling. **Note:** *The pressure will fluctuate – note the average between the minimum and maximum readings*

6 The fuel pressure in each case should be as specified at the beginning of this Chapter. **Note:** *For 2009-on models, Kawasaki only provide a pressure reading at engine idle speed.*

7 Turn the ignition OFF and disconnect the gauge and adapters, using a rag to catch any residual fuel as before. Connect the fuel hose (see Section 2).

8 If the pressure is too low, check for a leak in the fuel supply system, including the fuel rail and injectors. If there is no leakage the filter in the pump could be blocked or the pump could be faulty. Check the operation of the pump (see Section 5).

9 If the pressure is too high, either the fuel hose or injector(s) is/are clogged, or the pressure regulator is faulty. Remove the hose and blow through it with compressed air. Refer to Section 15 to inspect the fuel rail and injectors. If the pressure regulator is thought to be faulty a new pump will have to be fitted – the regulator is an integral part of the pump **(see illustration 5.18)**.

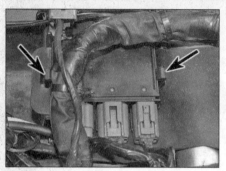

4.2a Release the clips (arrowed) ...

4.2b ... and lift out the relay box ...

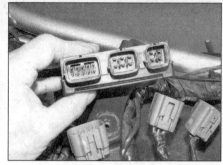

4.2c ... and disconnect the wiring connectors

4 Fuel pump relay

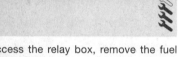

1 To access the relay box, remove the fuel tank and the fuel tank bracket (see Section 2).
2 Release the clips securing the relay box, lift it out of its rubber holder and disconnect the wiring connectors **(see illustrations)**.
3 Using a multimeter, check for continuity between terminals 7 and 8 on the relay **(see illustration)**. There should be no continuity. Now use jumper wires to connect the positive (+ve) terminal of a fully charged 12 volt battery to terminal 9 on the relay and the negative (-ve) battery terminal to relay terminal 10. There should now be continuity between terminals 7 and 8. If the relay fails either of the checks the relay box must be replaced with a new one – individual relays are not available.
4 If the relay is good, check for battery voltage between the red and brown/yellow wire terminals on the loom side of the wiring connector with the ignition and kill switch ON. If there is no voltage, check the circuit and its components, referring to the relevant wiring diagram at the end of Chapter 8. If voltage is present, check the wiring between the relay and the pump wiring connector for continuity. If all is good the ECU could be faulty (see Section 12).

5 Fuel pump assembly

 Warning: Refer to the precautions given in Section 1 before starting work.

Voltage check

1 The fuel pump is located inside the fuel tank. When the ignition is switched ON, it should be possible to hear the pump run for approximately 3 seconds until the system is up to pressure. If you can't hear anything, check the pump relay (see Section 4). If the relay is good, check the pump operating voltage as follows.
2 Remove the seat and the left-hand tank side panel (see Chapter 7).

3 Ensure the ignition is OFF.
4 Trace the wiring from the fuel pump to the connector **(see illustrations 2.6a and b)**. With the connector still connected, and using needle probes inserted into the pump side of the connector, connect the positive (+ve) lead of a voltmeter to the white/red wire terminal and the negative (-ve) lead to the black/yellow wire terminal. Turn the ignition ON – the meter should indicate battery voltage (12.9 volts or more) for approximately 3 seconds, and then zero volts. Turn the ignition OFF.
5 If the result is as described, the fuel pump circuit is operating correctly and the fuel pump itself is faulty and must be replaced with a new one (see Steps 15 to 23).
6 If no reading is obtained, check the white/red wire and connectors between the fuel pump and the pump relay for continuity using the wiring diagrams at the end of Chapter 8, and check for continuity to earth in the black/yellow wire.
7 If the reading permanently shows battery voltage, either the pump relay (see Section 4) or the ECU (see Section 12) is faulty.

Fuel flow rate check

Note: *A suitable calibrated container and length of fuel hose is required for this check.*
8 Follow the procedure in Section 2, Steps 1 to 5, to disconnect the fuel hose from the fuel pump union.
9 Connect a length of fuel hose to the union and place the open end in the calibrated container.
10 Turn the ignition ON – the pump should

operate for approximately 3 seconds and then stop. Turn the ignition OFF. Repeat this procedure until the fuel hose is filled with fuel. Now turn the ignition ON and note the amount of fuel discharged into the container during the time the pump is operating. Repeat the procedure several times, calculate the average amount of fuel discharged by the pump, then compare the result with the specification at the beginning of this Chapter.
11 If the fuel flow is below the specified minimum, first check the battery condition (see Chapter 8). If the battery is good, renew the fuel pump (see Steps 15 to 23).

Low fuel level warning sender

12 The low fuel level warning light in the instrument cluster should remain OFF until approximately 3.5 litres of fuel remains in the tank. If the light comes on when the tank is full it is likely the sender is faulty.
13 To check the operation of the sender, first remove the fuel pump (see Steps 15 to 17).
14 Connect a test light between the blue and black wire terminals in the fuel pump wiring connector – the light should come on. **Note:** *If the pump has just been removed from the tank it may take several minutes before the light comes on.* If the light does not come on, the sender is faulty and a new pump will have to be fitted – the sender is an integral part of the pump.

Removal

15 The fuel pump is located inside the fuel tank. If required, drain any fuel from the tank

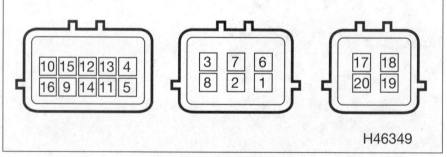

4.3 Relay box terminal numbering

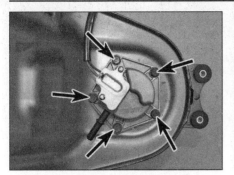

5.16 Undo the bolts (arrowed)

5.17a Lift out the fuel pump assembly

5.17b Note the location of the O-ring

using a commercially available pump, then remove the tank (see Section 2).

16 Turn the tank upside down and rest it on some clean rag to protect the paintwork. Note which way round the pump base plate is fitted, then undo the mounting bolts evenly in a criss-cross pattern **(see illustration)**.

17 Ease out the fuel pump assembly and discard the O-ring as a new one must be fitted on reassembly **(see illustrations)**.

18 Allow the filter to dry, then clean any sediment off its gauze with a soft brush or low pressure compressed air **(see illustration)**. The filter is an integral part of the pump – if the gauze is damaged, or if there is sediment inside the filter, a new pump will have to be fitted.

Installation

19 Make sure the wiring terminal screws are tight.

20 Ensure the mounting plate and tank surfaces are clean and dry, then fit the new O-ring **(see illustration 5.17b)**.

21 Install the pump carefully, ensuring it is the correct way round **(see illustration 5.17a)**.

22 Clean the threads of the pump mounting bolts and apply a suitable non-permanent thread-locking compound **(see illustration)**. Tighten the bolts finger-tight, then tighten them evenly and a little at a time in a criss-cross sequence to the torque setting specified at the beginning of this Chapter.

23 Install the fuel tank (see Section 2).

6 Fuel level gauge sensor – 2009-on models

Warning: Refer to the precautions given in Section 1 before starting work.

Removal

1 The fuel level gauge sensor is located inside the fuel tank. To access the sensor, first remove the tank (see Section 2) – if required, drain any fuel from the tank using a commercially available pump.

2 Turn the tank upside down and rest it on some clean rag to protect the paintwork. Note which way round the sensor base plate is

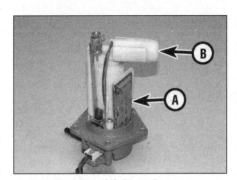

5.18 Fuel filter (A). Note the pressure regulator (B)

fitted, then undo the mounting bolts evenly in a criss-cross pattern.

3 Ease the sensor out of the tank, taking care not to damage the float arm **(see illustration)**. Discard the gasket as a new one must be fitted on reassembly.

Check

4 Check that the float arm moves up-and-down freely under its own weight **(see illustration)**.

5 To check the operation of the sensor, connect the probes of an ohmmeter to the terminals in the wiring connector and measure the resistance with the float in the raised (tank full) and lowered (tank empty) positions. Compare the results to the specifications at the beginning of this Chapter.

6 If the test shows the sensor is faulty, or if the

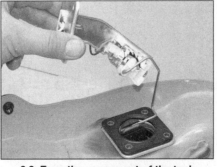

6.3 Ease the sensor out of the tank

5.22 Thread-lock the pump mounting bolts

resistance readings do not change smoothly, replace it with a new one.

7 If the tests show the sensor is good, refer to the relevant wiring diagram at the end of Chapter 8 and check the wiring circuit. If the wiring is good, have the fuel level display in the instrument cluster checked by a Kawasaki dealer.

Installation

8 Installation is the reverse of removal, noting the following:
● Fit a new gasket to the sensor base.
● Clean the threads of the mounting screws and apply a suitable non-permanent thread-locking compound.
● Tighten the bolts evenly to the torque setting specified at the beginning of this Chapter.
● Ensure the wiring connector is secure.

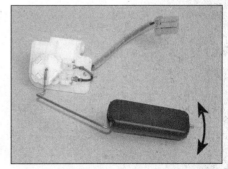

6.4 Ensure the float arm moves freely

7.3 Disconnect the crankcase breather hose (arrowed)

7.4 Disconnect the clean air system hose

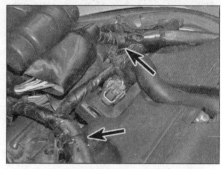

7.6 Release the clips (arrowed) securing the wiring loom

7 Air filter housing

Removal

1 Remove the fuel tank (see Section 2).
2 Remove the left-hand frame cover (see Chapter 7).
3 Release the clip and disconnect the crankcase breather hose from the union on the top of the case **(see illustration)**.
4 Pull the clean air system hose off the union on the filter housing **(see illustration)**.

5 Disconnect the intake air temperature sensor wiring connector **(see illustration 10.24)**.
6 Release the clips securing the wiring loom to the frame brackets and ease the loom away from the sides of the filter housing **(see illustration)**.
7 Undo the screws securing the housing cover and lift the cover off **(see illustrations)**.
8 Undo the screws securing the filter housing to the intake duct and remove them **(see illustration)** – it is advisable to block the throttle body intakes with clean rag to prevent the screws falling inside.

9 Ease the filter housing off, noting the routing of the drain hose **(see illustration)**.
10 If required, loosed the clamps securing the intake duct to the throttle body assembly and lift the intake duct off **(see illustration)**.

Installation

11 Installation is the reverse of removal, noting the following:
● Tighten the intake duct clamps securely.
● Tighten the filter housing screws securely.
● Ensure the intake air temperature sensor wiring connector is secure.
● Secure the crankcase breather hose to the union on the top of the case with its clip.

7.7a Undo the screws (arrowed) . . .

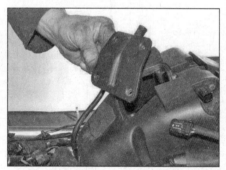

7.7b . . . and remove the housing cover

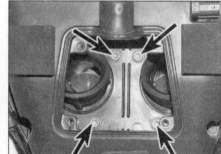

7.8 Undo the screws (arrowed) securing the filter housing

7.9 Lift the air filter housing off

7.10 Clamps (arrowed) secure the intake duct

7.11 Note the routing (arrowed) of the drain hose

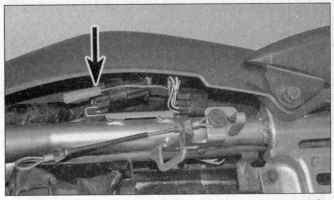

9.2 Location of the orange/black self diagnosis wire (arrowed)

● Make sure the drain hose is correctly routed and secured (see illustration).

8 Engine management system operation

1 The engine management system consists of the fuel system and the ignition circuit, controlled and co-ordinated by the electronic control unit (ECU). An overview of the engine management system can be found in Section 1.
2 To ensure optimum engine efficiency, the ECU monitors signals from the following sensors:
● Intake air temperature (IAT) sensor
● Intake air pressure (IAP) sensor
● Throttle position (TP) sensor
● Secondary throttle position (STP) sensor
● Speed sensor
● Crankshaft position (CKP) sensor
● Engine coolant temperature (ECT) sensor
● Tip-over (TO) sensor
● Oxygen sensor (where fitted)
3 The FI warning light in the instrument cluster should come on briefly when the ignition is switched ON, then go out – this serves as a check that the circuit is working correctly. If the light comes on and stays on, a fault has occurred. If the light does not come on at all, check the instrument cluster (see Chapter 8).
4 In the event of an abnormality in any of the sensor signals, the ECU will determine whether the engine can still be run safely. If it can, a back-up mode substitutes the sensor signal with a fixed signal, restricting performance but allowing the bike to be ridden home or to a dealer. In some cases the engine will continue to run after a fault has been registered, but once stopped the engine will not be able to be restarted. If the fault is serious, the fuel and ignition systems will be shut down and the engine will not run.
5 After the engine has been stopped, the appropriate self-diagnostic fault code can be accessed. See Section 9 for fault diagnosis.
6 The system incorporates two safety circuits. When the ignition is switched ON, the fuel pump runs for three seconds and pressurises

the system. Thereafter the pump automatically switches off until the engine is started. The second circuit incorporates a tip-over sensor, which automatically switches off the fuel pump and cuts power to the ignition and injection circuits if the motorcycle falls over.

9 Engine management system fuel diagnosis

1 The self diagnosis system has three modes:
● User Mode (the standard mode), in which the fuel injection system (FI) warning light will come on and stay on to warn the rider that a fault has occurred.
● Dealer Mode 1, in which the FI light will emit a series of flashes to denote the current fault code or codes.
● Dealer Mode 2, in which the FI light will emit a series of flashes to denote any past fault codes stored in the ECU memory. Note: In the event of a serious fault resulting in the fuel and ignition systems being shut down, use Dealer Mode 2 to access the fault code(s).
2 If the FI warning light comes on, enter Dealer Mode 1 as follows to read the fault code. Remove the rider's seat (see Chapter 7), then identify the orange/black self diagnosis wire behind the seat cowling on the right-hand side (see illustration). The orange/black wire has a female bullet connector on the end.
3 Prepare an insulated auxiliary wire with male bullet connector on one end and bare wire at the other. Connect the auxiliary wire to the orange/black wire.
4 Turn the ignition ON. Connect the bare end of the auxiliary wire to the battery negative (-ve) terminal and keep it connected – after approximately 5 seconds the FI light should start to flash, denoting the fault code(s) as follows.
5 The FI warning light emits long (1 second) and short (0.5 second) flashes to denote the fault codes. One or more long flashes are used to denote the first digit of the fault code, and one or more short flashes are used to denote the second digit (all codes are double

digit – see the fault code table). There is a 1.5 second gap between long (1 sec) flashes and a a 0.5 second gap between the short (0.5 sec) flashes. For example, two long (1 sec) flashes followed by four short (0.5 sec) flashes denotes the fault code 24.
6 If there is more than one fault code, there will be a 3 second gap between each one. The codes are displayed in numerical order, lowest to highest. Keep the wire connected until you have finished reading the fault code(s).
7 Once all the codes have been displayed, they will be repeated for as long as the auxiliary wire is connected to the battery negative (-ve) terminal. Record the fault codes, then disconnect the wire and turn the ignition OFF.
8 Compare the codes with the fault code table to identify the faulty components, then refer to Section 10 (2006 to 2008 models) or Section 11 (2009-on models) for checking procedures.
9 Once the fault has been corrected, turn the ignition switch ON and check that the FI warning light does not stay on. Start the engine and ride the machine at a speed above 18 mph (30 kph) to confirm that the fault has been corrected.
10 To read any fault codes stored in the ECU memory, enter Dealer Mode 2. Follow the procedure in Steps 2 and 3 to connect the auxiliary wire to the self diagnosis wire, turn the ignition ON, then repeatedly connect and disconnect the bare end of the auxiliary wire to the battery negative (-ve) terminal five times or more within two seconds, then keep it connected – the FI light should start to flash if there are any stored fault codes (see Step 5). Note: To enter dealer mode 2 from dealer mode 1, you must first switch the ignition OFF, then ON again.
11 To clear the stored fault codes, first enter Dealer Mode 2 (see Step 10). Keep the auxiliary wire connected to the battery negative (-ve) terminal, pull the clutch lever in and hold it in for five seconds or more, then release it. Now repeatedly disconnect and connect the auxiliary wire to the battery terminal five times or more within two seconds, then keep it connected for at least two seconds more. Disconnect the wire and turn the ignition OFF.

Fault code table

Code	Faulty component – ECU response	Possible causes
11	Throttle position (TP) sensor – engine will continue to run but with reduced performance	Faulty wiring or wiring connector Faulty, damaged or improperly installed sensor
12	Intake air pressure (IAP) sensor – engine will run	Faulty wiring or wiring connector Faulty, damaged or improperly installed sensor Detached, pinched or blocked hose
13	Intake air temperature (IAT) sensor – engine will run, intake temperature signal fixed at 30°C	Faulty wiring or wiring connector Faulty, damaged or improperly installed sensor
14	Engine coolant temperature (ECT) sensor – engine will run, coolant temperature signal fixed at 80°C	Faulty wiring or wiring connector Faulty, damaged or improperly installed sensor
21	Crankshaft position (CKP) sensor – engine will not run	Faulty wiring or wiring connector Faulty, damaged or improperly installed sensor or timing rotor
24 and 25	Speed sensor – engine will run, no reading on instrument cluster, gear position signal fixed at 6th	Faulty wiring or wiring connector Faulty damaged or improperly installed speed sensor
31	Tip-over (TO) sensor – engine will not run, fuel and ignition systems turned OFF	Machine overturned Faulty wiring or wiring connector Faulty damaged or improperly installed sensor
32	Secondary throttle position (STP) sensor – engine will run, sensor signal and secondary throttle fixed fully open	Faulty wiring or wiring connector Faulty, damaged or improperly installed sensor Faulty ECU
33*	Oxygen sensor not activated – engine will run, ECU stops sensor feedback signal	Faulty wiring or wiring connector Faulty, damaged or improperly installed sensor
51	No. 1 cylinder ignition coil – fuel supply to No. 1 cylinder cut, engine will run on cylinder No. 2	Faulty wiring or wiring connector Faulty or damaged ignition coil
52	No. 2 cylinder ignition coil – fuel supply to No. 2 cylinder cut, engine will run on cylinder No. 1	Faulty wiring or wiring connector Faulty or damaged ignition coil
56	Cooling fan relay	Faulty wiring or wiring connector Faulty relay
62	Secondary throttle actuator – engine will run, actuator disabled	Faulty wiring or wiring connector Faulty, damaged or improperly installed actuator
64	Clean air system control valve	Faulty wiring or wiring connector Faulty valve
67*	Oxygen sensor heater – engine will run, ECU stops power supply to heater	Faulty wiring or wiring connector Faulty, damaged or improperly installed sensor
94*	Oxygen sensor output voltage incorrect – engine will run, ECU stops sensor feedback signal	Faulty wiring or wiring connector Faulty, damaged or improperly installed sensor

Not US and Canada market models

10 Engine management system components – 2006 to 2008 models

Caution: Ensure the ignition is switched OFF before disconnecting/reconnecting any fuel injection system wiring connectors. If a connector is disconnected/reconnected with the ignition switched ON the ECU could be damaged.

1 If a fault is indicated on any of the system components, first check the wiring and connectors between the appropriate component and the ECU – see *Wiring Diagrams* at the end of Chapter 8. A continuity test of all wires will locate a break or short in any circuit. Inspect the terminals inside the wiring connectors and ensure that they are not loose or corroded. Spray the inside of the connectors with a proprietary electrical terminal cleaner before reconnection. Where appropriate, remove the sensor and check the sensor head and clean it if it is dirty – an accumulation of dirt could affect the signal it transmits.

2 It is possible to undertake some checks on system components using a multimeter and comparing the results with the specifications at the beginning of this Chapter. **Note:** *Different meters may give slightly different results to those specified even though the component being tested is not faulty – do not consign a component to the bin before having it double-checked.* Further tests can be undertaken using a multimeter and peak voltage adapter. Kawasaki provides a test meter (Part No. 57001-1394) and peak voltage adapter (Part No. 57001-1415) for this purpose. If the appropriate equipment is not available, the checks should be undertaken by a Kawasaki dealer.

3 If, after a thorough check, the source of a fault has not been identified, it is possible that the ECU itself is faulty. No test specifications are available for the ECU. In order to determine conclusively that the unit is defective, it should be substituted for a known good one (see

10.4 Location of the TP sensor (arrowed)

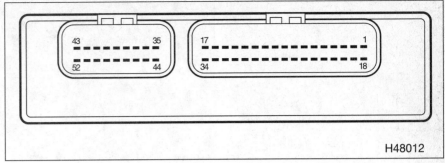

10.7 ECU connector terminal numbering – 2006 to 2008 models

Section 12). If the problem is then rectified, the original unit is faulty.

Throttle position (TP) sensor

4 The TP sensor is located on the left-hand end of the throttle body assembly **(see illustration)**.

5 To check the sensor input and output voltage you need either needle probes for your meter to back-probe the sensor connector terminals with the connector connected, or the Kawasaki test harness (Part No. 57001-1538) that fits between the sensor and its wiring loom.

6 Back-probe the blue wire terminal with the meter positive (+ve) probe and the brown/black wire terminal with the meter negative (-ve) probe. Alternatively, connect the positive (+ve) probe to the test harness red wire terminal and the negative (-ve) probe to the test harness black wire terminal. Turn the ignition ON and check the input voltage. Turn the ignition OFF. Compare the result with the specification at the beginning of this Chapter.

7 If the result is not as specified, disconnect the ECU multi-pin wiring connector (see Section 12). Check for continuity in the wiring between the TP sensor connector and the appropriate terminals in the ECU connector (blue wire to terminal 10, brown/black wire to terminal 28) **(see illustration)**. If the wiring is good, check the ECU earth (ground) connections and power supply (see Section 12).

8 If the input voltage is good, check the output voltage as follows. First warm up the engine and make sure the idle speed is correct (see Chapter 1), then turn the ignition OFF.

9 Back-probe the yellow/white wire terminal with the meter positive (+ve) probe and the brown/black wire terminal with the meter negative (-ve) probe. Alternatively, connect the positive (+ve) probe to the test harness red wire terminal and the negative (-ve) probe to the test harness white wire terminal. Turn the ignition ON and check the output voltage with the throttle closed, then with the throttle fully open. Turn the ignition OFF. Compare the results with the specifications at the beginning of this Chapter.

10 If the results are as specified, disconnect the ECU multi-pin wiring connector (see Section 12). Check for continuity in the wiring between the TP connector and the

appropriate terminals in the ECU connector (yellow/white wire to terminal 7, brown/black wire to terminal 28) **(see illustration 10.7)**. If the wiring is good, check the ECU earth (ground) connections and power supply (see Section 12).

11 If the output voltage is not as specified, disconnect the sensor wiring connector. Using a multi-meter set to the K-ohms scale, measure the resistance between the blue and brown/black wire terminals on the sensor side of the connector. If the resistance is outside the specified range the sensor is probably faulty – have it checked by a Kawasaki dealer. **Note:** *The TP sensor should not be removed from the throttle body assembly. It is an integral part of the assembly and is not available separately.*

Intake air pressure (IAP) sensor

Check

12 The IAP sensor is located on the left-hand side of the frame behind the left-hand fairing side panel **(see illustration)**. Remove the side panel for access (see Chapter 7).

13 To check the sensor input and output voltage you need needle probes for your meter to back-probe the ECU connector terminals with the connector connected. You also need needle probes to back-probe the sensor connector terminals with the connector connected, or the Kawasaki test harness (Part No. 57001-1561) that fits between the sensor and its wiring loom.

14 Remove the ECU from its mounting tray, then reconnect the wiring connectors (see

10.12 Location of the IAP sensor (A). Note the vacuum hose (B)

Section 12). Back-probe the ECU blue wire terminal 10 with the meter positive (+ve) probe and the brown/black wire terminal 28 with the meter negative (-ve) probe **(see illustration 10.7)**. Turn the ignition ON and check the input voltage. Turn the ignition OFF. Compare the result with the specification at the beginning of this Chapter.

15 If the result is not as specified, check the ECU earth (ground) connections and power supply (see Section 12).

16 If the input voltage is good, check the output voltage as follows. Back-probe the ECU yellow/blue wire terminal 8 with the meter positive (+ve) probe and the brown/black wire terminal 28 with the meter negative (-ve) probe. Turn the ignition ON and check the output voltage. Turn the ignition OFF. Compare the result with the specification at the beginning of this Chapter. **Note:** *The output voltage will vary according to local atmospheric pressure.*

17 If the output voltage is good, check the ECU earth (ground) connections and power supply (see Section 12).

18 If the result is not as specified, check the output voltage again at the IAP sensor connector as follows. Back-probe the yellow/blue wire terminal with the meter positive (+ve) probe and the brown/black wire terminal with the meter negative (-ve) probe. Alternatively, connect the positive (+ve) probe to the test harness green/white wire terminal and the negative (-ve) probe to the test harness black wire terminal. Turn the ignition ON and check the output voltage. Turn the ignition OFF. Compare the result with the specification at the beginning of this Chapter. **Note:** *The output voltage will vary according to local atmospheric pressure.*

19 If the output voltage is good, disconnect the IAP sensor wiring connector and the ECU multi-pin wiring connector (see Section 12). Check for continuity in the wiring between the IAP connector and the appropriate terminals in the ECU connector (yellow/blue wire to terminal 8, blue wire to terminal 10 and brown/black wire to terminal 28) **(see illustration 10.7)**.

20 If the result is not as specified, renew the sensor (see below).

Removal and installation

21 Remove the left-hand fairing side panel (see Chapter 7). Disconnect the sensor wiring

10.23 Ensure the vacuum hose is securely connected

10.24 Location of the IAT sensor (arrowed)

connector and detach the vacuum hose from the underside of the sensor (see illustration 10.12).

22 Undo the bolt securing the sensor bracket and remove the sensor.

23 Installation is the reverse of removal. Ensure the vacuum hose is in good condition and is securely connected to the throttle body assembly and the sensor (see illustration).

Intake air temperature (IAT) sensor

Check

24 The IAT sensor is located on the right-hand side of the air filter housing (see illustration). Remove the fuel tank for access (see Section 2).

25 To check the sensor output voltage you need needle probes for your meter to back-probe the ECU connector terminals with the connector connected.

26 Remove the ECU from its mounting tray, then reconnect the wiring connectors (see Section 12). Back-probe the ECU yellow wire terminal 26 with the meter positive (+ve)

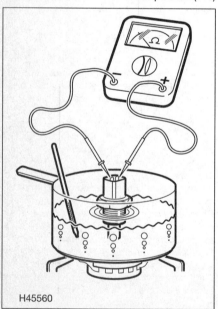

H45560

10.29 IAT sensor test set-up

probe and the brown/black wire terminal 28 with the meter negative (-ve) probe (see illustration 10.7). Turn the ignition ON and check the output voltage. Turn the ignition OFF. Compare the result with the specification at the beginning of this Chapter.

27 If the result is as specified, check the ECU earth (ground) connections and power supply (see Section 12). If they are good, it is likely the ECU is faulty – have it checked by a Kawasaki dealer.

28 If the output voltage is not as specified, disconnect the IAT sensor wiring connector and the ECU multi-pin wiring connector (see Section 12). Check for continuity in the wiring between the IAT connector and the appropriate terminals in the ECU connector (yellow wire to terminal 26, brown/black wire to terminal 28) (see illustration 10.7).

29 If the wiring is good, check the IAT sensor resistance as follows. Fill a small, heatproof container with oil and place it on a stove. Remove the sensor (see Steps 31 and 32). Using a multi-meter set to the K-ohms scale, connect the meter probes to the sensor terminals, and using some wire or other support, suspend the sensor in the oil so that just the sensing portion is submerged (see illustration). Also suspend a thermometer capable of reading temperatures up to 100°C in the oil so that its bulb is close to the sensor. Note: None of the components should be allowed to touch the container directly.

30 Check the meter reading and compare the result with the specifications at the beginning of this Chapter, then heat the oil slowly,

10.34 Location of the ECT sensor (arrowed)

stirring it gently. As the oil temperature rises the sensor resistance should fall. Check that the specified resistance is obtained at the correct temperature. If the readings obtained are different, or are obtained at different temperatures, the sensor is faulty and must be renewed. If the readings are as specified, it is likely the ECU is faulty – have it checked by a Kawasaki dealer.

Removal and installation

31 Remove the fuel tank (see Section 2).
32 Disconnect the IAT sensor wiring connector (see illustration 10.24). Undo the screw securing the sensor and draw it out of the air filter housing.
33 Installation is the reverse of removal.

Engine coolant temperature (ECT) sensor

34 The ECT sensor is located in the rear of the cylinder head on the left-hand side (see illustration). On EX650 models remove the left-hand fairing side panel for access (see Chapter 7).

35 To check the sensor output voltage you need needle probes for your meter to back-probe the ECU connector terminals with the connector connected.

36 Remove the ECU from its mounting tray, then reconnect the wiring connectors (see Section 12). Back-probe the ECU orange wire terminal 20 with the meter positive (+ve) probe and the brown/black wire terminal 28 with the meter negative (-ve) probe (see illustration 10.7). Turn the ignition ON and check the output voltage. Turn the ignition OFF. Compare the result with the specification at the beginning of this Chapter. Note: The output voltage will vary according to the coolant temperature.

37 If the result is as specified, check the ECU earth (ground) connections and power supply (see Section 12). If they are good, it is likely the ECU is faulty – have it checked by a Kawasaki dealer.

38 If the output voltage is not as specified, disconnect the ECT sensor wiring connector and the ECU multi-pin wiring connector (see Section 12). Check for continuity in the wiring between the ECT connector and the appropriate terminals in the ECU connector (orange wire to terminal 20, brown/black wire to terminal 28) (see illustration 10.7).

39 If the wiring is good, remove the ECT sensor and check the resistance as described in Chapter 3, Section 3. If the resistance is as specified, it is likely the ECU is faulty – have it checked by a Kawasaki dealer.

Crankshaft position (CKP) sensor

Note: In the event of a serious fault use Dealer Mode 2 to access the fault code.

Check

40 Remove the belly panel, the right-hand fuel tank side panel and the right-hand frame cover (see Chapter 7). Trace the CKP sensor

10.40a Trace the CKP sensor wiring (arrowed) . . .

10.40b . . . and disconnect it at the connector (arrowed)

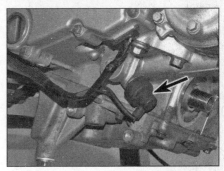

10.47a Displace the rubber boot (arrowed) . . .

10.47b . . . and disconnect the wiring connector

wiring from the front of the clutch cover and disconnect it at the connector **(see illustrations)**.

41 Using a multi-meter set to the ohms scale, measure the resistance between the black and yellow wire terminals on the sensor side of the connector. Compare the result with the specification at the beginning of this Chapter. Now check for continuity between each wire terminal and earth (ground) – there should be no continuity (infinite resistance). If the resistance varies greatly from the specification the sensor is faulty and must be renewed. Otherwise, check the sensor peak voltage as follows.

42 To check the CKP sensor peak voltage you will need a peak voltage adapter compatible with your voltmeter. Kawasaki produce a meter (Part No. 57001-1394) and a peak voltage adapter (Part No. 57001-1415).

43 If not already done, disconnect the sensor wiring connector. Set the voltmeter to the 10 volts DC scale and connect it to the peak voltage adapter. Connect the red positive (+ve) adapter lead to the black wire terminal on the sensor side of the connector and the black negative (-ve) adapter lead to the yellow wire terminal. Turn the ignition switch ON, turn the engine over on the starter motor for 4 to 5 seconds and note the peak voltage reading obtained. Repeat the procedure five more times.

44 Compare the results with the specification at the beginning of this Chapter – if the peak voltage is below the specified minimum, the sensor is faulty.

45 If the peak voltage is good, disconnect the ECU multi-pin wiring connector (see Section 12). Check for continuity in the wiring between the CKP sensor connector and the appropriate terminals in the ECU connector (red/black wire to terminal 13, yellow/black wire to terminal 30) **(see illustration 10.7)**. If the wiring is good, check the ECU earth (ground) connections and power supply (see Section 12).

Removal

46 Remove the belly panel, the right-hand fuel tank side panel and the right-hand frame cover (see Chapter 7).

47 Trace the CKP sensor wiring from the front of the clutch cover and disconnect it at the connector **(see illustration 10.40a and b)**. Release the wiring from any clips and feed it back to the clutch cover, noting its routing. Pull the rubber boot off the oil pressure switch, undo the terminal screw and detach the wire **(see illustrations)**.

48 Remove the clutch cover (see Chapter 2).

49 Undo the sensor mounting bolts, then ease the wiring grommet from the cut-out in the casing and remove the sensor along with the wiring **(see illustrations)**.

Installation

50 Remove all traces of old sealant from the clutch cover, crankcase and wiring grommet. Apply a smear of sealant around the grommet and press it into the cut-out, align the sensor with its mounting holes and tighten the bolts to the torque setting specified at the beginning of the chapter **(see illustrations 10.49b and a)**.

51 Install the clutch cover (see Chapter 2).

52 Route the wiring back to the connector and reconnect it **(see illustration 10.40b)**. Reconnect the oil pressure switch wire and fit the rubber boot **(see illustration 10.47b and a)**.

53 Install the remaining components in the reverse order of removal.

Speed sensor

Check

54 The speed sensor is mounted on a bracket behind the front sprocket cover **(see illustration)**. Remove the cover for access (see Chapter 6). On EX650 models, remove the left-hand fairing side panel (see Chapter 7).

55 To check the sensor input and output voltage you need either needle probes for your meter to back-probe the sensor connector terminals with the connector connected, or the

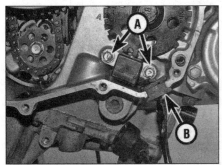

10.49a Undo the mounting bolts (A), noting the grommet (B) . . .

10.49b . . . then remove the CKP sensor

10.54 Location of the speed sensor – trace the wiring . . .

10.56 ... to the connector

Kawasaki test harness (Part No. 57001-1400) that fits between the sensor and its wiring loom.

56 Trace the wiring from the sensor to the wiring connector **(see illustration)**. Back-probe the pink wire terminal with the meter positive (+ve) probe and the black/yellow wire terminal with the meter negative (-ve) probe. Alternatively, connect the positive (+ve) probe to the test harness blue wire terminal and the negative (-ve) probe to the test harness black wire terminal. Turn the ignition ON and check the input voltage. Turn the ignition OFF. Compare the result with the specification at the beginning of this Chapter.

57 If the result is not as specified, check the sensor wiring for damage and check the instrument cluster (see Chapter 8).

58 If the input voltage is good, support the machine on an auxiliary stand so that the rear wheel is off the ground and check the output voltage as follows. Back-probe the light green/red wire terminal with the meter positive (+ve) probe and the black/yellow wire terminal with the meter negative (-ve) probe. Alternatively, connect the positive (+ve) probe to the test harness yellow/white wire terminal and the negative (-ve) probe to the test harness black wire terminal.

59 Turn the ignition ON and note the output voltage. Now rotate the rear wheel by hand

to check that the output voltage rises and falls within the specifications shown at the beginning of this Chapter. Turn the ignition OFF.

60 If the results are not as specified, disconnect the ECU multi-pin wiring connector (see Section 12). Check for continuity in the wiring between the speed sensor and the appropriate terminal in the ECU connector (light green/red wire to terminal 6) **(see illustration 10.7)**. If the wiring is good it is likely the sensor is faulty – have it checked by a Kawasaki dealer.

61 If the output voltage is good, check the ECU earth (ground) connections and power supply (see Section 12).

Removal and installation

62 Remove the front sprocket cover (see Chapter 6). On EX650 models, remove the left-hand fairing side panel (see Chapter 7).

63 Trace the wiring from the speed sensor and disconnect it at the connector **(see illustration 10.56)**. Release the wiring from any clips and feed it back to the sensor, noting its routing.

64 Undo the bolt securing the sensor to its bracket and lift it off **(see illustration)**.

65 Installation is the reverse of removal, noting the following:

● Clean the threads of the mounting bolt and apply a suitable non-permanent thread-locking compound.
● Tighten the mounting bolt to the torque setting specified at the beginning of this Chapter.
● Secure the wiring as noted on removal.

Tip-over (TO) sensor

Check

66 The TO sensor is located on the right-hand side of the frame below the rear shock absorber upper mounting **(see illustration)**. Remove the right-hand frame side panel (see Chapter 7) and, if required, the rear shock for access (see Chapter 5).

67 To check the sensor input and output voltage you need needle probes for your meter to back-probe the sensor connector terminals with the connector connected.

68 Back-probe the blue wire terminal with the meter positive (+ve) probe and the brown/black wire terminal with the meter negative (-ve) probe. Turn the ignition ON and check the input voltage. Turn the ignition OFF. Compare the result with the specification at the beginning of this Chapter.

69 If the input voltage is less than specified, disconnect the ECU multi-pin wiring connector (see Section 12). Check for continuity in the wiring between the TO sensor connector and the appropriate terminals in the ECU connector (blue wire to terminal 10, yellow/green wire to terminal 11, brown/black wire to terminal 28) **(see illustration 10.7)**. If the wiring is good, check the ECU earth (ground) connections and power supply (see Section 12).

70 If the input voltage is good, displace the sensor but do not disconnect the connector. Back-probe the yellow/green wire terminal with the meter positive (+ve) probe and the brown/black wire terminal with the meter negative (-ve) probe. Hold the sensor vertically (UP arrow pointing upwards), turn the ignition ON and note the output voltage. Now tilt the sensor 60 to 70° to the left, return it to the vertical position and note the output voltage. Turn the ignition OFF. Repeat the test, this time tilting the sensor to the right. Turn the ignition OFF. Compare the results with the specification at the beginning of this Chapter.

71 If the results are not as specified the TO sensor is faulty.

72 If the output voltage is good, disconnect the ECU multi-pin wiring connector (see Section 12). Check for continuity in the wiring between the TO sensor connector and the appropriate terminals in the ECU connector (blue wire to terminal 10, yellow/green wire to terminal 11, brown/black wire to terminal 28) **(see illustration 10.7)**. If the wiring is good,

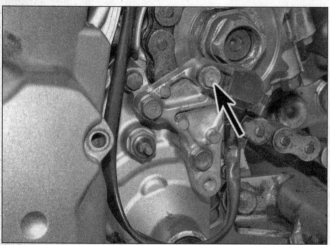

10.64 Undo the speed sensor mounting bolt (arrowed)

10.66 Location of the TO sensor

check the ECU earth (ground) connections and power supply (see Section 12).

Removal and installation

73 Remove the right-hand frame side panel (see Chapter 7) and, if required, the rear shock for access (see Chapter 5).
74 Disconnect the sensor wiring connector **(see illustration 10.66)**.
75 The sensor is secured by rubber grommets – ease the sensor off the grommets to remove it.
76 Installation is the reverse of removal, noting the following:
● Kawasaki advise that the mounting grommets should be renewed.
● Ensure that the sensor is fitted with its UP arrow pointing upwards.

Secondary throttle position (STP) sensor

Check

77 The STP sensor is located on the left-hand end of the throttle body assembly **(see illustration)**. Remove the air filter housing to access the sensor wiring connector (see Section 7) **(see illustration)**.
78 To check the sensor input and output voltage you need either needle probes for your meter to back-probe the sensor connector terminals with the connector connected, or the Kawasaki test harness (Part No. 57001-1400) that fits between the sensor and its wiring loom.
79 Back-probe the blue wire terminal with the meter positive (+ve) probe and the brown/black wire terminal with the meter negative (-ve) probe. Alternatively, connect the positive (+ve) probe to the test harness blue wire terminal and the negative (-ve) probe to the test harness black wire terminal. Turn the ignition ON and check the input voltage. Turn the ignition OFF. Compare the result with the specification at the beginning of this Chapter.
80 If the result is not as specified, disconnect the ECU multi-pin wiring connector (see Section 12). Check for continuity in the wiring between the STP sensor connector and the appropriate terminals in the ECU connector (blue wire to terminal 10, brown/black wire to terminal 28) **(see illustration 10.7)**. If the wiring is good, check the ECU earth (ground) connections and power supply (see Section 12).
81 If the input voltage is good, check the output voltage as follows. Back-probe the blue/white wire terminal with the meter positive (+ve) probe and the brown/black wire terminal with the meter negative (-ve) probe. Alternatively, connect the positive (+ve) probe to the test harness yellow wire terminal and the negative (-ve) probe to the test harness black wire terminal.
82 Ensure the secondary throttle valve is fully closed – close it by hand if necessary. Turn the ignition ON and note the output voltage, then open the throttle valve fully and note the output

10.77a Location of the STP sensor . . .

voltage again – the voltage should rise as the throttle valve is opened. Turn the ignition OFF. Compare the results with the specifications at the beginning of this Chapter.
83 If the results are as specified, disconnect the ECU multi-pin wiring connector (see Section 12). Check for continuity in the wiring between the STP connector and the appropriate terminals in the ECU connector (blue/white wire to terminal 24, brown/black wire to terminal 28) **(see illustration 10.7)**. If the wiring is good, check the ECU earth (ground) connections and power supply (see Section 12).
84 If the output voltage is not as specified, disconnect the sensor wiring connector. Using a multimeter set to the K-ohms scale, measure the resistance between the blue and black wire terminals on the sensor side of the connector. If the resistance is outside the specified range the sensor is probably faulty – have it checked by a Kawasaki dealer. **Note:** *The STP sensor should not be removed from the throttle body assembly. It is an integral part of the assembly and is not available separately.*

Oxygen sensor

85 The oxygen sensor is located in the silencer front pipe on the left-hand side **(see illustration)**. Remove the belly panel for access (see Chapter 7).

Fault code 33

86 To check the sensor output voltage

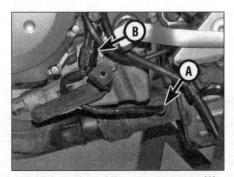

10.85 Location of the oxygen sensor (A) and sensor wiring connector (B)

10.77b . . . and the STP sensor wiring connector

you need needle probes for your meter to back-probe the sensor connector terminals with the connector connected.
87 Start the engine and run it until the cooling fan comes on, then turn it off. Trace the wiring from the sensor to the connector **(see illustration 10.85)**. Back-probe the blue/yellow wire terminal with the meter positive (+ve) probe and the brown/black wire terminal with the meter negative (-ve) probe.
88 Release the clip securing the clean air system hose to the union on the reed valve cover and disconnect the hose **(see illustration)**. Block-off the union with a suitable plug
89 Start the engine, note the output voltage at idle speed, then turn the engine off. Remove the plug from the union and repeat the test. Compare the results with the specifications at the beginning of this Chapter.
90 If the results are not as specified, disconnect the ECU multi-pin wiring connector (see Section 12). Check for continuity in the wiring between the oxygen sensor and the appropriate terminals in the ECU connector (blue/yellow wire to terminal 5, brown/black wire to terminal 28) **(see illustration 10.7)**. If the wiring is good the sensor is faulty.
91 If the output voltage is good, check the ECU earth (ground) connections and power supply (see Section 12).

Fault code 67

92 Trace the wiring from the sensor

10.88 Disconnect the clean air system hose (arrowed)

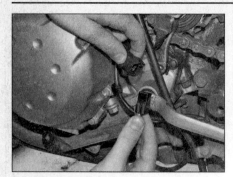

10.92 Disconnect the oxygen sensor wiring connector

10.110 Location of the STV actuator

10.111 Check the operation of the secondary throttle valves (arrowed)

and disconnect it at the connector **(see illustration)**.
93 Using a multimeter set to the ohms scale, measure the sensor heater resistance between the two black wire terminals on the sensor side of the connector. Compare the result with the specification at the beginning of this Chapter.
94 If the result is not as specified the sensor is faulty.
95 If the resistance is good, check the sensor heater power supply as follows. You will need a needle probe for your meter to back-probe the sensor connector terminal with the connector connected.
96 Back-probe the white/yellow wire terminal with the meter positive (+ve) probe and connect the meter negative (-ve) probe to the battery negative (-ve) terminal. Turn the ignition ON and check the supply voltage – battery voltage should be shown. Turn the ignition OFF.
97 If the voltage is good it is likely the ECU is faulty – have it checked by a Kawasaki dealer.
98 If the result is not as specified, first check the oxygen sensor heater fuse in the fusebox (see Chapter 8). Next, refer to *Wiring Diagrams* at the end of Chapter 8 and check the sensor heater power supply wiring. Finally, disconnect the ECU multi-pin wiring connector (see Section 12). Check for continuity in the wiring between the oxygen sensor connector and the appropriate terminal in the ECU connector (pink/black wire to terminal 29) **(see illustration 10.7)**. If the wiring is good, check the ECU earth (ground) connections and power supply (see Section 12).

Fault code 94

99 Follow the procedure in Steps 86 to 89 and check the oxygen sensor output voltage.
100 If the results are not as specified, check the fuel pressure (Section 3) and the injectors (Section 15). If they are good, the sensor is faulty.
101 If the output voltage is good, check the ECU earth (ground) connections and power supply (see Section 12).

Removal and installation

102 Remove the belly panel (see Chapter 7).

103 Disconnect the oxygen sensor wiring connector, then free the wiring from the clip **(see illustration 10.92)**.
104 Unscrew the sensor carefully to avoid damage. Take care not to drop the sensor and avoid handling the sensor tip.
105 Installation is the reverse of removal, noting the following:
● DO NOT apply oil or grease to the sensor threads.
● If available, use a special sensor spanner to tighten it to the torque setting specified at the beginning of this Chapter.
● Secure the wiring as noted on removal.

Ignition coils

106 The ignition coils are integral with the spark plug caps. For full details refer to Section 13.

Cooling fan relay

107 To access the relay box, remove the fuel tank and the fuel tank bracket (see Section 2). To check the operation of the relay, refer to Chapter 3, Section 2.
108 If the relay is good, check for battery voltage between the green and pink/blue wire terminals on the loom side of the wiring connector with the ignition and kill switch ON. If there is no voltage, check the circuit and its components, referring to the relevant wiring diagram at the end of Chapter 8. If voltage is present, check the wiring between the relay and the fan wiring connector and between the relay and the ECU (pink/blue wire to terminal 45) for continuity.
109 If the wiring is good, check the ECU earth (ground) connections and power supply (see Section 12).

Secondary throttle valve (STV) actuator

Check

110 The STV actuator is located on the left-hand end of the throttle body assembly **(see illustration)**. Remove the air filter housing cover to check the operation of the secondary throttle valves (see Section 7).

111 Turn the ignition ON and check that the secondary throttle valves (the uppermost set of valves in the throttle bodies) open and close – this is part of the engine start-up procedure **(see illustration)**.
112 If the valves don't move, remove the air filter housing (see Section 7), then disconnect the actuator wiring connector **(see illustration)**. Using a multimeter set to the ohms scale, measure the resistance between the black and pink wire terminals on the actuator side of the connector, then between the green and white/blue wire terminals.
113 Compare the results with the specifications at the beginning of this Chapter. If the resistance is outside the specified range the STV actuator is probably faulty – have it checked by a Kawasaki dealer. **Note:** *The STV actuator should not be removed from the throttle body assembly. It is an integral part of the assembly and is not available separately.*
114 If the results are good, check the actuator input voltage as follows. You will need needle probes to back-probe the actuator connector terminals with the connector connected. You will also need a peak voltage adapter compatible with your voltmeter. Kawasaki produce a meter (Part No. 57001-1394) and a peak voltage adapter (Part No. 57001-1415).
115 Working on the loom side of the connector, back-probe the black/blue wire terminal with the adapter positive (+ve) probe and the pink wire terminal with the adapter

10.112 STV actuator wiring connector

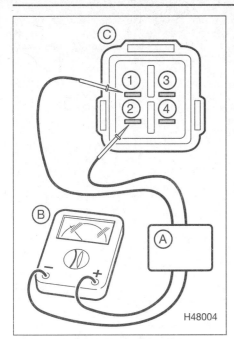

10.115 Set-up for testing the STV actuator input voltage. Peak voltage adapter (A), voltmeter (B) and loom side wiring connector (C)

1 *Black/blue wire terminal*
2 *Pink wire terminal*
3 *White/blue wire terminal*
4 *Green/yellow wire terminal*

negative (-ve) probe **(see illustration)**. Turn the ignition ON and check the input voltage. Turn the ignition OFF.

116 Now back-probe the white/blue wire terminal with the adapter positive (+ve) probe and the green/yellow wire terminal with the adapter negative (-ve) probe **(see illustration 10.115)**. Turn the ignition ON and check the input voltage. Turn the ignition OFF.

117 Compare the results with the specification at the beginning of this Chapter. If the input voltage is good, but the valves don't move, the STV actuator is probably faulty – have it checked by a Kawasaki dealer (see **Note** in Step 113).

118 If the results are outside the specified range, disconnect the ECU multi-pin wiring

10.120b ... and disconnect the wiring connector

10.119 Location of the clean air system control valve

connector (see Section 12). Check for continuity in the wiring between the STV actuator connector and the appropriate terminals in the ECU connector (black/blue wire to terminal 1, green/yellow wire to terminal 2, pink wire to terminal 18, white/blue wire to terminal 19) **(see illustration 10.7)**. If the wiring is good, check the ECU earth (ground) connections and power supply (see Section 12).

Clean air system control valve

119 The control valve is located in front of the air filter housing **(see illustration)**. Remove the fuel tank for access (see Section 2).
120 To remove the control valve, first pull off the inlet hose and disconnect the wiring connector **(see illustrations)**. Pull the valve off the outlet hose, noting how the valve holder locates on a bracket on the frame **(see illustration)**.
121 Using a multimeter set to the ohms scale, measure the resistance between the control valve terminals. Compare the result with the specification at the beginning of this Chapter.
122 If the result is not as specified the control valve is faulty.
123 To check the operation of the valve, blow into the inlet union and ensure air flows out the outlet union **(see illustration)**. Now connect a 12 volt battery across the valve wiring terminals, blow into the inlet union and ensure air does not flow out the outlet union.
124 If the control valve does not perform as described it should be renewed.
125 If the control valve is good, disconnect the ECU multi-pin wiring connector (see

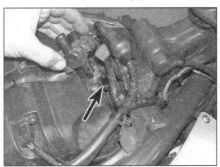

10.120c Pull the valve off the outlet hose (arrowed)

10.120a Pull off the air hose ...

Section 12). Check for continuity in the wiring between the control valve connector and the appropriate terminal in the ECU connector (red/blue wire to terminal 40) **(see illustration 10.7)**. If the wiring is good, check the ECU earth (ground) connections and power supply (see Section 12). Check for continuity between the control valve connector and the ECU main relay in the relay box (see *Wiring Diagrams* at the end of Chapter 8).

11 Engine management system components – 2009-on models	

Caution: Ensure the ignition is switched OFF before disconnecting/reconnecting any fuel injection system wiring connectors. If a connector is disconnected/reconnected with the ignition switched ON the ECU could be damaged.

1 If a fault is indicated on any of the system components, first check the wiring and connectors between the appropriate component and the ECU – see *Wiring Diagrams* at the end of Chapter 8. A continuity test of all wires will locate a break or short in any circuit. Inspect the terminals inside the wiring connectors and ensure that they are not loose or corroded. Spray the inside of the connectors with a proprietary electrical terminal cleaner before reconnection. Where appropriate, remove the sensor and check the sensor head and clean it if it is dirty – an accumulation of dirt could affect the signal it transmits.

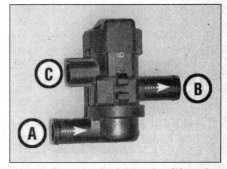

10.123 Control valve inlet union (A), outlet union (B) and wiring connectors (C)

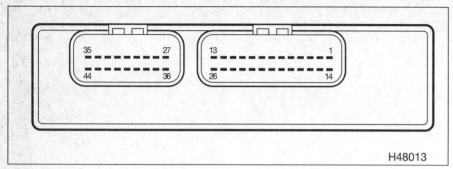

11.7 ECU connector terminal numbering – 2009-on models

2 It is possible to undertake some checks on system components using a multimeter and comparing the results with the specifications at the beginning of this Chapter. **Note:** *Different meters may give slightly different results to those specified even though the component being tested is not faulty – do not consign a component to the bin before having it double-checked.* Further tests can be undertaken using a multimeter and peak voltage adapter. Kawasaki provides a test meter (Part No. 57001-1394) and peak voltage adapter (Part No. 57001-1415) for this purpose. If the appropriate equipment is not available, the checks should be undertaken by a Kawasaki dealer.

3 If, after a thorough check, the source of a fault has not been identified, it is possible that the ECU itself is faulty. No test specifications are available for the ECU. In order to determine conclusively that the unit is defective, it should be substituted for a known good one (see Section 12). If the problem is then rectified, the original unit is faulty.

Throttle position (TP) sensor

4 The TP sensor is located on the left-hand end of the throttle body assembly (see illustration 10.4).

5 To check the sensor input and output voltage you need either needle probes for your meter to back-probe the sensor connector terminals with the connector connected, or the Kawasaki test harness (Part No. 57001-1538) that fits between the sensor and its wiring loom.

6 Back-probe the blue wire terminal with the meter positive (+ve) probe and the brown/black wire terminal with the meter negative (-ve) probe. Alternatively, connect the positive (+ve) probe to the test harness black wire terminal and the negative (-ve) probe to the test harness white wire terminal. Turn the ignition ON and check the input voltage. Turn the ignition OFF. Compare the result with the specification at the beginning of this Chapter.

7 If the result is not as specified, disconnect the ECU multi-pin wiring connector (see Section 12). Check for continuity in the wiring between the TP sensor connector and the appropriate terminals in the ECU connector (blue wire to terminal 8, brown/black wire to terminal 22) **(see illustration)**. If the wiring is good, check

the ECU earth (ground) connections and power supply (see Section 11).

8 If the input voltage is good, check the output voltage as follows. First warm up the engine and make sure the idle speed is correct (see Chapter 1), then turn the ignition OFF.

9 Back-probe the yellow/white wire terminal with the meter positive (+ve) probe and the brown/black wire terminal with the meter negative (-ve) probe. Alternatively, connect the positive (+ve) probe to the test harness red wire terminal and the negative (-ve) probe to the test harness white wire terminal. Turn the ignition ON and check the output voltage with the throttle closed, then with the throttle fully open. Turn the ignition OFF. Compare the results with the specifications at the beginning of this Chapter.

10 If the results are as specified, disconnect the ECU multi-pin wiring connector (see Section 12). Check for continuity in the wiring between the TP connector and the appropriate terminals in the ECU connector (yellow/white wire to terminal 6, brown/black wire to terminal 22) **(see illustration 11.7)**. If the wiring is good, check the ECU earth (ground) connections and power supply (see Section 11).

11 If the output voltage is not as specified, disconnect the sensor wiring connector. Using a multi-meter set to the K-ohms scale, measure the resistance between the blue and brown/black wire terminals on the sensor side of the connector. If the resistance is outside the specified range the sensor is probably faulty – have it checked by a Kawasaki dealer. **Note:** *The TP sensor should not be removed from the throttle body assembly. It is an integral part of the assembly and is not available separately.*

Intake air pressure (IAP) sensor

Check

12 The IAP sensor is located on the left-hand side of the frame behind the left-hand fairing side panel **(see illustration 10.12)**. Remove the side panel for access (see Chapter 7).

13 To check the sensor input and output voltage you need either needle probes for your meter to back-probe the sensor connector terminals with the connector connected, or the Kawasaki test harness (Part No. 57001-1700)

that fits between the sensor and its wiring loom.

14 Back-probe the blue wire terminal with the meter positive (+ve) probe and the brown/black wire terminal with the meter negative (-ve) probe. Alternatively, connect the positive (+ve) probe to the test harness red wire terminal and the negative (-ve) probe to the test harness black wire terminal. Turn the ignition ON and check the input voltage. Turn the ignition OFF. Compare the result with the specification at the beginning of this Chapter.

15 If the result is not as specified, disconnect the ECU multi-pin wiring connector (see Section 12). Check for continuity in the wiring between the IAP connector and the appropriate terminals in the ECU connector (blue wire to terminal 8, brown/black wire to terminal 22) **(see illustration 11.7)**. If the wiring is good, check the ECU earth (ground) connections and power supply (see Section 12).

16 If the input voltage is good, check the output voltage as follows. Back-probe the yellow/blue wire terminal with the meter positive (+ve) probe and the brown/black wire terminal with the meter negative (-ve) probe. Alternatively, connect the positive (+ve) probe to the test harness white wire terminal and the negative (-ve) probe to the test harness black wire terminal. Turn the ignition ON and check the output voltage. Turn the ignition OFF. Compare the result with the specification at the beginning of this Chapter. **Note:** *The output voltage will vary according to local atmospheric pressure.*

17 If the result is not as specified, renew the sensor (see Steps 20 to 22).

18 If the output voltage is good, disconnect the ECU multi-pin wiring connector (see Section 12). Check for continuity in the wiring between the IAP connector and the appropriate terminals in the ECU connector (yellow/blue wire to terminal 7, brown/black wire to terminal 22) **(see illustration 11.7)**.

19 If the wiring is good, have the sensor checked by a Kawasaki dealer.

Removal and installation

20 Remove the left-hand fairing side panel (see Chapter 7). Disconnect the sensor wiring connector and detach the vacuum hose from the underside of the sensor **(see illustration 10.12)**.

21 Undo the bolt securing the sensor bracket and remove the sensor.

22 Installation is the reverse of removal. Ensure the vacuum hose is in good condition and is securely connected to the throttle body assembly and the sensor **(see illustration 10.23)**.

Intake air temperature (IAT) sensor

Check

23 The IAT sensor is located on the right-hand side of the air filter housing **(see illustration 10.24)**. Remove the fuel tank for access (see Section 2).

24 To check the sensor output voltage you need either needle probes for your meter to back-probe the sensor connector terminals with the connector connected, or the Kawasaki test harness (Part No. 57001-1700) that fits between the sensor and its wiring loom.

25 Back-probe the yellow wire terminal with the meter positive (+ve) probe and the brown/black wire terminal with the meter negative (-ve) probe. Alternatively, connect the positive (+ve) probe to the test harness red wire terminal and the negative (-ve) probe to the test harness black wire terminal. Turn the ignition ON and check the output voltage. Turn the ignition OFF. Compare the result with the specification at the beginning of this Chapter.

26 If the result is as specified, check the ECU earth (ground) connections and power supply (see Section 12). If they are good, it is likely the ECU is faulty – have it checked by a Kawasaki dealer.

27 If the output voltage is not as specified, disconnect the ECU multi-pin wiring connector (see Section 12). Check for continuity in the wiring between the IAT connector and the appropriate terminals in the ECU connector (yellow wire to terminal 20, brown/black wire to terminal 22) **(see illustration 11.7)**.

28 If the wiring is good, check the IAT sensor resistance as follows. Fill a small, heatproof container with oil and place it on a stove. Remove the sensor (see Steps 30 to 32). Using a multi-meter set to the K-ohms scale, connect the meter probes to the sensor terminals, and using some wire or other support, suspend the sensor in the oil so that just the sensing portion is submerged **(see illustration 10.29)**. Also suspend a thermometer capable of reading temperatures up to 100°C in the oil so that its bulb is close to the sensor. **Note:** *None of the components should be allowed to touch the container directly.*

29 Check the meter reading and compare the result with the specifications at the beginning of this Chapter, then heat the oil slowly, stirring it gently. As the oil temperature rises the sensor resistance should fall. Check that the specified resistance is obtained at the correct temperature. If the readings obtained are different, or are obtained at different temperatures, the sensor is faulty and must be renewed. If the readings are as specified, it is likely the ECU is faulty – have it checked by a Kawasaki dealer.

Removal and installation

30 Remove the fuel tank (see Section 2).

31 Disconnect the IAT sensor wiring connector **(see illustration 10.24)**.

32 Undo the screw securing the sensor and draw it out of the air filter housing.

33 Installation is the reverse of removal.

Engine coolant temperature (ECT) sensor

34 The ECT sensor is located in the rear of the cylinder head on the left-hand side **(see illustration 10.34)**. On EX650models remove

the left-hand fairing side panel for access (see Chapter 7).

35 To check the sensor output voltage you need either needle probes for your meter to back-probe the sensor connector terminals with the connector connected, or the Kawasaki test harness (Part No. 57001-1700) that fits between the sensor and its wiring loom.

36 Back-probe the orange wire terminal with the meter positive (+ve) probe and the brown/black wire terminal with the meter negative (-ve) probe. Alternatively, connect the positive (+ ve) probe to the test harness red wire terminal and the negative (- ve) probe to the test harness black wire terminal. Turn the ignition ON and check the output voltage. Turn the ignition OFF. Compare the result with the specification at the beginning of this Chapter. **Note:** *The output voltage will vary according to the coolant temperature.*

37 If the result is as specified, check the ECU earth (ground) connections and power supply (see Section 12). If they are good, it is likely the ECU is faulty – have it checked by a Kawasaki dealer.

38 If the output voltage is not as specified, disconnect the ECU multi-pin wiring connector (see Section 12). Check for continuity in the wiring between the ECT connector and the appropriate terminals in the ECU connector (orange wire to terminal 17, brown/black wire to terminal 22) **(see illustration 11.7)**.

39 If the wiring is good, remove the ECT sensor and check the resistance as described in Chapter 3, Section 3). If the resistance is as specified, it is likely the ECU is faulty – have it checked by a Kawasaki dealer.

Crankshaft position (CKP) sensor

Note: *In the event of a serious fault use Dealer Mode 2 to access the fault code.*

Check

40 Remove the belly panel, the right-hand fuel tank side panel and the right-hand frame cover (see Chapter 7). Trace the CKP sensor wiring from the front of the clutch cover and disconnect it at the connector **(see illustrations 10.40a and b)**.

41 Using a multi-meter set to the ohms scale, measure the resistance between the black and yellow wire terminals on the sensor side of the connector. Compare the result with the specification at the beginning of this Chapter. Now check for continuity between each wire terminal and earth (ground) – there should be no continuity (infinite resistance). If the result of either test varies greatly from the specification the sensor is faulty and must be renewed. Otherwise, check the sensor peak voltage as follows.

42 To check the CKP sensor peak voltage you will need a peak voltage adapter compatible with your voltmeter. Kawasaki produce a meter (Part No. 57001-1394) and a peak voltage adapter (Part No. 57001-1415).

43 If not already done, disconnect the sensor

wiring connector. Set the voltmeter to the 10 volts DC scale and connect it to the peak voltage adapter. Connect the red positive (+ve) adapter lead to the black wire terminal on the sensor side of the connector and the black negative (-ve) adapter lead to the yellow wire terminal. Turn the ignition switch ON, turn the engine over on the starter motor for 4 to 5 seconds and note the peak voltage reading obtained. Repeat the procedure five more times.

44 Compare the results with the specification at the beginning of this Chapter – if the peak voltage is below the specified minimum, the sensor is faulty.

45 If the peak voltage is good, disconnect the ECU multi-pin wiring connector (see Section 12). Check for continuity in the wiring between the CKP sensor connector and the appropriate terminals in the ECU connector (red/black wire to terminal 11, yellow/black wire to terminal 24) **(see illustration 11.7)**. If the wiring is good, check the ECU earth (ground) connections and power supply (see Section 12).

Removal

46 Remove the belly panel, the right-hand fairing side panel and the right-hand frame cover (see Chapter 7).

47 Trace the CKP sensor wiring from the front of the clutch cover and disconnect it at the connector **(see illustration 10.40a and b)**. Release the wiring from any clips and feed it back to the clutch cover, noting its routing. Pull the rubber boot off the oil pressure switch, undo the terminal screw and detach the wire **(see illustrations 10.47a and b)**.

48 Remove the clutch cover (see Chapter 2).

49 Undo the sensor mounting bolts, then ease the wiring grommet from the cut-out in the casing and remove the sensor along with the wiring **(see illustrations 10.49a and b)**.

Installation

50 Remove all traces of old sealant from the clutch cover, crankcase and wiring grommet. Apply a smear of sealant around the grommet and press it into the cut-out, align the sensor with its mounting holes and tighten the bolts to the torque setting specified at the beginning of the chapter **(see illustration 10.49b and a)**.

51 Install the clutch cover (see Chapter2).

52 Route the wiring back to the connector and reconnect it **(see illustration 10.40b)**. Reconnect the oil pressure switch wire and fit the rubber boot **(see illustration 10.47b and a)**.

53 Install the remaining components in the reverse order of removal.

Speed sensor

Check

54 The speed sensor is mounted on a bracket behind the front sprocket cover **(see illustration 10.54)**. Remove the cover for access (see Chapter 6). On EX650 models, remove the left-hand fairing side panel (see Chapter 7).

55 To check the sensor input and output voltage you need either needle probes for your meter to back-probe the sensor connector terminals with the connector connected, or the Kawasaki test harness (Part No. 57001-1400) that fits between the sensor and its wiring loom.

56 Trace the wiring from the sensor to the wiring connector **(see illustration 10.56)**. Back-probe the pink wire terminal with the meter positive (+ve) probe and the black wire terminal with the meter negative (-ve) probe. Alternatively, connect the positive (+ve) probe to the test harness blue wire terminal and the negative (-ve) probe to the test harness black /blue wire terminal. Turn the ignition ON and check the input voltage. Turn the ignition OFF. Compare the result with the specification at the beginning of this Chapter.

57 If the result is not as specified, check the sensor wiring for damage and check the instrument cluster (see Chapter 8).

58 If the input voltage is good, support the machine on an auxiliary stand so that the rear wheel is off the ground and check the output voltage as follows. Back-probe the yellow wire terminal with the meter positive (+ve) probe and the black wire terminal with the meter negative (-ve) probe. Alternatively, connect the positive (+ve) probe to the test harness yellow/white wire terminal and the negative (-ve) probe to the test harness black/blue wire terminal.

59 Turn the ignition ON and note the output voltage. Now rotate the rear wheel by hand to check that the output voltage rises and falls within the specifications shown at the beginning of this Chapter. Turn the ignition OFF.

60 If the results are not as specified, disconnect the ECU multi-pin wiring connector (see Section 12). Check for continuity in the wiring between the speed sensor and the appropriate terminal in the ECU connector (light green/red wire to terminal 5) **(see illustration 11.7)**. If the wiring is good it is likely the sensor is faulty – have it checked by a Kawasaki dealer.

61 If the output voltage is good, check the ECU earth (ground) connections and power supply (see Section 12).

Removal and installation

62 Remove the front sprocket cover (see Chapter 6).

63 Trace the wiring from the speed sensor and disconnect it at the connector **(see illustration 10.56)**. Release the wiring from any clips and feed it back to the sensor, noting its routing.

64 Undo the bolt securing the sensor to its bracket and lift it off **(see illustration 10.64)**.

65 Installation is the reverse of removal, noting the following:
● Clean the threads of the mounting bolt and apply a suitable non-permanent thread-locking compound.

● Tighten the mounting bolt to the torque setting specified at the beginning of this Chapter.
● Secure the wiring as noted on removal.

Tip-over (TO) sensor

Check

66 The TO sensor is located on the right-hand side of the frame below the rear shock absorber upper mounting **(see illustration 10.66)**. Remove the right-hand frame side panel (see Chapter 7) and, if required, the rear shock for access (see Chapter 5).

67 To check the sensor input and output voltage you need needle probes for your meter to back-probe the sensor connector terminals with the connector connected.

68 Back-probe the blue wire terminal with the meter positive (+ve) probe and the brown/ black wire terminal with the meter negative (-ve) probe. Turn the ignition ON and check the input voltage. Turn the ignition OFF. Compare the result with the specification at the beginning of this Chapter.

69 If the input voltage is less than specified, disconnect the ECU multi-pin wiring connector (see Section 12). Check for continuity in the wiring between the TO sensor connector and the appropriate terminals in the ECU connector (blue wire to terminal 8, yellow/ green wire to terminal 9, brown/black wire to terminal 22) **(see illustration 11.7)**. If the wiring is good, check the ECU earth (ground) connections and power supply (see Section 12).

70 If the input voltage is good, displace the sensor but do not disconnect the connector. Back-probe the yellow/green wire terminal with the meter positive (+ve) probe and the brown/black wire terminal with the meter negative (-ve) probe. Hold the sensor vertically (UP arrow pointing upwards), turn the ignition ON and note the output voltage. Now tilt the sensor 60 to 70° to the left, return it to the vertical position and note the output voltage. Turn the ignition OFF. Repeat the test, this time tilting the sensor to the right. Turn the ignition OFF. Compare the results with the specification at the beginning of this Chapter.

71 If the results are not as specified the TO sensor is faulty.

72 If the output voltage is good, disconnect the ECU multi-pin wiring connector (see Section 12). Check for continuity in the wiring between the TO sensor connector and the appropriate terminals in the ECU connector (blue wire to terminal 8, yellow/green wire to terminal 9, brown/black wire to terminal 22) **(see illustration 11.7)**. If the wiring is good, check the ECU earth (ground) connections and power supply (see Section 12).

Removal and installation

73 Remove the right-hand frame side panel (see Chapter 7) and, if required, the rear shock for access (see Chapter 5).

74 Disconnect the sensor wiring connector **(see illustration 10.66)**.

75 The sensor is secured by rubber grommets – ease the sensor off the grommets to remove it.

76 Installation is the reverse of removal, noting the following:
● Kawasaki advise that the mounting grommets should be renewed.
● Ensure that the sensor is fitted with its UP arrow pointing upwards.

Secondary throttle position (STP) sensor

Check

77 The STP sensor is located on the left-hand end of the throttle body assembly **(see illustration 10.77a)**. Remove the air filter housing to access the sensor wiring connector (see Section 7) **(see illustration 10.77b)**.

78 To check the sensor input and output voltage you need either needle probes for your meter to back-probe the sensor connector terminals with the connector connected, or the Kawasaki test harness (Part No. 57001-1400) that fits between the sensor and its wiring loom.

79 Back-probe the blue wire terminal with the meter positive (+ve) probe and the black wire terminal with the meter negative (-ve) probe. Alternatively, connect the positive (+ve) probe to the test harness blue wire terminal and the negative (-ve) probe to the test harness black/ blue wire terminal. Turn the ignition ON and check the input voltage. Turn the ignition OFF. Compare the result with the specification at the beginning of this Chapter.

80 If the result is not as specified, disconnect the ECU multi-pin wiring connector (see Section 12). Check for continuity in the wiring between the STP sensor connector and the appropriate terminals in the ECU connector (blue wire to terminal 8, brown/black wire to terminal 22) **(see illustration 11.7)**. If the wiring is good, check the ECU earth (ground) connections and power supply (see Section 12).

81 If the input voltage is good, check the output voltage as follows. Back-probe the yellow wire terminal with the meter positive (+ve) probe and the black wire terminal with the meter negative (-ve) probe. Alternatively, connect the positive (+ve) probe to the test harness yellow/white wire terminal and the negative (-ve) probe to the test harness black/ blue wire terminal.

82 Ensure the secondary throttle valve is fully closed – close it by hand if necessary. Turn the ignition ON and note the output voltage, then open the throttle valve fully and note the output voltage again – the voltage should rise as the throttle valve is opened. Turn the ignition OFF. Compare the results with the specifications at the beginning of this Chapter.

83 If the results are as specified, disconnect the ECU multi-pin wiring connector (see Section 12). Check for continuity in the wiring between the STP connector and the appropriate terminals in the ECU connector (brown wire to terminal 19, brown/black wire to terminal 22) **(see illustration 11.7)**. If the wiring is good, check the ECU earth (ground) connections and power supply (see Section 12).

84 If the output voltage is not as specified, disconnect the sensor wiring connector. Using a multimeter set to the K-ohms scale, measure the resistance between the blue and black wire terminals on the sensor side of the connector. If the resistance is outside the specified range the sensor is probably faulty – have it checked by a Kawasaki dealer. **Note:** *The STP sensor should not be removed from the throttle body assembly. It is an integral part of the assembly and is not available separately.*

Oxygen sensor

85 The oxygen sensor is located in the silencer front pipe on the left-hand side **(see illustration 10.85)**. Remove the belly panel for access (see Chapter 7).

Fault code 33

86 To check the sensor output voltage you need either needle probes for your meter to back-probe the sensor connector terminals with the connector connected, or the Kawasaki test harness (Part No. 57001-1682) that fits between the sensor and its wiring loom.

87 Start the engine and run it until the cooling fan comes on, then turn it off. Trace the wiring from the sensor to the connector **(see illustration 10.85)**. Back-probe the blue wire terminal with the meter positive (+ve) probe and the white wire terminal with the meter negative (-ve) probe. Alternatively, connect the positive (+ve) probe to the test harness blue wire terminal and the negative (-ve) probe to the test harness brown wire terminal.

88 Release the clip securing the clean air system hose to the union on the reed valve cover and disconnect the hose **(see illustration 10.88)**. Block-off the union with a suitable plug

89 Start the engine, note the output voltage at idle speed, then turn the engine off. Remove the plug from the union and repeat the test. Compare the results with the specifications at the beginning of this Chapter.

90 If the results are not as specified, disconnect the ECU multi-pin wiring connector (see Section 12). Check for continuity in the wiring between the oxygen sensor and the appropriate terminals in the ECU connector (blue/yellow wire to terminal 4, brown/black wire to terminal 22) **(see illustration 11.7)**. If the wiring is good the sensor is faulty.

91 If the output voltage is good, check the ECU earth (ground) connections and power supply (see Section 12).

Fault code 67

92 Trace the wiring from the sensor and disconnect it at the connector **(see illustration 10.92)**.

93 Using a multimeter set to the ohms scale, measure the sensor heater resistance

between the two black wire terminals on the sensor side of the connector. Compare the result with the specification at the beginning of this Chapter.

94 If the result is not as specified the sensor is faulty.

95 If the resistance is good, check the sensor heater power supply as follows. You will need either a needle probe for your meter to back-probe the sensor connector terminal with the connector connected, or the Kawasaki test harness (Part No. 57001-1682) that fits between the sensor and its wiring loom.

96 Back-probe the white/yellow wire terminal with the meter positive (+ve) probe and connect the meter negative (-ve) probe to the battery negative (-ve) terminal. Alternatively, connect the positive (+ve) probe to the test harness white wire terminal and the negative (-ve) probe to the battery negative (-ve) terminal. Turn the ignition ON and check the supply voltage – battery voltage should be shown. Turn the ignition OFF.

97 If the voltage is good it is likely the ECU is faulty – have it checked by a Kawasaki dealer.

98 If the result is not as specified, first check the oxygen sensor heater fuse in the fusebox (see Chapter 8). Next, refer to *Wiring Diagrams* at the end of Chapter 8 and check the sensor heater power supply wiring. Finally, disconnect the ECU multi-pin wiring connector (see Section 12). Check for continuity in the wiring between the oxygen sensor connector and the appropriate terminal in the ECU connector (pink/black wire to terminal 23) **(see illustration 11.7)**. If the wiring is good, check the ECU earth (ground) connections and power supply (see Section 11).

Fault code 94

99 Follow the procedure in Steps 86 to 89 and check the oxygen sensor output voltage.

100 If the results are not as specified, check the fuel pressure (Section 3) and the injectors (Section 15). If they are good, the sensor is faulty.

101 If the output voltage is good, check the ECU earth (ground) connections and power supply (see Section 12).

Removal and installation

102 Remove the belly panel (see Chapter 7).

103 Disconnect the oxygen sensor wiring connector, then fee the wiring from the clip **(see illustration 10.92)**.

104 Unscrew the sensor carefully to avoid damage. Take care not to drop the sensor and avoid handling the sensor tip.

105 Installation is the reverse of removal, noting the following:

● DO NOT apply oil or grease to the sensor threads.
● If available, use a special sensor spanner to tighten it to the torque setting specified at the beginning of this Chapter.
● Secure the wiring as noted on removal.

Ignition coils

106 The ignition coils are integral with the

spark plug caps. For full details refer to Section 13.

Cooling fan relay

107 To access the relay box, remove the fuel tank and the fuel tank bracket (see Section 2). To check the operation of the relay, refer to Chapter 3, Section 2.

108 If the relay is good, check for battery voltage between the green and pink/blue wire terminals on the loom side of the wiring connector with the ignition and kill switch ON. If there is no voltage, check the circuit and its components, referring to the relevant wiring diagram at the end of Chapter 8. If voltage is present, check the wiring between the relay and the fan wiring connector and between the relay and the ECU (pink/blue wire to terminal 37) for continuity.

109 If the wiring is good, check the ECU earth (ground) connections and power supply (see Section 12).

Secondary throttle valve (STV) actuator

Check

110 The STV actuator is located on the left-hand end of the throttle body assembly **(see illustration 10.110)**. Remove the air filter housing cover to check the operation of the secondary throttle valves (see Section 7).

111 Turn the ignition ON and check that the secondary throttle valves (the uppermost set of valves in the throttle bodies) open and close – this is part of the engine start-up procedure **(see illustration 10.111)**.

112 If the valves don't move, remove the air filter housing (see Section 7), then disconnect the actuator wiring connector **(see illustration 10.112)**. Using a multimeter set to the ohms scale, measure the resistance between the black and pink wire terminals on the actuator side of the connector, then between the green and white/blue wire terminals.

113 Compare the results with the specifications at the beginning of this Chapter. If the resistance is outside the specified range the STV actuator is probably faulty – have it checked by a Kawasaki dealer. **Note:** *The STV actuator should not be removed from the throttle body assembly. It is an integral part of the assembly and is not available separately.*

114 If the results are good, check the actuator input voltage as follows. You will need either needle probes to back-probe the actuator connector terminals with the connector connected, or the Kawasaki test harness (Part No. 57001-1700) that fits between the actuator and its wiring loom. You will also need a peak voltage adapter compatible with your voltmeter. Kawasaki produce a meter (Part No. 57001-1394) and a peak voltage adapter (Part No. 57001-1415).

115 Working on the loom side of the connector, back-probe the pink wire terminal with the adapter positive (+ve) probe and the black/blue wire terminal with the adapter

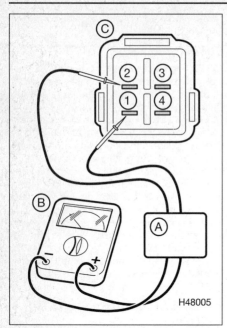

11.115 Set-up for testing the STV actuator input voltage. Peak voltage adapter (A), voltmeter (B) and loom side wiring connector (C)

1 *Pink wire terminal*
2 *Black/blue wire terminal*
3 *White/blue wire terminal*
4 *Green/yellow wire terminal*

negative (-ve) probe **(see illustration)**. Alternatively, connect the positive (+ ve) probe to the test harness red wire terminal and the negative (- ve) probe to the test harness black wire terminal. Turn the ignition ON and check the input voltage. Turn the ignition OFF.

116 Now back-probe the white/blue wire terminal with the adapter positive (+ve) probe and the green/yellow wire terminal with the adapter negative (-ve) probe **(see illustration 11.115)**. Alternatively, connect the positive (+ ve) probe to the test harness white wire terminal and the negative (- ve) probe to the test harness yellow wire terminal. Turn the ignition ON and check the input voltage. Turn the ignition OFF.

117 Compare the results with the specification at the beginning of this Chapter. If the input

voltage is good, but the valves don't move, the STV actuator is probably faulty – have it checked by a Kawasaki dealer (see **Note** in Step 113).

118 If the results are outside the specified range, disconnect the ECU multi-pin wiring connector (see Section 12). Check for continuity in the wiring between the STV actuator connector and the appropriate terminals in the ECU connector (black/ blue wire to terminal 1, green/yellow wire to terminal 2, pink wire to terminal 14, white/blue wire to terminal 15) **(see illustration 11.7)**. If the wiring is good, check the ECU earth (ground) connections and power supply (see Section 12).

Clean air system control valve

119 The control valve is located in front of the air filter housing **(see illustration 10.119)**. Remove the fuel tank for access (see Section 2).

120 To remove the control valve, first pull off the inlet hose and disconnect the wiring connector **(see illustrations 10.120a and b)**. Pull the valve off the outlet hose, noting how the valve holder locates on a bracket on the frame **(see illustration 10.120c)**.

121 Using a multimeter set to the ohms scale, measure the resistance between the control valve terminals. Compare the result with the specification at the beginning of this Chapter.

122 If the result Is not as specified the control valve is faulty.

123 To check the operation of the valve, blow into the inlet union and ensure air flows out the outlet union **(see illustration 10.123)**. Now connect a 12 volt battery across the valve wiring terminals, blow into the inlet union and ensure air does not flow out the outlet union.

124 If the control valve does not perform as described it should be renewed.

125 If the control valve is good, disconnect the ECU multi-pin wiring connector (see Section 12). Check for continuity in the wiring between the control valve connector and the appropriate terminal in the ECU connector (red/blue wire to terminal 32) **(see illustration 11.7)**. If the wiring is good, check the ECU earth (ground) connections and power supply (see Section 12). Check for continuity between the control valve connector and the ECU main

relay in the relay box (see *Wiring Diagrams* at the end of Chapter 8).

12 Electronic control unit (ECU) and ECU relay

ECU

Check – 2006 to 2008 models

1 Remove the ECU (see Steps 19 to 23).

2 Inspect the wiring connectors and the terminals in the ECU for dust and corrosion and clean them carefully if necessary **(see illustrations)**. Check for cracked or damaged connectors and bent or broken terminal pins and replace the main wiring harness or ECU with new ones if necessary.

3 Check the ECU earth (ground) connections as follows. Using a multimeter set to the ohms scale, check for continuity between the black/yellow wire terminals (terminals 34, 50 and 51) in the ECU connectors and the battery negative (-ve) terminal. Next, check for continuity between the engine earth terminal and the battery negative (-ve) terminal. There should be continuity (zero resistance).

4 If there is no continuity in any of the checks, inspect the wiring and the engine earth lead for damage and renew as necessary.

5 Reconnect the ECU wiring connectors and check the power supply as follows. Using a multimeter set to the volts DC scale, back-probe the brown/white wire terminal 16 with the meter positive (+ve) probe and connect the meter negative (-ve) probe to the battery negative (-ve) terminal. With the ignition switch OFF there should be zero volts. With the ignition switch ON there should be battery voltage. Turn the ignition OFF.

6 Now back-probe the white/black wire terminal 17 with the meter positive (+ve) probe and connect the meter negative (-ve) probe to the battery negative (-ve) terminal. With the ignition switch OFF and ON there should be battery voltage. Turn the ignition OFF.

7 If the results are not as stated, check the main fuse and the ECU fuse, then refer to the *Wiring Diagrams* and check the ECU power supply circuit (see Chapter 8).

8 Check the ECU relay (see below).

9 If the fuses, wiring and relay are good, it is likely the ECU is faulty – have it checked by a Kawasaki dealer.

Check – 2009-on models

10 Remove the ECU (see Steps 19 to 23).

11 Inspect the connectors and the terminals in the ECU for dust and corrosion and clean them carefully if necessary **(see illustrations 12.2a and b)**. Check for cracked or damaged connectors and bent or broken terminal pins and replace the main wiring harness or ECU with new ones if necessary.

12 Check the ECU earth (ground) connections as follows. Using a multimeter set to the ohms scale, check for continuity between

12.2a Inspect the terminals in the wiring connectors . . .

12.2b . . . and in the ECU sockets

12.21 Lower the ECU carrier (arrowed)

12.22a Draw the ECU rearwards . . .

12.22b . . . and disconnect the wiring connectors

the black/yellow wire terminals (terminals 26, 42 and 43) in the ECU connectors and the battery negative (-ve) terminal. Next, check for continuity between the engine earth terminal and the battery negative (-ve) terminal. There should be continuity (zero resistance).

13 If there is no continuity in any of the checks, inspect the wiring and the engine earth lead for damage and renew as necessary.

14 Reconnect the ECU wiring connectors and check the power supply as follows. Using a multimeter set to the volts DC scale, back-probe the brown/white wire terminal 12 with the meter positive (+ve) probe and connect the meter negative (-ve) probe to the battery negative (-ve) terminal. With the ignition switch OFF there should be zero volts. With the ignition (main) switch ON there should be battery voltage. Turn the ignition OFF.

15 Now back-probe the white/black wire terminal 27 with the meter positive (+ve) probe and connect the meter negative (-ve) probe to the battery negative (-ve) terminal. With the ignition switch OFF and ON there should be battery voltage. Turn the ignition OFF.

16 If the results are not as stated, check the main fuse and the ECU fuse, then refer to the *Wiring Diagrams* and check the ECU power supply circuit (see Chapter 8).

17 Check the ECU relay (see below).

18 If the fuses, wiring and relay are good, it is likely the ECU is faulty – have it checked by a Kawasaki dealer.

Removal and installation

19 Remove the seat cowling then undo the

rear mudguard fixings and lower the rear mudguard and under-seat panel assembly (see Chapter 7).

20 Ensure the ignition is OFF.

21 Undo the bolts securing the ECU carrier and lower the carrier **(see illustration)**.

22 Draw the ECU out rearwards, lift the rubber flap and disconnect the ECU multi-pin wiring connectors **(see illustrations)**.

23 If required, draw the ECU out of its rubber holder

24 Installation is the reverse of removal. Don't forget to fit the ECU into its rubber holder.

ECU relay

25 To access the relay box, remove the fuel tank and the fuel tank bracket (see Section 2). Release the clips securing the relay box, lift it out of its rubber holder and disconnect the wiring connectors **(see illustration 4.2a, b and c)**.

26 Using a multimeter, check for continuity between terminals 6 and 7 on the relay **(see illustration 4.3)**. There should be no continuity. Now use jumper wires to connect the positive (+ve) terminal of a fully charged 12 volt battery to terminal 4 on the relay and the negative (-ve) battery terminal to relay terminal 5. There should now be continuity between terminals 6 and 7. If the relay fails either of the checks the relay box must be replaced with a new one – individual relays are not available.

27 If the relay is good, check for battery voltage between the black/yellow and brown wire terminals on the loom side of the wiring connector with the ignition and kill switch ON.

If there is no voltage, check the circuit and its components, referring to *Wiring Diagrams* at the end of Chapter 8. If voltage is present, check the wiring between the relay and the ECU wiring connector for continuity. If all is good it is likely the ECU is faulty (see Steps 1 to 6 or 10 to 15 as appropriate).

13 Ignition coils

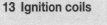

Removal

Note: *To avoid damaging the wiring, always disconnect the connectors before removing the coils. Do not attempt to lever the coil/caps off the plugs or pull them off with pliers. Do not drop the coils.*

1 Make sure the ignition is switched OFF.

2 Remove the air filter housing (Section 7).

3 Check that the cylinder location is marked on the coil's wiring sleeve, then disconnect the coil wiring connector **(see illustrations)**.

4 Clean the area around the coil seal to prevent any dirt falling into the spark plug channel, then pull the coil off the spark plug **(see illustration)**. Mark the cylinder location on each coil.

Check

5 Working on one coil at a time, ensure the primary circuit terminals in the top of the coil and the spark plug terminal inside are

13.3a Check cylinder numbering on the connector wiring (arrowed)

13.3b Disconnect the coil wiring connector

13.4 Pull the coil off the spark plug

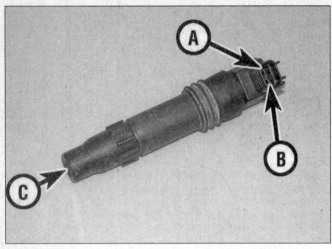

13.5 Check the negative (A) and positive (B) primary circuit terminals and the spark plug terminal (C)

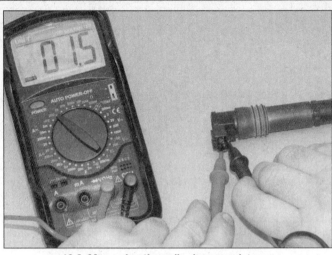

13.6 Measuring the coil primary resistance

undamaged and free from corrosion **(see illustration)**.

6 Using multimeter set to the ohms scale, measure the coil primary resistance between the primary circuit **terminals (see illustration)**. Compare the result with the specifications at the beginning of this Chapter.

7 Now set the meter to the K-ohms scale and measure the coil secondary resistance between the negative (-ve) primary circuit terminal and the spark plug terminal **(see illustration)**. Compare the result with the specifications at the beginning of this Chapter.

8 If either of the results are not as specified the coil is probably faulty – have it checked by a Kawasaki dealer. Otherwise, check the primary peak voltage as follows.

9 To check the ignition coil peak voltage you will need a peak voltage adapter compatible with your voltmeter. Kawasaki produce a meter (Part No. 57001-1394), peak voltage adapter (Part No. 57001-1415) and wiring loom adapter (Part No. 57001-1449).

10 Install a new spark plug into both coils. On the coil to be checked, connect the wiring loom adapter between the coil wiring connector and the coil itself.

11 On 2006 to 2008 models, connect the positive (+ve) lead of the voltmeter and peak

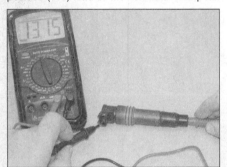

13.7 Measuring the coil secondary resistance

voltage adapter to the white wire terminal on the harness adapter, and connect the negative (-ve) lead to the red wire terminal.

12 On 2009-on models, connect the positive (+ve) lead of the voltmeter and peak voltage adapter to the red wire terminal on the harness adapter, and connect the negative (-ve) lead to the white wire terminal.

13 On the other coil, connect the coil wiring connector. Ensure both spark plugs are earthed onto the engine.

14 Turn the ignition switch ON, turn the engine over on the starter motor for 4 to 5 seconds and note the peak voltage reading obtained. Repeat the procedure five more times.

15 Compare the results with the specification at the beginning of this Chapter – if the peak voltage is below the specified value, check the coil input voltage as follows.

16 Follow the procedure in Section 12 to access the ECU wiring connectors, but do not disconnect the connectors. Use needle probes to back-probe the ECU connector terminals.

2006 to 2008 models

17 To check the No. 1 coil input voltage, back-probe the black wire terminal 43 with the meter positive (+ve) probe and the black/yellow wire terminal 51 with the meter negative (-ve) probe **(see illustration 10.7)**. Turn the ignition ON and check for battery voltage. Turn the ignition OFF.

18 To check the No. 2 coil input voltage, back-probe the black/green wire terminal 52 with the meter positive (+ve) probe and the black/yellow wire terminal 51 with the meter negative (-ve) probe. Turn the ignition ON and check for battery voltage. Turn the ignition OFF. Now go to Step 21.

2009-on models

19 To check the No. 1 coil input voltage, back-probe the black wire terminal 35 with the meter positive (+ve) probe and the black/yellow wire terminal 43 with the meter negative (-ve) probe **(see illustration 11.7)**. Turn the

ignition ON and check for battery voltage. Turn the ignition OFF.

20 To check the No. 2 coil input voltage, back-probe the black/green wire terminal 44 with the meter positive (+ve) probe and the black/yellow wire terminal 43 with the meter negative (-ve) probe. Turn the ignition ON and check for battery voltage. Turn the ignition OFF.

All models

21 If the result is not as specified, check for continuity in the wiring between the components in the ignition coil circuit. If the wiring is good, check the ECU earth (ground) connections and power supply (see Section 12).

22 Check the crankshaft position (CKP) sensor (see Section 10 or 11).

Installation

23 Ensure the spark plug channels are free from any obstructions and press the coils fully home onto the spark plugs.

24 Ensure the wiring connectors are reconnected correctly (see Step 3).

25 Installation the remaining components in the reverse order of removal.

14 Throttle bodies

 Warning: Refer to the precautions given in Section 1 before starting work.

Removal

1 On EX650 models, remove the fairing side panels (see Chapter 7).

2 Remove the air filter housing (see Section 7).

3 Disconnect the hose from the intake air pressure (IAP) sensor **(see illustration 10.23)**.

4 Disconnect the throttle position (TP) sensor wiring connector **(see illustration 10.4)**.

5 Disconnect the wiring connectors for the

14.6 Fuel injector wiring connectors (arrowed)

14.7 Location of the idle speed adjuster knob – EX650 models

14.8a Loosen the throttle body clamp screws (arrowed) . . .

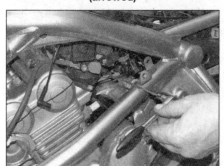

14.8b . . . using a long-reach Allen key if available

14.9 Lift off the throttle body assembly

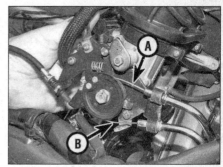

14.11 Decelerator cable (A) and accelerator cable (B)

secondary throttle valve (STV) actuator and the secondary throttle position (STP) sensor **(see illustrations 10.112 and 10.77b)**.

6 Disconnect the fuel injector wiring connectors **(see illustration)**.

7 On EX650 models, release the idle speed adjuster knob from the bracket on the top of the clutch cover **(see illustration)**.

8 Loosen the clamp screws securing the throttle body assembly to the intake manifolds – if available, use a long-reach Allen key to do this **(see illustrations)**.

9 Ease the throttle body assembly off the intake manifolds **(see illustration)**.

10 Detach the throttle cables from the twistgrip pulley (see Section 16).

11 Note the arrangement of the throttle inner cables on the throttle body pulley – the upper cable is the decelerator (throttle closing) cable and the lower cable is the accelerator (throttle opening) cable **(see illustration)**. Disconnect the cable ends from the pulley and lift the throttle body assembly off.

Caution: Tape over or stuff clean rag into the cylinder head intake manifolds after removing the throttle body assembly to prevent anything from falling inside.

Inspection

Caution: The throttle body assembly must be treated as a complete unit. Do not loosen any nuts/bolts/screws other than as directed here or in the next Section as they are pre-set at the factory to ensure correct operation. The only components on the assembly which are serviceable are the fuel rail and injectors (see Section 15).

12 Note the location of the clamps on the intake manifolds – if they are corroded or damaged they must be renewed **(see illustration)**. If the manifolds are hardened or split new ones should be fitted (see Chapter 2, Section 10).

14.12 Check the clamps (arrowed) on the intake manifolds

14.13b . . . and draw the hose elbow off the fuel rail union

13 Ease open the fuel hose connector clip and draw the hose elbow off the union on the fuel rail **(see illustrations)**. Inspect the seal in the elbows at both ends of the fuel hose **(see illustrations)**. If they are damaged or hardened a new fuel hose must be fitted.

14.13a Release the fuel hose connector clip . . .

14.13c Inspect the fuel hose seals (arrowed)

14.14a Loosen the clamps (arrowed) . . .

14.14b . . . and remove the intake duct

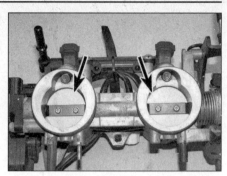

14.17 Check the operation of the throttle valves (arrowed)

14 If required, loosen the clamps securing the intake duct to the throttle body assembly and lift the intake duct off **(see illustrations)**.

15 Inspect the throttle body vacuum hose and blanking caps for signs of damage or deterioration and replace them with new ones if any are loose or deteriorated.

16 Check the throttle bodies for cracks or any other damage which may result in air getting in.

17 Check that the throttle valves move smoothly and freely in the bodies **(see illustration)**. Inspect the valve shafts and throttle bodies for wear. Check the condition of the valve shaft springs.

18 Inspect the TP sensor, STP sensor, STV actuator, associated wiring and wiring connectors for damage **(see illustration)**. All these components are integral with the throttle body assembly – they should not be removed. If any damage is found a new throttle body assembly will have to be fitted.

Installation

19 Installation is the reverse of removal, noting the following:
● Remove the tape/plugs from the intake manifolds.
● Connect the throttle cables before installing the throttle bodies.
● Ensure the throttle bodies are fully engaged with the intake manifolds before tightening the clamps.
● Refer to Chapter 1 and adjust throttle cable freeplay.

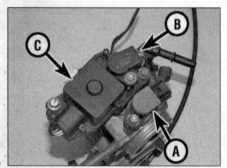

14.18 TP sensor (A), STP sensor (B) and STV actuator (C)

● Make sure all hoses and wiring connectors are securely connected.
● Check the engine idle speed and adjust as necessary (see Chapter 1).

15 Fuel rail and injectors

⚠️ *Warning: Refer to the precautions given in Section 1 before starting work.*

Check

1 If the engine runs, start it and allow it to idle. Check the operation of each fuel injector in the throttle bodies using a sounding rod – an injector will emit a 'clicking' noise when functioning. If an injector is silent, either the injector or its wiring harness is faulty.

2 If the engine does not run, remove the air filter housing (Section 7). Disconnect the wiring connector from each fuel injector. Using a multimeter set to the ohms scale, measure the resistance between the injector terminals **(see illustration)**. Compare the result with the specifications at the beginning of this Chapter.

3 If the result is not as specified the injector is faulty and must be renewed. If the resistance is good, check the injector power supply as follows.

2006 to 2008 models

4 Follow the procedure in Section 12 to

15.2 Measure the resistance between the injector terminals (arrowed)

access the ECU wiring connectors, but do not disconnect the connectors. You will need a needle probe for your meter to back-probe the ECU wiring connector.

5 Back-probe the brown/white wire terminal 16 with the meter positive (+ve) probe and connect the meter negative (-ve) probe to the battery negative (-ve) terminal. Turn the ignition ON – the meter should indicate battery voltage (12.8 volts or more). Turn the ignition OFF.

6 If the result is not as specified, check the main fuse (see Chapter 8) and the fuel pump relay (see Section 4). Check for continuity in the wiring between the ECU, the fuel pump relay and the fuel injectors (see *Wiring Diagrams* at the end of Chapter 8).

7 If the power supply is good, check the injector output voltage as follows.

8 Use a needle probe to back-probe the ECU connector terminals. To check the No. 1 injector output voltage, back-probe the blue/red wire terminal 42 with the meter positive (+ve) probe and connect the meter negative (-ve) probe to the battery negative (-ve) terminal. Turn the ignition ON – the meter should indicate battery voltage (12.8 volts or more). Turn the ignition OFF.

9 Repeat the procedure to check the No. 2 injector output voltage – this time back-probe the blue/green wire terminal 41 with the meter positive (+ve) probe.

10 If the result is not as specified, disconnect the ECU multi-pin wiring connector (see Section 12). Check for continuity in the wiring between the fuel injector connectors and the appropriate terminals in the ECU connector (fuel injector No. 1 blue/red wire to terminal 42, fuel injector No. 2 blue/green wire to terminal 41) **(see illustration 10.7)**. If the wiring is good, check the ECU earth (ground) connections and power supply (see Section 12).

11 If the output voltage is good, check the injector signal as follows.

12 Prepare two test lights with male wire terminals **(see illustration)**. Disconnect the injector wiring connectors and connect the test lights to the loom side of the injector wiring connectors. Turn the ignition ON, turn

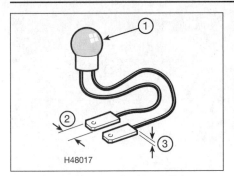

15.12 Injector signal test light

1   12 volt 3.4 W bulb
2   Terminal width 1.8 mm
3   Terminal thickness 0.8 mm

the engine over on the starter motor and check
that the test lights flicker at regular intervals.
13 If the result is as stated, the ECU injector
circuit and wiring are good and it is likely one
or both fuel injectors are faulty – have them
checked by a Kawasaki dealer. If the test
lights don't flicker, inspect the wiring and
connectors again (see Step 10). If no fault can
be found it is likely the ECU is faulty – have it
checked by a Kawasaki dealer.

2009-on models

14 You will need either a needle probe for your
meter to back-probe the injector connector
terminal with the connector connected, or the
Kawasaki test harness (Part No. 57001-1700)
that fits between the injector and its wiring
loom.
15 Back-probe the white/red wire terminal
with the meter positive (+ve) probe and
connect the meter negative (-ve) probe to the
battery negative (-ve) terminal. Alternatively,
connect the positive (+ve) probe to the test
harness red wire terminal and the negative
(-ve) probe to the battery negative (-ve)
terminal. Turn the ignition ON – the meter
should indicate battery voltage (12.9 volts or
more) for approximately 3 seconds, and then
zero volts. Turn the ignition OFF.
16 If the power supply does not turn off after
3 seconds, check the fuel pump relay (see
Section 4). If the relay is good, check the ECU
earth (ground) connections and power supply
(see Section 12).
17 If there is no battery voltage, check the

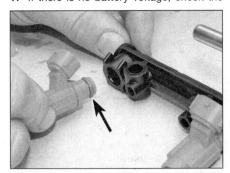

**15.27 Remove each injector and discard
the O-ring (arrowed)**

15.26a Undo the screws (arrowed) . . .

ECU relay and fuel pump relay (see Sections 12 and 4). If the relays are good, check
for continuity in the wiring between the
components in the fuel injector circuit. If the
wiring is good, check the ECU earth (ground)
connections and power supply (see Section 12).
18 If the power supply is good, check the
injector output voltage as follows.
19 Follow the procedure in Section 12 to
access the ECU wiring connectors, but do
not disconnect the connectors. Use a needle
probe to back-probe the ECU connector
terminals. To check the No. 1 injector output
voltage, back-probe the blue/red wire terminal
34 with the meter positive (+ve) probe and
connect the meter negative (-ve) probe to
the battery negative (-ve) terminal. Turn the
ignition ON – the meter should indicate battery
voltage (12.9 volts or more) for approximately
3 seconds, and then zero volts. Turn the
ignition OFF.
20 Repeat the procedure to check the No. 2
injector output voltage – this time back-probe
the blue/green wire terminal 33 with the meter
positive (+ve) probe.
21 If the output voltage is good, check the
ECU earth (ground) connections and power
supply (see Section 12).
22 If the result is not as specified, disconnect
the ECU multi-pin wiring connector (see
Section 11). Check for continuity in the wiring
between the fuel injector connectors and the
appropriate terminals in the ECU connector
(fuel injector No. 1 blue/red wire to terminal
34, fuel injector No. 2 blue/green wire to

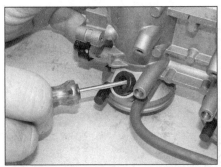

**15.28 Remove the seals from the injector
seats**

**15.26b . . . and draw the fuel rail and
injector assembly off**

terminal 33) **(see illustration 11.7)**. If the
wiring is good, check the ECU earth (ground)
connections and power supply (see Section 12).

Removal

23 Remove the throttle body assembly (see
Section 14).
24 If not already done, disconnect the fuel
hose from the fuel rail **(see illustrations
14.13a and b)**.
25 Release the cable-tie securing the wiring
to the fuel rail.
26 Undo the fuel rail screws **(see illustration)**.
Carefully lift off the fuel rail and injector
assembly **(see illustration)**.
27 Note the alignment of the injectors with
the fuel rail, then remove the injectors from
the fuel rail **(see illustration)**. Remove and
discard the O-rings – they must be replaced
with new ones.
28 Remove the seals from the injector seats
in the throttle bodies **(see illustration)**.
Discard them as new ones must be used.
29 Inspect the end of each fuel injector for
accumulations of carbon and signs of damage
(see illustration). Check that the terminals in
the wiring connectors are clean.
30 Modern fuels contain detergents which
should keep the injectors clean and free
of gum or varnish from fuel residue. If an
injector is suspected of being blocked, clean
it through with injector cleaner. If the injector
is clean but its performance is suspect, take it
to a Kawasaki dealer for assessment.

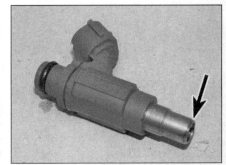

**15.29 Inspect the end of the injector
(arrowed)**

Installation

Note: *Apply a smear of engine oil to the new seals and O-rings before reassembly.*

31 Installation is the reverse of removal, noting the following:

● Ensure the injectors are correctly aligned with the fuel rail before installation.
● Install the new seals in the injector seats and press the injectors in firmly.
● Tighten the fuel rail screws securely.
● Secure the wiring to the fuel rail as noted on removal.
● Start the engine and check that there are no fuel leaks.

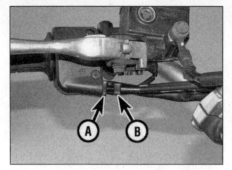

16.2 Accelerator cable lockring (A) and adjuster (B)

16.3 Location of the decelerator cable adjuster (arrowed)

16 Throttle cables

> ⚠️ **Warning:** *Refer to the precautions given in Section 1 before proceeding.*

Removal

1 Remove the fuel tank (see Section 2). On EX650 models, remove the right-hand fairing side panel (see Chapter 7).
2 Loosen the lockring on the accelerator (throttle opening) cable and turn the adjuster in to increase freeplay in the cable **(see illustration)**.
3 Displace the coolant reservoir (see Chapter 3). Locate the adjuster on the decelerator (throttle closing) cable **(see illustration)**. **Note:** *On models equipped with ABS it may be necessary to displace the brake system pipes to access the decelerator cable adjuster.* Ensure the throttle twistgrip is fully closed, then loosen the lockring and turn the adjuster to increase freeplay.

4 Undo the handlebar twistgrip housing screws and separate the halves, noting how the pin in the front half locates in the hole in the handlebar **(see illustrations)**.
5 Lift out the accelerator cable elbow and detach the inner cable end from the twistgrip pulley **(see illustrations)**.
6 Displace the rear half of the twistgrip housing, noting the location of the decelerator cable elbow, then detach the inner cable end from the twistgrip pulley, noting how it fits **(see illustrations)**.

7 Follow the procedure in Section 14 to displace the throttle body assembly and detach the cables from the pulley.
8 Draw the cables off the machine, noting the correct routing of each cable.

Installation

9 Route the cables correctly between the handlebar and the throttle bodies. The cables must not interfere with any other component and should not be kinked or bent sharply. Lubricate the cable ends lightly with multi-purpose grease.
10 Fit the cables to the twistgrip pulley first. Locate the decelerator inner cable end in the rear hole in the pulley, wrap the cable around the pulley and install the cable elbow in the rear half of the twistgrip housing **(see illustrations**

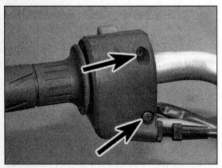

16.4a Undo the twistgrip housing screws (arrowed)

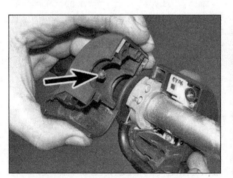

16.4b Note the location of the pin (arrowed)

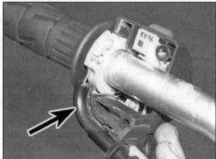

16.5a Lift out the accelerator cable elbow (arrowed) . . .

16.5b . . . and detach the inner cable end from the pulley

16.6a Separate the decelerator cable elbow from the housing . . .

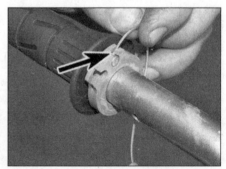

16.6b . . . and detach the inner cable end from the pulley

16.6b and a). Ensure the decelerator cable is correctly located **(see illustration)**.

11 Locate the accelerator inner cable end in the front hole in the pulley, wrap the cable around the pulley and install the cable elbow in the rear half of the twistgrip housing **(see illustration 16.5b)**. Ensure the accelerator cable is correctly located **(see illustration 16.5a)**.

12 Install the front half of the twistgrip housing, making sure the pin locates in the hole in the handlebar **(see illustration 16.4b)**. Ensure the two halves of the twistgrip housing are correctly assembled **(see illustration)**, then install the screws and tighten them securely.

13 Follow the procedure in Section 14 to fit the cables to the throttle body pulley and install the throttle body assembly.

14 Adjust the throttle cable freeplay (see Chapter 1).

15 Install the remaining components in the reverse order of removal.

16 Start the engine and check that the idle speed does not rise as the handlebars are turned. If it does, the throttle cables are routed incorrectly. Correct the problem before riding the motorcycle.

17 Exhaust system

Warning: If the engine has been running the exhaust system will be very hot. Allow the system to cool before carrying out any work.

16.10 Installed position of the decelerator cable

HAYNES HINT *Exhaust system clamp bolts tend to become corroded and seized. It is advisable to spray them with WD40 or a similar product before attempting to slacken them.*

Silencer
Removal

1 Remove the right-hand footrest bracket (see Chapter 5). Remove the belly panel (see Chapter 7).

2 Trace the wiring from the oxygen sensor and disconnect it at the connector **(see illustrations 10.92)**.

3 Loosen the silencer clamp bolt **(see illustration)**.

4 Undo the short silencer mounting bolt

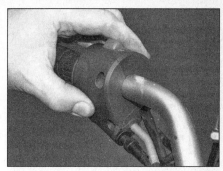

16.12 Ensure the correct assembly of the twistgrip housing

– note the location of the washer located in the mounting grommet and remove it for safekeeping if it is loose **(see illustration)**.

5 Undo the nut on the long mounting bolt and remove the washer if it is loose **(see illustration)**.

6 Support the silencer and withdraw the long mounting bolt, then draw the silencer off the downpipe assembly **(see illustrations)**. Remove the washer located in the mounting grommet if it is loose. **Note:** *On models fitted with a catalytic converter, handle the silencer carefully. If the silencer is dropped the catalytic converter could be damaged.*

7 Remove the sealing ring from the silencer or downpipe assembly – a new one must be fitted on installation **(see illustration)**.

8 Check the condition of the rubber grommets in the mounting bracket and replace them with new ones if necessary.

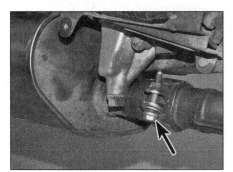

17.3 Silencer clamp bolt (arrowed)

17.4 Undo the short mounting bolt

17.5 Undo the nut on the long mounting bolt (arrowed)

17.6a Withdraw the long mounting bolt . . .

17.6b . . . then draw the silencer off the downpipe

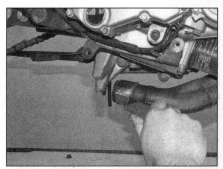

17.7 If necessary, cut the old sealing ring off with a craft knife

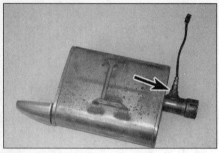

17.9 Location of the oxygen sensor (arrowed)

17.10 Fit a new sealing ring . . .

17.11 . . . and install the clamp

9 Note the location of the oxygen sensor (see illustration).

Installation

10 Fit a new sealing ring inside the silencer frontpipe (see illustration).
11 If removed, fit the silencer clamp onto the frontpipe (see illustration).
12 Slide the silencer over the end of the downpipe and align the mounting holes with the holes in the frame bracket (see illustration). Ensure the washers are installed in the grommets, then install the long mounting bolt and nut, and the short mounting bolt (see illustrations 17.6a, 5 and 4). Tighten the bolts finger-tight.
13 Tighten the silencer clamp bolt securely.
14 Tighten the mounting bolts to the torque setting specified at the beginning of this Chapter.
15 Connect the oxygen sensor wiring connector.
16 Install the remaining components in the reverse order of removal.

Downpipe assembly

Removal

17 Remove the silencer (see Steps 1 to 6).
18 On EX650 models, if required, remove the fairing side panels (see Chapter 7).
19 Undo the nuts securing the header pipe flanges to the cylinder head (see illustration).
20 Draw the flanges off the studs (see illustration). Manoeuvre the downpipe assembly off the cylinder head and remove it.
21 Remove the sealing ring from each port in the cylinder head or from each pipe and discard them as new ones must be used (see illustration 17.22).

Installation

22 Installation is the reverse of removal, noting the following:

• Lubricate the exhaust stud threads with a smear of copper-based grease.
• Fit a new sealing ring onto each header pipe (see illustration).
• Fit the downpipe assembly and silencer leaving all fasteners finger-tight.
• Check the alignment of the system, then tighten the downpipe nuts first.
• Tighten all fasteners to the torque settings specified at the beginning of this Chapter.
• Don't forget to connect the oxygen sensor wiring connector.
• Run the engine up to normal temperature and check that there are no exhaust gas leaks.

18 Catalytic converter

General information

1 A catalytic converter is incorporated in the exhaust system of all models except those intended for sale in the US and Canada. The catalytic converter is located inside the silencer.
2 The catalytic converter consists of a canister containing a fine mesh impregnated with a catalyst material, over which the hot exhaust gases pass. The catalyst speeds up the oxidation of harmful carbon monoxide, unburned hydrocarbons and soot, effectively reducing the quantity of harmful products released into the atmosphere via the exhaust gases.

Precautions

3 The catalytic converter is a reliable and simple device which needs no maintenance

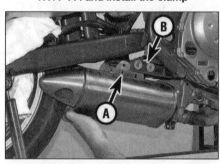

17.12 Align the mounting holes (A) with the holes in the bracket (B)

in itself, but there are some facts of which an owner should be aware if the converter is to function properly for its full service life.
• DO NOT use leaded or lead replacement petrol (gasoline) – the additives will coat the precious metals, reducing their converting efficiency and will eventually destroy the catalytic converter.
• Always keep the ignition and fuel systems well-maintained in accordance with the manufacturer's schedule – if the fuel/air mixture is suspected of being incorrect have it checked on an exhaust gas analyser.
• If the engine develops a misfire, do not ride the bike at all (or at least as little as possible) until the fault is cured.
• DO NOT use fuel or engine oil additives – these may contain substances harmful to the catalytic converter.
• DO NOT continue to use the bike if the engine burns oil to the extent of leaving a visible trail of blue smoke.
• Avoid bump-starting the bike unless absolutely necessary.

17.19 Nuts (arrowed) secure header pipe flanges

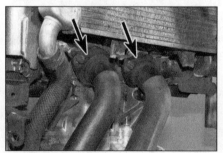

17.20 Draw the flanges (arrowed) off the studs

17.22 Install new sealing rings on the header pipes

Chapter 5
Frame and suspension

Contents

Degrees of difficulty

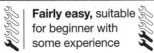

Easy, suitable for novice with little experience	**Fairly easy,** suitable for beginner with some experience	**Fairly difficult,** suitable for competent DIY mechanic	**Difficult,** suitable for experienced DIY mechanic	**Very difficult,** suitable for expert DIY or professional

Specifications

Front forks

Fork oil type	Kayaba KHL34-G10 or Showa SS-8 (both 10W)

Fork oil capacity (approx.)

At oil change

ER650A and B (2006 to 2008)	390 ml
ER650C (2009-on)	405 ml
ER650D (2009-on)	400 ml
EX650A (2006 to 2008)	415 ml
EX650B (2006 to 2008)	420 ml
EX650C (2009-on)	400 ml
EX650D (2009-on)	405 ml

At overhaul

ER650A (2006 to 2008)	458 ± 4 ml
ER650B (2006 to 2008)	462 ± 4 ml
ER650C (2009-on)	478 ± 4 ml
ER650D (2009-on)	471 ± 4 ml
EX650A (2006 to 2008)	489 ml ± 4 ml
EX650B (2006 to 2008)	498 ml ± 4 ml
EX650C (2009-on)	469 ml ± 4 ml
EX650D (2009-on)	478 ml ± 4 ml

Fork oil level*

ER650A (2006 to 2008)	115 ± 2 mm
ER650B (2006 to 2008)	111 ± 2 mm
ER650C (2009-on)	96 ± 2 mm
ER650D (2009-on)	103 ± 2 mm
EX650A (2006 to 2008)	98 ± 2 mm
EX650B (2006 to 2008)	89 ± 2 mm
EX650C (2009-on)	114 ± 2 mm
EX650D (2009-on)	105 ± 2 mm

*Oil level is measured from the top of the inner tube with the fork spring removed and the leg fully compressed.

Front forks (continued)

Fork spring free length

ER650A/B and EX650A/B (2006 to 2008)		
Standard	....	277.8 mm
Service limit	....	272 mm
ER650C (2009-on)		
Standard	....	291.3 mm
Service limit	....	285 mm
ER650D (2009-on)		
Standard	....	291.7 mm
Service limit	....	286 mm
EX650C (2009-on)		
Standard	....	294.7 mm
Service limit	....	289 mm
EX650D (2009-on)		
Standard	....	296.2 mm
Service limit	....	290 mm

Torque settings

Clutch lever bracket clamp bolts	....	8 Nm
Footrest bracket bolts	....	34 Nm
Fork damper bolt	....	30 Nm
Fork top bolt	....	25 Nm
Fork yoke clamp bolts	....	20 Nm
Handlebar clamp bolts	....	25 Nm
Rear brake pedal pivot bolt	....	9 Nm
Sidestand pivot bolt	....	44 Nm
Sidestand switch bolt	....	9 Nm
Steering head bearing adjuster nut		
Initial setting (pre-load)	....	39 Nm
Final setting	....	20 Nm
Steering stem bolt	....	108 Nm
Shock absorber mounting bolts	....	59 Nm
Swingarm pivot bolt nut	....	108 Nm

1 General information

All models have a tubular steel frame which uses the engine as a stressed member.

Front suspension is by a pair of oil-damped telescopic forks. The forks have a conventional damper and are non-adjustable.

At the rear, a box-section swingarm made of steel acts on a single shock absorber. The shock absorber is adjustable for spring pre-load.

2 Frame

1 The frame should not require attention unless accident damage has occurred. In most cases, fitting a new frame is the only satisfactory remedy for such damage. A few frame specialists have the jigs and other equipment necessary for straightening frames to the required standard of accuracy, but even then there is no simple way of assessing to what extent the frame may have been over stressed.

2 After a high mileage, examine the frame closely for signs of cracking or splitting at the welded joints. Loose engine mounting bolts can cause ovaling or fracturing of the mounting points. Minor damage can often be repaired by specialised welding, depending on the extent and nature of the damage.

3 Remember that a frame that is out of alignment will cause handling problems. If, as the result of an accident, misalignment is suspected, it will be necessary to strip the machine completely so the frame can be thoroughly checked by a specialist using a frame alignment jig.

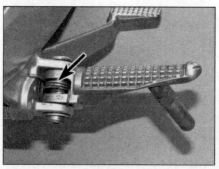

3.1a Location of footrest return spring (arrowed)

3 Footrests, brake pedal and gearchange lever

Rider's footrests

Removal

1 Note the location of the footrest return spring **(see illustration)**. Remove the E-clip from the bottom of the footrest pivot pin, then withdraw the pivot pin and remove the footrest **(see illustration)**. Discard the E-clip if it is damaged and fit a new one on reassembly.

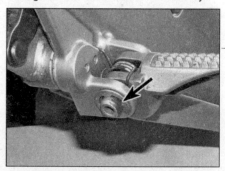

3.1b Pivot pin is secured by E-clip (arrowed)

3.2 Footrest rubbers are secured by screws (arrowed)

3.5a Undo the bolts (arrowed) . . .

3.5b . . . and lift the footrest bracket off

3.8a Remove the split pin (arrowed) . . .

3.8b . . . securing the clevis pin . . .

3.8c . . . then withdraw the clevis pin from the end of the pushrod (arrowed)

2 Rubbers are fitted to the footrests on 2009-on models. Undo the screws on the underside of the footrest to remove the rubbers **(see illustration)**.

Installation

3 Installation is the reverse of removal, noting the following:
● Ensure the return spring is fitted correctly.
● Lubricate the pivot pin with a smear of grease.

Footrest brackets

Removal

4 To remove the left-hand footrest bracket, first remove the frame cover and draw it off (see Chapter 7).
5 Undo the bolts securing the footrest bracket and lift it off **(see illustrations)**.
6 To remove the right-hand footrest bracket,

first remove the frame cover (see Chapter 7).
7 Trace the wiring from the rear brake light switch and disconnect it at the connector. Release the wiring from any clips or ties and feed it through to the back of the footrest bracket.
8 Remove the split pin securing the rear brake pedal clevis pin, then remove the clevis pin and separate the brake pedal from the master cylinder pushrod **(see illustrations)**.
9 Undo the bolts securing the rear brake master cylinder and displace the master cylinder **(see illustrations)**.
10 Undo the bolts securing the footrest bracket and lift it off **(see illustration)**. Note the location of the brake light switch on the rear of the bracket **(see illustration)**. If required, unhook the brake light switch spring and unscrew the switch from the lug on the back of the bracket.

Installation

11 Installation is the reverse of removal, noting the following:
● Tighten the footrest bracket bolts to the

3.9a Undo the bolts (arrowed) . . .

3.9b . . . and displace the master cylinder

3.10a Bolts (arrowed) secure footrest bracket

3.10b Location of rear brake light switch (arrowed)

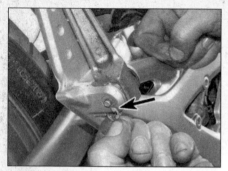

3.12a Remove the E-clip (arrowed) . . .

3.12b . . . then withdraw the pivot pin

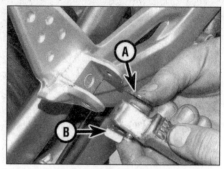

3.12c Note the location of the washer (A) and detent plate (B)

torque setting specified at the beginning of this Chapter.
● Tighten the rear brake master cylinder mounting bolts to the specified torque setting (see Chapter 6).
● Lubricate the clevis pin with a smear of grease.
● Use a new split pin to secure the brake pedal clevis pin.
● Check the operation of the rear brake light switch (see Chapter 1).

Passenger's footrests

12 Remove the E-clip from the bottom of the footrest pivot pin, then withdraw the pivot pin **(see illustrations)**. Remove the footrest carefully, noting the fitting of the washer, detent plate, balls and springs – take care not to loose the balls and springs **(see illustrations)**. Discard the E-clip if it is damaged and fit a new one on reassembly.
13 Installation is the reverse of removal, noting the following:
● Lubricate all the components with a smear of grease.
● Ensure the springs, balls and detent plate are assembled correctly.
● Don't forget to install the washer.

Brake pedal
Removal

14 If required, for ease of access, follow the procedure in Steps 6 and 10 and displace the right-hand footrest bracket. Support the

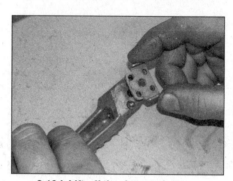

3.12d Lift off the detent plate . . .

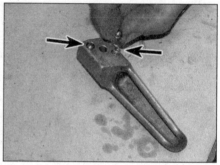

3.12e . . . and remove the balls and springs (arrowed)

bracket to avoid straining the brake hose or brake light wiring.
15 Follow the procedure in Step 8 to separate the brake pedal from the master cylinder pushrod.
16 Unhook the brake light switch spring and the brake pedal return spring, then unscrew the brake pedal pivot bolt **(see illustration)**.

Installation

17 Installation is the reverse of removal, noting the following:
● Lubricate the brake pedal pivot bolt with a smear of grease
● Tighten the pivot bolt to the torque setting specified at the beginning of this Chapter.
● Use a new split pin to secure the brake pedal clevis pin.
● Lubricate the clevis pin with a smear of grease.

● Check the rear brake pedal height (see Chapter 1).
● Check the operation of the rear brake light switch (see Chapter 1).

Gearchange lever
Removal

18 Note the alignment marks on the gearchange shaft and gearchange lever – if no marks are visible, make your own so that the lever can be correctly aligned on installation **(see illustration)**.
19 Undo the lever pinch bolt and draw the lever off **(see illustration)**.
20 Inspect the splines in the lever and on the end of the shaft – if they are damaged new components will have to be fitted (see Chapter 2, Section 18).

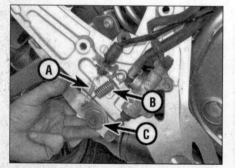

3.16 Brake light switch spring (A), brake pedal return spring (B) and brake pedal pivot bolt (C)

3.18 Note the alignment marks (arrowed)

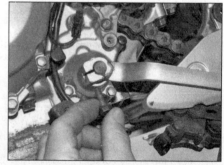

3.19 Undo the lever pinch bolt

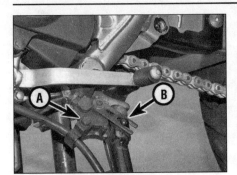

4.4 Undo the bolt (A) noting location of lever (B)

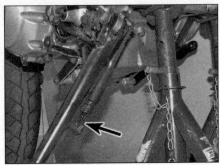

4.5 Ease lower ends of springs off the lug (arrowed)

4.6 Sidestand pivot bolt (arrowed)

Installation

21 Installation is the reverse of removal, noting the following:
● Align the marks made on removal to return the lever to its original position.
● Tighten the lever pinch bolt securely.

4 Sidestand

1 The sidestand pivots on a bracket on the frame. Springs between the stand and the frame ensure that it is held in the retracted or extended position as required.

Removal

2 Support the bike on an auxiliary stand.
3 Remove the left-hand footrest bracket (see Section 3).
4 Undo the bolt securing the sidestand switch and displace the switch, noting how the switch lever locates on the stand **(see illustration)**.
5 Ease the lower ends of the springs off the lug on the stand, then remove the springs, noting how they fit **(see illustration)**.
6 Unscrew the locknut from the pivot bolt, then undo the pivot bolt and remove the stand **(see illustration)**.
7 Clean the stand, bracket and pivot bolt and inspect them for damage and wear. Renew the pivot bolt if necessary.

Installation

8 Prior to installation, lubricate the bracket and pivot bolt with a smear of grease.
9 Fit the stand onto the bracket, install the pivot bolt and tighten it to the torque setting specified at the beginning of this Chapter. Tighten the locknut securely. Check that the stand pivots freely around the bolt.
10 Hook the upper ends of the springs over the lug on the bracket, then pull the springs down and hook them over the lug on the stand. **Note:** *It is essential that the springs are in good condition and are capable of holding the stand up when not in use.*
11 Clean the threads of the sidestand switch bolt and apply a suitable non-permanent thread-locking compound. Position the switch on the bracket, ensure the lever is correctly

located on the stand, then tighten the switch mounting bolt to the specified torque setting **(see illustration 4.4)**.

5 Handlebars and levers

Handlebars

Note: *The handlebars can be displaced from the top yoke for access to the steering stem bolt without displacing or removing the front brake master cylinder, clutch lever, cables or switch housings.*

Removal

1 Support the machine securely in an upright position.

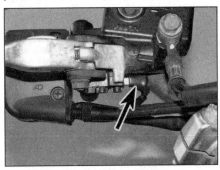

5.4 Front brake light switch wiring connector

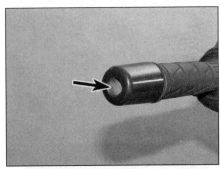

5.6 Handlebar end-weights are secured by screws

2 Remove the fuel tank to avoid damaging its paintwork (see Chapter 4).
3 On ER650 models, remove the mirrors (see Chapter 7).
4 Disconnect the front brake light switch wiring connector **(see illustration)**.
5 Undo the front brake master cylinder clamp bolts and remove the back of the clamp **(see illustration)**. Secure the master cylinder assembly clear of the handlebar and ensure no strain is placed on the brake hose. Keep the fluid reservoir upright to prevent air entering the system.
6 Undo each handlebar end-weight screws and remove the weights **(see illustration)**.
7 Detach the throttle cables from the twistgrip pulley (see Chapter 4). Slide the twistgrip off the handlebar.
8 Disconnect the clutch switch wiring connector **(see illustration)**.
9 Undo the clutch lever clamp bolts, remove

5.5 Front brake master cylinder clamp bolts

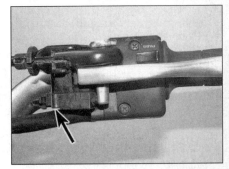

5.8 Clutch switch wiring connector (arrowed)

5.9 Clutch lever clamp bolts (arrowed)

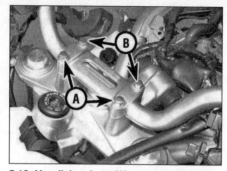

5.13 Handlebar front (A) and rear (B) clamp bolts

5.14a Align handlebar punch mark (arrowed) as described

5.14b Align clutch lever clamp joint with punch mark (arrowed)

5.15 Front brake lever pivot screw (arrowed)

5.17 Clutch lever pivot bolt (arrowed)

the back of the clamp and lift the lever off the handlebar **(see illustration)**.

10 Separate the two halves of the left-hand switch housing (see Chapter 8). Position the housing clear of the handlebar.

11 Pull the left-hand grip off the handlebar. **Note:** *The grip will probably be stuck in place – it may be necessary to slit it with a sharp knife in order to remove it.*

12 Release any ties securing the wiring to the handlebars.

13 Loosen the handlebar clamp bolts, then support the handlebars and remove the clamp **(see illustration)**. Lift the handlebars off. If the bars are only being displaced, rest them on a cushion of rag behind the top yoke.

Installation

14 Installation is the reverse of removal, noting the following:

● Align the punch mark on the back of the handlebars with the outer edge of the left-hand bracket **(see illustration)**.

● Tighten the clamp bolts to the torque setting specified at the beginning of this Chapter – tighten the front bolts first leaving any gap at the rear.

● Align the clutch lever clamp joint with the punch mark on the top of the handlebar **(see illustration)**.

● Refer to Chapter 8 for installation of the left-hand switch housing.

● If a new handlebar grip is being fitted, secure it using a suitable adhesive.

● Refer to Chapter 4 for installation of the throttle cables and twistgrip.

● Refer to Chapter 6 for installation of the front brake master cylinder.

● Clean the threads of the handlebar end-weight screws and apply a suitable non-permanent thread-locking compound. Tighten the screws securely.

● Check the operation of the throttle, clutch and brake levers, and the front brake light switch and clutch switch before riding the motorcycle.

Handlebar levers

15 To remove the front brake lever, undo the pivot screw locknut on the underside of the lever, then undo the pivot screw and remove the lever **(see illustration)**.

16 To remove the clutch lever, first disconnect the cable from the lever (see Chapter 2, Section 17).

17 Undo the pivot bolt locknut on the underside of the lever, then unscrew the pivot bolt and remove the lever **(see illustration)**. Note the collar in the lever and remove it for safekeeping. Note how the lever span adjuster, spring and lever locate together.

18 Installation is the reverse of removal, noting the following:

● When fitting the brake lever apply silicone grease to the contact area between the master cylinder pushrod tip and the brake lever, to the pivot screw and the contact areas between the lever and its bracket. Tighten the pivot screw lightly, then counter-hold it and tighten the locknut.

● When fitting the clutch lever apply silicone grease to the pivot screw and the contact

areas between the lever and its bracket. Adjust clutch cable freeplay (see Chapter 1).

6 Fork removal and installation

Removal

1 On EX650 models, remove the fairing side panels (see Chapter 7).

2 Remove the front wheel and, on machines equipped with ABS, displace the front wheel sensor (see Chapter 6). Remove the front mudguard (see Chapter 7).

3 Work on one fork leg at a time. If both legs are being removed, note which side they fit and mark them accordingly. Note the routing of any cables, hoses and wiring around the forks.

4 Loosen the fork clamp bolt in the top yoke **(see illustration)**. If the fork leg is to

6.4 Upper fork clamp bolt (arrowed)

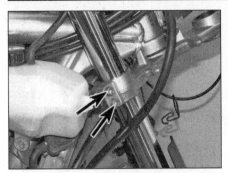

6.5a Lower fork clamp bolts (arrowed)

6.5b Twist and pull the fork leg downwards

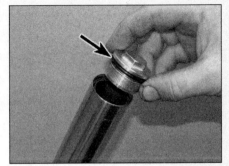

7.3 Unscrew the top bolt. Note the O-ring (arrowed)

be disassembled, or if the fork oil is being changed, loosen the fork top bolt at this stage.
5 Loosen the fork clamp bolts in the bottom yoke, then remove the fork leg by twisting it and pulling it downwards **(see illustrations)**.

HAYNES HiNT *If the fork legs are seized in the yokes, spray the area with penetrating oil and allow time for it to soak in before trying again.*

Installation

6 Remove all traces of corrosion from the fork inner tube and the yokes. Slide the fork leg up through the bottom yoke and into the top yoke, making sure all cables, hoses and wiring are routed on the correct side of the leg.
7 Align the top of the fork inner tube with the upper surface of the top yoke, with the rim of the top bolt above the yoke.
8 Tighten the fork clamp bolts in the bottom yoke evenly and a little at a time to the torque setting specified at the beginning of this Chapter **(see illustration 6.5a)**.
9 If the fork leg has been dismantled or if the fork oil was changed, tighten the fork top bolt to the specified torque setting. Now tighten the fork clamp bolt in the top yoke to the specified torque **(see illustration 6.4)**.
10 Install the remaining components in the reverse order of removal.
11 Check the operation of the front forks and brake before taking the machine out on the road.

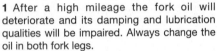

7 Fork oil change

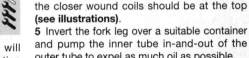

1 After a high mileage the fork oil will deteriorate and its damping and lubrication qualities will be impaired. Always change the oil in both fork legs.
2 Remove the fork leg (see Section 6) – make sure the top bolt is loosened while the leg is still clamped in the bottom yoke.
3 Support the leg upright and unscrew the top bolt from the top of the inner tube, noting that it is under pressure from the spring – it is best to use a ratchet tool and to keep constant downward pressure on the top bolt while unscrewing it **(see illustration)**. Check the condition of the top bolt O-ring – if it is deformed or deteriorated, fit a new one on reassembly.
4 Compress the inner tube into the outer

tube and remove the spacer, spring seat and spring, noting which way up the spring fits – the closer wound coils should be at the top **(see illustrations)**.
5 Invert the fork leg over a suitable container and pump the inner tube in-and-out of the outer tube to expel as much oil as possible.
6 Allow the fork leg to drain for several minutes. Wipe any excess oil off the spring and spacer. If the oil contains metal particles, disassemble the leg and inspect the fork components for signs of wear (see Section 8).
7 When the oil has drained, support the leg upright with the inner tube compressed into the outer tube. Slowly pour in the quantity and type of fork oil as specified at the beginning of this Chapter **(see illustration)**.
8 Pump the inner tube up-and-down several times to expel any trapped air **(see illustration)**. Secure the fork leg upright with the inner tube compressed into the outer tube,

7.4a Remove the spacer . . .

7.4b . . . spring seat . . .

7.4c . . . and spring noting how it fits

7.7 Pour the fork oil in slowly

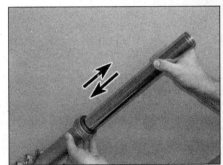

7.8 Pump the inner tube up-and-down to expel trapped air

7.9 Measure the fork oil level

7.11 Lubricate the O-ring with fork oil

8 Fork overhaul

Disassembly

1 Remove the fork leg (see Section 6) – make sure the top bolt is loosened while the leg is still clamped in the bottom yoke.

2 Always dismantle the fork legs separately to avoid interchanging parts. Store all components in separate, clearly marked containers **(see illustration)**.

3 Remove the fork protector from the top of the outer tube, noting how it locates **(see illustrations)**. When dismantling the right-hand leg, remove the axle clamp bolt. If required, remove the front mudguard brackets on 2006 to 2008 models, and the guide for the ABS speed sensor wire where fitted **(see illustrations)**.

4 Before dismantling the fork leg, loosen the damper bolt in the bottom of the outer tube. To do this, turn the leg upside down, compress the leg so that the fork spring exerts pressure on the internal damper assembly, then loosen the bolt **(see illustration)**. Alternatively, use an air wrench to loosen the bolt, or use a holding tool as described in Step 6.

5 Follow the procedure in Section 7 to remove the top bolt, spacer, spring seat and spring, then drain the fork oil.

6 Remove the previously loosened damper bolt and its sealing washer from the bottom of the outer tube. Discard the washer as a

and let it to stand for several minutes to allow the oil level to stabilise.

9 Measure the oil level from the top of the inner tube **(see illustration)**. Add or subtract oil until it is at the level specified at the beginning of this Chapter.

10 When the oil level is correct, pull the inner tube out to its full extension and install the spring, with its closer wound coils at the top, followed by the spring seat and spacer **(see illustrations 7.4c, b and a)**.

11 Lubricate the top bolt O-ring with a smear of fork oil **(see illustration)**. Thread the top bolt into the inner tube, making sure it is not cross-threaded, and tighten securely. **Note:** *The top bolt can be tightened to the specified torque setting once the fork leg has been installed on the bike and is securely held in the bottom yoke.*

12 Install the fork leg (see Section 6).

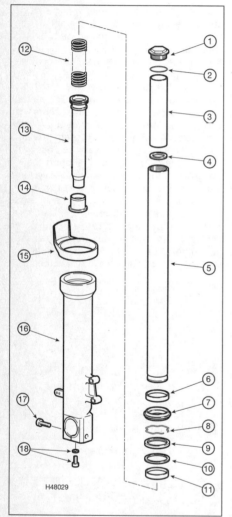

H48029

8.2 Front fork components

1 Top bolt	11 Top bush
2 O-ring	12 Spring
3 Spacer	13 Damper
4 Spring seat	14 Damper seat
5 Inner tube	15 Fork protector
6 Bottom bush	16 Outer tube
7 Dust seal	17 Axle clamp
8 Retaining clip	bolt
9 Oil seal	18 Damper bolt and
10 Washer	sealing washer

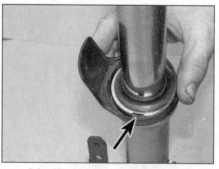

8.3a Note the location of the tab (arrowed) . . .

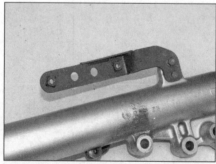

8.3c Note the location of the mudguard brackets . . .

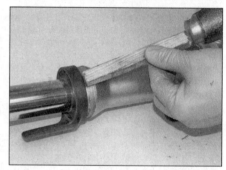

8.3b . . . then tap the fork protector off carefully

8.3d . . . and the speed sensor wire guide (arrowed)

8.4 Loosen the damper bolt

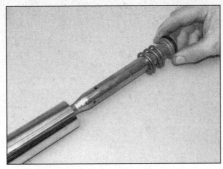
8.7 Withdraw the damper and rebound spring

8.8 Prise out the dust seal

new one must be fitted on reassembly. If the bolt could not be loosened earlier, a length of metal bar or wood dowel can be passed down through the fork inner tube and pressed hard against the top of the damper to hold it while the bolt is undone. Kawasaki produce service tools (Part Nos. 57001-183 and 57001-1057) to do this.

7 Withdraw the damper and rebound spring from the fork leg **(see illustration)**.

8 Using a small flat-bladed screwdriver, prise out the dust seal from the top of the outer tube – discard the seal as a new one must be fitted on reassembly **(see illustration)**.

9 Ease out the oil seal retaining clip, taking care not to scratch the surface of the inner tube **(see illustrations)**.

10 To separate the inner and outer tubes it is necessary to displace the oil seal and top

bush. To do this, first push the inner tube into the outer tube, then pull the tubes sharply apart so that the bottom bush on the inner tube strikes the top bush in the outer tube – repeat this procedure until the seal and top bush are displaced and the inner tube can be withdrawn completely **(see illustrations)**.

11 With the inner tube removed, slide off the oil seal, washer and top bush, noting how they fit. New oil seals must be fitted on reassembly, but the old ones can be used to aid installation. Do not remove the bottom bush unless it is to be replaced with a new one.

12 Tip the damper seat out of the outer tube.

Inspection

13 Clean all parts in a suitable solvent

and blow them dry with compressed air, if available.

14 Check the surface of the fork inner tube for score marks, scratches, pitting and flaking of the finish, and excessive or abnormal wear. Look for dents in the tube and renew the tubes in both fork legs if any are found.

15 Check the inner tubes for runout using V-blocks and a dial gauge. If the condition of either inner tube is suspect, have it checked by a Kawasaki dealer or suspension specialist. Kawasaki provides no specifications for runout.

16 Inspect the inside surface of the outer tube and the working surface of each bush for score marks, scratches and signs of excessive wear **(see illustrations)**. Renew the bushes as a set, particularly if excessive movement has been felt between the fork tubes (see

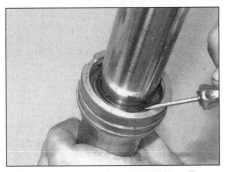
8.9a Ease out the oil seal retaining clip . . .

8.9b . . . noting how it fits

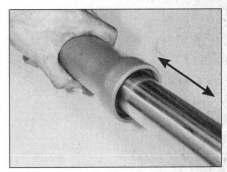
8.10a Pull the tubes apart sharply . . .

8.10b . . . to displace the oil seal (1), washer (2), top bush (3) and bottom bush (4)

8.16a Inspect the inside surface of the outer tube . . .

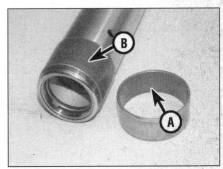
8.16b . . . the inner surface (A) of the top bush and the outer surface (B) of the bottom bush

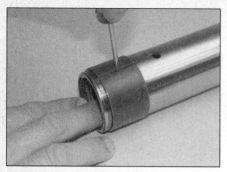

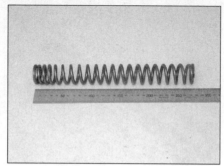

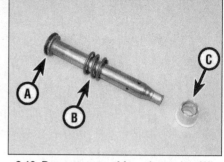

8.16c Prise the ends of the bottom bush apart to remove it

8.18 Measure the spring free length

8.19 Damper assembly – piston ring (A), rebound spring (B) and damper seat (C)

Chapter 1, Sections 16 and 17). To remove the bottom bush, prise it apart at the slit using a flat-bladed screwdriver and slide it off **(see illustration)**. Make sure the new bushes seat properly.

17 Check the fork oil seal seat for nicks, gouges and scratches. If damage is evident, leaks will occur. Also check the oil seal washer for damage or distortion and replace it with a new one if necessary.

18 Check the springs for cracks and other damage. Measure the spring free length and compare the result to the specifications at the beginning of this Chapter **(see illustration)**. If the spring is defective or has sagged below the service limit, fit new springs in both forks. Never fit only one new spring.

19 Check the damper and its piston ring for damage and wear, and renew them if

necessary **(see illustration)**. Ensure the small spring is secure inside the damper seat.

Reassembly

20 Make sure the bottom bush is correctly located in its recess in the bottom of the inner tube.

21 Slide the damper into the inner tube so its bottom end protrudes from the bottom of the tube. Fit the damper seat onto the bottom of the damper, then push them up into the bottom of the tube **(see illustrations)**.

22 Lubricate the bottom bush and the inner surface of the outer tube with the specified fork oil. Slide the inner tube all the way into the outer tube.

23 Clean the threads of the damper bolt, fit a new sealing washer and apply a few drops

of a suitable non-permanent thread-locking compound **(see illustration)**. Fit the bolt into the bottom of the outer tube, thread it into the bottom of the damper rod and tighten it to the torque setting specified at the beginning of this Chapter. If the damper rotates as you tighten the bolt, hold it with spring pressure or a metal bar or wood dowel as on disassembly (see Step 6).

24 Hold the fork leg upright. Lubricate the top bush with fork oil, slide it down the inner tube and press it as far as possible into its seat in the top of the outer tube **(see illustration)**. Install the washer and, if necessary, tap the top bush fully home with a small punch **(see illustrations)**. **Note:** *Take care not to mark the inner tube during reassembly. Keep it pushed fully into the outer tube so that any accidental scratching is confined to the area above the oil seal.*

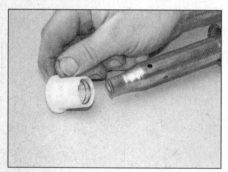

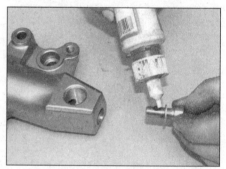

8.21a Fit the damper and the damper seat . . .

8.21b . . . then push them into the bottom of the tube

8.23 Fit a new sealing washer and thread-lock the damper bolt

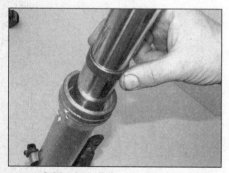

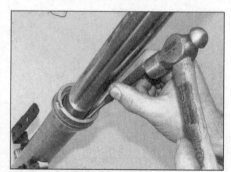

8.24a Install the top bush . . .

8.24b . . . and washer . . .

8.24c . . . and tap them into place with a small punch

8.25a Prepare the old oil seal as described . . .

8.25b . . . then use it to drive in the new seal . . .

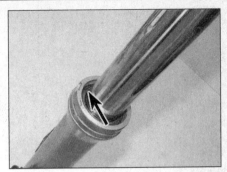

8.25c . . . until the groove (arrowed) is visible

25 Lubricate the new oil seal with fork oil and slide it down the inner tube with its markings facing upwards. Press the seal squarely into the outer tube as far as possible by hand. Cut away the inside lip of the old oil seal, then use this, together with a small block of wood and a hammer, to tap the new seal fully home (see illustrations). Remove the old seal and check that the retaining clip groove is visible above the new seal (see illustration).
26 Fit the retaining clip, making sure it is correctly located in its groove (see illustration 8.9b).
27 Lubricate the inside of the new dust seal, then slide it down the inner tube and press it into position (see illustration 8.8).
28 Fill the leg with the specified amount and type of oil, then install the spring, spring seat, spacer and top bolt (see Section 7).

29 Fit the fork protector to the top of the outer tube (see illustration 8.3a).
30 Fit the axle clamp bolt in the bottom of the right-hand outer tube. Install the remaining components in the reverse order of removal.
31 Install the fork leg (see Section 6).

9 Steering stem

Removal

1 Remove the fairing and fairing side panels on all models (see Chapter 7).
2 Displace the handlebars (see Section 5).
3 On EX650 models, note the location of the brake hose and wire guides secured by the horn bracket mounting bolts, then remove the horn (see illustration).
4 On ER650 models, remove the headlight panel brackets from the top and bottom yokes (see Chapter 7).
5 Remove the front fork legs (see Section 6).
6 If the top yoke is being removed from the bike rather than just being displaced, trace the wiring from the ignition switch and disconnect it at the connector. Release the wiring from any clips or ties and feed it through to the yoke, noting its routing.
7 Remove the plug from the steering stem bolt (see illustration). Unscrew the bolt and remove the washer, then lift the top yoke up off the steering stem (see illustrations).
8 Bend the upward-pointing lockwasher tabs out of the notches in the locknut and unscrew the locknut using a C-spanner located in one of the notches (see illustration).

9.3 Note the location of the guides secured by the horn bracket bolts

9.7a Remove the plug . . .

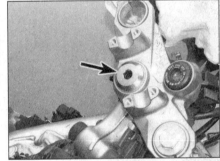

9.7b . . . then unscrew the steering stem bolt (arrowed)

9.7c Remove the bolt and washer

9.7d Lift off the top yoke

9.8 Remove the locknut

9.10a Unscrew the adjuster nut . . .

9.10b . . . and lift off the bearing cover

9.11 Lift off the upper bearing inner race

9 Remove the lockwasher, noting how the downward-pointing tabs locate in the adjuster nut – discard the lockwasher as a new one must be fitted.

10 Support the bottom yoke and unscrew the adjuster nut, then lift off the bearing cover

9.12a Withdraw the steering stem from the steering head . . .

(see illustrations).

11 Lower the bottom yoke and lift the upper bearing inner race off the steering stem **(see illustration).**

12 Withdraw the steering stem from the steering head and remove the upper bearing from the top of the steering head **(see illustrations).** Remove the lower bearing from the base of the steering stem **(see illustration).** **Note:** *Do not attempt to remove the outer races from the steering head or the lower bearing inner race from the steering stem unless new bearings are being installed (see Section 10).*

13 Remove all traces of old grease from the bearings and races and check them for wear and damage (see Section 10).

Installation

14 Apply general purpose grease to the bearing outer races in the steering head, and

work grease well into both the upper and lower bearings. Fit the lower bearing on the steering stem **(see illustration 9.12c).**

15 Carefully lift the steering stem up through the steering head and support it there. Fit the upper bearing into the top of the steering head, then slide the inner race down the stem and press it firmly over the bearing **(see illustrations).** Fit the bearing cover.

16 Thread the adjuster nut onto the steering stem **(see illustration 9.10a).**

17 If a suitable peg spanner (which can be made by cutting castellations into an old deep socket or box spanner) is available, tighten the adjuster nut to the initial torque setting specified at the beginning of the Chapter to pre-load the bearings **(see illustration).** Next, loosen the adjuster nut until it just turns lightly, and finally tighten it to the final torque setting.

18 Alternatively, tighten the adjuster nut using a C-spanner **(see illustration).** Tighten the nut

9.12b . . . and remove the upper bearing

9.12c Remove the lower bearing

9.15a Fit the upper bearing (arrowed) into the top of the steering head . . .

9.15b . . . then press the inner race (arrowed) over the bearing

9.17 Use a peg spanner to tighten the adjuster to the specified torque

9.18 Using a C-spanner to tighten the adjuster nut

9.20a Locate the new lockwasher on the underside of the locknut

9.20b Align outward facing tabs (arrowed) with notches in adjuster nut . . .

9.20c . . . then bend tabs down into the notches

until movement of the bottom yoke becomes stiff, then slacken it off. Now tighten the nut so that there is no front-to-back freeplay in the bearings.

19 When correctly adjusted, the steering should be able to move freely from lock to lock, but without front-to-back freeplay (see Chapter 1, Section 16).

Caution: Take great care not to apply excessive pressure because this will cause premature failure of the bearings.

20 Fit the new lockwasher to the underside of the locknut with the bent tabs located in the notches in the nut **(see illustration)**. Thread the locknut onto the steering stem until the lockwasher contacts the adjuster nut. Continue to turn the locknut until the outward facing tabs on the lockwasher align with notches in the adjuster nut, then bend the tabs down into the notches **(see illustrations)**.

21 Fit the top yoke on the steering stem and install the washer and steering stem bolt finger-tight **(see illustrations 9.7d and c)**. Temporarily install one of the fork legs to align the top and bottom yokes and secure it by tightening the bottom yoke clamp bolts only. Tighten the steering stem bolt to the torque setting specified at the beginning of this Chapter, then fit the plug **(see illustrations 9.7b and a)**.

22 If applicable, feed the ignition switch wiring through to its connector, making sure it is correctly routed, and connect the wiring.

23 Install the remaining components in the reverse order of removal. Prior to installing the handlebars, check of the steering head bearing adjustment as described in Chapter 1 Section 16, and if necessary re-adjust.

10 Steering head bearings

Inspection

1 Remove the steering stem (see Section 9).
2 Remove all traces of old grease from the bearings and races and check them for wear or damage.
3 The races should be polished and free from indentations – check the outer races in

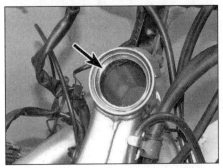

10.3a Inspect the outer races (arrowed) . . .

the steering head and the inner races on the steering stem **(see illustrations)**. Inspect the bearing balls for signs of wear, pitting or discoloration, and examine the bearing cages for cracks or splits. If there are any signs of wear or damage on any of the bearing components, both upper and lower bearing assemblies must be renewed as a set. **Note:** *Do not attempt to remove the outer races from the steering head or the lower bearing inner race from the steering stem unless new bearings are being installed.*

Renewal

4 The outer races are an interference fit in the steering head and can be tapped out using a suitable drift located in the recesses provided **(see illustration)**. Tap firmly and evenly around each race to ensure that it is driven out squarely.
5 Lubricate the new outer races with grease

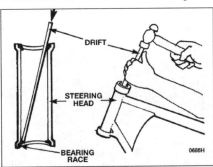

10.4 Drive the bearing outer races out with a drift as shown

10.3b . . . and the inner races

and install them both at the same time using a drawbolt arrangement **(see illustration)**. Ensure that the upper and lower drawbolt washers bear on the outer edges of the races only and do not contact the bearing surfaces.

> **HAYNES HINT** *Installation of new bearing outer races is made much easier if the races are left overnight in the freezer. This causes them to contract slightly making them a looser fit. Alternatively, use a freeze spray.*

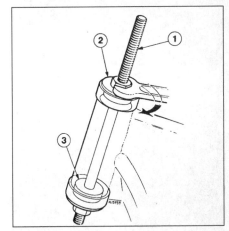

10.5 Drawbolt arrangement for fitting steering head bearing outer races

1 Long bolt or threaded bar
2 Thick washer
3 Guide for lower outer race

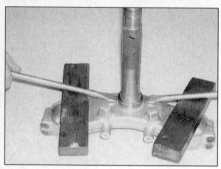

10.6a Lever off the lower bearing inner race . . .

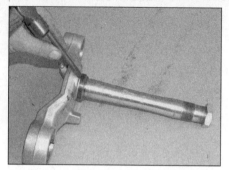

10.6b . . . or tap it free using a chisel

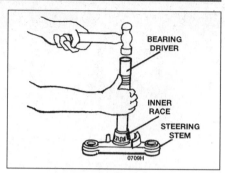

10.8 Installing the lower bearing inner race using a suitable driver

6 Only remove the lower bearing inner race from the steering stem if a new one is being fitted. To remove the race, use two screwdrivers placed on opposite sides to work it free, or tap under it using a cold chisel **(see illustrations)**. If the race is firmly in place it will be necessary to split it using an angle grinder – take care not to nick or gouge the steering stem
7 Remove the dust seal from the bottom of the stem and replace it with a new one.
8 Grease the inside of the new inner race, then slide it down the steering stem. Tap the race into position using a length of tubing with an internal diameter slightly larger than the steering stem **(see illustration)**. Ensure that the tubing bears only on the inner edge of the race and does not contact the bearing surface.
9 Install the steering stem (see Section 9).

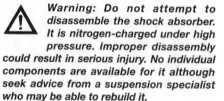

11 Rear shock absorber

⚠️ *Warning: Do not attempt to disassemble the shock absorber. It is nitrogen-charged under high pressure. Improper disassembly could result in serious injury. No individual components are available for it although seek advice from a suspension specialist who may be able to rebuild it.*

Removal

1 Support the motorcycle securely in an upright position with no weight on the rear wheel – if necessary, place a support under the wheel so that the swingarm does not drop when the shock absorber is removed.

2 Counter-hold the lower mounting bolt and undo the nut and washer, then support the shock absorber and withdraw the bolt **(see illustrations)**.
3 Prise off the cap from the upper mounting **(see illustration)**. Loosen the upper mounting bolt, then support the shock and withdraw the bolt **(see illustration)**. Manoeuvre the shock out **(see illustration)**.

Inspection

4 Inspect the shock absorber for obvious physical damage and oil leakage, and the coil spring for looseness, cracks or signs of fatigue **(see illustration)**. Ensure the spring pre-load adjuster turns freely.
5 If the shock is in any way damaged or worn a new one must be fitted. Take the old shock to a Kawasaki dealer for safe disposal.
6 Check the bush in the upper end of the shock absorber for wear and deterioration.

11.2a Undo the nut and washer . . .

11.2b . . . then withdraw the lower mounting bolt

11.3a Prise off the cap

11.3b Remove the upper mounting bolt (arrowed) . . .

11.3c . . . and lift out the shock absorber

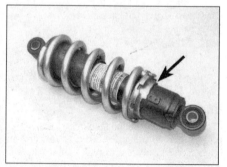

11.4 Inspect the shock for damage – note the pre-load adjuster (arrowed)

11.7a Remove the bearing seals . . .

11.7b . . . and press out the inner sleeve . . .

11.7c . . . to inspect the needle bearing (arrowed)

If necessary a new one can be fitted using the drawbolt method – refer to *Tools and workshop Tips (Section 5)* in the Reference section.

7 Check the needle bearing in the lower end of the shock absorber – prise off the seals and press out the inner sleeve **(see illustrations)**. Clean the components with a suitable solvent to remove all traces of dirt and grease. Remove any corrosion from the sleeve using steel wool. If the bearing is worn or pitted a new one should be fitted – refer to *Tools and Workshop Tips (Section 5)* in the Reference section. Renew the seals if they are damaged.

8 Inspect the mounting bolts for wear and renew them if necessary.

Installation

9 Installation is the reverse of removal, noting the following:

- Lubricate the lower bearing with multi-purpose grease and fit the seals.
- Lubricate the mounting bolts with a smear of grease.
- Install the upper and lower mounting bolts, and the nut and washer on the lower bolt, then tighten them to the torque setting specified at the beginning of this Chapter.

12 Swingarm

Removal

1 Support the motorcycle securely in an upright position – if required, remove the exhaust silencer (see Chapter 4) and place supports under the rear of the frame.

2 Remove the frame covers, the chainguard and, where fitted, the rear hugger (see Chapter 7).

3 On ABS equipped machines, trace the wiring from the rear wheel speed sensor and disconnect it at the connector. Feed the wiring back to the wheel through the guides on the swingarm **(see illustration)**.

4 Disconnect the brake hose from the rear caliper and plug the openings to prevent leakage (see Chapter 6). Feed the hose through the guides on the swingarm **(see illustrations)**.

5 Remove the drive chain and the rear wheel (see Chapter 6). Lift off the rear brake caliper bracket.

6 Withdraw the chain adjusters from the ends of the swingarm **(see illustration)**.

7 Support the swingarm and remove the rear shock absorber (see Section 11).

8 Unscrew the nut on the left-hand end of the pivot bolt **(see illustration)**.

12.3 Feed the speed sensor wiring back through the guides

12.4a Feed the brake hose through the guides (arrowed) . . .

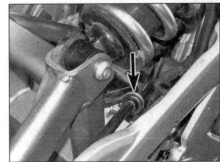

12.4b . . . along the swingarm

12.6 Remove the chain adjusters

12.8 Undo the pivot bolt nut

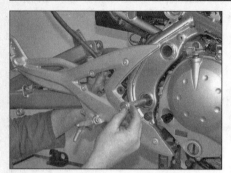

12.9a Withdraw the pivot bolt . . .

12.9b . . . and manoeuvre the swingarm out

12.12a Undo the screw . . .

12.12b . . . and remove the chain slider

12.15a Remove the right-hand spacer . . .

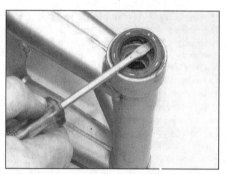

12.15b . . . then prise out the seal

9 Support the swingarm, then withdraw the pivot bolt and manoeuvre the swingarm out of the frame **(see illustrations)**.

Inspection

10 Clean the swingarm with a suitable solvent, removing all traces of dirt, corrosion and grease. If, during the course of inspection, any component is found to be worn or damaged, it must be renewed.

11 Inspect the swingarm closely, looking for obvious signs of wear such as heavy scoring, and cracks or distortion due to accident damage.

12 Check the upper and lower edges of the chain slider for wear. Undo the screw securing the chain slider and lift it off **(see illustrations)**.

13 Clean the swingarm pivot bolt and remove any corrosion using wire wool. Check that it is straight by rolling it on a flat surface such as a piece of plate glass.

14 Lay the swingarm on the work surface and support it so that the pivot end is level (check this with a spirit level). Install the chain adjusters and the wheel axle and check that the axle is also level – if not, the swingarm is out of true and must be replaced with a new one.

15 Lift the spacer out of the seal on the right-hand end of the swingarm pivot, then prise out the seal **(see illustrations)**.

16 Prise the seal out from the left-hand end of the swingarm pivot, then withdraw the bearing sleeve **(see illustrations)**. Discard both seals as new ones must be fitted.

17 The swingarm is fitted with two needle bearings in the left-hand pivot and an inner needle bearing and outer caged ball bearing in the right-hand pivot **(see illustrations)**. Check that the ball bearing turns smoothly. Apply

clean oil to the bearing sleeve, install it in the swingarm and check that it turns smoothly in the needle bearings. Slide the pivot bolt into place and check for any freeplay in the bearings.

12.16a Remove the left-hand seal . . .

12.16b . . . and withdraw the bearing sleeve

12.17a Left-hand needle bearings (arrowed)

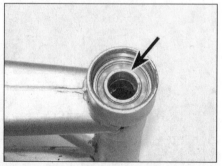

12.17b Right-hand ball bearing and needle bearing

12.18 Ball bearing is retained by circlip

A Inner left-hand
   bearing
B Outer left-hand
   bearing
C Inner right-hand
   bearing
D Inset 23.5 mm
E Inset 6 mm (2006
   to 2008 models),
   5.5 mm (2009-on
   models)
F Inset 25 mm

12.19 Installation of swingarm needle bearings

H48016

18 If the bearings do not turn smoothly and freely, or if there is excessive freeplay, they must be replaced with new ones – refer to *Tools and Workshop Tips (Section 5)* in the Reference section. Note that the ball bearing is retained by a circlip **(see illustration)**.
19 The needle bearings are installed at specific depths, measured from the outside edge of the swingarm pivot **(see illustration)**. Study the diagram before installing the bearings and check the installed depths with a Vernier caliper. The new needle bearings should be pressed or drawn into their bores rather than driven into position. In the absence of a press, a suitable drawbolt tool can be made up as described in *Tools and Workshop Tips* .
20 The ball bearing fits against a shoulder inside the swingarm pivot. Don't forget to fit a new circlip to secure the bearing **(see illustration 12.18)**.

Installation

21 Lubricate the bearing sleeve with clean engine oil and install in the swingarm from the left-hand side **(see illustration 12.16b)**. **Note:** *The swingarm bearings are all of the sealed type and require no grease lubrication.* Smear multi-purpose grease on the inside edge of the

12.21a Install the new left-hand seal

new left-hand seal and press it into the end of the swingarm pivot **(see illustration)**. Smear multi-purpose grease on the inside edge of the new right-hand seal and press it into the end of the swingarm pivot – if necessary, drive the seal home with a suitably-sized socket **(see illustrations)**. Press the spacer into the seal **(see illustration 12.15a)**.
22 Install the chain slider **(see illustrations 12.12b and a)**.
23 Clean the frame around the swingarm mountings, then support the swingarm in position and install the pivot bolt from the right-hand side **(see illustrations 12.9a)**. Counter-hold the pivot bolt and tighten the nut

12.21b Install the new right-hand seal . . .

to the torque setting specified at the beginning of this Chapter **(see illustration)**. Check that the swingarm moves freely up-and-down.
24 Install the rear shock absorber (see Section 11).
25 Install the remaining components in the reverse order of the removal. Follow the procedure in Chapter 6 to bleed the rear brake hydraulic circuit after reconnecting the brake hose.
26 Check and adjust the drive chain slack (see Chapter 1).
27 Check the operation of the rear suspension and brake before taking the machine on the road.

12.21c . . . and drive it in with a suitably-sized socket

12.23 Tighten the pivot bolt nut to the specified torque

13.2 Rear shock spring pre-load adjuster ring (arrowed)

13.3 Seats in the adjuster ring locate under tab (arrowed)

13 Rear shock absorber adjustment

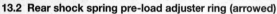

1 The rear shock absorber is adjustable for spring pre-load.

2 The pre-load is adjusted by turning the adjuster ring on the top of the spring with a suitable C-spanner – one is provided in the bike's tool kit **(see illustration)**.

3 There are seven settings, each identified by seats in the adjuster ring which locate under the tab on the shock body **(see illustration)**. The lowest seat is the softest setting, the second seat the standard setting, the highest seat is the hardest setting.

Chapter 6
Brakes, wheels and final drive

Contents

Degrees of difficulty

Easy, suitable for novice with little experience	**Fairly easy,** suitable for beginner with some experience	**Fairly difficult,** suitable for competent DIY mechanic	**Difficult,** suitable for experienced DIY mechanic	**Very difficult,** suitable for expert DIY or professional

Specifications

Front brakes

Brake fluid type	DOT 4
Disc thickness	
Non-ABS	
Standard.	4.3 to 4.7mm
Service limit	4.0 mm
ABS models	
Standard.	4.8 to 5.2 mm
Service limit	4.5 mm
Disc maximum runout	0.3 mm

Rear brake

Brake fluid type	DOT 4
Disc thickness	
Standard.	4.8 to 5.2 mm
Service limit	4.5 mm
Disc maximum runout	0.3 mm

ABS system
Sensor air gap . . . .   1.0 mm

Wheels
Maximum wheel runout (front and rear)
  Axial (side-to-side) . . . .   1.0 mm
  Radial (out-of-round) . . . .   1.0 mm
Maximum axle runout (front and rear) . . . .   0.2 mm

Tyres
Tyre pressures . . . .   see *Pre-ride checks*
Tyre sizes*
  Front . . . .   120/70-ZR17 (58W) Radial
  Rear . . . .   160/60-ZR17 (69W) Radial
*Refer to the owners handbook or the tyre information label on the swingarm for approved tyre brands.

Final drive
Drive chain slack and lubricant . . . .   see Chapter 1
Drive chain
  2006 to 2008 models
    Type . . . .   Enuma EK520MVXL1
    Length. . . . .   114 links
  2009-on models
    Type . . . .   Daido DID 520VP2-T
    Length. . . . .   114 links
Sprocket sizes
  Front (engine) sprocket. . . . .   15 tooth
  Rear (wheel) sprocket. . . . .   46 tooth

Torque settings
Brake system bleed valves. . . . .   8 Nm
Brake disc bolts . . . .   27 Nm
Brake hose banjo bolts. . . . .   25 Nm
Brake pipe gland nuts (ABS models) . . . .   18 Nm
Front axle . . . .   108 Nm
Front axle clamp bolt . . . .   34 Nm
Front brake caliper mounting bolts . . . .   34 Nm
Front brake master cylinder clamp bolts . . . .   11 Nm
Front sprocket nut . . . .   127 Nm
Rear axle nut . . . .   108 Nm
Rear brake caliper mounting bolts
  Front . . . .   34 Nm
  Rear . . . .   25 Nm
Rear master cylinder mounting bolts . . . .   25 Nm
Rear sprocket nuts . . . .   59 Nm
Speed sensor bracket bolts . . . .   10 Nm

---

1 General information

All models have hydraulically operated disc brakes, with twin discs at the front and a single disc at the rear. The front brake has twin piston sliding calipers, and the rear has a single piston sliding caliper. ABS (anti-lock brake system) was fitted as an option to all models covered in this manual.

The drive to the rear wheel is by chain and sprockets. The rear wheel hub incorporates a 'cush-drive'.

All models are fitted with cast alloy wheels designed for tubeless tyres only.

Caution: Disc brake components rarely require disassembly. Do not disassemble components unless absolutely necessary. If an hydraulic brake hose is loosened or disconnected, the union sealing washers must be replaced with new ones and the system must be bled upon reassembly. Do not use solvents on internal brake components. Solvents will cause the seals to swell and distort. Use only clean DOT 4 brake fluid. Use care when working with brake fluid as it can injure your eyes and it will damage painted surfaces and plastic parts.

2 Front brake pads

 Warning: The dust created by the brake system may contain asbestos, which is harmful to your health. Never blow it out with compressed air and don't inhale any of it. An approved filtering mask should be worn when working on the brakes.

Removal

1 Work on one caliper at a time.

2.2a Unscrew the mounting bolts (arrowed) . . .

2.2b . . . and slide the caliper off the disc

2 Unscrew the caliper mounting bolts and slide the caliper off the disc **(see illustrations)**. **Note:** *Do not operate the brake lever while the caliper is off the disc.*

3 Remove the R-clip from the pad pin and pull the pin out **(see illustrations)**.

4 Pivot the inner pad around its post and slide it off, then remove the outer pad, noting how it locates against the pad plate and tab on the caliper bracket **(see illustrations)**.

5 Note the location of the pad spring inside the caliper **(see illustration)**.

Inspection

6 Inspect the surface of each pad for contamination and check that the friction material has not worn beyond its service limit (see Chapter 1, Section 2). If any pad is worn down to, or beyond, the service limit, is fouled with oil or grease, or heavily scored or damaged, fit a complete set of new pads. **Note:** *It is not possible to degrease the friction material; if the pads are contaminated in any way they must be replaced with new ones.*

7 If the pads are in good condition clean them carefully, using a fine wire brush which is completely free of oil and grease to remove all traces of road dirt and corrosion. Using a pointed instrument, dig out any embedded particles of foreign matter. If required, spray with a dedicated brake cleaner to remove any dust.

8 Remove all traces of corrosion from the pad pin and check it for wear and damage. Renew the R-clip if it is deformed or corroded.

9 If required, spray the inside of the caliper with a dedicated brake cleaner to remove any dust. **Note:** *If the caliper bracket or pad spring are badly corroded, follow the procedure in Section 3 to disassemble the caliper and clean them.*

10 Check the condition of the brake disc (see Section 4).

2.3a Remove the R-clip . . .

2.3b . . . and pull out the pad pin

2.4a Pivot the inner pad around its post . . .

2.4b . . . and slide it off

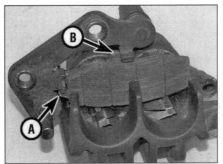

2.4c Note how the outer pad locates against the pad plate (A) and tab (B)

2.5 Location of the pad spring (arrowed)

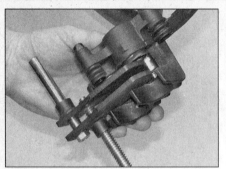

2.11 Using a piston spreader tool

3.1 Release the brake hose from the clips (arrowed)

3.2a Note the alignment of the union (arrowed) with the caliper

3.2b Note the location of the sealing washers (arrowed)

3.2c Note the arrangement of the twin brake hoses

Installation

11 If new pads are being fitted, create room for them by pushing the pistons back into the caliper with a piece of wood. If the pistons are difficult to push back, temporarily install the old pads. Insert a large flat-bladed screwdriver between the pads and lever them apart to retract the pistons. Alternatively, use a commercially available piston spreader tool **(see illustration)**. If the brake master cylinder reservoir is full, it is advisable to remove the cover, plate and diaphragm and siphon out some fluid (see *Pre-ride checks*).

12 If any piston appears seized, it will be necessary to overhaul the caliper (see Section 3).

13 Ensure the pad spring is located inside the caliper **(see illustration 2.5)**. Smear the backs of the pad backing material with copper-based grease, making sure none gets on the friction material. Also smear the pad post and pad pin.

14 Insert the pads into the caliper ensuring the friction material on each pad faces the other. Fit the outer pad first – push the tabbed end under the pad plate and press the pad back against the pistons **(see illustration 2.4c)**. Slide the inner pad onto its post then pivot it around into the caliper **(see illustrations 2.4b and a)**.

15 Press both pads down against the spring to align the holes for the pad pin with the holes in the caliper. Insert the pin and secure it with the R-clip **(see illustrations 2.3b and a)**. Ensure there is sufficient space between the pads to fit the caliper over the brake disc.

16 Slide the caliper onto the disc making sure the pads locate correctly on each side **(see illustration 2.2b)**. Fit the caliper mounting bolts and tighten them to the torque setting specified at the beginning of this Chapter **(see illustration 2.2a)**.

17 Operate the brake lever until the pads contact the disc. Check the level of fluid in the master cylinder reservoir and top-up if necessary (see *Pre-ride checks*).

18 Check the operation of the front brake before riding the motorcycle.

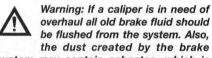

3 Front brake calipers

⚠ *Warning: If a caliper is in need of overhaul all old brake fluid should be flushed from the system. Also, the dust created by the brake system may contain asbestos, which is harmful to your health. Never blow it out with compressed air and do not inhale any of it. An approved filtering mask should be worn when working on the brakes. Overhaul of the brake caliper must be done in a spotlessly clean work area to avoid contamination and possible failure of the brake hydraulic system components. Do not, under any circumstances, use petroleum-based solvents to clean brake parts. Use clean DOT 4 brake fluid, dedicated brake cleaner or denatured alcohol only, as described. To prevent damage from spilled brake fluid, always cover paintwork when working on the braking system.*

Removal

Note: *If the caliper is being overhauled (usually due to sticking pistons or fluid leaks) read through the entire procedure first and make sure that you have obtained all the new parts required, and some new DOT 4 brake fluid.*

1 If the caliper is just being displaced, unscrew the caliper mounting bolts and slide the caliper off the disc (see Section 2). If required, release the brake hose from the clips on the front mudguard **(see illustration)**. Secure the caliper to the motorcycle with a cable-tie to avoid straining the brake hose. Note: *Do not operate the brake lever while either caliper is off the disc.*

2 If the caliper is being completely removed, note the alignment of the brake hose banjo union with the caliper **(see illustration)**. Unscrew the banjo bolt and detach the union – note the location of the sealing washers and discard them as new ones must be fitted **(see illustration)**. Note the twin hose arrangement on the right-hand side **(see illustration)**. **Note:** *If you are planning to overhaul the caliper and don't have a source of compressed air to blow out the pistons, just loosen the banjo bolt, then retighten it lightly at this stage. The brake system can be used to force the pistons out of the body once the caliper has been displaced.*

3 Wrap a small plastic bag around the banjo union and secure the hose in an upright position to minimise fluid loss.

4 Unscrew the caliper mounting bolts, slide the caliper off the disc and remove the brake pads (see Section 2).

Overhaul

5 Clean the exterior of the caliper with denatured alcohol or brake system cleaner. Have some clean rag ready to catch any spilled brake fluid.

6 Slide the caliper off its bracket **(see**

3.6a Slide the caliper off its bracket

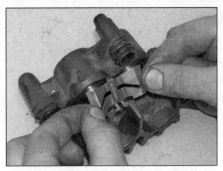

3.6b Note the location of the pad spring

3.6c Location of the pad plate (arrowed) on the caliper bracket

3.7 Check the pin boots (arrowed) for cracks and splits

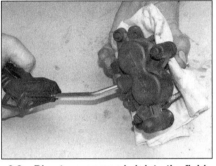

3.8a Direct compressed air into the fluid inlet

3.8b Block one piston with a piece of wood

illustration). Note the location of the pad spring inside the caliper and the pad plate on the caliper bracket and remove them if required for cleaning or renewal **(see illustrations)**.

7 Clean all traces of corrosion and hardened grease off the slider pins and examine the pin boots for cracks and splits. Replace the boots with new ones on reassembly if necessary **(see illustration)**.

8 Displace the pistons as far as possible from the caliper body, either by pumping them out by operating the brake lever, or by easing them out using compressed air. If compressed air is used, place a wad of rag inside of the caliper to act as a cushion and direct the air into the

fluid inlet on the caliper **(see illustration)**. Use only low pressure and make sure the pistons are displaced evenly, using a small piece of wood to block one while the other moves if necessary **(see illustration)**. Have some rag ready to catch any spilled brake fluid.

9 If a piston is stuck in its bore due to corrosion, the caliper should be replaced with a new one. Do not try to remove a piston by levering it out or by using pliers or grips.

10 Mark each piston and the caliper body to ensure that the pistons can be matched to their original bores on reassembly.

11 Remove the outer dust seals and inner piston seals from the caliper bores using a

soft wooden or plastic tool to avoid scratching the bores **(see illustration)**. Discard the seals as new ones must be fitted on reassembly.

12 Clean the pistons and bores with clean brake fluid. If compressed air is available, blow it through the fluid galleries in the caliper to ensure they are clear (make sure the air is filtered and unlubricated).

Caution: Do not, under any circumstances, use a petroleum-based solvent to clean brake parts.

13 Inspect the caliper bores and pistons for signs of corrosion, nicks and burrs and loss of plating **(see illustration)**. If surface defects are present, the pistons and/or the caliper must

3.11 Remove the seals carefully to avoid scratching the bores

3.13 Inspect the bores (arrowed) for damage

3.14 Install the new piston seals (A) and dust seals (B)

3.15a Install the pistons closed end first . . .

be replaced with new ones. If one caliper is in poor condition, the other front caliper and the master cylinder should also be checked.

14 Lubricate the new piston seals with clean brake fluid and fit them into their grooves in the caliper bores, then follow the same procedure to install the new dust seals **(see illustration)**.

15 Lubricate the pistons with clean brake fluid and fit them, closed-end first, into the caliper bores, taking care not to displace the seals **(see illustration)**. Using your thumbs, push the pistons all the way in, making sure they enter the bores squarely. **(see illustration)**.

16 Fit the pad spring into the caliper, ensuring it is the correct way round – the spring should be a tight fit, otherwise renew it **(see illustration 3.6b)**. Make sure the slider pin boots are secure **(see illustration 3.7)**.

17 Make sure the pad plate is located securely on the caliper bracket and lubricate the slider pins with a smear of silicone based grease **(see illustration 3.6c)**.

18 Slide the caliper onto its bracket **(see illustration 3.6a)**.

Installation

19 If removed, install the brake pads (see Section 2).

20 Slide the caliper onto the disc and tighten the mounting bolts to the torque setting specified at the beginning of this Chapter (see Section 2).

21 If removed, connect the brake hose(s) to the caliper using new sealing washers on each side of each banjo fitting – you need three washers for the two hoses on the right-hand side **(see illustration 3.2b or c)**. Align the hose(s) correctly. Tighten the banjo bolt to the specified torque setting.

22 Secure the brake hose with the clips on the front mudguard **(see illustrations 3.1)**.

23 Top-up the master cylinder reservoir with new DOT 4 brake fluid (see *Pre-ride checks*) and bleed the system as described in Section 11. Check that there are no fluid leaks.

24 Check the operation of the front brake before riding the motorcycle.

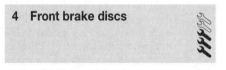

4   Front brake discs

Inspection

1 Inspect the surface of the discs for score marks and other damage. Light scratches are normal after use and won't affect brake operation, but deep grooves and heavy score marks will reduce braking efficiency and

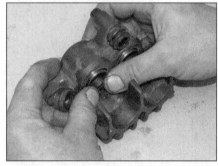

3.15b . . . and push them all the way in

accelerate pad wear. If a disc is badly grooved it must be replaced with a new one.

2 The disc must not be machined or allowed to wear down to a thickness less than the service limit listed in *Specifications* at the beginning of this Chapter. The minimum thickness is also stamped on the disc **(see illustration)**. Check the thickness of the disc with a micrometer and replace it with a new one if necessary **(see illustration)**.

3 To check if the disc is warped, position the bike on an auxiliary stand with the front wheel raised off the ground. Mount a dial gauge to the fork leg, with the gauge plunger touching the surface of the disc about 10 mm from its outer edge **(see illustration)**. Rotate the wheel

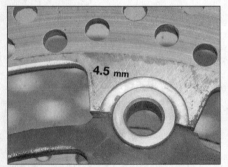

4.2a Minimum thickness is stamped on the disc

4.2b Measuring disc thickness with a micrometer

4.3 Set-up for checking brake disc runout

4.5 Front brake disc retaining bolts (arrowed)

5.2 Disconnect the front brake light switch (arrowed)

5.3 Unscrew the bolts (arrowed) and remove the back of the clamp

and watch the gauge needle, comparing the reading with the limit listed in *Specifications*. If the runout is greater than the service limit, check the wheel bearings for play (see Chapter 1). If the bearings are worn, install new ones (see Section 19) and repeat this check. If the disc runout is still excessive, a new disc will have to be fitted.

Removal

4 Remove the wheel (see Section 17).
Caution: Don't lay the wheel down and allow it to rest on the disc – the disc could become warped. Set the wheel on wood blocks so the wheel rim supports the weight of the wheel.
5 If you are not replacing the disc with a new one, mark the relationship of the disc to the wheel, so it can be installed in the same position and on the same side as originally fitted. Unscrew the disc retaining bolts, loosening them evenly and a little at a time in a criss-cross pattern to avoid distorting the disc, then remove the disc **(see illustration)**. On ABS equipped models note the sensor rotor fitted on the outside of the left-hand disc.
6 Note the location of the gasket behind the disc and discard it – a new one must be fitted.

Installation

7 Before installing the disc, make sure there is no dirt or corrosion where the disc seats on the hub. If the disc does not sit flat when it is

bolted down, it will appear to be warped when checked or when the front brake is used.
8 Fit a new gasket onto the wheel, aligning the holes. Fit the disc on the wheel with its marked side facing out, aligning the previously applied matchmarks if applicable.
9 Clean the threads of the disc mounting bolts, then apply a suitable non-permanent thread locking compound. Install the bolts and tighten them evenly and a little at a time in a criss-cross pattern to the torque setting specified at the beginning of this Chapter. Clean the disc using acetone or brake system cleaner. If a new disc has been installed, remove any protective coating from its working surfaces and fit new brake pads.
10 Install the front wheel (see Section 17).
11 Operate the brake lever several times to bring the pads into contact with the disc. Check the operation of the front brake before riding the motorcycle.

5 Front brake master cylinder

> **Warning: If the brake master cylinder is in need of overhaul all old brake fluid should be flushed from the system. Overhaul of the brake master cylinder must be done in a spotlessly clean work area to avoid contamination and possible failure of the brake hydraulic system components. Do not, under any circumstances, use**

petroleum-based solvents to clean brake parts. Use clean DOT 4 brake fluid, dedicated brake cleaner or denatured alcohol only, as described. To prevent damage from spilled brake fluid, always cover paintwork when working on the braking system.
Note: *If the master cylinder is being overhauled (usually due to sticking or poor action, or fluid leaks) read through the entire procedure first and make sure that you have obtained all the new parts required, including some new DOT 4 brake fluid.*

Removal

1 On ER650 models, remove the mirrors (see Chapter 7).
2 Disconnect the brake light switch wiring connectors **(see illustration)**.
3 If the master cylinder is just being displaced from the handlebar, make sure the fluid reservoir cover is secure. Unscrew the master cylinder clamp bolts and remove the back of the clamp, noting how it fits **(see illustration)**. Secure the master cylinder assembly clear of the handlebar and ensure no strain is placed on the brake hose. Keep the fluid reservoir upright to prevent air entering the system.
4 If the master cylinder is being overhauled, loosen, but do not remove the reservoir cover.
5 Note the alignment of the brake hose banjo union with the master cylinder **(see illustration)**. Unscrew the banjo bolt and detach the union – note the location of the sealing washers and discard them as new ones must be fitted **(see illustration)**.
6 Wrap a small plastic bag around the banjo union and secure the hose in an upright position to minimise fluid loss.
7 Unscrew the master cylinder clamp bolts and remove the back of the clamp, noting how it fits **(see illustration 5.3)**. Lift the master cylinder assembly off the handlebar
8 Undo the reservoir cover screws and remove the cover, diaphragm plate and the diaphragm (see *Pre-ride checks*). Drain the brake fluid from the reservoir into a suitable container. Wipe out any remaining fluid with a clean rag.
9 Undo the brake lever pivot screw locknut

5.5a Note the alignment of the brake hose banjo union (arrowed)

5.5b Note the location of the sealing washers (arrowed)

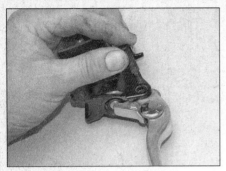

5.9a Undo the pivot screw . . .

5.9b . . . and remove the brake lever

5.9c Screw (arrowed) secures brake light switch

5.10 Pull off the dust boot

5.11a Remove the circlip . . .

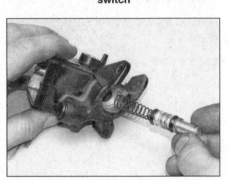

5.11b . . . then draw out the piston assembly and spring

on the underside of the lever, then undo the pivot screw and remove the lever **(see illustrations)**. If required, undo the screw

securing the brake light switch to the bottom of the master cylinder and remove the switch **(see illustration)**.

5.14 Front brake master cylinder rebuild kit

1 Dust boot
2 Circlip
3 Piston
4 Spring
5 Primary seal
6 Secondary seal

Overhaul

10 Remove the rubber boot from the master cylinder piston **(see illustration)**.

11 Depress the piston and use circlip pliers to remove the circlip, then slide out the piston assembly and the spring, noting how they fit **(see illustrations)**. If the piston is difficult to remove, apply low pressure compressed air to the brake fluid outlet. Lay the parts out in the proper order to prevent confusion during reassembly.

12 Clean the inside of the master cylinder and reservoir with clean brake fluid. If compressed air is available, blow it through the fluid galleries to ensure they are clear (make sure the air is filtered and unlubricated).

Caution: Do not, under any circumstances, use a petroleum-based solvent to clean brake parts.

13 Check the master cylinder bore for corrosion, scratches, nicks and score marks. If damage or wear is evident, the master cylinder must be replaced with a new one. If the master cylinder is in poor condition, then the calipers should be checked as well.

14 The dust boot, circlip, piston and its seals, and the spring, are all included in the master cylinder rebuild kit **(see illustration)**. Use all of the new parts, regardless of the apparent condition of the old ones.

15 If the seals are not fitted to the piston, first lubricate them with clean brake fluid. Ease the thinner secondary seal into its groove in the middle of the piston, wide end first **(see illustrations)**. Now ease the thicker primary seal into its groove in the inner end of the

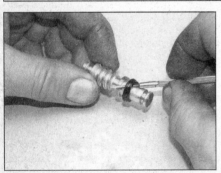

5.15a Install the secondary seal . . .

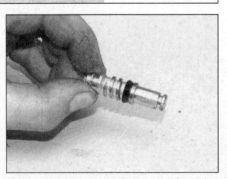

5.15b . . . in its groove in the middle of the piston

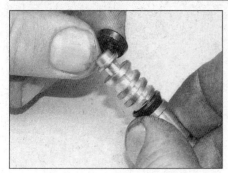

5.15c Install the primary seal . . .

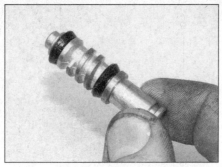

5.15d . . . in its groove in the end of the piston

5.18 Installation of the boot around the outer end (arrowed) of the piston

piston, narrow end first (see illustrations). Note: *When the piston is inserted into the master cylinder, the wider ends of the seals should go in first.*

16 Lubricate the master cylinder bore and the piston assembly with brake fluid. Fit the narrow end of the spring onto the piston, then carefully slide the assembly into the master cylinder (see illustration 5.11b).

17 Push the piston all the way in, compressing the spring, and fit the new circlip, making sure it locates properly in its groove (see illustration 5.11a).

18 Smear the inside of the rubber boot with silicone grease, fit it over the end of the piston and press the wide rim into the master cylinder against the circlip (see illustration 5.10). The outer rim of the boot should locate in the groove in the outer end of the piston (see illustration).

19 Inspect the fluid reservoir diaphragm and fit a new one if it is damaged or deteriorated.

Installation

20 If removed, fit the brake light switch onto the bottom of the master cylinder and tighten the screw securely (see illustration 5.9c). Install the brake lever and secure it with the pivot bolt, then tighten the pivot bolt locknut securely.

21 Attach the master cylinder to the handlebar, fit the back of the clamp with its UP mark facing up and align the clamp joint with the punch mark on the top of the handlebar (see illustration). Tighten the upper clamp bolt to the torque setting specified at the beginning of this Chapter, followed by the lower bolt so that any gap is at the bottom of the clamp joint.

22 Connect the brake hose to the master

cylinder, using new sealing washers on both sides of the banjo union (see illustration 5.5b). Align the hose as noted on removal, then tighten the banjo bolt to the specified torque setting.

23 Connect the brake light switch wiring connectors (see illustration 5.2). If applicable, fit the mirrors (see chapter 7).

24 Fill the fluid reservoir with new DOT 4 brake fluid (see *Pre-ride checks*) and bleed the system as described in Section 11. Check that there are no fluid leaks.

25 Check the operation of the front brake before riding the motorcycle.

6 Rear brake pads

⚠ Warning: The dust created by the brake system may contain asbestos, which is harmful to your health. Never blow it out with compressed air and don't inhale any of it. An approved filtering mask should be worn when working on the brakes.

Removal

1 Unscrew the caliper mounting bolts and slide the caliper off the disc (see illustration). Note: *Do not operate the brake pedal while the caliper is off the disc.*

2 Remove the R-clip from the pad pin and pull the pin out (see illustrations).

3 Pivot the inner pad around its post and slide

5.21 Align the clamp joint with the punch mark (arrowed)

6.1 Unscrew the caliper mounting bolts (arrowed)

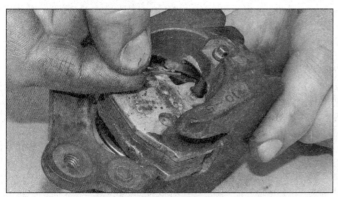

6.2a Remove the R-clip . . .

6.2b . . . and pull out the pad pin

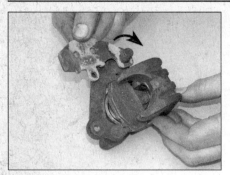

6.3a Pivot the inner pad around its post

6.3b Note how the outer pad locates against the pad plate (A) and tab (B)

6.4 Location of the pad spring (arrowed)

it off, then remove the outer pad, noting how it locates against the pad plate and tab on the caliper bracket **(see illustrations)**.

4 Note the location of the pad spring inside the caliper **(see illustration)**.

Inspection

5 Inspect the surface of each pad for contamination and check that the friction material has not worn beyond its service limit (see Chapter 1, Section 2). If any pad is worn down to, or beyond, the service limit, is fouled with oil or grease, or heavily scored or damaged, fit a set of new pads. **Note:** *It is not possible to degrease the friction material; if the pads are contaminated in any way they must be replaced with new ones.*

6 If the pads are in good condition clean them carefully, using a fine wire brush which is completely free of oil and grease to remove all traces of road dirt and corrosion. Using a pointed instrument, dig out any embedded particles of foreign matter. If required, spray with a dedicated brake cleaner to remove any dust.

7 Remove all traces of corrosion from the pad pin and check it for wear and damage. Renew the R-clip if it is deformed or corroded.

8 If required, spray the inside of the caliper with a dedicated brake cleaner to remove any dust. **Note:** *If the caliper bracket or pad spring are badly corroded, follow the procedure in Section 7 to disassemble the caliper and clean them.*

9 Check the condition of the brake disc (see Section 8).

6.14a Align the holes for the pad pin

Installation

10 If new pads are being fitted, create room for them by pushing the piston back into the caliper with a piece of wood. If the piston is difficult to push back, temporarily install the old pads. Insert a large flat-bladed screwdriver between the pads and lever them apart to retract the piston. Alternatively, use a commercially available piston spreader tool **(see illustration 2.11)**. If the brake master cylinder reservoir is full, it is advisable to remove the cap, plate and diaphragm and siphon out some fluid (see *Pre-ride checks*).

11 If the piston appears seized, it will be necessary to overhaul the caliper (see Section 7).

12 Ensure the pad spring is located inside the caliper **(see illustration 6.4)**. Smear the backs of the pad backing material with copper-based grease, making sure none gets on the friction material. Also smear the pad post and pad pin.

13 Insert the pads into the caliper ensuring the friction material on each pad faces the other. Fit the outer pad first – push the tabbed end against the pad plate, press the pad into the caliper against the pad spring and back against the piston so that the tab on its lower edge locates against the tab on the caliper bracket **(see illustration 6.3b)**. Slide the inner pad onto its post then pivot it around into the caliper **(see illustration 6.3a)**.

14 Press both pads down against the spring to align the holes for the pad pin with the holes in the caliper **(see illustration)**. Insert the pin and secure it with the R-clip **(see illustrations**

6.14b Allow space between the pads for the brake disc

6.2b and a). Ensure there is sufficient space between the pads to fit the caliper over the brake disc **(see illustration)**.

15 Slide the caliper onto the disc making sure the pads locate correctly on each side. Fit the caliper mounting bolts and tighten them to the torque setting specified at the beginning of this Chapter **(see illustration 6.1)**.

16 Operate the brake pedal until the pads contact the disc. Check the level of fluid in the master cylinder reservoir and top-up if necessary (see *Pre-ride checks*).

17 Check the operation of the rear brake before riding the motorcycle.

7 Rear brake caliper

 Warning: If a caliper is in need of overhaul all old brake fluid should be flushed from the system. Also, the dust created by the brake system may contain asbestos, which is harmful to your health. Never blow it out with compressed air and do not inhale any of it. An approved filtering mask should be worn when working on the brakes. Overhaul must be done in a spotlessly clean work area to avoid contamination and possible failure of the brake hydraulic system components. Do not, under any circumstances, use petroleum-based solvents to clean brake parts. Use clean DOT 4 brake fluid, dedicated brake cleaner or denatured alcohol only, as described. To prevent damage from spilled brake fluid, always cover paintwork when working on the braking system.

Removal

Note: *If the caliper is being overhauled (usually due to a sticking piston or fluid leak) read through the entire procedure first and make sure that you have obtained all the new parts required, including some new DOT 4 brake fluid.*

1 If the caliper is just being displaced, unscrew the caliper mounting bolts and slide the caliper off the disc (see Section 6). Secure the caliper to the motorcycle with a cable-tie

7.2a Note the alignment of the union (arrowed) with the caliper

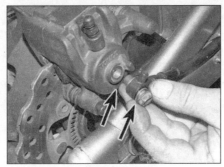

7.2b Note the location of the sealing washers (arrowed)

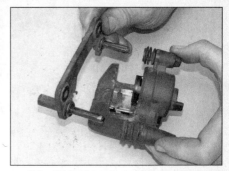

7.6a Slide the caliper off its bracket

to avoid straining the brake hose. **Note:** *Do not operate the brake pedal while either caliper is off the disc.*

2 If the caliper is being completely removed, note the alignment of the brake hose banjo union with the caliper **(see illustration)**. Unscrew the banjo bolt and detach the union – note the location of the sealing washers and discard them as new ones must be fitted **(see illustration)**.

3 Wrap a small plastic bag around the banjo union and secure the hose in an upright position to minimise fluid loss – if required, feed the hose back through the guides on the swingarm.

4 Unscrew the caliper mounting bolts, slide the caliper off the disc and remove the brake pads (see Section 6).

Overhaul

5 Clean the exterior of the caliper with denatured alcohol or brake system cleaner. Have some clean rag ready to catch any spilled brake fluid.

6 Slide the caliper off its bracket **(see illustration)**. Withdraw the insert from the piston **(see illustration)**. Note the location of the pad spring inside the caliper and the pad plate on the caliper bracket and remove them if required for cleaning or renewal **(see illustrations)**.

7 Clean all traces of corrosion and hardened grease off the slider pins and examine the pin boots for cracks and splits. Replace the boots with new ones on reassembly if necessary **(see illustration)**.

8 Place a wad of rag inside the caliper to act

as a cushion and to catch any spilled brake fluid, then insert a suitable drift into the fluid inlet and press the piston out by hand **(see illustration)**. If the piston sticks in its bore due to corrosion, the caliper should be replaced with a new one. Do not try to remove the piston by driving it out or by using pliers or grips.

9 Remove the outer dust seal and inner piston seal from the piston bore using a soft wooden or plastic tool to avoid scratching the bore **(see illustration)**. Discard the seals as new ones must be fitted on reassembly.

10 Clean the piston and bore with clean brake fluid. If compressed air is available, blow it through the fluid passages in the caliper to ensure they are clear (make sure the air is filtered and unlubricated).

7.6b Remove the piston insert

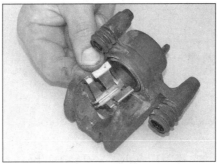

7.6c Note the location of the pad spring

7.6d Location of the pad plate (arrowed) on the caliper bracket

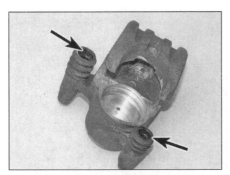

7.7 Check the pin boots (arrowed) for cracks and splits

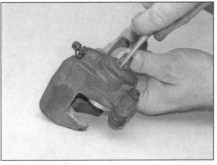

7.8 Press the piston out of the caliper

7.9 Remove the seals carefully to avoid scratching the bore

7.11 Inspect the bore (arrowed) for damage

7.12 Install the new piston seal and dust seal

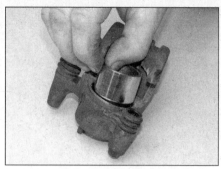

7.13a Install the piston closed end first . . .

Caution: Do not, under any circumstances, use a petroleum-based solvent to clean brake parts.

11 Inspect the caliper bore and piston for signs of corrosion, nicks and burrs and loss of plating **(see illustration)**. If surface defects are present, the piston and/or the caliper must be replaced with new ones. If the caliper is in poor condition, the master cylinder should also be checked.

12 Lubricate the new piston seal with clean brake fluid and fit it into its groove in the caliper bore, then follow the same procedure to install the new dust seal **(see illustration)**.

13 Lubricate the piston with clean brake fluid and fit it, closed-end first, into the caliper bore, taking care not to displace the seals **(see illustration)**. Using your thumbs, push the piston all the way in, making sure it enters the bore squarely **(see illustration)**.

14 Fit the pad spring into the caliper, ensuring it is the correct way round – the spring should be a tight fit, otherwise renew it **(see illustration 7.6c)**. Make sure the slider pin boots are secure. Fit the insert into the piston **(see illustration 7.6b)**.

15 Make sure the pad plate is located securely on the caliper bracket and lubricate the slider pins with a smear of silicone based grease **(see illustration 7.6d)**.

16 Slide the caliper onto its bracket **(see illustration 7.6a)**.

Installation

17 If removed, install the brake pads (see Section 6).

18 Slide the caliper onto the disc and tighten the mounting bolts to the torque setting specified at the beginning of this Chapter **(see illustration)**.

19 If removed, connect the brake hose to the caliper using new sealing washers on each side of each banjo fitting **(see illustration 7.2b)**. Ensure the hose is routed through the guides on the swingarm. Align the hose correctly, then tighten the banjo bolt to the specified torque setting.

20 Top-up the master cylinder reservoir with new DOT 4 brake fluid (see *Pre-ride checks*) and bleed the system as described in Section 11. Check that there are no fluid leaks.

21 Check the operation of the rear brake before riding the motorcycle.

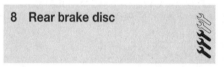

8 Rear brake disc

Inspection

1 Refer to Section 4 of this Chapter. On the machine used to illustrate this procedure, the disc minimum thickness was cast into the wheel hub. When checking disc runout, the dial gauge should be attached to the swingarm.

Removal

2 Remove the rear wheel (see Section 16).
Caution: Don't lay the wheel down and allow it to rest on the disc or sprocket – they could become warped. Set the wheel

on wood blocks so the wheel rim supports the weight of the wheel.

3 If you are not replacing the disc with a new one, mark the relationship of the disc to the wheel so it can be installed in the same position. Unscrew the disc retaining bolts, loosening them evenly and a little at a time in a criss-cross pattern to avoid distorting the disc, then remove the disc – on ABS equipped models note the sensor rotor fitted on the outside of the disc **(see illustration)**.

4 Note the location of the gasket behind the disc and discard it – a new one must be fitted.

Installation

5 Before installing the disc, make sure there is no dirt or corrosion where the disc seats on the hub. If the disc does not sit flat when it is bolted down, it will appear to be warped when checked or when the rear brake is used.

6 Fit a new gasket onto the wheel, aligning the holes. Fit the disc on the wheel with its marked side facing out, aligning the previously applied matchmarks if applicable – on ABS models the sensor rotor should be facing out.

7 Clean the threads of the disc mounting bolts, then apply a suitable non-permanent thread locking compound. Install the bolts and tighten them evenly and a little at a time in a criss-cross pattern to the torque setting specified at the beginning of this Chapter. Clean the disc using acetone or brake system cleaner. If a new disc has been installed, remove any protective coating from its working surfaces and fit new brake pads.

7.13b . . . and push it all the way in

7.18 Install the caliper and tighten the bolts to the specified torque

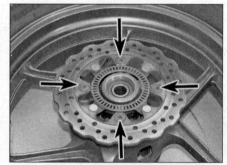

8.3 Rear brake disc retaining bolts (arrowed)

Brakes, wheels and final drive 6•13

9.1a Remove the split pin (arrowed) . . .

9.1b . . . securing the clevis pin . . .

9.1c . . . then withdraw the clevis pin from the end of the pushrod

8 Install the rear wheel (see Section 16).
9 Operate the brake pedal several times to bring the pads into contact with the disc. Check the operation of the rear brake before riding the motorcycle.

9 Rear brake master cylinder

⚠️ **Warning: If the brake master cylinder is in need of overhaul all old brake fluid should be flushed from the system. Overhaul must be done in a spotlessly clean work area to avoid contamination and possible failure of the brake hydraulic system components. Do not, under any circumstances, use petroleum-based solvents to clean brake parts. Use clean DOT 4 brake fluid, dedicated brake cleaner or denatured alcohol only, as described. To prevent damage from spilled brake fluid, always cover paintwork when working on the braking system.**

Note: *If the master cylinder is being overhauled (usually due to sticking or poor action, or fluid leaks) read through the entire procedure first and make sure that you have obtained all the new parts required, including some new DOT 4 brake fluid.*

Removal

1 Remove the split pin securing the rear brake

9.2a Undo the bolts (arrowed) . . .

9.2b . . . and displace the master cylinder

pedal clevis pin, then remove the clevis pin and separate the brake pedal from the master cylinder pushrod **(see illustrations)**.
2 Undo the bolts securing the rear brake master cylinder and displace the master cylinder **(see illustrations)**. If the master cylinder is just being displaced, secure it with a cable tie to ensure no strain is placed on the brake hose.
3 If the master cylinder is being removed completely, remove the seat (see Chapter 7).
4 Remove the brake fluid reservoir cap, diaphragm plate and diaphragm (see *Pre-ride checks*).
5 Release the clip securing the reservoir hose to the union on the master cylinder, detach the hose and drain the brake fluid into a suitable container **(see illustration)**. Wrap some rag around the end of the hose

to catch any residual brake fluid. Wipe any remaining fluid out of the reservoir with a clean rag.
6 Note the alignment of the brake hose banjo union with the master cylinder, then undo the banjo bolt and detach the union **(see illustration)**. If required, thread a suitable bolt into one of the master cylinder mountings to make it easier to hold. Note the location of the sealing washers and discard them as new ones must be fitted
7 Wrap a small plastic bag around the banjo union and secure the hose in an upright position to minimise fluid loss.
8 Remove the right-hand fuel tank side panel (see Chapter 7). Undo the bolt securing the fluid reservoir and lift the reservoir out, noting the routing of the reservoir hose **(see illustration)**.

9.5 Detach the reservoir hose (arrowed)

9.6 Undo the banjo bolt noting the sealing washers (arrowed)

9.8 Bolt (arrowed) secures brake fluid reservoir

9.10a Remove the circlip . . .

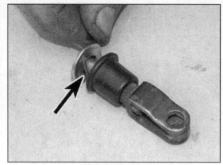

9.10b . . . and remove the pushrod assembly. Note the circlip (arrowed)

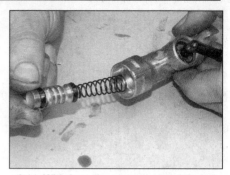

9.11 Withdraw the piston assembly and spring

9.12a Remove the circlip . . .

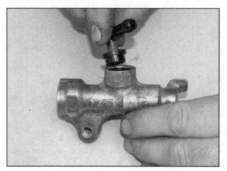

9.12b . . . and lift out the fluid reservoir hose union . . .

9.12c . . . noting the location of the O-ring

Overhaul

9 Pull back the rubber boot on the master cylinder pushrod.

10 Depress the pushrod and use circlip pliers to remove the circlip, then remove the pushrod assembly **(see illustrations)**.

11 Withdraw the piston assembly and spring, noting how they fit **(see illustration)**. If the piston is difficult to remove, apply low pressure compressed air to the brake fluid outlet. Lay the parts out in the proper order to prevent confusion during reassembly.

12 If required, remove the circlip securing the fluid reservoir hose union and detach it from the master cylinder **(see illustrations)**. Discard the O-ring as a new one must be

used. Inspect the reservoir hose for cracks or splits and replace it with a new one if necessary.

13 Clean the inside of the master cylinder and reservoir with clean brake fluid. If compressed air is available, blow it through the fluid galleries to ensure they are clear (make sure the air is filtered and unlubricated).

Caution: Do not, under any circumstances, use a petroleum-based solvent to clean brake parts.

14 Check the master cylinder bore for corrosion, scratches, nicks and score marks. If damage or wear is evident, the master cylinder must be replaced with a new one. If the master cylinder is in poor condition, then the caliper should be checked as well.

15 The piston, its seals and the spring are

all included in the master cylinder rebuild kit **(see illustration)**. Use all of the new parts, regardless of the apparent condition of the old ones.

16 The pushrod assembly and rubber boot are also available as a set if required, and the circlip is available separately **(see illustration 9.10b)**.

17 If the seals are not fitted to the piston, first lubricate them with clean brake fluid. Ease the thinner secondary seal into its groove in the outer end of the piston, wide end first **(see illustration)**. Now ease the thicker primary seal into its groove in the inner end of the piston, narrow end first **(see illustration)**. **Note:** *When the piston is inserted into the master cylinder, the wider ends of the seals should go in first.*

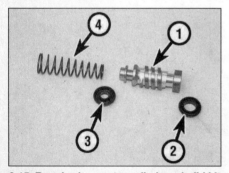

9.15 Rear brake master cylinder rebuild kit

1 Piston
2 Secondary seal
3 Primary seal
4 Spring

9.17a Install the secondary seal wide end first

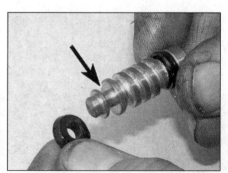

9.17b Install the primary seal into its groove (arrowed)

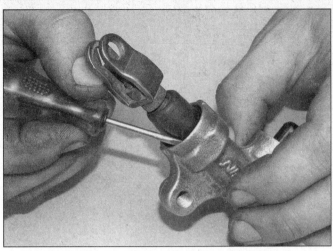

9.21 Ensure the rubber boot is correctly installed

9.28 Bend the ends of the split pin (arrowed) around the clevis pin

18 Lubricate the master cylinder bore and the piston assembly with brake fluid. Fit the narrow end of the spring onto the piston, then carefully slide the assembly into the master cylinder **(see illustrations 9.11)**. Push the piston all the way in.

19 Fit a new circlip onto the pushrod assembly and smear the pushrod and the inside of the rubber boot with silicone grease.

20 Press the pushrod down onto the piston, compressing the spring, until the washer on the pushrod is below the circlip groove inside the master cylinder. Fit the circlip into the groove, making sure it locates properly **(see illustration 9.10a)**.

21 Press the wide rim of the rubber boot into the master cylinder against the circlip **(see illustration)**.

22 If removed, fit a new fluid reservoir hose union O-ring smeared with brake fluid, then press the union into the master cylinder and secure it with the circlip.

23 Inspect the fluid reservoir diaphragm and fit a new one if it is damaged or deteriorated.

Installation

24 If removed, install the fluid reservoir. Ensure the hose is secured with its clip – fit a new clip if the old one is corroded.

25 Connect the brake hose to the master cylinder, using new sealing washers on each side of the banjo union **(see illustration 9.6)**. Align the hose as noted on removal, then tighten the banjo bolt to the torque setting specified at the beginning of this Chapter.

26 Connect the reservoir hose to its union on the master cylinder and secure it with the clip – fit a new clip if necessary **(see illustration 9.5)**.

27 Locate the master cylinder on the inside of the footrest bracket and tighten the mounting bolts to the torque setting specified at the beginning of this Chapter **(see illustration 9.2a)**.

28 Lubricate the clevis pin with grease. Align the clevis on the master cylinder pushrod with

the brake pedal, then insert the clevis pin and secure it with a new split pin, bending the ends as shown see illustration).

29 Fill the fluid reservoir with new DOT 4 brake fluid (see *Pre-ride checks*) and bleed the system as described in Section 11. Check that there are no fluid leaks.

30 Check the brake pedal height (see Chapter 1, Section 2).

31 Check the operation of the rear brake before riding the motorcycle.

10 Brake hoses, pipes and fittings

Inspection

1 Brake hose condition should be checked regularly and the hoses replaced with new ones at the specified interval (see Chapter 1).

2 Twist and flex the hoses while looking for cracks, bulges and seeping brake fluid. Check extra carefully around the areas where the hoses connect with the banjo unions, as these are common areas for hose failure.

3 Inspect the banjo unions – if they are rusted, scratched or cracked, fit new hoses.

4 On models with ABS remove the fuel tank (see Chapter 4) and check the brake pipes, the pipe joints and the ABS control unit for signs of fluid leakage and for any dents or cracks in the pipes (see Section 14).

5 Inspect the pipe joints – if they are rusted, fit new pipes.

Removal and installation

6 Most brake hoses have banjo unions on both ends. Cover the surrounding area with plenty of rags and unscrew the banjo bolt at each end of the hose, noting the alignment of the union with the master cylinder or brake caliper **(see illustrations 5.5a and 7.2a)**. Free the hose from any clips or guides and remove it, noting its routing. Discard the sealing

washers. **Note:** *Do not operate the brake lever or pedal while a brake hose is disconnected.*

7 Position the new hose, making sure it isn't twisted or otherwise strained, and ensure that it is correctly routed through any clips or guides and is clear of all moving components.

8 Check that the unions align correctly, then install the banjo bolts, using new sealing washers on both sides of the unions **(see illustration 5.5b and 7.2b)**. Tighten the banjo bolts to the torque setting specified at the beginning of this Chapter.

9 On models with ABS, some of the hoses join to pipes that connect the system components to the ABS control unit. The joints between the hoses and pipes, and where the pipes connect to the hydraulic unit are held by gland nuts (see Section 14).

10 Where applicable, hold the joint to prevent it twisting, then unscrew the gland nut to separate the hose or pipe from the union, or to detach a pipe from the control unit. There are no sealing washers.

11 When refitting them, tighten the nuts to the specified torque setting if the correct tools are available.

12 Flush the old brake fluid from the system, refill with new DOT 4 brake fluid (see *Pre-ride checks*) and bleed the air from the system (see Section 11).

13 Check the operation of the brakes before riding the motorcycle.

11 Brake system bleeding and fluid change

Bleeding

1 Bleeding the brakes is simply the process of removing air from the brake fluid reservoir, the hose and the brake caliper. Bleeding is necessary whenever a brake system hydraulic connection is loosened, after a component or hose is replaced with a new one, or when the

11.2a Set-up for bleeding the front brake

11.2b Set-up for bleeding the rear brake

master cylinder or caliper is overhauled. Leaks in the system may also allow air to enter, but leaking brake fluid will reveal their presence and warn you of the need for repair.

2 To bleed the brakes, you will need some new DOT 4 brake fluid, a length of clear vinyl or plastic hose, a small container partially filled with clean brake fluid, some rags and a spanner to fit the brake caliper bleed valve **(see illustrations)**. **Note:** *If bleeding the system using the conventional method*

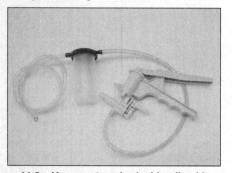

11.2c Vacuum-type brake bleeding kit

described does not work sufficiently well, use a vacuum-type brake bleeding kit **(see illustration)**. *Follow the manufacturer's instructions for using the kit. It is particularly important to ensure that the hose is a tight fit on the bleed valve and doesn't allow air to be draw in around the bleed valve head.*

3 Cover painted components to prevent damage in the event that brake fluid is spilled.
4 Refer to 'Pre-ride checks' at the beginning of the manual and remove the reservoir cover or cap, diaphragm plate and diaphragm, and slowly pump the brake lever (front brake) or pedal (rear brake) a few times, until no air bubbles can be seen floating up from the holes in the bottom of the reservoir. This bleeds the air from the master cylinder end of the line. Temporarily refit the reservoir cover or cap.
5 Pull the dust cap off the bleed valve **(see illustration)**. Attach one end of the clear hose to the bleed valve and submerge the other end in the clean brake fluid in the container **(see illustration 11.2a or b)**. **Note:** *To avoid damaging the bleed valve during the procedure, loosen it and then*

tighten it temporarily with a ring spanner before attaching the hose. With the hose attached, the valve can then be opened and closed either with an open-ended spanner, or by leaving the ring spanner located on the valve and fitting the hose above it **(see illustration)**.
6 When bleeding the front brakes, bleed the right-hand caliper first.
7 Check the fluid level in the reservoir. Do not allow the fluid level to drop below the lower mark during the procedure.
8 Carefully pump the brake lever or pedal three or four times, then hold it in (front) or down (rear) and open the bleed valve. When the valve is opened, brake fluid will flow out of the caliper into the clear hose, and the lever will move toward the handlebar, or the pedal will move down. If there is air in the system there will be air bubbles in the brake fluid coming out of the caliper.
9 Tighten the bleed valve, then release the brake lever or pedal gradually. Top-up the reservoir and repeat the process until no air bubbles are visible in the brake fluid leaving

11.5a Remove the bleed valve dust cap

11.5b Using a ring spanner to open and close the bleed valve

11.9 Look for air bubbles in the brake fluid

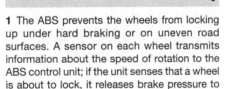

12.5 Location of the grey ABS self-diagnosis terminal (arrowed)

the caliper, and the lever or pedal is firm when applied **(see illustration)**. On completion, disconnect the hose, then tighten the bleed valve to the torque setting specified at the beginning of this Chapter and install the dust cap.

HAYNES HINT *If it is not possible to produce a firm feel to the lever or pedal, the fluid may be aerated. Let the brake fluid in the system stabilise for a few hours and then repeat the procedure when the tiny bubbles in the system have settled out.*

10 Top-up the reservoir, then install the diaphragm, diaphragm plate, and cover/cap (see *Pre-ride checks*). Wipe up any spilled brake fluid. Check the entire system for fluid leaks.
11 Check the operation of the brakes before riding the motorcycle.

Fluid change

12 Changing the brake fluid is a similar process to bleeding the brakes and requires the same materials plus a suitable tool for siphoning the fluid out of the reservoir. Also ensure that the container is large enough to take all the old fluid when it is flushed out of the system.
13 Follow Steps 3 and 5, then remove the reservoir cover/cap, diaphragm plate and diaphragm and siphon the old fluid out of the reservoir. Fill the reservoir with new brake fluid, then carefully pump the brake lever or pedal three or four times and hold it in (front) or down (rear) while opening the caliper bleed valve. When the valve is opened, brake fluid will flow out of the caliper into the clear hose, and the lever will move toward the handlebar, or the pedal will move down.
14 Tighten the bleed valve, then release the brake lever or pedal gradually. Keep the

HAYNES HINT *Old brake fluid is invariably much darker in colour than new fluid, making it easy to see when all old fluid has been expelled from the system.*

reservoir topped-up with new fluid to above the LOWER level at all times or air may enter the system and greatly increase the length of the task. Repeat the process until new fluid can be seen emerging from the caliper bleed valve.
15 Disconnect the hose, then make sure the bleed valve is tightened to the specified torque setting and install the dust cap.
16 Top-up the reservoir, then install the diaphragm, diaphragm plate, and cover/cap (see *Pre-ride checks*). Wipe up any spilled brake fluid. Check the entire system for fluid leaks.
17 Check the operation of the brakes before riding the motorcycle.

12 ABS fault finding

1 The ABS prevents the wheels from locking up under hard braking or on uneven road surfaces. A sensor on each wheel transmits information about the speed of rotation to the ABS control unit; if the unit senses that a wheel is about to lock, it releases brake pressure to that wheel momentarily, preventing a skid.
2 The ABS is self-checking and is activated when the ignition (main) switch is turned on – the ABS indicator light in the instrument cluster will come on and will remain on until road speed increases above 3 mph (5 kph) at which point, if the ABS is normal, the light will go off. **Note:** *If the ABS indicator light does not come on initially there is a fault in the system - see Section 13).*
3 If the indicator light remains on, or comes on while the machine is being ridden, there is a fault in the system and the ABS function will be switched off – the brakes will still operate but take extra care when using them. **Note:** *The ABS control unit may diagnose a fault if tyre sizes other than those specified by Kawasaki are fitted, if the tyre pressures are incorrect or if the machine has been run continuously over bumpy roads. A fault may also be diagnosed if the front wheel is lifted off the ground under acceleration or if the rear wheel turns while the engine is running with the machine on an auxilliary stand. Under these circumstances,*

stop the bike and turn the ignition OFF, then restart and ride the bike – the indicator light may not come on again. If it does, the fault code must be erased as described below.
4 If a fault is indicated, details will be stored as a code in the control unit memory. To access the fault codes, first remove the seat (see Chapter 7).
5 Ensure the ignition (main) switch is OFF. Identify the ABS self-diagnosis (grey wire) terminal behind the right-hand seat cowling **(see illustration)**. Using an insulated jumper wire, temporarily connect the self-diagnosis terminal to the battery negative (-ve) terminal.
6 Turn the ignition (main) switch ON. The ABS indicator light will come on initially for approximately 2 seconds, then go off for approximately 3 seconds. It will then display the fault code in a series of flashes.
7 All fault codes are represented by two-digit numbers (see Section 13). The 'tens' are represented by a series of 0.6 second flashes, the 'ones' are represented by a series of 0.3 second flashes. There is a delay of 0.9 seconds between the 'tens' and the 'ones' . Eg. fault code 14 will appear as 0.6 second flash followed by a 0.9 second delay followed by four 0.3 second flashes. The fault code will be repeated after a further 3.3 second delay.
8 If there is more than one fault, the flashes will appear in groups in ascending order, with a 3.3 second delay between each group. Note that the start code 12 appears at the beginning of each group of codes. If only start code 12 is displayed there is no fault with the ABS.
9 Up to six fault codes can be stored in the control unit memory. If there are further faults, they will be displayed after the first six have been corrected and the codes deleted. The codes cannot be deleted by switching the ignition OFF or disconnecting the battery or ABS control unit.
10 Record the code(s) and identify the fault(s) from the table in Section 13. Turn the ignition (main) switch OFF.
11 Once the faults have been corrected, reset the control unit memory to delete the old fault codes as follows.
12 Ensure that the ignition (main) switch is OFF and that the ABS self-diagnosis terminal is connected to the battery negative (-ve) terminal (see Step 5).
13 Turn the ignition (main) switch ON. The ABS indicator light will flash twice and then stay on – disconnect the self diagnosis terminal, then connect and disconnect it at least three times in a series of one second intervals. Turn the ignition (main) switch OFF.
14 Follow the procedure in Steps 5 and 6 to confirm that the old fault codes have been deleted – if so, only start code 12 will be displayed. Turn the ignition (main) switch OFF. Disconnect the jumper wire from the battery negative (-ve) terminal and the ABS self-diagnosis terminal. Install the seat (see Chapter 7).
15 Check that the ABS is operating normally (see Step 2).

13 ABS system checks

1 If a fault is indicated in the ABS, first check that the battery is fully charged, then check the ignition 10A fuse in the main fusebox (see Chapter 8).

2 Unless specified otherwise, carry-out all checks with the ignition (main) switch OFF.

3 Refer to Chapter 8, Section 2, for general fault finding procedures and equipment.

4 If, after a thorough check, the source of a fault has not been identified, have the ABS control unit tested by a Kawasaki dealer.

ABS indicator light does not come on

5 On ER650 models, remove the front fairing (see Chapter 7) and the instrument cover (see Chapter 8) to access the connector. Displace the rubber boot on the connector **(see illustrations)**. On EX650 models, remove the windshield and the cockpit trim panels to access the instrument cluster wiring connector (see Chapter 7).

6 Turn the ignition ON. Backprobe the orange/black and black/yellow wire terminals in the connector and test for voltage – there should be approximately 9 volts. If there is voltage it is likely the instrument cluster is faulty – have it tested by a Kawasaki dealer. Turn the ignition OFF.

7 If the voltage is outside the specification, disconnect the instrument cluster wiring connector. Remove the battery carrier (see Chapter 8) to gain access to the ABS control unit wiring connector **(see illustration)**. Make sure the ignition is OFF, then lift the catch on the wiring connector and disconnect it **(see illustrations)**.

8 Check for continuity between the orange/black wire terminal in the instrument cluster wiring connector and the orange/black wire terminal 12 in the ABS control unit connector **(see illustration)**. If there is no continuity, inspect the wire for damage and renew or repair the loom.

9 If there is continuity, connect the ABS control unit wiring connector, then identify the Kawasaki multi-pin self-diagnosis system

Fault code/flashes	Faulty component - symptoms	Possible causes
Light does not come on	No voltage at instrument cluster No voltage at control unit	Faulty instrument cluster Faulty wiring or wiring connector Faulty control unit
Light stays on continuously	No voltage at intrument cluster ABS wiring harness No voltage at control unit	Faulty instrument cluster Faulty wiring or wiring connector Faulty control unit
12	Start code	No fault
13	Rear inlet solenoid valve	Faulty control unit
14	Rear outlet solenoid valve	Faulty control unit
17	Front inlet solenoid valve	Faulty control unit
18	Front outlet solenoid valve	Faulty control unit
19	ABS solenoid valve relay	Damaged fuse Faulty control unit Faulty wiring or wiring connector
25	Front or rear tyre Front or rear wheel Front or rear wheel speed sensor	Incorrect tyre size/tyre pressure Damaged wheel Damaged rotor
35	ABS pump motor relay	Damaged fuse Faulty control unit Faulty wiring or wiring connector
42	Front wheel speed sensor	Dirty or damaged sensor Damaged rotor Faulty control unit
43	Front wheel speed sensor wiring Front wheel speed sensor	Faulty wiring or wiring connector Damaged sensor Faulty control unit
44	Rear wheel speed sensor	Dirty or damaged sensor Damaged rotor Faulty control unit
45	Rear wheel speed sensor wiring Rear wheel speed sensor	Faulty wiring or wiring connector Damaged sensor Faulty control unit
52	Power supply voltage too low	Faulty wiring or wiring connector Faulty battery Faulty control unit
53	Power supply voltage too high	Faulty wiring or wiring connector Faulty regulator/rectifier Faulty control unit
55	ABS control unit	Internal fault

13.5a Instrument cluster wiring connector – ER650 models

13.5b Instrument cluster wiring connector – EX650 models

13.7a ABS control unit wiring connector (arrowed)

13.7b Disconnect the connector – note the catch (arrowed)

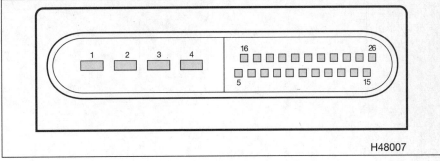

H48007

13.8 ABS control unit connector terminal numbering

connector located behind the right-hand seat cowling **(see illustration)**. Reconnect the battery. Turn the ignition ON and test for voltage between the brown wire terminal in the system connector and earth (ground) – there should be approximately 9.6 volts. If the voltage is good, it is likely the ABS control unit is faulty – have it tested by a Kawasaki dealer. If the voltage is low, check the battery condition (see Chapter 8).

ABS indicator light stays on continuously

10 Follow the procedure in Step 5 to access the instrument cluster wiring connector. Backprobe the orange/black and black/yellow wire terminals in the connector and test for voltage – there should be approximately 9 to 12 volts. If the voltage is outside the specification it is likely the instrument cluster is faulty – have it tested by a Kawasaki dealer.
11 If the voltage is good, follow the procedure in Step 7 and disconnect the ABS control unit wiring connector. Check for voltage between the orange/black wire terminal 12 and black/yellow wire terminal 4 in the connector **(see illustration 13.8)**. If there is no voltage it is likely the ABS control unit is faulty – have it tested by a Kawasaki dealer. If the voltage is between 9 to 12 volts the wiring loom is damaged and must be repaired or renewed.

Fault codes 13, 14, 17 and 18 – solenoid valves

12 First check the brake system, the brake discs, wheels and wheel bearings as described in Chapter 1.

13 If no problems are found, erase the fault code (see Section 12), then start and ride the bike and check if the indicator light comes on again. If it does not, the fault was temporary and the system is now working normally. If it does, follow the procedure to access the fault code. If the same code is displayed it is likely the ABS control unit is faulty – have it tested by a Kawasaki dealer.

Fault code 19 – solenoid valve relay

14 Remove the seat (see Chapter 7). The 25 A solenoid valve relay fuse is located behind the left-hand seat cowling **(see illustration)**. Unclip the top of the fuseholder and pull out the fuse **(see illustration)**. Refer to Chapter 8 to check the fuse.
15 If the fuse has blown, follow the procedure in Step 7 and disconnect the ABS control unit wiring connector. Check for continuity between the white/red wire terminal 3 and black/yellow wire terminal 4 on the unit side of the connector **(see illustration 13.8)**. There should be no continuity (infinite resistance). If there is continuity it is likely the ABS control unit is faulty – have it tested by a Kawasaki dealer.
16 Now check for continuity between the white/red wire terminal in the loom side of the connector and the white/red wire terminal in the fuseholder – if there is no continuity, inspect the wire for damage and renew or repair the loom.
17 If the fuse is good, check for battery voltage between the white/red wire terminal in

the fuseholder and earth (ground). If there is no voltage, check for continuity between the white/red wire terminal in the loom side of the control unit connector and the battery positive (+ve) lead. If there is no continuity, inspect the white/red wire for damage and renew or repair the loom.
18 If there is voltage, delete the fault code (see Section 12), then start and ride the bike and check if the indicator light comes on again. If it does not, the fault was temporary and the system is now working normally. If it does, follow the procedure to access the fault code. If the same code is displayed the solenoid valve relay inside the control unit is faulty and a new control unit will have to be fitted.

Fault code 25 – tyres, wheels and speed sensor rotors

19 First check the tyre pressures (see *Pre-ride checks*), then check that the correct tyres are fitted (see *Specifications* at the beginning of this Chapter). Check the tyres for deformation and damage. Check the wheel bearings for wear (see Chapter 1) and the wheels for damage and runout (see Section 15).
20 Inspect the front and rear speed sensor rotors for damage and dirt lodged between the slots in the rotor (see Steps 28 and 42).
21 If no problems are found, delete the fault code, then start and ride the bike and check if the indicator light comes on again. If it does not, the fault was temporary and the system is now working normally. If it does, follow the procedure to access the fault code. If the same

13.9 Location of the multi-pin self-diagnosis system connector

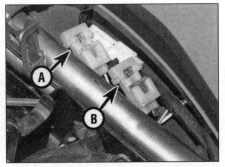

13.14a ABS solenoid valve relay fuse (A) and pump motor relay fuse (B)

13.14b Remove the solenoid valve fuse for checking

13.22 Remove the pump motor fuse for checking

13.27 Measuring the front wheel speed sensor air gap

13.30 Release the speed sensor wiring from the clips (arrowed)

code is displayed it is likely the ABS control unit is faulty – have it tested by a Kawasaki dealer.

Fault code 35 – pump motor relay

22 Remove the seat (see Chapter 7). The 30 A pump motor relay fuse is located behind the left-hand seat cowling **(see illustration 13.14a)**. Unclip the top of the fuseholder and pull out the fuse **(see illustration)**. Refer to Chapter 8 to check the fuse.

23 If the fuse has blown, follow the procedure in Step 7 and disconnect the ABS control unit wiring connector. Check for continuity between the red/white wire terminal 2 and black/yellow wire terminal 4 on the unit side of the connector **(see illustration 13.8)**. There should be no continuity (infinite resistance). If there is continuity it is likely the ABS control unit is faulty – have it tested by a Kawasaki dealer.

24 Now check for continuity between the red/white wire terminal in the loom side of the connector and the red/white wire terminal in the fuseholder – if there is no continuity, inspect the wire for damage and renew or repair the loom.

25 If the fuse is good, test for battery voltage between the red/white wire terminal in the fuseholder and earth (ground). If there is no voltage, check for continuity between the red/white wire terminal in the loom side of the control unit connector and the battery positive (+ve) lead. If there is no continuity, inspect the

red/white wire for damage and renew or repair the loom.

26 If there is voltage, delete the fault code (see Section 12), then start and ride the bike and check if the indicator light comes on again. If it does not, the fault was temporary and the system is now working normally. If it does, follow the procedure to access the fault code. If the same code is displayed the pump motor relay inside the control unit is faulty and a new control unit will have to be fitted.

Fault code 42 – front wheel speed sensor and rotor

Check

27 Measure the air gap between the speed sensor and the rotor with a feeler gauge, then compare the result with the specification at the beginning of this Chapter **(see illustration)**. Rotate the wheel to a new position and measure the air gap again to ensure the rotor is not out-of-true.

28 The gap is not adjustable – if it is outside the specification, check that the speed sensor and rotor fixings are tight, that the components are not damaged and that there is no dirt on the sensor tip or between the slots in the rotor **(see illustrations 13.31b and 34)**. If any of the components are damaged they must be renewed.

29 If no problems are found, delete the fault code (see Section 12), then start and ride the bike and check if the indicator light comes on again. If it does not, the fault was temporary and the system is now working normally. If it

does, follow the procedure to access the fault code. If the same code is displayed it is likely the ABS control unit is faulty – have it tested by a Kawasaki dealer.

Removal and installation

30 Remove the air filter housing (see Chapter 4). Trace the speed sensor wiring to the connector and disconnect it. Release the wiring from any clips or ties, noting its routing **(see illustration)**.

31 Undo the bolt securing the speed sensor to its mounting bracket and withdraw the sensor **(see illustrations)**.

32 Install the new speed sensor and tighten the mounting bolt securely. Feed the wiring up the front fork and secure it as noted on removal. Connect the wiring connector.

33 Check the air gap (see Step 27). Install the components in the reverse order of removal.

34 The speed sensor rotor is integral with the left-hand front brake disc **(see illustration)**. If the rotor is damaged a new disc will have to be fitted (see Section 4).

Fault code 43 – front wheel speed sensor wiring

35 Trace the speed sensor wiring to the connector and disconnect it (see Step 30). Follow the procedure in Step 7 and disconnect the ABS control unit wiring connector.

36 Using a jumper wire, bridge the white wire terminal 16 and black wire terminal 5 in the loom side of the control unit wiring connector, then check for continuity between the terminals on the loom side of the speed

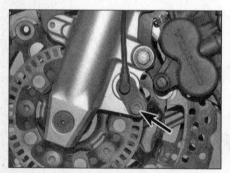

13.31a Undo the bolt (arrowed) . . .

13.31b . . . and remove the speed sensor

13.34 Sensor rotor is integral with the left-hand front disc

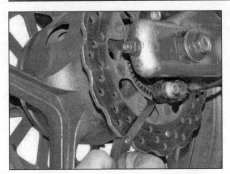

13.39 Measuring the rear wheel speed sensor air gap

13.41 Feed the wiring through the guides on the swingarm

13.42 Undo the bolt and remove the speed sensor

sensor connector (see illustration 13.8). If there is no continuity, inspect the wiring for damage and renew or repair the loom.

37 Check for continuity between the white and black wire terminals on the sensor side of the sensor connector and earth (ground) – there should be no continuity (infinite resistance). If there is continuity, the front wheel speed sensor is faulty and must be renewed.

38 If no problems are found, delete the fault code (see Section 12), then start and ride the bike and check if the indicator light comes on again. If it does not, the fault was temporary and the system is now working normally. If it does, follow the procedure to access the fault code. If the same code is displayed it is likely the ABS control unit is faulty – have it tested by a Kawasaki dealer.

Fault code 44 – rear wheel speed sensor and rotor

Check

39 Follow the procedure in Steps 27 and 28 and check the sensor air gap (see illustration), then check the sensor and rotor for damage (see illustrations 13.42 and 45). If any of the components are damaged they must be renewed.

40 If no problems are found, delete the fault code (see Section 12), then start and ride the bike and check if the indicator light comes on again. If it does not, the fault was temporary and the system is now working normally. If it does, follow the procedure to access the fault code. If the same code is displayed it is likely

13.45 Sensor rotor is integral with the rear disc

the ABS control unit is faulty – have it tested by a Kawasaki dealer.

Removal and installation

41 Remove the seat (see Chapter 7). Remove the air filter housing (see Chapter 4). Trace the speed sensor wiring to the connector and disconnect it. Release the wiring from any clips or ties and feed it back to the swingarm, noting its routing. Feed the wiring through the guides on the swingarm (see illustration).

42 Undo the bolt securing the speed sensor to the caliper bracket and withdraw the sensor (see illustration).

43 Install the new speed sensor and tighten the mounting bolt securely. Feed the wiring up the swingarm and secure it as noted on removal. Connect the wiring connector.

44 Check the air gap (see illustration 13.39). Install the components in the reverse order of removal.

45 The speed sensor rotor is integral with the rear brake disc (see illustration). If the rotor is damaged a new disc will have to be fitted (see Section 8).

Fault code 45 – rear wheel speed sensor wiring

46 Trace the speed sensor wiring to the connector and disconnect it (see Step 41). Follow the procedure in Step 7 and disconnect the ABS control unit wiring connector.

47 Using a jumper wire, bridge the red wire terminal 7 and green wire terminal 19 in the loom side of the control unit wiring connector, then check for continuity between the terminals on the loom side of the speed sensor connector (see illustration 13.8). If there is no continuity, inspect the wiring for damage and renew or repair the loom.

48 Check for continuity between the white and black wire terminals on the sensor side of the sensor connector and earth (ground) – there should be no continuity (infinite resistance). If there is continuity, the rear wheel speed sensor is faulty and must be renewed.

49 If no problems are found, delete the fault code (see Section 12), then start and ride the bike and check if the indicator light comes on again. If it does not, the fault was temporary and the system is now working normally. If it does, follow the procedure to access the fault code. If the same code is displayed it is likely

the ABS control unit is faulty – have it tested by a Kawasaki dealer.

Fault code 52 – power supply voltage too low

50 Follow the procedure in Step 7 and disconnect the ABS control unit wiring connector. Identify the Kawasaki self-diagnosis system connector (see Step 9).

51 Check for continuity between the brown wire terminal 18 in the ABS control unit connector and the brown wire terminal in the system connector. If there is no continuity, inspect the wire for damage and renew or repair the loom.

52 Connect the ABS control unit wiring connector. Reconnect the battery. Turn the ignition ON and test for voltage between the brown wire terminal in the system connector and earth (ground) – there should be 9.6 volts or more. If the voltage is lower, check the battery condition (see Chapter 8).

53 If the voltage is good, erase the fault code (see Section 12), then start and ride the bike and check if the indicator light comes on again. If it does not, the fault was temporary and the system is now working normally. If it does, follow the procedure to access the fault code. If the same code is displayed it is likely the ABS control unit is faulty – have it tested by a Kawasaki dealer.

Fault code 53 – power supply voltage too high

54 Follow the procedure in Step 7 and disconnect the ABS control unit wiring connector. Identify the Kawasaki self-diagnosis system connector (see Step 9).

55 Check for continuity between the brown wire terminal 18 in the ABS control unit connector and the brown wire terminal in the system connector. If there is no continuity, inspect the wire for damage and renew or repair the loom.

56 Connect the ABS control unit wiring connector. Turn the ignition ON and test for voltage between the brown wire terminal in the system connector and earth (ground) – there should be 16.6 volts or less. If the voltage is outside the specification, check the battery condition and the charging system (see Chapter 8).

14.8a Disconnect the pipes (arrowed) from the top . . .

57 If the voltage is good, erase the fault code (see Section 12), then start and ride the bike and check if the indicator light comes on again. If it does not, the fault was temporary and the system is now working normally. If it does, follow the procedure to access the fault code. If the same code is displayed it is likely the ABS control unit is faulty – have it tested by a Kawasaki dealer.

Fault code 55 – ABS control unit

58 Erase the fault code (see Section 12), then start and ride the bike and check if the indicator light comes on again. If it does not, the fault was temporary and the system is now working normally. If it does, follow the procedure to access the fault code. If the same code is displayed it is likely the ABS control unit is faulty – have it tested by a Kawasaki dealer.

14 ABS control unit

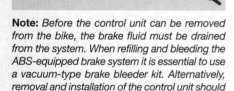

Note: *Before the control unit can be removed from the bike, the brake fluid must be drained from the system. When refilling and bleeding the ABS-equipped brake system it is essential to use a vacuum-type brake bleeder kit. Alternatively, removal and installation of the control unit should be entrusted to a Kawasaki dealer.*

1 Remove the left-hand frame cover (see Chapter 7).
2 Remove the battery and the battery carrier (see Chapter 8).

14.9a Left-hand mounting bracket bolt (arrowed)

14.8b . . . and the right-hand side of the ABS control unit

3 Remove the rear wheel (see Section 18).
4 Remove the rear shock absorber (see Chapter 5).
5 Remove the regulator/rectifier (see Chapter 8).
6 Refer to the procedure in Section 11 for changing the brake fluid – siphon the fluid out of the front and rear reservoirs and pump any residual fluid out through the brake calipers, but do not refill the system at this stage.
7 Disconnect the control unit wiring connector **(see illustration 13.7a and b)**.
8 Cover the area around the control unit with clean rag to catch any spilled brake fluid, then undo the brake pipe gland nuts and disconnect the pipes from the control unit, noting how they fit **(see illustrations)**. Plug the openings in the control unit to prevent dirt entering. Wrap small plastic bags around the ends of the brake pipes to catch any residual fluid.
9 Undo the left-hand mounting bracket bolt **(see illustration)**. Undo the rear mounting bracket bolt **(see illustration)** and manoeuvre the assembly out.
10 Installation is the reverse of removal, noting the following:
● Tighten the brake pipe gland nuts to the torque setting specified at the beginning of this Chapter.
● Ensure the control unit wiring connector is secure.
● Follow the procedure in Section 11 to refill and bleed the brake system.
● Check the operation of both brakes carefully before riding the motorcycle.

14.9b Rear mounting bracket bolt (arrowed)

15 Wheel inspection and repair

1 In order to carry out a proper inspection of the wheels, it is necessary to support the bike upright so that the wheel being inspected is raised off the ground. Position the motorcycle on an auxiliary stand. Clean the wheels thoroughly to remove mud and dirt that may interfere with the inspection procedure or mask defects. Make a general check of the wheels (see Chapter 1) and tyres (see *Pre-ride checks*).
2 Attach a dial gauge to the fork or the swingarm and position its tip against the side of the wheel rim. Spin the wheel slowly and check the axial (side-to-side) runout of the rim **(see illustration)**.
3 In order to accurately check radial (out of round) runout with the dial gauge, remove the wheel from the machine, and the tyre from the wheel. With the axle clamped in a vice and the dial gauge positioned on the top of the rim, the wheel can be rotated to check the runout **(see illustration 15.2)**.
4 An easier, though slightly less accurate, method is to attach a stiff wire pointer to the fork or the swingarm and position the end a fraction of an inch from the wheel rim where the wheel and tyre join. If the wheel is true, the distance from the pointer to the rim will be constant as the wheel is rotated. Note: *If wheel runout is excessive, check the wheel bearings very carefully before renewing the wheel.*
5 The wheels should also be inspected for cracks, flat spots on the rim and other damage. Look very closely for dents in the area where the tyre bead contacts the rim. Dents in this area may prevent complete sealing of the tyre against the rim, which leads to deflation of the tyre over a period of time. If damage is evident, or if runout in either direction is excessive, the wheel will have to be renewed. Never attempt to repair a damaged cast alloy wheel.

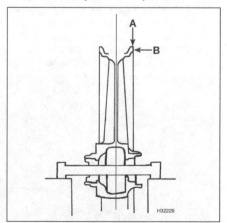

15.2 Check the wheel for radial (out-of-round) runout (A) and axial (side-to-side) runout (B)

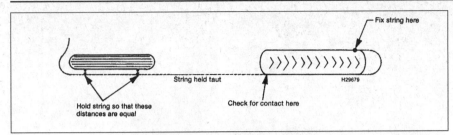

16.5 Wheel alignment check using string

16 Wheel alignment check

1 Misalignment of the wheels due to a bent frame or forks can cause strange and possibly serious handling problems. If the frame or forks are at fault, repair by a frame specialist or renewal are the only options.
2 To check wheel alignment you will need an assistant, a length of string or a perfectly straight piece of wood and a ruler. A plumb bob or spirit level for checking that the wheels are vertical will also be required.
3 In order to make a proper check of the wheels it is necessary to support the bike in an upright position, using an auxiliary stand. First ensure that the chain adjuster markings coincide on each side of the swingarm (see Chapter 1, Section 1). Next, measure the width of both tyres at their widest points. Subtract the smaller measurement from the larger measurement, then divide the difference by two. The result is the amount of offset that should exist between the front and rear tyres on both sides of the machine.
4 If a string is used, have your assistant hold one end of it about halfway between the floor and the rear axle, with the string touching the back edge of the rear tyre sidewall.
5 Run the other end of the string forward and pull it tight so that it is roughly parallel to the floor. Slowly bring the string into contact with the front edge of the rear tyre sidewall, then turn the front wheel until it is parallel with the string. Measure the distance from the front tyre sidewall to the string (see illustration).
6 Repeat the procedure on the other side of the motorcycle. The distance from the front

tyre sidewall to the string should be equal on both sides.
7 As previously mentioned, a perfectly straight length of wood or metal bar may be substituted for the string (see illustration).
8 If the distance between the string and tyre is greater on one side, or if the rear wheel appears to be out of alignment, have your machine checked by a Kawasaki dealer or frame specialist.
9 If the front-to-back alignment is correct, the wheels still may be out of alignment vertically.
10 Using a plumb bob or spirit level, check the rear wheel to make sure it is vertical. To do this, hold the string of the plumb bob against the tyre upper sidewall and allow the weight to settle just off the floor. If the string touches both the upper and lower tyre sidewalls and is perfectly straight, the wheel is vertical. If it is not, adjust the stand until it is.
11 Once the rear wheel is vertical, check the front wheel in the same manner. If both wheels are not perfectly vertical, the frame and/or major suspension components are bent.

17 Front wheel

Removal

Special tool: *A 14 mm Hex key is required to unscrew and/or tighten the axle. If a special tool is not available you can make one using suitable nuts and bolts.*

1 Using an auxiliary stand, support the motorcycle securely in an upright position with the front wheel off the ground.

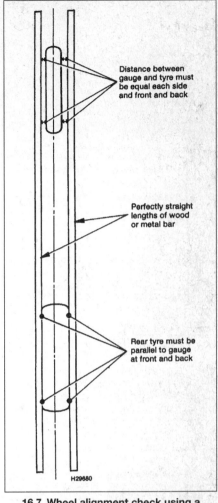

16.7 Wheel alignment check using a straight-edge

2 On ABS-equipped machines displace the front wheel sensor (see Section 13).
3 Displace the front brake calipers (see Section 3). **Note:** *Do not operate the brake lever while the calipers are off the discs.*
4 Loosen the axle clamp bolt on the bottom of the right-hand fork (see illustrations).
5 Support the wheel, then unscrew the axle using the special tool and withdraw it from the right-hand side (see illustration).

17.4a Axle clamp bolt – 2006 to 2008 models

17.4b Axle clamp bolt – 2009-on models

17.5 Unscrew the axle from the right-hand side

17.6a Note direction of rotation arrow (arrowed)

17.6b Remove spacers from both sides of the hub

18.5 Remove the axle nut and washer (arrowed)

6 Remove the wheel from between the forks, noting the direction of rotation arrow **(see illustration)**. Remove the spacers from the both sides of the hub **(see illustration)**.
Caution: Don't lay the wheel down and allow it to rest on a disc – the disc could become warped. Set the wheel on wood blocks so the disc doesn't support the weight of the wheel.

Inspection

7 Clean the axle and remove any corrosion using steel wool. Check the axle is straight by rolling it on a flat surface such as a piece of plate glass. If available, place the axle in V-blocks and check for runout using a dial gauge. Renew the axle if it is bent.
8 Wipe any old grease off the bearing seals and check the condition of the seals and the wheel bearings (see Section 19).
9 Clean the spacers and remove any corrosion using steel wool.

Installation

10 Lubricate the axle and the lips of the bearing seals with a smear of grease. Install the spacers on both sides of the hub **(see illustration 17.6b)**.
11 Manoeuvre the wheel into position between the forks, making sure the directional arrow is pointing in the direction of normal rotation **(see illustration 17.6a)**.
12 Lift the wheel and slide the axle through from the right-hand side **(see illustration 17.5)**. Ensure the axle is aligned with the hole in the left-hand outer fork tube and thread it in carefully using the special tool. Tighten the axle to the torque setting specified at the beginning of this Chapter.
13 Move the motorcycle off the stand and place a block of wood in front of the wheel. Bounce the front forks up-and-down a few times to settle the axle in position, then tighten the clamp bolt to the specified torque setting.

14 Install the front brake calipers (see Section 3).
15 On ABS-equipped machines install the front wheel sensor (see Section 13).
16 Check the operation of the front brake before riding the motorcycle.

18 Rear wheel

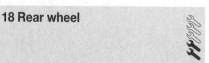

Removal

1 Support the motorcycle securely in an upright position with the rear wheel off the ground.
2 On ABS-equipped machines displace the rear wheel sensor (see Section 13).
3 Displace the rear brake caliper (see Section 7). **Note:** *Do not operate the brake pedal while the caliper is off the disc.*
4 Slacken the drive chain (see Chapter 1).
5 Remove the axle nut and washer **(see illustration)**.
6 Support the wheel, withdraw the axle and lower the wheel to the ground **(see illustration)**.
7 Disengage the chain from the sprocket **(see illustration)**.
8 Draw the wheel back out of the swingarm. Detach the caliper bracket from the swingarm, noting how it locates **(see illustrations)**.
9 Remove the spacers from both sides of the hub, noting how they fit **(see illustration)**.

18.6 Withdraw the axle noting the washer (arrowed)

18.7 Disengage the chain from the sprocket

18.8a Remove the caliper bracket . . .

18.8b . . . noting how it locates on the swingarm bracket (arrowed)

18.9 Remove the spacers from both sides of the hub

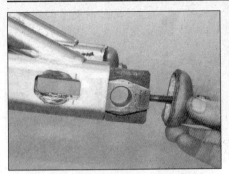

18.10 Note the location of the chain adjusters

19.2 Levering out the bearing seal

19.3 Check that the bearing turns smoothly

10 Note the location of the chain adjusters in the ends of the swingarm (see illustration). *Caution: Do not lay the wheel down and allow it to rest on the disc or the sprocket – they could become warped. Set the wheel on wood blocks so the disc or the sprocket doesn't support the weight of the wheel. Do not operate the brake pedal with the wheel removed.*

Inspection

11 Slide the washer off the axle. Clean the axle and remove any corrosion using steel wool. Check the axle is straight by rolling it on a flat surface such as a piece of plate glass. If available, place the axle in V-blocks and check for runout using a dial gauge. Renew the axle if it is bent.
12 Wipe any old grease off the bearing seals and check the condition of the seals and the wheel bearings (see Section 19).
13 Clean the spacers and remove any corrosion using steel wool.
14 Check that the sprocket coupling is a firm fit in the dampers in the wheel hub (see Section 23).

Installation

15 Lubricate the axle and the lips of the bearing seals with a smear of grease. Install the washer onto the axle. Press the spacers into the seals (see illustration 18.9).
16 Push the chain adjusters fully into the ends of the swingarm and install the caliper bracket (see illustrations 18.10, 8b and a).
17 Manoeuvre the wheel into position

between the ends of the swingarm and engage the drive chain with the sprocket (see illustration 18.7).
18 Lift the wheel into position, making sure the caliper bracket and spacers stay in place, and slide the axle through from the right-hand side (see illustration 18.6).
19 Check that everything is correctly aligned, then fit the washer and tighten the axle nut finger-tight (see illustration 18.5).
20 Adjust the chain slack, tighten the axle nut to the specified torque setting and secure it with a new split pin (see Chapter 1).
21 Install the rear brake caliper (see Section 7). Operate the brake pedal several times to bring the pads into contact with the disc.
22 On ABS-equipped machines install the rear wheel sensor (see Section 13).
23 Check the operation of the rear brake before riding the motorcycle.

19 Wheel bearings

Caution: Don't lay the wheel down and allow it to rest on either disc (front) or the disc/sprocket (rear) – they could become warped. Set the wheel on wood blocks so the wheel rim supports the weight of the wheel. Don't operate the brake lever/pedal with the wheel removed.
Note: *Always renew the wheel bearings in sets, never individually. Avoid using a high pressure cleaner on the wheel bearing area.*

Front wheel bearings

1 Remove the wheel (see Section 17).
2 Lever out the bearing seal from each side of the hub using a flat-bladed screwdriver or a seal hook (see illustration). Take care not to damage the hub. Discard the seals as new ones must be fitted on reassembly.
3 Inspect the bearings – check that the inner race turns smoothly **without binding or grating** and that the outer race is a tight fit in the hub (see illustration).
4 Only remove the bearings if they are damaged or worn and new ones are going to be fitted. Preferably, use an internal expanding puller with slide-hammer attachment, which can be obtained commercially (see illustration).
5 Alternatively, insert a drift through the centre of the upper bearing and tap evenly around the inner race of the lower bearing to drive it from the hub (see illustrations).
6 Once one bearing has been removed, remove the bearing spacer from the centre of the hub, then turn the wheel over and remove the other bearing. If required, heat the bearing housings with a hot air gun to assist removal. Refer to *Tools and Workshop Tips (Section 5)* in the Reference section for more information on bearing removal and installation.
7 Clean the hub area of the wheel thoroughly with a suitable solvent and inspect the bearing seats for scoring and wear. If the seats are damaged, consult a Kawasaki dealer before reassembling the wheel.

19.4 Using a puller with slide-hammer attachment

19.5a Using a drift to take out the bearing . . .

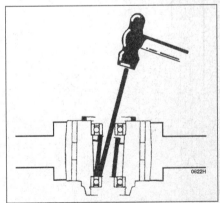

19.5b . . . locate the drift as shown

19.10a Press the new seal into place . . .

19.10b . . . and level it with the rim of the hub

19.12 Pull the sprocket coupling out of the hub

8 Use a drawbolt arrangement (see *Tools and Workshop Tips*), a bearing driver or suitable socket to install the new bearings. Ensure that the drawbolt washer or driver (as applicable) bears only on the outer edge of the bearing race and does not contact the bearing seat.

9 Install the bearings with the marked side facing out and don't forget to install the spacer between the bearings. **Note:** *The bearings are packed with grease and sealed during manufacture – no further lubrication is required.*

10 Lubricate the new seals with a smear of grease, then press them into the hub **(see illustration)**. Use a small block of wood to level the seals with the rim of the hub **(see illustration)**.

11 Clean the brake discs using acetone or brake system cleaner, then install the wheel (see Section 17).

Rear wheel bearings

12 Remove the wheel (see Section 18). Lift the sprocket coupling out of the hub **(see illustration)**. Note the location of the coupling dampers (see Section 23).

13 Note the location of the hub O-ring and discard it as a new one must be fitted on reassembly **(see illustration)**.

14 Lever out the bearing seal from the right-hand side of the hub using a flat-bladed screwdriver **(see illustration)**. Take care not to damage the hub. Discard the seal as a new one should be fitted.

15 Inspect the bearings in both sides of the hub – check that the inner race turns smoothly without binding or grating and that the outer race is a tight fit in the hub **(see illustration)**.

16 Only remove the bearings if they are damaged or worn and new ones are going to be fitted. Preferably, use an internal expanding puller with slide-hammer attachment,

which can be obtained commercially **(see illustration 19.4)**.

17 Alternatively, insert a drift through the centre of the upper bearing and tap evenly around the inner race of the lower bearing to drive it from the hub **(see illustrations 19.5a and b)**.

18 Once one bearing has been removed, remove the bearing spacer from the centre of the hub, then turn the wheel over and remove the other bearing. If required, heat the bearing housings with a hot air gun to assist removal. Refer to *Tools and Workshop Tips (Section 5)* in the Reference section for more information on bearing removal and installation.

19 Clean the hub area of the wheel thoroughly with a suitable solvent and inspect the bearing seats for scoring and wear. If the seats are damaged, consult a Kawasaki dealer before reassembling the wheel.

20 Use a drawbolt arrangement (see *Tools and Workshop Tips*), a bearing driver or suitable socket to install the new bearings. Ensure that the drawbolt washer or driver (as applicable) bears only on the outer edge of the bearing race and does not contact the bearing seat.

21 Install the bearings with the marked side facing out and don't forget to install the spacer between the bearings. **Note:** *The bearings are packed with grease and sealed during manufacture – no further lubrication is required.*

22 Lubricate the new seal with a smear of grease, then press it into the right-hand side of the hub **(see illustrations)**. Use a small

19.13 Note the location of the hub O-ring (arrowed)

19.14 Levering out the rear wheel bearing seal

19.15 Check that the bearing turns smoothly

19.22a Lubricate the new seal . . .

19.22b . . . then press it into the hub

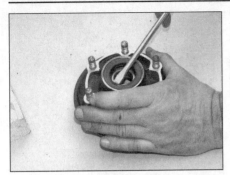

19.29 Levering out the sprocket coupling bearing seal

19.30 Note the location of the spacer (arrowed)

19.32a Remove the circlip from the outside . . .

19.32b . . . then drive the bearing out from the inside

19.34a Using a socket to drive in the new bearing

19.34b Ensure the circlip (arrowed) fits in its groove

block of wood to level the seal with the rim of the hub **(see illustration 19.10b)**.

23 Clean the brake disc using acetone or brake system cleaner.

24 Lubricate the new hub O-ring with a smear of grease, then fit it into the groove in the hub **(see illustration 19.13)**.

25 If required, check the sprocket coupling dampers (see Section 23).

26 Lubricate the inner end of the spacer inside the sprocket coupling with a smear of grease, then press the coupling into the hub. Install the wheel (see Section 18).

Sprocket coupling bearing

27 Remove the wheel (see Section 18). Lift the sprocket coupling out of the hub **(see illustration 19.12)**.

28 If required, remove the rear sprocket (see Section 22).

29 Lever out the bearing seal on the outside

of the coupling using a flat-bladed screwdriver **(see illustration)**. Take care not to damage the rim of the coupling. Discard the seal as a new one should be fitted on reassembly.

30 Note the location of the spacer inside the sprocket coupling bearing **(see illustration)**. Support the coupling, sprocket side up, and tap the spacer out using a suitably sized socket.

31 Inspect the bearing – check that the inner race turns smoothly **without binding or grating** and that the outer race is a tight fit in the coupling **(see illustration 19.15)**.

32 Only remove the bearing if it is worn and a new one is going to be fitted. First, use circlip pliers to remove the circlip securing the bearing, then turn the coupling over, support it on wooden blocks and drive the bearing out from the inside using a bearing driver or suitable socket **(see illustrations)**.

33 Clean the bearing seat thoroughly with

a suitable solvent and inspect it for scoring and wear. If the seat is damaged, consult a Kawasaki dealer before reassembling the wheel.

34 Install the new bearing with the marked side facing out, using a bearing driver or suitable socket **(see illustration)**. Ensure that the driver or socket bears only on the outer bearing race. Install a new circlip, ensuring it is fitted securely in its groove **(see illustration)**.

35 Lubricate the new seal with a smear of grease, then press it into the coupling **(see illustration)**. Use a small block of wood to level the seal with the rim of the coupling **(see illustration 19.10b)**.

36 Press the spacer into the bearing from the inside **(see illustration)**. Lubricate the inner end of the spacer with a smear of grease.

37 If removed, install the sprocket (see Section 22).

38 Fit a new hub O-ring (see Step 24).

39 If required, check the sprocket coupling dampers (see Section 23).

40 Press the sprocket coupling into the hub, then install the wheel (see Section 18).

20 Tyres

General information

1 The wheels fitted to all models are designed to take tubeless tyres only. Tyre sizes are given in the Specifications at the beginning of this chapter.

19.35 Press the new seal into place

19.36 Install the spacer from the inside

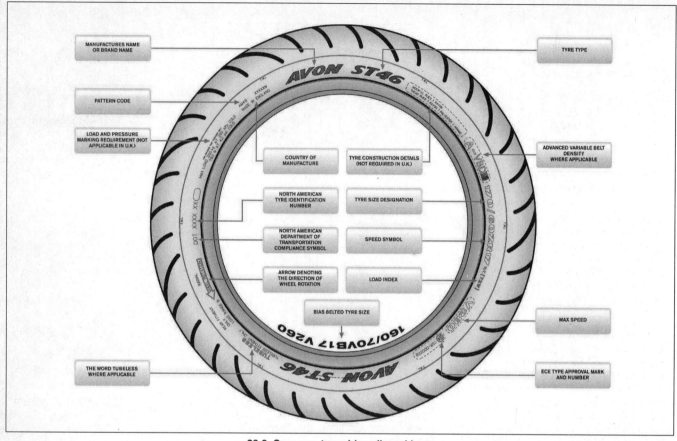

MANUFACTURES NAME OR BRAND NAME

PATTERN CODE

LOAD AND PRESSURE MARKING REQUIREMENT (NOT APPLICABLE IN U.K.)

TYRE TYPE

ADVANCED VARIABLE BELT DENSITY WHERE APPLICABLE

COUNTRY OF MANUFACTURE

TYRE CONSTRUCTION DETAILS (NOT REQUIRED IN U.K.)

NORTH AMERICAN TYRE IDENTIFICATION NUMBER

TYRE SIZE DESIGNATION

NORTH AMERICAN DEPARTMENT OF TRANSPORTATION COMPLIANCE SYMBOL

SPEED SYMBOL

ARROW DENOTING THE DIRECTION OF WHEEL ROTATION

LOAD INDEX

BIAS BELTED TYRE SIZE

MAX SPEED

THE WORD TUBELESS WHERE APPLICABLE

ECE TYPE APPROVAL MARK AND NUMBER

20.3 Common tyre sidewall markings

2 Refer to the *Pre-ride checks* listed at the beginning of this manual for tyre maintenance.

Fitting new tyres

3 When selecting new tyres, refer to the tyre information in the Owner's Handbook. Ensure that front and rear tyre types are compatible, the correct size and correct speed rating; if necessary seek advice from a Kawasaki dealer or tyre fitting specialist **(see illustration)**.
4 It is recommended that tyres are fitted by a motorcycle tyre specialist rather than attempted in the home workshop. This is particularly relevant in the case of tubeless

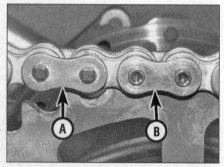

21.3 Standard chain link (A) and riveted soft link (B)

tyres because the force required to break the seal between the wheel rim and tyre bead is substantial, and is usually beyond the capabilities of an individual working with normal tyre levers. Additionally, the specialist will be able to balance the wheels after tyre fitting.
5 Note that punctured tubeless tyres can in some cases be repaired. Repairs must be carried out by a motorcycle tyre fitting specialist. Kawasaki advise that a repaired tyre should not be used at speeds above 50 mph (80 kmh) for the first 24 hours, and not above 80 mph (130 kmh) thereafter.

21 Drive chain

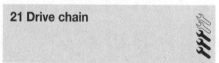

⚠️ *Warning: NEVER install a drive chain which uses a clip-type (split) master link. ONLY use the correct tools to secure the riveted soft link – if you do not have access to such tools or do not have the skill to operate them correctly, have the chain installed by a Kawasaki dealer.*

Removal

Special tool: *A drive chain cutting/staking*

tool is absolutely necessary for this procedure (see Step 3).
1 Remove the front sprocket cover (see Section 22).
2 Remove the chain guard (see Chapter 7).
3 The drive chain has a riveted soft link which must be split before the chain can be removed **(see illustration)**. Refer to *Tools and Workshop Tips (Section 8)* in the Reference section for details of how to identify the soft link, then split the chain at the soft link using the chain breaking tool. Note the chain's routing around the swingarm, then remove the chain from the bike.
Note: *If the chain and sprockets are being renewed, loosen the front sprocket nut before removing the rear wheel or splitting the chain – refer to Section 22.*

Installation

4 Loosen the rear wheel axle nut, then loosen the locknuts and adjuster nuts on both chain adjusters and push them forwards in the swingarm (see Chapter 1).
5 Fit the drive chain through the swingarm and around the sprockets, leaving the two ends in a convenient position to work on.
6 Assemble the new soft link, O-rings and sideplate and rivet the assembly as described in *Tools and Workshop Tips (Section 8)*.
7 On 2006 to 2008 models, if fitting the

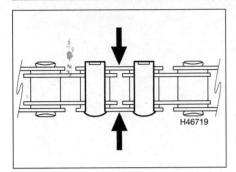

21.7 Check the width across the outer edges of the sideplates

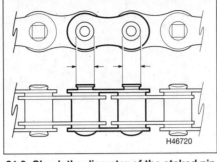

21.9 Check the diameter of the staked pin ends

22.1a Undo the bolts (arrowed) . . .

original equipment Enuma chain, Kawasaki specifies that the sideplate must be pressed into place so that the width across the outer edges of the chain measures 17.25 to 17.45 mm **(see illustration)**. On 2009-on models, if fitting the original equipment Daido chain, Kawasaki specifies that the sideplate must be pressed into place so that the width across the outer edges of the chain measures 17.25 to 17.55 mm.

8 After the soft link pins have been riveted in place, check the staked pin ends for any signs of cracking. If either of the pins have cracked the chain must be disassembled and another new soft link and O-rings fitted.

9 On all models, if fitting the original equipment chain, Kawasaki specifies that the diameter of the staked pin ends should be 5.7 to 6.0 mm **(see illustration)**.

10 Install the chain guard (see Chapter 7) and

the front sprocket cover (see Section 22).

11 On completion, adjust and lubricate the chain (see Chapter 1).

22 Sprockets

Front sprocket

Removal

1 Undo the bolts securing the front sprocket cover and remove the cover **(see illustrations)**.

2 Undo the bolts securing the speed sensor bracket and displace the bracket **(see illustration)**.

3 Bend back the lockwasher on the sprocket nut using a suitable tool **(see illustration)**.

4 Shift the transmission into gear. Have an assistant apply the rear brake, then undo the front sprocket nut and remove the nut and washer **(see illustrations)**. Discard the washer as a new one must be fitted on installation.

5 Slacken the drive chain (see Chapter 1). Draw the sprocket and chain off the gearbox output shaft and remove the sprocket **(see illustration)**. If the sprocket is going to be refitted, mark the outside face so that it can be fitted the same way round.

Installation

6 Engage the sprocket with the chain and slide it onto the gearbox shaft **(see illustration 22.5)**. If the original sprocket is being refitted, ensure it is installed the same way around as on removal.

7 Fit a new lockwasher and hand-tighten the sprocket nut. Adjust the chain (see Chapter 1).

22.1b . . . and remove the front sprocket cover

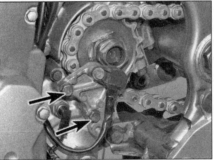

22.2 Bolts (arrowed) secure speed sensor bracket

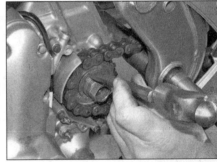

22.3 Bend back the lockwasher

22.4a Undo the front sprocket nut . . .

22.4b . . . and remove the lockwasher

22.5 Draw the sprocket off the gearbox output shaft

22.8 Bend up one side of the lockwasher

22.12 Undo the nuts securing the sprocket

22.13 Ensure that the sprocket studs (arrowed) are tight

8 Tighten the sprocket nut to the torque setting specified at the beginning of this Chapter, using the rear brake to prevent the sprocket turning. Bend up one side of the washer against a flat on the nut to lock it **(see illustration)**.
9 Install the speed sensor bracket and tighten the bracket bolts to the specified torque setting **(see illustration 22.2)**.
10 Install the sprocket cover and tighten the cover bolts securely.

Rear sprocket
Removal
11 Remove the rear wheel (see Section 18). If required, lift the sprocket coupling out of the hub **(see illustration 19.12)**.
12 Undo the nuts securing the sprocket to the sprocket coupling, then remove the sprocket, noting which way round it fits **(see illustration)**.

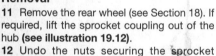

22.15 Nut flanges (arrowed) must be against the sprocket

13 Ensure that the sprocket studs are a tight fit in the coupling **(see illustration)**. If any of the studs have become loose, unscrew them completely and clean the threads. Before installing a stud, lock two nuts together on the upper end and apply a suitable thread-locking compound on the lower end. Install the stud and tighten it securely with a spanner on the locked nuts, then remove the locked nuts.
14 Fit the sprocket onto the coupling with any stamped mark denoting number of teeth facing out. If the original sprocket is being refitted, ensure it is installed the same way around as on removal.
15 Fit the nuts, ensuring the flanges are against the sprocket **(see illustration)**. Tighten the nuts evenly and in a criss-cross sequence to the torque setting specified at the beginning of this Chapter.
16 If removed, press the sprocket coupling

23.2 Check the sprocket coupling for rotational freeplay

into the hub, not forgetting to fit a new hub O-ring, then install the wheel (see Section 18).

23 Rear sprocket coupling dampers

1 Remove the rear wheel (see Section 18).
2 The sprocket coupling should be a firm fit between the dampers in the hub, with no rotational freeplay – if there is freeplay, the damper segments have compressed and should be replaced with a new set **(see illustration)**.
3 Pull the sprocket coupling out of the hub leaving the dampers in position **(see illustrations)**. Note the location of the O-ring and discard it as a new one must be fitted on reassembly.
4 Check the coupling for cracks and damage.
5 Lift the damper segments from the hub, noting how they fit **(see illustration)**. Inspect the dampers for cracks, hardening and general deterioration and renew them as a set if necessary.
6 Follow the procedure in Section 19 to check and renew the coupling bearing.
7 Ensure the dampers are pressed firmly into the hub **(see illustrations 23.3b)**.
8 Lubricate the new hub O-ring with a smear of grease, then fit it into the groove in the hub **(see illustration 23.3b)**.
9 Lubricate the inner end of the coupling bearing spacer with a smear of grease. Press the coupling firmly into the hub **(see illustration 23.3a)**.
10 Install the rear wheel (see Section 18).

23.3a Pull the sprocket coupling out of the hub . . .

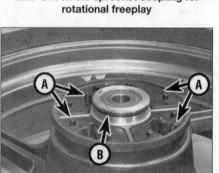

23.3b . . . leaving the dampers (A) in position. Note the O-ring (B)

23.5 Lift out the damper segments

Chapter 7
Bodywork

Contents

Degrees of difficulty

Easy, suitable for novice with little experience	**Fairly easy,** suitable for beginner with some experience	**Fairly difficult,** suitable for competent DIY mechanic	**Difficult,** suitable for experienced DIY mechanic	**Very difficult,** suitable for expert DIY or professional

Specifications

Torque settings

Belly panel bracket bolts . . . . 10 Nm
Front mudguard bracket bolts . . . . 9 Nm

1 General information

This Chapter covers the procedures necessary to remove and install the bodywork. Since many service and repair operations on these motorcycles require the removal of the body panels, the procedures are grouped here and referred to from other Chapters.

In the case of damage to the bodywork, it is usually necessary to remove the broken component and replace it with a new (or used) one. The material that the body panels are composed of doesn't lend itself to conventional repair techniques. Note that there are however some companies that specialise in 'plastic welding' and there are a number of bodywork repair kits now available for motorcycles.

When attempting to remove any body panel, first study it closely, noting any fasteners and associated fittings, to be sure of returning everything to its correct place on installation. In some cases the aid of an assistant will be required when removing panels, to help avoid the risk of damage to paintwork. Once the evident fasteners have been removed, try to withdraw the panel as described but DO NOT FORCE IT – if it will not release, check that all fasteners have been removed and try again.

When installing a body panel, first study it closely, noting any fasteners and associated fittings removed with it, to be sure of returning everything to its correct place. Check that all fasteners are in good condition, including the trim clips and damping/rubber mounts; replace any faulty fasteners with new ones before the panel is reassembled. Check also that all mounting brackets are straight and repair them or replace them with new ones if necessary before attempting to install the panel.

Tighten the fasteners securely, but be careful not to overtighten any of them or the panel may break (not always immediately) due to the uneven stress.

Trim clips

1 Two types of plastic trim clip are used. The most common type has a centre pin which is pushed into the body of the clip to

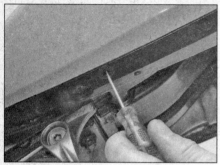

1.1a Push the centre into the body . . .

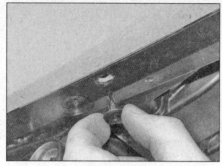

1.1b . . . then draw the body out

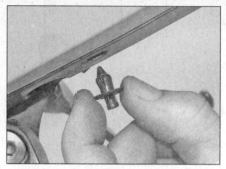

1.2a Reset the clip by drawing the centre out then fit the body

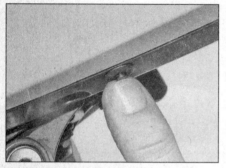

1.2b . . . and push the centre in flush to secure it

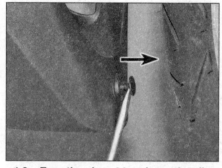

1.3a Ease the pin out to release the clip

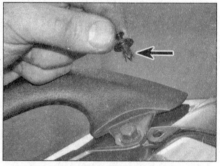

1.3b Note the position of the pawls (arrowed)

allow it to be drawn out of the panel **(see illustrations)**.

2 Before installing the clip, depress the pawls by drawing the centre pin out so that it extends from the body. Fit the clip into its hole, then push the centre pin in so that it is flush with the clip head **(see illustrations)**. The clip should now be locked in place.

3 The other type of trim clip (found on the belly panel on EX650 models and, on 2006 to 2008 models, the seat cowling centre panel) has a protruding centre pin. Ease the pin out of the body of the clip to allow the clip to be drawn out of the panel **(see illustrations)**. To install the clip, press the pawls together to fit

the clip into its hole, then push the centre pin in. The clip should now be locked in place.

2 Seat

1 Insert the ignition key into the seat lock on the left-hand side and turn it anti-clockwise to unlock the seat **(see illustration)**.
2 Lift the back of the seat and draw it rearwards to disengage the catches and lift the seat off **(see illustration)**. Note how the tab on the front of the seat locates under the bracket on the back edge of the fuel tank.

3 Installation is the reverse of removal. Align the tab on the front of the seat with the bracket, then press the seat forwards and down to engage the catches. Push down hard on the rear of the seat to engage the latch with the lock.

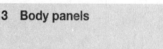

3 Body panels

Fuel tank side panels

1 Remove the seat (see Section 2).
2 On 2006 to 2008 models, undo the screw

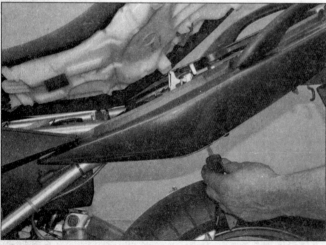

2.1 Turn the key to unlock the seat

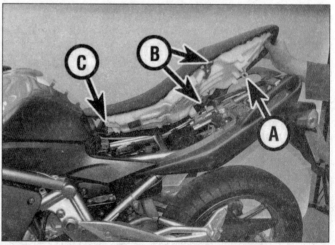

2.2 Seat latch (A), catches (B) and tab (C)

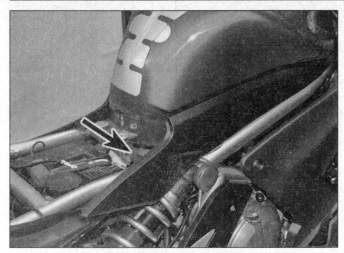

3.2a Undo the screw (arrowed)

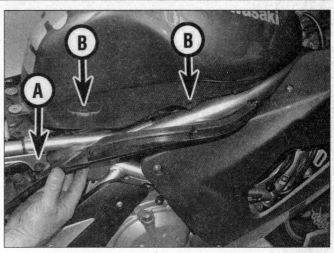

3.2b Location of grommets in frame bracket (A) and tank (B)

3.3a Release the trim clip

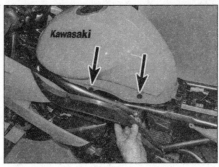

3.3b Release the pegs from the grommets (arrowed)

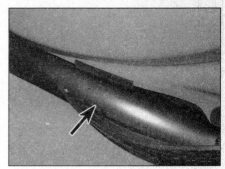

3.3c Note how tab (arrowed) locates under lower edge of tank

securing the side panel to the fuel tank bracket **(see illustration)**. Ease the panel away evenly to release the pegs on the back of the panel from the grommets in the frame bracket and the side of the tank **(see illustration)**.

3 On 2009-on models, follow the procedure in Section 1 to release the trim clip securing the side panel to the seat cowling **(see illustration)**. Ease the panel away evenly to release the two pegs on the back of the panel from the grommets in the tank – note how the tab on the front of the panel locates under lower edge of the fuel tank **(see illustrations)**.

4 Installation is the reverse of removal.

Frame covers

5 On 2006 to 2008 models, undo the screw securing the cover **(see illustration)**. Ease the cover away evenly to release the pegs on the back of the cover from the grommets in the footrest bracket **(see illustration)**.

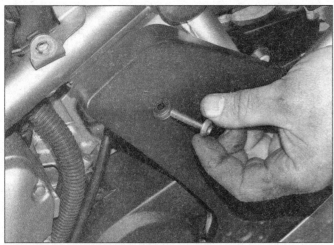

3.5a Undo the screw . . .

3.5b . . . then release the pegs from the grommets (arrowed)

3.6a Undo the screw (arrowed)

3.6b Location of grommets in frame (arrowed)

3.8a Undo the screws . . .

3.8b . . . securing the belly panel . . .

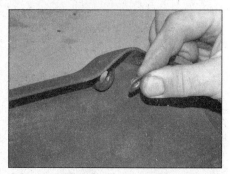

3.8c . . . noting the location of the spacers

6 On 2009-on models, undo the screw securing the cover **(see illustration)**. Ease the cover away evenly to release the pegs on the back of the cover from the grommets in the frame **(see illustration)**.

7 Installation is the reverse of removal.

Belly panel

ER650 models

8 Undo the screws on both sides securing the belly panel and lift the panel off **(see illustrations)**. Note the location of the spacers in the panel mounting holes **(see illustration)**. If required, undo the bolts securing the mounting brackets and remove the brackets **(see illustration)**.

9 Installation is the reverse of removal, noting the following:

● Tighten the bracket mounting bolts to the torque setting specified at the beginning of this Chapter.

● Don't forget to install the spacers in the panel mounting holes.

EX650 models

10 The belly panel is a two-piece assembly – remove one half at a time.

11 On 2006 to 2008 models, follow the procedure in Section 1 to release the trim clips securing the two halves of the panel together **(see illustration)**.

12 Undo the screws securing the top edge

3.8d Bolts (arrowed) secure mounting brackets

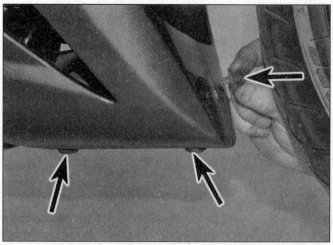

3.11 Release the trim clips (arrowed)

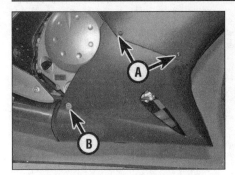

3.12a Undo the screws (A) and (B)

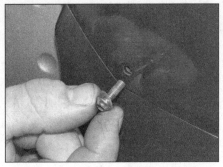

3.12b . . . noting the plastic washers (on screws A) . . .

3.12c . . . and washer and spacer (on screw B)

of the panel, noting the location of the plastic washers **(see illustrations)**. Undo the screw securing the rear edge of the panel, noting the location of the plastic washer and spacer **(see illustration)**.

13 Lower the belly panel to release the tabs on the fairing side panel from the slots in the top edge **(see illustration)**. If required, undo the bolts securing the mounting bracket and remove the bracket **(see illustration 3.8d)**.

14 Installation is the reverse of removal. Ensure that the wellnuts in the top edge of the panel are secure and renew them if necessary (see Section 4, Step 31).

15 On 2009-on models, follow the procedure in Section 1 to release the trim clips securing the two halves of the panel together **(see illustration)**.

16 Undo the screws securing the top and rear edges of the panel **(see illustration)**. Note the location of the plastic washers and the plastic washer and spacer **(see illustrations 3.12b and c)**.

17 Lower the belly panel to release the tabs

on the fairing side panel from the slots in the top edge **(see illustration)**. If required, undo the bolts securing the mounting bracket and remove the bracket **(see illustration 3.8d)**.

18 Installation is the reverse of removal, noting the following:

● Tighten the bracket mounting bolts to the torque setting specified at the beginning of this Chapter.

● Ensure that the wellnuts in the top edge of the panel are secure and renew them if necessary (see Section 4, Step 31).

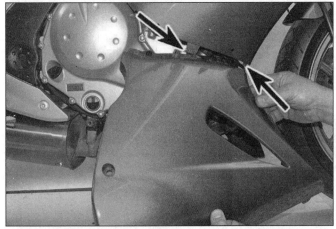

3.13 Release the tabs (arrowed) from the belly panel

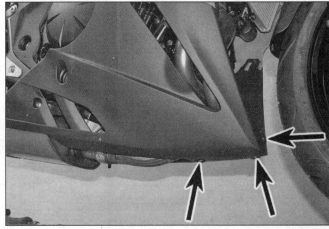

3.15 Release the trim clips (arrowed)

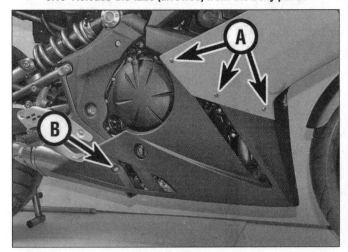

3.16 Screws (A) secure top edge, screw (B) secures rear edge

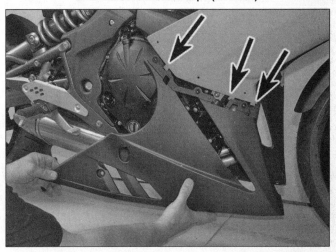

3.17 Lower the belly panel to release the tabs (arrowed)

4.1a Undo the screws (arrowed) ...

4.1b ... securing the side panel

4.2 Release the peg from the grommet (arrowed)

4 Fairing panels

4.3a Disconnect the wiring connector

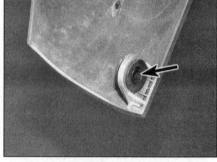

4.3b Note the sleeve (arrowed)

ER650

Side panels

1 Undo the upper and lower screws securing the side panel, noting the location of the plastic washers **(see illustrations)**.

2 Ease the panel away to release the peg on the inside from the grommet in the frame bracket **(see illustration)**.

3 Disconnect the turn signal wiring connector and lift the panel off **(see illustration)**. Note the location of the sleeve inside the grommet on the lower mounting **(see illustration)**.

4 If required, remove the turn signal assemblies (see Chapter 8).

5 Installation is the reverse of removal. Ensure the turn signal wiring connector is secure.

6 Check the operation of the turn signals before riding the motorcycle.

Headlight panel

7 On 2009-on models, follow the procedure in Section 1 to release the trim clips securing the top panel and lift the panel off.

8 Undo the upper and lower screws securing the panel on both sides **(see illustrations)**.

9 Lift the panel off and disconnect the wiring connectors for the headlights and sidelight **(see illustration)**. If required remove the headlight assembly (see Chapter 8).

10 Note the location of the sleeved washers inside the grommets on the panel mountings **(see illustration)**.

11 The upper panel mounting bracket also supports the instrument cluster. To remove the bracket, first remove the instrument cluster

(see Chapter 8), then release the wiring from the ties and guides on the bracket, noting how it fits. Undo the bolts securing the bracket to the underside of the fork top yoke and lift it off **(see illustration)**.

12 If required, undo the bolts securing the

4.8a Undo the upper ...

4.8b ... and lower mounting screws ...

4.9 ... and lift the panel off

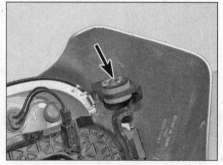

4.10 Note the sleeved washers (arrowed)

4.11 Release the wiring and undo the upper mounting bolts (arrowed)

4.12 Remove the lower mounting bracket (arrowed)

4.16 Undo the screw (arrowed)

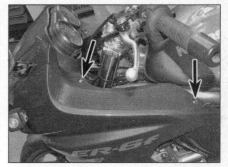

4.17a Undo the screws (arrowed) . . .

lower mounting bracket to the fork bottom yoke and lift it off **(see illustration)**.

13 Installation is the reverse of removal. Ensure the headlight and sidelight wiring connectors are secure.

14 Check the operation of the headlights and sidelight before riding the motorcycle

EX650 (2006 to 2008)

Side panels

15 Remove the belly panel (see Section 3).

16 Working on one side panel at a time, undo the screw under the front edge of the panel, noting the location of the plastic washer **(see illustration)**.

17 Undo the screws securing the cockpit trim panel and lift the panel out **(see illustrations)**. Disconnect the turn signal wiring connector and release the wiring from the guides inside the panel **(see illustration)**.

4.17b . . . and remove the trim panel

18 Undo the screws on both sides securing the instrument cluster panel and lift the panel off **(see illustrations)**.

19 Undo the screw securing the rear edge of the side panel, noting the location of the washer and spacer **(see illustrations)**.

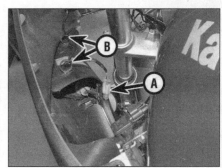

4.17c Turn signal wiring connector (A) and guides (B)

20 Undo the screw securing the upper edge of the panel to the mounting bracket **(see illustration)**.

21 Ease the lower edge of the panel away to release the peg on the inside from the grommet in the frame bracket **(see illustration)**.

4.18a Undo the screws on both sides . . .

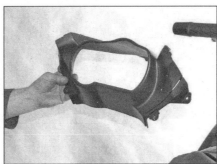

4.18b . . . and remove the instrument cluster panel

4.19a Undo the screw (arrowed) . . .

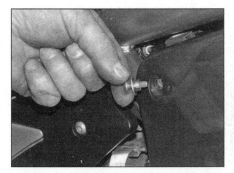

4.19b . . . noting the washer and spacer

4.20 Screw secures upper edge of panel to mounting bracket

4.21 Release peg from grommet (arrowed)

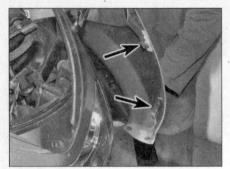

4.22a Tabs (arrowed) on side panel . . .

4.22b . . . locate in slots in headlight panel

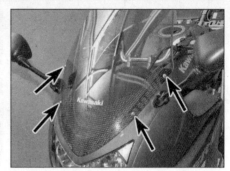

4.26a Undo the screws (arrowed) . . .

22 Draw the side panel forwards to disengage the tabs on the upper inside edge from the slots in the headlight panel **(see illustrations)**.

If required, remove the turn signal assemblies (see Chapter 8).
23 Installation is the reverse of removal.

Ensure the turn signal wiring connector is secure.
24 Check the operation of the turn signals before riding the motorcycle.

Headlight panel

25 Remove the left and right-hand side panels (see Steps 15 to 22).
26 Undo the screws securing the windshield, noting the location of the plastic washers, and lift the windshield off **(see illustrations)**.
27 Undo the nuts securing the left and right-hand mirrors and lift them off **(see illustrations)**.
28 Disconnect the wiring connectors for the headlights and sidelight (see Chapter 8).
29 Release the wiring from the clips on the back of the headlight unit, then lift the headlight panel off the mirror brackets **(see illustrations)**.
30 Note the location of the rubber dampers on the mirror brackets and renew them if they are damaged or deteriorated **(see illustration)**.
31 Inspect the wellnuts in the panel – if they are loose new ones must be fitted **(see illustration)**. Apply a smear of grease to the screw threads on installation.
32 If required remove the headlight assembly (see Chapter 8).
33 The headlight panel mounting bracket also supports the instrument cluster. To remove the bracket, first remove the instrument cluster (see Chapter 8), then release the wiring from the ties on the bracket, noting how it fits. Undo

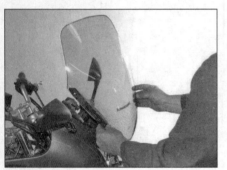

4.26b . . . and remove the windshield

4.27a Undo the nuts (arrowed) . . .

4.27b . . . and remove the mirrors

4.29a Release the wiring from the clips . . .

4.29b . . . then lift the headlight panel off

4.30 Note the location of the rubber dampers

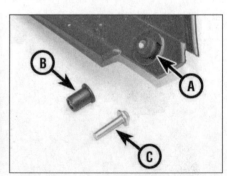

4.31 Installed wellnut (A), wellnut (B) and screw (C)

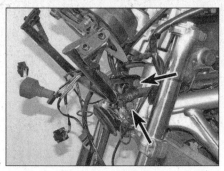

4.33 Headlight panel bracket mounting bolts (arrowed)

4.37a Undo the screws . . .

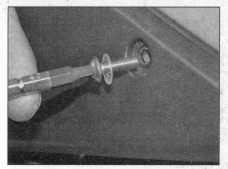

4.37b . . . noting the plastic washers

the bolts securing the bracket to the frame steering head and lift it off **(see illustration)**.
34 Installation is the reverse of removal. Ensure the headlight and sidelight wiring connectors are secure.
35 Check the operation of the headlights before riding the motorcycle

EX650 (2009-on)

Fairing assembly

36 Remove the belly panel (see Section 3).
37 Undo the screws securing the left and right-hand fairing covers, noting the location of the plastic washers, and draw the covers off **(see illustrations)**. Note how the tabs on the top edge locate in the slots and how the pegs on the inside locate in the grommets in the frame brackets **(see illustrations)**.

4.37c Note how the tabs locate in the slots (arrowed) . . .

4.37d . . . and how the pegs locate in the grommets (arrowed)

38 Undo the screws securing the windshield, noting the location of the plastic washers, and lift the windshield off **(see illustrations)**.
39 Follow the procedure in Section 1 to

release the trim clips securing the fairing top cover and lift the cover off, noting how it fits **(see illustrations)**.
40 Release the trim clip and undo the screw

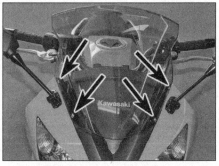

4.38a Undo the screws . . .

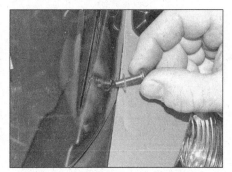

4.38b . . . noting the plastic washers . . .

4.38c . . . and remove the windshield

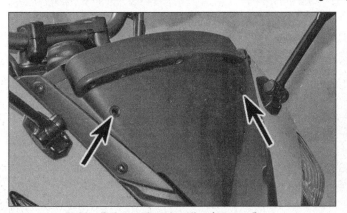

4.39a Release the trim clips (arrowed) . . .

4.39b . . . and lift the fairing top cover off

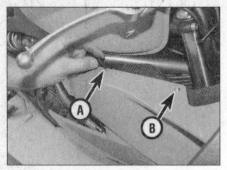

4.40a Release the trim clip (A) and undo the screw (B) . . .

4.40b . . . then lift out the trim panel

4.41a Disconnect the wiring connector . . .

4.41b . . . then undo the screws (arrowed) . . .

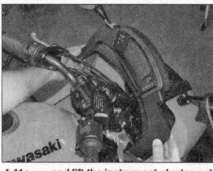

4.41c . . . and lift the instrument cluster out

4.42a Undo the nuts . . .

on both sides securing the cockpit trim panels and lift the panels out **(see illustrations)**.

41 Pull back the boot and disconnect the instrument cluster wiring connector **(see illustration)**. Undo the screws securing the instrument cluster and lift it out **(see illustrations)**.

42 If required, undo the nuts securing the left and right-hand mirrors and lift them off **(see illustrations)**.

43 Disconnect the wiring connectors for the headlights, sidelight and turn signals. Release the wiring from any clips or ties on the fairing bracket **(see illustrations)**.

44 Undo the screws securing the left and right-hand sides of the fairing **(see illustration)**. Ease the sides of the fairing away to release the pegs on the inside from

4.42b . . . and remove the mirrors

4.43a Disconnect the wiring connectors – turn signal shown

the grommets in the frame brackets **(see illustration)**.

45 Undo the bolts securing the fairing top

bracket to the frame bracket, then draw the fairing forwards and off the machine **(see illustrations)**.

4.43b Release the wiring clips from the fairing bracket

4.44a Undo the screws (arrowed) on both sides

4.44b Release the pegs from the grommets in the frame brackets

4.45a Bolts (arrowed) secure fairing top bracket to frame bracket

4.45b Lift the fairing off the frame bracket . . .

4.45c . . . then draw it forwards and off

4.46 Note the location of the small brackets

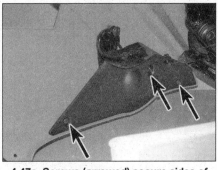

4.47a Screws (arrowed) secure sides of fairing inner panel

Section 1 to release the trim clip securing the centre section of the fairing inner panel, then unclip the two halves and lift them off **(see illustrations)**.

48 Undo the screws securing the left and right-hand sides of the fairing assembly to the centre joining panel and separate them carefully, noting how the tabs fit **(see illustration)**.

49 If required, remove the turn signal assemblies (see Chapter 8).

50 Inspect the wellnuts in the panels – if they are loose new ones must be fitted **(see illustration 4.31)**. Apply a smear of grease to the screw threads on installation.

51 The fairing frame bracket is fixed to the steering head **(see illustration)**. To remove the bracket, first release the wiring from any ties, then undo the bolts securing the bracket and lift it off.

52 Installation is the reverse of removal. Ensure the headlight, sidelight and turn signal wiring connectors are secure.

53 Check the operation of the headlights before riding the motorcycle

46 If required, the fairing assembly can be separated into two halves. If not already done, remove the mirrors (see Step 42). Remove the headlight assembly (see Chapter 8). Note how the brackets on the two upper headlight

mounting bolts secure the fairing top bracket **(see illustration)**.

47 Undo the screws securing the left and right-hand sides of the fairing inner panel **(see illustration)**. Follow the procedure in

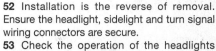

5 Mirrors

ER650

1 To remove the mirror and extension bracket (where fitted), first prise out the plug from the top of the mounting bolt **(see illustration)**.

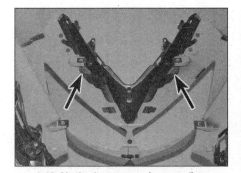

4.47b Release the trim clip (arrowed) . . .

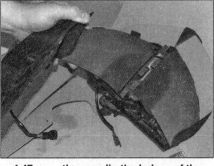

4.47c . . . then unclip the halves of the fairing inner panel

4.48 Undo the screws (arrowed) to separate the panels

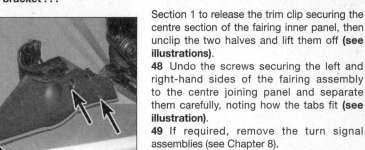

4.51 Release the wiring before removing the frame bracket

5.1 Prise out the plug

5.2 Note the location of the spacer (arrowed)

5.3a Using two spanners . . .

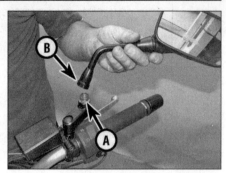

5.3b . . . counter-hold nut (A) and undo nut (B)

2 Undo the mounting bolt and lift off the bracket and mirror assembly, noting the location of the spacer **(see illustration)**.
3 To remove the mirror only, counter-hold the lower nut on the mirror stem and unscrew the upper nut **(see illustrations)**.
4 Installation is the reverse of removal.

When installing the mirror only, thread the upper stem nut on finger-tight, position the mirror as required, then tighten the upper nut.

EX650

5 To remove the mirrors on 2006 to 2008

models, first remove the cockpit trim panels and instrument cluster panel (see Section 4, Steps 17 and 18). Undo the nuts securing the mirrors and lift them off **(see illustrations 4.27a and b)**.
6 To remove the mirrors on 2009-on models, first remove the windshield, fairing top cover, cockpit trim panels and instrument cluster (see Section 4, Steps 38 to 41. Undo the nuts securing the mirrors and lift them off **(see illustrations 4.42a and b)**.
7 Installation is the reverse of removal.

6 Seat cowling

2006 to 2008 models

1 Remove the seat (see Section 2).
2 Follow the procedure in Section 1 to release the trim clips securing the centre panel and lift it off, noting how it fits **(see illustrations)**.
3 Remove the bridging piece **(see illustration)**. The seat cowling can now be removed in two halves.
4 Where fitted, undo the bolts securing the grab handle, noting the location of the washers, and lift the handle off **(see illustrations)**. Note which way round the handles fit – they are marked L (left-hand) and R (right-hand) on the underside of the front bracket **(see illustration)**.
5 Release the trim clip securing the underside

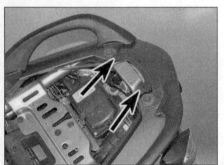

6.2a Release the trim clips (arrowed) . . .

6.2b . . . and lift off the centre panel

6.3 Remove the bridging piece

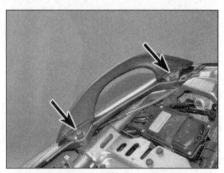

6.4a Undo the bolts (arrowed) . . .

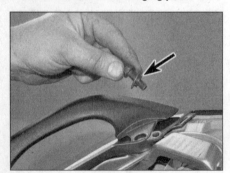

6.4b . . . noting the location of the washers . . .

6.4c . . . and lift the handle off

6.4d Handles are left and right-hand fit – L (left) shown

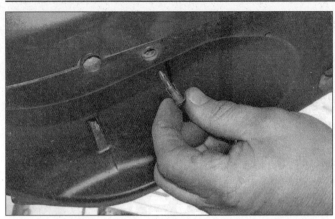

6.5 Trim clip secures underside of cowling to mudguard

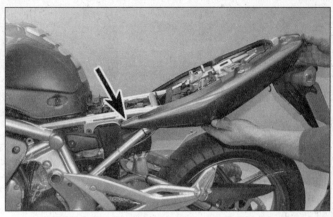

6.6a Release the peg from the grommet (arrowed)

of the cowling to the mudguard **(see illustration)**.

6 Ease the front of the cowling away to release the peg on the inside from the grommet in the frame bracket, then unhook the rear of the cowling from the tab on the tail light assembly and lift the cowling off **(see illustrations)**.

7 Installation is the reverse of removal. Ensure the rear of the cowling is hooked over the tab on the tail light assembly and the lower edge is correctly aligned with the edge of the mudguard before pressing the peg into the grommet.

2009-on models

8 Remove the seat (see Section 2).

9 Where fitted, undo the bolts securing the grab handles, noting the location of the spacers, and lift the handles off **(see illustrations)**.

10 Follow the procedure in Section 1 to release the trim clips securing the centre panel and lift it off **(see illustrations)**.

11 Undo the screw securing the top edge of the cowling, noting the washer **(see illustration)**.

12 Release the trim clip securing the underside of the cowling to the mudguard **(see illustration)**.

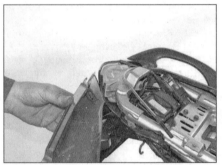

6.6b Unhook the rear of the cowling . . .

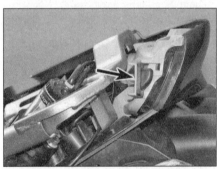

6.6c . . . from the tab on the tail light assembly

6.9a Undo the bolts (arrowed) . . .

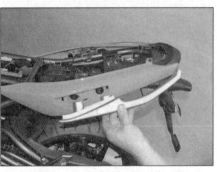

6.9b . . . and lift the handle off

6.10a Release the trim clips (arrowed) . . .

6.10b . . . and lift the centre panel off

6.11 Undo the screw securing the top edge of the cowling

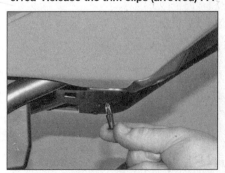

6.12 Trim clip secures underside of cowling to mudguard

13 Release the trim clip securing the front of the cowling to the fuel tank side panel **(see illustration 3.3a)**.

14 Ease the front of the cowling away to release the peg on the inside from the grommet in the frame bracket, then pull the tab on the inside rear of the cowling out of the mounting rubber on the tail light assembly and lift the cowling off **(see illustrations)**.

15 Installation is the reverse of removal. Ensure the tab on the rear of the cowling is pressed into the rubber on the tail light assembly and the lower edge is correctly aligned with the edge of the mudguard before pressing the peg into the grommet.

6.14a Release the peg from the grommet (arrowed)

6.14b Unhook the tab from the tail light assembly

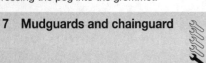

7 Mudguards and chainguard

Front mudguard

2006 to 2008 models

1 Release the brake hose clips from the mudguard by squeezing the ends together and pulling the clips out **(see illustration)**.

2 Undo the screws securing the mudguard on both sides, noting the location of the washers and rubber bushes in the mudguard **(see illustration)**.

3 Lift the mudguard forwards and off **(see illustration)**. Note the location of the mudguard brackets – if necessary undo the

bolts on the inside of the fork legs and remove the brackets.

4 Installation is the reverse of removal.

2009-on models

5 Undo the screws securing the mudguard on both sides **(see illustration)**. Note how the brake hose clips are retained by the rear screws.

6 Draw the mudguard forwards and off.

7 Installation is the reverse of removal.

Rear mudguard

8 Remove the seat cowling (see Section 6).

9 Trace the wiring from the licence plate light and the turn signal assemblies and disconnect it at the connectors **(see illustration)**. Release the wiring from any clips or ties and feed it

through to the underside of the under-seat panel.

10 To remove the mudguard, undo the bolts securing it to the frame and to the under-seat panel **(see illustration)**. Lift the mudguard off, together with the licence plate light and the turn signal assemblies. If required, remove the licence plate light and the turn signal assemblies (see Chapter 8).

11 Installation is the reverse of removal.

12 Check the operation of the licence plate light and the turn signals before riding the motorcycle

Chainguard and rear hugger

2006 to 2008 models

13 Follow the procedure in Section 1 to

7.1 Release the brake hose clips from the mudguard

7.2 Undo the screws securing the mudguard

7.3 Lift the mudguard forwards and off

7.5 Undo the screws securing the mudguard

7.9 Disconnect the wiring connectors (arrowed)

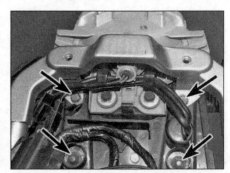

7.10 Bolts (arrowed) secure the rear mudguard

7.13 Removing the chainguard – 2006 to 2008 models

7.15 Remove the trim clip (A) and right-hand mounting screw (B)

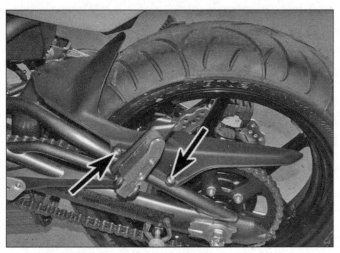

7.16a Remove the left-hand mounting screws . . .

7.16c . . . and lift the chainguard/hugger off – 2009-on models

release the trim clip securing the front of the chainguard, then undo the screw and lift the chainguard off (see illustration).

14 Installation is the reverse of removal.

2009-on models

15 Follow the procedure in Section 1 to release the trim clip securing the front of the combined chainguard and rear hugger (see illustration).

16 Undo the screws on both sides and lift the chainguard/hugger off (see illustrations).

17 Installation is the reverse of removal.

Chapter 8
Electrical system

Contents

Degrees of difficulty

Easy, suitable for novice with little experience	**Fairly easy,** suitable for beginner with some experience 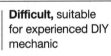	**Fairly difficult,** suitable for competent DIY mechanic
Difficult, suitable for experienced DIY mechanic	**Very difficult,** suitable for expert DIY or professional	

Specifications

Battery

Type	YTX12-BS
Capacity	12 V, 10 Ah
Voltage fully-charged	
2006 to 2008 models	min 12.8 V
2009-on models	min 12.6 V
Charging rate	
Normal	1.2 A for 5 to 10 hrs
Quick	5 A for 1 hr

Charging system

Alternator stator coil resistance	0.18 to 0.27 ohms
Alternator unregulated output	min 42 volts AC @ 4000 rpm
Regulated voltage output	14.2 to 15.2 volts DC
Current leakage	2 mA (max)

Starter motor

Brush length	
Standard	12 mm
Service limit (min)	
Engine numbers up to AE046804	6 mm
Engine numbers from AE046805-on	6.5 mm
Commutator diameter – engine numbers up to AE046804	
Standard	28 mm
Service limit (min)	27 mm

Fuses

Main fuse	30 A
ECU (engine management) fuse	15 A
Fan fuse	15 A
Oxygen sensor heater fuse	10 A
Turn signal relay fuse	10 A
Headlight fuse	10 A
Tail light fuse	10 A
Ignition fuse	10 A
Horn fuse	10 A
ABS solenoid valve relay fuse	25 A
ABS pump motor relay fuse	30 A

Bulbs

Headlights	55 W x 2 quartz halogen
Brake/tail light	
2006 to 2008	21/5W
2009-on	LED
Licence plate light	5 W
Sidelight	
2006 to 2008	5 W
2009-on	5 W x 2
Turn signal lights	
2006 to 2008	21 W x 4
2009-on	10 W x 4
Instrument and warning lights	LED

Torque settings

Alternator cover bolts	10 Nm
Alternator rotor bolt	
Initial torque	20 Nm
Final torque (2006 to 2008 models)	157 Nm
Final torque (2009-on models)	155 Nm
Alternator stator bolts	12 Nm
Neutral switch	15 Nm
Oil pressure switch	15 Nm
Sidestand switch bolt	9 Nm
Speed sensor bolt	8 Nm
Starter motor mounting bolts	10 Nm

1 General information

All models have a 12 volt electrical system charged by a three-phase alternator with a separate regulator/rectifier.

The regulator maintains the charging system output within the specified range to prevent overcharging, and the rectifier converts the ac (alternating current) output of the alternator to dc (direct current) to power the lights and other components and to charge the battery. The alternator rotor is mounted on the left-hand end of the crankshaft.

The starter motor is mounted on the top of the crankcase behind the cylinders. The starting system includes the motor, the battery, the relay and the various wires and switches. Some of the switches are part of a starter safety interlock system – see Chapter 1, Section 13, for further information.

Note: *Keep in mind that electrical parts, once purchased, often cannot be returned. To avoid unnecessary expense, make very sure the faulty component has been positively identified before buying a replacement part.*

2 Electrical system fault finding

⚠️ *Warning: To prevent the risk of short circuits, the ignition switch must always be OFF and the battery negative (-ve) terminal should be disconnected before any of the bike's other electrical components are disturbed. Don't forget to reconnect the terminal securely once work is finished or if battery power is needed for circuit testing.*

1 A typical electrical circuit consists of an electrical component, the switches, relays, etc, related to that component and the wiring and connectors that link the component to the battery and the frame.

2 Before tackling any troublesome electrical circuit, first study the wiring diagram thoroughly to get a complete picture of what makes up that individual circuit. Trouble spots, for instance, can often be narrowed down by noting if other components related to that circuit are operating properly or not. If several components or circuits fail at one time, chances are the fault lies either in the fuse or in the common earth (ground) connection, as several circuits are often routed through the same fuse and earth (ground) connections.

3 Electrical problems often stem from simple causes, such as loose or corroded connections or a blown fuse. Prior to any electrical fault finding, always check the condition of the fuse, wires and connections in the problem circuit. Intermittent failures can be especially frustrating, since you can't always duplicate the failure when it's convenient to test. In such situations, a good practice is to clean all connections in the affected circuit, whether or not they appear to be good – where possible use a dedicated electrical cleaning spray along with sandpaper, wire wool or other abrasive material to remove corrosion, and a dedicated electrical protection spray to prevent further problems. All of the connections and wires should also be wiggled to check for looseness which can cause intermittent failure.

4 If you don't have a multimeter it is highly advisable to obtain one – they are not expensive and will enable a full range of electrical tests to be made. Go for a modern digital one with LCD display as they are easier to use. A continuity tester and/or test light are useful for certain electrical checks

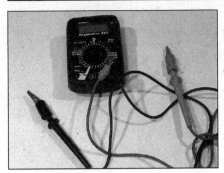

2.4a A digital multimeter can be used for all electrical tests

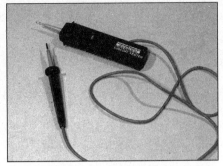

2.4b A battery powered continuity tester

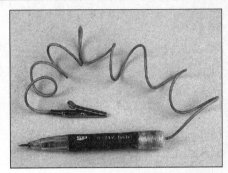

2.4c A simple test light can be used for voltage checks

as an alternative, though are limited in their usefulness compared to a multimeter **(see illustrations)**.

Continuity checks

5 The term continuity describes the uninterrupted flow of electricity through an electrical circuit. Continuity can be checked with a multimeter set either to its continuity function (a beep is emitted when continuity is found), or to the resistance (ohms / Ω) function, or with a dedicated continuity tester. Both instruments are powered by an internal battery, therefore the checks are made with the ignition OFF. As a safety precaution, always disconnect the battery negative (-ve) lead before making continuity checks, particularly if ignition switch checks are being made.

6 If using a multimeter, select the continuity function if it has one, or the resistance (ohms) function. Touch the meter probes together and check that a beep is emitted or the meter reads zero, which indicates continuity. If there is no continuity there will be no beep or the meter will show infinite resistance. After using the meter, always switch it OFF to conserve its battery.

7 A continuity tester can be used in the same way – its light should come on or it should beep to indicate continuity in the switch ON position, but should be off or silent in the OFF position.

8 Note that the polarity of the test probes

doesn't matter for continuity checks, although care should be taken to follow specific test procedures if a diode or solid-state component is being checked.

Switch continuity checks

9 If a switch is at fault, trace its wiring to the wiring connectors. Separate the connectors and inspect them for security and condition. A build-up of dirt or corrosion here will most likely be the cause of the problem – clean up and apply a water dispersant such as WD40, or alternatively use a dedicated contact cleaner and protection spray.

10 If using a multimeter, select the continuity function if it has one, or the resistance (ohms) function, and connect its probes to the terminals in the connector **(see illustration)**. Simple ON/OFF type switches, such as brake light switches, only have two wires whereas combination switches, like the handlebar switches, have many wires. Study the wiring diagram to ensure that you are connecting to the correct pair of wires. Continuity should be indicated with the switch ON and no continuity with it OFF.

Wiring continuity checks

11 Many electrical faults are caused by damaged wiring, often due to incorrect routing or chaffing on frame components. Loose, wet or corroded wire connectors can also be the cause of electrical problems.

12 A continuity check can be made on a single length of wire by disconnecting it at each end and connecting the meter or .continuity tester probes to each end of the

wire **(see illustration)**. Continuity (low or no resistance – zero ohms) should be indicated if the wire is good. If no continuity (high resistance) is shown, suspect a broken wire.

13 To check for continuity to earth in any earth wire connect one probe of your meter or tester to the earth wire terminal in the connector and the other to the frame, engine, or battery earth (-ve) terminal. Continuity (low or no resistance – zero ohms) should be indicated if the wire is good. If no continuity (high resistance) is shown, suspect a broken wire or corroded or loose earth point (see below).

Voltage checks

14 A voltage check can determine whether power is reaching a component. Use a multimeter set to the dc voltage scale, or a test light. The test light is the cheaper component, but the meter has the advantage of being able to give a voltage reading.

15 Connect the meter or test light in parallel, i.e. across the load **(see illustration)**.

16 First identify the relevant wiring circuit by referring to the wiring diagram at the end of this manual. If other electrical components share the same power supply (i.e. are fed from the same fuse), take note whether they are working correctly – this is useful information in deciding where to start checking the circuit.

17 If using a meter, check first that the meter leads are plugged into the correct terminals on the meter (red to positive (+ve), black to negative (-ve). Set the meter to the dc volts function, where necessary at a range suitable for the battery voltage – 0 to 20 V dc. Connect

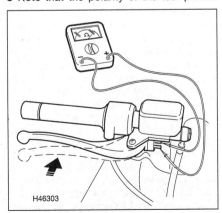

2.10 Testing a brake light switch for continuity

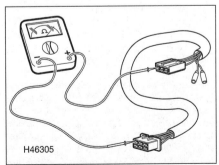

2.12 Testing for continuity in a wiring loom

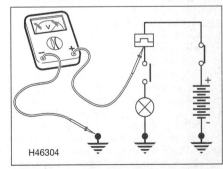

2.15 Connect the multimeter in parallel, or across the load, as shown

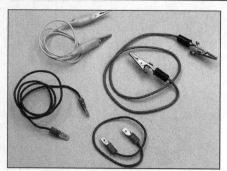

2.23 A selection of jumper wires for making earth (ground) checks

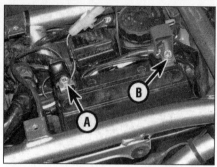

3.3a Battery negative (-ve) terminal (A) and positive (+ve) terminal (B)

3.3b Disconnect the negative (-ve) terminal first

the meter red probe (+ve) to the power supply wire and the black probe to a good metal earth (ground) on the motorcycle's frame or directly to the battery negative (-ve) terminal. Battery voltage should be shown on the meter with the ignition switch, and if necessary any other relevant switch, ON.

18 If using a test light, connect its positive (+ve) probe to the power supply terminal and its negative (-ve) probe to a good earth (ground) on the motorcycle's frame. With the switch, and if necessary any other relevant switch, ON, the test light should illuminate.

19 If no voltage is indicated, work back towards the fuse continuing to check for voltage. When you reach a point where there is voltage, you know the problem lies between that point and your last check point.

Earth (ground) checks

20 Earth connections are made either directly to the engine or frame (such as neutral switch, oil pressure switch etc. which only have a positive feed) or by a separate wire into the earth circuit of the wiring harness. Alternatively a short earth wire is sometimes run from the component directly to the motorcycle's frame.

21 Corrosion is a common cause of a poor earth connection, as is a loose earth terminal fastener.

22 If total or multiple component failure is experienced, check the security of the main earth lead from the negative (-ve) terminal of the battery, the earth lead bolted to the engine, and the main earth point(s) on the frame. If corroded, dismantle the connection and clean all surfaces back to bare metal. Remake the connection and prevent further corrosion from forming by smearing battery terminal grease over the connection.

23 To check the earth of a component, use an insulated jumper wire to temporarily bypass its earth connection **(see illustration)** – connect one end of the jumper wire to the earth terminal or metal body of the component and the other end to the motorcycle's frame. If the circuit works with the jumper wire installed, the earth circuit is faulty.

24 To check an earth wire first check for corroded or loose connections, then check the wiring for continuity (Step 13) between each connector in the circuit in turn, and then to its earth point, to locate the break.

HAYNES HiNT *Remember that all electrical circuits are designed to conduct electricity from the battery, through the wires, switches, relays, etc. to the electrical component (light bulb, starter motor, etc). From there it is directed to the frame (earth) where it is passed back to the battery. Electrical problems are basically an interruption in the flow of electricity from the battery or back to it.*

3 Battery

Caution: Be extremely careful when handling or working around the battery. The electrolyte is very caustic and an explosive gas (hydrogen) is given off when the battery is charging. Always disconnect the battery negative (-ve) lead first, and reconnect it last.

Removal and installation

1 Make sure the ignition is switched OFF. Remove the seat (see Chapter 7).

2 On the machine used to illustrate this procedure, the fuel tank bracket restricted access to the battery. If necessary, remove the fuel tank and bracket (see Chapter 4).

3 Pull back the black insulating cover, unscrew the negative (-ve) terminal bolt and disconnect the lead from the battery **(see illustrations)**.

4 Next, lift up the red insulating cover,

3.5 Lift out the battery

unscrew the positive (+ve) terminal bolt and disconnect the lead **(see illustration 3.3a)**.

5 Lift the battery out of its holder **(see illustration)**.

6 Prior to installation, ensure the battery terminals and lead ends are clean (see Step 10). Ensure the battery is fitted the correct way round, then reconnect the leads, connecting the positive (+ve) terminal first.

HAYNES HiNT *Battery corrosion can be kept to a minimum by applying a layer of battery terminal grease or petroleum jelly (Vaseline) to the terminals after the leads have been connected. DO NOT use a mineral based grease.*

7 Install the remaining components in the reverse order of removal.

Inspection and maintenance

8 The battery is of the maintenance free (sealed) type – however, the following checks should still be performed.

9 Check the battery condition by measuring the voltage at the terminals. Connect the voltmeter positive (+ve) probe to the battery positive (+ve) terminal, and the negative (-ve) probe to the battery negative (-ve) terminal **(see illustration)**. When fully-charged there should be 12.6 volts or more present. If the voltage falls below that level, remove the battery and recharge it (see Steps 14 to 18).

10 Check the battery terminals and leads are tight and free of corrosion. If corrosion is evident, remove the battery and clean the

3.9 Checking the battery voltage

3.16 Ensure the charging rate is safe

3.25 Undo the screw (arrowed)

3.26 Release the wiring loom from the clip

terminals and lead ends with a wire brush, knife or steel wool.

11 Keep the battery case clean to prevent current leakage, which can discharge the battery over a period of time (especially when it sits unused). If necessary, wash the outside of the case with a solution of baking soda and water. Rinse the battery thoroughly, then dry it.

12 Look for cracks in the case and replace the battery with a new one if any are found. If acid has been spilled on the frame or battery housing, neutralise it with a baking soda and water solution, dry it thoroughly, then touch up any damaged paint.

13 If the motorcycle sits unused for long periods of time, disconnect the leads from the battery terminals, negative (-ve) terminal first. Check the battery condition regularly and charge the battery once every month to six weeks.

Charging

14 Ensure the battery charger is suitable for charging a 12 volt battery.

15 Remove the battery (see Steps 1 to 5). Before switching the charger ON, connect it to the battery, making sure that the positive (+ve) lead on the charger is connected to the positive (+ve) terminal on the battery, and the negative (-ve) lead is connected to the negative (-ve) terminal.

16 Kawasaki recommend that the battery is charged at a rate of 1.2 amps for 5 to 10 hours. Exceeding this figure can cause the battery to overheat, buckling the plates and rendering it useless. Few owners will have access to an expensive current controlled charger, so if a normal domestic charger is used, check that after a possible initial peak, the charge rate falls to a safe level **(see illustration)**.

17 If the battery becomes hot during charging **STOP**. Further charging will cause damage. **Note:** *In emergencies the battery can be charged at a maximum rate of 5.0 amps for a period of 1 hour. However, this is not recommended and the low amp charge is by far the safer method of charging the battery.*

18 After charging, allow the battery to stand for 30 minutes, then measure its terminal voltage (see Step 9). If the voltage is below 12.6 volts, charge the battery again and repeat the voltage measuring process. If the voltage

is still low, the battery is failing and should be replaced with a new one.

19 Install the battery (see Steps 6 and 7).

20 If the recharged battery discharges rapidly when left disconnected, it is likely that an internal short caused by physical damage or sulphation has occurred. A new battery will be required. A good battery will tend to lose its charge at about 1% per day.

Battery carrier

21 To remove the battery carrier, first remove the seat cowling (see Chapter 7).

22 Remove the battery – remove the fuel tank bracket for this procedure (see Steps 1 to 5).

23 Displace the relay box – it is not necessary to disconnect the wiring connectors (see Chapter 3, Section 2).

24 Unclip the starter relay/main fuse holder from the left-hand side of the battery carrier (see Section 4).

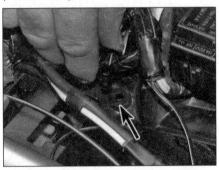
3.27 Unclip the wiring loom from the battery carrier

3.29 Release the trim clip securing the rear of the battery carrier

25 Undo the screw securing the rear brake reservoir to the battery carrier **(see illustration)**.

26 Release the wiring loom from the clip on the left-hand side of the frame **(see illustration)**.

27 Release the wiring loom from the clip on the battery carrier **(see illustration)**.

28 Unclip the fusebox from the inside of the battery carrier **(see illustration)**.

29 Follow the procedure in Chapter 7, Section 1, to release the trim clip securing the rear of the battery carrier to the frame **(see illustration)**.

30 Ease the battery carrier out, taking care not to damage or strain any components on the wiring loom **(see illustration)**.

31 Installation is the reverse of removal. Ensure the wiring connectors for the components mounted on the carrier are secure.

3.28 Unclip the fusebox from inside the battery carrier

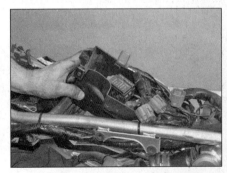
3.30 Ease the battery carrier out

4.2a Fuse function and rating is marked on fusebox lid

4.2b Unclip fusebox lid for access – note spare fuses

4 Fuses

1 The electrical systems are protected by fuses of different ratings. The circuit fuses are housed in the fusebox which is underneath the seat – remove the seat for access (see Chapter 7)

2 Unclip the fusebox lids to access the fuses as marked on the lids (see illustrations). Note the location of the spare fuses.

3 The main fuse is integral with the starter relay which is mounted on the left-hand side of the battery carrier – remove the left-hand fuel tank side panel for access (see Chapter 7, Section 3). Undo the screw securing the relay cover, unclip the relay/main fuse holder from the battery carrier, then unclip

the wiring connector to access the fuse (see illustrations).

4 On ABS-equipped machines the ABS solenoid valve and pump motor fuses are located in holders mounted on the left-hand side of the rear subframe underneath the seat (see Chapter 6, Section 13).

5 The fuses can be removed and checked visually. If you can't pull the fuse out with your fingertips, use a pair of needle-nose pliers. A blown fuse is easily identified by a break in the element (see illustration). Each fuse is clearly marked with its rating and must only be renewed by a fuse of the correct rating. A spare fuse of each rating is housed in the fusebox or fuse holder. A spare main fuse is housed with the starter relay on 2009-on models. If a spare fuse is used, always replace it with a new one so that a spare of each rating is carried on the bike at all times.

 Warning: Never put in a fuse of a higher rating or bridge the terminals with any other substitute, however temporary it may be. Serious damage may be done to the circuit, or a fire may start.

6 If a fuse blows, be sure to check the wiring circuit very carefully for evidence of a short-circuit. Look for bare wires and chafed, melted or burned insulation. If the fuse is renewed before the cause is located, the new fuse will blow immediately.

7 Occasionally a fuse will blow or cause an open-circuit for no obvious reason. Corrosion of the fuse ends and fusebox terminals may occur and cause poor fuse contact. If this happens, remove the corrosion with a wire brush or wire wool, then spray the fuse ends and terminals with electrical contact cleaner.

5 Lighting circuit checks

1 The battery provides power for operation of the lights. If none of the lights work, always check battery voltage before proceeding. Low battery voltage indicates either a faulty battery or a defective charging system. Refer to Section 3 for battery checks and Section 24 for charging system tests. Also, check the condition of the fuses (see Section 4) – if there is more than one problem at the same time, it is likely to be a fault relating to a multi-function component, such as one of the fuses governing more than one circuit, or the ignition switch. When checking for a blown filament in a bulb, it is advisable to back up a visual check with a continuity test of the filament as it is not always apparent that a bulb has blown. When testing for continuity, remember that on single terminal bulbs it is the metal body of the bulb that is the earth (ground).

Headlight

2 All models have two single filament bulbs. If one bulb fails to work, first check the bulb and the bulb terminals (see Section 6). If both bulbs fail to work check the headlight fuse (see Section 4), and then the relay (see

4.3a Undo the relay cover

4.3b Draw the relay out . . .

4.3c . . . and disconnect the wiring connector . . .

4.3d . . . to access the main fuse (arrowed)

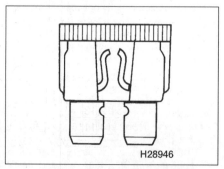

H28946

4.5 A blown fuse can be identified by a break in its element

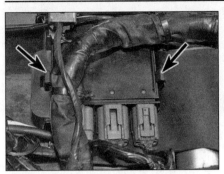
5.6a Release the clips (arrowed) . . .

5.6b . . . and lift out the relay box . . .

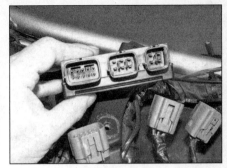
5.6c . . . and disconnect the wiring connectors

Step 6). If the high beam bulb fails to work check the dimmer switch (see Section 15).

3 Next disconnect the relevant headlight bulb wiring connector (see Section 7), and check for battery voltage on the supply side of the connector – connect the negative probe of a multimeter to the black/yellow wire (earth), and the positive probe to the red/black wire for the high beam bulb connector and the blue/yellow wire for the low beam bulb connector, with the ignition switch ON. Don't forget to select either high or low beam as appropriate at the dimmer switch while conducting this test.

4 If no voltage is indicated, check for continuity between the black/yellow wire connector terminal and earth (ground). If there is no continuity, check the earth (ground) circuit for an open or poor connection.

5 If the earth circuit is good, check the wiring between the headlight connector, dimmer switch, headlight relay (see Step 6), and the ignition switch, referring to *Wiring Diagrams* at the end of this chapter, then check the switches themselves.

6 To check the headlight relay, first remove the fuel tank and the fuel tank bracket (see Chapter 4). Release the clips securing the relay box, lift it out of its rubber holder and disconnect the wiring connectors **(see illustrations)**.

7 Using a multimeter, check for continuity between terminals 1 and 3 on the relay **(see illustration)**. There should be no continuity. Now use jumper wires to connect the positive (+ve) terminal of a fully charged 12 volt battery to terminal 2 on the relay and the negative (-ve) battery terminal to relay terminal 11. There should now be continuity between terminals 1 and 3. If the relay fails either of the checks the relay box must be replaced with a new one – individual relays are not available.

8 If the relay is good, check the diodes in the circuit using an ohmmeter. First connect the positive (+ve) probe to terminal 1 and the negative (-ve) to terminal 11 and note the result. Now reverse the probes – the resistance should be low in one direction and more than ten times as much in the other. Repeat the test between terminals 2 and 11. If the results are not as stated, replace the relay box with a new one.

Sidelight

9 If the sidelight(s) fail(s) to work, first check the bulb(s), the bulb terminals and wiring connector(s) (see Section 6). Check the tail light fuse (see Section 4).

10 Next, disconnect the wiring connector and check for battery voltage at the red wire terminal on the supply side of the connector, with the ignition switch ON.

11 If no voltage is indicated, check the wiring between the sidelight and the ignition switch, then check the switch (see Section 14).

12 If voltage is indicated, check for continuity between the wiring connector terminals on the sidelight side of the wiring connector and the corresponding terminals in the bulbholder – no continuity indicates a break in the circuit. If continuity is present, check for continuity between the black/yellow wire terminal in the loom side of the connector and earth (ground). If there is no continuity, check the earth (ground) circuit for a broken or poor connection.

Tail light

2006 to 2008 models

13 If the tail light fails to work, first check the bulb and the bulb terminals (see Section 8). Check the tail light fuse (see Section 4). Check the wiring connector

14 Next, disconnect the wiring connector and check for battery voltage at the red wire terminal on the supply side of the connector, with the ignition switch ON.

15 If no voltage is indicated, check the wiring between the tail light connector and the ignition switch, then check the switch (see Section 14).

16 If voltage is indicated, check for continuity between the terminals on the tail light side of the wiring connector and the corresponding terminals in the bulbholder – no continuity indicates a break in the circuit. If continuity is present, check for continuity between the black/yellow wire terminal in the loom side of the connector and earth (ground). If there is no continuity, check the earth (ground) circuit for a broken or poor connection.

2009-on models

17 The tail light consists of a number of LEDs in a sealed unit. When a single LED fails it cannot be replaced with a new one, however the failure of one LED will not affect the function of the others. If enough LEDs have failed so as to impair the safe operation of the motorcycle, replace the tail light unit with a new one (see Section 8).

18 If the tail light fails to work completely, first check the fuse (see Section 4), then the wiring connector (see Section 8). Next disconnect the wiring connector and check for battery voltage at the red wire terminal on the supply side of the connector, with the ignition switch ON.

19 If no voltage is indicated, check the wiring between the tail light connector and the ignition switch, then check the switch itself (see Section 14).

20 If voltage is indicated, check for continuity between the black/yellow wire terminal in the loom side of the connector and earth (ground). If there is no continuity, check the earth (ground) circuit for a broken or poor connection.

Brake light

2006 to 2008 models

21 If the brake light fails to work, first check the bulb and the bulb terminals (see Section 8). Check the tail light fuse (see Section 4). Check the wiring connector.

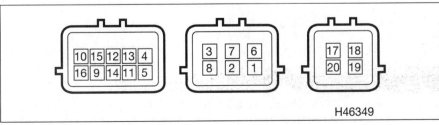
H46349

5.7 Relay box terminal numbering

22 Next, disconnect the wiring connector and check for battery voltage at the blue wire terminal on the supply side of the connector with the ignition switch ON and the brake lever or pedal applied.

23 If no voltage is indicated, check the brake light switches (see Section 11), then the wiring between the tail light connector and the switches.

24 If voltage is indicated, check for continuity between the terminals on the tail light side of the wiring connector and the corresponding terminals in the bulbholder – no continuity indicates a break in the circuit. If continuity is present, check for continuity between the black/yellow wire terminal in the loom side of the connector and earth (ground). If there is no continuity, check the earth (ground) circuit for a broken or poor connection.

2009-on models

25 The brake light consists of a number of LEDs in a sealed unit. When a single LED fails it cannot be replaced with a new one, however the failure of one LED will not affect the function of the others. If enough LEDs have failed so as to impair the safe operation of the motorcycle, replace the tail light unit with a new one (see Section 8).

26 If the brake light fails to work completely, first check the tail light fuse (see Section 4), then the wiring connector (see Section 8). Next, disconnect the wiring connector and check for battery voltage at the blue wire terminal on the supply side of the connector, with the ignition switch ON and the brake lever or pedal applied.

27 If no voltage is indicated, check the brake

light switches (see Section 11), then the wiring between the connector and the switches.

28 If voltage is indicated, check for continuity between the black/yellow wire terminal in the loom side of the connector and earth (ground). If there is no continuity, check the earth (ground) circuit for a broken or poor connection.

Licence plate light

29 If the light fails to work, first check the bulb and the bulb terminals (see Section 8). Check the tail light fuse (see Section 4). Check the wiring connector (see Section 8).

30 Next, disconnect the wiring connector and check for battery voltage at the red wire terminal on the supply side of the connector with the ignition switch ON.

31 If no voltage is indicated, check the wiring between the connector and the ignition switch, then check the switch itself (see Section 14).

32 If voltage is indicated, check for continuity between the terminals on the licence plate light side of the wiring connector and the corresponding terminals in the bulbholder – no continuity indicates a break in the circuit. If continuity is present, check for continuity between the black/yellow wire terminal in the loom side of the connector and earth (ground). If there is no continuity, check the earth (ground) circuit for a broken or poor connection.

Turn signal lights

33 If one light fails to work, check the bulb and the bulb terminals (see Section 9), then the wiring connector. If none of the turn signals work, check the turn signal relay fuse (see Section 4).

34 If the fuse is good, check the turn signal relay (see Section 10).

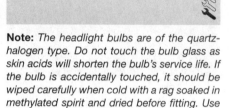

6 Headlight bulbs and sidelight bulbs

Note: *The headlight bulbs are of the quartz-halogen type. Do not touch the bulb glass as skin acids will shorten the bulb's service life. If the bulb is accidentally touched, it should be wiped carefully when cold with a rag soaked in methylated spirit and dried before fitting. Use a paper towel or dry cloth when handling new bulbs to prevent injury if the bulb should break and to increase bulb life.*

ER650 (2006 to 2008)

Headlight

1 Remove the headlight panel (see Chapter 7, Section 4).

2 Remove the rubber cover, noting how it fits **(see illustration)**.

3 Release the bulb retaining clip, then remove the bulbholder **(see illustrations)**.

4 Pull the old bulb out of the holder and fit the new one into it, bearing in mind the information in the **Note** above **(see illustration)**.

5 Fit the bulbholder into the headlight, making sure it locates correctly, and secure it in position with the retaining clip **(see illustration)**.

6 Fit the rubber cover with the TOP mark uppermost – ensure the cover is pressed all the way on **(see illustration)**.

6.2 Remove the rubber cover

6.3a Release the bulb retaining clip . . .

6.3b . . . and lift out the bulbholder

6.4 Pull the bulb out of the holder

6.5 Secure the bulb with the clip

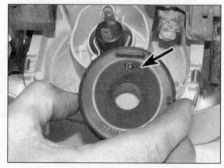

6.6 Cover TOP mark (arrowed) should face up

7 Connect the wiring connectors **(see illustration)**. Support the headlight panel and check the operation of the headlight, then install the headlight panel.

Sidelight

8 Remove the headlight panel (see Chapter 7, Section 4).
9 Pull the bulbholder out from the back of the headlight, then carefully pull the bulb out of the holder **(see illustrations)**.
10 Fit the new bulb into the bulbholder then press the holder firmly into the headlight.
11 Connect the wiring connector **(see illustration)**. Support the headlight panel and check the operation of the sidelight, then install the headlight panel.

ER650 (2009-on)

Headlight

12 Remove the headlight panel (see Chapter 7, Section 4).
13 Remove the rubber cover, noting how it fits.
14 Turn the bulb anti-clockwise to release it from the socket in the headlight and draw it out.
15 Fit the new bulb, bearing in mind the information in the **Note** above. Align the tabs on the bulb with the cut-outs in the socket, then turn the bulb clockwise to secure it.
16 Fit the rubber cover – ensure the cover is pressed all the way on.
17 Connect the wiring connector. Support the headlight panel and check the operation of the headlight, then install the headlight panel.

Sidelight

18 Follow the procedure in Steps 8 to 11 – note that two sidelights are fitted to these models.

EX650 (2006 to 2008)

Headlight

19 Follow the procedure in Chapter 7, Section 4, to remove the cockpit trim panels and instrument cluster panel.
20 Disconnect the wiring connector **(see illustration)**.
21 Remove the rubber cover, noting how it fits **(see illustration)**.

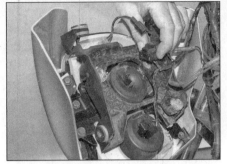

6.7 Connect the wiring connectors

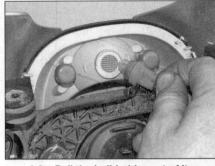

6.9a Pull the bulbholder out of its socket . . .

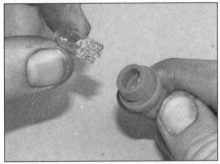

6.9b . . . then pull out the bulb

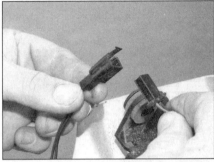

6.11 Connect the sidelight wiring connector

22 Release the bulb retaining clip, noting how it fits, then remove the bulbholder **(see illustrations)**.
23 Pull the old bulb out of the holder and fit the new one into it, bearing in mind the information in the **Note** above **(see illustration)**.
24 Fit the bulbholder into the headlight, making sure it locates correctly, and secure it in position with the retaining clip.

6.20 Disconnect the wiring connector . . .

6.21 . . . and remove the rubber cover

6.22a Release the bulb retaining clip . . .

6.22b . . . and lift out the bulbholder

6.23 Pull the bulb out of the holder

6.25 Ensure the cover is pressed all the way on

6.29a Location of the sidelight bulbholder (arrowed)

6.29b Pull out the bulbholder . . .

6.29c . . . then pull the bulb out of the holder

6.36 Release the retaining clip and lift out the bulb

25 Fit the rubber cover – ensure the cover is pressed all the way on **(see illustration)**.
26 Connect the wiring connector and check the operation of the headlight.
27 Install the remaining components in the reverse order of removal.

Sidelight

28 Follow the procedure in Chapter 7, Section 4, to remove the cockpit trim panels and instrument cluster panel.
29 Pull the bulbholder out from the back of the headlight, then carefully pull the bulb out of the holder **(see illustrations)**.
30 Fit the new bulb into the bulbholder then press the holder firmly into the headlight.
31 Check the operation of the sidelight.
32 Install the remaining components in reverse order of bolts.

EX650 (2009-on)

Headlight

33 Follow the procedure in Chapter 7, Section 4, to remove the windshield, fairing top cover, cockpit trim panels and instrument cluster panel.
34 Disconnect the wiring connector **(see illustration 6.20)**.
35 Remove the rubber cover, noting how it fits **(see illustration 6.21)**.
36 Release the bulb retaining clip, noting how it fits, then remove the bulb **(see illustration)**.
37 Fit the new bulb, bearing in mind the information in the **Note** above. Align the tab on the bulb with the cut-out in the socket, and secure it in position with the retaining clip.
38 Fit the rubber cover with the TOP mark

uppermost – ensure the cover is pressed all the way on **(see illustration)**.
39 Connect the wiring connector and check the operation of the headlight.
40 Install the remaining components in the reverse order of removal.

Sidelight

41 Follow the procedure in Chapter 7, Section 4, to remove the windshield, fairing top cover, cockpit trim panels and instrument cluster panel.
42 Pull the bulbholder out from the back of the headlight, then carefully pull the bulb out of the holder – note that two sidelights are fitted to these models **(see illustrations)**.
43 Fit the new bulb into the bulbholder then press the holder firmly into the headlight.
44 Check the operation of the sidelight.
45 Install the remaining components in the reverse order of removal.

---

7 Headlight assembly and headlight aim

Headlight assembly

Removal

1 On ER650 models, remove the headlight panel; on 2009-on EX650 models, remove the fairing assembly (see Chapter 7).
2 On ER650 models, unscrew the bolts

6.38 TOP mark (arrowed) must be uppermost

6.42a Pull the bulbholder out . . .

6.42b . . . then pull the bulb out of the holder

7.2 Bolts (arrowed) secure headlight assembly – ER650

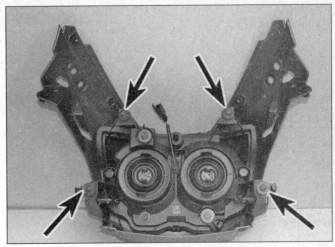

7.3 Bolts (arrowed) secure headlight assembly – 2006 to 2008 EX650

securing the headlight assembly to the headlight panel and lift it out **(see illustration)**. Note the location of the U-clips on the panel lugs. The clips should be a tight fit – renew any that are sprained.

3 On 2006 to 2008 EX650 models, unscrew the bolts securing the headlight panel, noting the location of the wiring guides on the two lower bolts **(see illustration)**. Lift out the headlight assembly. Note the location of the U-clips on the panel lugs. The clips should be a tight fit – renew any that are sprained. Note the location of the spacers and grommets on the headlight mounting lugs – if any of the grommets are damaged replace them with new ones.

4 On 2009-on EX650 models, unscrew the bolts securing the headlight assembly to the headlight panel **(see illustration)**. Note the location of the brackets on the upper mounting bolts and the spacers and grommets in the brackets **(see illustration)**. If any of the grommets are damaged replace them with

new ones. Lift out the headlight assembly. Note the location of the U-clips on the panel lugs. The clips should be a tight fit – renew any that are sprained.

Installation

5 Installation is the reverse of removal. Make sure all the wiring is correctly routed, connected and secured. Check the operation of the headlights and sidelight(s). Check the headlight aim.

Headlight aim

Note: *An improperly adjusted headlight may cause problems for oncoming traffic or provide poor, unsafe illumination of the road ahead. Before adjusting the headlight aim, be sure to consult with local traffic laws and regulations – for UK models refer to MOT Test Checks in the Reference section.*

6 Before making any adjustment, check that the tyre pressures are correct and the

suspension is adjusted as required. Make any adjustments to the headlight aim with the machine on level ground, with the fuel tank half full and with an assistant sitting on the seat. If the bike is usually ridden with a passenger on the back, have a second assistant to do this.

7 The headlight beam can adjusted both horizontally and vertically. On ER650 models and 2006 to 2008 EX650 models, adjustment is made either using a spanner on the adjuster hex, or using a suitable cross-head screwdriver under the notched rim of the adjuster – a slot is provided in the back of the headlight to locate the tip of the screwdriver. On 2009-on EX650 models, adjustment is made by turning the adjuster knobs by hand. On all models, the adjusters are located on the back of the headlight assembly.

8 On 2006 to 2008 ER650 models, horizontal adjustment is made by turning the adjuster on the upper left-hand side of the headlight and vertical adjustment is made by turning the adjuster on the lower right-hand side **(see**

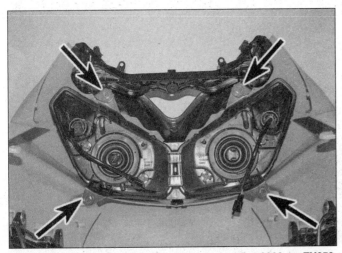

7.4a Bolts (arrowed) secure headlight assembly – 2009-on EX650

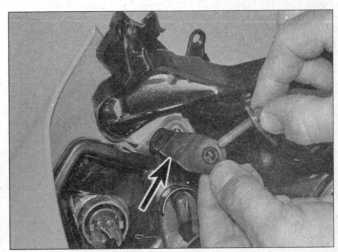

7.4b Note the location of the brackets (arrowed)

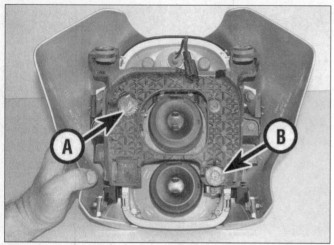

7.8 Horizontal beam adjuster (A) and vertical beam adjuster (B) – ER650

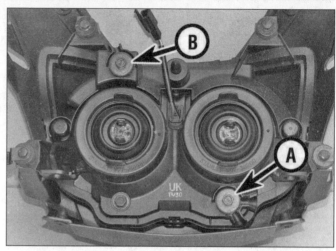

7.9 Horizontal beam adjuster (A) and vertical beam adjuster (B) – 2006 to 2008 EX650

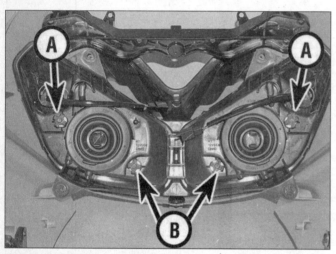

7.10 Horizontal beam adjuster (A) and vertical beam adjuster (B) – 2009-on EX650

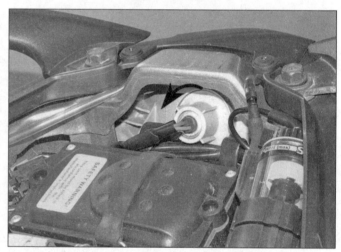
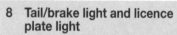

8.2a Turn the bulbholder anti-clockwise . . .

illustration). On 2009-on ER650 models, horizontal adjustment is made by turning the adjuster on the lower right-hand side of the headlight and vertical adjustment is made by turning the adjuster on the lower left-hand side.

9 On 2006 to 2008 EX650 models, horizontal adjustment is made by turning the adjuster on the lower right-hand side of the headlight and vertical adjustment is made by turning the adjuster on the upper left-hand side of the headlight (see illustration).

10 On 2009 EX650 models, the high beam (left-hand) and low beam (right-hand) lights are adjusted separately. Horizontal adjustment is made by turning the adjuster on the upper outside of the bulb location, and vertical adjustment is made by turning the adjuster on the lower inside of the bulb location (see illustration).

8 Tail/brake light and licence plate light

Note: *It is a good idea to use a paper towel or dry cloth when removing and installing bulbs to prevent injury if the bulb should break and to increase bulb life.*

Tail/brake light

Bulb

1 On all 2006 to 2008 models the tail/brake light is illuminated by a bulb. To access the bulb, first remove the seat (see Chapter 7).
2 Turn the bulbholder anti-clockwise and withdraw it from the tail light (see illustrations).
3 Push the bulb into the bulbholder and twist it anti-clockwise to remove it (see illustration).

8.2b . . . and remove it from the tail light unit

8.3 Push the bulb in and twist it anti-clockwise

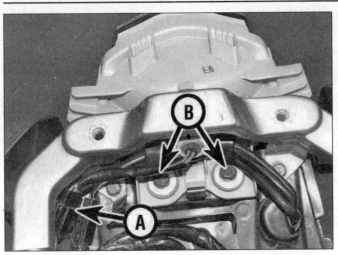

8.10 Tail light wiring connector (A) and mounting bolts (B)

8.14a Undo the screws (arrowed) . . .

4 Check the terminals in the bulbholder for corrosion and clean them if necessary.
5 Line up the pins of the new bulb with the slots in the holder, then push the bulb in and turn it clockwise until it locks into place. Check the operation of the tail/brake light.
6 Insert the bulbholder into the tail light and turn it clockwise to lock it in place.
7 Install the seat (see Chapter 7).
8 On 2009-on models the tail/brake light consists of a number of LEDs in a sealed unit. If enough LEDs have failed so as to impair the safe operation of the motorcycle, replace the tail light unit with a new one (see Steps 9 to 13).

Removal and installation

9 Remove the seat cowling (see Chapter 7).
10 Trace the wiring from the light unit and disconnect it at the connector **(see illustration)**.
11 Release the wiring from the clips secured by the light unit mounting bolts then undo the bolts **(see illustration 8.10)**. Lift the tail/brake light unit off.
12 Note the location of the spacers and grommets on the light unit mounting lugs – if either of the grommets are damaged replace them with new ones.
13 Installation is the reverse of removal. Make sure all the wiring is correctly routed,

connected and secured. Check the operation of the tail light and brake light.

Licence plate light

Bulb

14 Undo the lens housing screws and remove the housing **(see illustrations)**.
15 On 2006 to 2008 models, push the bulb into the holder and twist it anti-clockwise to remove it **(see illustration)**.
16 On 2009 models, the bulb is the capless type – do not twist the bulb, pull it out of the holder carefully **(see illustration)**.

8.14b . . . and remove the housing – 2006 to 2008 models

17 Check the terminals in the bulbholder for corrosion and clean them if necessary.
18 On 2006 to 2008 models, line up the pins of the new bulb with the slots in the holder, then push the bulb in and turn it clockwise until it locks into place.
19 On 2009-on models, push the new bulb into the bulbholder.
20 Fit the lens housing and tighten the screws.

Removal and installation

21 Remove the rear mudguard (see Chapter 7).
22 Undo the screws securing the licence plate

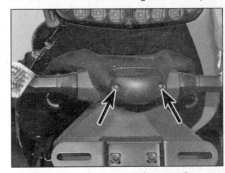

8.14c Undo the screws (arrowed) . . .

8.14d . . . and remove the housing – 2009-on models

8.15 Push the bulb in and twist it anti-clockwise – 2006 to 2008 models

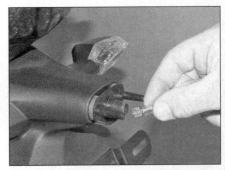

8.16 Pull the bulb out carefully – 2009-on models

light on the inside of the mudguard, noting the location of the washers, and remove the light.
23 Note the location of the spacers and grommets in the mudguard mountings – if either of the grommets are damaged replace them with new ones.
24 Installation is the reverse of removal. Make sure all the wiring is correctly routed, connected and secured. Check the operation of the licence plate light.

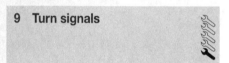

9 Turn signals

Note: *It is a good idea to use a paper towel or dry cloth when removing and installing bulbs to prevent injury if the bulb should break and to increase bulb life.*

Bulbs

ER650

1 To access the front turn signal bulbs, first follow the procedure in Chapter 7, Section 4, and remove the relevant side panel.
2 Turn the bulbholder anti-clockwise and withdraw it from the back of the signal assembly **(see illustrations)**.
3 Push the bulb into the bulbholder and twist it anti-clockwise to remove it **(see illustration)**.
4 Check the terminals in the bulbholder for corrosion and clean them if necessary.

9.2a Turn the bulbholder anti-clockwise . . .

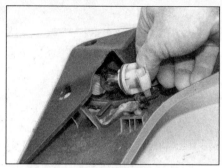

9.2b . . . and remove it from the signal assembly

5 Line up the pins of the new bulb with the slots in the holder, then push the bulb in and turn it clockwise until it locks into place.
6 Insert the bulbholder into the signal assembly and turn it clockwise to lock it in place. Reconnect the wiring connector and check the operation of the turn signal.
7 Install the side panel (see Chapter 7).
8 To access the rear turn signal bulbs on 2006 to 2008 models, undo the screw securing the lens on the underside of the assembly and draw the lens off, noting how it fits **(see illustrations)**.
9 Push the bulb into the bulbholder and twist it anti-clockwise to remove it **(see illustration)**.
10 Check the terminals in the bulbholder for corrosion and clean them if necessary.
11 Line up the pins of the new bulb with

the slots in the holder, then push the bulb in and turn it clockwise until it locks into place. Check the operation of the turn signal.
12 Install the lens and secure it with the screw. Do not over-tighten the screw as it is easy to strip the threads or crack the lens.
13 To access the rear turn signal bulbs on 2009-on models, undo the screw securing the lens on the rear of the assembly and draw the lens off, noting how it fits **(see illustrations)**.
14 Follow the procedure in Steps 9 to 12 to renew the bulb and install the lens.

EX650 (2006 to 2008)

15 To access the front turn signal bulbs, first follow the procedure in Chapter 7, Section 4, and remove the relevant cockpit trim panel.

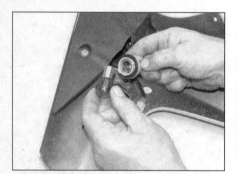

9.3 Push the bulb in and twist it anti-clockwise

9.8a Undo the screw (arrowed) . . .

9.8b . . . and remove the lens

9.9 Push the bulb in and twist it anti-clockwise

9.13a Undo the screw (arrowed) . . .

9.13b . . . and remove the lens

9.16a Turn the bulbholder anti-clockwise . . .

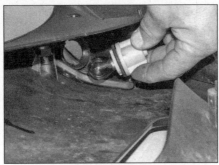

9.16b . . . and remove it from the signal assembly

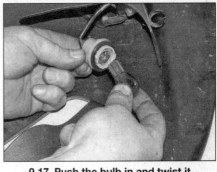

9.17 Push the bulb in and twist it anti-clockwise

16 Turn the bulbholder anti-clockwise and withdraw it from the back of the signal assembly **(see illustrations)**.
17 Push the bulb into the bulbholder and twist it anti-clockwise to remove it **(see illustration)**.
18 Check the terminals in the bulbholder for corrosion and clean them if necessary.
19 Line up the pins of the new bulb with the slots in the holder, then push the bulb in and turn it clockwise until it locks into place.
20 Insert the bulbholder into the signal assembly and turn it clockwise to lock it in place. Reconnect the wiring connector and check the operation of the turn signal.
21 Install the cockpit trim panel (see Chapter 7).
22 To access the rear turn signal bulbs, follow the procedure in Steps 8 to 12.

EX650 (2009-on)

23 To access the front turn signal bulbs, first follow the procedure in Chapter 7, Section 4, and remove the belly panel, working on the appropriate side of the machine only. Next, remove the fairing cover and the screws securing the side of the fairing, then ease the side of the fairing away from the frame.
24 Disconnect the turn signal wiring connector **(see illustration)**.
25 Undo the screws securing the fairing inner panel and ease the panel back to access the

9.24 Disconnect the wiring connector

turn signal bulbholder – turn the bulbholder anti-clockwise and withdraw it from the back of the signal assembly **(see illustrations)**.
26 Push the bulb into the bulbholder and twist it anti-clockwise to remove it **(see illustration)**.
27 Check the terminals in the bulbholder for corrosion and clean them if necessary.
28 Line up the pins of the new bulb with the slots in the holder, then push the bulb in and turn it clockwise until it locks into place.
29 Insert the bulbholder into the signal assembly and turn it clockwise to lock it in place. Reconnect the wiring connector and check the operation of the turn signal.

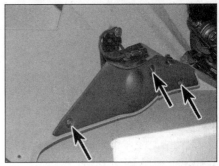

9.25a Undo the inner panel screws (arrowed)

30 Install the fairing inner panel screws, then install the remaining components in the reverse order of removal.
31 To access the rear turn signal bulbs, follow the procedure in Steps 13 and 14.

Turn signal assemblies

ER650

32 To remove the front turn signal assemblies, first follow the procedure in Chapter 7, Section 4, and remove the relevant side panel. Remove the bulbholder (see Step 2).
33 Undo the screws securing the fairing inner panel and lift the panel off, then lift the

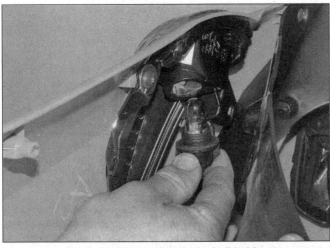

9.25b Turn and withdraw the bulbholder

9.26 Push the bulb in and twist it anti-clockwise

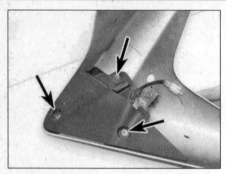

9.33a Undo the screws (arrowed) . . .

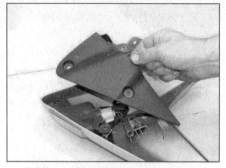

9.33b . . . lift out the inner panel . . .

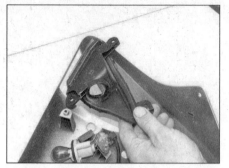

9.33c . . . and remove the signal assembly

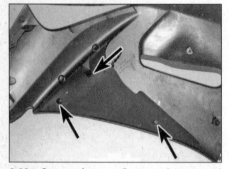

9.39a Screws (arrowed) secure inner panel

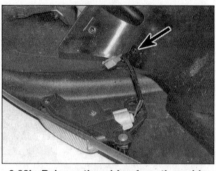

9.39b Release the wiring from the guide (arrowed)

10 Turn signal circuit check

Circuit

1 Most turn signal problems are the result of a burned out bulb or corroded bulbholder. This is especially true when the turn signals function properly in one direction, but fail to flash in the other direction. If this is the case, first check the bulbs, the bulbholders and the wiring connectors.

2 If all the turn signals fail to work, first check the turn signal relay fuse (see Section 4), and then the relay (see Steps 5 to 7). **3** If the fuse and relay are good, the problem lies in the wiring or connectors, or the switch. Check the orange wire for continuity between the relay and the left-hand switch housing, and repair or renew the wiring or connectors as required (see *Wiring Diagrams* at the end of this Chapter). Refer to Section 15 and test the switch.

4 If all is good so far, or if the signals work on one side but not the other, check the wiring between the left-hand switch housing and the turn signals themselves. Repair or renew the wiring or connectors as necessary.

signal assembly out of the side panel **(see illustrations)**.

34 Installation is the reverse of removal. Check the operation of the turn signals.

35 To remove the rear turn signal assemblies, first follow the procedure in Chapter 7, Section 7, and remove the rear mudguard.

36 Undo the screw securing the signal assembly on the inside of the mudguard, noting the location of the mounting plates. Remove the mounting plates and lift the signal assembly off.

37 Installation is the reverse of removal. Check the operation of the turn signals.

EX650 (2006 to 2008)

38 To remove the front turn signal assemblies, first follow the procedure in Chapter 7, Section 4, and remove the relevant side panel.

39 Undo the screws securing the fairing inner panel, release the wiring from the guide on the inside of the inner panel and lift the panel off **(see illustrations)**.

40 Undo the screw securing the signal assembly to the inside of the fairing side panel then lift the signal assembly out of the side panel **(see illustration)**.

41 Installation is the reverse of removal. Check the operation of the turn signals.

42 To remove the rear turn signal assemblies follow the procedure in Steps 35 and 36.

EX650 (2009-on)

43 To remove the front turn signal assemblies, first follow the procedure in Chapter 7, Section 4, and remove the fairing assembly. Remove the fairing inner panel.

44 Undo the screws securing the signal assembly to the inside of the fairing side panel, noting the location of the washers, then lift the signal assembly out of the side panel **(see illustration)**.

45 Installation is the reverse of removal. Check the operation of the turn signals.

46 To remove the rear turn signal assemblies follow the procedure in Steps 35 and 36.

Turn signal relay

5 The relay is located on the left-hand side of the frame behind the left-hand fairing side panel **(see illustration)**. Remove the side panel for access (see Chapter 7).

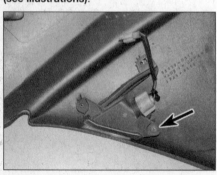

9.40 Screw (arrowed) secures signal assembly

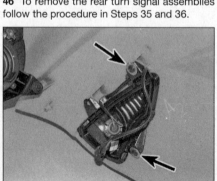

9.44 Screws (arrowed) secure signal assembly

10.5 Location of the turn signal relay

11.2 Location of the front brake light switch

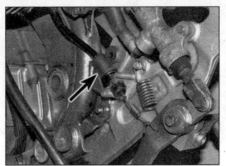

11.4a Location of the rear brake light switch

11.4b Rear brake light switch wiring connector

6 Displace the relay and disconnect the wiring connector. Check for battery voltage at the brown/yellow wire terminal on the loom side of the connector with the ignition ON. If no voltage is present, check the wiring from the connector to the ignition switch (via the fuse) for continuity (see *Wiring Diagrams* at the end of this Chapter).

7 If voltage is present, bridge the terminals in the connector using an insulated jumper wire. Turn the ignition ON and operate the turn signal switch. If the signals come on (they will not flash), the relay is confirmed faulty and must be replaced with a new one.

11 Brake light switches

Check

1 Before checking the switches, and if not already done, check the brake light circuit (see Section 5).

2 The front brake light switch is mounted on the underside of the brake master cylinder. Disconnect the wiring connectors from the switch **(see illustration)**.

3 Using a continuity tester, connect the probes to the terminals of the switch **(see illustration 2.10)**. With the brake lever at rest, there should be no continuity. With the brake lever applied, there should be continuity. The switch is not adjustable – if it fails to operate as described it is faulty and must be renewed.

4 The rear brake light switch is mounted on

the inside of the right-hand footrest bracket **(see illustration)**. Remove the left-hand frame side panel (see Chapter 7), then trace the wiring from the switch and disconnect it at the connector **(see illustration)**.

5 Using a continuity tester, connect the probes to the terminals on the switch side of the wiring connector. With the brake pedal at rest, there should be no continuity. With the brake pedal applied, there should be continuity. If the switch fails to operate as described, check the adjustment (see Chapter 1, Section 2). If it still fails to operate properly, replace it with a new one.

6 If the switches are good, check for voltage at the red/blue wire on the loom side of the connector with the ignition switch ON – there should be battery voltage. If there's no voltage present, check the wiring between the connector and the fuse, and then from the fuse to the ignition switch (see *Wiring Diagrams* at the end of this Chapter). If voltage is present, check the blue/red wire for continuity from the switch wiring connector to the brake light connector. Repair or renew the wiring as necessary.

Removal and installation

Front brake switch

7 The switch is mounted on the underside of the brake master cylinder. Disconnect the wiring connector(s) from the switch **(see illustration 11.2)**.

8 Follow the procedure in Chapter 6, Section 5, to remove and install the switch.

Rear brake switch

9 The rear brake light switch is mounted on the inside of the right-hand footrest bracket – disconnect the wiring connector and feed the wiring down to the switch (see Step 4).

10 Follow the procedure in Chapter 5, Section 3, to remove the footrest bracket. Secure the bracket with a cable tie to avoid straining the rear brake hoses.

11 Detach the switch spring from the brake pedal, then thread the switch out of its adjustment nut **(see illustration)**.

12 Installation is the reverse of removal. Check the operation of the rear brake switch (see Chapter 1, Section 2).

12 Instrument cluster

Note: *Handle the instrument cluster with care. If it is removed from the machine, store it right way up – if it is left on its side or upside down for a period of time it may malfunction.*

Removal and installation

ER650

1 On 2006 to 2008 models, follow the procedure in Chapter 7, Section 4, to remove the headlight panel. Undo the screws securing the instrument cluster front cover and draw the cover off, noting how it fits **(see illustrations)**.

2 On 2009-on models, follow the procedure in Chapter 7, Section 1, to release the trim clips securing the headlight top panel and lift

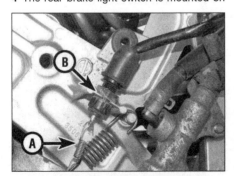

11.11 Brake switch spring (A) and adjustment nut (B)

12.1a Undo the screws (arrowed) . . .

12.1b . . . and remove the cover

12.3 Disconnect the wiring connector

12.4 Screws (arrowed) secure instrument cluster

12.8 Disconnect the wiring connector

the panel off. Undo the screws securing the instrument cluster front cover and draw the cover off.

3 Pull the rubber boot off the wiring connector and disconnect it from the instrument cluster **(see illustration)**.

4 Undo the screws securing the instrument cluster, noting the location of the washers, and lift the instrument cluster off **(see illustration)**.

5 Check the grommets in the mounting bracket – if they are damaged or deteriorated, replace them with new ones.

6 Installation is the reverse of removal. Make sure the pegs on the underside of the instrument cluster locate correctly in the grommets. Tighten the screws securely. Ensure the wiring connector is secure and cover it with the rubber boot.

EX650 (2006 to 2008)

7 Follow the procedure in Chapter 7, Section 4, to remove the cockpit trim panels, instrument cluster panel and the windshield.

8 Pull the rubber boot off the wiring connector and disconnect it from the instrument cluster **(see illustration)**.

9 Undo the nuts securing the instrument cluster and lift the instrument cluster and mounting plate off **(see illustration)**.

10 Check the grommets in the mounting bracket – if they are damaged or deteriorated and replace them with new ones.

11 Installation is the reverse of removal. Fit the mounting plate over the bracket, then install the instrument cluster and tighten the nuts securely. Ensure the wiring connector is secure and cover it with the rubber boot.

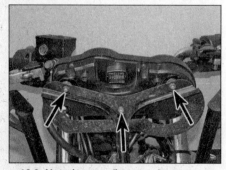

12.9 Nuts (arrowed) secure instrument cluster

EX650 (2009-on)

12 Follow the procedure in Chapter 7, Section 4, to remove the windshield, fairing top cover, cockpit trim panels and instrument cluster panel.

13 Undo the screws securing the instrument cluster in the panel, noting the location of the washers, and lift the instrument cluster out.

14 Check the grommets in the panel – if they are damaged or deteriorated and replace them with new ones.

15 Installation is the reverse of removal. Make sure the pegs on the underside of the instrument cluster locate correctly in the grommets. Tighten the screws securely. Follow the procedure in Chapter 7 to install the instrument cluster panel. Ensure the wiring connector is secure and cover it with the rubber boot.

Power check

16 If none of the instruments or displays are working, first check the ignition fuse (see Section 4).

17 If the fuse is good, remove the fairing (see Chapter 7) and check the instrument cluster wiring connector for loose or broken connections **(see illustration 12.3 or 12.8)**.

18 To check the power input wire, connect the positive (+ve) probe of a voltmeter to the brown/white wire terminal on the loom side of the wiring connector, and the negative (-ve) probe to a good earth (ground). There should be battery voltage with the ignition switch ON. If there is no voltage, refer to the wiring diagrams and check the wire between the instrument cluster, the ignition fuse and the

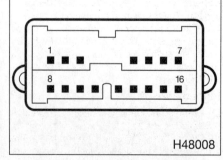

12.23 Instrument cluster terminal numbering – 2006 to 2008 ER650

H48008

ignition switch for loose or broken connections or a damaged wire, then check the white wire from the switch to the main fuse and battery.

19 To check the back-up power wire, connect the positive (+ve) probe of a voltmeter to the white/black wire terminal on the loom side of the wiring connector, and the negative (-ve) probe to a good earth (ground). Check for battery voltage with the ignition switch OFF. There should be battery voltage. If there is no voltage, refer to the wiring diagrams and check the wire between the instrument cluster and the engine management fuse for loose or broken connections or a damaged wire, then check the white wire from the fuse to the main fuse and battery.

20 If there is voltage, and to check the earth (ground) wire, check for continuity between the black/yellow wire terminal on the loom side of the wiring connector and earth (ground). If there is no continuity, check the circuit for loose or broken connections or a damaged wire and repair as necessary.

21 If the power input and earth wires are good, but there is no display or instrument function, check the individual instrument functions as follows.

Instrument check – ER650 (2006 to 2008 models)

Note: *If the instrument cluster fails any of the following checks have it tested by a Kawasaki dealer to confirm your findings before buying a replacement part. The instrument cluster covers and printed circuit board (PCB) are available separately (see Steps 82 to 85).*

22 Remove the instrument cluster (see above).

23 Using a fully charged 12 V battery, connect the positive (+ve) battery terminal to connector terminal 1 and the negative (-ve) battery terminal to terminal 3 **(see illustration)**. The display should remain inactive. Now use an insulated jumper wire to connect terminal 2 to terminal 1. The tachometer needle should move momentarily and the LCD panel and LED warning lights should come on. If the result is not as described the instrument cluster is faulty.

Mode and reset button

24 Connect the battery and jumper wires as in Step 23, then press the MODE button to

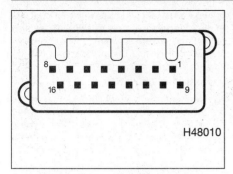

12.38 Instrument cluster terminal numbering – 2009-on ER650

scroll through the CLOCK, FUEL (if low fuel level has been indicated), ODO, TRIP A and TRIP B displays in the lower section of the LCD display. Next, select the ODO mode, hold the MODE button on and press the RESET button to change the ODO display between mph (miles) and km/h (kilometres). If the display function does not work, the instrument cluster is faulty.

Speedometer

25 Connect the battery and jumper wires as in Step 23. Using a voltmeter set to the 25 V DC scale, connect the positive (+ve) meter probe to connector terminal 10 and the negative (-ve) probe to terminal 3. If the recorded voltage is less than 9 V the instrument cluster is faulty.

26 Refer to Chapter 4, Section 10, to check the speed sensor. **Note:** *A failure of the speed sensor signal to the ECU will be identified as a fuel injection system fault (codes 24 and 25) – see Chapter 4.*

Tachometer

27 Connect the battery and jumper wires as in Step 23. Using a second jumper wire, momentarily connect and disconnect terminal 2 and terminal 6 several times. The tachometer needle should flick up-and-down – if not the instrument cluster is faulty.

Warning/indicator lights

28 Connect the battery and jumper wires as in Step 23. Using a second jumper wire, connect the battery terminals and instrument cluster connector terminals as follows. If the appropriate light does not come on the instrument cluster is faulty.

29 Engine coolant temperature warning light – connect the battery negative (-ve) terminal to connector terminal 7.

30 Oil pressure warning light – connect the battery negative (-ve) terminal to connector terminal 8.

31 Fuel level warning light – connect the battery negative (-ve) terminal to connector terminal 9.

32 High beam indicator light – connect the battery positive (+ve) terminal to connector terminal 11.

33 Neutral indicator light – connect the battery negative (-ve) terminal to connector terminal 12.

34 Right turn signal indicator light – connect the battery positive (+ve) terminal to connector terminal 14.

35 Left turn signal indicator light – connect the battery positive (+ve) terminal to connector terminal 15.

36 Fuel injection warning light – connect the battery negative (-ve) terminal to connector terminal 16.

37 On machines fitted with ABS, connect the battery negative (-ve) terminal to connector terminal 13. If the warning light comes on and remains on, the instrument cluster is faulty.

Instrument check – ER650 (2009-on models)

Note: *If the instrument cluster fails any of the following checks have it tested by a Kawasaki dealer to confirm your findings before buying a replacement part. The instrument cluster covers and printed circuit board (PCB) are available separately (see Steps 82 to 85).*

38 Remove the instrument cluster (see above). Using a fully charged 12 V battery, connect the positive (+ve) battery terminal to connector terminal 1 and the negative (-ve) battery terminal to terminal 3 **(see illustration)**. The display should remain inactive. Now use an insulated jumper wire to connect terminal 2 to terminal 1. The speedometer needle should move momentarily and the LCD panel, the LED coolant temperature warning light and the LED instrument light should come on. If the result is not as described the instrument cluster is faulty.

Mode and reset button

39 Connect the battery and jumper wires as in Step 38, then press the MODE button to scroll through the CLOCK, FUEL (if low fuel level has been indicated), ODO, TRIP A and TRIP B displays in the lower section of the LCD display. Next, select the ODO mode, hold the MODE button on and press the RESET button to change the ODO display between mph (miles) and km/h (kilometres). If the display function does not work the instrument cluster is faulty.

Speedometer

40 Connect the battery and jumper wires as in Step 38. Using a voltmeter set to the 25 V DC scale, connect the positive (+ve) meter probe to connector terminal 4 and the negative (-ve) probe to terminal 3. If the recorded voltage is less than 9 V the instrument cluster is faulty.

41 Refer to Chapter 4, Section 11, to check the speed sensor. **Note:** *A failure of the speed sensor signal to the ECU will be identified as a fuel injection system fault (codes 24 and 25) – see Chapter 4.*

Tachometer

42 Connect the battery and jumper wires as in Step 38.

43 When terminal 2 and terminal 1 are connected with the jumper wire the tachometer display should go from minimum to maximum and back again. Using a second jumper wire,

momentarily connect and disconnect terminal 2 and terminal 6 several times. The tachometer display should flick up-and-down – if not the instrument cluster is faulty.

Warning/indicator lights

44 Connect the battery and jumper wires as in Step 38. Using a second jumper wire, connect the battery terminals and instrument cluster connector terminals as follows. If the appropriate light does not come on the instrument cluster is faulty.

45 Engine coolant temperature warning light – connect the battery negative (-ve) terminal to connector terminal 10.

46 Oil pressure warning light – connect the battery negative (-ve) terminal to connector terminal 15.

47 High beam indicator light – connect the battery positive (+ve) terminal to connector terminal 11.

48 Neutral indicator light – connect the battery negative (-ve) terminal to connector terminal 14.

49 Right turn signal indicator light – connect the battery positive (+ve) terminal to connector terminal 13.

50 Left turn signal indicator light – connect the battery positive (+ve) terminal to connector terminal 12.

51 Fuel injection warning light – connect the battery negative (-ve) terminal to connector terminal 9.

52 On machines fitted with ABS, connect the battery negative (-ve) terminal to connector terminal 16. If the warning light comes on and remains on, the instrument cluster is faulty.

Instrument check – EX650 (2006 to 2008 models)

Note: *If the instrument cluster fails any of the following checks have it tested by a Kawasaki dealer to confirm your findings before buying a replacement part. The instrument cluster covers and printed circuit board (PCB) are available separately (see Steps 82 to 85).*

53 Remove the instrument cluster (see above). Using a fully charged 12 V battery, connect the positive (+ve) battery terminal to connector terminal 10 and the negative (-ve) battery terminal to terminal 9 **(see illustration)**. The speedometer and tachometer needles should move momentarily. Now use an insulated

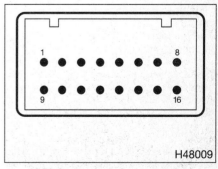

12.53 Instrument cluster terminal numbering – 2006 to 2008 EX650

jumper wire to connect terminal 1 to terminal 10. The LCD panel and the LED warning lights on the face of the speedometer and tachometer should come on. If the result is not as described the instrument cluster is faulty.

Mode and reset button

54 Connect the battery and jumper wires as in Step 53, then press the MODE button to scroll through the CLOCK, FUEL (if low fuel level has been indicated), ODO, TRIP A and TRIP B displays in the LCD display.

Speedometer

55 Connect the battery and jumper wires as in Step 53. Using a voltmeter set to the 25 V DC scale, connect the positive (+ve) meter probe to connector terminal 12 and the negative (-ve) probe to terminal 9. If the recorded voltage is less than 8 V the instrument cluster is faulty.
56 Refer to Chapter 4, Section 10, to check the speed sensor. **Note:** *A failure of the speed sensor signal to the ECU will be identified as a fuel injection system fault (codes 24 and 25) – see Chapter 4.*

Tachometer

57 Connect the battery and jumper wires as in Step 53. Using a second jumper wire, momentarily connect and disconnect terminal 1 and terminal 7 several times. The tachometer needle should flick up-and-down – if not the instrument cluster is faulty.

Warning/indicator lights

58 Connect the battery and jumper wires as in Step 53. Using a second jumper wire, connect the battery terminals and instrument cluster connector terminals as follows. If the appropriate light does not come on the instrument cluster is faulty.
59 Engine coolant temperature warning light – connect the battery negative (-ve) terminal to connector terminal 8.
60 Oil pressure warning light – connect the battery negative (-ve) terminal to connector terminal 11.
61 Fuel level warning light – connect the battery negative (-ve) terminal to connector terminal 2.
62 High beam indicator light – connect the battery positive (+ve) terminal to connector terminal 15.
63 Neutral indicator light – connect the battery negative (-ve) terminal to connector terminal 5.
64 Right turn signal indicator light – connect the battery positive (+ve) terminal to connector terminal 13.
65 Left turn signal indicator light – connect the battery positive (+ve) terminal to connector terminal 14.
66 Fuel injection warning light – connect the battery negative (-ve) terminal to connector terminal 6.
67 On machines fitted with ABS, connect the battery negative (-ve) terminal to connector terminal 3. If the warning light comes on and remains on, the instrument cluster is faulty.

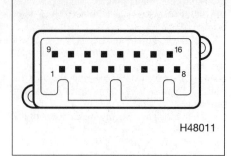

H48011

12.68 Instrument cluster terminal numbering – 2009 EX650

Instrument check – EX650 (2009-on models)

Note: *If the instrument cluster fails any of the following checks have it tested by a Kawasaki dealer to confirm your findings before buying a replacement part. The instrument cluster covers and printed circuit board (PCB) are available separately (see Steps 82 to 85).*
68 Remove the instrument cluster (see above). Using a fully charged 12 V battery, connect the positive (+ve) battery terminal to connector terminal 7 and the negative (-ve) battery terminal to terminal 8 **(see illustration)**. The display should remain inactive. Now use an insulated jumper wire to connect terminal 16 to terminal 7. The full LCD panel and the coolant temperature LED warning light should come on for 3 seconds. On machines fitted with ABS, the ABS warning light should also come on. If the result is not as described the instrument cluster is faulty.

Mode and reset button

69 Connect the battery and jumper wires as in Step 68, then press the MODE button to scroll through the FUEL (if low fuel level has been indicated), ODO, TRIP A and TRIP B displays in the LCD display. Nest, select the ODO mode, hold the MODE button on and press the RESET button to change the ODO and speedometer displays between mph (miles) and km/h (kilometres). If the display function does not work the instrument cluster is faulty.

Speedometer

70 Connect the battery and jumper wires as in Step 68. Using a voltmeter set to the 25 V DC scale, connect the positive (+ve) meter probe to connector terminal 15 and the negative (-ve) probe to terminal 8. If the recorded voltage is less than 9 V the instrument cluster is faulty.
71 Refer to Chapter 4, Section 11, to check the speed sensor. **Note:** *A failure of the speed sensor signal to the ECU will be identified as a fuel injection system fault (codes 24 and 25) – see Chapter 4.*

Tachometer

72 Connect the battery and jumper wires as in Step 68. When the LCD panel comes on the tachometer display should go from minimum to maximum and back again twice, then go off. Using a second jumper wire, momentarily connect and disconnect terminal 16 and terminal 4 several times. The tachometer display should flick up-and-down – if not the instrument cluster is faulty.

Warning/indicator lights

73 Connect the battery and jumper wires as in Step 68. Using a second jumper wire, connect the battery terminals and instrument cluster connector terminals as follows. If the appropriate light does not come on the instrument cluster is faulty.
74 Engine coolant temperature warning light – connect the battery negative (-ve) terminal to connector terminal 14.
75 Oil pressure warning light – connect the battery negative (-ve) terminal to connector terminal 6.
76 High beam indicator light – connect the battery positive (+ve) terminal to connector terminal 1.
77 Neutral indicator light – connect the battery negative (-ve) terminal to connector terminal 9.
78 Right turn signal indicator light – connect the battery positive (+ve) terminal to connector terminal 10.
79 Left turn signal indicator light – connect the battery positive (+ve) terminal to connector terminal 13.
80 Fuel injection warning light – connect the battery negative (-ve) terminal to connector terminal 2.
81 On machines fitted with ABS, connect the battery negative (-ve) terminal to connector terminal 5. If the warning light comes on and remains on, the instrument cluster is faulty.

Disassembly and printed circuit board (PCB) renewal

82 Remove the instrument cluster (see the relevant procedure at the beginning of this section).
83 Undo the rear cover screws and lift the cover off. Lift the PCB out of the front cover, noting how it locates.
84 All meters, instrument and warning lights are part of the PCB and are not available individually.
85 Installation is the reverse of removal. Make sure the PCB locates correctly and do not over-tighten the screws.

13 Oil pressure switch

1 The oil pressure warning light should come on when the ignition switch is turned ON, and should go out when the engine is started. If the warning light is thought to be faulty, follow the procedure in Section 12 to check it.
2 If the warning light does not go out when the engine is started, or if it comes on when the engine is running, low oil pressure is indicated – stop the engine immediately and carry out an oil level check (see *Pre-ride checks*).

13.4 Location of the oil pressure switch

13.5 Detach the wiring connector from the switch

3 If the oil level is good, check the operation of the oil pressure switch as follows.

Check

4 The oil pressure switch is screwed into the right-hand side of the crankcase **(see illustration)**. Remove the belly panel for access (see Chapter 7).
5 Pull back the rubber boot, loosen the screw and detach the wiring connector from the switch **(see illustration)**.
6 Turn the ignition ON and check for voltage at the wiring connector. If there is voltage, earth (ground) the connector on the crankcase and check that the oil warning light comes on.
7 Now touch the connector to the terminal on the switch and check that the oil warning light comes on. If the warning light does not come on, the switch must be assumed faulty and a new one must be fitted.

Removal and installation

8 If not already done, remove the belly panel and detach the wiring connector from the switch (see Steps 4 and 5).
9 Position a suitable container below the engine to catch any residual oil, then unscrew the switch and withdraw it from the crankcase.
10 Apply a suitable sealant to the threads on the switch body, then install it in the crankcase and tighten it to the torque setting specified at the beginning of this Chapter.
11 Attach the wiring connector and tighten the screw securely.

12 Check the engine oil level and refill as necessary (see *Pre-ride Checks*).
13 Start the engine and check the operation of the switch. Check that there are no oil leaks around the switch.
14 Install the belly panel.

14 Ignition switch

> ⚠ **Warning: To prevent the risk of short circuits, disconnect the battery negative (–) lead before making any ignition switch checks.**

Check

1 Remove the fuel tank (see Chapter 4). Trace the wiring from the ignition switch and disconnect it at the connector.
2 Using an ohmmeter or a continuity tester, check the continuity of the connector terminal pairs (see *Wiring Diagrams* at the end of this Chapter). Continuity should exist between the terminals connected by a solid line on the diagram when the switch is in the indicated position.
3 If the switch fails any of the tests, replace it with a new one.

Removal and installation

Note: *For security the ignition switch is held by two shear-head bolts – new bolts of the same type should be obtained before starting work.*

4 Disconnect the ignition switch wiring connector (see Step 1).
5 Remove the front fork top yoke (see Chapter 5, Section 9).
6 Use a centre punch and hammer to undo the shear-head bolts securing the ignition switch to the underside of the top yoke, then remove the switch **(see illustration)**.
7 Installation is the reverse of removal. Tighten the new bolts until their heads shear off. Make sure the wiring is correctly routed and securely connected.

15 Handlebar switches

Check

1 Generally speaking, the switches are reliable and trouble-free. Most problems, when they do occur, are caused by dirty or corroded contacts, but wear and breakage of internal parts is a possibility that should not be overlooked. If breakage does occur, the entire switch and related wiring harness will have to be replaced with a new one, as individual parts are not available.
2 The switches can be checked for continuity using an ohmmeter or continuity tester. Always disconnect the battery negative (-ve) lead, which will prevent the possibility of a short circuit, before making the checks.
3 The switch wiring connectors are located in front of the air filter housing inside protective boots. Remove the fuel tank for access (see Chapter 4).
4 Trace the wiring from the switch in question and disconnect it at the connector **(see illustration)**. Check for continuity between the terminals of the connector on the switch side, with the switch in various positions (i.e. switch OFF – no continuity, switch ON – continuity). Refer to the switch boxes in *Wiring Diagrams* at the end of this Chapter. Continuity should exist between the terminals connected by a solid line in the boxes when the switch is in the indicated position.
5 If the continuity check indicates a problem exists, displace the switch housing (see below) and spray the switch contacts with electrical contact cleaner **(see illustration)**. If they are

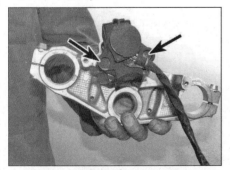

14.6 Ignition switch is secured by shear-head bolts (arrowed)

15.4 Location of the handlebar switch wiring connectors

15.5 Inspect the switch contacts (arrowed)

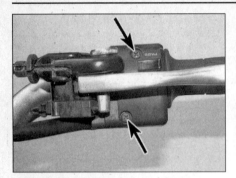

15.11a Undo the switch housing screws (arrowed)

15.11b Note how pin (A) locates in hole (B)

accessible, the contacts can be scraped clean with a small knife and polished with crocus cloth. If switch components are damaged or broken, it will be obvious when the switch is disassembled.

Removal and installation

6 Remove the fuel tank to access the switch wiring connectors (see Chapter 4). Trace the wiring from the switch and disconnect it at the connector **(see illustration 15.4)**. Feed the wiring back to the switch, freeing it from any clips and ties and noting its routing.

Right-hand switch

7 The right-hand switch is integral with the throttle twistgrip housing. Follow the procedure in Chapter 4, Section 16, to disconnect the throttle cables from the twistgrip.
8 Disconnect the wiring connectors from the brake light switch **(see illustration 11.2)**. Lift the rear half of the housing off.
9 Installation is the reverse of removal. Refer to Chapter 4 for installation of the throttle cables. Don't forget to connect the brake light switch connectors. Secure the wiring with any ties as noted on removal. Check the operation of the switches.

Left-hand switch

10 Disconnect the wiring connector from the clutch switch **(see illustration 18.2)**.
11 Undo the switch housing screws and separate the halves of the housing, noting how the pin in the front half locates in the hole in the handlebar **(see illustrations)**.
12 Installation is the reverse of removal.

Make sure the locating pin in the switch housing locates in the hole in the handlebar **(see illustration 15.11b)**. Tighten the housing screws securely. Don't forget to connect the clutch switch connector. Secure the wiring with any ties as noted on removal. Check the operation of the switches.

16 Neutral switch

1 The neutral switch is part of the starter safety interlock circuit which prevents or stops the engine running if the transmission is in gear whilst the sidestand is down, and prevents the engine from starting if the transmission is in gear unless the sidestand is up and the clutch lever is pulled in.
2 The switch is located on the left-hand side of the transmission casing below the speed sensor bracket **(see illustration)**. Remove the front sprocket cover for access (see Chapter 6).

Check

3 Make sure the transmission is in neutral. Detach the wiring connector from the switch terminal **(see illustration)**. Check for continuity between the switch terminal and the crankcase. With the transmission in neutral, there should be continuity. With the transmission in gear, there should be no continuity. If the results are not as stated the

switch is faulty and must be renewed (see Steps 7 to 12).
4 If the switch is good, check for battery voltage in the wiring connector with the ignition ON. If there's no voltage present, check the wire between the connector and the instrument cluster (see *Wiring Diagrams* at the end of this Chapter).
5 If there is voltage, with the connector disconnected, ensure that the neutral light is out – if not, the wire between the connector and instrument cluster must be earthed (grounded) at some point. If the light is out, earth (ground) the connector on the crankcase and check that the neutral light comes on. Turn the ignition OFF.
6 If the switch and wiring are good, the LED in the instrument cluster could be faulty (see Section 12). **Note:** *If a starter circuit problem cannot be traced to the neutral switch, check the other components in the starter circuit – the sidestand switch (Section 17), clutch switch (Section 18), and the starter circuit relay and diodes (Section 19).*

Removal and installation

7 If not already done, remove the front sprocket cover (see Chapter 6).
8 Make sure the transmission is in neutral. Detach the wiring connector from the switch.
9 Clean the area around the switch, then unscrew it from the gearchange mechanism cover **(see illustration)**. Discard the sealing washer as a new one should be used.
10 Install the switch using a new washer and tighten it to the torque setting specified at the beginning of this Chapter.
11 Connect the wiring connector and check the operation of the neutral light.
12 Install the front sprocket cover.

17 Sidestand switch

1 The sidestand switch is part of the starter safety interlock circuit which prevents or stops the engine running if the transmission is in gear whilst the sidestand is down, and prevents the engine from starting if the transmission is in gear unless the sidestand is up and the clutch lever is pulled in.

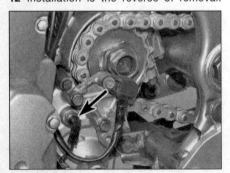

16.2 Location of the neutral switch (arrowed)

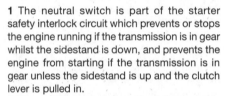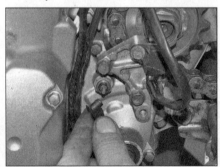

16.3 Detach the switch wiring connector

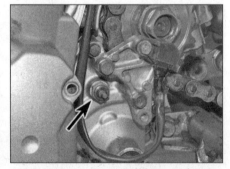

16.9 Unscrew the switch (arrowed) from the cover

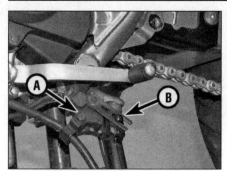

17.2 Location of the sidestand switch – note the mounting bolt (A) and lever (B)

17.3a Trace the wiring from the switch . . .

17.3b . . . and disconnect it at the connector

2 The switch is mounted on the stand bracket **(see illustration)**. Remove the left-hand footrest bracket for access (see Chapter 5).

Check

3 Remove the left-hand frame cover (see Chapter 7). Trace the wiring from the switch and disconnect it at the wiring connector **(see illustrations)**. If required, remove the ducting from around the wiring to help identification.
4 Check for continuity between the terminals on the switch side of the connector. With the sidestand up there should be continuity (zero resistance) and with the stand down there should be no continuity (infinite resistance).
5 If the results are not as stated the switch is faulty and must be replaced with a new one (see Steps 9 to 15).
6 If the switch is good, check for battery voltage at the green/white wire terminal on the loom side of the connector with the ignition ON. If there's no voltage present, check the wire between the connector and the starter circuit relay (see *Wiring Diagrams* at the end of this Chapter).
7 If there is voltage, check for continuity to earth at the black/yellow wire terminal on the loom side of the connector.
Note: *If a starter circuit problem cannot be traced to the sidestand switch, check the other components in the starter circuit – the neutral switch (Section 16), clutch switch (Section 18), and the starter circuit relay and diodes (Section 19).*

Removal and installation

8 If not already done, remove the left-hand footrest bracket (see Chapter 5).
9 Remove the front sprocket cover (see Chapter 6).
10 Remove the ducting from around the wiring, trace the wiring from the switch and disconnect it at the wiring connector **(see illustration 17.3b)**. Feed the wiring back to the switch, freeing it from any clips and ties and noting its routing.
11 Undo the switch mounting bolt, noting the location of the fuel tank drain hose guide **(see illustration 17.2)**. Remove the switch, noting how the lever locates on the peg on the sidestand.
12 Install the switch, making sure the lever

locates correctly on the peg on the stand. Clean the mounting bolt threads and apply a suitable non-permanent thread-locking compound, then tighten the bolt to the torque setting specified at the beginning of this Chapter. Secure the fuel tank drain hose with its guide.
13 Feed the wiring up to its connector, making sure it is correctly routed and secured by any clips, and install the ducting.
14 Connect the wiring connector and check the operation of the sidestand switch.
15 Install the remaining components in the reverse order of removal.

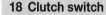

18 Clutch switch

1 The clutch switch is part of the starter safety interlock circuit which prevents or stops the engine running if the transmission is in gear whilst the sidestand is down, and prevents the engine from starting if the transmission is in gear unless the sidestand is up and the clutch lever is pulled in.
2 The switch is mounted on the underside of the clutch lever bracket **(see illustration)**.

Check

3 Disconnect the wiring connector from the switch and check for continuity between the terminals on the switch. With the clutch lever pulled in there should be continuity (zero resistance) and with the lever out there should be no continuity (infinite resistance).

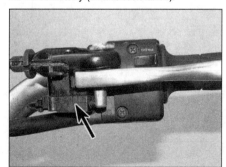

18.2 Location of the clutch switch

4 If the results are not as stated the switch is faulty and must be replaced with a new one (see Steps 8 to 10).
5 If the switch is good, check for battery voltage at the black/red wire terminal in the connector with the ignition switch ON. If there's no voltage present, check the green/white wire between the connector and the starter circuit relay (see *Wiring Diagrams* at the end of this Chapter).
6 If there is voltage, check for continuity in the black wire (changing to red/green) between the connector, the ECU and the starter circuit relay (see *Wiring Diagrams* at the end of this Chapter). **Note:** *If a starter circuit problem cannot be traced to the clutch switch, check the other components in the starter circuit – the neutral switch (Section 16), sidestand switch (Section 17), and the starter circuit relay and diodes (Section 19).*

Removal and installation

7 If not already done, disconnect the wiring connector from the switch **(see illustration 18.2)**.
8 Undo the screws securing the switch and remove it, noting how it fits.
9 Installation is the reverse of removal. Make sure the switch is correctly located.
10 Connect the wiring connector and check the operation of the clutch switch.

19 Starter safety interlock circuit relay and diodes

1 The starter circuit relay and diodes are housed in the relay box. Remove the fuel tank and the fuel tank bracket for access (see Chapter 4).
2 Release the clips securing the relay box, lift it out of its rubber holder and disconnect the wiring connectors **(see illustrations 5.6a, b and c)**.
3 Using a multimeter, check for continuity between terminals 11 and 16, and terminals 11 and 12, on the relay **(see illustration 5.7)**. There should be no continuity. Now use jumper wires to connect the positive (+ve) terminal of a fully charged 12 volt battery to terminal 16 on the relay and the negative (-ve) battery

20.1 Location of the horn – ER650 models

20.2 Location of the horn – EX650 models

20.4 Disconnect the wiring connectors

terminal to relay terminal 12. Set the meter to the volts DC scale and check for battery voltage between terminals 11 and 12. If the relay fails either of the checks the relay box must be replaced with a new one – individual relays are not available.

4 If the relay is good, check the diodes in the circuit using an ohmmeter. First connect the positive (+ve) probe to terminal 12 and the negative (-ve) probe to terminal 13 and note the result. Now reverse the probes – the resistance should be low in one direction and more than ten times as much in the other. Repeat the test between terminals 12 and 15, 12 and 16, 13 and 14, 13 and 15. Don't forget to reverse the probes and check the resistance in both directions on each pair of terminals. If the results are not as stated, replace the relay box with a new one.

20 Horn

1 On ER650 models, the horn is mounted behind the left-hand fairing side panel (see illustration). Remove the side panel for access (see Chapter 7).
2 On EX650 models, the horn is mounted on the front fork lower yoke (see illustration). If required, remove the fairing or fairing side panel for access (see Chapter 7).

Check
3 If the horn fails to work, first check the horn circuit fuse (see Section 4).
4 Disconnect the wiring connectors from the horn (see illustration). Ensure the horn terminals are clean, then, using two jumper wires, apply battery voltage directly to the terminals. If the horn doesn't sound, replace it with a new one.
5 If the horn sounds, check for battery voltage at the brown/black wire connector with the ignition ON. If there is no voltage, check the brown/black wire from the switch to the fusebox (see Wiring Diagrams at the end of this Chapter).
6 If there is voltage, check the black/white wire connector for continuity to earth (ground) with the horn button pressed.
7 If there is no continuity, check the switch (see Section 15) and the wiring.

Removal and installation
8 Remove the appropriate fairing panel for access (see Steps 1 and 2).
9 Disconnect the wiring connectors from the horn (see illustration 20.4).
10 Undo the nut securing the horn to its bracket and lift it off (see illustration). Note the insulating rubber grommet on the horn bracket and renew it if it is damaged or distorted.
11 Installation is the reverse of removal. Connect the wiring connectors and check the operation of the horn.

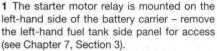

21 Starter motor relay

Removal
1 The starter motor relay is mounted on the left-hand side of the battery carrier – remove the left-hand fuel tank side panel for access (see Chapter 7, Section 3).
2 Disconnect the battery negative (-ve) terminal (see Section 3).
3 Undo the screw securing the relay cover, unclip the relay/main fuse holder from the battery carrier, then unclip the wiring connector (see illustrations 4.3a, b and c).
4 Pull back the rubber boot and undo the bolts securing the battery and starter motor leads to the relay, noting how they fit (see illustration). Remove the relay.

Check
5 Set a multimeter to the ohms x 1 scale and connect it across the starter motor and battery lead terminals on the relay (see illustration). There should be no continuity (infinite resistance).
6 Using a fully-charged 12 volt battery and two insulated jumper wires, connect the positive (+ve) battery terminal to the yellow/red wire terminal of the relay, and the negative (-ve) battery terminal to the black/yellow

20.10 Horn is secured by nut (arrowed)

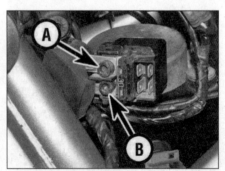

21.4 Battery lead (A) and starter motor lead (B)

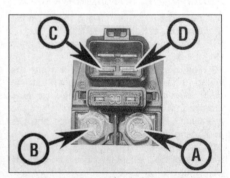

21.5 Starter relay terminal identification – starter motor (A), battery (B), yellow/red wire (C), black/yellow wire (D)

21.6 Set-up for checking the starter relay continuity

22.3a Undo the starter motor mounting bolts (arrowed)

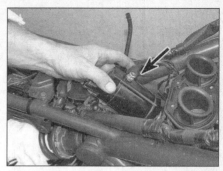

22.3b Lift the starter motor to access the terminal (arrowed)

wire terminal of the relay **(see illustration)**. The relay should be heard to click and the multimeter should indicate continuity (zero ohms). Disconnect the battery.

7 If the results are not as stated the relay is faulty and must be renewed.

8 If the relay is good, check for battery voltage at the yellow/red wire terminal in the relay wiring connector with the ignition ON, the kill switch in the RUN position, gearbox in neutral, and the starter button pressed. If there is no voltage, check the wiring between the connector and the relay box, then check the starter circuit relay (Section 19).

9 If there is voltage, check the black/yellow wire terminal for continuity to earth (ground).

Installation

10 Installation is the reverse of removal. Connect the starter motor and battery leads as noted on removal **(see illustration 21.4).** Cover the terminals with the rubber boot. If a new relay is being fitted, don't forget to install a new main fuse. Ensure the wiring connector is secure. Reconnect the battery negative (-ve) terminal last.

22 Starter motor removal and installation

Removal

1 The starter motor is mounted on the crankcase behind the cylinders. Remove the

seat and frame side panels (see Chapter 7). Remove the air filter housing (see Chapter 4)

2 Disconnect the battery negative (-ve) lead.

3 On machines with engine numbers up to AE046804, undo the two bolts securing the starter motor to the crankcase **(see illustration)**. Draw the starter motor out of the crankcase and lift it up to gain access to the terminal **(see illustration)**. Note the position of the starter motor lead. Peel back the rubber boot, undo the nut securing the starter lead, disconnect the lead and lift the motor off **(see illustration)**.

4 On machines with engine numbers from AE046805-on, peel back the rubber boot, undo the nut securing the starter lead and disconnect the lead **(see illustration)**. Undo the two bolts securing the starter motor to the crankcase **(see illustration)**. Draw the starter motor out of the crankcase and lift it off **(see illustration)**.

22.3c Disconnect the starter motor lead

5 Remove the O-ring on the end of the starter motor and discard it as a new one must be used **(see illustration)**.

Installation

6 Fit a new O-ring to the end of the starter motor, making sure it is seated in its groove **(see illustration 22.5)**. Apply a smear of engine oil to the O-ring. Make sure the bottom of the mounting lugs on the motor and tops of the mounts on the crankcase are clean.

7 On machines with engine numbers up to AE046804, connect the starter lead to the terminal and secure it with the nut **(see illustration 22.3c)**. Ensure the lead runs towards the rear of the machine. Fit the rubber boot over the terminal.

8 On all machines, manoeuvre the motor into position and slide it into the crankcase **(see**

22.4a Disconnect the starter motor lead (arrowed)

22.4b Undo the starter motor mounting bolts (arrowed)

22.4c Draw the starter motor out of the crankcase

22.5 Renew the O-ring on reassembly

22.8 Slide the starter motor into the crankcase

23.2 Note the alignment marks (arrowed)

illustration). Ensure that the starter motor teeth mesh correctly with those of the starter clutch reduction gear. Clean the threads of the mounting bolts and apply a suitable non-permanent thread-locking compound, then tighten the bolts to the torque setting specified at the beginning of this Chapter **(see illustration 22.3a or 4b)**.

9 On machines with engine numbers from AE046805-on, connect the starter lead to the terminal and secure it with the nut **(see illustration 22.4a)**. Fit the rubber boot over the terminal.

10 Install the remaining components in the reverse order of removal.

23 Starter motor overhaul

Note: *Two designs of starter motor are fitted to the machines covered in this manual. Check your engine number before proceeding.*

Engine numbers up to AE046804

Disassembly

1 Remove the starter motor (see Section 22).
2 Note any alignment marks between the housing and the front and rear covers, or make your own if they aren't clear **(see illustration)**.
3 Unscrew the two long bolts, then remove the front cover and its sealing ring **(see illustrations)**. Discard the sealing ring as a new one must be fitted. Remove the tabbed

23.3a Unscrew the two long bolts . . .

23.3b . . . then remove the front cover . . .

23.3c . . . and the cover sealing ring

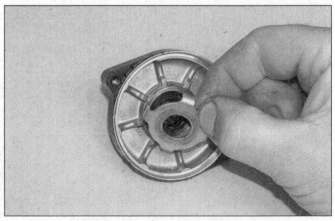

23.3d Remove the tabbed washer . . .

23.3e . . . and the shims

23.4a Remove the rear cover . . .

23.4b . . . the cover sealing ring . . .

23.4c . . . and the shims

washer (from the cover or the armature shaft) and slide the shims off the shaft (see illustrations).

4 Remove the rear cover and its sealing ring (see illustrations). Discard the sealing ring as a new one must be fitted. Slide the shims off the shaft (see illustration).

5 Note how the brushes locate on the commutator (see illustration). Ease the brush springs onto the top edges of the brush holders, then draw the housing off the armature – the armature is held by the attraction of the magnets inside the housing (see illustrations).

6 Note how the tab on the brush plate

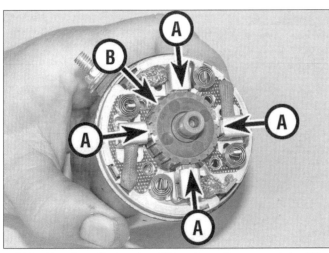

23.5a Note how the brushes (A) locate on the commutator (B)

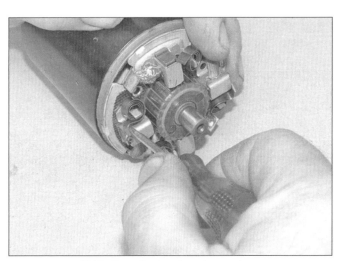

23.5b Ease the brush springs out . . .

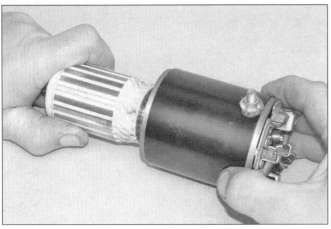

23.5c ... then draw the housing off the armature

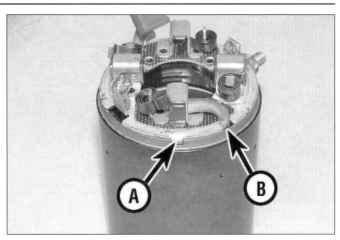

23.6 Note location of tab (A) and terminal wire (B)

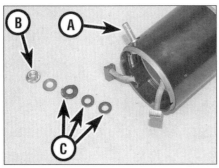

23.7 Terminal (A), terminal nut (B) and insulating washers (C)

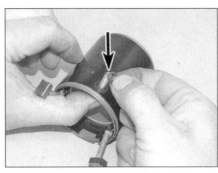

23.8 Renew the terminal O-ring (arrowed)

aligns with the cut-out in the housing and how the wires for the terminal brushes are routed through cut-outs in the brushplate, then ease the brush plate out (see illustration).

7 Undo the terminal nut and remove the washers from the terminal (see illustration). If any of the insulating washers are damaged they should be renewed on reassembly.

8 Remove the O-ring from the terminal and discard it as a new one must be fitted (see illustration).

9 Draw out the terminal, noting how it fits, then remove the terminal brush assembly and insulator (see illustrations).

Inspection

10 The parts of the starter motor that are most likely to require attention are the brushes. Measure the length of each brush and compare the results to the length listed in this Chapter's Specifications (see illustrations). If any of the brushes are worn beyond the service limit, renew the brushplate and terminal brush assemblies. If the brushes are not worn excessively, cracked, chipped, or otherwise damaged, they may be reused. If required, new brush springs are available individually.

11 Inspect the commutator bars on

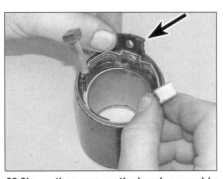

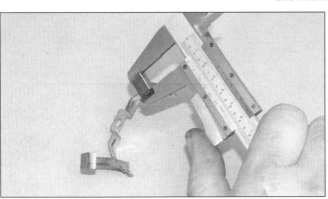

23.9a Draw out the terminal ...

23.9b ... then remove the brush assembly and insulator (arrowed)

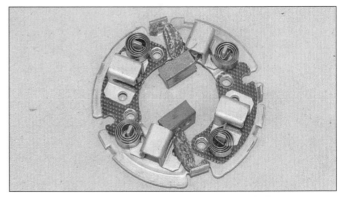

23.10a Measure the terminal brushes ...

23.10b ... and the brushes on the brushplate

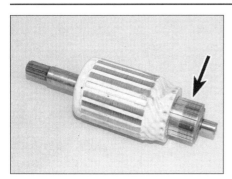

23.11 Inspect the commutator bars (arrowed)

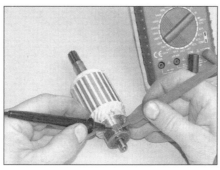

23.12a Checking for continuity between the commutator bars

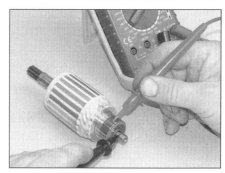

23.12b Checking for continuity between the commutator bars and the armature shaft

the armature for scoring, scratches and discoloration **(see illustration)**. The commutator can be cleaned and polished with crocus cloth, but do not use sandpaper or emery paper. After cleaning, wipe away any residue with a cloth soaked in electrical system cleaner, ensuring the grooves between the bars are free of dirt.

12 Using an ohmmeter or a continuity test light, check for continuity between the commutator bars **(see illustration)**. There should be continuity (zero resistance) between all the bars. Also, check for continuity between the commutator bars and the armature shaft **(see illustration)**. There should be no continuity (infinite resistance) between the commutator and the shaft. If

23.13 Check the armature shaft for worn, chipped or broken teeth

the results are not as stated, the armature is defective and a new starter motor must be fitted – the armature is not available separately.

13 Check the front end of the armature shaft for worn, chipped or broken teeth **(see illustration)**. If the shaft is damaged or worn, fit a new starter motor.

14 Inspect the front and rear covers for signs of cracks or wear. Check the oil seal and bearing in the front cover **(see illustration)** – they are not listed as being available separately, however if they need renewing, aftermarket seals and bearings are available from good suppliers.

Reassembly

15 Install the terminal brush assembly and insulator in the housing, then fit the terminal and a new O-ring **(see illustrations 23.9b, 9a and 8)**. Ensure the O-ring sits around the base of the terminal between it and the housing. Install the washers on the terminal and secure them with the nut **(see illustration 23.7)**.

16 Ease the brush springs onto the top edges of the brush holders **(see illustration)**. Install the brush plate in the housing as noted on removal **(see illustration 23.6)**. Fit the brushes into their holders ensuring the wires locate in the slots in the holders.

17 Insert the armature into the housing so that the commutator protrudes through the

brushplate, then ease the springs off the brush holders onto the brushes **(see illustration 23.5b and a)**. Check that each brush is pressed against the commutator by its spring.

18 Slide the shims onto the rear end of the shaft and lubricate the shaft with a smear of grease **(see illustration 23.4c)**. Fit a new sealing ring onto the housing, then install the rear cover aligning the marks made on removal **(see illustrations 23.4b and a)**.

19 Slide the shims onto the front end of the shaft **(see illustration 23.3e)**. Lubricate the front cover bearing with a smear of grease and install the tabbed washer **(see illustration 23.3d)**. Fit a new sealing ring onto the housing, then install the front cover aligning the marks made on removal **(see illustrations 23.3c and b)**.

20 Install the two long bolts and tighten them securely **(see illustration 23.3a)**.

21 Install the starter motor (see Section 22).

Engine numbers from AE046805-on

Disassembly

22 Remove the starter motor (see Section 22).

23 Note any alignment marks between the main housing and the front and rear covers, or make your own if they aren't clear **(see illustration)**.

24 Unscrew the two long bolts, noting the

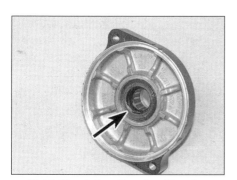

23.14 Check the oil seal and bearing (arrowed)

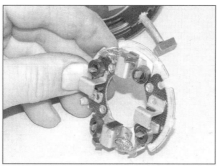

23.16 Position the brush springs on the top edges of the holders

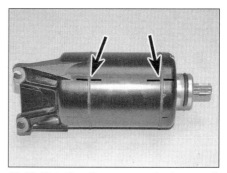

23.23 Note the alignment marks (arrowed)

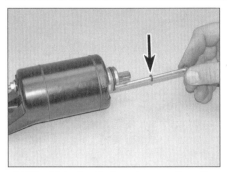

23.24a Note the O-rings (arrowed) on the long bolts

23.24b Lift off the front cover

23.25 Remove the rear cover and brushplate assembly

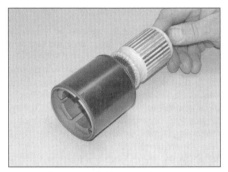

23.26a Draw the housing off the armature

23.26b New cover sealing rings must be fitted on reassembly

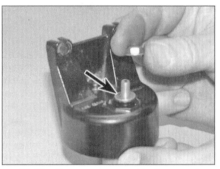

23.27a Remove the terminal nut and washer (arrowed)

location of the O-rings, then remove the front cover **(see illustrations)**.

25 Remove the rear cover and brushplate assembly **(see illustration)**.

26 Draw the housing off the armature – the armature is held by the attraction of the magnets inside the housing **(see illustration)**. Discard the front and rear cover sealing rings as new ones must be fitted **(see illustration)**.

27 Undo the terminal nut and remove the washer, insulator and O-ring from the terminal **(see illustrations)**. Note how the brushes locate inside the brush holder, then withdraw the terminal brush assembly **(see illustration)**.

28 Undo the screw securing the brush holder and lift out the brushplate assembly **(see illustrations)**.

23.27b Remove the insulator and O-ring (arrowed)

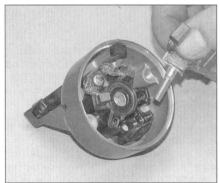

23.27c Remove the terminal brush assembly

23.28a Undo the screw . . .

23.28b . . . and lift out the brushplate assembly

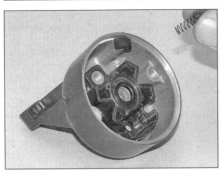

23.29a Remove the brush springs . . .

23.29b . . . then draw out the brush holder

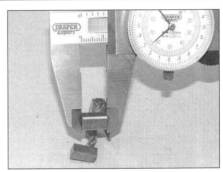

23.30a Measure the brush length

29 Lift the brush springs out of the brush holder, then draw the holder out of the rear cover **(see illustrations)**.

Inspection

30 The parts of the starter motor that are most likely to require attention are the brushes. Measure the length of each brush and compare the results to the length listed in this Chapter's Specifications **(see illustration)**. If any of the brushes are worn beyond the service limit, renew the brushplate and terminal bolt assemblies as a set **(see illustration)**. If the brushes are not worn excessively, chipped, or otherwise damaged, they may be reused. If required, new brush springs are available individually.

31 Inspect the commutator segments on the armature for scoring, scratches and discoloration **(see illustration)**.The face of the commutator can be cleaned and polished with crocus cloth, but do not use sandpaper

or emery paper. After cleaning, wipe away any residue with a cloth soaked in electrical system cleaner, ensuring the grooves between the bars are free of dirt.

32 Using an ohmmeter or a continuity test light, check for continuity between the commutator bars **(see illustration)**. There should be continuity (zero resistance) between all the bars. Also, check for continuity between the commutator bars and the armature shaft **(see illustration)**. There should be no continuity (infinite resistance) between the commutator and the shaft. If the results are not as stated, the armature is defective and a new starter motor must be fitted – the armature is not available separately.

33 Check the front end of the armature shaft for worn, cracked, chipped and broken teeth **(see illustration 23.13)**. If the shaft is damaged or worn, fit a new starter motor.

34 Inspect the front and rear covers for signs

of cracks or wear. Check the bearing in the front cover – it is not listed as being available separately, however if it needs renewing, aftermarket bearings are available from good suppliers.

Reassembly

35 Fit the brush holder into the rear cover, then install the brush springs **(see illustrations 23.29b and a)**. Install the brushplate assembly and secure it with the screw **(see illustrations 23.28b and a)**.

36 Install the terminal brush assembly, then fit the O-ring, insulator and washer onto the terminal and secure them with the nut **(see illustrations 23.27c, b and a)**.

37 Install new cover sealing rings onto the housing, then install the armature in the housing **(see illustrations 23.26b and a)**.

38 Check that the brushes slide freely in the holder. Lubricate the rear end of the shaft with a smear of grease, then install the rear cover, ensuring the brushes locate squarely on the commutator **(see illustrations 23.25)**. Align the marks made on removal **(see illustrations 23.23)**.

39 Install the front cover and align the marks made on removal.

40 Fit new O-rings on the two long bolts, then install the bolts and tighten them securely.

41 Install the starter motor (see Section 22).

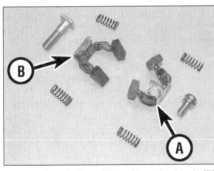

23.30b Brushplate (A) and terminal bolt (B) brush sets

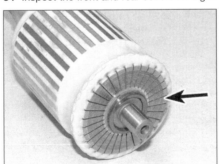

23.31 Inspect the commutator bars (arrowed)

24 Charging system testing

1 If the performance of the charging system is suspect, the system as a whole should be checked first, followed by testing of the individual components. **Note:** Before beginning the checks, make sure the battery is fully charged and that all system connections are clean and tight.

2 Checking the output of the charging system and the performance of the various components within the charging system requires the use of a multimeter (with voltage, current, resistance checking facilities). If a multimeter is not available, the job of checking the charging system should be left to a Kawasaki dealer.

23.32a Checking for continuity between the commutator bars

23.32b Checking for continuity between the commutator bars and the armature shaft

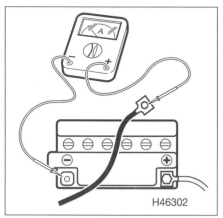

24.5 Current leakage check

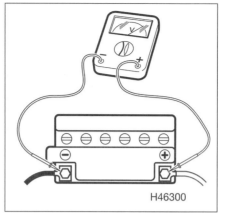

24.9 Regulated voltage output check

3 When making the checks, follow the procedures carefully to prevent incorrect connections or short circuits resulting in irreparable damage to electrical system components.

Leakage test

Caution: Always connect an ammeter in series, never in parallel with the battery, otherwise it will be damaged. Do not turn the ignition ON or operate the starter motor when the ammeter is connected – a sudden surge in current will blow the meter's fuse.
4 Ensure the ignition is OFF, then disconnect the battery negative (-ve) lead (see Section 3).
5 Set the multimeter to the Amps function and connect its negative (-ve) probe to the battery negative (-ve) terminal, and positive (+ve) probe to the disconnected negative (-ve) lead **(see illustration)**. Always set the meter to a high amps range initially and then bring it down to the mA (milli Amps) range; if there is a high current flow in the circuit it may blow the meter's fuse.
6 Battery current leakage should not exceed the maximum limit (see *Specifications* at the beginning of this Chapter). If a higher leakage rate is shown there is a short circuit in the wiring, although if an alarm is fitted its current draw should be taken into account. Disconnect the meter and reconnect the battery negative (-ve) lead.
7 If leakage is indicated, refer to *Wiring*

Diagrams at the end of this Chapter to systematically disconnect individual electrical components and repeat the test until the source is identified.

Output test

8 Refer to Section 3 for access to the battery terminals, then start the engine and warm it up.
9 To check the regulated (DC) voltage output, allow the engine to idle. Connect a multimeter set to the 0-20 volts DC scale across the terminals of the battery – connect the positive (+ve) meter probe to battery positive (+ve) terminal and the negative (-ve) meter probe to battery negative (-ve) terminal **(see illustration)**.
10 Slowly increase the engine speed and note the reading obtained – it should rise from normal battery voltage as engine speed increases, reaching a maximum as specified at the beginning of this Chapter. Repeat the test with the headlight wiring connectors disconnected (see Section 6). If the regulated voltage output is outside the specification, check the alternator and the regulator (see Sections 25 and 26).
11 To check the unregulated (AC) voltage output, first remove the left-hand frame cover (see Chapter 7).
12 Trace the wiring from the back of the alternator cover on the left-hand side of the engine to the three-pin wiring connector and

disconnect it **(see illustration)**. If required, remove the ducting from around the wiring to help identification.
13 Start the engine and increase the engine speed to 4000 rpm, then using a multimeter set to 0-250 volts AC scale, connect the meter probes to one pair of terminals at a time on the alternator side of the wiring connector **(see illustration)**. Note the three readings obtained.
14 Compare the results with the specification at the beginning of this Chapter. If the unregulated (AC) voltage output is outside the specification, check the alternator and the regulator (see Sections 25 and 26).

> **HAYNES HiNT** *Clues to a faulty regulator are constantly blowing bulbs, with brightness varying considerably with engine speed, and battery overheating.*

25 Alternator

Check

1 Remove the left-hand frame cover (see Chapter 7).
2 Trace the wiring from the back of the alternator cover on the left-hand side of the engine to the three-pin wiring connector and disconnect it **(see illustration 24.12)**. If required, remove the ducting from around the wiring to help identification.
3 Using a multimeter set to the ohms scale, connect the meter probes to one pair of terminals at a time on the alternator side of the wiring connector and measure the resistance between the terminals. Note the three readings obtained. Now check for continuity between each terminal and earth (ground).
4 If the stator coil windings are in good condition the three readings should be within the range shown in *Specifications* at the beginning of this Chapter and there should be no continuity (infinite resistance) between any of the terminals and earth (ground). If not, the alternator stator coil assembly is faulty and should be renewed. **Note:** *Before condemning*

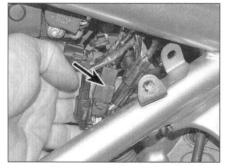

24.12 Alternator three-pin wiring connector (arrowed)

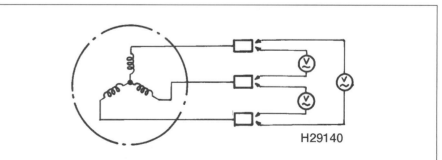

24.13 Alternator unregulated voltage test connections

25.9 Hold the rotor and unscrew the rotor bolt

25.10 Remove the bolt and washer (arrowed)

25.11 Install the rotor puller as described

the stator coils, check the fault is not due to damaged wiring between the connector and coils.

Removal

5 Remove the left-hand frame cover, the belly panel and, on EX650 models, the left-hand fairing side panel (see Chapter 7).

6 Drain the engine oil (see Chapter 1). Position a suitable receptacle underneath the alternator cover to catch any residual oil when the cover is removed.

7 Trace the wiring from the back of the alternator cover and disconnect it at the connector **(see illustration 24.12)**. Feed the wiring down to the cover, freeing it from any clips and noting its routing

8 Follow the procedure in Chapter 2, Section 15, to remove the alternator cover, then remove the starter idler and reduction gears.

9 To loosen the rotor bolt it is necessary to stop the rotor from turning. Kawasaki produces Service Tools (Part Nos. 57001-1658 and 57001-1591) to do this. Alternatively, use a commercially available rotor strap **(see illustration)**. Clean the outside of the rotor with a suitable solvent before installing the strap. If a rotor strap is not available, and the engine is in the frame, place the transmission in gear and have an assistant apply the rear brake hard.

10 With the rotor held, unscrew and remove

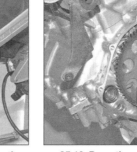

25.12 Turn the puller centre bolt to free the rotor

the bolt, noting the location of the washer **(see illustration)**. Keep the bolt and washer together so the washer is installed the same way round.

11 To remove the rotor from the crankshaft taper it is necessary to use a rotor puller. A Kawasaki Service Tool (Part No. 57001-1405) is available or an alternative which threads onto the external threads provided on the rotor boss. Thread a suitable bolt into the end of the crankshaft, then thread the body of the rotor puller fully onto the external threads on the rotor boss **(see illustration)**.

12 Using the same method employed to prevent the rotor from turning (see Step 9), turn

25.13 Draw the rotor off the crankshaft

the puller centre bolt clockwise until the rotor is free of the crankshaft taper **(see illustration)**.

13 Remove the puller, undo the bolt from the end of the crankshaft and remove the rotor **(see illustration)**. If the starter driven gear comes off with the alternator rotor, lay the rotor face down on the work bench, then lift the gear off the back of the rotor, rotating it anti-clockwise as you do to release it from the starter clutch (see Chapter 2, Section 15).

14 To remove the stator from the cover, first undo the bolt securing the wiring clamp and ease the wiring grommet out of the cover **(see illustration)**. Undo the bolts securing the stator and lift it out **(see illustration)**.

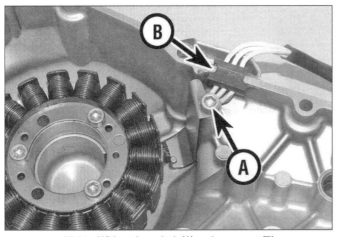

25.14a Wiring clamp bolt (A) and grommet (B)

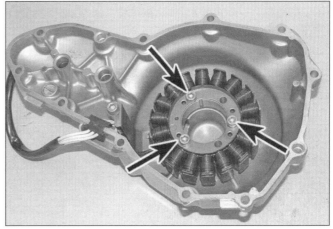

25.14b Alternator stator mounting bolts (arrowed)

25.19 Turn the starter driven gear to aid assembly

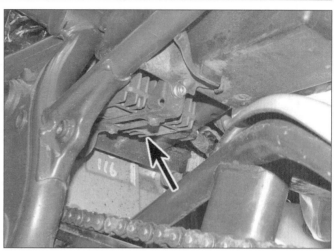

26.1a Location of the regulator/rectifier (arrowed)

Installation

15 Clean all traces of old gasket and sealant from the cover and crankcase mating surfaces. Clean the threads of the stator and clamp bolts.

16 Apply a suitable sealant to the wiring grommet, then fit the stator into the cover and press the grommet into the cut-out in the cover **(see illustration 25.14a)**. Install the wiring clamp. Apply a suitable non-permanent thread locking compound to the stator and wiring clamp bolts and tighten them to the torque setting specified at the beginning of this Chapter.

17 If removed, install the starter driven gear and large washer onto the crankshaft (see Chapter 2).

18 Clean the tapered end of the crankshaft and the corresponding mating surface on the inside of the rotor thoroughly with a suitable solvent.

19 Make sure that no metal objects have attached themselves to the magnet on the inside of the rotor. Slide the rotor onto the shaft and the starter driven gear, turning the gear clockwise as you do **(see illustration)**.

20 Lubricate the threads and seating surface of the rotor bolt with molybdenum disulphide oil (a 50/50 mixture of molybdenum disulphide grease and engine oil). Install the bolt with its washer and tighten it to the initial torque setting specified at the beginning of this Chapter, using the method employed on removal to prevent the rotor from turning **(see illustrations 25.10 and 9)**.

21 To check that the rotor has been correctly installed on the taper, now undo the bolt and washer. Follow the procedure in Step 11 to install the rotor puller and check that the puller centre bolt can be tightened to 20 Nm without the rotor being displaced – if so the rotor is correctly installed. If not, remove the rotor, clean the crankshaft and the corresponding mating surface on the inside of the rotor once more, then re-install the rotor.

22 Once the rotor has been correctly installed, tighten the rotor bolt to the final torque setting specified.

23 Follow the procedure in Chapter 2, Section 15, to install the starter gears and the alternator cover – don't forget to fit a new cover gasket.

24 Feed the wiring up to its connector, making sure it is correctly routed and secured by any clips, and install the ducting. Connect the wiring connector securely **(see illustration 24.12)**.

25 Refill the engine oil to the correct level (see Chapter 1 and *Pre-ride Checks*).

26 Install the remaining components in the reverse order of removal.

26 Regulator/rectifier

Removal and installation

1 The regulator/rectifier is located behind the engine unit **(see illustrations)**. Access is extremely restricted, especially on machines equipped with ABS – if required, remove the exhaust silencer (see Chapter 4) and the rear shock absorber (see Chapter 5).

2 Remove the right-hand frame side panel (see Chapter 7).

3 Disconnect the regulator/rectifier wiring connector **(see illustration)**. Check the connector terminals for corrosion.

4 Undo the bolts on the underside of the unit securing it to its mounting bracket and lift it off **(see illustration)**.

5 Installation is the reverse of removal. Ensure the wiring connector is secure.

Check

Note: *If the regulator/rectifier fails any of the following checks have it tested by a Kawasaki dealer to confirm your findings before buying a replacement part.*

6 Remove the regulator/rectifier (see Steps 1 to 4).

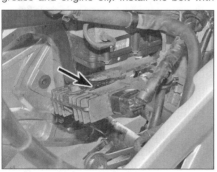

26.1b Location of the regulator/rectifier – ABS equipped machines

26.3 Disconnect the wiring connector

26.4 Location of the rear mounting bolt (arrowed)

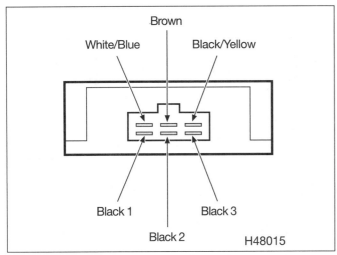

26.7 Regulator/rectifier terminal identification – 2006 to 2008 models

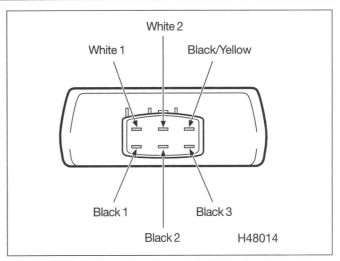

26.12 Regulator/rectifier terminal identification – 2009-on models

2006 to 2008 models

7 Check the rectifier circuits with an ohmmeter. Connect the positive (+ve) probe to the white/blue wire terminal and the negative (-ve) probe first to black wire terminal 1, then to black wire terminal 2, and then to black wire terminal 3 **(see illustration)**. Note the results. Now reverse the probes – the resistance should be low in one direction and more than ten times as much in the other.

8 Now repeat the test procedure between the black/yellow wire terminal and the black wire terminals.

9 If the resistance between any two terminals is either high or low in both directions the unit is faulty and a new one must be fitted.

10 Testing of the regulator circuit requires a fairly complex text arrangement, unlikely to be available in the home workshop. If the rectifier is good, refer to *Wiring Diagrams* at the end of this Chapter and check the wiring and connectors between the battery, ignition switch and regulator/rectifier for shorts,

breaks, and loose or corroded terminals.

11 Refer to Section 25, Steps 3 and 4, and perform the same test between the black wire terminals on the loom side of the regulator/rectifier wiring connector. If the results are not as specified, check the wiring between the regulator/rectifier connector and the alternator connector for continuity, and check for damaged or corroded terminals. If the wiring is good the stator coil windings could be faulty.

2009-on models

12 Check the rectifier circuits with an ohmmeter. Connect the positive (+ve) probe to white wire terminal 1 and the negative (-ve) probe first to black wire terminal 1, then to black wire terminal 2, and then to black wire terminal 3 **(see illustration)**. Note the results. Now reverse the probes – the resistance should be low in one direction and more than ten times as much in the other.

13 Now repeat the test procedure between

the black/yellow wire terminal and the black wire terminals.

14 If the resistance between any two terminals is either high or low in both directions the unit is faulty and a new one must be fitted.

15 Testing of the regulator circuit requires a fairly complex text arrangement, unlikely to be available in the home workshop. If the rectifier is good, refer to *Wiring Diagrams* at the end of this Chapter and check the wiring and connectors between the battery, ignition switch and regulator/rectifier for shorts, breaks, and loose or corroded terminals.

16 Refer to Section 25, Steps 3 and 4, and perform the same test between the black wire terminals on the loom side of the regulator/rectifier wiring connector. If the results are not as specified, check the wiring between the regulator/rectifier connector and the alternator connector for continuity, and check for damaged or corroded terminals. If the wiring is good the stator coil windings could be faulty.

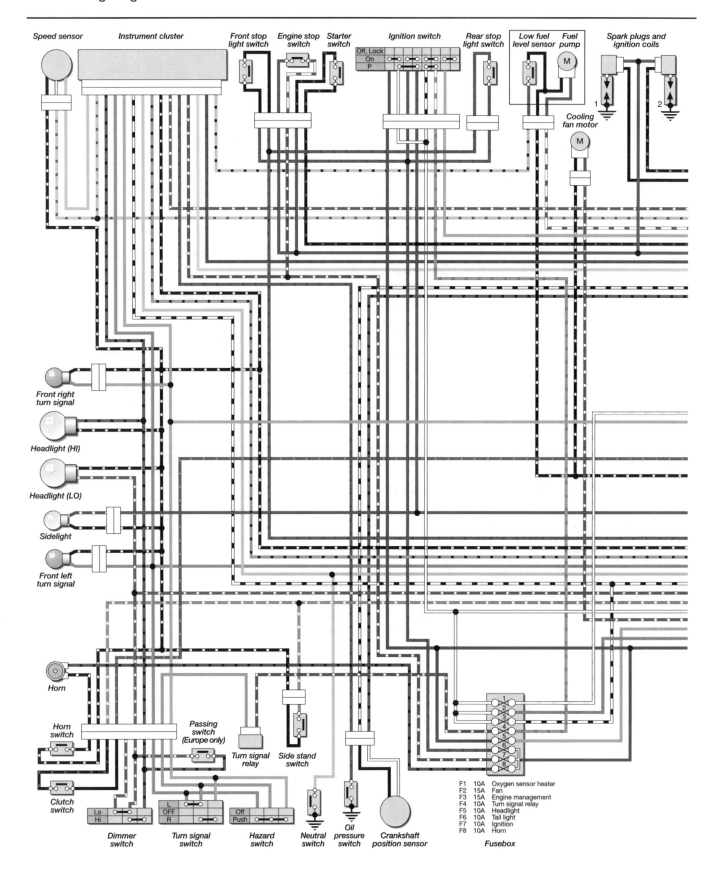

2006 to 2008 ER650A6-A8, EX650A6-A8, ER650B6-B8 (ABS) and EX650B6-B8 (ABS)

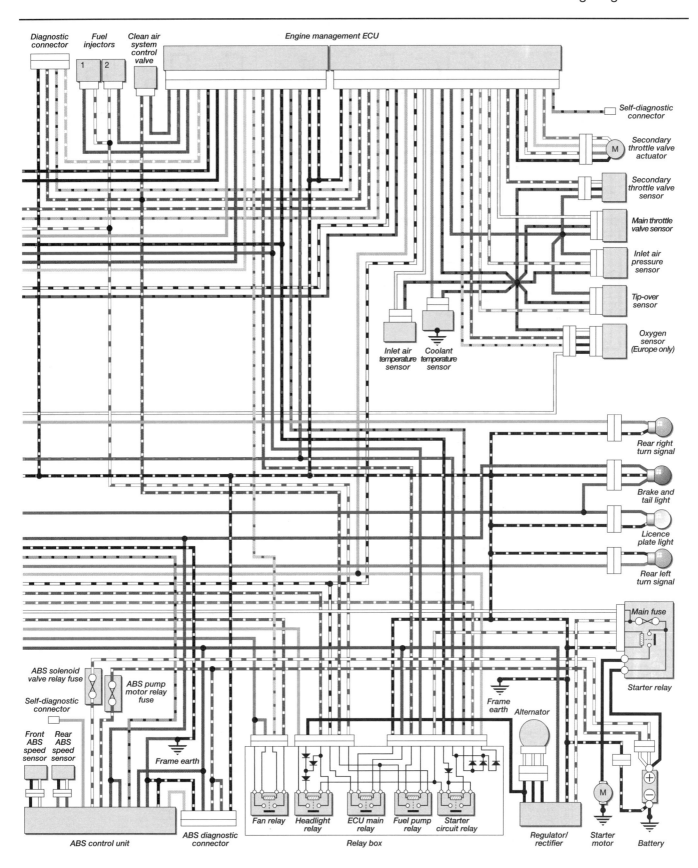

2006 to 2008 ER650A6-A8, EX650A6-A8, ER650B6-B8 (ABS) and EX650B6-B8 (ABS)

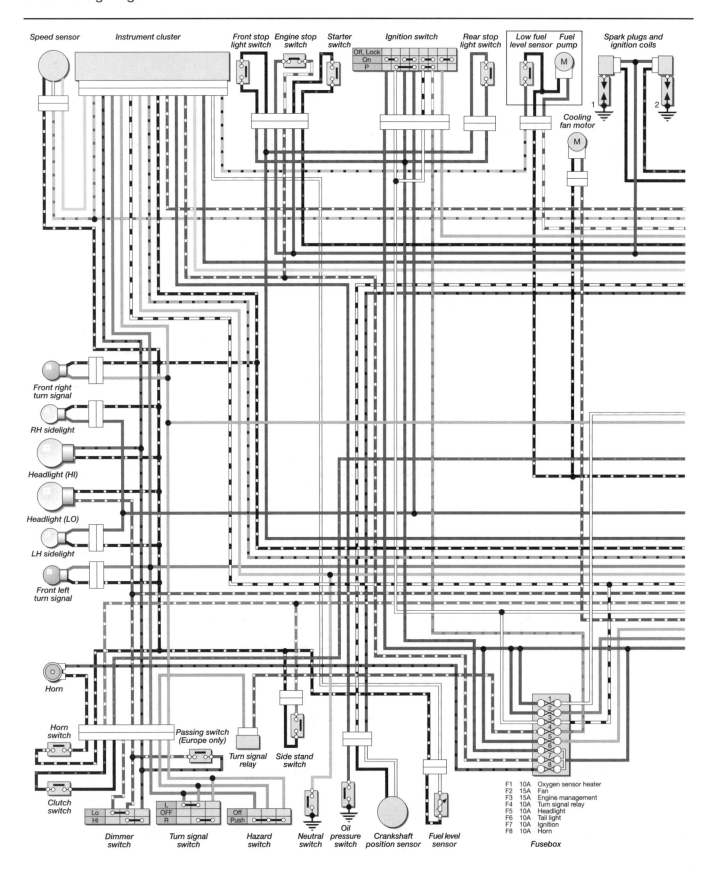

2009-on ER650C9/CA, EX650C9/CA, ER650D9/DA (ABS) and EX650D9/DA (ABS)

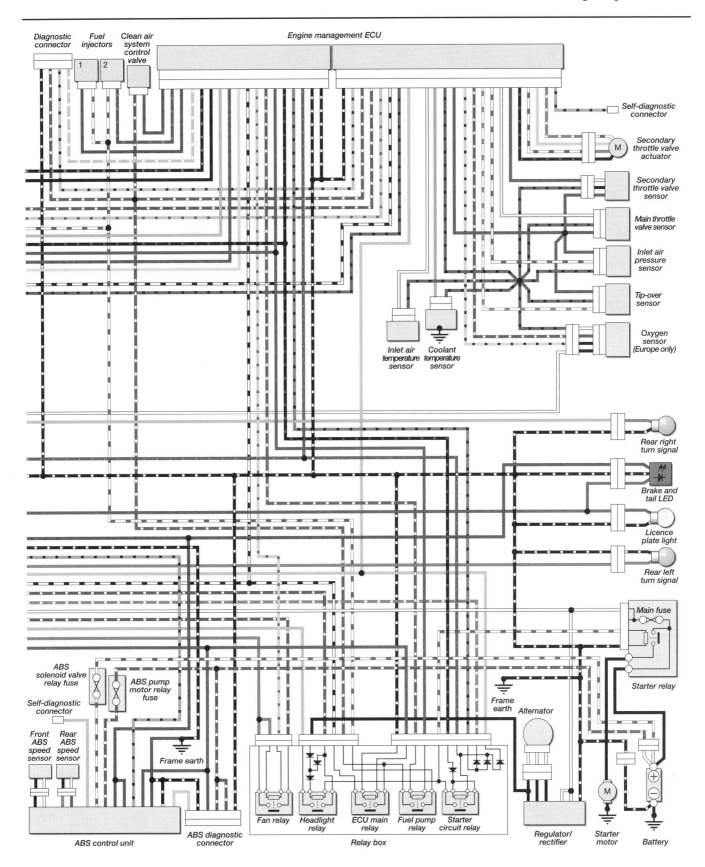

2009-on ER650C9/CA, EX650C9/CA, ER650D9/DA (ABS) and EX650D9/DA (ABS)

Reference

Tools and Workshop Tips

● Building up a tool kit and equipping your workshop ● Using tools ● Understanding bearing, seal, fastener and chain sizes and markings ● Repair techniques

Security

● Locks and chains ● U-locks ● Disc locks ● Alarms and immobilisers ● Security marking systems ● Tips on how to prevent bike theft

Lubricants and fluids

● Engine oils ● Transmission (gear) oils ● Coolant/anti-freeze ● Fork oils and suspension fluids ● Brake/clutch fluids ● Spray lubes, degreasers and solvents

Conversion Factors

$$34\ Nm \times 0.738$$
$$= 25\ lbf\ ft$$

● Formulae for conversion of the metric (SI) units used throughout the manual into Imperial measures

MOT Test Checks

● A guide to the UK MOT test ● Which items are tested ● How to prepare your motorcycle for the test and perform a pre-test check

Storage

● How to prepare your motorcycle for going into storage and protect essential systems ● How to get the motorcycle back on the road

Fault Finding

● Common faults and their likely causes ● Links to main chapters for testing or repair procedures

Technical Terms Explained

● Component names, technical terms and common abbreviations explained

Index

Buying tools

A toolkit is a fundamental requirement for servicing and repairing a motorcycle. Although there will be an initial expense in building up enough tools for servicing, this will soon be offset by the savings made by doing the job yourself. As experience and confidence grow, additional tools can be added to enable the repair and overhaul of the motorcycle. Many of the specialist tools are expensive and not often used so it may be preferable to hire them, or for a group of friends or motorcycle club to join in the purchase.

As a rule, it is better to buy more expensive, good quality tools. Cheaper tools are likely to wear out faster and need to be renewed more often, nullifying the original saving.

> ⚠️ **Warning: To avoid the risk of a poor quality tool breaking in use, causing injury or damage to the component being worked on, always aim to purchase tools which meet the relevant national safety standards.**

The following lists of tools do not represent the manufacturer's service tools, but serve as a guide to help the owner decide which tools are needed for this level of work. In addition, items such as an electric drill, hacksaw, files, soldering iron and a workbench equipped with a vice, may be needed. Although not classed as tools, a selection of bolts, screws, nuts, washers and pieces of tubing always come in useful.

For more information about tools, refer to the Haynes *Motorcycle Workshop Practice Techbook* (Bk. No. 3470).

Manufacturer's service tools

Inevitably certain tasks require the use of a service tool. Where possible an alternative tool or method of approach is recommended, but sometimes there is no option if personal injury or damage to the component is to be avoided. Where required, service tools are referred to in the relevant procedure.

Service tools can usually only be purchased from a motorcycle dealer and are identified by a part number. Some of the commonly-used tools, such as rotor pullers, are available in aftermarket form from mail-order motorcycle tool and accessory suppliers.

Maintenance and minor repair tools

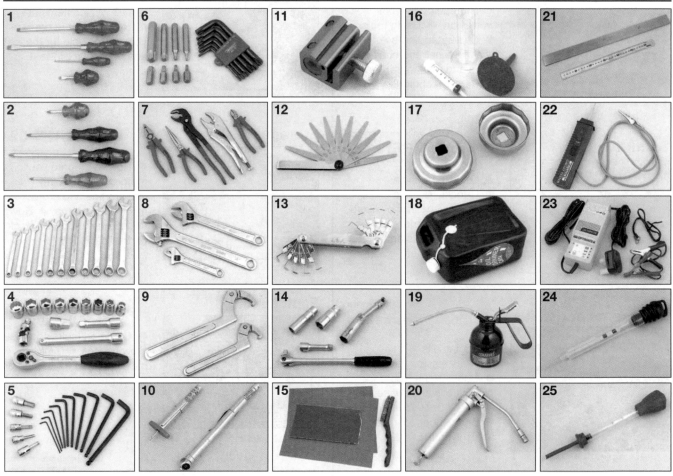

1 Set of flat-bladed screwdrivers
2 Set of Phillips head screwdrivers
3 Combination open-end and ring spanners
4 Socket set (3/8 inch or 1/2 inch drive)
5 Set of Allen keys or bits
6 Set of Torx keys or bits
7 Pliers, cutters and self-locking grips (Mole grips)
8 Adjustable spanners
9 C-spanners
10 Tread depth gauge and tyre pressure gauge
11 Cable oiler clamp
12 Feeler gauges
13 Spark plug gap measuring tool
14 Spark plug spanner or deep plug sockets
15 Wire brush and emery paper
16 Calibrated syringe, measuring vessel and funnel
17 Oil filter adapters
18 Oil drainer can or tray
19 Pump type oil can
20 Grease gun
21 Straight-edge and steel rule
22 Continuity tester
23 Battery charger
24 Hydrometer (for battery specific gravity check)
25 Anti-freeze tester (for liquid-cooled engines)

Repair and overhaul tools

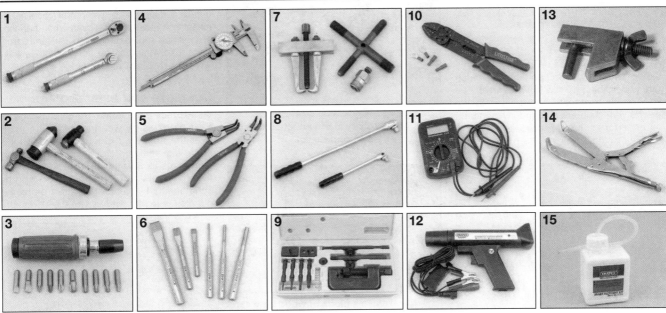

1 Torque wrench
   (small and mid-ranges)
2 Conventional, plastic or
   soft-faced hammers
3 Impact driver set

4 Vernier gauge
5 Circlip pliers (internal and
   external, or combination)
6 Set of cold chisels
   and punches

7 Selection of pullers
8 Breaker bars
9 Chain breaking/
   riveting tool set

10 Wire stripper and
   crimper tool
11 Multimeter (measures
   amps, volts and ohms)
12 Stroboscope (for
   dynamic timing checks)

13 Hose clamp
   (wingnut type shown)
14 Clutch holding tool
15 One-man brake/clutch
   bleeder kit

Specialist tools

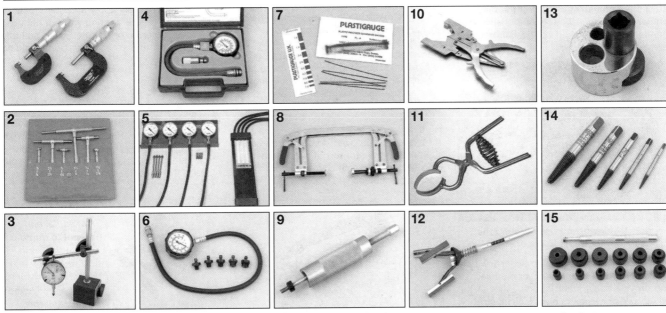

1 Micrometers
   (external type)
2 Telescoping gauges
3 Dial gauge

4 Cylinder
   compression gauge
5 Vacuum gauges (left) or
   manometer (right)
6 Oil pressure gauge

7 Plastigauge kit
8 Valve spring compressor
   (4-stroke engines)
9 Piston pin drawbolt tool

10 Piston ring removal and
   installation tool
11 Piston ring clamp
12 Cylinder bore hone
   (stone type shown)

13 Stud extractor
14 Screw extractor set
15 Bearing driver set

1 Workshop equipment and facilities

The workbench

● Work is made much easier by raising the bike up on a ramp - components are much more accessible if raised to waist level. The hydraulic or pneumatic types seen in the dealer's workshop are a sound investment if you undertake a lot of repairs or overhauls **(see illustration 1.1)**.

1.1 Hydraulic motorcycle ramp

● If raised off ground level, the bike must be supported on the ramp to avoid it falling. Most ramps incorporate a front wheel locating clamp which can be adjusted to suit different diameter wheels. When tightening the clamp, take care not to mark the wheel rim or damage the tyre - use wood blocks on each side to prevent this.
● Secure the bike to the ramp using tie-downs **(see illustration 1.2)**. If the bike has only a sidestand, and hence leans at a dangerous angle when raised, support the bike on an auxiliary stand.

1.2 Tie-downs are used around the passenger footrests to secure the bike

● Auxiliary (paddock) stands are widely available from mail order companies or motorcycle dealers and attach either to the wheel axle or swingarm pivot **(see illustration 1.3)**. If the motorcycle has a centrestand, you can support it under the crankcase to prevent it toppling whilst either wheel is removed **(see illustration 1.4)**.

1.3 This auxiliary stand attaches to the swingarm pivot

1.4 Always use a block of wood between the engine and jack head when supporting the engine in this way

Fumes and fire

● Refer to the Safety first! page at the beginning of the manual for full details. Make sure your workshop is equipped with a fire extinguisher suitable for fuel-related fires (Class B fire - flammable liquids) - it is not sufficient to have a water-filled extinguisher.
● Always ensure adequate ventilation is available. Unless an exhaust gas extraction system is available for use, ensure that the engine is run outside of the workshop.
● If working on the fuel system, make sure the workshop is ventilated to avoid a build-up of fumes. This applies equally to fume build-up when charging a battery. Do not smoke or allow anyone else to smoke in the workshop.

Fluids

● If you need to drain fuel from the tank, store it in an approved container marked as suitable for the storage of petrol (gasoline) **(see illustration 1.5)**. Do not store fuel in glass jars or bottles.

1.5 Use an approved can only for storing petrol (gasoline)

● Use proprietary engine degreasers or solvents which have a high flash-point, such as paraffin (kerosene), for cleaning off oil, grease and dirt - never use petrol (gasoline) for cleaning. Wear rubber gloves when handling solvent and engine degreaser. The fumes from certain solvents can be dangerous - always work in a well-ventilated area.

Dust, eye and hand protection

● Protect your lungs from inhalation of dust particles by wearing a filtering mask over the nose and mouth. Many frictional materials still contain asbestos which is dangerous to your health. Protect your eyes from spouts of liquid and sprung components by wearing a pair of protective goggles **(see illustration 1.6)**.

1.6 A fire extinguisher, goggles, mask and protective gloves should be at hand in the workshop

● Protect your hands from contact with solvents, fuel and oils by wearing rubber gloves. Alternatively apply a barrier cream to your hands before starting work. If handling hot components or fluids, wear suitable gloves to protect your hands from scalding and burns.

What to do with old fluids

● Old cleaning solvent, fuel, coolant and oils should not be poured down domestic drains or onto the ground. Package the fluid up in old oil containers, label it accordingly, and take it to a garage or disposal facility. Contact your local authority for location of such sites or ring the oil care hotline.

OIL CARE
FOLLOW THE CODE
OIL BANK LINE
0800 66 33 66
www.oilbankline.org.uk

Note: It is antisocial and illegal to dump oil down the drain. To find the location of your local oil recycling bank, call this number free.

In the USA, note that any oil supplier must accept used oil for recycling.

2 Fasteners -
screws, bolts and nuts

Fastener types and applications

Bolts and screws

● Fastener head types are either of hexagonal, Torx or splined design, with internal and external versions of each type (see illustrations 2.1 and 2.2); splined head fasteners are not in common use on motorcycles. The conventional slotted or Phillips head design is used for certain screws. Bolt or screw length is always measured from the underside of the head to the end of the item (see illustration 2.11).

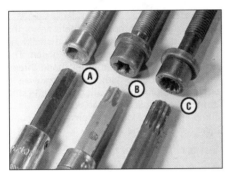

2.1 Internal hexagon/Allen (A), Torx (B) and splined (C) fasteners, with corresponding bits

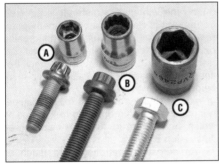

2.2 External Torx (A), splined (B) and hexagon (C) fasteners, with corresponding sockets

● Certain fasteners on the motorcycle have a tensile marking on their heads, the higher the marking the stronger the fastener. High tensile fasteners generally carry a 10 or higher marking. Never replace a high tensile fastener with one of a lower tensile strength.

Washers (see illustration 2.3)

● Plain washers are used between a fastener head and a component to prevent damage to the component or to spread the load when torque is applied. Plain washers can also be used as spacers or shims in certain assemblies. Copper or aluminium plain washers are often used as sealing washers on drain plugs.

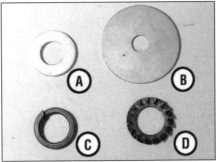

2.3 Plain washer (A), penny washer (B), spring washer (C) and serrated washer (D)

● The split-ring spring washer works by applying axial tension between the fastener head and component. If flattened, it is fatigued and must be renewed. If a plain (flat) washer is used on the fastener, position the spring washer between the fastener and the plain washer.

● Serrated star type washers dig into the fastener and component faces, preventing loosening. They are often used on electrical earth (ground) connections to the frame.

● Cone type washers (sometimes called Belleville) are conical and when tightened apply axial tension between the fastener head and component. They must be installed with the dished side against the component and often carry an OUTSIDE marking on their outer face. If flattened, they are fatigued and must be renewed.

● Tab washers are used to lock plain nuts or bolts on a shaft. A portion of the tab washer is bent up hard against one flat of the nut or bolt to prevent it loosening. Due to the tab washer being deformed in use, a new tab washer should be used every time it is disturbed.

● Wave washers are used to take up endfloat on a shaft. They provide light springing and prevent excessive side-to-side play of a component. Can be found on rocker arm shafts.

Nuts and split pins

● Conventional plain nuts are usually six-sided (see illustration 2.4). They are sized by thread diameter and pitch. High tensile nuts carry a number on one end to denote their tensile strength.

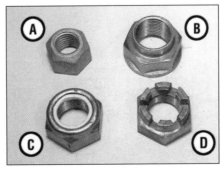

2.4 Plain nut (A), shouldered locknut (B), nylon insert nut (C) and castellated nut (D)

● Self-locking nuts either have a nylon insert, or two spring metal tabs, or a shoulder which is staked into a groove in the shaft - their advantage over conventional plain nuts is a resistance to loosening due to vibration. The nylon insert type can be used a number of times, but must be renewed when the friction of the nylon insert is reduced, ie when the nut spins freely on the shaft. The spring tab type can be reused unless the tabs are damaged. The shouldered type must be renewed every time it is disturbed.

● Split pins (cotter pins) are used to lock a castellated nut to a shaft or to prevent slackening of a plain nut. Common applications are wheel axles and brake torque arms. Because the split pin arms are deformed to lock around the nut a new split pin must always be used on installation - always fit the correct size split pin which will fit snugly in the shaft hole. Make sure the split pin arms are correctly located around the nut (see illustrations 2.5 and 2.6).

2.5 Bend split pin (cotter pin) arms as shown (arrows) to secure a castellated nut

2.6 Bend split pin (cotter pin) arms as shown to secure a plain nut

Caution: If the castellated nut slots do not align with the shaft hole after tightening to the torque setting, tighten the nut until the next slot aligns with the hole - never slacken the nut to align its slot.

● R-pins (shaped like the letter R), or slip pins as they are sometimes called, are sprung and can be reused if they are otherwise in good condition. Always install R-pins with their closed end facing forwards (see illustration 2.7).

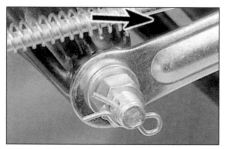

2.7 Correct fitting of R-pin. Arrow indicates forward direction

Circlips (see illustration 2.8)

● Circlips (sometimes called snap-rings) are used to retain components on a shaft or in a housing and have corresponding external or internal ears to permit removal. Parallel-sided (machined) circlips can be installed either way round in their groove, whereas stamped circlips (which have a chamfered edge on one face) must be installed with the chamfer facing away from the direction of thrust load **(see illustration 2.9)**.

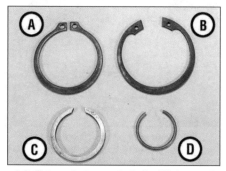

2.8 External stamped circlip (A), internal stamped circlip (B), machined circlip (C) and wire circlip (D)

● Always use circlip pliers to remove and install circlips; expand or compress them just enough to remove them. After installation, rotate the circlip in its groove to ensure it is securely seated. If installing a circlip on a splined shaft, always align its opening with a shaft channel to ensure the circlip ends are well supported and unlikely to catch **(see illustration 2.10)**.

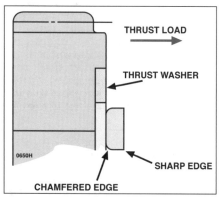

2.9 Correct fitting of a stamped circlip

THRUST LOAD

THRUST WASHER

SHARP EDGE

CHAMFERED EDGE

0650H

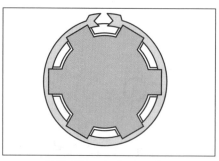

2.10 Align circlip opening with shaft channel

● Circlips can wear due to the thrust of components and become loose in their grooves, with the subsequent danger of becoming dislodged in operation. For this reason, renewal is advised every time a circlip is disturbed.

● Wire circlips are commonly used as piston pin retaining clips. If a removal tang is provided, long-nosed pliers can be used to dislodge them, otherwise careful use of a small flat-bladed screwdriver is necessary. Wire circlips should be renewed every time they are disturbed.

Thread diameter and pitch

● Diameter of a male thread (screw, bolt or stud) is the outside diameter of the threaded portion **(see illustration 2.11)**. Most motorcycle manufacturers use the ISO (International Standards Organisation) metric system expressed in millimetres, eg M6 refers to a 6 mm diameter thread. Sizing is the same for nuts, except that the thread diameter is measured across the valleys of the nut.

● Pitch is the distance between the peaks of the thread **(see illustration 2.11)**. It is expressed in millimetres, thus a common bolt size may be expressed as 6.0 x 1.0 mm (6 mm thread diameter and 1 mm pitch). Generally pitch increases in proportion to thread diameter, although there are always exceptions.

● Thread diameter and pitch are related for conventional fastener applications and the accompanying table can be used as a guide. Additionally, the AF (Across Flats), spanner or socket size dimension of the bolt or nut **(see illustration 2.11)** is linked to thread and pitch specification. Thread pitch can be measured with a thread gauge **(see illustration 2.12)**.

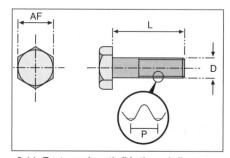

2.11 Fastener length (L), thread diameter (D), thread pitch (P) and head size (AF)

AF

L

D

P

2.12 Using a thread gauge to measure pitch

AF size	Thread diameter x pitch (mm)
8 mm	M5 x 0.8
8 mm	M6 x 1.0
10 mm	M6 x 1.0
12 mm	M8 x 1.25
14 mm	M10 x 1.25
17 mm	M12 x 1.25

● The threads of most fasteners are of the right-hand type, ie they are turned clockwise to tighten and anti-clockwise to loosen. The reverse situation applies to left-hand thread fasteners, which are turned anti-clockwise to tighten and clockwise to loosen. Left-hand threads are used where rotation of a component might loosen a conventional right-hand thread fastener.

Seized fasteners

● Corrosion of external fasteners due to water or reaction between two dissimilar metals can occur over a period of time. It will build up sooner in wet conditions or in countries where salt is used on the roads during the winter. If a fastener is severely corroded it is likely that normal methods of removal will fail and result in its head being ruined. When you attempt removal, the fastener thread should be heard to crack free and unscrew easily - if it doesn't, stop there before damaging something.

● A smart tap on the head of the fastener will often succeed in breaking free corrosion which has occurred in the threads **(see illustration 2.13)**.

● An aerosol penetrating fluid (such as WD-40) applied the night beforehand may work its way down into the thread and ease removal. Depending on the location, you may be able to make up a Plasticine well around the fastener head and fill it with penetrating fluid.

2.13 A sharp tap on the head of a fastener will often break free a corroded thread

● If you are working on an engine internal component, corrosion will most likely not be a problem due to the well lubricated environment. However, components can be very tight and an impact driver is a useful tool in freeing them (see illustration 2.14).

2.14 Using an impact driver to free a fastener

● Where corrosion has occurred between dissimilar metals (eg steel and aluminium alloy), the application of heat to the fastener head will create a disproportionate expansion rate between the two metals and break the seizure caused by the corrosion. Whether heat can be applied depends on the location of the fastener - any surrounding components likely to be damaged must first be removed (see illustration 2.15). Heat can be applied using a paint stripper heat gun or clothes iron, or by immersing the component in boiling water - wear protective gloves to prevent scalding or burns to the hands.

2.15 Using heat to free a seized fastener

● As a last resort, it is possible to use a hammer and cold chisel to work the fastener head unscrewed (see illustration 2.16). This will damage the fastener, but more importantly extreme care must be taken not to damage the surrounding component.

Caution: Remember that the component being secured is generally of more value than the bolt, nut or screw - when the fastener is freed, do not unscrew it with force, instead work the fastener back and forth when resistance is felt to prevent thread damage.

2.16 Using a hammer and chisel to free a seized fastener

Broken fasteners and damaged heads

● If the shank of a broken bolt or screw is accessible you can grip it with self-locking grips. The knurled wheel type stud extractor tool or self-gripping stud puller tool is particularly useful for removing the long studs which screw into the cylinder mouth surface of the crankcase or bolts and screws from which the head has broken off (see illustration 2.17). Studs can also be removed by locking two nuts together on the threaded end of the stud and using a spanner on the lower nut (see illustration 2.18).

2.17 Using a stud extractor tool to remove a broken crankcase stud

2.18 Two nuts can be locked together to unscrew a stud from a component

● A bolt or screw which has broken off below or level with the casing must be extracted using a screw extractor set. Centre punch the fastener to centralise the drill bit, then drill a hole in the fastener (see illustration 2.19). Select a drill bit which is approximately half to three-quarters the

2.19 When using a screw extractor, first drill a hole in the fastener . . .

diameter of the fastener and drill to a depth which will accommodate the extractor. Use the largest size extractor possible, but avoid leaving too small a wall thickness otherwise the extractor will merely force the fastener walls outwards wedging it in the casing thread.

● If a spiral type extractor is used, thread it anti-clockwise into the fastener. As it is screwed in, it will grip the fastener and unscrew it from the casing (see illustration 2.20).

2.20 . . . then thread the extractor anti-clockwise into the fastener

● If a taper type extractor is used, tap it into the fastener so that it is firmly wedged in place. Unscrew the extractor (anti-clockwise) to draw the fastener out.

⚠ *Warning: Stud extractors are very hard and may break off in the fastener if care is not taken - ask an engineer about spark erosion if this happens.*

● Alternatively, the broken bolt/screw can be drilled out and the hole retapped for an oversize bolt/screw or a diamond-section thread insert. It is essential that the drilling is carried out squarely and to the correct depth, otherwise the casing may be ruined - if in doubt, entrust the work to an engineer.

● Bolts and nuts with rounded corners cause the correct size spanner or socket to slip when force is applied. Of the types of spanner/socket available always use a six-point type rather than an eight or twelve-point type - better grip

2.21 Comparison of surface drive ring spanner (left) with 12-point type (right)

is obtained. Surface drive spanners grip the middle of the hex flats, rather than the corners, and are thus good in cases of damaged heads **(see illustration 2.21)**.

● Slotted-head or Phillips-head screws are often damaged by the use of the wrong size screwdriver. Allen-head and Torx-head screws are much less likely to sustain damage. If enough of the screw head is exposed you can use a hacksaw to cut a slot in its head and then use a conventional flat-bladed screwdriver to remove it. Alternatively use a hammer and cold chisel to tap the head of the fastener around to slacken it. Always replace damaged fasteners with new ones, preferably Torx or Allen-head type.

A dab of valve grinding compound between the screw head and screwdriver tip will often give a good grip.

Thread repair

● Threads (particularly those in aluminium alloy components) can be damaged by overtightening, being assembled with dirt in the threads, or from a component working loose and vibrating. Eventually the thread will fail completely, and it will be impossible to tighten the fastener.

● If a thread is damaged or clogged with old locking compound it can be renovated with a thread repair tool (thread chaser) **(see illustrations 2.22 and 2.23)**; special thread

2.22 A thread repair tool being used to correct an internal thread

2.23 A thread repair tool being used to correct an external thread

chasers are available for spark plug hole threads. The tool will not cut a new thread, but clean and true the original thread. Make sure that you use the correct diameter and pitch tool. Similarly, external threads can be cleaned up with a die or a thread restorer file **(see illustration 2.24)**.

2.24 Using a thread restorer file

● It is possible to drill out the old thread and retap the component to the next thread size. This will work where there is enough surrounding material and a new bolt or screw can be obtained. Sometimes, however, this is not possible - such as where the bolt/screw passes through another component which must also be suitably modified, also in cases where a spark plug or oil drain plug cannot be obtained in a larger diameter thread size.

● The diamond-section thread insert (often known by its popular trade name of Heli-Coil) is a simple and effective method of renewing the thread and retaining the original size. A kit can be purchased which contains the tap, insert and installing tool **(see illustration 2.25)**. Drill out the damaged thread with the size drill specified **(see illustration 2.26)**. Carefully retap the thread **(see illustration 2.27)**. Install the

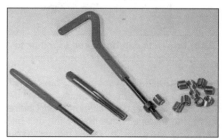

2.25 Obtain a thread insert kit to suit the thread diameter and pitch required

2.26 To install a thread insert, first drill out the original thread . . .

2.27 . . . tap a new thread . . .

2.28 . . . fit insert on the installing tool . . .

2.29 . . . and thread into the component . . .

2.30 . . . break off the tang when complete

insert on the installing tool and thread it slowly into place using a light downward pressure **(see illustrations 2.28 and 2.29)**. When positioned between a 1/4 and 1/2 turn below the surface withdraw the installing tool and use the break-off tool to press down on the tang, breaking it off **(see illustration 2.30)**.

● There are epoxy thread repair kits on the market which can rebuild stripped internal threads, although this repair should not be used on high load-bearing components.

Thread locking and sealing compounds

● Locking compounds are used in locations where the fastener is prone to loosening due to vibration or on important safety-related items which might cause loss of control of the motorcycle if they fail. It is also used where important fasteners cannot be secured by other means such as lockwashers or split pins.

● Before applying locking compound, make sure that the threads (internal and external) are clean and dry with all old compound removed. Select a compound to suit the component being secured - a non-permanent general locking and sealing type is suitable for most applications, but a high strength type is needed for permanent fixing of studs in castings. Apply a drop or two of the compound to the first few threads of the fastener, then thread it into place and tighten to the specified torque. Do not apply excessive thread locking compound otherwise the thread may be damaged on subsequent removal.

● Certain fasteners are impregnated with a dry film type coating of locking compound on their threads. Always renew this type of fastener if disturbed.

● Anti-seize compounds, such as copper-based greases, can be applied to protect threads from seizure due to extreme heat and corrosion. A common instance is spark plug threads and exhaust system fasteners.

3 Measuring tools and gauges

Feeler gauges

● Feeler gauges (or blades) are used for measuring small gaps and clearances (see illustration 3.1). They can also be used to measure endfloat (sideplay) of a component on a shaft where access is not possible with a dial gauge.

● Feeler gauge sets should be treated with care and not bent or damaged. They are etched with their size on one face. Keep them clean and very lightly oiled to prevent corrosion build-up.

3.1 Feeler gauges are used for measuring small gaps and clearances - thickness is marked on one face of gauge

● When measuring a clearance, select a gauge which is a light sliding fit between the two components. You may need to use two gauges together to measure the clearance accurately.

Micrometers

● A micrometer is a precision tool capable of measuring to 0.01 or 0.001 of a millimetre. It should always be stored in its case and not in the general toolbox. It must be kept clean and never dropped, otherwise its frame or measuring anvils could be distorted resulting in inaccurate readings.

● External micrometers are used for measuring outside diameters of components and have many more applications than internal micrometers. Micrometers are available in different size ranges, eg 0 to 25 mm, 25 to 50 mm, and upwards in 25 mm steps; some large micrometers have interchangeable anvils to allow a range of measurements to be taken. Generally the largest precision measurement you are likely to take on a motorcycle is the piston diameter.

● Internal micrometers (or bore micrometers) are used for measuring inside diameters, such as valve guides and cylinder bores. Telescoping gauges and small hole gauges are used in conjunction with an external micrometer, whereas the more expensive internal micrometers have their own measuring device.

External micrometer

Note: *The conventional analogue type instrument is described. Although much easier to read, digital micrometers are considerably more expensive.*

● Always check the calibration of the micrometer before use. With the anvils closed (0 to 25 mm type) or set over a test gauge (for

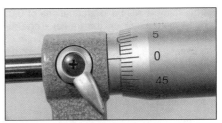

3.2 Check micrometer calibration before use

the larger types) the scale should read zero (see illustration 3.2); make sure that the anvils (and test piece) are clean first. Any discrepancy can be adjusted by referring to the instructions supplied with the tool. Remember that the micrometer is a precision measuring tool - don't force the anvils closed, use the ratchet (4) on the end of the micrometer to close it. In this way, a measured force is always applied.

● To use, first make sure that the item being measured is clean. Place the anvil of the micrometer (1) against the item and use the thimble (2) to bring the spindle (3) lightly into contact with the other side of the item (see illustration 3.3). Don't tighten the thimble down because this will damage the micrometer - instead use the ratchet (4) on the end of the micrometer. The ratchet mechanism applies a measured force preventing damage to the instrument.

● The micrometer is read by referring to the linear scale on the sleeve and the annular scale on the thimble. Read off the sleeve first to obtain the base measurement, then add the fine measurement from the thimble to obtain the overall reading. The linear scale on the sleeve represents the measuring range of the micrometer (eg 0 to 25 mm). The annular scale

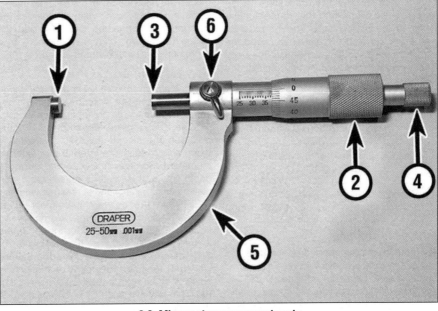

3.3 Micrometer component parts

| 1 Anvil | 3 Spindle | 5 Frame |
| 2 Thimble | 4 Ratchet | 6 Locking lever |

on the thimble will be in graduations of 0.01 mm (or as marked on the frame) - one full revolution of the thimble will move 0.5 mm on the linear scale. Take the reading where the datum line on the sleeve intersects the thimble's scale. Always position the eye directly above the scale otherwise an inaccurate reading will result.

In the example shown the item measures 2.95 mm (see illustration 3.4):

Linear scale	2.00 mm
Linear scale	0.50 mm
Annular scale	0.45 mm
Total figure	**2.95 mm**

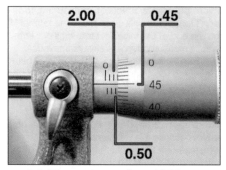

3.4 Micrometer reading of 2.95 mm

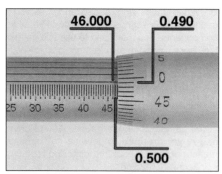

3.5 Micrometer reading of 46.99 mm on linear and annular scales . . .

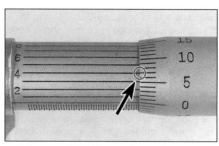

3.6 . . . and 0.004 mm on vernier scale

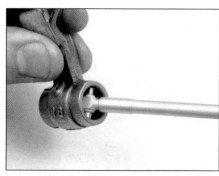

3.7 Expand the telescoping gauge in the bore, lock its position . . .

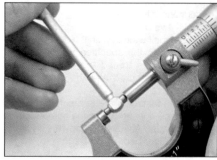

3.8 . . . then measure the gauge with a micrometer

3.9 Expand the small hole gauge in the bore, lock its position . . .

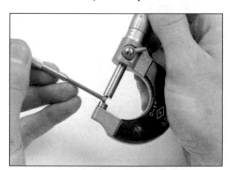

3.10 . . . then measure the gauge with a micrometer

Most micrometers have a locking lever (6) on the frame to hold the setting in place, allowing the item to be removed from the micrometer.
● Some micrometers have a vernier scale on their sleeve, providing an even finer measurement to be taken, in 0.001 increments of a millimetre. Take the sleeve and thimble measurement as described above, then check which graduation on the vernier scale aligns with that of the annular scale on the thimble **Note:** *The eye must be perpendicular to the scale when taking the vernier reading - if necessary rotate the body of the micrometer to ensure this.* Multiply the vernier scale figure by 0.001 and add it to the base and fine measurement figures.

In the example shown the item measures 46.994 mm (see illustrations 3.5 and 3.6):

Linear scale (base)	46.000 mm
Linear scale (base)	00.500 mm
Annular scale (fine)	00.490 mm
Vernier scale	00.004 mm
Total figure	**46.994 mm**

Internal micrometer

● Internal micrometers are available for measuring bore diameters, but are expensive and unlikely to be available for home use. It is suggested that a set of telescoping gauges and small hole gauges, both of which must be used with an external micrometer, will suffice for taking internal measurements on a motorcycle.
● Telescoping gauges can be used to measure internal diameters of components. Select a gauge with the correct size range, make sure its ends are clean and insert it into the bore. Expand the gauge, then lock its position and withdraw it from the bore (see illustration 3.7). Measure across the gauge ends with a micrometer (see illustration 3.8).
● Very small diameter bores (such as valve guides) are measured with a small hole gauge. Once adjusted to a slip-fit inside the component, its position is locked and the gauge withdrawn for measurement with a micrometer (see illustrations 3.9 and 3.10).

Vernier caliper
Note: *The conventional linear and dial gauge type instruments are described. Digital types are easier to read, but are far more expensive.*
● The vernier caliper does not provide the precision of a micrometer, but is versatile in being able to measure internal and external diameters. Some types also incorporate a depth gauge. It is ideal for measuring clutch plate friction material and spring free lengths.
● To use the conventional linear scale vernier, slacken off the vernier clamp screws (1) and set its jaws over (2), or inside (3), the item to be measured (see illustration 3.11). Slide the jaw into contact, using the thumb-wheel (4) for fine movement of the sliding scale (5) then tighten the clamp screws (1). Read off the main scale (6) where the zero on the sliding scale (5) intersects it, taking the whole number to the left of the zero; this provides the base measurement. View along the sliding scale and select the division which

lines up exactly with any of the divisions on the main scale, noting that the divisions usually represents 0.02 of a millimetre. Add this fine measurement to the base measurement to obtain the total reading.

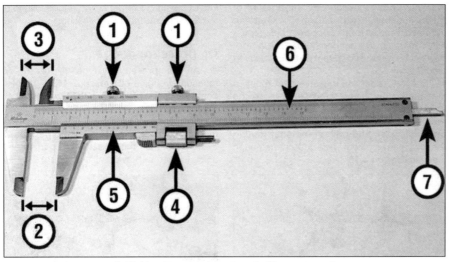

3.11 Vernier component parts (linear gauge)

1	Clamp screws	3	Internal jaws	5	Sliding scale	7 Depth gauge
2	External jaws	4	Thumbwheel	6	Main scale	

In the example shown the item measures 55.92 mm **(see illustration 3.12)**:

Base measurement	55.00 mm
Fine measurement	00.92 mm
Total figure	**55.92 mm**

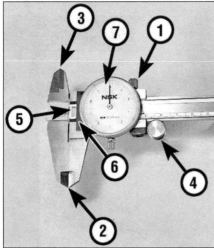

3.12 Vernier gauge reading of 55.92 mm

● Some vernier calipers are equipped with a dial gauge for fine measurement. Before use, check that the jaws are clean, then close them fully and check that the dial gauge reads zero. If necessary adjust the gauge ring accordingly. Slacken the vernier clamp screw (1) and set its jaws over (2), or inside (3), the item to be measured **(see illustration 3.13)**. Slide the jaws into contact, using the thumbwheel (4) for fine movement. Read off the main scale (5) where the edge of the sliding scale (6) intersects it, taking the whole number to the left of the zero; this provides the base measurement. Read off the needle position on the dial gauge (7) scale to provide the fine measurement; each division represents 0.05 of a millimetre. Add this fine measurement to the base measurement to obtain the total reading.

In the example shown the item measures 55.95 mm **(see illustration 3.14)**:

Base measurement	55.00 mm
Fine measurement	00.95 mm
Total figure	**55.95 mm**

3.14 Vernier gauge reading of 55.95 mm

3.13 Vernier component parts (dial gauge)

1	Clamp screw
2	External jaws
3	Internal jaws
4	Thumbwheel
5	Main scale
6	Sliding scale
7	Dial gauge

Plastigauge

● Plastigauge is a plastic material which can be compressed between two surfaces to measure the oil clearance between them. The width of the compressed Plastigauge is measured against a calibrated scale to determine the clearance.

● Common uses of Plastigauge are for measuring the clearance between crankshaft journal and main bearing inserts, between crankshaft journal and big-end bearing inserts, and between camshaft and bearing surfaces. The following example describes big-end oil clearance measurement.

● Handle the Plastigauge material carefully to prevent distortion. Using a sharp knife, cut a length which corresponds with the width of the bearing being measured and place it carefully across the journal so that it is parallel with the shaft **(see illustration 3.15)**. Carefully install both bearing shells and the connecting rod. Without rotating the rod on the journal tighten its bolts or nuts (as applicable) to the specified torque. The connecting rod and bearings are then disassembled and the crushed Plastigauge examined.

3.15 Plastigauge placed across shaft journal

● Using the scale provided in the Plastigauge kit, measure the width of the material to determine the oil clearance **(see illustration 3.16)**. Always remove all traces of Plastigauge after use using your fingernails.

> **Caution: Arriving at the correct clearance demands that the assembly is torqued correctly, according to the settings and sequence (where applicable) provided by the motorcycle manufacturer.**

3.16 Measuring the width of the crushed Plastigauge

Dial gauge or DTI (Dial Test Indicator)

● A dial gauge can be used to accurately measure small amounts of movement. Typical uses are measuring shaft runout or shaft endfloat (sideplay) and setting piston position for ignition timing on two-strokes. A dial gauge set usually comes with a range of different probes and adapters and mounting equipment.

● The gauge needle must point to zero when at rest. Rotate the ring around its periphery to zero the gauge.

● Check that the gauge is capable of reading the extent of movement in the work. Most gauges have a small dial set in the face which records whole millimetres of movement as well as the fine scale around the face periphery which is calibrated in 0.01 mm divisions. Read off the small dial first to obtain the base measurement, then add the measurement from the fine scale to obtain the total reading.

In the example shown the gauge reads 1.48 mm **(see illustration 3.17)**:

Base measurement	1.00 mm
Fine measurement	0.48 mm
Total figure	**1.48 mm**

3.17 Dial gauge reading of 1.48 mm

● If measuring shaft runout, the shaft must be supported in vee-blocks and the gauge mounted on a stand perpendicular to the shaft. Rest the tip of the gauge against the centre of the shaft and rotate the shaft slowly whilst watching the gauge reading **(see illustration 3.18)**. Take several measurements along the length of the shaft and record the

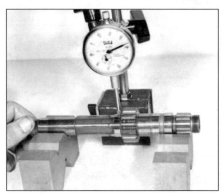

3.18 Using a dial gauge to measure shaft runout

maximum gauge reading as the amount of runout in the shaft. **Note:** *The reading obtained will be total runout at that point - some manufacturers specify that the runout figure is halved to compare with their specified runout limit.*

● Endfloat (sideplay) measurement requires that the gauge is mounted securely to the surrounding component with its probe touching the end of the shaft. Using hand pressure, push and pull on the shaft noting the maximum endfloat recorded on the gauge **(see illustration 3.19)**.

3.19 Using a dial gauge to measure shaft endfloat

● A dial gauge with suitable adapters can be used to determine piston position BTDC on two-stroke engines for the purposes of ignition timing. The gauge, adapter and suitable length probe are installed in the place of the spark plug and the gauge zeroed at TDC. If the piston position is specified as 1.14 mm BTDC, rotate the engine back to 2.00 mm BTDC, then slowly forwards to 1.14 mm BTDC.

Cylinder compression gauges

● A compression gauge is used for measuring cylinder compression. Either the rubber-cone type or the threaded adapter type can be used. The latter is preferred to ensure a perfect seal against the cylinder head. A 0 to 300 psi (0 to 20 Bar) type gauge (for petrol/gasoline engines) will be suitable for motorcycles.

● The spark plug is removed and the gauge either held hard against the cylinder head (cone type) or the gauge adapter screwed into the cylinder head (threaded type) **(see illustration 3.20)**. Cylinder compression is measured with the engine turning over, but not running - carry out the compression test as described in

3.20 Using a rubber-cone type cylinder compression gauge

Fault Finding Equipment. The gauge will hold the reading until manually released.

Oil pressure gauge

● An oil pressure gauge is used for measuring engine oil pressure. Most gauges come with a set of adapters to fit the thread of the take-off point **(see illustration 3.21)**. If the take-off point specified by the motorcycle manufacturer is an external oil pipe union, make sure that the specified replacement union is used to prevent oil starvation.

3.21 Oil pressure gauge and take-off point adapter (arrow)

● Oil pressure is measured with the engine running (at a specific rpm) and often the manufacturer will specify pressure limits for a cold and hot engine.

Straight-edge and surface plate

● If checking the gasket face of a component for warpage, place a steel rule or precision straight-edge across the gasket face and measure any gap between the straight-edge and component with feeler gauges **(see illustration 3.22)**. Check diagonally across the component and between mounting holes **(see illustration 3.23)**.

3.22 Use a straight-edge and feeler gauges to check for warpage

3.23 Check for warpage in these directions

- Checking individual components for warpage, such as clutch plain (metal) plates, requires a perfectly flat plate or piece or plate glass and feeler gauges.

4 Torque and leverage

What is torque?

- Torque describes the twisting force about a shaft. The amount of torque applied is determined by the distance from the centre of the shaft to the end of the lever and the amount of force being applied to the end of the lever; distance multiplied by force equals torque.
- The manufacturer applies a measured torque to a bolt or nut to ensure that it will not slacken in use and to hold two components securely together without movement in the joint. The actual torque setting depends on the thread size, bolt or nut material and the composition of the components being held.
- Too little torque may cause the fastener to loosen due to vibration, whereas too much torque will distort the joint faces of the component or cause the fastener to shear off. Always stick to the specified torque setting.

Using a torque wrench

- Check the calibration of the torque wrench and make sure it has a suitable range for the job. Torque wrenches are available in Nm (Newton-metres), kgf m (kilograms-force metre), lbf ft (pounds-feet), lbf in (inch-pounds). Do not confuse lbf ft with lbf in.
- Adjust the tool to the desired torque on the scale (see illustration 4.1). If your torque wrench is not calibrated in the units specified, carefully convert the figure (see *Conversion Factors*). A manufacturer sometimes gives a torque setting as a range (8 to 10 Nm) rather than a single figure - in this case set the tool midway between the two settings. The same torque may be expressed as 9 Nm ± 1 Nm. Some torque wrenches have a method of locking the setting so that it isn't inadvertently altered during use.

4.1 Set the torque wrench index mark to the setting required, in this case 12 Nm

- Install the bolts/nuts in their correct location and secure them lightly. Their threads must be clean and free of any old locking compound. Unless specified the threads and flange should be dry - oiled threads are necessary in certain circumstances and the manufacturer will take this into account in the specified torque figure. Similarly, the manufacturer may also specify the application of thread-locking compound.
- Tighten the fasteners in the specified sequence until the torque wrench clicks, indicating that the torque setting has been reached. Apply the torque again to double-check the setting. Where different thread diameter fasteners secure the component, as a rule tighten the larger diameter ones first.
- When the torque wrench has been finished with, release the lock (where applicable) and fully back off its setting to zero - do not leave the torque wrench tensioned. Also, do not use a torque wrench for slackening a fastener.

Angle-tightening

- Manufacturers often specify a figure in degrees for final tightening of a fastener. This usually follows tightening to a specific torque setting.
- A degree disc can be set and attached to the socket (see illustration 4.2) or a protractor can be used to mark the angle of movement on the bolt/nut head and the surrounding casting (see illustration 4.3).

4.2 Angle tightening can be accomplished with a torque-angle gauge . . .

4.3 . . . or by marking the angle on the surrounding component

Loosening sequences

- Where more than one bolt/nut secures a component, loosen each fastener evenly a little at a time. In this way, not all the stress of the joint is held by one fastener and the components are not likely to distort.
- If a tightening sequence is provided, work in the REVERSE of this, but if not, work from the outside in, in a criss-cross sequence (see illustration 4.4).

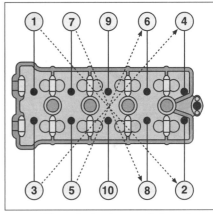

4.4 When slackening, work from the outside inwards

Tightening sequences

- If a component is held by more than one fastener it is important that the retaining bolts/nuts are tightened evenly to prevent uneven stress build-up and distortion of sealing faces. This is especially important on high-compression joints such as the cylinder head.
- A sequence is usually provided by the manufacturer, either in a diagram or actually marked in the casting. If not, always start in the centre and work outwards in a criss-cross pattern (see illustration 4.5). Start off by securing all bolts/nuts finger-tight, then set the torque wrench and tighten each fastener by a small amount in sequence until the final torque is reached. By following this practice,

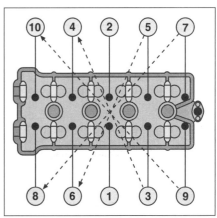

4.5 When tightening, work from the inside outwards

the joint will be held evenly and will not be distorted. Important joints, such as the cylinder head and big-end fasteners often have two- or three-stage torque settings.

Applying leverage

● Use tools at the correct angle. Position a socket wrench or spanner on the bolt/nut so that you pull it towards you when loosening. If this can't be done, push the spanner without curling your fingers around it **(see illustration 4.6)** - the spanner may slip or the fastener loosen suddenly, resulting in your fingers being crushed against a component.

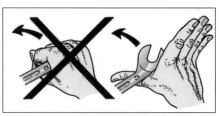

4.6 If you can't pull on the spanner to loosen a fastener, push with your hand open

● Additional leverage is gained by extending the length of the lever. The best way to do this is to use a breaker bar instead of the regular length tool, or to slip a length of tubing over the end of the spanner or socket wrench.
● If additional leverage will not work, the fastener head is either damaged or firmly corroded in place (see *Fasteners*).

5 Bearings

Bearing removal and installation

Drivers and sockets

● Before removing a bearing, always inspect the casing to see which way it must be driven out - some casings will have retaining plates or a cast step. Also check for any identifying markings on the bearing and if installed to a certain depth, measure this at this stage. Some roller bearings are sealed on one side - take note of the original fitted position.
● Bearings can be driven out of a casing using a bearing driver tool (with the correct size head) or a socket of the correct diameter. Select the driver head or socket so that it contacts the outer race of the bearing, not the balls/rollers or inner race. Always support the casing around the bearing housing with wood blocks, otherwise there is a risk of fracture. The bearing is driven out with a few blows on the driver or socket from a heavy mallet. Unless access is severely restricted (as with wheel bearings), a pin-punch is not recommended unless it is moved around the bearing to keep it square in its housing.

● The same equipment can be used to install bearings. Make sure the bearing housing is supported on wood blocks and line up the bearing in its housing. Fit the bearing as noted on removal - generally they are installed with their marked side facing outwards. Tap the bearing squarely into its housing using a driver or socket which bears only on the bearing's outer race - contact with the bearing balls/rollers or inner race will destroy it **(see illustrations 5.1 and 5.2)**.
● Check that the bearing inner race and balls/rollers rotate freely.

5.1 Using a bearing driver against the bearing's outer race

5.2 Using a large socket against the bearing's outer race

Pullers and slide-hammers

● Where a bearing is pressed on a shaft a puller will be required to extract it **(see illustration 5.3)**. Make sure that the puller clamp or legs fit securely behind the bearing and are unlikely to slip out. If pulling a bearing

5.3 This bearing puller clamps behind the bearing and pressure is applied to the shaft end to draw the bearing off

off a gear shaft for example, you may have to locate the puller behind a gear pinion if there is no access to the race and draw the gear pinion off the shaft as well **(see illustration 5.4)**.

> *Caution: Ensure that the puller's centre bolt locates securely against the end of the shaft and will not slip when pressure is applied. Also ensure that puller does not damage the shaft end.*

5.4 Where no access is available to the rear of the bearing, it is sometimes possible to draw off the adjacent component

● Operate the puller so that its centre bolt exerts pressure on the shaft end and draws the bearing off the shaft.
● When installing the bearing on the shaft, tap only on the bearing's inner race - contact with the balls/rollers or outer race with destroy the bearing. Use a socket or length of tubing as a drift which fits over the shaft end **(see illustration 5.5)**.

5.5 When installing a bearing on a shaft use a piece of tubing which bears only on the bearing's inner race

● Where a bearing locates in a blind hole in a casing, it cannot be driven or pulled out as described above. A slide-hammer with knife-edged bearing puller attachment will be required. The puller attachment passes through the bearing and when tightened expands to fit firmly behind the bearing **(see illustration 5.6)**. By operating the slide-hammer part of the tool the bearing is jarred out of its housing **(see illustration 5.7)**.
● It is possible, if the bearing is of reasonable weight, for it to drop out of its housing if the casing is heated as described opposite. If this

5.6 Expand the bearing puller so that it locks behind the bearing . . .

5.7 . . . attach the slide hammer to the bearing puller

method is attempted, first prepare a work surface which will enable the casing to be tapped face down to help dislodge the bearing - a wood surface is ideal since it will not damage the casing's gasket surface. Wearing protective gloves, tap the heated casing several times against the work surface to dislodge the bearing under its own weight **(see illustration 5.8)**.

5.8 Tapping a casing face down on wood blocks can often dislodge a bearing

● Bearings can be installed in blind holes using the driver or socket method described above.

Drawbolts

● Where a bearing or bush is set in the eye of a component, such as a suspension linkage arm or connecting rod small-end, removal by drift may damage the component. Furthermore, a rubber bushing in a shock absorber eye cannot successfully be driven out of position. If access is available to a engineering press, the task is straightforward. If not, a drawbolt can be fabricated to extract the bearing or bush.

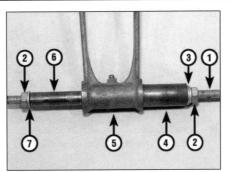

5.9 Drawbolt component parts assembled on a suspension arm

1 Bolt or length of threaded bar
2 Nuts
3 Washer (external diameter greater than tubing internal diameter)
4 Tubing (internal diameter sufficient to accommodate bearing)
5 Suspension arm with bearing
6 Tubing (external diameter slightly smaller than bearing)
7 Washer (external diameter slightly smaller than bearing)

5.10 Drawing the bearing out of the suspension arm

● To extract the bearing/bush you will need a long bolt with nut (or piece of threaded bar with two nuts), a piece of tubing which has an internal diameter larger than the bearing/bush, another piece of tubing which has an external diameter slightly smaller than the bearing/bush, and a selection of washers **(see illustrations 5.9 and 5.10)**. Note that the pieces of tubing must be of the same length, or longer, than the bearing/bush.
● The same kit (without the pieces of tubing) can be used to draw the new bearing/bush back into place **(see illustration 5.11)**.

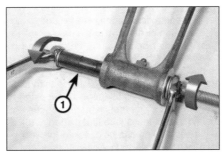

5.11 Installing a new bearing (1) in the suspension arm

Temperature change

● If the bearing's outer race is a tight fit in the casing, the aluminium casing can be heated to release its grip on the bearing. Aluminium will expand at a greater rate than the steel bearing outer race. There are several ways to do this, but avoid any localised extreme heat (such as a blow torch) - aluminium alloy has a low melting point.
● Approved methods of heating a casing are using a domestic oven (heated to 100°C) or immersing the casing in boiling water **(see illustration 5.12)**. Low temperature range localised heat sources such as a paint stripper heat gun or clothes iron can also be used **(see illustration 5.13)**. Alternatively, soak a rag in boiling water, wring it out and wrap it around the bearing housing.

> ⚠ **Warning: All of these methods require care in use to prevent scalding and burns to the hands. Wear protective gloves when handling hot components.**

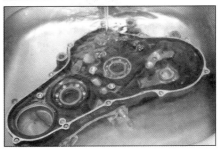

5.12 A casing can be immersed in a sink of boiling water to aid bearing removal

5.13 Using a localised heat source to aid bearing removal

● If heating the whole casing note that plastic components, such as the neutral switch, may suffer - remove them beforehand.
● After heating, remove the bearing as described above. You may find that the expansion is sufficient for the bearing to fall out of the casing under its own weight or with a light tap on the driver or socket.
● If necessary, the casing can be heated to aid bearing installation, and this is sometimes the recommended procedure if the motorcycle manufacturer has designed the housing and bearing fit with this intention.

● Installation of bearings can be eased by placing them in a freezer the night before installation. The steel bearing will contract slightly, allowing easy insertion in its housing. This is often useful when installing steering head outer races in the frame.

Bearing types and markings

● Plain shell bearings, ball bearings, needle roller bearings and tapered roller bearings will all be found on motorcycles (see illustrations 5.14 and 5.15). The ball and roller types are usually caged between an inner and outer race, but uncaged variations may be found.

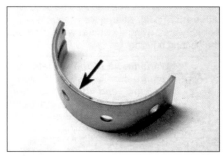

5.14 Shell bearings are either plain or grooved. They are usually identified by colour code (arrow)

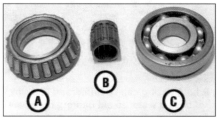

5.15 Tapered roller bearing (A), needle roller bearing (B) and ball journal bearing (C)

● Shell bearings (often called inserts) are usually found at the crankshaft main and connecting rod big-end where they are good at coping with high loads. They are made of a phosphor-bronze material and are impregnated with self-lubricating properties.

● Ball bearings and needle roller bearings consist of a steel inner and outer race with the balls or rollers between the races. They require constant lubrication by oil or grease and are good at coping with axial loads. Taper roller bearings consist of rollers set in a tapered cage set on the inner race; the outer race is separate. They are good at coping with axial loads and prevent movement along the shaft - a typical application is in the steering head.

● Bearing manufacturers produce bearings to ISO size standards and stamp one face of the bearing to indicate its internal and external diameter, load capacity and type (see illustration 5.16).

● Metal bushes are usually of phosphor-bronze material. Rubber bushes are used in suspension mounting eyes. Fibre bushes have also been used in suspension pivots.

5.16 Typical bearing marking

Bearing fault finding

● If a bearing outer race has spun in its housing, the housing material will be damaged. You can use a bearing locking compound to bond the outer race in place if damage is not too severe.

● Shell bearings will fail due to damage of their working surface, as a result of lack of lubrication, corrosion or abrasive particles in the oil (see illustration 5.17). Small particles of dirt in the oil may embed in the bearing material whereas larger particles will score the bearing and shaft journal. If a number of short journeys are made, insufficient heat will be generated to drive off condensation which has built up on the bearings.

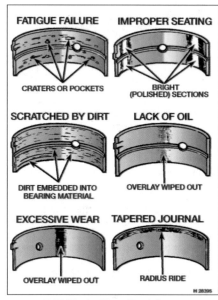

5.17 Typical bearing failures

● Ball and roller bearings will fail due to lack of lubrication or damage to the balls or rollers. Tapered-roller bearings can be damaged by overloading them. Unless the bearing is sealed on both sides, wash it in paraffin (kerosene) to remove all old grease then allow it to dry. Make a visual inspection looking to dented balls or rollers, damaged cages and worn or pitted races (see illustration 5.18).

● A ball bearing can be checked for wear by listening to it when spun. Apply a film of light oil to the bearing and hold it close to the ear - hold the outer race with one hand and spin the inner

5.18 Example of ball journal bearing with damaged balls and cages

5.19 Hold outer race and listen to inner race when spun

race with the other hand (see illustration 5.19). The bearing should be almost silent when spun; if it grates or rattles it is worn.

6 Oil seals

Oil seal removal and installation

● Oil seals should be renewed every time a component is dismantled. This is because the seal lips will become set to the sealing surface and will not necessarily reseal.

● Oil seals can be prised out of position using a large flat-bladed screwdriver (see illustration 6.1). In the case of crankcase seals, check first that the seal is not lipped on the inside, preventing its removal with the crankcases joined.

6.1 Prise out oil seals with a large flat-bladed screwdriver

● New seals are usually installed with their marked face (containing the seal reference code) outwards and the spring side towards the fluid being retained. In certain cases, such as a two-stroke engine crankshaft seal, a double lipped seal may be used due to there being fluid or gas on each side of the joint.

● Use a bearing driver or socket which bears only on the outer hard edge of the seal to install it in the casing - tapping on the inner edge will damage the sealing lip.

Oil seal types and markings

● Oil seals are usually of the single-lipped type. Double-lipped seals are found where a liquid or gas is on both sides of the joint.
● Oil seals can harden and lose their sealing ability if the motorcycle has been in storage for a long period - renewal is the only solution.
● Oil seal manufacturers also conform to the ISO markings for seal size - these are moulded into the outer face of the seal (see illustration 6.2).

6.2 These oil seal markings indicate inside diameter, outside diameter and seal thickness

7 Gaskets and sealants

Types of gasket and sealant

● Gaskets are used to seal the mating surfaces between components and keep lubricants, fluids, vacuum or pressure contained within the assembly. Aluminium gaskets are sometimes found at the cylinder joints, but most gaskets are paper-based. If the mating surfaces of the components being joined are undamaged the gasket can be installed dry, although a dab of sealant or grease will be useful to hold it in place during assembly.
● RTV (Room Temperature Vulcanising) silicone rubber sealants cure when exposed to moisture in the atmosphere. These sealants are good at filling pits or irregular gasket faces, but will tend to be forced out of the joint under very high torque. They can be used to replace a paper gasket, but first make sure that the width of the paper gasket is not essential to the shimming of internal components. RTV sealants should not be used on components containing petrol (gasoline).
● Non-hardening, semi-hardening and hard setting liquid gasket compounds can be used with a gasket or between a metal-to-metal joint. Select the sealant to suit the application: universal non-hardening sealant can be used on virtually all joints; semi-hardening on joint faces which are rough or damaged; hard setting sealant on joints which require a permanent bond and are subjected to high temperature and pressure. **Note:** *Check first if the paper gasket has a bead of sealant*

impregnated in its surface before applying additional sealant.
● When choosing a sealant, make sure it is suitable for the application, particularly if being applied in a high-temperature area or in the vicinity of fuel. Certain manufacturers produce sealants in either clear, silver or black colours to match the finish of the engine. This has a particular application on motorcycles where much of the engine is exposed.
● Do not over-apply sealant. That which is squeezed out on the outside of the joint can be wiped off, whereas an excess of sealant on the inside can break off and clog oilways.

Breaking a sealed joint

● Age, heat, pressure and the use of hard setting sealant can cause two components to stick together so tightly that they are difficult to separate using finger pressure alone. Do not resort to using levers unless there is a pry point provided for this purpose (see illustration 7.1) or else the gasket surfaces will be damaged.
● Use a soft-faced hammer (see illustration 7.2) or a wood block and conventional hammer to strike the component near the mating surface. Avoid hammering against cast extremities since they may break off. If this method fails, try using a wood wedge between the two components.

Caution: If the joint will not separate, double-check that you have removed all the fasteners.

7.1 If a pry point is provided, apply gently pressure with a flat-bladed screwdriver

7.2 Tap around the joint with a soft-faced mallet if necessary - don't strike cooling fins

Removal of old gasket and sealant

● Paper gaskets will most likely come away complete, leaving only a few traces stuck on

Most components have one or two hollow locating dowels between the two gasket faces. If a dowel cannot be removed, do not resort to gripping it with pliers - it will almost certainly be distorted. Install a close-fitting socket or Phillips screwdriver into the dowel and then grip the outer edge of the dowel to free it.

the sealing faces of the components. It is imperative that all traces are removed to ensure correct sealing of the new gasket.
● Very carefully scrape all traces of gasket away making sure that the sealing surfaces are not gouged or scored by the scraper (see illustrations 7.3, 7.4 and 7.5). Stubborn deposits can be removed by spraying with an aerosol gasket remover. Final preparation of

7.3 Paper gaskets can be scraped off with a gasket scraper tool . . .

7.4 . . . a knife blade . . .

7.5 . . . or a household scraper

7.6 Fine abrasive paper is wrapped around a flat file to clean up the gasket face

7.7 A kitchen scourer can be used on stubborn deposits

the gasket surface can be made with very fine abrasive paper or a plastic kitchen scourer **(see illustrations 7.6 and 7.7)**.

● Old sealant can be scraped or peeled off components, depending on the type originally used. Note that gasket removal compounds are available to avoid scraping the components clean; make sure the gasket remover suits the type of sealant used.

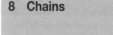

8 Chains

Breaking and joining final drive chains

● Drive chains for all but small bikes are continuous and do not have a clip-type connecting link. The chain must be broken using a chain breaker tool and the new chain securely riveted together using a new soft rivet-type link. Never use a clip-type connecting link instead of a rivet-type link, except in an emergency. Various chain breaking and riveting tools are available, either as separate tools or combined as illustrated in the accompanying photographs - read the instructions supplied with the tool carefully.

> ⚠ **Warning: The need to rivet the new link pins correctly cannot be overstressed - loss of control of the motorcycle is very likely to result if the chain breaks in use.**

● Rotate the chain and look for the soft link. The soft link pins look like they have been

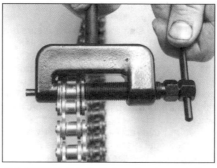

8.1 Tighten the chain breaker to push the pin out of the link . . .

8.2 . . . withdraw the pin, remove the tool . . .

8.3 . . . and separate the chain link

deeply centre-punched instead of peened over like all the other pins **(see illustration 8.9)** and its sideplate may be a different colour. Position the soft link midway between the sprockets and assemble the chain breaker tool over one of the soft link pins **(see illustration 8.1)**. Operate the tool to push the pin out through the chain **(see illustration 8.2)**. On an O-ring chain, remove the O-rings **(see illustration 8.3)**. Carry out the same procedure on the other soft link pin.

> **Caution: Certain soft link pins (particularly on the larger chains) may require their ends to be filed or ground off before they can be pressed out using the tool.**

● Check that you have the correct size and strength (standard or heavy duty) new soft link - do not reuse the old link. Look for the size marking on the chain sideplates **(see illustration 8.10)**.

● Position the chain ends so that they are engaged over the rear sprocket. On an O-ring

8.4 Insert the new soft link, with O-rings, through the chain ends . . .

8.5 . . . install the O-rings over the pin ends . . .

8.6 . . . followed by the sideplate

chain, install a new O-ring over each pin of the link and insert the link through the two chain ends **(see illustration 8.4)**. Install a new O-ring over the end of each pin, followed by the sideplate (with the chain manufacturer's marking facing outwards) **(see illustrations 8.5 and 8.6)**. On an unsealed chain, insert the link through the two chain ends, then install the sideplate with the chain manufacturer's marking facing outwards.

● Note that it may not be possible to install the sideplate using finger pressure alone. If using a joining tool, assemble it so that the plates of the tool clamp the link and press the sideplate over the pins **(see illustration 8.7)**. Otherwise, use two small sockets placed over

8.7 Push the sideplate into position using a clamp

8.8 Assemble the chain riveting tool over one pin at a time and tighten it fully

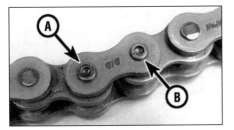

8.9 Pin end correctly riveted (A), pin end unriveted (B)

the rivet ends and two pieces of the wood between a G-clamp. Operate the clamp to press the sideplate over the pins.

● Assemble the joining tool over one pin (following the maker's instructions) and tighten the tool down to spread the pin end securely **(see illustrations 8.8 and 8.9)**. Do the same on the other pin.

> **Warning: Check that the pin ends are secure and that there is no danger of the sideplate coming loose. If the pin ends are cracked the soft link must be renewed.**

Final drive chain sizing

● Chains are sized using a three digit number, followed by a suffix to denote the chain type **(see illustration 8.10)**. Chain type is either standard or heavy duty (thicker sideplates), and also unsealed or O-ring/X-ring type.

● The first digit of the number relates to the pitch of the chain, ie the distance from the centre of one pin to the centre of the next pin **(see illustration 8.11)**. Pitch is expressed in eighths of an inch, as follows:

8.10 Typical chain size and type marking

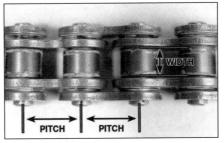

8.11 Chain dimensions

Sizes commencing with a 4 (eg 428) have a pitch of 1/2 inch (12.7 mm)
Sizes commencing with a 5 (eg 520) have a pitch of 5/8 inch (15.9 mm)
Sizes commencing with a 6 (eg 630) have a pitch of 3/4 inch (19.1 mm)

● The second and third digits of the chain size relate to the width of the rollers, again in imperial units, eg the 525 shown has 5/16 inch (7.94 mm) rollers **(see illustration 8.11)**.

9 Hoses

Clamping to prevent flow

● Small-bore flexible hoses can be clamped to prevent fluid flow whilst a component is worked on. Whichever method is used, ensure that the hose material is not permanently distorted or damaged by the clamp.

a) A brake hose clamp available from auto accessory shops **(see illustration 9.1)**.
b) A wingnut type hose clamp **(see illustration 9.2)**.

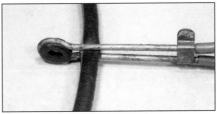

9.1 Hoses can be clamped with an automotive brake hose clamp . . .

9.2 . . . a wingnut type hose clamp . . .

c) Two sockets placed each side of the hose and held with straight-jawed self-locking grips **(see illustration 9.3)**.
d) Thick card each side of the hose held between straight-jawed self-locking grips **(see illustration 9.4)**.

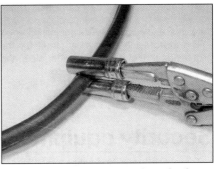

9.3 . . . two sockets and a pair of self-locking grips . . .

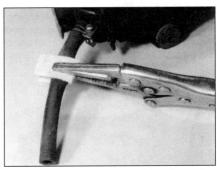

9.4 . . . or thick card and self-locking grips

Freeing and fitting hoses

● Always make sure the hose clamp is moved well clear of the hose end. Grip the hose with your hand and rotate it whilst pulling it off the union. If the hose has hardened due to age and will not move, slit it with a sharp knife and peel its ends off the union **(see illustration 9.5)**.

● Resist the temptation to use grease or soap on the unions to aid installation; although it helps the hose slip over the union it will equally aid the escape of fluid from the joint. It is preferable to soften the hose ends in hot water and wet the inside surface of the hose with water or a fluid which will evaporate.

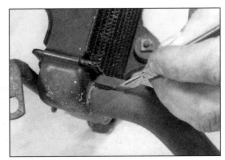

9.5 Cutting a coolant hose free with a sharp knife

Introduction

In less time than it takes to read this introduction, a thief could steal your motorcycle. Returning only to find your bike has gone is one of the worst feelings in the world. Even if the motorcycle is insured against theft, once you've got over the initial shock, you will have the inconvenience of dealing with the police and your insurance company.

The motorcycle is an easy target for the professional thief and the joyrider alike and the official figures on motorcycle theft make for depressing reading; on average a motorcycle is stolen every 16 minutes in the UK!

Motorcycle thefts fall into two categories, those stolen 'to order' and those taken by opportunists. The thief stealing to order will be on the look out for a specific make and model and will go to extraordinary lengths to obtain that motorcycle. The opportunist thief on the other hand will look for easy targets which can be stolen with the minimum of effort and risk.

Whilst it is never going to be possible to make your machine 100% secure, it is estimated that around half of all stolen motorcycles are taken by opportunist thieves. Remember that the opportunist thief is always on the look out for the easy option: if there are two similar motorcycles parked side-by-side, they will target the one with the lowest level of security. By taking a few precautions, you can reduce the chances of your motorcycle being stolen.

Security equipment

There are many specialised motorcycle security devices available and the following text summarises their applications and their good and bad points.

Once you have decided on the type of security equipment which best suits your needs, we recommended that you read one of the many equipment tests regularly carried out by the motorcycle press. These tests compare the products from all the major manufacturers and give impartial ratings on their effectiveness, value-for-money and ease of use.

No one item of security equipment can provide complete protection. It is highly recommended that two or more of the items described below are combined to increase the security of your motorcycle (a lock and chain plus an alarm system is just about ideal). The more security measures fitted to the bike, the less likely it is to be stolen.

Ensure the lock and chain you buy is of good quality and long enough to shackle your bike to a solid object

Lock and chain

Pros: *Very flexible to use; can be used to secure the motorcycle to almost any immovable object. On some locks and chains, the lock can be used on its own as a disc lock (see below).*

Cons: *Can be very heavy and awkward to carry on the motorcycle, although some types* will be supplied with a carry bag which can be strapped to the pillion seat.

● Heavy-duty chains and locks are an excellent security measure **(see illustration 1)**. Whenever the motorcycle is parked, use the lock and chain to secure the machine to a solid, immovable object such as a post or railings. This will prevent the machine from being ridden away or being lifted into the back of a van.

● When fitting the chain, always ensure the chain is routed around the motorcycle frame or swingarm **(see illustrations 2 and 3)**. Never merely pass the chain around one of the wheel rims; a thief may unbolt the wheel and lift the rest of the machine into a van, leaving you with just the wheel! Try to avoid having excess chain free, thus making it difficult to use cutting tools, and keep the chain and lock off the ground to prevent thieves attacking it with a cold chisel. Position the lock so that its lock barrel is facing downwards; this will make it harder for the thief to attack the lock mechanism.

Pass the chain through the bike's frame, rather than just through a wheel . . .

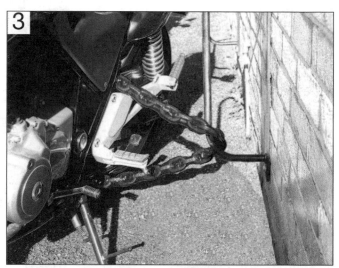

. . . and loop it around a solid object

U-locks

Pros: *Highly effective deterrent which can be used to secure the bike to a post or railings. Most U-locks come with a carrier which allows the lock to be easily carried on the bike.*

Cons: *Not as flexible to use as a lock and chain.*

● These are solid locks which are similar in use to a lock and chain. U-locks are lighter than a lock and chain but not so flexible to use. The length and shape of the lock shackle limit the objects to which the bike can be secured **(see illustration 4)**.

Disc locks

Pros: *Small, light and very easy to carry; most can be stored underneath the seat.*

Cons: *Does not prevent the motorcycle being lifted into a van. Can be very embarrassing if you*

U-locks can be used to secure the bike to a solid object – ensure you purchase one which is long enough

A typical disc lock attached through one of the holes in the disc

forget to remove the lock before attempting to ride off!

● Disc locks are designed to be attached to the front brake disc. The lock passes through one of the holes in the disc and prevents the wheel rotating by jamming against the fork/brake caliper **(see illustration 5)**. Some are equipped with an alarm siren which sounds if the disc lock is moved; this not only acts as a theft deterrent but also as a handy reminder if you try to move the bike with the lock still fitted.

● Combining the disc lock with a length of cable which can be looped around a post or railings provides an additional measure of security **(see illustration 6)**.

Alarms and immobilisers

Pros: *Once installed it is completely hassle-free to use. If the system is 'Thatcham' or 'Sold Secure-approved', insurance companies may give you a discount.*

Cons: *Can be expensive to buy and complex to install. No system will prevent the motorcycle from being lifted into a van and taken away.*

● Electronic alarms and immobilisers are available to suit a variety of budgets. There are three different types of system available: pure alarms, pure immobilisers, and the more expensive systems which are combined alarm/immobilisers **(see illustration 7)**.

● An alarm system is designed to emit an audible warning if the motorcycle is being tampered with.

● An immobiliser prevents the motorcycle being started and ridden away by disabling its electrical systems.

● When purchasing an alarm/immobiliser system, check the cost of installing the system unless you are able to do it yourself. If the motorcycle is not used regularly, another consideration is the current drain of the system. All alarm/immobiliser systems are powered by the motorcycle's battery; purchasing a system with a very low current drain could prevent the battery losing its charge whilst the motorcycle is not being used.

A disc lock combined with a security cable provides additional protection

A typical alarm/immobiliser system

Indelible markings can be applied to most areas of the bike – always apply the manufacturer's sticker to warn off thieves

Chemically-etched code numbers can be applied to main body panels . . .

. . . again, always ensure that the kit manufacturer's sticker is applied in a prominent position

Security marking kits

Pros: *Very cheap and effective deterrent. Many insurance companies will give you a discount on your insurance premium if a recognised security marking kit is used on your motorcycle.*

Cons: *Does not prevent the motorcycle being stolen by joyriders.*

● There are many different types of security marking kits available. The idea is to mark as many parts of the motorcycle as possible with a unique security number (see illustrations 8, 9 and 10). A form will be included with the kit to register your personal details and those of the motorcycle with the kit manufacturer. This register is made available to the police to help them trace the rightful owner of any motorcycle or components which they recover should all other forms of identification have been removed. Always apply the warning stickers provided with the kit to deter thieves.

Ground anchors, wheel clamps and security posts

Pros: *An excellent form of security which will deter all but the most determined of thieves.*

Cons: *Awkward to install and can be expensive.*

● Whilst the motorcycle is at home, it is a good idea to attach it securely to the floor or a solid wall, even if it is kept in a securely locked garage. Various types of ground anchors, security posts and wheel clamps are available for this purpose (see illustration 11). These security devices are either bolted to a solid concrete or brick structure or can be cemented into the ground.

Permanent ground anchors provide an excellent level of security when the bike is at home

Security at home

A high percentage of motorcycle thefts are from the owner's home. Here are some things to consider whenever your motorcycle is at home:

✔ Where possible, always keep the motorcycle in a securely locked garage. Never rely solely on the standard lock on the garage door, these are usual hopelessly inadequate. Fit an additional locking mechanism to the door and consider having the garage alarmed. A security light, activated by a movement sensor, is also a good investment.

✔ Always secure the motorcycle to the ground or a wall, even if it is inside a securely locked garage.

✔ Do not regularly leave the motorcycle outside your home, try to keep it out of sight wherever possible. If a garage is not available, fit a motorcycle cover over the bike to disguise its true identity.

✔ It is not uncommon for thieves to follow a motorcyclist home to find out where the bike is kept. They will then return at a later date. Be aware of this whenever you are returning

home on your motorcycle. If you suspect you are being followed, do not return home, instead ride to a garage or shop and stop as a precaution.

✔ When selling a motorcycle, do not provide your home address or the location where the bike is normally kept. Arrange to meet the buyer at a location away from your home. Thieves have been known to pose as potential buyers to find out where motorcycles are kept and then return later to steal them.

Security away from the home

As well as fitting security equipment to your motorcycle here are a few general rules to follow whenever you park your motorcycle.
✔ Park in a busy, public place.
✔ Use car parks which incorporate security features, such as CCTV.

✔ At night, park in a well-lit area, preferably directly underneath a street light.
✔ Engage the steering lock.
✔ Secure the motorcycle to a solid, immovable object such as a post or railings with an additional lock. If this is not possible,

secure the bike to a friend's motorcycle. Some public parking places provide security loops for motorcycles.
✔ Never leave your helmet or luggage attached to the motorcycle. Take them with you at all times.

Lubricants and fluids

A wide range of lubricants, fluids and cleaning agents is available for motor-cycles. This is a guide as to what is available, its applications and properties.

Four-stroke engine oil

● Engine oil is without doubt the most important component of any four-stroke engine. Modern motorcycle engines place a lot of demands on their oil and choosing the right type is essential. Using an unsuitable oil will lead to an increased rate of engine wear and could result in serious engine damage. Before purchasing oil, always check the recommended oil specification given by the manufacturer. The manufacturer will state a recommended 'type or classification' and also a specific 'viscosity' range for engine oil.

● The oil 'type or classification' is identified by its API (American Petroleum Institute) rating. The API rating will be in the form of two letters, e.g. SG. The S identifies the oil as being suitable for use in a petrol (gasoline) engine (S stands for spark ignition) and the second letter, ranging from A to J, identifies the oil's performance rating. The later this letter, the higher the specification of the oil; for example API SG oil exceeds the requirements of API SF oil. **Note:** *On some oils there may also be a second rating consisting of another two letters, the first letter being C, e.g. API SF/CD. This rating indicates the oil is also suitable for use in a diesel engines (the C stands for compression ignition) and is thus of no relevance for motorcycle use.*

● The 'viscosity' of the oil is identified by its SAE (Society of Automotive Engineers) rating. All modern engines require multigrade oils and the SAE rating will consist of two numbers, the first followed by a W, e.g. 10W/40. The first number indicates the viscosity rating of the oil at low temperatures (W stands for winter – tested at –20°C) and the second number represents the viscosity of the oil at high temperatures (tested at 100°C). The lower the number, the thinner the oil. For example an oil with an SAE 10W/40 rating will give better cold starting and running than an SAE 15W/40 oil.

● As well as ensuring the 'type' and 'viscosity' of the oil match the recommendations, another consideration to make when buying engine oil is whether to purchase a standard mineral-based oil, a semi-synthetic oil (also known as a synthetic blend or synthetic-based oil) or a fully-synthetic oil. Although all oils will have a similar rating and viscosity, their cost will vary considerably; mineral-based oils are the cheapest, the fully-synthetic oils the most expensive with the semi-synthetic oils falling somewhere in-between. This decision is very much up to the owner, but it should be noted that modern synthetic oils have far better lubricating and cleaning qualities than traditional mineral-based oils and tend to retain these properties for far longer. Bearing in mind the operating conditions inside a modern, high-revving motorcycle engine it is highly recommended that a fully synthetic oil is used. The extra expense at each service could save you money in the long term by preventing premature engine wear.

● As a final note always ensure that the oil is specifically designed for use in motorcycle engines. Engine oils designed primarily for use in car engines sometimes contain additives or friction modifiers which could cause clutch slip on a motorcycle fitted with a wet-clutch.

Two-stroke engine oil

● Modern two-stroke engines, with their high power outputs, place high demands on their oil. If engine seizure is to be avoided it is essential that a high-quality oil is used. Two-stroke oils differ hugely from four-stroke oils. The oil lubricates only the crankshaft and piston(s) (the transmission has its own lubricating oil) and is used on a total-loss basis where it is burnt completely during the combustion process.

● The Japanese have recently introduced a classification system for two-stroke oils, the JASO rating. This rating is in the form of two letters, either FA, FB or FC – FA is the lowest classification and FC the highest. Ensure the oil being used meets or exceeds the recommended rating specified by the manufacturer.

● As well as ensuring the oil rating matches the recommendation, another consideration to make when buying engine oil is whether to purchase a standard mineral-based oil, a semi-synthetic oil (also known as a synthetic blend or synthetic-based oil) or a fully-synthetic oil. The cost of each type of oil varies considerably; mineral-based oils are the cheapest, the fully-synthetic oils the most expensive with the semi-synthetic oils falling somewhere in-between. This decision is very much up to the owner, but it should be noted that modern synthetic oils have far better lubricating properties and burn cleaner than traditional mineral-based oils. It is therefore recommended that a fully synthetic oil is used. The extra expense could save you money in the long term by preventing premature engine wear, engine performance will be improved, carbon deposits and exhaust smoke will be reduced.

● Always ensure that the oil is specifically designed for use in an injector system. Many high quality two-stroke oils are designed for competition use and need to be pre-mixed with fuel. These oils are of a much higher viscosity and are not designed to flow through the injector pumps used on road-going two-stroke motorcycles.

Transmission (gear) oil

● On a two-stroke engine, the transmission and clutch are lubricated by their own separate oil bath which must be changed in accordance with the Maintenance Schedule.
● Although the engine and transmission units of most four-strokes use a common lubrication supply, there are some exceptions where the engine and gearbox have separate oil reservoirs and a dry clutch is used.
● Motorcycle manufacturers will either recommend a monograde transmission oil or a four-stroke multigrade engine oil to lubricate the transmission.
● Transmission oils, or gear oils as they are often called, are designed specifically for use in transmission systems. The viscosity of these oils is represented by an SAE number, but the scale of measurement applied is different to that used to grade engine oils. As a rough guide a SAE90 gear oil will be of the same viscosity as an SAE50 engine oil.

Shaft drive oil

● On models equipped with shaft final drive, the shaft drive gears are will have their own oil supply. The manufacturer will state a recommended 'type or classification' and also a specific 'viscosity' range in the same manner as for four-stroke engine oil.
● Gear oil classification is given by the number which follows the API GL (GL standing for gear lubricant) rating, the higher the number, the higher the specification of the oil, e.g. API GL5 oil is a higher specification than API GL4 oil. Ensure the oil meets or

exceeds the classification specified and is of the correct viscosity. The viscosity of gear oils is also represented by an SAE number but the scale of measurement used is different to that used to grade engine oils. As a rough guide an SAE90 gear oil will be of the same viscosity as an SAE50 engine oil.
● If the use of an EP (Extreme Pressure) gear oil is specified, ensure the oil purchased is suitable.

Fork oil and suspension fluid

● Conventional telescopic front forks are hydraulic and require fork oil to work. To ensure the forks function correctly, the fork oil must be changed in accordance with the Maintenance Schedule.
● Fork oil is available in a variety of viscosities, identified by their SAE rating; fork oil ratings vary from light (SAE 5) to heavy (SAE 30). When purchasing fork oil, ensure the viscosity rating matches that specified by the manufacturer.
● Some lubricant manufacturers also produce a range of high-quality suspension fluids which are very similar to fork oil but are designed mainly for competition use. These fluids may have a different viscosity rating system which is not to be confused with the SAE rating of normal fork oil. Refer to the manufacturer's instructions if in any doubt.

Brake and clutch fluid

● All disc brake systems and some clutch systems are hydraulically operated. To ensure correct operation, the hydraulic fluid must be changed in accordance with the Maintenance Schedule.
● Brake and clutch fluid is classified by its DOT rating with most motorcycle manufacturers specifying DOT 3 or 4 fluid. Both fluid types are glycol-based and can be mixed together without adverse effect; DOT 4 fluid exceeds the requirements of DOT 3

fluid. Although it is safe to use DOT 4 fluid in a system designed for use with DOT 3 fluid, never use DOT 3 fluid in a system which specifies the use of DOT 4 as this will adversely affect the system's performance. The type required for the system will be marked on the fluid reservoir cap.
● Some manufacturers also produce a DOT 5 hydraulic fluid. DOT 5 hydraulic fluid is silicone-based and is not compatible with the glycol-based DOT 3 and 4 fluids. Never mix DOT 5 fluid with DOT 3 or 4 fluid as this will seriously affect the performance of the hydraulic system.

Coolant/antifreeze

● When purchasing coolant/antifreeze, always ensure it is suitable for use in an aluminium engine and contains corrosion inhibitors to prevent possible blockages of the internal coolant passages of the system. As a general rule, most coolants are designed to be used neat and should not be diluted whereas antifreeze can be mixed with distilled water to provide a coolant solution of the required strength. Refer to the manufacturer's instructions on the bottle.
● Ensure the coolant is changed in accordance with the Maintenance Schedule.

Chain lube

● Chain lube is an aerosol-type spray lubricant specifically designed for use on motorcycle final drive chains. Chain lube has two functions, to minimise friction between the final drive chain and sprockets and to prevent corrosion of the chain. Regular use of a good-quality chain lube will extend the life of the drive chain and sprockets and thus maximise the power being transmitted from the transmission to the rear wheel.
● When using chain lube, always allow some time for the solvents in the lube to evaporate before riding the motorcycle. This will minimise the amount of lube which will

'fling' off from the chain when the motorcycle is used. If the motorcycle is equipped with an 'O-ring' chain, ensure the chain lube is labelled as being suitable for use on 'O-ring' chains.

Degreasers and solvents

● There are many different types of solvents and degreasers available to remove the grime and grease which accumulate around the motorcycle during normal use. Degreasers and solvents are usually available as an aerosol-type spray or as a liquid which you apply with a brush. Always closely follow the manufacturer's instructions and wear eye protection during use. Be aware that many solvents are flammable and may give off noxious fumes; take adequate precautions when using them (see Safety First!).

● For general cleaning, use one of the many solvents or degreasers available from most motorcycle accessory shops. These solvents are usually applied then left for a certain time before being washed off with water.

Brake cleaner is a solvent specifically designed to remove all traces of oil, grease and dust from braking system components. Brake cleaner is designed to evaporate quickly and leaves behind no residue.

Carburettor cleaner is an aerosol-type solvent specifically designed to clear carburettor blockages and break down the hard deposits and gum often found inside carburettors during overhaul.

Contact cleaner is an aerosol-type solvent designed for cleaning electrical components. The cleaner will remove all traces of oil and dirt from components such as switch contacts or fouled spark plugs and then dry, leaving behind no residue.

Gasket remover is an aerosol-type solvent designed for removing stubborn gaskets from engine components during overhaul. Gasket remover will minimise the amount of scraping required to remove the gasket and therefore reduce the risk of damage to the mating surface.

Spray lubricants

● Aerosol-based spray lubricants are widely available and are excellent for lubricating lever pivots and exposed cables and switches. Try to use a lubricant which is of the dry-film type as the fluid evaporates, leaving behind a dry-film of lubricant. Lubricants which leave behind an oily residue will attract dust and dirt which will increase the rate of wear of the cable/lever.

● Most lubricants also act as a moisture dispersant and a penetrating fluid. This means they can also be used to 'dry out' electrical components such as wiring connectors or switches as well as helping to free seized fasteners.

Greases

● Grease is used to lubricate many of the pivot-points. A good-quality multi-purpose grease is suitable for most applications but some manufacturers will specify the use of specialist greases for use on components such as swingarm and suspension linkage bushes. These specialist greases can be purchased from most motorcycle (or car) accessory shops; commonly specified types include molybdenum disulphide grease, lithium-based grease, graphite-based grease, silicone-based grease and high-temperature copper-based grease.

Gasket sealing compounds

● Gasket sealing compounds can be used in conjunction with gaskets, to improve their sealing capabilities, or on their own to seal metal-to-metal joints. Depending on their type, sealing compounds either set hard or stay relatively soft and pliable.

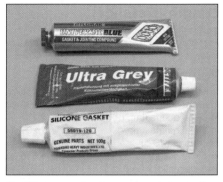

● When purchasing a gasket sealing compound, ensure that it is designed specifically for use on an internal combustion engine. General multi-purpose sealants available from DIY stores may appear visibly similar but they are not designed to withstand the extreme heat or contact with fuel and oil encountered when used on an engine (see 'Tools and Workshop Tips' for further information).

Thread locking compound

● Thread locking compounds are used to secure certain threaded fasteners in position to prevent them from loosening due to vibration. Thread locking compounds can be purchased from most motorcycle (and car) accessory shops. Ensure the threads of the both components are completely clean and dry before sparingly applying the locking compound (see 'Tools and Workshop Tips' for further information).

Fuel additives

● Fuel additives which protect and clean the fuel system components are widely available. These additives are designed to remove all traces of deposits that build up on the carburettors/injectors and prevent wear, helping the fuel system to operate more efficiently. If a fuel additive is being used, check that it is suitable for use with your motorcycle, especially if your motorcycle is equipped with a catalytic converter.

● Octane boosters are also available. These additives are designed to improve the performance of highly-tuned engines being run on normal pump-fuel and are of no real use on standard motorcycles.

Length (distance)

Inches (in)	x 25.4	= Millimetres (mm)	x 0.0394	= Inches (in)
Feet (ft)	x 0.305	= Metres (m)	x 3.281	= Feet (ft)
Miles	x 1.609	= Kilometres (km)	x 0.621	= Miles

Volume (capacity)

Cubic inches (cu in; in³)	x 16.387	= Cubic centimetres (cc; cm³)	x 0.061	= Cubic inches (cu in; in³)
Imperial pints (Imp pt)	x 0.568	= Litres (l)	x 1.76	= Imperial pints (Imp pt)
Imperial quarts (Imp qt)	x 1.137	= Litres (l)	x 0.88	= Imperial quarts (Imp qt)
Imperial quarts (Imp qt)	x 1.201	= US quarts (US qt)	x 0.833	= Imperial quarts (Imp qt)
US quarts (US qt)	x 0.946	= Litres (l)	x 1.057	= US quarts (US qt)
Imperial gallons (Imp gal)	x 4.546	= Litres (l)	x 0.22	= Imperial gallons (Imp gal)
Imperial gallons (Imp gal)	x 1.201	= US gallons (US gal)	x 0.833	= Imperial gallons (Imp gal)
US gallons (US gal)	x 3.785	= Litres (l)	x 0.264	= US gallons (US gal)

Mass (weight)

Ounces (oz)	x 28.35	= Grams (g)	x 0.035	= Ounces (oz)
Pounds (lb)	x 0.454	= Kilograms (kg)	x 2.205	= Pounds (lb)

Force

Ounces-force (ozf; oz)	x 0.278	= Newtons (N)	x 3.6	= Ounces-force (ozf; oz)
Pounds-force (lbf; lb)	x 4.448	= Newtons (N)	x 0.225	= Pounds-force (lbf; lb)
Newtons (N)	x 0.1	= Kilograms-force (kgf; kg)	x 9.81	= Newtons (N)

Pressure

Pounds-force per square inch (psi; lbf/in²; lb/in²)	x 0.070	= Kilograms-force per square centimetre (kgf/cm²; kg/cm²)	x 14.223	= Pounds-force per square inch (psi; lbf/in²; lb/in²)
Pounds-force per square inch (psi; lbf/in²; lb/in²)	x 0.068	= Atmospheres (atm)	x 14.696	= Pounds-force per square inch (psi; lbf/in²; lb/in²)
Pounds-force per square inch (psi; lbf/in²; lb/in²)	x 0.069	= Bars	x 14.5	= Pounds-force per square inch (psi; lbf/in²; lb/in²)
Pounds-force per square inch (psi; lbf/in²; lb/in²)	x 6.895	= Kilopascals (kPa)	x 0.145	= Pounds-force per square inch (psi; lbf/in²; lb/in²)
Kilopascals (kPa)	x 0.01	= Kilograms-force per square centimetre (kgf/cm²; kg/cm²)	x 98.1	= Kilopascals (kPa)
Millibar (mbar)	x 100	= Pascals (Pa)	x 0.01	= Millibar (mbar)
Millibar (mbar)	x 0.0145	= Pounds-force per square inch (psi; lbf/in²; lb/in²)	x 68.947	= Millibar (mbar)
Millibar (mbar)	x 0.75	= Millimetres of mercury (mmHg)	x 1.333	= Millibar (mbar)
Millibar (mbar)	x 0.401	= Inches of water (inH₂O)	x 2.491	= Millibar (mbar)
Millimetres of mercury (mmHg)	x 0.535	= Inches of water (inH₂O)	x 1.868	= Millimetres of mercury (mmHg)
Inches of water (inH₂O)	x 0.036	= Pounds-force per square inch (psi; lbf/in²; lb/in²)	x 27.68	= Inches of water (inH₂O)

Torque (moment of force)

Pounds-force inches (lbf in; lb in)	x 1.152	= Kilograms-force centimetre (kgf cm; kg cm)	x 0.868	= Pounds-force inches (lbf in; lb in)
Pounds-force inches (lbf in; lb in)	x 0.113	= Newton metres (Nm)	x 8.85	= Pounds-force inches (lbf in; lb in)
Pounds-force inches (lbf in; lb in)	x 0.083	= Pounds-force feet (lbf ft; lb ft)	x 12	= Pounds-force inches (lbf in; lb in)
Pounds-force feet (lbf ft; lb ft)	x 0.138	= Kilograms-force metres (kgf m; kg m)	x 7.233	= Pounds-force feet (lbf ft; lb ft)
Pounds-force feet (lbf ft; lb ft)	x 1.356	= Newton metres (Nm)	x 0.738	= Pounds-force feet (lbf ft; lb ft)
Newton metres (Nm)	x 0.102	= Kilograms-force metres (kgf m; kg m)	x 9.804	= Newton metres (Nm)

Power

Horsepower (hp)	x 745.7	= Watts (W)	x 0.0013	= Horsepower (hp)

Velocity (speed)

Miles per hour (miles/hr; mph)	x 1.609	= Kilometres per hour (km/hr; kph)	x 0.621	= Miles per hour (miles/hr; mph)

Fuel consumption*

Miles per gallon (mpg)	x 0.354	= Kilometres per litre (km/l)	x 2.825	= Miles per gallon (mpg)

Temperature

Degrees Fahrenheit = (°C x 1.8) + 32

Degrees Celsius (Degrees Centigrade; °C) = (°F - 32) x 0.56

It is common practice to convert from miles per gallon (mpg) to litres/100 kilometres (l/100km), where mpg x l/100 km = 282

About the MOT Test

In the UK, all vehicles more than three years old are subject to an annual test to ensure that they meet minimum safety requirements. A current test certificate must be issued before a machine can be used on public roads, and is required before a road fund licence can be issued. Riding without a current test certificate will also invalidate your insurance.

For most owners, the MOT test is an annual cause for anxiety, and this is largely due to owners not being sure what needs to be checked prior to submitting the motorcycle for testing. The simple answer is that a fully roadworthy motorcycle will have no difficulty in passing the test.

This is a guide to getting your motorcycle through the MOT test. Obviously it will not be possible to examine the motorcycle to the same standard as the professional MOT tester, particularly in view of the equipment required for some of the checks. However, working through the following procedures will enable you to identify any problem areas before submitting the motorcycle for the test.

It has only been possible to summarise the test requirements here, based on the regulations in force at the time of printing. Test standards are becoming increasingly stringent, although there are some exemptions for older vehicles. More information about the MOT test can be obtained from the TSO publications, *How Safe is your Motorcycle* and *The MOT Inspection Manual for Motorcycle Testing*.

Many of the checks require that one of the wheels is raised off the ground. If the motorcycle doesn't have a centre stand, note that an auxiliary stand will be required. Additionally, the help of an assistant may prove useful.

Certain exceptions apply to machines under 50 cc, machines without a lighting system, and Classic bikes - if in doubt about any of the requirements listed below seek confirmation from an MOT tester prior to submitting the motorcycle for the test.

Check that the frame number is clearly visible.

Electrical System

Lights, turn signals, horn and reflector

✔ With the ignition on, check the operation of the following electrical components. **Note:** *The electrical components on certain small-capacity machines are powered by the generator, requiring that the engine is run for this check.*

a) *Headlight and tail light. Check that both illuminate in the low and high beam switch positions.*

b) *Position lights. Check that the front position (or sidelight) and tail light illuminate in this switch position.*

c) *Turn signals. Check that all flash at the correct rate, and that the warning light(s) function correctly. Check that the turn signal switch works correctly.*

d) *Hazard warning system (where fitted). Check that all four turn signals flash in this switch position.*

e) *Brake stop light. Check that the light comes on when the front and rear brakes are independently applied. Models first used on or after 1st April 1986 must have a brake light switch on each brake.*

f) *Horn. Check that the sound is continuous and of reasonable volume.*

✔ Check that there is a red reflector on the rear of the machine, either mounted separately or as part of the tail light lens.

✔ Check the condition of the headlight, tail light and turn signal lenses.

Headlight beam height

✔ The MOT tester will perform a headlight beam height check using specialised beam setting equipment **(see illustration 1)**. This equipment will not be available to the home mechanic, but if you suspect that the headlight is incorrectly set or may have been maladjusted in the past, you can perform a rough test as follows.

✔ Position the bike in a straight line facing a brick wall. The bike must be off its stand, upright and with a rider seated. Measure the height from the ground to the centre of the headlight and mark a horizontal line on the wall at this height. Position the motorcycle 3.8 metres from the wall and draw a vertical

Headlight beam height checking equipment

line up the wall central to the centreline of the motorcycle. Switch to dipped beam and check that the beam pattern falls slightly lower than the horizontal line and to the left of the vertical line **(see illustration 2)**.

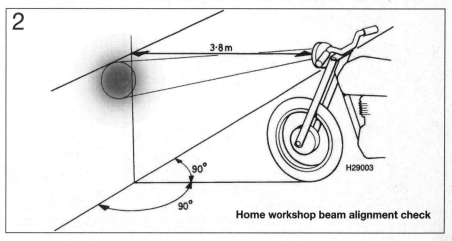

Home workshop beam alignment check

Exhaust System and Final Drive

Exhaust

✔ Check that the exhaust mountings are secure and that the system does not foul any of the rear suspension components.

✔ Start the motorcycle. When the revs are increased, check that the exhaust is neither holed nor leaking from any of its joints. On a linked system, check that the collector box is not leaking due to corrosion.

✔ Note that the exhaust decibel level ("loudness" of the exhaust) is assessed at the discretion of the tester. If the motorcycle was first used on or after 1st January 1985 the silencer must carry the BSAU 193 stamp, or a marking relating to its make and model, or be of OE (original equipment) manufacture. If the silencer is marked NOT FOR ROAD USE, RACING USE ONLY or similar, it will fail the MOT.

Final drive

✔ On chain or belt drive machines, check that the chain/belt is in good condition and does not have excessive slack. Also check that the sprocket is securely mounted on the rear wheel hub. Check that the chain/belt guard is in place.

✔ On shaft drive bikes, check for oil leaking from the drive unit and fouling the rear tyre.

Steering and Suspension

Steering

✔ With the front wheel raised off the ground, rotate the steering from lock to lock. The handlebar or switches must not contact the fuel tank or be close enough to trap the rider's hand. Problems can be caused by damaged lock stops on the lower yoke and frame, or by the fitting of non-standard handlebars.

✔ When performing the lock to lock check, also ensure that the steering moves freely without drag or notchiness. Steering movement can be impaired by poorly routed cables, or by overtight head bearings or worn bearings. The tester will perform a check of the steering head bearing lower race by mounting the front wheel on a surface plate, then performing a lock to lock check with the weight of the machine on the lower bearing (see illustration 3).

✔ Grasp the fork sliders (lower legs) and attempt to push and pull on the forks (see

Front wheel mounted on a surface plate for steering head bearing lower race check

illustration 4). Any play in the steering head bearings will be felt. Note that in extreme cases, wear of the front fork bushes can be misinterpreted for head bearing play.

✔ Check that the handlebars are securely mounted.

✔ Check that the handlebar grip rubbers are secure. They should by bonded to the bar left end and to the throttle cable pulley on the right end.

Front suspension

✔ With the motorcycle off the stand, hold the front brake on and pump the front forks up and down (see illustration 5). Check that they are adequately damped.

Checking the steering head bearings for freeplay

Hold the front brake on and pump the front forks up and down to check operation

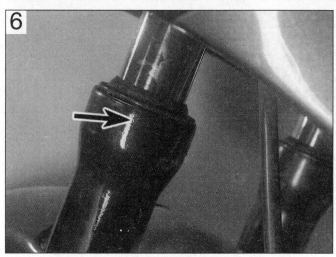

Inspect the area around the fork dust seal for oil leakage (arrow)

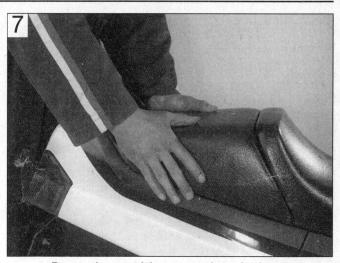

Bounce the rear of the motorcycle to check rear suspension operation

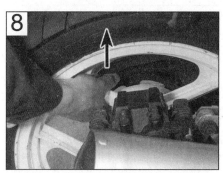

Checking for rear suspension linkage play

✔ Inspect the area above and around the front fork oil seals (see illustration 6). There should be no sign of oil on the fork tube (stanchion) nor leaking down the slider (lower leg). On models so equipped, check that there is no oil leaking from the anti-dive units.

✔ On models with swingarm front suspension, check that there is no freeplay in the linkage when moved from side to side.

Rear suspension

✔ With the motorcycle off the stand and an assistant supporting the motorcycle by its handlebars, bounce the rear suspension (see illustration 7). Check that the suspension components do not foul on any of the cycle parts and check that the shock absorber(s) provide adequate damping.

✔ Visually inspect the shock absorber(s) and check that there is no sign of oil leakage from its damper. This is somewhat restricted on certain single shock models due to the location of the shock absorber.

✔ With the rear wheel raised off the ground, grasp the wheel at the highest point and attempt to pull it up (see illustration 8). Any play in the swingarm pivot or suspension linkage bearings will be felt as movement. Note: Do not confuse play with actual suspension movement. Failure to lubricate suspension linkage bearings can lead to bearing failure (see illustration 9).

✔ With the rear wheel raised off the ground, grasp the swingarm ends and attempt to move the swingarm from side to side and forwards and backwards - any play indicates wear of the swingarm pivot bearings (see illustration 10).

Worn suspension linkage pivots (arrows) are usually the cause of play in the rear suspension

Grasp the swingarm at the ends to check for play in its pivot bearings

Brake pad wear can usually be viewed without removing the caliper. Most pads have wear indicator grooves (1) and some also have indicator tangs (2)

On drum brakes, check the angle of the operating lever with the brake fully applied. Most drum brakes have a wear indicator pointer and scale.

Brakes, Wheels and Tyres

Brakes

✔ With the wheel raised off the ground, apply the brake then free it off, and check that the wheel is about to revolve freely without brake drag.

✔ On disc brakes, examine the disc itself. Check that it is securely mounted and not cracked.

✔ On disc brakes, view the pad material through the caliper mouth and check that the pads are not worn down beyond the limit **(see illustration 11)**.

✔ On drum brakes, check that when the brake is applied the angle between the operating lever and cable or rod is not too great **(see illustration 12)**. Check also that the operating lever doesn't foul any other components.

✔ On disc brakes, examine the flexible hoses from top to bottom. Have an assistant hold the brake on so that the fluid in the hose is under pressure, and check that there is no sign of fluid leakage, bulges or cracking. If there are any metal brake pipes or unions, check that these are free from corrosion and damage. Where a brake-linked anti-dive system is fitted, check the hoses to the anti-dive in a similar manner.

✔ Check that the rear brake torque arm is secure and that its fasteners are secured by self-locking nuts or castellated nuts with split-pins or R-pins **(see illustration 13)**.

✔ On models with ABS, check that the self-check warning light in the instrument panel works.

✔ The MOT tester will perform a test of the motorcycle's braking efficiency based on a calculation of rider and motorcycle weight. Although this cannot be carried out at home, you can at least ensure that the braking systems are properly maintained. For hydraulic disc brakes, check the fluid level, lever/pedal feel (bleed of air if its spongy) and pad material. For drum brakes, check adjustment, cable or rod operation and shoe lining thickness.

Wheels and tyres

✔ Check the wheel condition. Cast wheels should be free from cracks and if of the built-up design, all fasteners should be secure. Spoked wheels should be checked for broken, corroded, loose or bent spokes.

✔ With the wheel raised off the ground, spin the wheel and visually check that the tyre and wheel run true. Check that the tyre does not foul the suspension or mudguards.

✔ With the wheel raised off the ground, grasp the wheel and attempt to move it about the axle (spindle) **(see illustration 14)**. Any play felt here indicates wheel bearing failure.

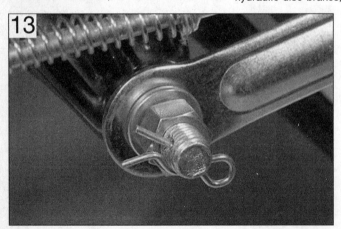

Brake torque arm must be properly secured at both ends

Check for wheel bearing play by trying to move the wheel about the axle (spindle)

Checking the tyre tread depth

Tyre direction of rotation arrow can be found on tyre sidewall

Castellated type wheel axle (spindle) nut must be secured by a split pin or R-pin

Two straightedges are used to check wheel alignment

✔ Check the tyre tread depth, tread condition and sidewall condition (see illustration 15).
✔ Check the tyre type. Front and rear tyre types must be compatible and be suitable for road use. Tyres marked NOT FOR ROAD USE, COMPETITION USE ONLY or similar, will fail the MOT.

✔ If the tyre sidewall carries a direction of rotation arrow, this must be pointing in the direction of normal wheel rotation (see illustration 16).
✔ Check that the wheel axle (spindle) nuts (where applicable) are properly secured. A self-locking nut or castellated nut with a split-pin or R-pin can be used (see illustration 17).
✔ Wheel alignment is checked with the motorcycle off the stand and a rider seated. With the front wheel pointing straight ahead, two perfectly straight lengths of metal or wood and placed against the sidewalls of both tyres (see illustration 18). The gap each side of the front tyre must be equidistant on both sides. Incorrect wheel alignment may be due to a cocked rear wheel (often as the result of poor chain adjustment) or in extreme cases, a bent frame.

General checks and condition

✔ Check the security of all major fasteners, bodypanels, seat, fairings (where fitted) and mudguards.

✔ Check that the rider and pillion footrests, handlebar levers and brake pedal are securely mounted.

✔ Check for corrosion on the frame or any load-bearing components. If severe, this may affect the structure, particularly under stress.

Sidecars

A motorcycle fitted with a sidecar requires additional checks relating to the stability of the machine and security of attachment and swivel joints, plus specific wheel alignment (toe-in) requirements. Additionally, tyre and lighting requirements differ from conventional motorcycle use. Owners are advised to check MOT test requirements with an official test centre.

Preparing for storage

Before you start

If repairs or an overhaul is needed, see that this is carried out now rather than left until you want to ride the bike again.

Give the bike a good wash and scrub all dirt from its underside. Make sure the bike dries completely before preparing for storage.

Engine

● Remove the spark plug(s) and lubricate the cylinder bores with approximately a teaspoon of motor oil using a spout-type oil can **(see illustration 1)**. Reinstall the spark plug(s). Crank the engine over a couple of times to coat the piston rings and bores with oil. If the bike has a kickstart, use this to turn the engine over. If not, flick the kill switch to the OFF position and crank the engine over on the starter **(see illustration 2)**. If the nature on the ignition system prevents the starter operating with the kill switch in the OFF position,

remove the spark plugs and fit them back in their caps; ensure that the plugs are earthed (grounded) against the cylinder head when the starter is operated **(see illustration 3)**.

⚠️ **Warning: It is important that the plugs are earthed (grounded) away from the spark plug holes otherwise there is a risk of atomised fuel from the cylinders igniting.**

HAYNES HiNT *On a single cylinder four-stroke engine, you can seal the combustion chamber completely by positioning the piston at TDC on the compression stroke.*

● Drain the carburettor(s) otherwise there is a risk of jets becoming blocked by gum deposits from the fuel **(see illustration 4)**.

● If the bike is going into long-term storage, consider adding a fuel stabiliser to the fuel in the tank. If the tank is drained completely, corrosion of its internal surfaces may occur if left unprotected for a long period. The tank can be treated with a rust preventative especially for this purpose. Alternatively, remove the tank and pour half a litre of motor oil into it, install the filler cap and shake the tank to coat its internals with oil before draining off the excess. The same effect can also be achieved by spraying WD40 or a similar water-dispersant around the inside of the tank via its flexible nozzle.

● Make sure the cooling system contains the correct mix of antifreeze. Antifreeze also contains important corrosion inhibitors.

● The air intakes and exhaust can be sealed off by covering or plugging the openings. Ensure that you do not seal in any condensation; run the engine until it is hot,

Squirt a drop of motor oil into each cylinder

Flick the kill switch to OFF . . .

. . . and ensure that the metal bodies of the plugs (arrows) are earthed against the cylinder head

Connect a hose to the carburettor float chamber drain stub (arrow) and unscrew the drain screw

Exhausts can be sealed off with a plastic bag

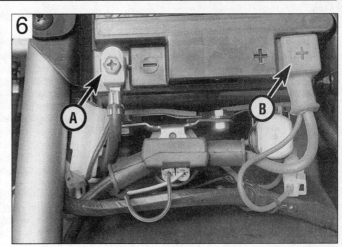

Disconnect the negative lead (A) first, followed by the positive lead (B)

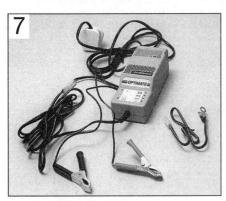

Use a suitable battery charger - this kit also assess battery condition

then switch off and allow to cool. Tape a piece of thick plastic over the silencer end(s) **(see illustration 5)**. Note that some advocate pouring a tablespoon of motor oil into the silencer(s) before sealing them off.

Battery

● Remove it from the bike - in extreme cases of cold the battery may freeze and crack its case **(see illustration 6)**.

● Check the electrolyte level and top up if necessary (conventional refillable batteries). Clean the terminals.
● Store the battery off the motorcycle and away from any sources of fire. Position a wooden block under the battery if it is to sit on the ground.
● Give the battery a trickle charge for a few hours every month **(see illustration 7)**.

Tyres

● Place the bike on its centrestand or an auxiliary stand which will support the motorcycle in an upright position. Position wood blocks under the tyres to keep them off the ground and to provide insulation from damp. If the bike is being put into long-term storage, ideally both tyres should be off the ground; not only will this protect the tyres, but will also ensure that no load is placed on the steering head or wheel bearings.
● Deflate each tyre by 5 to 10 psi, no more or the beads may unseat from the rim, making subsequent inflation difficult on tubeless tyres.

Pivots and controls

● Lubricate all lever, pedal, stand and footrest pivot points. If grease nipples are fitted to the rear suspension components, apply lubricant to the pivots.
● Lubricate all control cables.

Cycle components

● Apply a wax protectant to all painted and plastic components. Wipe off any excess, but don't polish to a shine. Where fitted, clean the screen with soap and water.
● Coat metal parts with Vaseline (petroleum jelly). When applying this to the fork tubes, do not compress the forks otherwise the seals will rot from contact with the Vaseline.
● Apply a vinyl cleaner to the seat.

Storage conditions

● Aim to store the bike in a shed or garage which does not leak and is free from damp.
● Drape an old blanket or bedspread over the bike to protect it from dust and direct contact with sunlight (which will fade paint). This also hides the bike from prying eyes. Beware of tight-fitting plastic covers which may allow condensation to form and settle on the bike.

Getting back on the road

Engine and transmission

● Change the oil and replace the oil filter. If this was done prior to storage, check that the oil hasn't emulsified - a thick whitish substance which occurs through condensation.
● Remove the spark plugs. Using a spout-type oil can, squirt a few drops of oil into the cylinder(s). This will provide initial lubrication as the piston rings and bores comes back into contact. Service the spark plugs, or fit new ones, and install them in the engine.

● Check that the clutch isn't stuck on. The plates can stick together if left standing for some time, preventing clutch operation. Engage a gear and try rocking the bike back and forth with the clutch lever held against the handlebar. If this doesn't work on cable-operated clutches, hold the clutch lever back against the handlebar with a strong elastic band or cable tie for a couple of hours **(see illustration 8)**.
● If the air intakes or silencer end(s) were blocked off, remove the bung or cover used.
● If the fuel tank was coated with a rust

Hold clutch lever back against the handlebar with elastic bands or a cable tie

preventative, oil or a stabiliser added to the fuel, drain and flush the tank and dispose of the fuel sensibly. If no action was taken with the fuel tank prior to storage, it is advised that the old fuel is disposed of since it will go off over a period of time. Refill the fuel tank with fresh fuel.

Frame and running gear

● Oil all pivot points and cables.
● Check the tyre pressures. They will definitely need inflating if pressures were reduced for storage.
● Lubricate the final drive chain (where applicable).
● Remove any protective coating applied to the fork tubes (stanchions) since this may well destroy the fork seals. If the fork tubes weren't protected and have picked up rust spots, remove them with very fine abrasive paper and refinish with metal polish.
● Check that both brakes operate correctly. Apply each brake hard and check that it's not possible to move the motorcycle forwards, then check that the brake frees off again once released. Brake caliper pistons can stick due to corrosion around the piston head, or on the sliding caliper types, due to corrosion of the slider pins. If the brake doesn't free after repeated operation, take the caliper off for examination. Similarly drum brakes can stick

due to a seized operating cam, cable or rod linkage.
● If the motorcycle has been in long-term storage, renew the brake fluid and clutch fluid (where applicable).
● Depending on where the bike has been stored, the wiring, cables and hoses may have been nibbled by rodents. Make a visual check and investigate disturbed wiring loom tape.

Battery

● If the battery has been previously removal and given top up charges it can simply be reconnected. Remember to connect the positive cable first and the negative cable last.
● On conventional refillable batteries, if the battery has not received any attention, remove it from the motorcycle and check its electrolyte level. Top up if necessary then charge the battery. If the battery fails to hold a charge and a visual checks show heavy white sulphation of the plates, the battery is probably defective and must be renewed. This is particularly likely if the battery is old. Confirm battery condition with a specific gravity check.
● On sealed (MF) batteries, if the battery has not received any attention, remove it from the motorcycle and charge it according to the information on the battery case - if the battery fails to hold a charge it must be renewed.

Starting procedure

● If a kickstart is fitted, turn the engine over a couple of times with the ignition OFF to distribute oil around the engine. If no kickstart is fitted, flick the engine kill switch OFF and the ignition ON and crank the engine over a couple of times to work oil around the upper cylinder components. If the nature of the ignition system is such that the starter won't work with the kill switch OFF, remove the spark plugs, fit them back into their caps and earth (ground) their bodies on the cylinder head. Reinstall the spark plugs afterwards.
● Switch the kill switch to RUN, operate the choke and start the engine. If the engine won't start don't continue cranking the engine - not only will this flatten the battery, but the starter motor will overheat. Switch the ignition off and try again later. If the engine refuses to start, go through the fault finding procedures in this manual. **Note:** *If the bike has been in storage for a long time, old fuel or a carburettor blockage may be the problem. Gum deposits in carburettors can block jets - if a carburettor cleaner doesn't prove successful the carburettors must be dismantled for cleaning.*
● Once the engine has started, check that the lights, turn signals and horn work properly.
● Treat the bike gently for the first ride and check all fluid levels on completion. Settle the bike back into the maintenance schedule.

This Section provides an easy reference-guide to the more common faults that are likely to afflict your machine. Obviously, the opportunities are almost limitless for faults to occur as a result of obscure failures, and to try and cover all eventualities would require a book. Indeed, a number have been written on the subject.

Successful troubleshooting is not a mysterious 'black art' but the application of a bit of knowledge combined with a systematic and logical approach to the problem. Approach any troubleshooting by first accurately identifying the symptom and then checking through the list of possible causes, starting with the simplest or most obvious and progressing in stages to the most complex.

Take nothing for granted, but above all apply liberal quantities of common sense.

The main symptom of a fault is given in the text as a major heading below which are listed the various systems or areas which may contain the fault. Details of each possible cause for a fault and the remedial action to be taken are given, in brief, in the paragraphs below each heading. Further information should be sought in the relevant Chapter.

1 Engine doesn't start or is difficult to start

- [ ] Starter motor doesn't rotate
- [ ] Starter motor rotates but engine does not turn over
- [ ] No fuel flow
- [ ] Engine flooded
- [ ] No spark or weak spark
- [ ] Compression low
- [ ] Stalls after starting
- [ ] Rough idle

2 Poor running at low speed

- [ ] Spark weak
- [ ] Fuel/air mixture incorrect
- [ ] Compression low
- [ ] Poor acceleration

3 Poor running or no power at high speed

- [ ] Firing incorrect
- [ ] Fuel/air mixture incorrect
- [ ] Compression low
- [ ] Knocking or pinking
- [ ] Miscellaneous causes

4 Overheating

- [ ] Engine overheats
- [ ] Firing incorrect
- [ ] Fuel/air mixture incorrect
- [ ] Compression too high
- [ ] Engine load excessive
- [ ] Lubrication inadequate
- [ ] Miscellaneous causes

5 Clutch problems

- [ ] Clutch slipping
- [ ] Clutch not disengaging completely

6 Gearchanging problems

- [ ] Doesn't go into gear, or lever doesn't return
- [ ] Jumps out of gear
- [ ] Overselects

7 Abnormal engine noise

- [ ] Knocking or pinking
- [ ] Piston slap or rattling
- [ ] Valve noise
- [ ] Other noise

8 Abnormal driveline noise

- [ ] Clutch noise
- [ ] Transmission noise
- [ ] Final drive noise

9 Abnormal frame and suspension noise

- [ ] Front end noise
- [ ] Shock absorber noise
- [ ] Brake noise

10 Oil pressure warning light comes on

- [ ] Engine lubrication system
- [ ] Electrical system

11 Excessive exhaust smoke

- [ ] White smoke
- [ ] Black smoke
- [ ] Brown smoke

12 Poor handling or stability

- [ ] Handlebar hard to turn
- [ ] Handlebar shakes or vibrates excessively
- [ ] Handlebar pulls to one side
- [ ] Poor shock absorbing qualities

13 Braking problems

- [ ] Brakes are spongy, don't hold
- [ ] Brake lever or pedal pulsates
- [ ] Brakes drag

14 Electrical problems

- [ ] Battery dead or weak
- [ ] Battery overcharged

1 Engine doesn't start or is difficult to start

Starter motor doesn't rotate

- [ ] Engine kill switch OFF.
- [ ] Fuse blown. Check main fuse (Chapter 8).
- [ ] Battery voltage low. Check and recharge battery (Chapter 8).
- [ ] Starter motor defective. Make sure the wiring to the starter is secure. Make sure the starter relay clicks when the start button is pushed. If the relay clicks, then the fault is in the wiring or motor (Chapter 8).
- [ ] Starter switch not contacting. The contacts could be wet, corroded or dirty. Disassemble and clean the switch (Chapter 8).
- [ ] Wiring open or shorted. Check all wiring connections and harnesses to make sure that they are dry, tight and not corroded. Also check for broken or frayed wires that can cause a short to ground (earth) (see *Wiring diagrams*, Chapter 8).
- [ ] Ignition switch defective. Check the switch and replace with a new one if it is defective (Chapter 8).
- [ ] Engine kill switch defective. Check for wet, dirty or corroded contacts. Clean or replace the switch with a new one as necessary (Chapter 8).
- [ ] Faulty neutral switch, sidestand switch or clutch switch. Check the wiring to each switch and the switch itself (Chapter 8).
- [ ] Faulty starter circuit relay or diode (Chapter 8).
- [ ] Fuel injection system shutdown due to system fault (Chapter 4).

Starter motor rotates but engine does not turn over

- [ ] Starter clutch defective. Inspect and repair or replace with a new one (Chapter 2).
- [ ] Damaged idler or starter gears. Inspect and replace the damaged parts (Chapter 2).

No fuel flow

- [ ] No fuel in tank.
- [ ] Fuel tank breather hose obstructed.
- [ ] Faulty fuel pump relay. Check the relay (Chapter 4).
- [ ] Fuel pump faulty, or the fuel filter is blocked (Chapter 4).
- [ ] Fuel hose clogged. Remove the fuel hose and carefully blow through it.
- [ ] Fuel rail or injector clogged. For both injectors to be clogged, either a very bad batch of fuel with an unusual additive has been used, or some other foreign material has entered the tank. In some cases, if a machine has been unused for several months, the fuel turns to a varnish-like liquid which can cause an injector needle to stick to its seat. Drain the tank and fuel system (Chapter 4).

Engine flooded

- [ ] Injector needle valve worn or stuck open. A piece of dirt, rust or other debris can cause the needle to seat improperly, causing excess fuel to be admitted to the throttle body. In this case, the injector should be cleaned and the needle and seat inspected (Chapter 4). If the needle and seat are worn, then the leaking will persist and the parts should be renewed.
- [ ] Starting technique incorrect. Under normal circumstances (i.e. if all the components of the fuel injection system are good) the machine should start with the throttle closed.

No spark or weak spark

- [ ] Ignition switch OFF.
- [ ] Engine kill switch turned to the OFF position.
- [ ] Ignition or kill switch shorted. This is usually caused by water, corrosion, damage or excessive wear. The switches can be disassembled and cleaned with electrical contact cleaner. If cleaning does not help, replace the switches (Chapter 8).
- [ ] Battery voltage low. Check and recharge the battery as necessary (Chapter 8).
- [ ] Ignition coils not making good contact. Make sure that the coils fit snugly over the plug ends.

- [ ] Spark plugs dirty, defective or worn out. Locate reason for fouled plugs using spark plug condition chart on the inside back cover and follow the plug maintenance procedures (Chapter 1).
- [ ] Incorrect spark plugs. Wrong type or heat range. Check and install correct plugs (Chapter 1)
- [ ] Ignition coil defective. Test and renew if necessary (Chapter 4).
- [ ] Fuel injection system shutdown due to system fault (Chapter 4).
- [ ] Crankshaft position (CKP) sensor defective (Chapter 4).
- [ ] Engine control unit (ECU) defective (Chapter 4).
- [ ] Wiring shorted or broken between:
    - a) *Ignition switch and engine kill switch (or blown fuse)*
    - b) *ECU and engine kill switch*
    - c) *ECU and ignition coils*
    - d) *ECU and CKP sensor*
- [ ] Make sure that all wiring connections are clean, dry and tight. Look for chafed and broken wires (Chapters 4 and 8).

Compression low

- [ ] Spark plugs loose. Remove the plugs and inspect their threads. Reinstall and tighten securely (Chapter 1).
- [ ] Cylinder head not sufficiently tightened down. If the cylinder head is suspected of being loose, then there's a chance that the gasket or head is damaged if the problem has persisted for any length of time. The head bolts should be tightened to the proper torque and in the correct sequence (Chapter 2).
- [ ] Improper valve clearance. This means that the valve is not closing completely and compression pressure is leaking past the valve. Check and adjust the valve clearances (Chapter 1).
- [ ] Cylinder and/or piston worn. Excessive wear will cause compression pressure to leak past the rings. This is usually accompanied by worn rings as well. A top-end overhaul is necessary (Chapter 2).
- [ ] Piston rings worn, weak, broken, or sticking. Broken or sticking piston rings usually indicate a lubrication or fuelling problem that causes excess carbon deposits to form on the pistons and rings. Top-end overhaul is necessary (Chapter 2).
- [ ] Piston ring-to-groove clearance excessive. This is caused by excessive wear of the piston ring lands. Piston renewal is necessary (Chapter 2).
- [ ] Cylinder head gasket damaged. If a head is allowed to become loose, or if excessive carbon build-up on the piston crown and combustion chamber causes extremely high compression, the head gasket may leak. Retorquing the head is not always sufficient to restore the seal, so a new gasket is necessary (Chapter 2).
- [ ] Cylinder head warped. This is caused by overheating or improperly tightened head bolts. Machine shop resurfacing or head renewal is necessary (Chapter 2).
- [ ] Valve spring broken or weak. Caused by component failure or wear; the springs must be renewed (Chapter 2).
- [ ] Valve not seating properly. This is caused by a bent valve (from over-revving or improper valve adjustment), burned valve or seat (improper fuelling) or an accumulation of carbon deposits on the seat. The valves must be cleaned and/or renewed and the seats serviced (Chapter 2).

Stalls after starting

- [ ] Engine idle speed incorrect. Turn idle adjusting screw until the engine idles at the specified rpm (Chapter 1).
- [ ] Ignition malfunction (Chapter 4).
- [ ] Fuel injection system malfunction (Chapter 4).
- [ ] Fuel contaminated. The fuel can be contaminated with either dirt or water, or can change chemically if the machine has been unused for several months. Drain the tank and fuel system (Chapter 4).
- [ ] Intake air leak. Check for loose throttle body-to-intake manifold connections, loose or damaged air system vacuum hose or missing vacuum gauge blanking caps (Chapter 4).

1 Engine doesn't start or is difficult to start (continued)

Rough idle

☐ Idle speed incorrect (Chapter 1).
☐ Ignition fault (Chapter 4).
☐ Throttle bodies not synchronised. Adjust them as described in Chapter 1.
☐ Fuel injection system malfunction (Chapter 4).
☐ Fuel contaminated. The fuel can be contaminated with either dirt or water, or can change chemically if the machine has been

unused for several months. Drain the tank and the fuel system (Chapter 4).
☐ Intake air leak. Check for loose throttle body-to-intake manifold connections, loose or damaged air system vacuum hose or missing vacuum gauge blanking caps (Chapter 4).
☐ Air filter clogged. Clean the air filter element or replace it with a new one (Chapter 1).

2 Poor running at low speeds

Spark weak

☐ Battery voltage low. Check and recharge battery (Chapter 8).
☐ Ignition coils not making good contact. Make sure that the coils fit snugly over the plug ends.
☐ Spark plugs dirty, defective or worn out. Locate reason for fouled plugs using spark plug condition chart on the inside back cover and follow the plug maintenance procedures (Chapter 1).
☐ Incorrect spark plugs. Wrong type or heat range. Check and install correct plugs (see Chapter 1).
☐ Ignition coil defective. Test and renew if necessary (Chapter 4).

Fuel/air mixture incorrect

☐ Fuel tank breather hose obstructed.
☐ Fuel pump faulty, or the fuel filter is blocked (Chapter 4).
☐ Fuel hose clogged. Remove the fuel hose and carefully blow through it.
☐ Fuel rail or injector clogged. For both injectors to be clogged, either a very bad batch of fuel with an unusual additive has been used, or some other foreign material has entered the tank. In some cases, if a machine has been unused for several months, the fuel turns to a varnish-like liquid which can cause an injector needle to stick to its seat. Drain the tank and fuel system (Chapter 4).
☐ Intake air leak. Check for loose throttle body-to-intake manifold connections, loose or damaged vacuum hose or missing vacuum gauge blanking caps (Chapter 4).
☐ Air filter clogged. Clean the air filter element or replace it with a new one (Chapter 1).

Compression low

☐ Spark plugs loose. Remove the plugs and inspect their threads. Reinstall and tighten securely (see Chapter 1).
☐ Cylinder head not sufficiently tightened down. If the cylinder head is suspected of being loose, then there's a chance that the gasket or head is damaged if the problem has persisted for any length of time. The head bolts should be tightened to the proper torque and in the correct sequence (Chapter 2).
☐ Improper valve clearance. This means that the valve is not closing completely and compression pressure is leaking past the valve. Check and adjust the valve clearances (Chapter 1).

☐ Cylinder and/or piston worn. Excessive wear will cause compression pressure to leak past the rings. This is usually accompanied by worn rings as well. A top-end overhaul is necessary (Chapter 2).
☐ Piston rings worn, weak, broken, or sticking. Broken or sticking piston rings usually indicate a lubrication or fuelling problem that causes excess carbon deposits to form on the pistons and rings. Top-end overhaul is necessary (Chapter 2).
☐ Piston ring-to-groove clearance excessive. This is caused by excessive wear of the piston ring lands. Piston renewal is necessary (Chapter 2).
☐ Cylinder head gasket damaged. If the head is allowed to become loose, or if excessive carbon build-up on the piston crown and combustion chamber causes extremely high compression, the head gasket may leak. Retorquing the head is not always sufficient to restore the seal, so a new gasket is necessary (Chapter 2).
☐ Cylinder head warped. This is caused by overheating or improperly tightened head bolts. Machine shop resurfacing or head renewal is necessary (Chapter 2).
☐ Valve spring broken or weak. Caused by component failure or wear; the springs must be renewed (Chapter 2).
☐ Valve not seating properly. This is caused by a bent valve (from over-revving or improper valve adjustment), burned valve or seat (improper fuelling) or an accumulation of carbon deposits on the seat (from fuelling or lubrication problems). The valves must be cleaned and/or renewed and the seats serviced (Chapter 2).

Poor acceleration

☐ Timing not advancing. The crankshaft position sensor (CKP) or the electronic control unit (ECU) may be defective (Chapter 4). If so, they must be renewed.
☐ Engine oil viscosity too high. Using a heavier oil than that recommended in Pre-ride checks can damage the oil pump or lubrication system and cause drag on the engine.
☐ Brakes dragging. Usually caused by debris which has entered the brake caliper piston seals, or from a warped disc or bent axle (Chapter 6).

3 Poor running or no power at high speed

Firing incorrect

☐ Ignition coil not making good contact. Make sure that the coils fit snugly over the plug ends and that the wiring is secure.

☐ Spark plugs dirty, defective or worn out. Locate reason for fouled plugs using spark plug condition chart on the inside back cover and follow the plug maintenance procedures (Chapter 1).

☐ Incorrect spark plugs. Wrong type or heat range. Check and install correct plugs (Chapter 1).

☐ Ignition coil defective. Test and renew if necessary (Chapter 4).

☐ Faulty ECU (Chapter 4).

Fuel/air mixture incorrect

☐ Fuel tank breather hose obstructed.

☐ Fuel pump faulty, or the fuel filter is blocked (Chapter 4).

☐ Fuel hose clogged. Remove the fuel hose and carefully blow through it.

☐ Fuel rail or injector clogged. For both injectors to be clogged, either a very bad batch of fuel with an unusual additive has been used, or some other foreign material has entered the tank. In some cases, if a machine has been unused for several months, the fuel turns to a varnish-like liquid which can cause an injector needle to stick to its seat. Drain the tank and fuel system (Chapter 4).

☐ Intake air leak. Check for loose throttle body-to-intake manifold connections, loose or damaged vacuum hose or missing vacuum gauge blanking caps (Chapter 4).

☐ Air filter clogged. Clean the air filter element or replace it with a new one (Chapter 1).

Compression low

☐ Spark plugs loose. Remove the plugs and inspect their threads. Reinstall and tighten securely (Chapter 1).

☐ Cylinder head not sufficiently tightened down. If the cylinder head is suspected of being loose, then there's a chance that the gasket or head is damaged if the problem has persisted for any length of time. The head bolts should be tightened to the proper torque and in the correct sequence (Chapter 2).

☐ Improper valve clearance. This means that the valve is not closing completely and compression pressure is leaking past the valve. Check and adjust the valve clearances (Chapter 1).

☐ Cylinder and/or piston worn. Excessive wear will cause compression pressure to leak past the rings. This is usually accompanied by worn rings as well. A top-end overhaul is necessary (Chapter 2).

☐ Piston rings worn, weak, broken, or sticking. Broken or sticking piston rings usually indicate a lubrication or fuelling problem that causes excess carbon deposits to form on the pistons and rings. Top-end overhaul is necessary (Chapter 2).

☐ Piston ring-to-groove clearance excessive. This is caused by excessive wear of the piston ring lands. Piston renewal is necessary (Chapter 2).

☐ Cylinder head gasket damaged. If a head is allowed to become loose, or if excessive carbon build-up on the piston crown and combustion chamber causes extremely high compression, the head gasket may leak. Retorquing the head is not always sufficient to restore the seal, so a new gasket is necessary (Chapter 2).

☐ Cylinder head warped. This is caused by overheating or improperly tightened head bolts. Machine shop resurfacing or head renewal is necessary (Chapter 2).

☐ Valve spring broken or weak. Caused by component failure or wear; the springs must be replaced with new ones (Chapter 2).

☐ Valve not seating properly. This is caused by a bent valve (from over-revving or improper valve adjustment), burned valve or seat (improper fuelling) or an accumulation of carbon deposits on the seat (from fuelling or lubrication problems). The valves must be cleaned and/or renewed and the seats serviced (Chapter 2).

Knocking or pinking

☐ Carbon build-up in combustion chamber. Use of a fuel additive that will dissolve the adhesive bonding the carbon particles to the piston crown and chamber is the easiest way to remove the build-up. Otherwise, the cylinder head will have to be removed and decarbonised (Chapter 2).

☐ Incorrect or poor quality fuel. Old or improper grades of fuel can cause detonation. This causes the piston to rattle, thus the knocking or pinking sound. Drain old fuel and always use the recommended fuel grade.

☐ Spark plug heat range incorrect. Uncontrolled detonation indicates the plug heat range is too hot. The plug in effect becomes a glow plug, raising cylinder temperatures. Install the proper heat range plug (Chapter 1).

☐ Improper air/fuel mixture. This will cause the cylinders to run hot, which leads to detonation. A blockage in the fuel system or an air leak can cause this imbalance (Chapter 4).

Miscellaneous causes

☐ Throttle valve doesn't open fully. Adjust the throttle twistgrip freeplay (Chapter 1).

☐ Clutch slipping due loose or worn clutch components (Chapter 2).

☐ Timing not advancing. The CKP or ECU may be defective (Chapter 4). If so, they must be replaced with new ones.

☐ Engine oil viscosity too high. Using a heavier oil than the one recommended in Chapter 1 can damage the oil pump or lubrication system and cause drag on the engine.

☐ Brakes dragging. Usually caused by debris which has entered the brake caliper piston seals, or from a warped disc or bent axle (Chapter 6).

4 Overheating

Engine overheats

- ☐ Coolant level low. Check and add coolant (see *Pre-ride checks*).
- ☐ Leak in cooling system. Check cooling system hoses and radiator for leaks and other damage. Repair system or renew parts as necessary (Chapter 3).
- ☐ Faulty thermostat. Check and renew as described in Chapter 3.
- ☐ Faulty radiator cap. Remove the cap and have it pressure tested.
- ☐ Coolant passages clogged. Have the entire system drained and flushed, then refill with fresh coolant.
- ☐ Water pump defective. Remove the pump and check the components (Chapter 3).
- ☐ Clogged or damaged radiator fins (Chapter 3).
- ☐ Faulty cooling fan, ECT sensor or relay (Chapter 3).

Firing incorrect

- ☐ Wrongly connected ignition coil wiring.
- ☐ Spark plugs dirty, defective or worn out. Locate reason for fouled plugs using spark plug condition chart on the inside back cover and follow the plug maintenance procedures (Chapter 1).
- ☐ Incorrect spark plugs. Wrong type or heat range. Check and install correct plugs (Chapter 1).
- ☐ Ignition coil defective. Test and replace with a new one if necessary (Chapter 4).
- ☐ Faulty ECU (Chapter 4).

Fuel/air mixture incorrect

- ☐ Fuel tank breather hose obstructed.
- ☐ Fuel pump faulty, or the fuel filter is blocked (Chapter 4).
- ☐ Fuel hose clogged. Remove the fuel hose and carefully blow through it.
- ☐ Fuel rail or injector clogged. For both injectors to be clogged, either a very bad batch of fuel with an unusual additive has been used, or some other foreign material has entered the tank. In some cases, if a machine has been unused for several months, the fuel turns to a varnish-like liquid which can cause an injector needle to stick to its seat. Drain the tank and fuel system (Chapter 4).
- ☐ Intake air leak. Check for loose throttle body-to-intake manifold connections, loose or damaged air system vacuum hose or missing vacuum gauge blanking caps (Chapter 4).
- ☐ Air filter clogged. Clean the air filter element or replace it with a new one (Chapter 1).

Compression too high

- ☐ Carbon build-up in combustion chamber. Use of a fuel additive that will dissolve the adhesive bonding the carbon particles to the piston crown and chamber is the easiest way to remove the build-up. Otherwise, the cylinder head will have to be removed and decarbonised (Chapter 2).
- ☐ Improperly machined head surface or installation of incorrect gasket during engine assembly.

Engine load excessive

- ☐ Clutch slipping due loose or worn clutch components (Chapter 2).
- ☐ Engine oil level too high. Too much oil will cause pressurisation of the crankcase and inefficient engine operation. Check the level (see *Pre-ride checks*).
- ☐ Engine oil viscosity too high. Using a heavier oil than the one recommended in Chapter 1 can damage the oil pump or lubrication system as well as cause drag on the engine.
- ☐ Brakes dragging. Usually caused by debris which has entered the brake caliper piston seals, or from a warped disc or bent axle (Chapter 6).

Lubrication inadequate

- ☐ Engine oil level too low. Friction caused by intermittent lack of lubrication or from oil that is overworked can cause overheating. The oil provides a definite cooling function in the engine. Check the oil level (see *Pre-ride checks*).
- ☐ Low engine oil pressure. Check the pressure (Chapter 2).
- ☐ Blocked oil filter (Chapter 1).
- ☐ Poor quality engine oil or incorrect viscosity or type. Oil is rated not only according to viscosity but also according to type. Some oils are not rated high enough for use in this engine. Check the Specifications section and change to the correct oil (see *Pre-ride checks*).

Miscellaneous causes

- ☐ Modification to exhaust system. Most aftermarket exhaust systems cause the engine to run leaner, which make them run hotter. When installing an accessory exhaust system, always check with the manufacturer/supplier as to whether adjustments are necessary.

5 Clutch problems

Clutch slipping

- ☐ Insufficient clutch cable freeplay. Check and adjust (Chapter 1).
- ☐ Clutch plates worn or warped. Overhaul the clutch assembly (Chapter 2).
- ☐ Clutch springs broken or weak. Old or heat-damaged (from slipping clutch) springs should be renewed (Chapter 2).
- ☐ Faulty clutch release mechanism. Replace any defective parts with new ones (Chapter 2).
- ☐ Clutch centre or housing unevenly worn. This causes improper engagement of the plates. Replace the damaged or worn parts (Chapter 2).
- ☐ Use of a motor oil designed for car engines. Always use oils packaged as being suitable for motorcycle engines.

Clutch not disengaging completely

- ☐ Excessive clutch cable freeplay. Check and adjust (Chapter 1).
- ☐ Clutch plates warped or damaged. This will cause clutch drag, which in turn will cause the machine to creep. Overhaul the clutch assembly (Chapter 2).
- ☐ Clutch springs fatigued or broken. Check and renew the springs (Chapter 2).
- ☐ Engine oil deteriorated. Old, thin oil will not provide proper lubrication for the plates, causing the clutch to drag. Renew the oil and filter (Chapter 1).
- ☐ Engine oil viscosity too high. Using a heavier oil than recommended in Chapter 1 can cause the plates to stick together. Change to the correct weight oil.
- ☐ Clutch housing bearing seized on the transmission input shaft. Lack of lubrication, severe wear or damage can cause the bearing to seize. Overhaul of the clutch, and perhaps transmission, may be necessary to repair system the damage (Chapter 2).
- ☐ Faulty clutch release mechanism. Renew any defective parts (Chapter 2).
- ☐ Loose clutch centre nut. Causes housing and centre misalignment putting a drag on the engine. Engagement adjustment continually varies. Overhaul the clutch assembly (Chapter 2).

6 Gearchanging problems

Doesn't go into gear or lever doesn't return

- ☐ Clutch not disengaging (see above).
- ☐ Gearchange mechanism stopper arm spring weak or broken, or arm roller broken or worn. Replace the spring or arm with a new one (Chapter 2).
- ☐ Selector fork(s) bent, worn or seized. Overhaul the transmission (Chapter 2).
- ☐ Gear(s) stuck on shaft. Most often caused by a lack of lubrication or excessive wear in transmission bearings and bushes. Overhaul the transmission (Chapter 2).
- ☐ Selector drum binding. Caused by lubrication failure or excessive wear. Replace the drum and/or its bearing with a new one (Chapter 2).
- ☐ Gearchange mechanism return spring weak or broken (Chapter 2).
- ☐ Gearchange linkage arm broken. Splines stripped out of arm or shaft, caused by a loose linkage arm pinch bolt or from dropping the machine (Chapter 2).

Jumps out of gear

- ☐ Selector fork(s) worn (Chapter 2).
- ☐ Selector fork groove(s) in selector drum worn (Chapter 2).
- ☐ Gear pinion dogs or dog slots worn or damaged. The gear pinions should be inspected and renewed. No attempt should be made to repair the worn parts.

Overselects

- ☐ Gearchange mechanism stopper arm spring weak or broken, or arm roller broken or worn. Renew the spring or arm (Chapter 2).
- ☐ Gearchange mechanism return spring weak or broken (Chapter 2).

7 Abnormal engine noise

Knocking or pinking

☐ Carbon build-up in combustion chamber. Use of a fuel additive that will dissolve the adhesive bonding the carbon particles to the piston crown and chamber is the easiest way to remove the build-up. Otherwise, the cylinder head will have to be removed and decarbonised (Chapter 2).

☐ Incorrect or poor quality fuel. Old or improper grades of fuel can cause detonation. This causes the piston to rattle, thus the knocking or pinking sound. Drain old fuel and always use the recommended fuel grade.

☐ Spark plug heat range incorrect. Uncontrolled detonation indicates the plug heat range is too hot. The plug in effect becomes a glow plug, raising cylinder temperatures. Install the proper heat range plug (Chapter 1).

☐ Improper air/fuel mixture. This will cause the cylinders to run hot, which leads to detonation. A blockage in the fuel system or an air leak can cause this imbalance (Chapter 4).

Piston slap or rattling

☐ Cylinder-to-piston clearance excessive. Cylinder and/or piston worn, usually accompanied by worn rings as well. A top-end overhaul is necessary (Chapter 2).

☐ Piston ring(s) worn, broken or sticking. Overhaul the top-end (Chapter 2).

☐ Piston pin, piston pin bore or connecting rod small-end worn from high mileage or seized due to lack of lubrication (Chapter 2).

☐ Piston seizure damage. Usually from lack of lubrication or overheating. Replace the pistons and cylinder block, as necessary (Chapter 2).

☐ Connecting rod big-end clearance excessive. Caused by excessive wear or lack of lubrication. Replace worn parts.

☐ Connecting rod bent. Caused by over-revving, trying to start a badly flooded engine or from ingesting a foreign object into the combustion chamber. Replace the damaged parts (Chapter 2).

Valve noise

☐ Incorrect valve clearances – check and adjust (Chapter 1).

☐ Valve spring broken or weak. Check and replace weak valve springs with new ones (Chapter 2).

☐ Camshaft or camshaft journals in the cylinder head worn or damaged. Lubrication failure at high rpm is usually the cause of damage due to insufficient oil or failure to change the oil at the recommended intervals. Since there are no replaceable bearings in the head, the head itself will have to be replaced with a new one (Chapter 2).

Other noise

☐ Cylinder head gasket leaking. Check around the joint for blowing with the engine running.

☐ Exhaust pipe leaking at cylinder head connection. Caused by incorrect fit of pipe(s), loose exhaust flange or damaged gasket. All exhaust system fasteners should be tightened evenly and carefully to avoid leaks (Chapter 4).

☐ Crankshaft runout excessive. Caused by a bent crankshaft (from over-revving) or damage from an upper cylinder component failure. Can also be attributed to dropping the machine on either of the crankshaft ends.

☐ Engine mounting bolts loose – ensure all the bolts are tightened to the specified torque settings (Chapter 2).

☐ Crankshaft bearings worn (Chapter 2).

☐ Cam chain rattle, due to worn chain or defective tensioner. Also worn chain tensioner/guide blades (Chapter 2).

8 Abnormal driveline noise

Clutch noise

- [ ] Clutch housing/friction plate clearance excessive (Chapter 2).
- [ ] Wear between the clutch housing splines and input shaft splines (Chapter 2).
- [ ] Worn release bearing (Chapter 2).

Transmission noise

- [ ] Bearings worn. Also includes the possibility that the shafts are worn. Overhaul the transmission (Chapter 2).
- [ ] Gears worn or chipped (Chapter 2).
- [ ] Metal chips jammed in gear teeth. Probably pieces from a broken clutch, gear or selector mechanism that were picked up by the gears. This will cause early bearing failure (Chapter 2).
- [ ] Engine oil level too low. Causes a howl from transmission. Also affects engine power and clutch operation (see *Pre-ride checks*).

Final drive noise

- [ ] Chain not adjusted properly (Chapter 1).
- [ ] Front or rear sprocket loose. Tighten fasteners (Chapter 6).
- [ ] Sprockets and/or chain worn. Fit new sprockets and chain (Chapter 6).
- [ ] Rear sprocket warped. Fit a new sprocket (Chapter 6).
- [ ] Rubber dampers in rear wheel worn (Chapter 6).

9 Abnormal frame and suspension noise

Front end noise

- [ ] Low fluid level or improper viscosity oil in forks. This can sound like spurting and is usually accompanied by irregular fork action (Chapter 5).
- [ ] Spring weak or broken. Makes a clicking or scraping sound. Fork oil, when drained, will have a lot of metal particles in it (Chapter 5).
- [ ] Steering head bearings loose or damaged. Clicks when braking. Check and adjust or replace with new ones as necessary (Chapters 1 and 5).
- [ ] Fork yoke clamp bolts loose – ensure all the bolts are tightened to the specified torque (Chapter 6).
- [ ] Forks bent. Good possibility if machine has been dropped. Replace the inner tubes with new ones as required (Chapter 5).
- [ ] Front axle or axle pinch bolts loose. Tighten them to the specified torque (Chapter 6).
- [ ] Loose or worn wheel bearings. Check and replace with new ones as needed (Chapters 1 and 6).

Shock absorber noise

- [ ] Fluid level incorrect. Indicates a leak caused by defective seal. Shock will be covered with oil. Replace shock with a new one or seek advice on repair from a suspension specialist (Chapter 5).
- [ ] Defective shock absorber with internal damage. This is in the body of the shock and can't be remedied. The shock must be replaced with a new one or rebuilt (Chapter 5).
- [ ] Bent or damaged shock body. Replace the shock with a new one (Chapter 5).
- [ ] Loose or worn mounting bolts. Check and replace with new ones as necessary (Chapter 5).

Brake noise

- [ ] Squeal caused by dust on brake pads. Usually found in combination with glazed pads. Clean using brake cleaning solvent (Chapter 6).
- [ ] Pads glazed. Caused by excessive heat from prolonged hard use or from contamination. DO NOT use sandpaper, emery cloth, carborundum cloth or any other abrasive to roughen the pad surfaces as abrasives will stay in the pad material and damage the disc. A very fine flat file can be used, but new pads is the best remedy (Chapter 6).
- [ ] Contamination of brake pads. Oil or brake fluid can cause the brake pads to chatter or squeal. Fit new pads. Identify the cause of the contamination, especially check the caliper piston seals for leaking fluid. Clean disc thoroughly with brake system cleaner (Chapter 6).
- [ ] Disc warped. Can cause a chattering, clicking or intermittent squeal. Usually accompanied by a pulsating lever and uneven braking. Replace the disc with new one (Chapter 6).
- [ ] Loose or worn wheel bearings. Check and replace with new ones as needed (Chapters 1 and 6).

10 Oil pressure warning light comes on

Engine lubrication system

- [ ] Engine oil level low. Inspect for leak or other problem causing low oil level and add recommended oil (see *Pre-ride checks*).
- [ ] Engine oil pump defective, blocked oil filter or oil strainer gauze or failed pressure relief valve. Carry out an oil pressure check (Chapter 2).
- [ ] Engine oil viscosity too low. Very old, thin oil or an improper weight of oil used in the engine. Change to correct oil (see Chapter 1 and *Pre-ride checks*).
- [ ] Camshaft or crankshaft journals worn. Excessive wear causing drop in oil pressure. Abnormal wear could be caused by oil starvation at high rpm from low oil level or improper weight or type of oil (Chapter 1).

Electrical system

- [ ] Oil pressure switch defective. Check the switch according to the procedure in Chapter 8. Replace it with a new one if it is defective.
- [ ] Oil pressure warning LED or circuit defective. Check for pinched, shorted, disconnected or damaged wiring (Chapter 8).

11 Excessive exhaust smoke

White smoke

- [ ] Piston rings worn or broken, causing oil from the crankcase to be pulled past the piston into the combustion chamber. Replace the rings with new ones (Chapter 2).
- [ ] Cylinders worn or scored. Caused by overheating or oil starvation. Install a new cylinder block (Chapter 2).
- [ ] Valve stem oil seal damaged or worn. Replace the oil seals with new ones (Chapter 2).
- [ ] Valve guide worn. Perform a complete valve job (Chapter 2).
- [ ] Engine oil level too high, which causes the oil to be forced past the rings. Drain oil to the proper level (see *Pre-ride checks*).
- [ ] Head gasket broken between oil return and cylinder. Causes oil to be pulled into the combustion chamber. Replace the head gasket with a new one and check the head for warpage (Chapter 2).
- [ ] Abnormal crankcase pressurisation which forces oil past the rings, usually caused by a clogged breather.

Black smoke

- [ ] Air filter clogged. Clean the air filter element or replace it with a new one (Chapter 1).
- [ ] Fuel injection system malfunction (Chapter 4).

Brown smoke

- [ ] Air filter poorly sealed or not installed (Chapter 1).
- [ ] Fuel injection system malfunction (Chapter 4).

12 Poor handling or stability

Handlebars hard to turn

☐ Steering head bearing adjuster nut too tight. Check adjustment as described in Chapter 1.

☐ Bearings damaged. Roughness can be felt as the bars are turned from side-to-side. Replace the bearings with new ones (Chapter 5).

☐ Races dented or worn. Denting results from wear in only one position (e.g. straight ahead), from a collision or hitting a pothole or from dropping the machine. Replace the bearings with new ones (Chapter 5).

☐ Steering stem lubrication inadequate. Causes are grease getting hard from age or being washed out by high pressure car washes. Disassemble steering head and repack bearings (Chapter 5).

☐ Steering stem bent. Caused by a collision, hitting a pothole or by dropping the machine. Replace damaged part. Don't try to straighten the steering stem (Chapter 5).

☐ Front tyre air pressure too low (see *Pre-ride checks*).

Handlebar shakes or vibrates excessively

☐ Tyres worn or out of balance (Chapter 6).

☐ Swingarm bearings worn. Replace the bearings with new ones (Chapter 5).

☐ Wheel rim(s) warped or damaged. Inspect wheels for runout (Chapter 6).

☐ Wheel bearings worn. Worn front or rear wheel bearings can cause poor tracking. Worn front bearings will cause wobble (Chapters 1 and 6).

☐ Fork yoke clamp bolts or handlebar clamp bolts loose. Tighten them to the specified torque (Chapter 5).

☐ Engine mounting bolts loose. Will cause excessive vibration with increased engine rpm – ensure all the bolts are tightened to the specified torque settings (see Chapter 2).

Machine pulls to one side

☐ Frame bent. Definitely suspect this if the machine has been dropped. May or may not be accompanied by cracking near the steering head, swingarm mountings or engine mountings. Replace the frame with a new one (Chapter 5).

☐ Wheels out of alignment. Caused by improper location of axle spacers or from bent steering stem or frame (Chapter 5).

☐ Forks bent. Disassemble the forks and replace the damaged parts (Chapter 5).

☐ Swingarm bent or twisted. Replace the swingarm with a new one (Chapter 5).

☐ Fork oil level uneven. Check and add or drain as necessary (Chapter 5).

Poor shock absorbing qualities

☐ Too hard:
   a) *Rear suspension setting incorrect.*
   b) *Fork oil level excessive (Chapter 5).*
   c) *Fork oil viscosity too high (Chapter 5).*
   d) *Fork inner tube bent. Causes a harsh, sticking feeling (Chapter 5).*
   e) *Fork internal damage (Chapter 5).*
   f) *Shock shaft or body bent or damaged (Chapter 5).*
   g) *Shock internal damage.*
   h) *Tyre pressure too high (see Pre-ride checks).*

☐ Too soft:
   a) *Rear suspension setting incorrect.*
   b) *Fork oil level too low (Chapter 5).*
   c) *Fork oil viscosity too light (Chapter 5).*
   d) *Fork springs weak or broken (Chapter 5).*
   e) *Fork or shock oil leaking (Chapter 5).*
   f) *Shock internal damage (Chapter 5).*

13 Braking problems

Brakes are spongy, don't hold

☐ Low brake fluid level (see *Pre-ride checks*).
☐ Air in hydraulic system. Caused by inattention to master cylinder fluid level or by leakage. Locate problem and bleed brakes (Chapter 6).
☐ Pad or disc worn (Chapters 1 and 6).
☐ Contaminated pads. Caused by contamination with oil, grease, brake fluid, etc. Fit new pads. Identify the cause of the contamination, especially check the caliper piston seals for leaking fluid. Clean disc thoroughly with brake system cleaner (Chapter 6).
☐ Brake fluid deteriorated. Fluid is old or contaminated. Drain system, replenish with new fluid and bleed the system (Chapter 6).
☐ Master cylinder internal seals worn or damaged causing fluid to bypass (Chapter 6).
☐ Master cylinder bore scratched by foreign material or broken spring. Fit a new master cylinder (Chapter 6).
☐ Disc warped. Replace disc with new one (Chapter 6).

Brake lever or pedal pulsates

☐ Disc warped. Replace disc with new one (Chapter 6).

☐ Axle bent. Replace axle with new one (Chapter 6).
☐ Brake caliper bolts loose – tighten the bolts to the specified torque (Chapter 6).
☐ Wheel warped or otherwise damaged (Chapter 6).
☐ Wheel bearings damaged or worn (Chapters 1 and 6).

Brakes drag

☐ Master cylinder piston seized. Caused by wear or damage to piston or cylinder bore (Chapter 6).
☐ Lever balky or stuck. Check pivot and lubricate (Chapter 6).
☐ Brake caliper piston seized in bore. Caused by corrosion or ingestion of dirt past deteriorated seal (Chapter 6).
☐ Caliper sticking on slider pins due to corrosion. Clean and lubricate pins and check dust boots (Chapter 6).
☐ Brake pad damaged. Pad material separated from backing plate. Usually caused by faulty manufacturing process or from contact with chemicals. Fit new pads (Chapter 6).
☐ Pads improperly installed (Chapter 6).
☐ Brake caliper incorrectly installed (Chapter 6).

ABS indicator light comes on

☐ If the light remains on after start-up or comes on while riding, investigate the fault (Chapter 6).

14 Electrical problems

Battery dead or weak

☐ Battery faulty. Caused by sulphated plates which are shorted through sedimentation. Confirm with battery condition check (Chapter 8).
☐ Broken battery terminal making only occasional contact.
☐ Battery leads making poor contact (Chapter 8).
☐ Load excessive. Caused by addition of high wattage lights or other electrical accessories.
☐ Ignition switch defective. Switch either grounds (earths) internally or fails to shut off system. Renew the switch (Chapter 8).
☐ Regulator/rectifier defective (Chapter 8).
☐ Alternator stator coil open or shorted (Chapter 8).

☐ Charging system fault. Check for excessive current leakage (Chapter 8).
☐ Wiring faulty. Wiring grounded (earthed) or connections loose in ignition, charging or lighting circuits (Chapter 8).

Battery overcharged

☐ Regulator/rectifier defective. Overcharging is noticed when battery gets excessively warm (Chapter 8).
☐ Battery faulty. Confirm with battery condition check (Chapter 8).
☐ Battery amperage too low, wrong type or size of battery. Install manufacturer's specified amp-hour battery to handle charging load (Chapter 8).

A

ABS (Anti-lock braking system) A system, usually electronically controlled, that senses incipient wheel lockup during braking and relieves hydraulic pressure at wheel which is about to skid.

Aftermarket Components suitable for the motorcycle, but not produced by the motorcycle manufacturer.

Allen key A hexagonal wrench which fits into a recessed hexagonal hole.

Alternating current (ac) Current produced by an alternator. Requires converting to direct current by a rectifier for charging purposes.

Alternator Converts mechanical energy from the engine into electrical energy to charge the battery and power the electrical system.

Ampere (amp) A unit of measurement for the flow of electrical current. Current = Volts ÷ Ohms.

Ampere-hour (Ah) Measure of battery capacity.

Angle-tightening A torque expressed in degrees. Often follows a conventional tightening torque for cylinder head or main bearing fasteners **(see illustration)**.

Angle-tightening cylinder head bolts

Antifreeze A substance (usually ethylene glycol) mixed with water, and added to the cooling system, to prevent freezing of the coolant in winter. Antifreeze also contains chemicals to inhibit corrosion and the formation of rust and other deposits that would tend to clog the radiator and coolant passages and reduce cooling efficiency.

Anti-dive System attached to the fork lower leg (slider) to prevent fork dive when braking hard.

Anti-seize compound A coating that reduces the risk of seizing on fasteners that are subjected to high temperatures, such as exhaust clamp bolts and nuts.

API American Petroleum Institute. A quality standard for 4-stroke motor oils.

Asbestos A natural fibrous mineral with great heat resistance, commonly used in the composition of brake friction materials. Asbestos is a health hazard and the dust created by brake systems should never be inhaled or ingested.

ATF Automatic Transmission Fluid. Often used in front forks.

ATU Automatic Timing Unit. Mechanical device for advancing the ignition timing on early engines.

ATV All Terrain Vehicle. Often called a Quad.

Axial play Side-to-side movement.

Axle A shaft on which a wheel revolves. Also known as a spindle.

B

Backlash The amount of movement between meshed components when one component is held still. Usually applies to gear teeth.

Ball bearing A bearing consisting of a hardened inner and outer race with hardened steel balls between the two races.

Bearings Used between two working surfaces to prevent wear of the components and a build-up of heat. Four types of bearing are commonly used on motorcycles: plain shell bearings, ball bearings, tapered roller bearings and needle roller bearings.

Bevel gears Used to turn the drive through 90°. Typical applications are shaft final drive and camshaft drive **(see illustration)**.

Bevel gears are used to turn the drive through 90°

BHP Brake Horsepower. The British measurement for engine power output. Power output is now usually expressed in kilowatts (kW).

Bias-belted tyre Similar construction to radial tyre, but with outer belt running at an angle to the wheel rim.

Big-end bearing The bearing in the end of the connecting rod that's attached to the crankshaft.

Bleeding The process of removing air from an hydraulic system via a bleed nipple or bleed screw.

Bottom-end A description of an engine's crankcase components and all components contained there-in.

BTDC Before Top Dead Centre in terms of piston position. Ignition timing is often expressed in terms of degrees or millimetres BTDC.

Bush A cylindrical metal or rubber component used between two moving parts.

Burr Rough edge left on a component after machining or as a result of excessive wear.

C

Cam chain The chain which takes drive from the crankshaft to the camshaft(s).

Canister The main component in an evaporative emission control system (California market only); contains activated charcoal granules to trap vapours from the fuel system rather than allowing them to vent to the atmosphere.

Castellated Resembling the parapets along the top of a castle wall. For example, a castellated wheel axle or spindle nut.

Catalytic converter A device in the exhaust system of some machines which converts certain pollutants in the exhaust gases into less harmful substances.

Charging system Description of the components which charge the battery, ie the alternator, rectifier and regulator.

Circlip A ring-shaped clip used to prevent endwise movement of cylindrical parts and shafts. An internal circlip is installed in a groove in a housing; an external circlip fits into a groove on the outside of a cylindrical piece such as a shaft. Also known as a snap-ring.

Clearance The amount of space between two parts. For example, between a piston and a cylinder, between a bearing and a journal, etc.

Coil spring A spiral of elastic steel found in various sizes throughout a vehicle, for example as a springing medium in the suspension and in the valve train.

Compression Reduction in volume, and increase in pressure and temperature, of a gas, caused by squeezing it into a smaller space.

Compression damping Controls the speed the suspension compresses when hitting a bump.

Compression ratio The relationship between cylinder volume when the piston is at top dead centre and cylinder volume when the piston is at bottom dead centre.

Continuity The uninterrupted path in the flow of electricity. Little or no measurable resistance.

Continuity tester Self-powered bleeper or test light which indicates continuity.

Cp Candlepower. Bulb rating commonly found on US motorcycles.

Crossply tyre Tyre plies arranged in a criss-cross pattern. Usually four or six plies used, hence 4PR or 6PR in tyre size codes.

Cush drive Rubber damper segments fitted between the rear wheel and final drive sprocket to absorb transmission shocks **(see illustration)**.

Cush drive rubbers dampen out transmission shocks

D

Degree disc Calibrated disc for measuring piston position. Expressed in degrees.

Dial gauge Clock-type gauge with adapters for measuring runout and piston position. Expressed in mm or inches.

Diaphragm The rubber membrane in a master cylinder or carburettor which seals the upper chamber.

Diaphragm spring A single sprung plate often used in clutches.

Direct current (dc) Current produced by a dc generator.

Decarbonisation The process of removing carbon deposits - typically from the combustion chamber, valves and exhaust port/system.

Detonation Destructive and damaging explosion of fuel/air mixture in combustion chamber instead of controlled burning.

Diode An electrical valve which only allows current to flow in one direction. Commonly used in rectifiers and starter interlock systems.

Disc valve (or rotary valve) A induction system used on some two-stroke engines.

Double-overhead camshaft (DOHC) An engine that uses two overhead camshafts, one for the intake valves and one for the exhaust valves.

Drivebelt A toothed belt used to transmit drive to the rear wheel on some motorcycles. A drivebelt has also been used to drive the camshafts. Drivebelts are usually made of Kevlar.

Driveshaft Any shaft used to transmit motion. Commonly used when referring to the final driveshaft on shaft drive motorcycles.

E

Earth return The return path of an electrical circuit, utilising the motorcycle's frame.

ECU (Electronic Control Unit) A computer which controls (for instance) an ignition system, or an anti-lock braking system.

EGO Exhaust Gas Oxygen sensor. Sometimes called a Lambda sensor.

Electrolyte The fluid in a lead-acid battery.

EMS (Engine Management System) A computer controlled system which manages the fuel injection and the ignition systems in an integrated fashion.

Endfloat The amount of lengthways movement between two parts. As applied to a crankshaft, the distance that the crankshaft can move side-to-side in the crankcase.

Endless chain A chain having no joining link. Common use for cam chains and final drive chains.

EP (Extreme Pressure) Oil type used in locations where high loads are applied, such as between gear teeth.

Evaporative emission control system Describes a charcoal filled canister which stores fuel vapours from the tank rather than allowing them to vent to the atmosphere. Usually only fitted to California models and referred to as an EVAP system.

Expansion chamber Section of two-stroke engine exhaust system so designed to improve engine efficiency and boost power.

F

Feeler blade or gauge A thin strip or blade of hardened steel, ground to an exact thickness, used to check or measure clearances between parts.

Final drive Description of the drive from the transmission to the rear wheel. Usually by chain or shaft, but sometimes by belt.

Firing order The order in which the engine cylinders fire, or deliver their power strokes, beginning with the number one cylinder.

Flooding Term used to describe a high fuel level in the carburettor float chambers, leading to fuel overflow. Also refers to excess fuel in the combustion chamber due to incorrect starting technique.

Free length The no-load state of a component when measured. Clutch, valve and fork spring lengths are measured at rest, without any preload.

Freeplay The amount of travel before any action takes place. The looseness in a linkage, or an assembly of parts, between the initial application of force and actual movement. For example, the distance the rear brake pedal moves before the rear brake is actuated.

Fuel injection The fuel/air mixture is metered electronically and directed into the engine intake ports (indirect injection) or into the cylinders (direct injection). Sensors supply information on engine speed and conditions.

Fuel/air mixture The charge of fuel and air going into the engine. See **Stoichiometric ratio**.

Fuse An electrical device which protects a circuit against accidental overload. The typical fuse contains a soft piece of metal which is calibrated to melt at a predetermined current flow (expressed as amps) and break the circuit.

G

Gap The distance the spark must travel in jumping from the centre electrode to the side electrode in a spark plug. Also refers to the distance between the ignition rotor and the pickup coil in an electronic ignition system.

Gasket Any thin, soft material - usually cork, cardboard, asbestos or soft metal - installed between two metal surfaces to ensure a good seal. For instance, the cylinder head gasket seals the joint between the block and the cylinder head.

Gauge An instrument panel display used to monitor engine conditions. A gauge with a movable pointer on a dial or a fixed scale is an analogue gauge. A gauge with a numerical readout is called a digital gauge.

Gear ratios The drive ratio of a pair of gears in a gearbox, calculated on their number of teeth.

Glaze-busting see **Honing**

Grinding Process for renovating the valve face and valve seat contact area in the cylinder head.

Gudgeon pin The shaft which connects the connecting rod small-end with the piston. Often called a piston pin or wrist pin.

H

Helical gears Gear teeth are slightly curved and produce less gear noise that straight-cut gears. Often used for primary drives.

Installing a Helicoil thread insert in a cylinder head

Helicoil A thread insert repair system. Commonly used as a repair for stripped spark plug threads **(see illustration)**.

Honing A process used to break down the glaze on a cylinder bore (also called glaze-busting). Can also be carried out to roughen a rebored cylinder to aid ring bedding-in.

HT (High Tension) Description of the electrical circuit from the secondary winding of the ignition coil to the spark plug.

Hydraulic A liquid filled system used to transmit pressure from one component to another. Common uses on motorcycles are brakes and clutches.

Hydrometer An instrument for measuring the specific gravity of a lead-acid battery.

Hygroscopic Water absorbing. In motorcycle applications, braking efficiency will be reduced if DOT 3 or 4 hydraulic fluid absorbs water from the air - care must be taken to keep new brake fluid in tightly sealed containers.

I

lbf ft Pounds-force feet. An imperial unit of torque. Sometimes written as ft-lbs.

lbf in Pound-force inch. An imperial unit of torque, applied to components where a very low torque is required. Sometimes written as in-lbs.

IC Abbreviation for Integrated Circuit.

Ignition advance Means of increasing the timing of the spark at higher engine speeds. Done by mechanical means (ATU) on early engines or electronically by the ignition control unit on later engines.

Ignition timing The moment at which the spark plug fires, expressed in the number of crankshaft degrees before the piston reaches the top of its stroke, or in the number of millimetres before the piston reaches the top of its stroke.

Infinity (∞) Description of an open-circuit electrical state, where no continuity exists.

Inverted forks (upside down forks) The sliders or lower legs are held in the yokes and the fork tubes or stanchions are connected to the wheel axle (spindle). Less unsprung weight and stiffer construction than conventional forks.

J

JASO Quality standard for 2-stroke oils.

Joule The unit of electrical energy.

Journal The bearing surface of a shaft.

K

Kickstart Mechanical means of turning the engine over for starting purposes. Only usually fitted to mopeds, small capacity motorcycles and off-road motorcycles.

Kill switch Handlebar-mounted switch for emergency ignition cut-out. Cuts the ignition circuit on all models, and additionally prevent starter motor operation on others.

km Symbol for kilometre.

kmh Abbreviation for kilometres per hour.

L

Lambda (λ) sensor A sensor fitted in the exhaust system to measure the exhaust gas oxygen content (excess air factor).

Lapping see **Grinding**.

LCD Abbreviation for Liquid Crystal Display.

LED Abbreviation for Light Emitting Diode.

Liner A steel cylinder liner inserted in a aluminium alloy cylinder block.

Locknut A nut used to lock an adjustment nut, or other threaded component, in place.

Lockstops The lugs on the lower triple clamp (yoke) which abut those on the frame, preventing handlebar-to-fuel tank contact.

Lockwasher A form of washer designed to prevent an attaching nut from working loose.

LT Low Tension Description of the electrical circuit from the power supply to the primary winding of the ignition coil.

M

Main bearings The bearings between the crankshaft and crankcase.

Maintenance-free (MF) battery A sealed battery which cannot be topped up.

Manometer Mercury-filled calibrated tubes used to measure intake tract vacuum. Used to synchronise carburettors on multi-cylinder engines.

Micrometer A precision measuring instrument that measures component outside diameters **(see illustration)**.

Tappet shims are measured with a micrometer

MON (Motor Octane Number) A measure of a fuel's resistance to knock.

Monograde oil An oil with a single viscosity, eg SAE80W.

Monoshock A single suspension unit linking the swingarm or suspension linkage to the frame.

mph Abbreviation for miles per hour.

Multigrade oil Having a wide viscosity range (eg 10W40). The W stands for Winter, thus the viscosity ranges from SAE10 when cold to SAE40 when hot.

Multimeter An electrical test instrument with the capability to measure voltage, current and resistance. Some meters also incorporate a continuity tester and buzzer.

N

Needle roller bearing Inner race of caged needle rollers and hardened outer race. Examples of uncaged needle rollers can be found on some engines. Commonly used in rear suspension applications and in two-stroke engines.

Nm Newton metres.

NOx Oxides of Nitrogen. A common toxic pollutant emitted by petrol engines at higher temperatures.

O

Octane The measure of a fuel's resistance to knock.

OE (Original Equipment) Relates to components fitted to a motorcycle as standard or replacement parts supplied by the motorcycle manufacturer.

Ohm The unit of electrical resistance. Ohms = Volts ÷ Current.

Ohmmeter An instrument for measuring electrical resistance.

Oil cooler System for diverting engine oil outside of the engine to a radiator for cooling purposes.

Oil injection A system of two-stroke engine lubrication where oil is pump-fed to the engine in accordance with throttle position.

Open-circuit An electrical condition where there is a break in the flow of electricity - no continuity (high resistance).

O-ring A type of sealing ring made of a special rubber-like material; in use, the O-ring is compressed into a groove to provide the sealing action.

Oversize (OS) Term used for piston and ring size options fitted to a rebored cylinder.

Overhead cam (sohc) engine An engine with single camshaft located on top of the cylinder head.

Overhead valve (ohv) engine An engine with the valves located in the cylinder head, but with the camshaft located in the engine block or crankcase.

Oxygen sensor A device installed in the exhaust system which senses the oxygen content in the exhaust and converts this information into an electric current. Also called a Lambda sensor.

P

Plastigauge A thin strip of plastic thread, available in different sizes, used for measuring clearances. For example, a strip of Plastigauge is laid across a bearing journal. The parts are assembled and dismantled; the width of the crushed strip indicates the clearance between journal and bearing.

Polarity Either negative or positive earth (ground), determined by which battery lead is connected to the frame (earth return). Modern motorcycles are usually negative earth.

Pre-ignition A situation where the fuel/air mixture ignites before the spark plug fires. Often due to a hot spot in the combustion chamber caused by carbon build-up. Engine has a tendency to 'run-on'.

Pre-load (suspension) The amount a spring is compressed when in the unloaded state. Preload can be applied by gas, spacer or mechanical adjuster.

Premix The method of engine lubrication on older two-stroke engines. Engine oil is mixed with the petrol in the fuel tank in a specific ratio. The fuel/oil mix is sometimes referred to as "petroil".

Primary drive Description of the drive from the crankshaft to the clutch. Usually by gear or chain.

PS Pfedestärke - a German interpretation of BHP.

PSI Pounds-force per square inch. Imperial measurement of tyre pressure and cylinder pressure measurement.

PTFE Polytetrafluroethylene. A low friction substance.

Pulse secondary air injection system A process of promoting the burning of excess fuel present in the exhaust gases by routing fresh air into the exhaust ports.

Q

Quartz halogen bulb Tungsten filament surrounded by a halogen gas. Typically used for the headlight **(see illustration)**.

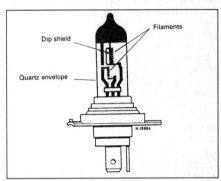

Quartz halogen headlight bulb construction

R

Rack-and-pinion A pinion gear on the end of a shaft that mates with a rack (think of a geared wheel opened up and laid flat). Sometimes used in clutch operating systems.

Radial play Up and down movement about a shaft.

Radial ply tyres Tyre plies run across the tyre (from bead to bead) and around the circumference of the tyre. Less resistant to tread distortion than other tyre types.

Radiator A liquid-to-air heat transfer device designed to reduce the temperature of the coolant in a liquid cooled engine.

Rake A feature of steering geometry - the angle of the steering head in relation to the vertical **(see illustration)**.

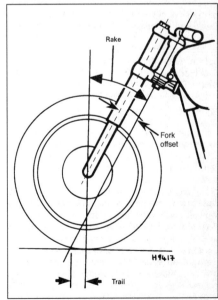

Steering geometry

Rebore Providing a new working surface to the cylinder bore by boring out the old surface. Necessitates the use of oversize piston and rings.

Rebound damping A means of controlling the oscillation of a suspension unit spring after it has been compressed. Resists the spring's natural tendency to bounce back after being compressed.

Rectifier Device for converting the ac output of an alternator into dc for battery charging.

Reed valve An induction system commonly used on two-stroke engines.

Regulator Device for maintaining the charging voltage from the generator or alternator within a specified range.

Relay A electrical device used to switch heavy current on and off by using a low current auxiliary circuit.

Resistance Measured in ohms. An electrical component's ability to pass electrical current.

RON (Research Octane Number) A measure of a fuel's resistance to knock.

rpm revolutions per minute.

Runout The amount of wobble (in-and-out movement) of a wheel or shaft as it's rotated. The amount a shaft rotates 'out-of-true'. The out-of-round condition of a rotating part.

S

SAE (Society of Automotive Engineers) A standard for the viscosity of a fluid.

Sealant A liquid or paste used to prevent leakage at a joint. Sometimes used in conjunction with a gasket.

Service limit Term for the point where a component is no longer useable and must be renewed.

Shaft drive A method of transmitting drive from the transmission to the rear wheel.

Shell bearings Plain bearings consisting of two shell halves. Most often used as big-end and main bearings in a four-stroke engine. Often called bearing inserts.

Shim Thin spacer, commonly used to adjust the clearance or relative positions between two parts. For example, shims inserted into or under tappets or followers to control valve clearances. Clearance is adjusted by changing the thickness of the shim.

Short-circuit An electrical condition where current shorts to earth (ground) bypassing the circuit components.

Skimming Process to correct warpage or repair a damaged surface, eg on brake discs or drums.

Slide-hammer A special puller that screws into or hooks onto a component such as a shaft or bearing; a heavy sliding handle on the shaft bottoms against the end of the shaft to knock the component free.

Small-end bearing The bearing in the upper end of the connecting rod at its joint with the gudgeon pin.

Spalling Damage to camshaft lobes or bearing journals shown as pitting of the working surface.

Specific gravity (SG) The state of charge of the electrolyte in a lead-acid battery. A measure of the electrolyte's density compared with water.

Straight-cut gears Common type gear used on gearbox shafts and for oil pump and water pump drives.

Stanchion The inner sliding part of the front forks, held by the yokes. Often called a fork tube.

Stoichiometric ratio The optimum chemical air/fuel ratio for a petrol engine, said to be 14.7 parts of air to 1 part of fuel.

Sulphuric acid The liquid (electrolyte) used in a lead-acid battery. Poisonous and extremely corrosive.

Surface grinding (lapping) Process to correct a warped gasket face, commonly used on cylinder heads.

T

Tapered-roller bearing Tapered inner race of caged needle rollers and separate tapered outer race. Examples of taper roller bearings can be found on steering heads.

Tappet A cylindrical component which transmits motion from the cam to the valve stem, either directly or via a pushrod and rocker arm. Also called a cam follower.

TCS Traction Control System. An electronically-controlled system which senses wheel spin and reduces engine speed accordingly.

TDC Top Dead Centre denotes that the piston is at its highest point in the cylinder.

Thread-locking compound Solution applied to fastener threads to prevent slackening. Select type to suit application.

Thrust washer A washer positioned between two moving components on a shaft. For example, between gear pinions on gearshaft.

Timing chain See **Cam Chain.**

Timing light Stroboscopic lamp for carrying out ignition timing checks with the engine running.

Top-end A description of an engine's cylinder block, head and valve gear components.

Torque Turning or twisting force about a shaft.

Torque setting A prescribed tightness specified by the motorcycle manufacturer to ensure that the bolt or nut is secured correctly. Undertightening can result in the bolt or nut coming loose or a surface not being sealed. Overtightening can result in stripped threads, distortion or damage to the component being retained.

Torx key A six-point wrench.

Tracer A stripe of a second colour applied to a wire insulator to distinguish that wire from another one with the same colour insulator. For example, Br/W is often used to denote a brown insulator with a white tracer.

Trail A feature of steering geometry. Distance from the steering head axis to the tyre's central contact point.

Triple clamps The cast components which extend from the steering head and support the fork stanchions or tubes. Often called fork yokes.

Turbocharger A centrifugal device, driven by exhaust gases, that pressurises the intake air. Normally used to increase the power output from a given engine displacement.

TWI Abbreviation for Tyre Wear Indicator. Indicates the location of the tread depth indicator bars on tyres.

U

Universal joint or U-joint (UJ) A double-pivoted connection for transmitting power from a driving to a driven shaft through an angle. Typically found in shaft drive assemblies.

Unsprung weight Anything not supported by the bike's suspension (ie the wheel, tyres, brakes, final drive and bottom (moving) part of the suspension).

V

Vacuum gauges Clock-type gauges for measuring intake tract vacuum. Used for carburettor synchronisation on multi-cylinder engines.

Valve A device through which the flow of liquid, gas or vacuum may be stopped, started or regulated by a moveable part that opens, shuts or partially obstructs one or more ports or passageways. The intake and exhaust valves in the cylinder head are of the poppet type.

Valve clearance The clearance between the valve tip (the end of the valve stem) and the rocker arm or tappet/follower. The valve clearance is measured when the valve is closed. The correct clearance is important - if too small the valve won't close fully and will burn out, whereas if too large noisy operation will result.

Valve lift The amount a valve is lifted off its seat by the camshaft lobe.

Valve timing The exact setting for the opening and closing of the valves in relation to piston position.

Vernier caliper A precision measuring instrument that measures inside and outside dimensions. Not quite as accurate as a micrometer, but more convenient.

VIN Vehicle Identification Number. Term for the bike's engine and frame numbers.

Viscosity The thickness of a liquid or its resistance to flow.

Volt A unit for expressing electrical "pressure" in a circuit. Volts = current x ohms.

W

Water pump A mechanically-driven device for moving coolant around the engine.

Watt A unit for expressing electrical power. Watts = volts x current.

Wear limit see **Service limit**

Wet liner A liquid-cooled engine design where the pistons run in liners which are directly surrounded by coolant **(see illustration).**

Wet liner arrangement

Wheelbase Distance from the centre of the front wheel to the centre of the rear wheel.

Wiring harness or loom Describes the electrical wires running the length of the motorcycle and enclosed in tape or plastic sheathing. Wiring coming off the main harness is usually referred to as a sub harness.

Woodruff key A key of semi-circular or square section used to locate a gear to a shaft. Often used to locate the alternator rotor on the crankshaft.

Wrist pin Another name for gudgeon or piston pin.

Note: *References throughout this index are in the form - "Chapter number" • "Page number"*

Haynes Motorcycle Manuals – The Complete List

Title	Book No
APRILIA RS50 (99 - 06) & RS125 (93 - 06)	4298
Aprilia RSV1000 Mille (98 - 03)	♦ 4255
Aprilia SR50	4755
BMW 2-valve Twins (70 - 96)	♦ 0249
BMW F650	♦ 4761
BMW K100 & 75 2-valve Models (83 - 96)	♦ 1373
BMW R850, 1100 & 1150 4-valve Twins (93 - 04)	♦ 3466
BMW R1200 (04 - 06)	♦ 4598
BSA Bantam (48 - 71)	0117
BSA Unit Singles (58 - 72)	0127
BSA Pre-unit Singles (54 - 61)	0326
BSA A7 & A10 Twins (47 - 62)	0121
BSA A50 & A65 Twins (62 - 73)	0155
Chinese Scooters	4768
DUCATI 600, 620, 750 and 900 2-valve V-Twins (91 - 05)	♦ 3290
Ducati MK III & Desmo Singles (69 - 76)	♦ 0445
Ducati 748, 916 & 996 4-valve V-Twins (94 - 01)	♦ 3756
GILERA Runner, DNA, Ice & SKP/Stalker (97 - 07)	4163
HARLEY-DAVIDSON Sportsters (70 - 08)	♦ 2534
Harley-Davidson Shovelhead and Evolution Big Twins (70 - 99)	♦ 2536
Harley-Davidson Twin Cam 88 (99 - 03)	♦ 2478
HONDA NB, ND, NP & NS50 Melody (81 - 85)	◊ 0622
Honda NE/NB50 Vision & SA50 Vision Met-in (85 - 95)	◊ 1278
Honda MB, MBX, MT & MTX50 (80 - 93)	0731
Honda C50, C70 & C90 (67 - 03)	0324
Honda XR80/100R & CRF80/100F (85 - 04)	2218
Honda XL/XR 80, 100, 125, 185 & 200 2-valve Models (78 - 87)	0566
Honda H100 & H100S Singles (80 - 92)	◊ 0734
Honda CB/CD125T & CM125C Twins (77 - 88)	◊ 0571
Honda CG125 (76 - 07)	0433
Honda NS125 (86 - 93)	3056
Honda CBR125R (04 - 07)	4620
Honda MBX/MTX125 & MTX200 (83 - 93)	◊ 1132
Honda CD/CM185 200T & CM250C 2-valve Twins (77 - 85)	0572
Honda XL/XR 250 & 500 (78 - 84)	0567
Honda XR250L, XR250R & XR400R (86 - 03)	2219
Honda CB250 & CB400N Super Dreams (78 - 84)	◊ 0540
Honda CR Motocross Bikes (86 - 01)	2222
Honda CRF250 & CRF450 (02 - 06)	2630
Honda CBR400RR Fours (88 - 99)	◊ ♦ 3552
Honda VFR400 (NC30) & RVF400 (NC35) V-Fours (89 - 98)	◊ ♦ 3496
Honda CB500 (93 - 02) & CBF500 03 - 08	◊ ♦ 3753
Honda CB400 & CB550 Fours (73 - 77)	0262
Honda CX/GL500 & 650 V-Twins (78 - 86)	0442
Honda CBX550 Four (82 - 86)	◊ 0940
Honda XL600R & XR600R (83 - 08)	♦ 2183
Honda XL600/650V Transalp & XRV750 Africa Twin (87 to 07)	♦ 3919
Honda CBR600F1 & 1000F Fours (87 - 96)	♦ 1730
Honda CBR600F2 & F3 Fours (91 - 98)	♦ 2070
Honda CBR600F4 (99 - 06)	♦ 3911
Honda CB600F Hornet & CBF600 (98 - 06)	◊ ♦ 3915
Honda CBR600RR (03 - 06)	♦ 4590
Honda CB650 sohc Fours (78 - 84)	0665
Honda NTV600 Revere, NTV650 and NT650V Deauville (88 - 05)	◊ ♦ 3243
Honda Shadow VT600 & 750 (USA) (88 - 03)	2312
Honda CB750 sohc Four (69 - 79)	0131
Honda V45/65 Sabre & Magna (82 - 88)	0820
Honda VFR750 & 700 V-Fours (86 - 97)	♦ 2101
Honda VFR800 V-Fours (97 - 01)	♦ 3703
Honda VFR800 V-Tec V-Fours (02 - 05)	♦ 4196
Honda CB750 & CB900 dohc Fours (78 - 84)	0535
Honda VTR1000 (FireStorm, Super Hawk) & XL1000V (Varadero) (97 - 08)	♦ 3744
Honda CBR900RR FireBlade (92 - 99)	♦ 2161
Honda CBR900RR FireBlade (00 - 03)	♦ 4060
Honda CBR1000RR Fireblade (04 - 07)	♦ 4604
Honda CBR1100XX Super Blackbird (97 - 07)	♦ 3901
Honda ST1100 Pan European V-Fours (90 - 02)	♦ 3384
Honda Shadow VT1100 (USA) (85 - 98)	2313
Honda GL1000 Gold Wing (75 - 79)	0309

Title	Book No
Honda GL1100 Gold Wing (79 - 81)	0669
Honda Gold Wing 1200 (USA) (84 - 87)	2199
Honda Gold Wing 1500 (USA) (88 - 00)	2225
KAWASAKI AE/AR 50 & 80 (81 - 95)	1007
Kawasaki KC, KE & KH100 (75 - 99)	1371
Kawasaki KMX125 & 200 (86 - 02)	◊ 3046
Kawasaki 250, 350 & 400 Triples (72 - 79)	0134
Kawasaki 400 & 440 Twins (74 - 81)	0281
Kawasaki 400, 500 & 550 Fours (79 - 91)	0910
Kawasaki EN450 & 500 Twins (Ltd/Vulcan) (85 - 07)	2053
Kawasaki EX500 (GPZ500S) & ER500 (ER-5) (87 - 08)	♦ 2052
Kawasaki ZX600 (ZZ-R600 & Ninja ZX-6) (90 - 06)	♦ 2146
Kawasaki ZX-6R Ninja Fours (95 - 02)	♦ 3541
Kawasaki ZX-6R (03 - 06)	♦ 4742
Kawasaki ZX600 (GPZ600R, GPX600R, Ninja 600R & RX) & ZX750 (GPX750R, Ninja 750R)	♦ 1780
Kawasaki 650 Four (76 - 78)	0373
Kawasaki 750 Air-cooled Fours (80 - 91)	0574
Kawasaki ZR550 & 750 Zephyr Fours (90 - 97)	♦ 3382
Kawasaki Z750 & Z1000 (03 - 08)	♦ 4762
Kawasaki ZX750 (Ninja ZX-7 & ZXR750) Fours (89 - 96)	♦ 2054
Kawasaki Ninja ZX-7R & ZX-9R (94 - 04)	♦ 3721
Kawasaki 900 & 1000 Fours (73 - 77)	0222
Kawasaki ZX900, 1000 & 1100 Liquid-cooled Fours (83 - 97)	♦ 1681
KTM EXC Enduro & SX Motocross (00 - 07)	♦ 4629
MOTO GUZZI 750, 850 & 1000 V-Twins (74 - 78)	0339
MZ ETZ Models (81 - 95)	◊ 1680
NORTON 500, 600, 650 & 750 Twins (57 - 70)	0187
Norton Commando (68 - 77)	0125
PEUGEOT Speedfight, Trekker & Vivacity Scooters (96 - 08)	◊ 3920
PIAGGIO (Vespa) Scooters (91 - 06)	3492
SUZUKI GT, ZR & TS50 (77 - 90)	◊ 0799
Suzuki TS50X (84 - 00)	◊ 1599
Suzuki 100, 125, 185 & 250 Air-cooled Trail bikes (79 - 89)	0797
Suzuki GP100 & 125 Singles (78 - 93)	◊ 0576
Suzuki GS, GN, GZ & DR125 Singles (82 - 05)	◊ 0888
Suzuki GS & 350 Twins (68 - 78)	0120
Suzuki GT250X7, GT200X5 & SB200 Twins (78 - 83)	◊ 0469
Suzuki GS/GSX250, 400 & 450 Twins (79 - 85)	0736
Suzuki GS500 Twin (89 - 06)	♦ 3238
Suzuki GS550 (77 - 82) & GS750 Fours (76 - 79)	0363
Suzuki GS/GSX550 4-valve Fours (83 - 88)	1133
Suzuki SV650 & SV650S (99 - 08)	♦ 3912
Suzuki GSX-R600 & 750 (96 - 00)	♦ 3553
Suzuki GSX-R600 (01 - 03), GSX-R750 (00 - 03) & GSX-R1000 (01 - 02)	♦ 3986
Suzuki GSX-R600/750 (04 - 05) & GSX-R1000 (03 - 06)	♦ 4382
Suzuki GSF600, 650 & 1200 Bandit Fours (95 - 06)	♦ 3367
Suzuki Intruder, Marauder, Volusia & Boulevard (85 - 06)	♦ 2618
Suzuki GS850 Fours (78 - 88)	0536
Suzuki GS1000 Four (77 - 79)	0484
Suzuki GSX-R750, GSX-R1100 (85 - 92), GSX600F, GSX750F, GSX1100F (Katana) Fours	♦ 2055
Suzuki GSX600/750F & GSX750 (98 - 02)	♦ 3987
Suzuki GS/GSX1000, 1100 & 1150 4-valve Fours (79 - 88)	0737
Suzuki TL1000S/R & DL1000 V-Strom (97 - 04)	♦ 4083
Suzuki GSF650/1250 (05 - 09)	♦ 4798
Suzuki GSX1300R Hayabusa (99 - 04)	♦ 4184
Suzuki GSX1400 (02 - 07)	♦ 4758
TRIUMPH Tiger Cub & Terrier (52 - 68)	0414
Triumph 350 & 500 Unit Twins (58 - 73)	0137
Triumph Pre-Unit Twins (47 - 62)	0251
Triumph 650 & 750 2-valve Unit Twins (63 - 83)	0122
Triumph Trident & BSA Rocket 3 (69 - 75)	0136
Triumph Bonneville (01 - 07)	♦ 4364
Triumph Daytona, Speed Triple, Sprint & Tiger (97 - 05)	♦ 3755
Triumph Triples and Fours (carburettor engines) (91 - 04)	♦ 2162
VESPA P/PX125, 150 & 200 Scooters (78 - 06)	0707
Vespa Scooters (59 - 78)	0126
YAMAHA DT50 & 80 Trail Bikes (78 - 95)	◊ 0800
Yamaha T50 & 80 Townmate (83 - 95)	◊ 1247

Title	Book No
Yamaha YB100 Singles (73 - 91)	◊ 0474
Yamaha RS/RXS100 & 125 Singles (74 - 95)	0331
Yamaha RD & DT125LC (82 - 95)	◊ 0887
Yamaha TZR125 (87 - 93) & DT125R (88 - 07)	◊ 1655
Yamaha TY50, 80, 125 & 175 (74 - 84)	◊ 0464
Yamaha XT & SR125 (82 - 03)	◊ 1021
Yamaha YBR125	4797
Yamaha Trail Bikes (81 - 00)	2350
Yamaha 2-stroke Motocross Bikes 1986 - 2006	2662
Yamaha YZ & WR 4-stroke Motocross Bikes (98 - 08)	2689
Yamaha 250 & 350 Twins (70 - 79)	0040
Yamaha XS250, 360 & 400 sohc Twins (75 - 84)	0378
Yamaha RD250 & 350LC Twins (80 - 82)	0803
Yamaha RD350 YPVS Twins (83 - 95)	1158
Yamaha RD400 Twin (75 - 79)	0333
Yamaha XT, TT & SR500 Singles (75 - 83)	0342
Yamaha XZ550 Vision V-Twins (82 - 85)	0821
Yamaha FJ, FZ, XJ & YX600 Radian (84 - 92)	2100
Yamaha XJ600S (Diversion, Seca II) & XJ600N Fours (92 - 03)	♦ 2145
Yamaha YZF600R Thundercat & FZS600 Fazer (96 - 03)	♦ 3702
Yamaha FZ-6 Fazer (04 - 07)	♦ 4751
Yamaha YZF-R6 (99 - 02)	♦ 3900
Yamaha YZF-R6 (03 - 05)	♦ 4601
Yamaha 650 Twins (70 - 83)	0341
Yamaha XJ650 & 750 Fours (80 - 84)	0738
Yamaha XS750 & 850 Triples (76 - 85)	0340
Yamaha TDM850, TRX850 & XTZ750 (89 - 99)	◊ ♦ 3540
Yamaha YZF750R & YZF1000R Thunderace (93 - 00)	♦ 3720
Yamaha FZR600, 750 & 1000 Fours (87 - 96)	♦ 2056
Yamaha XV (Virago) V-Twins (81 - 03)	♦ 0802
Yamaha XVS650 & 1100 Drag Star/V-Star (97 - 05)	♦ 4195
Yamaha XJ900F Fours (83 - 94)	♦ 3239
Yamaha XJ900S Diversion (94 - 01)	♦ 3739
Yamaha YZF-R1 (98 - 03)	♦ 3754
Yamaha YZF-R1 (04 - 06)	♦ 4605
Yamaha FZS1000 Fazer (01 - 05)	♦ 4287
Yamaha FJ1100 & 1200 Fours (84 - 96)	♦ 2057
Yamaha XJR1200 & 1300 (95 - 06)	♦ 3981
Yamaha V-Max (85 - 03)	♦ 4072

ATVs	Book No
Honda ATC70, 90, 110, 185 & 200 (71 - 85)	0565
Honda Rancher, Recon & TRX250EX ATVs	2553
Honda TRX300 Shaft Drive ATVs (88 - 00)	2125
Honda Foreman (95 - 07)	2465
Honda TRX300EX, TRX400EX & TRX450R/ER ATVs (93 - 06)	2318
Kawasaki Bayou 220/250/300 & Prairie 300 ATVs (86 - 03)	2351
Polaris ATVs (85 - 97)	2302
Polaris ATVs (98 - 06)	2508
Yamaha YFS200 Blaster ATV (88 - 06)	2317
Yamaha YFB250 Timberwolf ATVs (92 - 00)	2217
Yamaha YFM350 & YFM400 (ER and Big Bear) ATVs (87 - 03)	2126
Yamaha Banshee and Warrior ATVs (87 - 03)	2314
Yamaha Kodiak and Grizzly ATVs (93 - 05)	2567
ATV Basics	10450

TECHBOOK SERIES	Book No
Twist and Go (automatic transmission) Scooters Service and Repair Manual	4082
Motorcycle Basics TechBook (2nd Edition)	3515
Motorcycle Electrical TechBook (3rd Edition)	3471
Motorcycle Fuel Systems TechBook	3514
Motorcycle Maintenance TechBook	4071
Motorcycle Modifying	4272
Motorcycle Workshop Practice TechBook (2nd Edition)	3470

◊ = not available in the USA   ♦ = Superbike

The manuals on this page are available through good motorcycle dealers and accessory shops.
In case of difficulty, contact: **Haynes Publishing**
(UK) +44 1963 442030   (USA) +1 805 498 6703
(SV) +46 18 124016
(Australia/New Zealand) +61 3 9763 8100

MCL24.08/09

Haynes Manuals – The Complete UK Car List

Title	Book No.
ALFA ROMEO Alfasud/Sprint (74 - 88) up to F *	0292
Alfa Romeo Alfetta (73 - 87) up to E *	0531
AUDI 80, 90 & Coupe Petrol (79 - Nov 88) up to F	0605
Audi 80, 90 & Coupe Petrol (Oct 86 - 90) D to H	1491
Audi 100 & 200 Petrol (Oct 82 - 90) up to H	0907
Audi 100 & A6 Petrol & Diesel (May 91 - May 97) H to P	3504
Audi A3 Petrol & Diesel (96 - May 03) P to 03	4253
Audi A4 Petrol & Diesel (95 - 00) M to X	3575
Audi A4 Petrol & Diesel (01 - 04) X to 54	4609
AUSTIN A35 & A40 (56 - 67) up to F *	0118
Austin/MG/Rover Maestro 1.3 & 1.6 Petrol (83 - 95) up to M	0922
Austin/MG Metro (80 - May 90) up to G	0718
Austin/Rover Montego 1.3 & 1.6 Petrol (84 - 94) A to L	1066
Austin/MG/Rover Montego 2.0 Petrol (84 - 95) A to M	1067
Mini (59 - 69) up to H *	0527
Mini (69 - 01) up to X	0646
Austin/Rover 2.0 litre Diesel Engine (86 - 93) C to L	1857
Austin Healey 100/6 & 3000 (56 - 68) up to G *	0049
BEDFORD CF Petrol (69 - 87) up to E	0163
Bedford/Vauxhall Rascal & Suzuki Supercarry (86 - Oct 94) C to M	3015
BMW 316, 320 & 320i (4-cyl) (75 - Feb 83) up to Y *	0276
BMW 320, 320i, 323i & 325i (6-cyl) (Oct 77 - Sept 87) up to E	0815
BMW 3- & 5-Series Petrol (81 - 91) up to J	1948
BMW 3-Series Petrol (Apr 91 - 99) H to V	3210
BMW 3-Series Petrol (Sept 98 - 03) S to 53	4067
BMW 520i & 525e (Oct 81 - June 88) up to E	1560
BMW 525, 528 & 528i (73 - Sept 81) up to X *	0632
BMW 5-Series 6-cyl Petrol (April 96 - Aug 03) N to 03	4151
BMW 1500, 1502, 1600, 1602, 2000 & 2002 (59 - 77) up to S *	0240
CHRYSLER PT Cruiser Petrol (00 - 03) W to 53	4058
CITROËN 2CV, Ami & Dyane (67 - 90) up to H	0196
Citroën AX Petrol & Diesel (87 - 97) D to P	3014
Citroën Berlingo & Peugeot Partner Petrol & Diesel (96 - 05) P to 55	4281
Citroën BX Petrol (83 - 94) A to L	0908
Citroën C15 Van Petrol & Diesel (89 - Oct 98) F to S	3509
Citroën C3 Petrol & Diesel (02 - 05) 51 to 05	4197
Citroen C5 Petrol & Diesel (01-08) Y to 08	4745
Citroën CX Petrol (75 - 88) up to F	0528
Citroën Saxo Petrol & Diesel (96 - 04) N to 54	3506
Citroën Visa Petrol (79 - 88) up to F	0620
Citroën Xantia Petrol & Diesel (93 - 01) K to Y	3082
Citroën XM Petrol & Diesel (89 - 00) G to X	3451
Citroën Xsara Petrol & Diesel (97 - Sept 00) R to W	3751
Citroën Xsara Picasso Petrol & Diesel (00 - 02) W to 52	3944
Citroen Xsara Picasso (03-08)	4784
Citroën ZX Diesel (91 - 98) J to S	1922
Citroën ZX Petrol (91 - 98) H to S	1881
Citroën 1.7 & 1.9 litre Diesel Engine (84 - 96) A to N	1379
FIAT 126 (73 - 87) up to E *	0305
Fiat 500 (57 - 73) up to M *	0090
Fiat Bravo & Brava Petrol (95 - 00) N to W	3572
Fiat Cinquecento (93 - 98) K to R	3501
Fiat Panda (81 - 95) up to M	0793
Fiat Punto Petrol & Diesel (94 - Oct 99) L to V	3251
Fiat Punto Petrol (Oct 99 - July 03) V to 03	4066
Fiat Punto Petrol (03-07) 03 to 07	4746
Fiat Regata Petrol (84 - 88) A to F	1167
Fiat Tipo Petrol (88 - 91) E to J	1625
Fiat Uno Petrol (83 - 95) up to M	0923
Fiat X1/9 (74 - 89) up to G *	0273
FORD Anglia (59 - 68) up to G *	0001

Title	Book No.
Ford Capri II (& III) 1.6 & 2.0 (74 - 87) up to E *	0283
Ford Capri II (& III) 2.8 & 3.0 V6 (74 - 87) up to E	1309
Ford Cortina Mk I & Corsair 1500 ('62 - '66) up to D*	0214
Ford Cortina Mk III 1300 & 1600 (70 - 76) up to P *	0070
Ford Escort Mk I 1100 & 1300 (68 - 74) up to N *	0171
Ford Escort Mk I Mexico, RS 1600 & RS 2000 (70 - 74) up to N *	0139
Ford Escort Mk II Mexico, RS 1800 & RS 2000 (75 - 80) up to W *	0735
Ford Escort (75 - Aug 80) up to V *	0280
Ford Escort Petrol (Sept 80 - Sept 90) up to H	0686
Ford Escort & Orion Petrol (Sept 90 - 00) H to X	1737
Ford Escort & Orion Diesel (Sept 90 - 00) H to X	4081
Ford Fiesta (76 - Aug 83) up to Y	0334
Ford Fiesta Petrol (Aug 83 - Feb 89) A to F	1030
Ford Fiesta Petrol (Feb 89 - Oct 95) F to N	1595
Ford Fiesta Petrol & Diesel (Oct 95 - Mar 02) N to 02	3397
Ford Fiesta Petrol & Diesel (Apr 02 - 07) 02 to 57	4170
Ford Focus Petrol & Diesel (98 - 01) S to Y	3759
Ford Focus Petrol & Diesel (Oct 01 - 05) 51 to 05	4167
Ford Galaxy Petrol & Diesel (95 - Aug 00) M to W	3984
Ford Granada Petrol (Sept 77 - Feb 85) up to B *	0481
Ford Granada & Scorpio Petrol (Mar 85 - 94) B to M	1245
Ford Ka (96 - 02) P to 52	3570
Ford Mondeo Petrol (93 - Sept 00) K to X	1923
Ford Mondeo Petrol & Diesel (Oct 00 - Jul 03) X to 03	3990
Ford Mondeo Petrol & Diesel (July 03 - 07) 03 to 56	4619
Ford Mondeo Diesel (93 - 96) L to N	3465
Ford Orion Petrol (83 - Sept 90) up to H	1009
Ford Sierra 4-cyl Petrol (82 - 93) up to K	0903
Ford Sierra V6 Petrol (82 - 91) up to J	0904
Ford Transit Petrol (Mk 2) (78 - Jan 86) up to C	0719
Ford Transit Petrol (Mk 3) (Feb 86 - 89) C to G	1468
Ford Transit Diesel (Feb 86 - 99) C to T	3019
Ford Transit Diesel (00-06)	4775
Ford 1.6 & 1.8 litre Diesel Engine (84 - 96) A to N	1172
Ford 2.1, 2.3 & 2.5 litre Diesel Engine (77 - 90) up to H	1606
FREIGHT ROVER Sherpa Petrol (74 - 87) up to E	0463
HILLMAN Avenger (70 - 82) up to Y	0037
Hillman Imp (63 - 76) up to R *	0022
HONDA Civic (Feb 84 - Oct 87) A to E	1226
Honda Civic (Nov 91 - 96) J to N	3199
Honda Civic Petrol (Mar 95 - 00) M to X	4050
Honda Civic Petrol & Diesel (01 - 05) X to 55	4611
Honda CR-V Petrol & Diesel (01-06)	4747
Honda Jazz (01 - Feb 08) 51 - 57	4735
HYUNDAI Pony (85 - 94) C to M	3398
JAGUAR E Type (61 - 72) up to L *	0140
Jaguar MkI & II, 240 & 340 (55 - 69) up to H *	0098
Jaguar XJ6, XJ & Sovereign; Daimler Sovereign (68 - Oct 86) up to D	0242
Jaguar XJ6 & Sovereign (Oct 86 - Sept 94) D to M	3261
Jaguar XJ12, XJS & Sovereign; Daimler Double Six (72 - 88) up to F	0478
JEEP Cherokee Petrol (93 - 96) K to N	1943
LADA 1200, 1300, 1500 & 1600 (74 - 91) up to J	0413
Lada Samara (87 - 91) D to J	1610
LAND ROVER 90, 110 & Defender Diesel (83 - 07) up to 56	3017
Land Rover Discovery Petrol & Diesel (89 - 98) G to S	3016
Land Rover Discovery Diesel (Nov 98 - Jul 04) S to 04	4606
Land Rover Freelander Petrol & Diesel (97 - Sept 03) R to 53	3929
Land Rover Freelander Petrol & Diesel (Oct 03 - Oct 06) 53 to 56	4623

Title	Book No.
Land Rover Series IIA & III Diesel (58 - 85) up to C	0529
Land Rover Series II, IIA & III 4-cyl Petrol (58 - 85) up to C	0314
MAZDA 323 (Mar 81 - Oct 89) up to G	1608
Mazda 323 (Oct 89 - 98) G to R	3455
Mazda 626 (May 83 - Sept 87) up to E	0929
Mazda B1600, B1800 & B2000 Pick-up Petrol (72 - 88) up to F	0267
Mazda RX-7 (79 - 85) up to C *	0460
MERCEDES-BENZ 190, 190E & 190D Petrol & Diesel (83 - 93) A to L	3450
Mercedes-Benz 200D, 240D, 240TD, 300D & 300TD 123 Series Diesel (Oct 76 - 85)	1114
Mercedes-Benz 250 & 280 (68 - 72) up to L *	0346
Mercedes-Benz 250 & 280 123 Series Petrol (Oct 76 - 84) up to B *	0677
Mercedes-Benz 124 Series Petrol & Diesel (85 - Aug 93) C to K	3253
Mercedes-Benz A-Class Petrol & Diesel (98-04) S to 54	4748
Mercedes-Benz C-Class Petrol & Diesel (93 - Aug 00) L to W	3511
Mercedes-Benz C-Class (00-06)	4780
MGA (55 - 62) *	0475
MGB (62 - 80) up to W	0111
MG Midget & Austin-Healey Sprite (58 - 80) up to W *	0265
MINI Petrol (July 01 - 05) Y to 05	4273
MITSUBISHI Shogun & L200 Pick-Ups Petrol (83 - 94) up to M	1944
MORRIS Ital 1.3 (80 - 84) up to B	0705
Morris Minor 1000 (56 - 71) up to K	0024
NISSAN Almera Petrol (95 - Feb 00) N to V	4053
Nissan Almera & Tino Petrol (Feb 00 - 07) V to 56	4612
Nissan Bluebird (May 84 - Mar 86) A to C	1223
Nissan Bluebird Petrol (Mar 86 - 90) C to H	1473
Nissan Cherry (Sept 82 - 86) up to D	1031
Nissan Micra (83 - Jan 93) up to K	0931
Nissan Micra (93 - 02) K to 52	3254
Nissan Micra Petrol (03-07) 52 to 57	4734
Nissan Primera Petrol (90 - Aug 99) H to T	1851
Nissan Stanza (82 - 86) up to D	0824
Nissan Sunny Petrol (May 82 - Oct 86) up to D	0895
Nissan Sunny Petrol (Oct 86 - Mar 91) D to H	1378
Nissan Sunny Petrol (Apr 91 - 95) H to N	3219
OPEL Ascona & Manta (B Series) (Sept 75 - 88) up to F *	0316
Opel Ascona Petrol (81 - 88)	3215
Opel Astra Petrol (Oct 91 - Feb 98)	3156
Opel Corsa Petrol (83 - Mar 93)	3160
Opel Corsa Petrol (Mar 93 - 97)	3159
Opel Kadett Petrol (Nov 79 - Oct 84) up to B	0634
Opel Kadett Petrol (Oct 84 - Oct 91)	3196
Opel Omega & Senator Petrol (Nov 86 - 94)	3157
Opel Rekord Petrol (Feb 78 - Oct 86) up to D	0543
Opel Vectra Petrol (Oct 88 - Oct 95)	3158
PEUGEOT 106 Petrol & Diesel (91 - 04) J to 53	1882
Peugeot 205 Petrol (83 - 97) A to P	0932
Peugeot 206 Petrol & Diesel (98 - 01) S to X	3757
Peugeot 206 Petrol & Diesel (02 - 06) 51 to 06	4613
Peugeot 306 Petrol & Diesel (93 - 02) K to 02	3073
Peugeot 307 Petrol & Diesel (01 - 04) Y to 54	4147
Peugeot 309 Petrol (86 - 93) C to K	1266
Peugeot 405 Petrol (88 - 97) E to P	1559
Peugeot 405 Diesel (88 - 97) E to P	3198
Peugeot 406 Petrol & Diesel (96 - Mar 99) N to T	3394
Peugeot 406 Petrol & Diesel (Mar 99 - 02) T to 52	3982

* Classic reprint

Title	Book No.
Peugeot 505 Petrol (79 - 89) up to G	0762
Peugeot 1.7/1.8 & 1.9 litre Diesel Engine (82 - 96) up to N	0950
Peugeot 2.0, 2.1, 2.3 & 2.5 litre Diesel Engines (74 - 90) up to H	1607
PORSCHE 911 (65 - 85) up to C	0264
Porsche 924 & 924 Turbo (76 - 85) up to C	0397
PROTON (89 - 97) F to P	3255
RANGE ROVER V8 Petrol (70 - Oct 92) up to K	0606
RELIANT Robin & Kitten (73 - 83) up to A *	0436
RENAULT 4 (61 - 86) up to D *	0072
Renault 5 Petrol (Feb 85 - 96) B to N	1219
Renault 9 & 11 Petrol (82 - 89) up to F	0822
Renault 18 Petrol (79 - 86) up to D	0598
Renault 19 Petrol (89 - 96) F to N	1646
Renault 19 Diesel (89 - 96) F to N	1946
Renault 21 Petrol (86 - 94) C to M	1397
Renault 25 Petrol & Diesel (84 - 92) B to K	1228
Renault Clio Petrol (91 - May 98) H to R	1853
Renault Clio Diesel (91 - June 96) H to N	3031
Renault Clio Petrol & Diesel (May 98 - May 01) R to Y	3906
Renault Clio Petrol & Diesel (June '01 - '05) Y to 55	4168
Renault Espace Petrol & Diesel (85 - 96) C to N	3197
Renault Laguna Petrol & Diesel (94 - 00) L to W	3252
Renault Laguna Petrol & Diesel (Feb 01 - Feb 05) X to 54	4283
Renault Mégane & Scénic Petrol & Diesel (96 - 99) N to T	3395
Renault Mégane & Scénic Petrol & Diesel (Apr 99 - 02) T to 52	3916
Renault Megane Petrol & Diesel (Oct 02 - 05) 52 to 55	4284
Renault Scenic Petrol & Diesel (Sept 03 - 06) 53 to 06	4297
ROVER 213 & 216 (84 - 89) A to G	1116
Rover 214 & 414 Petrol (89 - 96) G to N	1689
Rover 216 & 416 Petrol (89 - 96) G to N	1830
Rover 211, 214, 216, 218 & 220 Petrol & Diesel (Dec 95 - 99) N to V	3399
Rover 25 & MG ZR Petrol & Diesel (Oct 99 - 04) V to 54	4145
Rover 414, 416 & 420 Petrol & Diesel (May 95 - 98) M to R	3453
Rover 45 / MG ZS Petrol & Diesel (99 - 05) V to 55	4384
Rover 618, 620 & 623 Petrol (93 - 97) K to P	3257
Rover 75 / MG ZT Petrol & Diesel (99 - 06) S to 06	4292
Rover 820, 825 & 827 Petrol (86 - 95) D to N	1380
Rover 3500 (76 - 87) up to E *	0365
Rover Metro, 111 & 114 Petrol (May 90 - 98) G to S	1711
SAAB 95 & 96 (66 - 76) up to R *	0198
Saab 90, 99 & 900 (79 - Oct 93) up to L	0765
Saab 900 (Oct 93 - 98) L to R	3512
Saab 9000 (4-cyl) (85 - 98) C to S	1686
Saab 9-3 Petrol & Diesel (98 - Aug 02) R to 02	4614
Saab 9-3 Petrol & Diesel (02-07) 52 to 57	4749
Saab 9-5 4-cyl Petrol (97 - 04) R to 54	4156
SEAT Ibiza & Cordoba Petrol & Diesel (Oct 93 - Oct 99) L to V	3571
Seat Ibiza & Malaga Petrol (85 - 92) B to K	1609
SKODA Estelle (77 - 89) up to G	0604
Skoda Fabia Petrol & Diesel (00 - 06) W to 06	4376
Skoda Favorit (89 - 96) F to N	1801
Skoda Felicia Petrol & Diesel (95 - 01) M to X	3505
Skoda Octavia Petrol & Diesel (98 - Apr 04) R to 04	4285
SUBARU 1600 & 1800 (Nov 79 - 90) up to H *	0995

Title	Book No.
SUNBEAM Alpine, Rapier & H120 (67 - 74) up to N *	0051
SUZUKI SJ Series, Samurai & Vitara (4-cyl) Petrol (82 - 97) up to P	1942
Suzuki Supercarry & Bedford/Vauxhall Rascal (86 - Oct 94) C to M	3015
TALBOT Alpine, Solara, Minx & Rapier (75 - 86) up to D	0337
Talbot Horizon Petrol (78 - 86) up to D	0473
Talbot Samba (82 - 86) up to D	0823
TOYOTA Avensis Petrol (98 - Jan 03) R to 52	4264
Toyota Carina E Petrol (May 92 - 97) J to P	3256
Toyota Corolla (80 - 85) up to C	0683
Toyota Corolla (Sept 83 - Sept 87) A to E	1024
Toyota Corolla (Sept 87 - Aug 92) E to K	1683
Toyota Corolla Petrol (Aug 92 - 97) K to P	3259
Toyota Corolla Petrol (July 97 - Feb 02) P to 51	4286
Toyota Hi-Ace & Hi-Lux Petrol (69 - Oct 83) up to A	0304
Toyota RAV4 Petrol & Diesel (94-06) L to 55	4750
Toyota Yaris Petrol (99 - 05) T to 05	4265
TRIUMPH GT6 & Vitesse (62 - 74) up to N *	0112
Triumph Herald (59 - 71) up to K *	0010
Triumph Spitfire (62 - 81) up to X	0113
Triumph Stag (70 - 78) up to T *	0441
Triumph TR2, TR3, TR3A, TR4 & TR4A (52 - 67) up to F *	0028
Triumph TR5 & 6 (67 - 75) up to P *	0031
Triumph TR7 (75 - 82) up to Y *	0322
VAUXHALL Astra Petrol (80 - Oct 84) up to B	0635
Vauxhall Astra & Belmont Petrol (Oct 84 - Oct 91) B to J	1136
Vauxhall Astra Petrol (Oct 91 - Feb 98) J to R	1832
Vauxhall/Opel Astra & Zafira Petrol (Feb 98 - Apr 04) R to 04	3758
Vauxhall/Opel Astra & Zafira Diesel (Feb 98 - Apr 04) R to 04	3797
Vauxhall/Opel Astra Petrol (04 - 08)	4732
Vauxhall/Opel Astra Diesel (04 - 08)	4733
Vauxhall/Opel Calibra (90 - 98) G to S	3502
Vauxhall Carlton Petrol (Oct 78 - Oct 86) up to D	0480
Vauxhall Carlton & Senator Petrol (Nov 86 - 94) D to L	1469
Vauxhall Cavalier Petrol (81 - Oct 88) up to F	0812
Vauxhall Cavalier Petrol (Oct 88 - 95) F to N	1570
Vauxhall Chevette (75 - 84) up to B	0285
Vauxhall/Opel Corsa Diesel (Mar 93 - Oct 00) K to X	4087
Vauxhall Corsa Petrol (Mar 93 - 97) K to R	1985
Vauxhall/Opel Corsa Petrol (Apr 97 - Oct 00) P to X	3921
Vauxhall/Opel Corsa Petrol & Diesel (Oct 00 - Sept 03) X to 53	4079
Vauxhall/Opel Corsa Petrol & Diesel (Oct 03 - Aug 06) 53 to 06	4617
Vauxhall/Opel Frontera Petrol & Diesel (91 - Sept 98) J to S	3454
Vauxhall Nova Petrol (83 - 93) up to K	0909
Vauxhall/Opel Omega Petrol (94 - 99) L to T	3510
Vauxhall/Opel Vectra Petrol & Diesel (95 - Feb 99) N to S	3396
Vauxhall/Opel Vectra Petrol & Diesel (Mar 99 - May 02) T to 02	3930
Vauxhall/Opel Vectra Petrol & Diesel (June 02 - Sept 05) 02 to 55	4618
Vauxhall/Opel 1.5, 1.6 & 1.7 litre Diesel Engine (82 - 96) up to N	1222
VW 411 & 412 (68 - 75) up to P *	0091
VW Beetle 1200 (54 - 77) up to S	0036
VW Beetle 1300 & 1500 (65 - 75) up to P	0039

Title	Book No.
VW 1302 & 1302S (70 - 72) up to L *	0110
VW Beetle 1303, 1303S & GT (72 - 75) up to P	0159
VW Beetle Petrol & Diesel (Apr 99 - 07) T to 57	3798
VW Golf & Jetta Mk 1 Petrol 1.1 & 1.3 (74 - 84) up to A	0716
VW Golf, Jetta & Scirocco Mk 1 Petrol 1.5, 1.6 & 1.8 (74 - 84) up to A	0726
VW Golf & Jetta Mk 1 Diesel (78 - 84) up to A	0451
VW Golf & Jetta Mk 2 Petrol (Mar 84 - Feb 92) A to J	1081
VW Golf & Vento Petrol & Diesel (Feb 92 - Mar 98) J to R	3097
VW Golf & Bora Petrol & Diesel (April 98 - 00) R to X	3727
VW Golf & Bora 4-cyl Petrol & Diesel (01 - 03) X to 53	4169
VW Golf & Jetta Petrol & Diesel (04 - 07) 53 to 07	4610
VW LT Petrol Vans & Light Trucks (76 - 87) up to E	0637
VW Passat & Santana Petrol (Sept 81 - May 88) up to E	0814
VW Passat 4-cyl Petrol & Diesel (May 88 - 96) E to P	3498
VW Passat 4-cyl Petrol & Diesel (Dec 96 - Nov 00) P to X	3917
VW Passat Petrol & Diesel (Dec 00 - May 05) X to 05	4279
VW Polo & Derby (76 - Jan 82) up to X	0335
VW Polo (82 - Oct 90) up to H	0813
VW Polo Petrol (Nov 90 - Aug 94) H to L	3245
VW Polo Hatchback Petrol & Diesel (94 - 99) M to S	3500
VW Polo Hatchback Petrol (00 - Jan 02) V to 51	4150
VW Polo Petrol & Diesel (02 - May 05) 51 to 05	4608
VW Scirocco (82 - 90) up to H *	1224
VW Transporter 1600 (68 - 79) up to V	0082
VW Transporter 1700, 1800 & 2000 (72 - 79) up to V *	0226
VW Transporter (air-cooled) Petrol (79 - 82) up to Y *	0638
VW Transporter (water-cooled) Petrol (82 - 90) up to H	3452
VW Type 3 (63 - 73) up to M *	0084
VOLVO 120 & 130 Series (& P1800) (61 - 73) up to M *	0203
Volvo 142, 144 & 145 (66 - 74) up to N *	0129
Volvo 240 Series Petrol (74 - 93) up to K	0270
Volvo 262, 264 & 260/265 (75 - 85) up to C *	0400
Volvo 340, 343, 345 & 360 (76 - 91) up to J	0715
Volvo 440, 460 & 480 Petrol (87 - 97) D to P	1691
Volvo 740 & 760 Petrol (82 - 91) up to J	1258
Volvo 850 Petrol (92 - 96) J to P	3260
Volvo 940 petrol (90 - 98) H to R	3249
Volvo S40 & V40 Petrol (96 - Mar 04) N to 04	3569
Volvo S40 & V50 Petrol & Diesel (Mar 04 - Jun 07) 04 to 07	4731
Volvo S60 Petrol & Diesel (01-08)	4793
Volvo S70, V70 & C70 Petrol (96 - 99) P to V	3573
Volvo V70 / S80 Petrol & Diesel (98 - 05) S to 55	4263

DIY MANUAL SERIES

Title	Book No.
The Haynes Air Conditioning Manual	4192
The Haynes Car Electrical Systems Manual	4251
The Haynes Manual on Bodywork	4198
The Haynes Manual on Brakes	4178
The Haynes Manual on Carburettors	4177
The Haynes Manual on Diesel Engines	4174
The Haynes Manual on Engine Management	4199
The Haynes Manual on Fault Codes	4175
The Haynes Manual on Practical Electrical Systems	4267
The Haynes Manual on Small Engines	4250
The Haynes Manual on Welding	4176

* Classic reprint

All the products featured on this page are available through most motor accessory shops, cycle shops and book stores. Our policy of continuous updating and development means that titles are being constantly added to the range. For up-to-date information on our complete list of titles, please telephone: (UK) +44 1963 442030 • (USA) +1 805 498 6703 • (Sweden) +46 18 124016 • (Australia) +61 3 9763 8100

CL24.08/09

Preserving Our Motoring Heritage

< The Model J Duesenberg Derham Tourster. Only eight of these magnificent cars were ever built – this is the only example to be found outside the United States of America

Almost every car you've ever loved, loathed or desired is gathered under one roof at the Haynes Motor Museum. Over 300 immaculately presented cars and motorbikes represent every aspect of our motoring heritage, from elegant reminders of bygone days, such as the superb Model J Duesenberg to curiosities like the bug-eyed BMW Isetta. There are also many old friends and flames. Perhaps you remember the 1959 Ford Popular that you did your courting in? The magnificent 'Red Collection' is a spectacle of classic sports cars including AC, Alfa Romeo, Austin Healey, Ferrari, Lamborghini, Maserati, MG, Riley, Porsche and Triumph.

A Perfect Day Out

Each and every vehicle at the Haynes Motor Museum has played its part in the history and culture of Motoring. Today, they make a wonderful spectacle and a great day out for all the family. Bring the kids, bring Mum and Dad, but above all bring your camera to capture those golden memories for ever. You will also find an impressive array of motoring memorabilia, a comfortable 70 seat video cinema and one of the most extensive transport book shops in Britain. The Pit Stop Cafe serves everything from a cup of tea to wholesome, home-made meals or, if you prefer, you can enjoy the large picnic area nestled in the beautiful rural surroundings of Somerset.

> John Haynes O.B.E., Founder and Chairman of the museum at the wheel of a Haynes Light 12.

< The 1936 490cc sohc-engined International Norton – well known for its racing success

The Museum is situated on the A359 Yeovil to Frome road at Sparkford, just off the A303 in Somerset. It is about 40 miles south of Bristol, and 25 minutes drive from the M5 intersection at Taunton.

Open 9.30am - 5.30pm (10.00am - 4.00pm Winter) 7 days a week, *except Christmas Day, Boxing Day and New Years Day*

Special rates available for schools, coach parties and outings Charitable Trust No. 292048